HOUSE OF WAR

HOUSE OF WAR

··

THE PENTAGON
AND THE
DISASTROUS RISE
OF AMERICAN
POWER

JAMES CARROLL

HOUGHTON MIFFLIN COMPANY

BOSTON · NEW YORK

2006

For information about permission to reproduce selections from
this book, write to Permissions, Houghton Mifflin Company,
215 Park Avenue South, New York, New York 10003.

Visit our Web site: www.houghtonmifflinbooks.com.

Library of Congress Cataloging-in-Publication Data

Carroll, James, date.
House of war : the Pentagon and the disastrous rise
of American power / James Carroll.
p.   cm.
Includes bibliographical references and index.
ISBN-13: 978-0-618-18780-5
ISBN-10: 0-618-18780-4
1. United States — Military policy. 2. Pentagon (Va.)
3. United States — Dept. of Defense. 4. Militarism — United
States — History — 20th century. 5. Militarism — United
States — History — 21st century. 6. Arms race — United States
— History — 20th century. 7. Arms race — United States —
History — 21st century. I. Title.
UA23.C274 2006
355'.033073'09045 — dc22   2005024014

Printed in the United States of America

Book design by Robert Overholtzer

QUM 10 9 8 7 6 5 4 3 2 1

Grateful acknowledgment is made to Rosanna Warren and
Daniel Berrigan for permission to quote from their poetry.

IN MEMORY OF
Lieutenant General Joseph F. Carroll

*   *   *

For Elizabeth Marshall Carroll
and
Patrick Marshall Carroll

The potential for the disastrous rise of misplaced power exists and will persist. We must never let the weight of this combination endanger our liberties or democratic processes. We should take nothing for granted.

— President Dwight D. Eisenhower,
farewell address, January 17, 1961

PROLOGUE

THE INVISIBLE BOY

The Building looms over the Potomac across sixty years of war and peace, through six decades of memory. A forbidden temple even now, when I am older—imagine how the sight of it hit the child who first came here with his dad.

What did I know? Young, pining at the slick, slanting terrazzo, I wanted nothing more than the place for my very own, the largest playhouse in the world. Five sides, five stories, five rings by alphabet, four moats, seven spokes, triple the square footage of the Empire State Building, covering thirty full acres, a mile in circumference, with seventeen and a half miles of looping corridors in which to run.[1] But the ramps were best, and at five sharp the workers made for their cars, like shells bumpedy-bumpedy after the tide. I watched them go, glad to have the place to myself, because my dad worked late. I tried counting the rush-hour refugees, but there were more people than any place outside China, which Dad was watching. When they were gone, with no chrome helmets in sight, I stepped out of my shoes for the slick glide of stocking feet down the ramps.

There were eighteen dining rooms that served sixty thousand meals a day. There were two barber shops, a drugstore, a vaccination clinic, five "beverage bars," each with more swivel stools than even a swift lad like me could set to spinning. There were six hundred drinking fountains, and I sipped from most of them. A clock room had the right time for every place right down to Moscow, Russia. Grown-up men rode three-wheeled bikes with baskets, messengers with their bells blasting — make way for secrets! In corners stood faded battle flags attached to spears, with streamers flowing from the blades. On the walls hung paintings of warplanes and horses, tanks and dead-eyed men. Parthenon, Pantheon — I couldn't keep the words straight. Call it Paradise. It was not so much to want for a lad of ten.

I was the invisible boy, keen, brimming with stealth, spying it all from my unnoted perch in the rush-hour throng, or standing stock-still against the wall, which was the color of a robin's egg. A boy could get lost, and I did. No windows to mark, no signs, just numbers and letters painted everywhere. It was dangerous to lose my way; they could shoot me for being a spy. Open no door, speak to no stranger. I will tell them, if asked, I am going to the john. Even if they torture me, I will not tell them about my father.

That was the real wonder — Dad worked here! He was uniformed, like all those others — tan or blue, depending on the season, but always hatless in the vast indoors. In the early morning, I would have watched him at the sink: slapping on after-shave, shining a shoe on the edge of the toilet bowl, adjusting the silver stars on the shoulders of his coat, making sure the points were aligned. And then, click — my father striding into the Building, taking salutes, returning them with the very fingers that snapped to the music of the car radio as we drove home.

Soon that primal identification of man and building would form the un-slippable knot of my young life, forever tying me to the mystical stake in the middle of the five-sided courtyard, if I could only find it. Corridors and Corregidors, dead ends and deadly force, hallway ramps and Pork Chop Hill — it was so easy to get lost looking for the center of the maze. At last a window! I ran to it. But that courtyard, seen from the window in the center ring, was always a surprise. In the hub of the world's fortress was grass, a patch of grass, green, vacant, growing there like a spillover plot from the cemetery on the hill. Even I knew that the proximity to Arlington made the Pentagon the largest tombstone in the world. As for the courtyard, its five little acres must have been God's to warrant such protection.

But I knew. That courtyard, stillpoint of the swirling Building, was also known as ground zero,[2] focus of the Soviet aiming device, the last grass when the next smoke clears. I thought grass in such a place was wrong, perhaps a provocation. They should pave it over, make it a parking lot for tanks, I thought. A helipad. A paratrooper's landing place. The enemy come at last. Invasion. I turned from the window with a secret of my own, my first, my center ring, my acre of God, my soul, my first fear, but not my last: Who is the enemy? Who the friend? And what, after all, is to be done?[3] I hustled, not quite running (*Don't let them know you don't belong here, fool!*), through the tiled

CONTENTS

forest, minefield, no man's land, searching for my Air Force father's office, looking for my dad.

The ceremonial groundbreaking for the Building's construction, on September 11, 1941,[4] took place sixty years, almost to the minute, before American Airlines flight 77 arrowed into the side of the Pentagon that faces Arlington Cemetery. As the world seemed to grasp on September 11, 2001, it turned out that there was a poignant vulnerability to the headquarters building of the American military establishment, by far the mightiest martial force in history. "Unmistakably marked for potential enemies from the air," the biographer of General George Marshall had written years before 9/11, "it seemed to invite attack as well as to radiate resistance to the foes of the United States."[5]

For square footage of floor space, the Pentagon would be surpassed only by New York's World Trade Center, in 1973. Once American flight 11 and United flight 175 had brought the twin towers down, the Pentagon, though wounded, resumed its place as the nation's largest building. But in the aftermath of the 9/11 attacks, the Building looked strangely fragile. Soon a kind of huge bandage was stretched into place, hiding the broken wall. An American flag was positioned over that construction tarp. As the nation's trauma centered on New York, the Pentagon moved to the margin of communal awareness, where it had always been.

When the Building was hit by flight 77, I recognized for the first time in years how the Pentagon had seared my soul when I was a boy. The universal grief and pain of September 11 was, in my case, centered on an ache attached to Arlington—an ache that tied the trauma to a line running through my life.

After my initial infatuation with the Pentagon, I had been conscripted into youthful criticism of America's wars, and therefore of the Building's work. September 11 could seem to be the American Cold War nightmare come a little late, an approximation of the mushroom cloud, complete with its own ground zero. That the terrorists had included the Pentagon in their assault seemed, even amid the outrage of that day's mayhem, somehow inevitable. American power was being attacked that day—economic power, military power, and, if the airliner downed in Pennsylvania had reached its target, thought to be the Capitol or the White House, political power. The haste with which the gap in the southern wall of the edifice in Arlington was covered up, and the efficiency with which Defense Department headquarters was moved to the edge of the field of national attention in the months and years after September 11, raised questions of their own, at least for me.

What does the Pentagon mean, actually, to the United States of America? How is its influence felt, its power exercised? Since ground was broken in

1941, what has the Building's effect been on the nation's sense of itself, its place in the world? How has the struggle for the American soul been won or lost here? Those questions, among others, form the spine of this book.

The story it tracks begins with one man, General Leslie Groves, who embodied the twin centers of a previously unimagined source of power. Another man, Secretary of War Henry Stimson, saw the new danger at once and warned of it, to no avail. After Stimson, dozens of others would sound alarms as the Pentagon usurped controls over the levers of the American economy and culture, over science, academia, and politics. "Disastrous rise" is Dwight Eisenhower's phrase, from his farewell address warning of what he dubbed the "military-industrial complex."

The Pentagon has been so much at the center of national life that one could write an entire history of the contemporary United States in its terms. This history aims at less, and will not take on large but tangential questions like the impact of Pentagon racial policies on the civil rights movement, or the restructuring of academia that resulted from the infusion of Pentagon funds into university budgets. The Pentagon had a powerful impact on the American media, but that, too, is beyond our interest here. Relations between the executive branch and the Congress were recast when the government's center of gravity moved across the Potomac, and that development will find its way into this story, but only indirectly.

Our subject concerns, more simply, the ways in which the accumulation of Pentagon power effected what amounted to a mutation in the meaning of American power, with cosmic consequences both at home and abroad. Harry Truman, Dean Acheson, and James Forrestal anchor one end of the narrative, with Ronald Reagan, Bill Clinton, Colin Powell, and George W. Bush tying down the other, with figures like George Kennan, Paul Nitze, Curtis LeMay, Robert McNamara, Donald Rumsfeld, Paul Wolfowitz, and Richard Cheney unspooling the line between. A classic saga, the story of the Pentagon's rise marks an ongoing melding of personal and public paranoia, of psychological and political stresses, a process by which unsubstantiated ephemera were again and again transformed into tangible reality, taking on heft and moral gravitas.[6]

Nuclear weapons inform the tale from start to finish, but more as the gods of a new religion than as mere instruments of war. Anti-Communism gives that religion its first theology, and its first heresy hunt. But America's bipolar mindset survives the disappearance of Communism, as the Cold War bleeds into the Global War on Terror, with "evil" making its stunning comeback in the new century, and appeals to religion becoming more overt than ever. Always, the Pentagon remains the nation's sacred temple. At the same time, the Pentagon remains an engine room, generating a current that flows inexorably toward the edge of an abyss. Until, finally, the Pentagon becomes the bull's-eye of a world target.

Ironies animate this history, as emergency measures designed to be temporary become permanent; as imagined enemies become real by virtue of having been imagined; as arms control initiatives themselves fuel the upward spiral of weapons accumulation; as intellectual brilliance is assigned second place (even by intellectuals) to technical expertise; as peacenik opposition to the draft leads to a professional military of the poor. At times, militarized belligerence defines the State Department more than the Defense Department, with generals embracing the diplomacy their martinet civilian overseers reject. The narrative's two great reversals come when, first, the most ideological Cold War figure of all finds a way to cooperate with his enemy to end that war, making a friend of the enemy to boot; and then, second, when a self-appointed peacemaker president keeps the Cold War going, even without that enemy. The story's tragic endpoint arrives like punctuation when a ragtag group of "insurgents" fights the most lavishly armed force in history to a virtual stalemate.

Korea, Berlin, Cuba, Vietnam, Yugoslavia, Somalia, Iraq, Iran, Korea again; the radioactive standoff with Moscow; the perennial false promise of technology; the U.S. Navy's war against, first, the U.S. Air Force; the U.S. Army twice carrying out orders for its own self-destruction; and, always, the frontier of space as the next battlefield—such are the markers of this story. It has its heroes: the Cold War leadership on both sides, who found it possible *not* to start World War III, as well as that legion of the unnamed who nobly fought the "limited" wars that had the unlimited consequence for many of them. There are also heroes among the counterbalancing throng, Gandhi's children, who demanded an end to those wars, calling time-out from the nuclear high noon.

This history has its villains, too: men who fell under the thrall of new machines, who lost the tie between means and ends, or who refused to acknowledge the limits of American power—and also innocence. These men launched the nation on unnecessary wars. They risked the very earth for a mere idea of it. Seeing threats, they put in place protections that did more damage than the threats ever could have. The spirit of revenge was set loose during World War II, and it found its niche in the American soul, surfacing with power after the September 11 attacks. And so also fear. Leaders who are afraid do terrible things, not least by making their nation afraid. That, too, is what happened here.

Mostly, though, the Pentagon's is a story of ordinary people who acted with good intentions, faced tragic dilemmas, and resisted what they saw happening right in front of them. One of those was my father, which makes me the chastened storyteller. I have the eyes of a soldier's son, through which, unfortunately, I see everything. This book travels a path through a forest of questions, the Pentagon itself a kind of dark woods. A child's questions have become a man's.

What happened when the impersonal forces of mass bureaucracy, the Building's own culture, were joined to the critical mass of nuclear power? What changes in the ethical norms of American military policy unfolded during the Pentagon's World War II years, during the martial anguish of the Cold War, and during the upward rush toward the ever elusive goal of nuclear dominance? Who were the men of the Pentagon, and how did their moral agency interact with the impersonal momentum of the arms race? How did the constitutional checks and balances in Washington withstand the fierce concentration of power and influence on the Virginia side of the river?

How did the Global War on Terror seize the American psyche so self-destructively? And how, finally, can this usurping center of principality and power be brought back under the control of ordinary citizens, beginning with the disenchanted man who grew from the Pentagon's invisible boy? To get out from under the weight of such questions — to find his way in the forest, to find his light in the dark, if no longer to find his dad — he is writing this book. It concerns the Building, the bomb, and the battle, still raging, for America.

ONE

ONE WEEK IN 1943

1. HELL'S BOTTOM

A year after the Al Qaeda attack, at a rededication ceremony on September 11, 2002, much was made of the post-9/11 repairs having been completed in a mere twelve months. No one seemed to know that the entire Building had been constructed from start to finish in less than sixteen months. It was made of cement for which 700,000 tons of sand were dredged from the Potomac riverbed next to the site. The river's edge is key to the Building's impression, evoking a forbidden temple of the timeless past, as if looming over the ancient Nile.[1] The picturesque lagoon that sets off the River Entrance, like a plaza waiting to receive the barge of Cleopatra, is a vestige of that dredging.[2]

Relatively little steel was used in the construction — those ramps instead of elevators — because it was needed just then for bullets, shells, and tanks. Planners took for granted that once the war emergency had passed, the hulking edifice would be handed over for civilian use: a depot for government records or — and this is what my mother told me, which is why I always believed it, even after learning it was a myth — a facility for the care of wounded and disabled veterans, the ramps built for wheelchairs and gurneys. The largest hospital in the world. My mother's devotion to this idea was sacralized when my brother Joe was stricken with polio, making her a haunter of hospitals, a connoisseur of ramps. Joe's polio, in turn, transformed into worship her devotion to the similarly stricken, but nobly unbowed, President Roosevelt. He was photographed visiting the Building just before its completion in January 1943, but there is no record of his using a wheelchair there.

In fact, Roosevelt was deeply conflicted about the Pentagon. As assistant secretary of the Navy during World War I, he had ordered the construction of barracks-like "tempos" all over Washington, and these eyesores were still there twenty years later, despoiling especially the Mall between the Lincoln Memorial and the Washington Monument. The structures were a source of self-rebuke to Roosevelt. The War Department alone occupied seventeen separate facilities around Washington. To consolidate the offices in one handsome place, FDR had personally overseen the construction of a new headquarters building at 21st Street in Foggy Bottom, but no sooner was it completed than World War II broke out. By mid-1941, the Army had mushroomed to a million and a half men; the new headquarters was instantly inadequate, and senior Army officials told the president they would never use it.[3] Though its entrance was decorated by a huge, undiplomatic martial mural — helmeted soldiers in combat — the building would become the headquarters of the State Department, which it remains to this day.

The size of the space was not the only issue. The freshly empowered Army wanted its new building to be set apart from the so-called Federal West Executive Area, apart from entanglements with, and the limits of, the seat of government. In a time of peril, the Army was not about to be treated as just another bureaucratic function, alongside Interior and Commerce and Indian Affairs. The Army would transcend. Senior military officials immediately began scouting sites outside the city — this despite the explicit terms of congressional appropriations for construction within Washington.[4] A site in Virginia appealed to the Army because, for one thing, District of Columbia architectural supervision would not hinder the mammoth scale envisioned by departmental planners. Yet even across the river the initial site selection proved controversial. The D.C. Fine Arts Commission, chaired by Roosevelt's cousin Frederick A. Delano, reached across the Potomac to denounce the "flagrant disregard"[5] of context in the Army's wish to build at the western end of Memorial Bridge. The site was then occupied by Arlington Farms, an agricultural research facility — all that was left of Robert E. Lee's original plantation, the rest of which had long before been seized by the federal government to serve as the national cemetery. Recovering from the punitive impulse of that requisition, Washington had, in the 1920s, established a symbol of reconciliation between North and South by aligning an axis along Memorial Bridge between Lee's becolumned mansion atop the hill at Arlington and the Lincoln Memorial, which was completed in 1922. Joined to Lincoln in this way, Lee was thus linked along the Mall to George Washington and the Capitol. The proposed new War Department building, just below the Lee mansion and directly on that axis, would destroy the geographic symbol of national reconciliation.

When that was pointed out to President Roosevelt, he ordered the War Department building moved about a mile downriver. At the same time, considering the architects' plans for the hulking structure, FDR ordered the size of the building reduced by half. Among other considerations, the president expressed concern for the psychological effect on those who would be employed amid such dominating impersonality.[6] He also affirmed that, after "the present emergency," the War Department headquarters would be returned to Washington where it belonged; no permanent headquarters building would be necessary in Virginia. Roosevelt found himself declaring that the Army could make do, as the Navy would, with yet more tempos. (The Navy Annex was constructed to be temporary, but to this day it sits on the Arlington ridge, above the Pentagon.) When the general in charge of the project objected to these terms, the president said, "My dear General, I'm still Commander-in-Chief of the Army."[7]

The general complied, but only partially. The new downriver site was accepted — an unsightly shack-ridden wasteland called Hell's Bottom. It was a former airfield and railroad yard littered with abandoned tin hangars and rusted-out boxcars. But without Roosevelt's knowledge, the general declined to reduce the size of the Building, and with the help of Virginia congressmen, he protected the appropriations needed to make the construction permanent. By then the Building's architects, led by G. Edwin Bergstrom, who had also designed the Hollywood Bowl, had completed drawings for the upriver site at Arlington Farms. The original design for that now abandoned location called for a simple rectangular footprint, but access roads required one corner of the rectangle to be cut off, leaving an asymmetrical five-sided building. What Bergstrom did was to even up the five sides, producing — voilà — the Pentagon. When the site was moved downriver, the polygonal shape was no longer required by the limits of the roadways, but such was the hurried pace of the project that the architects did not change the design. Eventually Bergstrom and others would mythologize the pentagonal form of the War Department headquarters as an echo of Napoleonic-era fortress architecture.[8] The true, entirely mundane origin of the design would be forgotten.

Over the next year, more than a hundred architects and nearly as many engineers worked around the clock in those abandoned airplane hangars, turning out drawings for the more than fifteen thousand laborers, who often didn't wait for specs. Pearl Harbor was attacked almost three months after groundbreaking, and from then on the already quickened pace of construction was redoubled. "How big should I make that beam across the third floor?" one architect asked another, who replied, "I don't know. They installed it yesterday."[9]

*   *   *

Supervising all of this work was a Corps of Engineers colonel named Leslie R. Groves, who was forty-five years old when appointed to head up Pentagon construction. He was a burly, corpulent man whose belly protruded like lips over his brass-buckled belt.[10] A man of the job, Groves was an important military manager. In charge of the Army's crash building program across the country (in 1940 the Corps's construction budget skyrocketed from $20 million to $10 billion), he had already purchased half the lumber in the United States.[11] Born into an Army family four years after the Battle of Wounded Knee, in 1890, which marked the end of the Indian wars, Groves had spent part of his childhood at Fort Apache, Arizona, living in the house of a man famous for killing Indians.[12] His lifelong hero was General William Tecumseh Sherman, whose "march to the sea" across Georgia legitimized the spirit of total war, which after the Civil War was unleashed on Native Americans.

Groves began as a student at the Massachusetts Institute of Technology, but when his older brother died in 1914 — of a disease contracted at the same Arlington Farms that would much later be the first site proposed for the Pentagon — Groves transferred to West Point. From then on he wore a mustache, which did nothing to soften his stern, unfriendly demeanor. Work in the Corps of Engineers was essentially a matter of management, and Groves proved himself again and again. By the time he was put in charge of Pentagon construction, his most notable prior service had been in Nicaragua, developing plans for a second (never undertaken) canal across the Central American isthmus.[13]

As the Pentagon neared completion, Groves was promoted to brigadier general, although for a reason having to do with his next project, not this one. Among his last decisions in Arlington was one that provided the new Building with separate eating and lavatory accommodations for "colored people" and whites. The dining areas for blacks would be in the basement, and on the other floors, at each corridor junction, double toilet facilities would be built, separated by race. When President Roosevelt visited the Building shortly before its dedication, he asked why there were so many lavatories (more than two hundred), and he was told that the Army was abiding by Virginia's racial laws. Roosevelt had issued an order prohibiting such discrimination throughout the U.S. military only six months earlier, and he told Groves to get rid of the Whites Only signs at once. Groves obeyed. Because he was overridden by the president, the Pentagon would for a long time be the only place in Virginia where segregation was not allowed.[14]

Within days of Roosevelt's visit to the new War Department headquarters, at an understated ceremony presided over by Secretary of War Henry L. Stimson, the Pentagon was dedicated. Wartime exigencies eclipsed such a formality in the memoirs and memories of witnesses. Honor guards would have mounted battle flags in mahogany stands, and portraits of former secretaries of war would have been unveiled. One imagines the Army band playing martial music. Perhaps a ribbon was cut. It was January 15, 1943.[15]

2. UNCONDITIONAL SURRENDER

The coincidence of dates — September 11 (on that day in 1944, American forces would first arrive at the German border, near Trier); January 15 (on that day in 1944, Allied forces would prepare to land at Anzio) — is precious to human beings because it creates the impression that underlying the randomness of everyday life is an orderly structure. The passage of time is not a mere matter of chance, and even things that seem unrelated are tied together, if not by links of causality, then by meaning. Perhaps instead of coincidence, what we are talking about is convergence, which implies more than the bumping together of dissimilar objects. Technically, convergence defines the movement of a person's eyes toward each other in order to look more closely at something. Two things become one, and connection itself becomes the point of focus. "Correspondence" is the word given to this sense of double events, how one event illuminates the other, and of course it provides the very architecture of memory — how present experience constantly evokes that of the past, so that the past may be more fully understood, while the present is more vividly brought to life.

In casting an eye — a pair of eyes — back over the terrain of the past, it may help to juxtapose seemingly disparate events, to expose the hidden connections that alone explain their full significance. Attention to such coincidences in time will characterize this work, beginning with an investigation of events that occurred in one week, from the fifteenth to the twenty-second of January. Things that happened across the world within days of the dedication of the new icon of military might on the shore of the Potomac were disparate events except for the way they set in motion currents of thought and deed that would eventually combine in a kind of chain reaction, transforming attitudes, actions, and ultimately the meaning of the Pentagon itself.

Franklin Roosevelt was not present at the dedication, not because he disapproved of it — although, as we have seen, in part he did — but because just then, on the first trip he took by air as president,[16] he had flown to Casablanca, Morocco. He was in the midst of an eight-day meeting with Prime Minister Winston Churchill, General Henri Giraud, head of state of French North Africa, and General Charles de Gaulle, chief of the "Fighting French." Joseph Stalin was not present at this urgent conference of Allied leaders because Soviet armies were just then throwing back the Germans at Leningrad, lifting a seventeen-month siege. At the same time, Stalin's forces were about to complete the destruction of the whole 300,000-man German army at Stalingrad, where the six-month battle would end on the last day of January. On the eastern front, the days coinciding with the Casablanca conference were the most decisive two weeks of the war, a turning of the tide against the Germans. "There has begun," Stalin said, "a massive expulsion of the enemy from the Soviet land."[17] Armed now with the initiative, Stalin's warmaking would be driven as much by revenge as by strategy, and his allies would have to accommodate it.[18]

At Casablanca, General Dwight Eisenhower was given command of the unified North African forces, and there, too, a tide turned. On January 23, the last day of the conference, the Eighth Army conquered Tripoli. "Rommel is still flying before them," Churchill declared[19] of the advance that marked the beginning of the rout of General Erwin Rommel, which would ultimately cost the Axis armies a million men captured or killed. In the same days of January, British methods of deciphering German military communications, based on a first-generation computer, were finally proving themselves. "Decrypts" of intercepted radio messages were stamped "Ultra Top Secret," which led to the name Ultra for the British reading of enemy messages. Because of Ultra, German U-boats could be readily located and Allied shipping rerouted to avoid them, while Allied air power could home in on the submerged vessels. After January 1943, no Allied merchant ship within range of air cover was sunk by a German submarine.[20] In 1944, the Ultra team forwarded more than forty thousand decoded German intercepts to Allied field commanders. Ultra, which in time laid bare Hitler's own orders to his generals,[21] would ensure Allied dominance over Germany from this month on.

By January 1943 the war in the Pacific had turned its corner, too. The Japanese, set on an invasion of Australia, had been defeated at the Battle of the Coral Sea the previous spring, an Allied triumph that was quickly followed by the Battle of Midway, where the Japanese lost four aircraft carriers and control of the Pacific. After the American conquest of Guadalcanal in August, one island after another fell as the Japanese began their steady retreat to the home islands. By January there was no longer any prospect of a Japanese recovery. All of these factors together made that month — indeed, that week of Casablanca, that week of the Pentagon — the hinge of the war, as Allied victory became a matter of *when* rather than *if*.

Roosevelt reflected this assurance at Casablanca when, overriding the instincts of Churchill, he insisted on defining the Allied war aim for the first time as the "unconditional surrender" of the Axis. The conference deliberated on the subject, but owing to differences between the president and the prime minister, there was no agreed plan to issue a declaration. Roosevelt spontaneously used the phrase in the postconference press briefing, claiming later that it was unintentional — a reference sparked, he said, by an odd thought that General Ulysses S. Grant had been called "Old Unconditional Surrender" — ". . . and the next thing I knew I had said it." Churchill recounts this in his memoir, then adds sarcastically, "I do not feel that this frank statement is in any way weakened by the fact that the phrase occurs in the notes from which he spoke."[22]

That Roosevelt and Churchill differed on this question may reflect nothing more than a pervasive difference between the New World and the Old, but even in America the tradition was less than absolute. Grant had not insisted on unconditional surrender with Robert E. Lee at Appomattox, accepting, for example, Lee's condition that his officers could keep their horses.[23] In Europe, modern wars had ended through the negotiation of conditions. The Crimean War (1853–1856) was concluded when Russia accepted conditions defined by the Vienna "Four Points." Before America entered World War I, Woodrow Wilson proposed conditions for settlement that he characterized as "peace without victory," a phrase he first used in a speech to the U.S. Senate on — coincidentally — January 22, 1916.[24] But America was not to be the mediator. German U-boats included American shipping in their attacks, bringing the United States into war against Germany on April 2, 1917 (although Washington did not declare war against Austria-Hungary until — coincidentally — December 7, 1917).[25] Yet even with this expansion of hostilities, negotiations aimed at defining conditions for ending the war continued. America's entry broke the stalemate, eventually forcing Germany to terms. An armistice with Austria-Hungary was agreed to on November 3, 1918, and with Germany on November 8. The conditions of the armistice were harsh, involving Germany's surrender of territory and of vast amounts of materiel (a long way from Wilson's "peace without victory"), but they were still conditions. Germany was by no means destroyed by the armistice (the subsequent terms of the Treaty of Versailles, signed the following June, were far harsher, leading to the myth of the "stab in the back").

What haunted Roosevelt more than twenty years later was that World War I had ended without the permanent destruction of Germany's capacity to recover as a war-waging nation.[26] In calling for unconditional surrender at Casablanca, his stated purpose was to ensure that Germany would not be able to repeat that recovery — or resuscitate the stab-in-the-back myth. Roosevelt rationalized the demand as aiming only at the prevention of a future war with Germany, and, tangentially, with Japan, but, cutting off what might have been a divisive debate in Congress over war goals, it had a domestic impact as well.

By sounding a note of unprecedented and even brutal determination, it is also likely that Roosevelt was trying to mollify Stalin, who was increasingly impatient for a British-American invasion of Europe. The Western allies' nightmare was that the Soviets, throwing back the Germans after Stalingrad, would enter into a separate peace with Berlin, as the new Soviet regime had done in World War I. The unconditional surrender demand was a signal to the Soviet leader that his Western allies were not going to do any such thing themselves.

In any case, the declaration carried grave implications for the war's duration, the war's conclusion, and the shape of the conflict that would follow the war. If Churchill opposed Roosevelt on this point, it was not because he was indifferent to shoring up Stalin, nor because he had learned history's lessons less well than Roosevelt, nor because he was softer — more "Wilsonian" — than his American counterpart. Churchill, after all, had spent the century up to his elbows in the blood of Britain's imperial wars. That was the experience he was drawing on. Churchill knew that by foreclosing any possible negotiations toward surrender, the Allies were making it more likely that the Axis powers would fight to the bitter end, at a huge cost in lives on both sides, resulting in a level of devastation that would itself be the seedbed of the next catastrophe. This was so because "unconditional surrender" could be taken by an enemy as promising the destruction not just of its armies but of its whole society. Indeed, Joseph Goebbels would tell Germans that this demand issued at Casablanca meant the Allies were set on making slaves of their entire nation.[27] To put such dread in the breast of an enemy population was to make inevitable a fight to the death — or, as Churchill had put it about his own people earlier in the war, when they faced the prospect of conquest by an ascendant Germany, a fight "on the beaches." Knowing of his own ferocious readiness to resist to the last breath, the last ounce of blood, Churchill might have cited Sun Tzu, the ancient Chinese theorist of war, who wrote, "When you surround an army leave an outlet free. Do not press a desperate foe too hard."[28]

"Unconditional surrender" meant that the enemy would have no reason to mitigate the ferocity of its resistance. It was an invitation to the Germans and the Japanese, as their likely defeat came closer, to fight back without restraint, preferring to take their chances even with the brutally immoral tactics of a last stand rather than to accept defeat at the hands of an enemy refusing to offer any terms whatsoever.

Roosevelt's demand for unconditional surrender immediately deprived secretly alienated members of the German high command of the main motive to overthrow the increasingly irrational Hitler. Because such a move could no longer be linked to a hope for some concession from the Allies, the assassination conspiracy that was already brewing among Hitler's staff — and within a few weeks would make its first attempt on Hitler's life — remained marginal and ultimately unsuccessful.[29] In other words, one obvious "condition" on which German leaders might well have sought an end to the war was the removal of Hitler. The Casablanca declaration helped protect the Führer from the rational and pragmatic element among his own staff. It reinforced the fanatics.

And it may have reinforced them in their most maniacal enterprise. "Unconditional surrender" meant that the Allies, aiming only at the complete and final destruction of the Nazi war machine, were not in a position to mitigate the Final Solution. Even if Roosevelt and Churchill at that point did not know the full horror of the genocide, they knew by the time of Casablanca that the systematic and industrialized murder of Jews was under way.[30] They knew, in other words, that Germany, under Hitler, was embarked on an extraordinary barbarity. For the remainder of the war, Roosevelt and other leaders insisted that the best rescue of Jews was the quick and complete defeat of the German military, but from "unconditional surrender" forward, that was, in fact, the only real option the Allies had.

It is not necessary to believe that Hitler would have softened his treatment of Jews had the Allies been willing to negotiate, nor to believe that an end to the genocide would have been a primary Allied demand in such negotiations, in order to grasp that the extremities of the war's denouement and the delay of the war's end enabled the Nazi death machine to do its worst. The policy of unconditional surrender, that is, guaranteed that the war would last long enough for the genocide nearly to succeed. The last savage months of war in Europe saw the deaths of millions of people, not merely the defeat of the Nazi war machine. In the end, there was a technical German surrender, by the military command after Hitler's suicide, but "surrender," unconditional or not, misses the point of what happened. Germany was simply destroyed, and with it much of Europe.

Ironically, Roosevelt would learn at Tehran, ten months after Casablanca, that Stalin, whom he hoped to encourage with the demand of unconditional surrender, was completely opposed to it. Even the harshest conditions, Stalin argued — and if he did not aim to enslave the German population, he certainly aimed to impoverish them — would bring about a settlement far sooner than none at all.[31] Stalin's army, imposing itself "unconditionally" on Germany from the east in the war's last months, would lose a million more men.

What is to be made of such horrors? In fact, there is an entire intellectual discipline devoted to parsing them. The war theorist Thomas Schelling has observed that "pain and shock, loss and grief, privation and horror are always in some terrible degree among the results of warfare, but in traditional military science they are incidental, they are not the object."[32] But "traditional military science" averts its eyes from the harshest fact of war — that it includes a savage momentum operating apart from the intentions of the warriors. In the modern age, that momentum is compounded by technology, when killing becomes both more efficient and more impersonal. When the distance between attacker and victim increases, the psychological effects of battle can become less restrained. Momentum and technology together erode the moralities of the battlefield, even as persons far from the killing continue to expound them. All of this, in addition to rational strategies, is built into the impulse to demand unconditional surrender.

Practical experience of war, winning or losing, trumps war room strategy. In the death struggle, winners and losers together enter a realm defined precisely by "pain and shock, loss and grief, privation and horror" as main objects, instead of as incidentals. This explains the "shrieking public enthusiasm"[33] with which the American populace picked up the cry of unconditional surrender. They, too, had entered the mortal zone.

January 1943 did not signify the moment of Allied victory, but it was clearly the first time — after Midway, Tripoli, and Stalingrad — that Allied leaders could confidently look forward to victory. A demand of unconditional surrender would otherwise have been absurd. The demand can be taken as a marker, therefore, of a shift in the Allied experience of the momentum of war — movement, in effect, toward a spirit of no quarter, no compromise, no stopping short of complete devastation. The death zone had been entered. In this sense, for Roosevelt, and perhaps for the others at Casablanca, that hinge week in January was the extreme boundary, the leaders' version of being at the front, the emergence at last from the fog of war into clarity, energy, and license.

"Unconditional surrender" is the signal of all this. Roosevelt had his rationale — putting the enemy on notice that they had lost — but a dreadful irrationality was at work, too. The demand suggests that the war's momentum had had its way with the war's great leader. While it is necessary to acknowledge among warriors the universal "totality" of the urge to kill at a certain point in combat, it is also important to note, as we have, that statesmen ordinarily avoid overt expressions of such extremity. But Roosevelt did not avoid it. His declaration of unconditional surrender, coming after Allied and Axis forces had been brutally at each other for two years, clearly implied an escalation of threat — a threat of violence carried to an extreme that would be limited, not by any restraint on the part of the Allies, but only by the abject and impotent surrender of the Axis nations.

"Unconditional surrender" was thus a threat of total war, a readiness to embark, if a stubborn enemy so invited it, on a program of total destruction. But destruction of what? The Axis armies? The Axis leadership? Or the entire Axis nations? Could the enemy expect, as Joseph Goebbels warned the Germans to expect, a horde of marauding invaders come to obliterate their society — this war ending as the infamous wars of old had? Children stolen, women turned into sex slaves, men cut to pieces, livestock left to rot.[34] In the Middle Ages, Christians distinguished between *bellum hostile,* which was war waged among Christians and according to the rules of chivalry, and *bellum Romanum,* which was war without regulation, the sort waged against infidels.[35] If the enemy could be defined as radically evil, then the restraints of morality did not apply.

The totality of destruction that was being threatened against the radically evil Axis powers at Casablanca was not specified, and it seems unlikely that Roosevelt consciously defined it for himself — although one wonders whether he would have had to if the far more ruthless Stalin had been present at the conference. The totality of destruction of which the Allied forces were just then becoming capable was probably not clear to Roosevelt either. Indeed, as we shall see shortly, two technological revolutions were even then redefining the meaning of "totality." This time, because of those technologies, the momentum of war unleashed by both the rhetoric and the decisions of Casablanca would be accelerated in ways no one could have imagined. The point is that Roosevelt's declaration, whether or not it marked an unconscious shift toward the pure, vengeful violence of a latent victor, prepared the way for such total violence, wreaked as always by war's own impersonal logic, but also by diabolical human inventiveness as never before.

Technology was about to force the old question: Should the violence of warfare be restricted to military forces, or can it extend to civilian populations? The time was long past when war was an enterprise of feudal elites, monarchs or mercenaries, exempting the peasantry and burgher class except as prizes. Since the rise of popular nationalist wars, beginning with Napoleon, and especially once societies were industrialized, entire nations were routinely mobilized as the source of warmaking power. In the new era, the labor of the whole nation, and its esprit, became crucial elements of national belligerence. The distinction between civilians and soldiers, that is, had been qualitatively different — far easier to maintain — in agrarian societies, where men of the hoe could ignore the battles raging on the hill between men of the horse. Even so, that distinction, in the commitments of statesmen on all sides, still held.

World War I was mainly a war of army against army. Indeed, so was the Civil War in the United States, with the notable exception of Sherman's march to the sea.[36] Sherman embodied the movement from violence for the sake of defeating an army's war-waging ability to violence for the sake of terrorizing a population on which the army depends and for which it fights. By authorizing the berserking of his own forces, setting them loose on civilians, Sherman found a way to turn what had always before been the purposeless violence of pillage and rampage into a highly purposeful campaign. His aim was to use the misery of noncombatants as a point of pressure against the army and its leaders. Sherman, in that sense, stopped being a soldier and became a political strategist — and a terrorist.[37]

In demanding unconditional surrender, Roosevelt surely knew he was setting up in his enemy the fear that soldiers would come at them like murderers. And if that fear, Roosevelt doubtless would have argued, led the enemy more quickly to conditionless surrender, good. Churchill yielded the point at Casablanca, but he opposed Roosevelt because he feared the threat of terrorism latent in the demand would stiffen the resistance not only of the enemy leadership but of whole peoples who would be its target. As it happened, the two revolutions in technology that would move all of this out of the realm of strategic abstraction and onto the field of battle — or into the air above — had their decisive beginnings that same week.

3. OPERATION POINTBLANK

All of the abstractions attached to the idea of unconditional surrender would be made concrete in the consequences of the other large decision that Roosevelt and Churchill made at Casablanca. It led immediately, on January 27, 1943, to the first bombing mission conducted by the U.S. Army Air Forces[38] against Germany proper, an assault by sixty-four B-17s against a submarine yard thirty miles up the Weser River from the North Sea. With this mission, the American air war against the Nazi homeland began. After the new orders issued at Casablanca, the main body of American bombers would be shifted from North Africa to England for air attacks across the Channel. It proved to be a defining moment in World War II, and in American history. At the stick of the lead plane on the January 27 raid was the commander of the 305th Bomber Group of the Eighth Air Force, a controversial young colonel named Curtis LeMay.

Winston Churchill had gone into the Casablanca conference determined to delay the invasion of northern Europe, an invasion for which Stalin, and to a lesser extent Roosevelt, were impatient. For Churchill, whose nightmare would be a repetition of the static trench-line stalemate of World War I, postponement was a simple matter of waiting until an overwhelmingly unstoppable Allied force could be assembled, and that logistical sine qua non was at least a year away. In the near term, British and American ground forces would begin their assault against the German-occupied territories, but through Sicily and Italy. The move against France would have to wait until 1944. But to prepare for that invasion, to mollify Stalin for its delay, and to satisfy American impatience for a direct blow against Hitler, Churchill was anxious for Roosevelt's agreement to an expansion of the air bombardment of Germany, which the Royal Air Force had been carrying on, with limited success, since 1940. Now that the tide had turned against Rommel in North Africa, and with U.S. factories producing tidal waves of new aircraft and bombs, the time had come for British and American flyers to join forces. For their part, the air commanders of both nations were eager to demonstrate that the devastating effects of concerted strategic bombing against Germany itself would make the land invasion of the Continent unnecessary. The air war would enshrine the air forces as the dominant military muscle of the new age. Roosevelt and Churchill were skeptical on the point, but for their own reasons they agreed to unleash the flyboys. At Casablanca, the two leaders took up Royal Air Force and Army Air Forces proposals for Operation Pointblank, aimed at the destruction of German industrial and economic capacity.

But here again, Churchill and Roosevelt had their differences, and at first glance they can seem to be opposite ones from what divided them on the question of unconditional surrender. This is so because a strategy of air bombardment aimed at a nation's warmaking capacity raised the question of the distinction between combatant and noncombatant. When the war had first broken out, FDR, speaking on September 9, 1939, had beseeched the war leaders on both sides to "under no circumstances undertake the bombardment from the air of civilian populations or of unfortified cities."[39] But when Churchill was elected prime minister on the following May 10, his island nation was mortally threatened, and the next day, as one of his first acts, he ordered the bombing of military targets in Germany.

Three days later, on May 13, 1940, the Luftwaffe began bombing Rotterdam, terrorizing the civilian population. A little over a month later, Churchill revised his order so that "military" targets could include civilian areas near industrial and transportation centers. In July, the idea of extermination found its way into Churchill's rhetoric: "But when I look round to see how we can win the war I see that there is only one sure path," he wrote to his minister of aircraft production, "and that is absolutely devastating, exterminating attack by very heavy bombers from this country upon the Nazi homeland."[40]

German retaliation could be anticipated, and it came that summer and fall in the form of the blitz.[41] The German raids against British cities were a savage assault, lasting six months and resulting in forty thousand civilian deaths, but it was an assault Churchill could welcome — though he surely regretted such carnage — since vengeful targeting of urban areas in England had the effect of sparing the vulnerable bases and irreplaceable aircraft of the Royal Air Force. The British and the Germans moved in synchrony toward terror bombing, although some historians emphasize Churchill's role as the originator of a strategy in which bombardment from the air, and against civilians, would be central.[42]

Winston Churchill had proven himself capable of arguing against "air bombing of the noncombatant populations for the purpose of slaughter,"[43] but by the time of Casablanca, moral distinctions between direct and indirect purposes, as with the lost distinctions between industry and industrial workers, their workplaces and their residences, military capability and national morale, had become a fog as impenetrable as London's. Or so it seemed in London. In Washington it still looked different, but that was certainly, in part at least, because Washington's very existence, unlike London's, was not felt to be at risk.[44]

At Casablanca, Americans wanted no part of British "area bombing," as the general attacks had become known. By and large, the AAF leaders, aware of the brutality of the entire enterprise, declined to make the argument for their approach in the language of morality. LeMay summed up that reluctance: "To worry about the *morality* of what we were doing — Nuts."[45] The U.S. preference for "precision bombing," carried out in daylight raids, as opposed to the British practice of attacking under cover of darkness,[46] was a practical matter, they said. The British assumption that German morale would crack under bombardment was wrong, the Americans thought, but strategic reasoning was even more important. Bombing raids, in the American view, should directly and quickly affect the battlefield. Thus, as one former AAF targeting officer told me in an interview, there was little point in taking out a steel factory, since that would have an impact on German fighting ability only in a year or so, the time it took for raw steel to be made into tanks. Hitting a fuel dump would deprive tanks of gasoline within weeks. Scaling targets in this way, the Americans had neither strategic nor tactical interest in purely civilian targets.[47]

The Americans knew that in 1941 the RAF bombing campaign had been so inept that more British flyers lost their lives than Germans on the ground. It was that frustration that had sparked the dropping of all pretense, in 1942, that military-civilian distinctions were to be drawn. But as the Americans knew, the "dehousing" of German industrial workers had not been successful.[48] Unescorted and lightly armed British bombers — the Lancaster, the Halifax, the Wellington — flew at night primarily because otherwise they would be shot down. And flying at night, especially in the early period before black-out precautions were perfected, made even partially glowing cities the obvious target.[49]

The Americans intended something very different. Well-armed B-17s, carrying high-explosive, as opposed to incendiary, bombs and using superior bomb sights in daylight, would pinpoint and destroy the factories and bases that the RAF night raids had missed. Indeed, even the most violent British raids — forty-five thousand Germans made homeless in one night in Cologne the previous May[50] — had little or no measurable impact on German industrial capacity, much less on battlefield readiness.[51]

Despite the strategic rationale in favor of precision bombing, and despite the hard-nosed language of the likes of LeMay, the moral repugnance against deliberate targeting of civilians that Roosevelt himself had expressed at the start of the war was strongly, if implicitly, characteristic of most AAF leaders. At Casablanca, it was General Ira C. Eaker, commander of the Eighth Air Force, who made the main, practical argument for precision versus area bombing, but his superior, the AAF's chief, General H. H. Arnold,[52] defined the American preference as a "spur to conscience," as "humanitarian but nonetheless practical." In addressing his officers not long after Casablanca, Arnold said, "War, no matter how it may be glorified, is unspeakably horrible in every form. The bomber simply adds to the extent of the horror, especially if not used with discretion; but when used with the proper degree of understanding, it becomes in effect, the most humane of all weapons."[53]

Eaker, Arnold, and Roosevelt carried the argument with Churchill, who accepted the American method — for the Americans. When, on January 21, 1943, Casablanca issued the order for Operation Pointblank, to be carried out by a newly established Combined Bomber Offensive, it was agreed that the RAF would conduct its area bombing at night, while the AAF would wage a campaign of precision bombing in daylight. Together, the Casablanca declaration said, the Allied air forces would bring about "the progressive destruction and dislocation of the German military, industrial and economic system, and the undermining of the morale of the German people to a point where their capacity for armed resistance is fatally weakened."

The American public could read reports of this decision without appreciating its inherent contradiction — industrial bombing and morale bombing were not the same thing — but they were also reading in that same month proposals from respectable quarters for a drastic shift in American air war strategy. As the historian Richard Rhodes points out, the January 1943 issue of *Harper's Magazine* carried an impassioned appeal for the firebombing of Japan's "matchbox" cities. "We must strike hard with everything we have at the spot where it will do the most damage to the enemy."[54]

But not in Europe. Not yet. American flyers would learn the hard way that "precision" was more fantasy than reality. "To find a target," a member of the postwar U.S. Strategic Bombing Survey observed, "was not necessarily to hit it. Nothing in World War II air operations was subject to such assault as open agricultural land."[55] The weather patterns over northern Europe, for one thing, guaranteed that bombers would rarely fly except through or over clouds. Targets were almost always impossible to see, and when they could be seen, the much-touted Norden bombsight turned out to be less impressive than its inventors claimed. In stateside training, air crews had routinely scored hits from fifteen thousand feet, landing dummy payloads within a few hundred feet of targets, but as the former AAF targeting officer told me, in actual conditions of combat bombardment, "we got ten percent of the bomb load within a mile of the aiming point. Some precision."[56]

That experience was in the future, and so was the punitive collapse of the distinction between combatants and noncombatants that would pile high the rubble of German cities and the ashes of Japanese cities in the spring and summer of 1945. As of January 1943, the American military still defined itself in terms of martial honor that refused to target innocents. This starting point of U.S. strategic doctrine has particular poignancy in the context of the career path of the young AAF targeting officer whom I have cited twice. His name is Carl Kaysen. He reported for service with the Eighth Air Force in London in that same early winter of 1943, and after two years of picking targets for American bombers flying into Germany, he would pursue a career as an academic economist that would bring him prominence. Later in this story we will see how, as a senior adviser to President Kennedy, Kaysen revisited the mortal question of targeting civilians from the air, but on a far deadlier scale — an experience that made him one of the Cold War's most important arms control advocates.

That first Casablanca debate between the RAF and the AAF was, in effect, a rehearsal for the arms control argument. General Arnold characterized the Casablanca order separating U.S. tactics and aims from those of the British as "a major victory, for we would bomb in accordance with American principles using methods for which our planes were designed."[57]

Henry Harley Arnold — "Hap," as he was known, a man of cheerful disposition — was chief of the Army Air Forces through most of the war, a responsibility he exercised mostly from his office in the Pentagon. Indeed, one of the innovations in this war was the way in which close military supervision was conducted far from the battle lines and across theaters, with George C. Marshall directing worldwide Army operations from the Building by the Potomac and Arnold directing the Air Forces from there, especially once the firebombing of Japan began. This distancing of military supervision from the battlefield is one consequence of the technological shift, noted above, that did so much to accelerate the momentum of killing.

General Marshall was Arnold's superior, of course, but the Army Air Forces had its own corridors in the Pentagon, and the airmen at once set out to gain independence. The Pentagon monumentalized the rivalry between the service branches, even as the politics of theater operations intensified it. The Army forever assumed the campaigns in Europe and the Pacific would be won by invasions. The AAF assumed bombing would bring victory, and when that did not happen in Germany, the bombing of Japan became more ferocious. If Navy admirals and Army generals criticized that bombing, it would not be, first, for reasons of morality.

The Navy, for its part, assumed that the decisive factor in the war would be blockade, and by the end admirals would criticize the morality of bombing and invasion both. But here, too, ethics came second to service self-interest, since a blockade is not known for sparing innocents. The Navy showed disdain for the other branches by refusing to move its command offices into the Pentagon, claiming a distance — and a freedom of operation — that foreshadowed the interservice conflicts after the war.[58] The leaders of the Army Air Forces, for their part, refused to do anything that might subordinate their purposes to the other service branches. For example, though a combination of air bombardment and mine laying had already proven itself effective against enemy submarines, Arnold declined to deploy his warplanes in anti-sub activity because to do so, submitting to Navy battle orders, took away from AAF autonomy. Such narrowly made decisions, in which interservice conflict took priority over conflict with the enemy, would negatively affect the conduct of the war and do much to shape the postwar world. The Pentagon was quick to embody, and enable, all of this.

4. LeMay

H. H. Arnold, cheerful disposition or no, was stricken by heart attacks five times during the war, and he retired not long after V-J Day. An American high school was named for him — which I attended — at the Air Force base in Wiesbaden, Germany, a base to which my father was assigned in the late 1950s. Wiesbaden was Air Force headquarters in Europe; as a hospital city in wartime, it had never been bombed. Nearby Mainz and Frankfurt were even then not fully cleared of Pointblank rubble. Wiesbaden, seventy miles from the Iron Curtain, was at the Cold War's epicenter, with its wings of nuclear-laden medium-range bombers poised to strike at Moscow and its secret hangar housing Francis Gary Powers's U-2 spy plane. From Wiesbaden, Curtis LeMay had overseen the Berlin airlift, the great Air Force triumph of 1948–49, when all the besieged city's needs were supplied with a round-the-clock run of C-54s and C-47s, lasting more than a year — an operation dubbed "the LeMay Coal and Feed Company."

From 1957 to 1959, Dad served as chief of staff of the U.S. Air Force in Europe, status that leaked onto me in a world that worshiped rank as much as it feared it. I had a blast in that school, playing football, having a cheerleader girlfriend, running for class president and winning, coming of age as a "Hap" myself. There was a portrait of General Arnold in the high school entryway. That he seemed our patron, our mascot even, gave me a feeling of connection with him that I still have. Attending his high school, loving it, sealed my identity as a son of the Air Force.

As my senior year began, the brass hats yanked on the tether tying my father to the Pentagon — except for the two years in Wiesbaden, he served his entire career in the Building — and he returned to Washington with the rest of my family. To my surprise and delight, my parents allowed me to stay on in Wiesbaden, living in the dormitory, to complete my senior year. I graduated from H. H. Arnold High School in 1960 and then returned to Washington to live with my brothers and parents on Generals' Row at Bolling Air Force Base, a few miles downriver from the Pentagon. By then Dad, wearing his third star, was inspector general of the Air Force.

One Friday night the summer after graduation, my buddy Pete and I went to the base theater for the movie; admission was a quarter. The film was the just released *Spartacus,* the Kirk Douglas–Tony Curtis account of a slave revolt in Rome. Pete and I, soon to enroll as freshmen at Georgetown, were decked out in button-down shirts and Ivy League chinos — cuffed cotton trousers with little belts in back, a style that disappeared soon after. Almost everyone else in the base theater was wearing tan fatigues. I loved going to movies there because the theater was always filled with rambunctious young airmen who hooted at the onscreen dames and hollered at the bad guys.

But sometimes everyone in the theater would grow quiet, and this was one of those nights. No sooner had the movie started than a pungent cloud of cigar smoke drifted forward from the back row. Since smoking was forbidden, everyone in the dark theater knew who it was, the one person on the base to whom such rules did not apply: General Curtis E. LeMay.

In 1960, LeMay, by then a four-star general, was vice chief of staff of the Air Force, living next door to my family's house on Generals' Row. From my place at the basketball hoop on the garage, I often glimpsed him going to his staff car, which sat purring at the curb, the blue-uniformed driver saluting at the door. LeMay, a large man with wavy salt-and-pepper hair, moved at a good clip. With his stocky bulk he had the hefty grace of a fullback and often carried a file folder under his arm like a football. His snarl was always organized around that cigar. Once in a while he'd glance my way, perhaps throw a bare nod in my direction, perhaps not.

To me, as to those airmen, LeMay was our Spartacus, our Ben-Hur, our Julius Caesar. And like Caesar, he was known to be ruthless. "I'll tell you what war is about" — here is a typical pronouncement of LeMay's, the sort of *mal mot* that would be quoted in whispers behind his back — "you've got to kill people, and when you've killed enough they stop fighting."[59]

In the military, a man assumed to be feared by the enemy can, by his comrades, be simultaneously held in great esteem — and equally feared. So as the telltale cigar smoke wafted through the dark, a cold silence descended on the theater. There was no hooting now. We took our cues from the radioactive presence behind us, silent too but for the general's odd, occasional grunt, which sparked stifled bursts of nervous laughter in the airmen. The film seemed to last forever. The crowd itched to be out. But as intimidated as we were by LeMay's presence, we were also awed. A much-told story had it that he had once approached a B-52 with a full payload on the flight line, lit cigar in his mouth. A bold air policeman said, "General, you'd better put that cigar out. The plane might explode." To which LeMay replied, "It wouldn't dare."

The B-17s that LeMay led into German airspace on January 27, 1943, flew in stepped formations, dozens of aircraft nested together and moving as one creature, a swarm. With crews of nine — four officers and five enlisted men — the planes were cramped, cold, dangerous. The men were young; it was not unusual for the command pilot to be nineteen or twenty years old.[60] The planes carried heavy machine guns on turrets in the belly, back, chin, nose, and tail of the fuselage. They carried three tons of bombs, which they released over targets at twenty thousand feet. But German antiaircraft guns had a range of up to that altitude, and superior German Messerschmitts scrambled to meet the formation of American bombers. The first time LeMay led a bombing mission, over France the previous November, he had ordered his group to take no evasive action, flying straight toward the targeted railway yards and going well below twenty thousand feet, under a canopy of clouds that blocked the bombsights. This was a break with the long-established RAF practice of staying high and of zigzag flying to avoid German flak and fighters, but those tactics often threw off navigators and bombardiers. LeMay wanted to hit what he was aiming at. But at his order to fly right through the flak, his men objected, "Sir, it can't be done."

"Yes, it can," he replied. "And you're going to see me do it." LeMay piloted the lead plane. And it worked. LeMay's group, his biographer reports, "had

put down twice as many bombs on the target as any other group. And none
of its planes were shot down. Within three weeks, every group in the 8th Air
Force was flying straight-and-level bomb runs, taking no evasive action over
the targets."[61] Eventually German gun batteries and pursuit planes adjusted to
this method, and the AAF's loss rate would climb, but because the Americans
were able to get their bombs closer to the "aiming points" than the evasion-
minded RAF, it took fewer missions to knock out targets. This meant that
while AAF losses were considerably lower over the long haul,[62] the peril of
each mission under LeMay increased.[63]

The B-17 missions were nightmarish under the best of circumstances.
The planes flew in close formation, with the most dangerous point being
flight through the "box" of antiaircraft fire that awaited almost every mission.
In addition to enemy fighters and flak to worry about, there was often panicked machine-gun fire coming from friendly B-17s on either side. In order to
accommodate the numerous portals for those machine guns, the fuselage was
open to the air, which was typically thirty or forty degrees below zero. The
crewmen's fleece-lined flight suits were heated with electrical wires, but they
often malfunctioned. "More men were disabled by frostbite," according to
one historian, "than by combat wounds."[64] Oxygen masks were essential, but
at that temperature moisture in the lines, commonly resulting from breath-
ing, could freeze. If that happened, the pilot would have to risk blackout or
suffocation for his affected crew member, or drop out of formation to a lower
altitude. But waiting German pursuit planes could easily pick off such a lone
bomber, and the more U.S. missions were flown into Germany, the better
those pursuit planes became.

More than seventy air bases from which bombers flew[65] dotted the English countryside. Returning B-17s were increasingly battered, and increasing
numbers did not return. Those carrying wounded airmen shot off flares as
they approached the base so that other planes would let them land first. Flight
surgeons reported that men who were not wounded were more apt to suffer
from "undue fatigue," which meant the trauma of fear.[66] As the campaign
progressed, LeMay was not happy. He began gathering his flyers in the base's
mess hall after each mission — every man in his group, enlisted and officer
alike. He closed the doors. What was said in the room would stay there. "We
want to know what went right, what went wrong, and why it went wrong," he
told them. "And each of you is in the act. Everybody has his say." Referring to
himself, he added, "If you think your group commander is a stupid son-of-a-
bitch, now is the time to say it. And why."[67] The permanent snarl on LeMay's
face was, in fact, caused by a mild case of Bell's palsy — what he was hiding
with that cigar — and he was not the mean bastard strangers took him for. He
was the son of unsuccessful parents, had grown up rootless and in poverty,

and paid his way through Ohio State as a steelworker. His stipend as an ROTC cadet was a crucial financial supplement, and his military experiences, including his time in Army flying school, gave his life meaning. He was commissioned as a flyer in 1929, and at last he knew who he was. He distinguished himself by a passionate focus on the methods of war fought from the air.

For all his brusqueness, he never considered himself better than the men under him, and they knew it. The main thing they saw was a commander who led from the front, who shared every risk. His determination to destroy enemy targets with utmost efficiency, they saw soon enough, was, in the long run if not the short, their best protection. They were afraid of him — and revered him.

A turning point in Curtis LeMay's attitudes came some months after that first late-January flight into Germany, when he was so sure that precision was as possible for American airmen as it was preferable. On August 17, 1943, an assault force of 146 B-17s was to bomb the Messerschmitt factory at Regensburg on the Danube, on the far side of Germany. To take out the source of Luftwaffe fighter planes — this would be the most important raid of the war so far. Flying that distance would certainly make it the most dangerous. Tension mounted as the day approached.

AAF doctrine proclaimed that the so-called Flying Fortress, unlike the British Lancaster, was a bomber that could protect itself, needing no fighter escorts with their considerably shorter ranges. Regensburg was final disproof of that, and the formation of B-17s, with LeMay at the stick of the lead plane, had to fight its way through endless clouds of flak — and, at times, body parts and broken bits of steel hurtling through the air from planes that were hit. German attack planes, defending the Messerschmitt factory as if it were their very cradle, took down 24 of the 146 American bombers. Losses from all AAF raids that day would total 60, a disaster compared with previous losses.[68] As the bombers were shot down, surviving planes moved forward to fill in the formation. In daylight, without taking evasive action, almost every plane was hit by the time the wing began its bomb run. The German fighters were low on fuel by then, and they dropped away. When the battered American force finally approached the well-defended target, antiaircraft fire opened up. Yet over the next twenty-two minutes, LeMay's planes scored direct hits on the Messerschmitt factory, "one of the most accurate bombardments of the war."[69]

LeMay, pushing fully across the continent and landing with his survivors in North Africa, had to have been staggered by the mission. Medical officers described such trauma in others as "a wasteland in which to wander, filled with shadows of theories, dusty slogans, and dire predictions."[70] But LeMay kept his reactions to himself. After a week of makeshift repairs at a desert air base, mechanics cannibalizing the worst-hit planes to restore the others, LeMay led his remnant force back to England, dropping 144 tons of bombs on a German air base at Bordeaux on the way.[71]

The assumption of the leaders of the Combined Bomber Offensive that was launched at Casablanca in 1943 was that bombers would deal a decisive blow to German military capability. Over the next two years it turned out to be true, but not in the way those leaders expected. As we have seen, most of the explosives dropped from Allied planes did little lasting damage to German fighting capacity. Industrial and military targets on the ground were missed or damaged only temporarily. Ironically, by destroying city centers the bombers often reinforced the economic sectors on which industry depended. Waiters and clerks in downtown restaurants and businesses "forcibly unemployed by the bombers flocked to the war plants to find work . . . The bombers had eased the labor shortage."[72]

The horrors inflicted on civilians also did little to deflate the nation's war-fighting morale; if anything, German morale was stiffened. But the effect of the Allied bomber offensive on the Luftwaffe was another matter, for it was not on the ground that Pointblank had its effect, but in the air. In a year and a half, the German air force exhausted itself in the attempt to impede or stop the American and British bombers, and *that* would be decisive. By the time of D-Day in June 1944, the dreaded Messerschmitts, having been taken down over Germany by P-51s, Thunderbolts, and the gunners of B-17s, were not a factor in the skies over Normandy. The Luftwaffe launched a mere 250 combat sorties on D-Day, compared with 8,722 American sorties. The Allied invasion succeeded because, after eighteen months of air battles over the fatherland, German air power could no longer resist it. If the Allies had intended this outcome, the Pointblank campaign would be regarded as strategic genius. It was unforeseen good luck, an after-the-fact justification of what would otherwise have been rank failure. General Eisenhower anticipated this advantage, telling his forces as they prepared to go ashore, "If you see fighting aircraft over you, they will be ours."[73]

5. THE WHIZ KID

LeMay would become controversial in the 1960s for his denunciations of the "swivel-chair intellectual types" with whom he had to work in the Pentagon, but in the same week that he set off on that first mission to Germany — the week of the Building's dedication, of Stalingrad, Tripoli, "unconditional surrender," and the Casablanca declaration launching the combined air offensive

— a brilliant young Harvard intellectual flew from the United States to England to work as a civilian consultant for LeMay's command in the Eighth Air Force.[74] He was a professor of statistical analysis at the Harvard Business School, and his job would be to use the disciplines of his new science to cut through "the shadows of theories, dusty slogans, and dire predictions" that were coming to characterize the strategic thinking of both the war-weary British Bomber Command and the upstart Eighth Air Force. Statistical analysis — "stat control" — would be key to the Eighth Air Force's ability not only to track inventories of materiel and ordnance and to weed out inefficiencies in supply and maintenance, but to evaluate the performance of its flyers. Full of confidence, the consultant set about using his objective methods of measurement and prediction to bring order to the escalating chaos of America's first air war.

The flyers of the Eighth Air Force resisted stat control's forms and questionnaires, and the professor's very presence, but that would not stop him. Soon enough commanders began to depend on him. His name was Robert S. McNamara.

"I worked alongside LeMay," McNamara told me in the winter of 2003. We were sitting in his office in Washington. He was an old man now, his hair still slicked back but very thin and white. Wary of interviews,[75] McNamara had agreed to see me, he said at the outset, because "I have great admiration for your father." My father had died in 1991, his death coinciding exactly with the start of the Gulf War. (In another of those coincidences, the 2003 Iraq War had begun on March 19, my late father's birthday.)

Instead of asking first about the time my father worked for McNamara in the Pentagon — we would get to that — I asked him about his experiences with LeMay that winter of 1943.

"At that time," McNamara said, "the abort rate was very high, both the abort rate and the loss rate . . . very, very high." The jargon of sixty years earlier came back to him. "Abort rate" referred to the percentage of bombers that had to return to their bases in England before reaching the target area; "loss rate" referred to the number of bombers brought down in combat. "We were bombing by daylight, as contrasted to the British bombing at night. We believed that you couldn't hit anything at night, and the British believed that while accuracy was much less at night, their casualties were much less because it was harder for fighters to bring the bombers down."

McNamara became animated as he remembered the challenge. He and his fellow stat control experts were assigned to analyze bomber performance in raids over Germany. The large question of area bombing versus precision bombing — embedded in day versus night bombing and the true separation between the AAF and the RAF — was not the point of McNamara's inquiry.

He was looking at what could be measured, counted, analyzed. "I think the Eighth Air Force abort rate was twenty percent — twenty percent of our planes weren't even getting to the target — and the question was, what was causing that? So we devised what was called, I think, a form 1-A, and the command required the flyers to fill it out after each mission. Did you get to the target? Did you hit the target? If you didn't hit the target, what was the cause?"

Reported causes included failure of the electric heaters in the flying seats: "therefore they were freezing and had to turn back. Another frequent cause was guns jammed . . . There was a whole list of these causes. And we went through all this stuff." After McNamara and his stat control wizards did their analysis, they came up with an explanation for the high abort rate that was not on form 1-A. "The answer," he told me, "was probably fear" — what the medical officers would soon be calling "undue fatigue."

The clue to understanding the abort rate was to look at the loss rate. "The loss rate was extremely high, four percent." Actually, by the time McNamara was doing his statistical analysis, the loss rate was approaching 7 percent, and the damage rate was more than 30 percent. On many missions, total losses approached 50 percent.[76] "The average for each flyer was twenty-five missions," McNamara went on. "Now that didn't mean that a hundred percent of everybody would be killed, but it meant that a hell of a lot of people were getting killed. So many of the crews were turning back out of fear. They conceived of reasons to justify turning back. But it was fear."[77]

I interviewed a man who had flown in a B-17 as a bombardier, perched in the plastic bubble in the nose of the plane. He told me that he and his fellow crew members never spoke of fear, but he recalled the lurch in his stomach every time these words came through his earphones from the navigator: "Okay, we're over enemy territory." Looking ahead at a sky full of black puffs, he thought, every time, "We'll never get through that."[78]

A 4 percent loss rate did not mean that a flyer had a 100 percent chance of dying over the course of twenty-five slated missions, but it did mean that many airmen failed to make the twenty-fifth flight. "It has come to be an accepted fact," one airman wrote at the time, "that you will be shot down eventually . . . It is impossible to complete a full tour of duty."[79] The airmen's fear was not only for themselves, however. LeMay interviewed one command pilot and reported finding that he "was not worried about himself. He had not gone yellow; he was perfectly willing to see himself expended . . . But he simply couldn't bring himself to the point of taking another crew into combat, and then losing some of them. It had happened too often."[80] As one squadron leader put it to AAF psychiatrists, he was "ghosted by his dead friends, who," the psychiatrists reported, "will not leave him alone or give him peace of mind."[81]

Whether judged harshly as "going yellow" or more compassionately as having empathy for fellow crewmen, the measurable incidence of fear as a main factor in mission failure was dismaying. McNamara reported his findings to LeMay, who responded by issuing new orders to his flyers. "'Our abort rate is too high,' LeMay's statement said, 'and the cause of it is fear. Therefore, I will be in the lead plane on these missions, and any crew that takes off, and that doesn't get to the target, will be court-martialed,'" McNamara said and shook his head slowly, remembering LeMay's declaration with evident admiration. Then McNamara added, "Well, the abort rate dropped."

The admiration was apparently mutual. LeMay's regard for this Harvard professor, and what his analysis could mean for the performance of his flyers, is evident in the fact that in March 1943, just weeks after being assigned to the Eighth Air Force as a civilian consultant, McNamara was commissioned directly as a captain. He rose quickly through the ranks to colonel and followed LeMay later in the war to the Pacific theater, where once again he brought his methods to bear on the performance of LeMay's bombers. Statistical analysis would not be used, however, to measure the consequences of the simultaneous American movement, about which we will see more, from precision to area bombing.

6. LESLIE GROVES DOES IT ALL

Technology was driving change — change in the way war was fought and change in the way war was thought about. The center of change was the Pentagon, and in that crucial week of January 1943, technology and the Building came together in one man, Leslie Groves. As we saw, he had supervised the construction of the new War Department headquarters, and now that that was completed he was ready for new duty. Groves was the son of an army chaplain and a man who loved Indian fighters and General Sherman. He had supervised the finish work on the new War Department headquarters — those Whites Only lavatories — but in that same period he had undertaken another, more momentous responsibility. Before the Building's January completion, Groves had already been dividing his time. In September 1942, he had just testified before a congressional committee on Army construction programs when a general stopped him in the hallway outside the hearing room. "The Secretary of War has selected you for a very important assignment," the general said, "and the President has approved the selection." Groves asked where, was told Washington, and he immediately protested that he wanted a combat assignment. "If you do the job right," the general said, "it will win the war."[82]

The job had begun in a laboratory. The nucleus of a uranium atom had first been split at the Kaiser Wilhelm Institute of Chemistry in Berlin in 1938, an event that would prompt Albert Einstein to send his much-noted 1939 letter to President Roosevelt warning of the German uranium bomb project.[83] Fear of the German program provided an urgent and ongoing motivation for physicists working in America. One of them, for example, went home for lunch every day through 1944 and 1945 to turn on his shortwave radio to London broadcasts just to see if the city was still there.[84] Two and a half years after Einstein's letter, scientists led by Enrico Fermi at the University of Chicago set in motion, on December 2, 1942, the first self-sustaining nuclear chain reaction, finally proving that an atomic bomb was feasible. If there was any reluctance among the scientists to proceed with the development of a bomb, it was undercut, especially for those who were Jewish, by a State Department bulletin issued that same day: two million Jews had already been systematically murdered by the Nazis, and many others were vulnerable.[85] Soon thereafter the Army's effort got serious, and the center of U.S. nuclear weapons research moved from Chicago to a new secret facility in the desert of New Mexico.

By the beginning of 1943, Leslie Groves, now director of the innocuously named Manhattan Engineer District,[86] had discreetly pulled back from the last phase of Pentagon construction and begun to inform himself about the supersecret work of the scientists. When the scientific director of the project, Vannevar Bush,[87] learned of Groves's appointment, he objected because the gruff Army colonel lacked, as Bush wrote, "sufficient tact for the job." But War Secretary Henry Stimson knew Groves from his work on the Pentagon, which provided proof enough of his competence. The Pentagon was the largest building project in history up until that time, but the Manhattan Project, simply as a management task, would far surpass it.[88] In fact, Groves would oversee the construction of an even larger building, the largest in the world: a plant for the manufacture of enriched uranium in Oak Ridge, Tennessee.[89] Within days of his hallway encounter with that general, Groves was promoted to general himself, and he moved back to the Washington side of the river. His office was in the so-called New War Department Building in Foggy Bottom, the Roosevelt-favored building that Groves's Pentagon had just trumped, in spades.

Among his first challenges was the large-scale recruitment of, and the imposition of strict discipline on, scientists who would inevitably disdain him. There was a profound clash of cultures: Philip Morrison, a young physicist brought into the project by his mentor J. Robert Oppenheimer, remembered the permanent jolt of having armed guards on duty in hallways outside the laboratories.[90] When Groves took in the scientists' concern about what their counterparts might be accomplishing in Nazi laboratories, his simple response was to propose the kidnapping and assassination of German physicists.[91] Soon the scientists came to admire what one of their leaders, I. I. Rabi, would call Groves's "eccentric administrative genius."[92] In the same momentous few days that saw the completion of the Pentagon, the demand of unconditional surrender, the liberation of Stalingrad, the taking of Tripoli, and the first American air attacks against Germany, the Manhattan Project was formally launched. Now that an atomic weapon was a real possibility, Groves took steps to guarantee an indefinite American monopoly on the secret, moving to exclude even the British, who had been partners until then in the theoretical work.[93] For our purposes, the point to emphasize is that the same hardscrabble genius that informed and enabled the feat of constructing the Pentagon now served as the manager of the world-changing atomic project.

In the figure of Groves we find another of those correspondences that already give resonance to this story. He can be claimed as the father of the Building that over the years came to symbolize, and to promote, a massive bureaucratic power center broken loose from the checks and balances of the government across the river. And judging from the testimony of many who tried to control it, apparently broken loose from the constraints of human will. That "Pentagon effect" on American governance and life is the subject of this book. It focuses on the question of how moral agency (for good and for ill) and impersonal forces beyond human control interact. It sounds like classical tragedy. But that ancient dilemma of agency and fate gained new power when mass bureaucracy and mechanization combined with group paranoia in the nuclear project presided over by Groves.

The American military establishment, in an era when traditional martial destructiveness was joined to nearly unlimited technological capacity, took on a dynamic of its own once it was centered in the Pentagon. Certainly the forces unleashed by World War II — unprecedented destruction, revolutionary technology — set that dynamic going, but soon enough it had a momentum that would never fully submit to controls no matter who applied them. Across the decades, this phenomenon transcended party and ideology. A Republican secretary of defense in a Democratic administration would compare the Building to the frenzied, anarchic Moby Dick, and himself to the doomed Ahab, lashed to the back of the runaway whale.[94] And it was a Republican president, a military hero, who most unforgettably, and most ominously, named the monster that the place had become: the unchecked behemoth, the "military-industrial complex."[95]

At the Pentagon, bureaucracy replaced battle order as the defining social structure of the military. One result was a vast leveling of its human component, the inadvertent creation of a culture that was the opposite of that which thrives on individual leadership, with civilians mixed in with officers, who were in turn mixed in, as members of the Building's anonymous throng, with enlisted men. This bureaucratic leveling solved an early problem of World War II and then made the solution permanent. In the rapid buildup of forces between 1940 and 1943 — the U.S. Army went from 250,000 to 8.3 million men in little more than two years[96] — the Army and Navy found themselves without anywhere near enough qualified officer candidates at all levels, and yet the leadership ranks had to be filled. In that situation, the necessary lowering of intellectual, educational, and personal standards was compensated for by the downplaying of individual quality, of initiative, of integrity. There were exceptions to this leveling on the battlefield, where men of lower rank bravely stepped into the places left vacant by their wounded or killed superiors, rescuing unit cohesiveness, but such individual distinction mattered less in the nascent bureaucracy in Washington. What the personnel lacked there, the organization would supply, which meant that institutional momentum would replace personal decisiveness as the key to American force.

We shall see how figures like Groves, LeMay, James Forrestal, George Kennan, Paul Nitze, and, later, Richard Cheney, Donald Rumsfeld, and Paul Wolfowitz, actively propelled this momentum. Others, like Henry Stimson, Robert McNamara, Carl Kaysen, Jimmy Carter, and, later, Ronald Reagan and Bill Clinton, attempted and failed to turn the tide. Yet this is not mainly a story of bad guys versus good ones, but more a drama of human responses to extreme danger, and the tragedy that follows when those responses make the danger worse.

For the purposes of war, in a time of emergency, this impersonal momentum could seem a good thing, because a bureaucracy driven by technology, and at the mercy of an unexamined energy, is capable of destructiveness far surpassing what one, two, or a dozen individual leaders will deliberately sponsor. And in war, destructiveness is the point. In the Pentagon, there was a leveling, that is, of conscience. Who decided, for example, to firebomb cities or to drop an atomic bomb on Japan or, finally, to link American foreign policy to nuclear force? Individual moral responsibility must always be insisted upon, but reckoning with an unprecedented impersonal force, it can also be said of each of these fateful choices that the Building made them.

*   *   *

And there go its occupants, all streaming down the same ramps in end-of-the-day stampedes, all standing at the same rows of urinals (since the only women here are typists), all (but the brass) eating off trays in the same cafeterias, all initialing the same endlessly circulated manila interoffice envelopes with their cord fasteners making figure eights around discs the color of dried blood. What the population of the Pentagon had in common was not the warrior's ethos but the functionary's.

Yet even while the Building's new culture was subtly civilizing the military — Pentagon regulations allowed, and would eventually encourage, officers to wear civilian clothes — the Pentagon was at the center of an implicit and more profound militarization of American society. Economic, political, martial, academic, scientific, technological, and cultural forces combined at the Pentagon — in some way *because* of the Pentagon — to create the new phenomenon that was well established by the time Eisenhower warned of it at the end of his presidency. In the twenty years after World War II, the Pentagon spent nearly $100 billion, ten times the federal expenditures devoted to all aspects of health, education, and welfare in the same period. By 1965, nearly six million Americans were employed in the enterprises administered from the Pentagon.[97] If business was transformed by defense contracts, so was academia, with the great American universities taking on, being enriched by, and becoming dependent on large research projects for the military establishment.[98] Indeed, much of the postwar boom that institutionalized the wealth of the United States was driven by engines in the Pentagon. No one knew this better than the politicians whose reelections were assured by defense spending in their districts, and who became, therefore, the self-appointed and self-perpetuating guardians of the gold-spewing temple on the Potomac.

For the first time in the country's history, military assumptions undergirded America's idea of itself. The combination of factors making this so had reached critical mass, an apt metaphor. The military-industrial-academic-political complex achieved a social fission, and the Pentagon was its reactor. An apt metaphor because the literal, one could say the radioactive, core of this unprecedented energy, what justified it, sanctioned it, mythologized it, even sanctified it, was the atomic bomb. And wasn't Leslie Groves its father, too?

Beginning in January 1943, an Army engineer in effect solved the existential problem with which the Air Force was left after the evaporation of its strategic bombing doctrine, and he did it with the nuclear weapon. The tremendous expenditures in treasure and lives of Operation Pointblank had bought little, as we saw, but an attrition campaign, not against Axis industrial might or morale but against the Luftwaffe. However effective that had turned out to

be as *a priori* tactical support of the D-Day invasion and the Army's subsequent march on Berlin, it represented a total failure of the Air Force's articulated mission. Not even the horrific incendiary raids of the spring of 1945
fulfilled what air war advocates had long predicted — not Operation Thunderclap in Germany and not the LeMay-led terror campaign against the
"matchbox" cities of Japan, about both of which we will see more. But strategic bombing's condition of drift and purposelessness changed instantly when
a transcendent explosive device, a product worthy of the AAF delivery system, came surprisingly into being on August 6, 1945.

   Not until Hiroshima did the "pain and shock, loss and grief, privation
and horror" of bombing, in Thomas Schelling's phrase, ever approach the
level of the "shock and awe," to use the term of art introduced by Pentagon
spokespersons during the opening salvos of the Iraq War in 2003, necessary to
shatter a whole nation's will. This was a matter of both strategic consequence
and myth. Before the atomic bomb, it was considered a tactical failure when a
bomber could reliably drop only a small proportion of its ordnance, and that
only "within a mile or so of the actual target," as Kaysen put it. After the
atomic bomb, a mile was fine. Devastation was total. But the larger issue was
the psychological, as opposed to the physical, effect of such a weapon. Its effect on the human mind, surpassing that of the almost equally violent incendiary raids that preceded Hiroshima, is what made the bomb "the absolute
weapon," as it was defined only a few months later.[99]

   After all, the level of destruction inflicted by a Hiroshima-type bomb was
not the innovation. Given the time, the power, and the heartlessness, one
group of human beings could inflict massive hurt on another using almost
anything. "Against defenseless people," as Schelling pointed out, "there is not
much that nuclear weapons can do that cannot be done with an ice pick." No,
the innovation of Hiroshima lay in its demonstration that "nuclear weapons
can do it quickly."[100] Rapid as was the firebombing of Tokyo on March 10,
1945 — up to a hundred thousand dead in a long night's series of attacks,
with wildfires sweeping through a paper city — the horror was not instantaneous.

   Nor was it transcendent, which is why the savageries of Hiroshima —
somewhere between 120,000 and 150,000 dead — transfigure the imagination,
while those of Tokyo mainly go unremembered.[101] The lasting effect was on
the human mind, in other words; on witnesses, on later investigators, on people who slowly came to appreciate what happened that week in August — first
at Hiroshima and then, three days later, at Nagasaki, where 70,000 to 80,000
died. The bomb was the absolute weapon in this sense: what human beings,
no matter how depraved, would never have had the moral capacity to do over

time and personally — with ice picks — they would do now with nary a second thought — in a second.

Hiroshima and Nagasaki, evoking the primal heroes of Leslie Groves, may have been "in the tradition of Sheridan against the Comanches and Sherman in Georgia,"[102] but they still marked the ultimate line of before-and-after in warfare. The atomic bomb obliterated distinctions between decisions and the rapidity with which they can be carried out, between the rear echelon and the front line, between military devastation and mass annihilation. Conversely, the atomic bomb established a connection between "unconditional surrender" and "unconditional destruction."[103]

As for Hiroshima, it was left with mere "deadness, the absolute essence of death," as one American investigator wrote from the city a month later, "in the sense of finality without hope of resurrection."[104] The psychological impact on slayer and slain alike is what made the weapon absolute. Its use eventually led to a kind of totemization, as if Hiroshima became a dark sacrament — a contemporary interruption in history, comparable to, say, the parting of the Red Sea.[105] "Never again" would become the twentieth century's great moral injunction, applying as much to Hiroshima as to Auschwitz. That mystification, more than the actual physical results of nuclear explosion, is what established the monumental taboo that, despite attempts to remove it (as we shall see, by the likes of LeMay and John Foster Dulles), kept nuclear weapons in a category apart. They remained there, "unthinkable," until they began to be "conventionalized" in the era of Secretary of Defense James Schlesinger, who sought ways to use tactical nuclear weapons against a conventional Soviet attack on Europe.[106] The same impulse to make nuclear weapons usable implicitly underwrote, across the decades, the pursuit of antiballistic missile systems and "intermediate" nuclear forces, but the most explicit conventionalizing of nukes would reach fruition only when George W. Bush became president early in the twenty-first century. We will see more of that, too.

So Leslie Groves, having built the Temple, supplied its holy of holies with the Ark. That is, having built a building that would transform the American martial imagination and the American economy, he then supervised the creation of the weapon that would not only "end the war," as that general in the congressional hallway had predicted it might, but change forever the way war itself is imagined. And not only war. The "sanctification of Hiroshima" indicates the nature of the spiritual crisis that the explosion of the fission weapon sparked. The "absolute essence of death" involved a plunge deeper into the ancient abyss of mortality. Now what was mortal, however, was not merely the human person but the human future. Yet mortality has itself served as the main human opening to transcendence. What does it mean that Trinity was the code name for the first atomic blast, on July 16, 1945? What infinite longing, by thwarting it, did that weapon express? And how, over the years, did it take on nothing less than holy status in the American psyche?

As a child, I carefully scissored out and mailed in the tops of Kix cereal boxes to obtain my own atomic bomb ring, with its lightning-blast design, its bombardier's insignia, its warhead, its sealed atom chamber in which I could see the green flash of "genuine atoms splitting to smithereens." That ring was less a toy to me than a relic, an object as sacramental as my rosary was, my crucifix. As a boy with ready access, through his dad, to the sacred precincts on the river, I also thought of that ring as a token of admission to the sanctuary, for I knew already what the real business of the Pentagon was.

Simple possession of the nuclear weapon had made the American military establishment, especially leaders of the Air Force like Dad, into nothing less than a priesthood — the very existence of which, with an almost irresistible tendency to elevate military power over civilian, put the Constitution itself on loose gravel, an unstable foundation on which, whether Americans know it or not, it still sits. The political sanctification of nuclear weapons, not the result of evil intentions, precisely, nor the creation of monster leaders, is the mortal knot in the narrative of ever-deepening predicament that is this book's subject. Like sacred mysteries, the bomb was exempt from doubt and questioning: one never asked about the relationship between Operation Pointblank and the Manhattan Protect, between the firebombing of Tokyo and the atomic bombing of Hiroshima. One never asked if the bomb's use against Japan had been proper, as one never asked if Roosevelt's unconditional-surrender demand in 1943 made Truman's decision to obliterate Hiroshima in 1945 inevitable. One never asked if threatening to use nuclear weapons against Moscow was proper, or if we would actually carry out the doomsday threat. And one never asked if the atomic arsenal was yet sufficiently stocked. Of course it never was.

One never asked, in sum, how America, a good nation if ever there was one, came to live so complacently with the bomb. Soon enough, the nuclear force, alone of all government enterprises, was exempt from the normal checks and balances of democratic politics. Without drawing undue attention, the bomb had left the realm of the merely utilitarian to take on a significance that transformed the nation's relationship to the world. As with me, it transformed every citizen's relationship — even a child's — to his or her existence. *Duck and Cover!* The gravest moments of my life, perhaps to this day, were those spent under my child-size desk in St. Mary's School, two or three miles downriver from Dad's ground zero. Arms clutching my head, eyes firmly shut against the flash, I waited, waited for the end of the only moments in which I ever thought of myself as dead. This book is nothing but tribute paid for the hostage-taking of Civil Defense, a product of "the stress," in Freud's phrase, "laid on the writer's memories of his childhood."[107] The nuns always told us it was a drill, but I for one knew otherwise.

That profoundly utilitarian engineer Leslie Groves, when he lifted his head from *his* Duck and Cover to see that the Trinity test explosion had worked on that July morning, turned to J. Robert Oppenheimer and said simply, "I am proud of you." Oppenheimer, as he would famously recount later, thought only of the line from the Bhagavad Gita: "Now I am become Death, the destroyer of worlds."[108] But Groves, as he reported to Secretary of War Stimson, his overseer on both his projects, would also think at once that his beloved Pentagon was no longer invulnerable — an intuition that itself made the link between the Building and the bomb.

Philip Morrison was at Trinity, announcing the countdown to the world-historic instant,[109] wondering if the atmosphere itself would ignite. Trinity base camp was ten miles from the site of the explosion — or, as Morrison said to me with a physicist's preciseness, "eighteen thousand yards."[110] He watched for the blast through welder's glasses, but when it came, as he told me, "it wasn't the sight that was impressive. It was the heat. The sound didn't come for a minute, so one didn't associate the sound. It was the heat. Instantaneous heat. Like a summer sunrise. Like dawn. How the sun is at first dawn. And right after the explosion, oh, within two or three minutes, the real sun rose."[111] As a child, Morrison was striken with polio, and the disease had left him lame. He died in the spring of 2005. When I interviewed him, at his home in Cambridge, Massachusetts, in the winter of 2003, he was eighty-eight years old, still deftly maneuvering his wheelchair around his paper-strewn desk. A long career as a theoretical physicist did nothing to alter his primary identity as a man who had helped launch the new era.

After Trinity, Morrison went from Los Alamos to Tinian Island in the northern Pacific to help in the final assembly of the bombs that were to be dropped on Hiroshima and Nagasaki.[112] He completed his "long witness to the entire tragedy" by immediately joining the damage assessment party in Hiroshima and Nagasaki. Morrison soon became one of the atomic physicists to turn against the bomb, and was an advocate of nuclear disarmament for the rest of his life. Even decades later, what he had seen in the ashes wrought by his own work lived like an after-flash in his eyes, like the ghost flame of a welder's torch, a blade of light a visitor could see. "What will people of the future think of us?" C. P. Snow asked of himself and his colleagues on the project. "Will they say, as Roger Williams said of some of the Massachusetts Indians, that we were wolves with the mind of men? Will they think that we resigned our humanity? They will have the right."[113]

7. THE OTHER SEPTEMBER 11S

Such were the events of that third week of January 1943. In that one week are directly joined the launching of American air warfare, the totality of unconditional surrender, the related shift of coercive hurt away from armies and toward whole enemy populations, the world-historic technological innovations that made all of this "absolute," the decision to maintain an American nuclear monopoly, and the Building that would organize this new spirit and symbolize it. The Building would also be the arena in which was conducted the decades-long argument — the Building against itself — all of these developments led to. The argument concerns the meaning of the Building's story. Or, to be more precise, what its story is. Has the Building been a bulwark against the tides of chaos and conflict? Or has it been the tidal engine? Is the production of weapons a strategy that secures or threatens? Does the paradox of deterrence — if it fails, we must destroy our enemy by destroying ourselves — already involve defeat? Which story is to be told? This book, in consulting the Building's inhabitants over the years, aims to discover that.

Coincidence gives us our starting point and a frame of reference, reminding us that history is a matter of the memory not of one thing but of one thing in relation to other things. To coincide, *Webster's* says, is to occupy the same place in space or in time. Thus apparent accidents of simultaneous chronology — unconditional surrender, Pointblank, the Manhattan Project — draw attention to the correspondence in character of the three narrative tracks initiated then, for together they changed the world forever. "Memory," the novelist Paul Auster says, is "the space in which a thing happens for the second time."[114] So our subject is less coincidence, as we saw, than convergence, the sense of how the energy of disparate events can drive along one axis, toward one inexorable outcome.

September 11, as the date of the Pentagon's groundbreaking in 1941, pulls the mind forward exactly sixty years to 2001, when the Building's vulnerability fulfilled Groves's nervous intuition at Trinity and the prophecy of those who had long seen the Pentagon as a bull's-eye on the earth. Beginning then, under President George W. Bush, America entered a new era characterized by the rhetoric of "dead or alive," by a new doctrine of "preventive war," by a recasting of nuclear policy, and by a radical new empowering of the Pentagon.

Convergence, as opposed to coincidence, prompts the question, Was all of this set in motion at the start?

But 2001 was not the only year with the ominous date. On September 11, 1944, the prince of Hesse, the principality in which Wiesbaden, site of my one-time boyhood home, is located, stood on a promontory of his property, his eyes fixed in the direction of the city of Darmstadt, fifteen kilometers distant: "The light grew and grew until the whole of the southern sky was glowing, shot through with red and yellow." The prince was seeing Allied bombers at work. It is almost certain that many more died that night from the action of airplanes than would from airplanes arrowing into Wall Street and Hell's Bottom fifty-seven years later.[115]

On September 11, 1973, twenty-eight years almost to the exact moment before American Airlines flight 77's explosive crash into the Pentagon, terrorists launched the violent overthrow of a democratic government in Chile, although in that case the result was the murder of the head of state, Salvador Allende, and the terrorists were sponsored not by an ad hoc nihilist group but by the United States.

On September 11, 1990, after Saddam Hussein's invasion of Kuwait, President George H. W. Bush, in a speech before Congress, declared what he called "a new world order," a phrase originating in Machiavelli[116] (and which appears, in Latin, on the one-dollar bill), a purpose his son would attempt to fulfill, beginning exactly eleven years later.

Such coincidences of dates and convergences of themes provide a context within which to consider the history of American attitudes toward war and peace, through the lens of my own experience, from 1943 forward: from Roosevelt's "unconditional surrender," to Truman's "decision," to Eisenhower's warning, to Kennedy's ambivalence, to the coming of arms control, to the belligerent Reagan's near breakthrough to "abolition," to the tragically missed opportunity of the Cold War's end, when America was given an unexpected chance to live without an enemy. At the end of the book, we will see what this history has to tell us about the place to which we have come in the new century, a place, apparently, where enemies abound.

But September 11 as an anniversary of savage violence pushes the mind also to September 11, 1945, the date that marks one of the great roads not taken, a bold stroke proposed by the man in charge of the Pentagon and the bomb both, Henry Stimson. The Stimson proposal, seeking to head off a nuclear arms race with the Soviet Union and thereby to undo the worst consequences of his own handiwork, was regarded as a naïve reach for the impossible, and perhaps it was. We will take up this question shortly.

Similarly, a study of the transformation of a nation's technological and psychological capacities to inflict hurt on a massive scale pushes us back in time to an event of another September 11, one more example of how one narrative track illuminates another. On September 11, 1906, more than three thousand men of Indian origin gathered at the Empire Theater in Johannesburg, South Africa, to denounce the Asiatic Law Amendment Ordinance, a new racial law condemning them to second-class citizenship. One of those who stood and took a God-invoking oath against obedience to such a law was a lawyer named Mohandas K. Gandhi. He recognized this joint commitment to a radically individual act — "a new principle," he later said, "had come into being" — as the creative spark of *satyagraha*, the "truth force" that would generate the great counterstory of nonviolence through the most violent century in history.[117]

Correspondences. What Paul Auster calls "the music of chance." But chance, of course, is entirely random, while music is anything but. Coincidental correspondences can reveal a hidden order, patterns of intelligibility in an apparently chaotic universe. Ordinarily we think of incidents in isolation, but there can be an archaeology of the calendar that uncovers harmonies in the layers of time. There are moments around which meanings orbit, and this book will be full of them, a spine that firms up the flux of an otherwise plotless narrative. We will be as attentive to the "time of the soul," in Paul Ricoeur's formulation, as to the time of physics. And speaking of physics, we will be attentive to what the Danish nuclear physicist Niels Bohr called "complementarity," which for him indicated the union between physics and philosophy, but also between realities that otherwise seem like contradictions.[118]

In this way we will bracket events against each other in order to gauge their full significance. Thus the meaning of the date December 7, 1941, as the beginning of America's great war (the attack on Pearl Harbor), can be transformed when it is paired with December 7, 1988, when that great war was, in effect, declared officially over by Mikhail Gorbachev. Speaking before the United Nations, he renounced the principle that had undergirded Soviet tyranny since the Red Army arrived at the Elbe River.[119] The mythic aura around December 7 had been equally bolstered a year earlier, in 1987, the date of Gorbachev's arrival in Washington to sign the Intermediate-Range Nuclear Forces Treaty with Ronald Reagan. With that, the United States and the Soviet Union agreed to the destruction of more than 2,600 nuclear missiles, the first act of real arms reduction. This date, Gorbachev said, "will be inscribed in the history books."[120] The Day of Infamy was no longer only that.

Similarly, what does it tell us about the forces set in motion on November 9, 1938, the "night of broken glass," when assaults against Jews spread from Berlin to every city in Germany, when they are measured against November 9, 1989, the night that mobs of East Germans jubilantly dismantled the Berlin

Wall? That velvet liberation, igniting a wave of nonviolent overthrow from Berlin to every corner of the Soviet empire, confounded those who believed in war as the only response to tyranny, and perhaps repaired, if it did not undo, the evil unleashed on the world on *Kristallnacht*.

History, in other words, is not a mere catalogue of events, not just a knowledge of their chronology. History is, rather, the appreciation of how events relate to each other, if not causally, then mythically. Objectively, but also personally. In this we are "close to Leonardo's universe where the painter said he saw actual lines connecting objects in a form of visible geometry."[121] If the past is a foreign country, then our concern is not only to map it but to understand its citizens.[122] Our concern is not only with what happened but how it felt, and how it set other things moving in the public realm and in the human heart. Can we pair the joyous fall of the Berlin Wall with the murderous destruction of the World Trade Center or the attack on the Pentagon? Can we pair 11/9, that is, with 9/11?

Thucydides, driven from Athens, wrote a history of the Peloponnesian Wars for "those who want to understand clearly the events which happened in the past and which (human nature being what it is) will at some time or other and in much the same ways be repeated in the future."[123] George W. Bush was not the first American president to contemplate preventive war, if he was the first to wage one. James Forrestal was the first secretary of defense — and the only one to commit suicide. Robert McNamara asked to see the Pentagon's war plans and was told by generals he lacked clearance. Aerospace manufacturers created for their enterprise an unchecked exceptionalism, salting the earth with an excess of nuclear warheads that has yet to be explained, or checked. Jimmy Carter wanted total disarmament too much, and Ronald Reagan nearly achieved it through his very belligerence. Bill Clinton was a war resister who could not find a way to resist the warrior ethos at a crucial moment. The brass hats were never univocal in their approach to questions of war and peace; indeed, they had regularly to restrain their civilian overseers, who came and went like seasonal birds. The nation, meanwhile, grew so dependent on the idea of imminent war as a source of identity — and prosperity — that the idea survived even when its animating enemy disappeared. Always the Building held fast to its purpose, which came closest to fulfillment with the arrival of Richard Cheney, Donald Rumsfeld, Paul Wolfowitz, and what became openly acknowledged as an American empire. The Pentagon, world capital of a twenty-first-century Pax Americana that assumed, like Thucydides, the permanence of war, at last had a function worthy of its monumentality. The future met its past.

How events coincide in time and place — as well as across time and space in the realm of meaning — is a matter of memory, which discerns the sig-

nificance of individual experience by seeing it in the context of the community's. The still unfolding story of American attitudes toward war under the
cloud of the absolute weapon begins in that January week of multiple transformations. Correspondence. Convergence. As a child of the Pentagon, I have
long known that this narrative defines the arc of my life, as the field of my
consciousness has constantly shifted from personal memory to political and
cultural history. My father in his prime as a prelate of the Cold War, fearlessly
tossing back salutes with me happily by his side, striding from the River Entrance toward the waiting blue staff car, my having to take two paces for his
one. I'd have reached for his hand, but it seemed he needed to snap his fingers
as he walked.

That memory defines the first bracket of my life. Even then I had the
sense that what I was being shown was incomplete. Secrets abounded in that
world, and I knew it. Would I ever uncover them? And what of the secrets I
was keeping from myself? What did it mean that Hap Arnold and Curt
LeMay made first marks on my measure of heroism? W. G. Sebald, the German writer whose last work chronicled the Allied bombing of his world, describes himself as a child of World War II, though he was only a year old
when it ended. "The horrors I did not experience," he wrote, "cast a shadow
over me . . . one from which I shall never entirely emerge."[124] And so also me.
Total war. Total victory. The coming Armageddon. *Peace is our profession.* Us
versus them. Dead or alive. I am identified from the start with the contradiction, fear, absurdity–and, yes, virtue — of American attitudes toward war. Is
war heroic, a proper source of meaning and identity? Or is war chaos, evil, a
threat to the very earth? I wrote this book hoping to emerge from the shadow
at last, but knowing I probably will not. No more than my worshiped father
did. The martial absolutism embodied in the Building where he spent the
best part of his life destroyed him, and that, too, is the story.

The second bracket that defines my life also involves the five-sided Building, but this time on my own. The correspondence here evokes an image of
protesters defiling the air above the River Entrance with curses — curses
aimed, by accident, at my father's office window, and I am one of them. Without knowing it, I am a party to his personal destruction. The date is October
22, 1967. I become myself, in a reversal worthy of Aristotle, by marching on
the Pentagon, to say *Hell no!* The act leaves me under not a shadow but a
curse. I wouldn't know it until years later, but my father fell under a curse
then, too, as if because of me. Within two years he was defeated — not by my
kind, whom he detested by then; not by pajama-clad enemies in the jungles
of Southeast Asia, who were defeating the Pentagon; but by enemies in offices
near his own, down various Pentagon corridors — Corregidors after all.

I have reflected on aspects of my father's fate before,[125] but I had to become the age he was when the catastrophe struck to understand that the five-sided megalith in Arlington is as much the ground zero of my territory as his, of the nation's as much as ours. Already a personal tragedy for us, the broader story of the Building as it belongs to history — 9/11/41 to 9/11/44 to 9/11/45 to 9/11/73 to 9/11/01 — awaits a fuller denouement. But it has been clear for most of my life that to tell my story, I had someday to tell as much of the Building's as I could.

It was the discovery of a first coincidence of dates that made all this plain, a chord struck by the music of chance that conscripted me into the work of the Pentagon's biography, an exploration of correspondence and convergence. Ever since I first heard of it years ago, I have thought of that low-key dedication ceremony, in the middle of that world-transforming week near the middle of the century, as the Pentagon's birthday: the third week of January 1943. I embarked on this work of political, military, and personal history — my nation's story, my father's story, and mine — because in that week, like the Building's twin, I, too, was born.[126]

THE ABSOLUTE WEAPON

1. "TRUMAN'S DECISION"

The phrase "Truman's decision" can refer to only one thing. Of all the many decisions Harry Truman made in his life — marrying Bess Wallace; leaving haberdashery for politics; taking bribes from the Pendergast machine; challenging, as a U.S. senator, congressional deference toward wartime military spending; accepting Roosevelt's invitation to join the national ticket; standing up to a Soviet envoy as a newly elected president; declining to run for reelection — none of them rank in importance with, or loom in the American memory like, the decision to use the atomic bomb against Japan.[1] The event was decisive, of course, not only for him but for his nation and the world. August 6, 1945, marks a defining moment, an instance of transformed consciousness, an absolute marker in time. Always before, evolution meant a gradual unfolding, and shifts in the essence of what it is to be human — the movement out of the jungle, say, into the savanna; a four-legged creature learning to walk upright — required eons to take effect and to be assimilated into understanding. No one human or set of humans could ever be aware of the radical transition as it occurred. Yet this time the meaning of dramatic change — a threshold crossed into complete moral responsibility for the very survival of the species — presented itself at once and to all who took notice, an epiphany as brightly unmissable as the flash of an explosion in the blue Japanese sky. Truman's decision was humankind's.

More narrowly, it instantly changed his nation's relationship to power. The United States had come out of World War I unscathed. The great empires of Europe had savaged each other. "Overseas," as we said, an entire generation of males had effectively committed suicide. That was the primary fact of the Great War, that of all modern nations, only America was left with young men, a demographic circumstance from which the century progressed. Britain maintained its grasp on financial markets and world empire, but its decline had begun. Relative to all other nations and by default, the United States was ascendant by the 1920s. Still, the American consciousness remained that of a minor state, which is why Washington, obsessing about being repaid its war loans by Europe, could then watch the emergence of fascism, Stalinism, and Nazism with detachment.

Washington consciously, deliberately assumed global power through the years of World War II, with the imperial vestiges once again suicidally self-destructive, but as the instant and near-total demobilization of the American fighting force after 1945 shows, the U.S. population still lacked the viscera of martial ambition. Yet in that one moment, August 6, 1945, the nation redefined itself — and it did so around an enterprise that was until then a secret closely held by a very few officials. As a mark on the arc of the history of power, that date surpasses even the day of the conversion of Constantine, when an ill-defined and harried religious sect became the Roman Empire. Just as that event gutted the meaning of the Church, changing it forever, so Hiroshima transformed America. Where before its evolving center had been the farm, the frontier, the factory, the city, now the American center was seized and occupied, as if by infiltration, by the nuclear weapon itself. From Hiroshima on, the bomb would be the defining note of the United States, changing everything, including the American capacity to know that this is what happened. Truman's decision, to repeat, was America's.[2]

A large literature exists about the decision, but before reviewing what that literature teaches, one must begin by acknowledging that, from the perspective of the person who ordered the atom bomb dropped, and most of those who carried out the order, there was no question about it. To reflect on the decision as an early mark in the narrative traced here is not to judge it moralistically, from hindsight, but to complicate the perhaps oversimplified way it is carried in the nation's memory. The aim is to examine the complexities of a choice that may have seemed at the time to be far less consequential than it was.

It was on July 24, at a borrowed manor house on Kaiserstrasse in Potsdam, that Truman is usually described as having issued the official order. He was in that suburb of Berlin for a meeting with Churchill, Stalin, and Chiang Kai-shek. Germany was defeated; the Japanese were holding on. But not for long. "The 509 Composite Group, 20th Air Force, will deliver its first special bomb," Truman's order read, "as soon as weather will permit visual bombing after about 3 August 1945 on one of the targets: Hiroshima, Kokura, Niigata, and Nagasaki."[3] The order is dated July 25, the next day. Truman did not sign it, but there is no doubt he approved the order as drafted.

"We have discovered the most terrible bomb in the history of the world," Truman wrote in his diary on July 25. "The weapon is to be used against Japan between now and August 10th . . . The target will be a purely military one."[4] In the years since that "decision," critics have second-guessed Truman, with objections coming in fairly regular waves, and we will consider the elements of such dissension. Among scholars, commentators, and the broad public a consensus of acceptance, if not approval, holds. Truman, according to this view, as one writer put it on the fiftieth anniversary of Hiroshima, "used the weapon he had. He did what he thought was right, and the war ended, the killing stopped . . . The bombing was cruel, but it ended a longer, greater cruelty."[5]

Those who have raised questions about Truman's decision — whether the bomb was necessary to force the Japanese surrender, whether the bomb was used more with an eye to Moscow than to Tokyo, and so on — are somewhat dismissively referred to as "revisionists."[6] The historiography of the decision (like that of the origins of the Cold War, of which we will see more later) has itself become complex. After the revisionists came the "postrevisionists," who were answered in turn by the "we now know" historians such as John Lewis Gaddis.[7] By the 1990s, triumphalist American claims had cycled back to the assertions of the early postwar historians. Through all of this, the ability of the most critical historians to reach objective judgments about the past use of the atomic bomb is called into question by their evident objection to present nuclear arsenals. "The critics have an agenda," a prominent newspaper columnist wrote, "not an ignoble agenda, but one that goes well beyond instructing us to face up to our true history. It is to repudiate the moral basis of nuclear weapons. If their use in the one situation where they were actually employed can be shown to be unnecessary, illegitimate, and even depraved, then a powerful change will have been wrought in the political culture in which strategic decisions and historical judgements are made."[8] This comment appeared in 1995. In effect, it uses against the idea of nuclear reconsideration the intuition that the world is still at risk of nuclear catastrophe. "Listen to me!" as the woman in *Hiroshima Mon Amour* says. "I know it will happen again."

There is an assumption that the revisionist questions were raised only later,[9] especially by the generation of historians who came of age in the 1970s and 1980s, but it isn't true. Kai Bird and Lawrence Lifschultz edited a collection of articles that were contemporaneous with the bomb's being used against Japan. Their book, *Hiroshima's Shadow,* demonstrates that doubts about the justification for Truman's action arose shortly after the bombs fell. The vast majority of American citizens told pollsters that they approved of the attacks,[10] but powerful voices were immediately raised in dissent. The day after Hiroshima, Albert Camus declared, "Technological civilization has just reached its final degree of savagery."[11] Within a few weeks, Dwight Macdonald wrote in *The New Yorker,* "What first appalled us was its blast."[12] The question of the "purely military" character of the target surfaced: "King Herod's slaughter of the innocents — an atrocity committed in the name of defense — destroyed no more than a few hundred children." This appeared in the *Christian Century* on August 29. "Today a single atomic bomb slaughters tens of thousands of children and their mothers and fathers. Newspapers and radio acclaim it a great victory. Victory for what?"[13] And in September, an editorial in the *Catholic World* defined the bomb's use as "atrocious and abominable . . . the most powerful blow ever delivered against Christian civilization and the moral law."[14]

The author of the editorial was Father James Gillis, a priest who would be a figure in my own life years later, when I joined the Catholic order of which he was a mythic figure. By the early 1960s, when I left the house on Generals' Row at Bolling Air Force Base to enter the Paulist Fathers, there was no debate in America about the justification for Truman's decision. Gillis's portrait — bald pate, stern visage, mission cross hooked in his cincture — hung in the Paulist common room, and in that company he was remembered as a champion of social justice, a friend to labor, and an enemy of racial segregation. But no one ever referred in my hearing to Gillis's dissent at the time of the dropping of the atomic bomb. Only in researching this book did I learn of it. His view obviously had not carried, and by my time would have been an embarrassment. Establishment historians, who beat back the revisionists of the 1970s and 1980s, likewise pretend that Truman's decision was unquestioned at the time.

It was taken for granted by the early sixties, and mainly still is, that dropping the bombs on Hiroshima and Nagasaki had spared legions of American soldiers from certain death. More than two million Japanese troops awaited the American invasion of their home islands. It was to be called Operation Downfall and was planned in two stages, for November 1945 and March 1946, but already soldiers and Marines, in island combat across the Pacific, had learned what to fear. On the small island of Okinawa, in April, May, and June 1945, more than a hundred thousand Japanese soldiers fought to the death, almost, of the last man. Infused with the samurai spirit, these diehards inflicted heavy casualties on Americans, including 20 percent of all Navy men killed and 14 percent of all Marines killed in the entire war.[15] A hundred and fifty

thousand civilians caught in the crossfire were killed. This one battle traumatized U.S. commanders, and it defined at least some expectations for the upcoming invasion of the home islands.

Truman wrote in his memoir nearly ten years after the fact that invading
Japan would have easily cost the lives of half a million young GIs and leather-
necks.[16] Speaking in 1945, just months after the decision, he put the figure at
half that: "It occurred to me that a quarter of a million of the flower of our
young manhood were worth a couple of Japanese cities, and I still think they
were and are." Truman cited George Marshall as his source for both figures,
disparate though they are.[17] When Winston Churchill took up the question in
his history of the war in 1953, he put the number of anticipated killed at a million American and 500,000 British soldiers.[18] Such figures in the litanies of
American justifications say nothing about the number of Japanese, civilian
and military alike, who would have been killed in the invasion that the two
bombs supposedly made unnecessary. Millions of dead in the one offensive
seemed likely.

A combat veteran turned writer later brought the abstraction of these
numbers down to the human level when, contemplating his own fate as one
of the invading force, he wrote, "Thank God for the Atomic Bomb."[19] When
another young soldier, later a writer, learned of the bombing of Hiroshima,
he wept with his fellow infantrymen with the same feeling: "We were going to
live. We were going to grow to adulthood after all."[20] In the time since this
particular platoon-level testimony in favor of the bombing appeared in the
New Republic in 1991, it has often been cited by Truman's defenders[21] because
it comes from the historian and critic Paul Fussell, whose writing otherwise
debunks every effort to glorify war.[22]

In the American memory, the fact that the Japanese started the war with
their attack on Pearl Harbor has also justified the brutalities of the war's end.
Just as death row inmates, by their crimes, have forfeited the right to any
mercy (or ethical treatment), in this view so with Tokyo. But the imaginative
identification with the young soldiers whose lives were spared because of the
lives lost at Hiroshima and Nagasaki has proved to be the enduring trump
card justifying the bomb's use. Even if the number of Americans who would
be killed in an invasion turned out to be far lower than stated estimates, there
is no brushing such casualties aside. Exactly how many would "grow to adulthood" because no invasion was needed is less important than the certainty
that they were granted a reprieve to do so, but their purported number continued to mount over the years. In 1991, President George H. W. Bush said
that the atomic bombs "spared millions of American lives."[23] The bomb was
the alternative to the invasion, and that was that.

2. STIMSON'S DEFENSE

The definitive assertion of this position was given in an article published in *Harper's Magazine* by Henry Stimson, secretary of war from 1940 to 1945.[24] As such, he was the man ultimately in charge of the manufacture and use of the atomic bomb. Stimson's article contributed to the myth of Truman's decision by using that word in its title: "The Decision to Use the Atomic Bomb." The article was featured on the *Harper's* cover in February 1947. Stimson could address that controversial subject, pretty much laying questions to rest for many years, because of an authority born of his distinction as an American statesman.

A childless patrician, he earned a fortune as a Wall Street lawyer and lived like a prince on a Long Island estate and, during his years of government service, in a Washington mansion near Rock Creek Park. He took his privilege so much for granted that he exuded an air of Victorian self-denial while surrounded by the trappings of extraordinary wealth. He was a dignified figure with a cavalier's erectness, a trim mustache, and a permanent waistcoat set off by a drooping gold watch fob. His glinting eye bespoke directness and integrity. Over his long career, he showed himself to be so sensitive to the human costs of power that one of his biographers could measure the moral meaning of the decision to use the atomic bomb by the standard of Stimson's own rectitude: "What is interesting about that conflict, in the context of 1945, is that even Stimson, who repeatedly demonstrated a far from common sensitivity to the moral outrages of war, should have seen no objection to opening the atomic Pandora's box and loosing its demons on the world."[25]

Before serving Roosevelt, and then Truman, Stimson was secretary of war (1911–1913) under William Howard Taft and secretary of state (1929–1933) under Herbert Hoover. His lack of arrogance is reflected in the fact that when World War I broke out, he left the cabinet to enlist in the Army he had until then overseen. Commanding an artillery battery in France and attaining the rank of colonel, he was pleased to be referred to by that title for the rest of his life, although he exercised authority over the great generals of World War II. As one of his biographers points out, his personal experience of war extended from surviving a Ute uprising in Colorado in 1887 to supervision of the production and use of the bombs against Hiroshima and Nagasaki.[26]

For our purposes, it is important to note that Stimson was the supervisor of General Leslie Groves, in the latter's work both as the builder of the Pentagon and as the manager of the Manhattan Project. Today, visitors to the office of the secretary of defense enter a space personally designed by Stimson, a broad rectangular room with high formal windows facing the Potomac River and Washington. Fluted panels, faux pillars, and elaborate wall molding give the room a classical feel without violating its patrician understatement. The office is a distillation of the aesthetic gravity that defines the whole Building. Impatient for its completion, Stimson was one of the first officials to occupy the Pentagon. In his office there in 1942 and 1943, he had countless meetings with Groves, going over blueprints and ledgers as both men struggled to keep pace with the massive project. They would next turn their attention to the one that would surpass it.

As construction of the new War Department headquarters in Virginia consumed Stimson's energy early in his tenure as secretary, completing the atomic bomb obsessed him through the last year of the war. Again Groves was at his elbow, poring over plans. Each monumental task, in its separate sphere, was unprecedented in reach and effect, and for both Stimson depended on the rotund engineer. In the end, however, the seventy-eight-year-old Stimson's health was failing, and he repeatedly considered retirement. If he clung to his position, it was, as he said of the atomic bomb in April 1945, to "devote all of my time to this particular project."[27] Groves's progress reports as the Manhattan Project entered its last, triumphant phase left Stimson feeling, as he said, "immensely cheered and braced up."[28]

In the same month, it was Stimson who first revealed the secret of the soon-to-be-completed superweapon to Truman, and he did so within hours of Truman's becoming president.[29] As a further measure of his authority over the project, it was Stimson who controlled the selection of the Japanese targets, and it was Stimson who, at Potsdam, presented Truman with the order to bomb them. But he did none of this without Groves, who operated behind the scenes. We will soon consider the question of whether it was Groves who directed the other players.

As with Stimson's memoir, published later, the *Harper's* article was written with McGeorge Bundy, the young son of Stimson's trusted aide Harvey Bundy, although the junior Bundy's work on the *Harper's* piece, unlike the memoir, was not disclosed. McGeorge Bundy, in 1947, was a rising star at Harvard and a protégé of its president, James B. Conant, who had served as scientific chief of the Manhattan Project and had participated in the final decision to use the weapon against an urban population. Though the American public continued its *ex post facto* support of the bombing of Hiroshima and Nagasaki, intellectual critics and religious leaders of the kind Conant cared about continued to raise questions of the sort we saw above.[30] Within weeks of the first anniversary of the bombings, *The New Yorker* published John

Hersey's "Hiroshima," a stirring description of the real effects of the weapon on human beings. That in turn prompted widespread comment, including a September article in the middlebrow *Saturday Review of Literature* by its influential editor Norman Cousins, who used the word "crime" to define the attacks.[31]

Conant was not just worried about his own reputation as one of the bomb's creators. He feared that a reversal in the public's attitude toward the weapon's use would undermine its broader moral legitimacy at a time when American nuclear politics with the Soviet Union (compounded by Communist electoral gains in Europe) were entering a critical phase. In Conant's view, Moscow had to believe in the American capacity and will to use the bomb again if it was going to come to terms on international atomic controls, such as those put forward in the Baruch Plan, to which we will return. Moralistic second-guessing of Hiroshima could undermine American resolve, and the Soviet perception of it, at the worst moment. That is why Conant urged Stimson, with young Bundy, to write a defense of the bomb's use against Japan. He wanted to stiffen American determination with a view to softening Russia's. This was the first time, but would not be the last, that justifications of U.S. nuclear policy in the past were tied to strategic requirements of the present. At stake in the debate was public acceptance of nuclear weapons as the normal and moral basis of deterrence. If Americans rejected the legitimacy of past nuclear use, the ability to keep the Soviet Union at bay by the threat of future use would be undercut. The manipulation of American memory regarding Hiroshima and Nagasaki became a key tool in legitimizing the nation's atomic policy.

The *Harper's* article did not shrink from the horrors of the atomic bomb or from its effect on the devastated Japanese cities. "The face of war is the face of death," Stimson wrote. As secretary of war in 1911, he had presided over an American army consisting of a few thousand men, deployed to fight Indian wars. By V-J Day, he had authority over fourteen million men. He understood exactly what that transformation meant. "Death is an inevitable part of every order a wartime leader gives. The decision to use the atomic bomb was a decision that brought death to over a hundred thousand Japanese. No explanation can change that fact and I do not wish to gloss it over." Indeed, by directly acknowledging those horrors, the Stimson article established the prevailing view of the Hiroshima-Nagasaki bombings as prime instances of the moral theory of the lesser evil: "This deliberate, premeditated destruction was our least abhorrent choice. The destruction of Hiroshima and Nagasaki put an end to the Japanese war. It stopped the fire raids, and the strangling blockade; it ended the ghastly specter of a clash of great land armies." War entailed mass destruction and carnage; the bomb put an end to that. But Stimson saw the terrible irony: "In this last great action of the Second World War we were given final proof that war is death."[32]

The Stimson article set the parameters within which the decision to drop the bombs continues to be discussed to this day — namely, that invasion was the alternative. After the shock of Hiroshima and Nagasaki, Stimson, like Truman before and Churchill after him, knew the importance of publicizing the costs of that alternative — for public relations reasons, not to wrestle with the morality of it. A detailed accounting of what the invasion would entail first appeared here: five million U.S. soldiers, combat lasting well into 1946, more than a million American casualties. What was the source of such projections? Stimson and Bundy did not get the estimates from the War Department. They decided instead to promulgate their own guessed-at but memorable numbers.[33]

Declassified documents, made available in the years since, suggest a somewhat different set of numbers, and they would probably have been provided to Stimson, and through him to Truman. The Joint War Plans Committee, the body responsible for providing the Joint Chiefs of Staff with information for all planning, offered an estimate on June 15, 1945, that the invasion of the Japanese homeland would result in 40,000 U.S. dead and 150,000 wounded. The brutal Battle of Okinawa had just ended, and the planners had a full appreciation of combat injuries and deaths. They also knew that the defenders of the Japanese home islands were already a shadow of the fighting forces American soldiers had encountered elsewhere. In Japan proper, the defenders lacked food, fuel, and raw materials because of the U.S. Navy's choking blockade, and their positions had been decimated by air bombardment. Indeed, leaders of the Navy and the AAF both assumed that the invasion would not be necessary. That same June, both General Marshall and General Douglas MacArthur, who would have shared command of the invasion, signed documents in agreement with the War Plans Committee estimates.[34] Despite these facts, it was Stimson's fabricated numbers that were branded on the American memory,[35] because the horrors of Hiroshima and Nagasaki, in order to have moral valence, had to be counterbalanced with a proportionate death toll in American lives. Only then could Americans feel an ethical equilibrium. To be sure, 40,000 U.S. dead is a horrendous number, representing family tragedies many times that, but it is far short of the figure on which American moral presumption, Truman to Bush, has come to depend.

Was invasion the alternative? Fussell's poignant testimony to the relief felt by putative invaders notwithstanding, there is reason to believe that the crucial

American choice in the summer of 1945 was not between invasion and the atomic bomb, nor even between invasion and the combination of Navy blockade and AAF conventional bombing. Rather, the choice was between, in the formulation of the historian Martin Sherwin, "various forms of warfare and diplomacy."[36] When Stimson briefed General Dwight Eisenhower at his headquarters in Germany in July, laying out the plan to use the atomic bomb against Japan, Eisenhower expressed, as he later put it, "my grave misgivings, first on the basis of my belief that Japan was already defeated and that dropping the bomb was completely unnecessary, and secondly because I thought that our nation should avoid shocking world opinion by use of a weapon whose employment was, I thought, no longer mandatory to save American lives."[37]

Eisenhower reports that Stimson was annoyed by his statement, but it reflected realities of which Stimson was all too aware, and which he was expressing himself. At that point, almost none of Truman's inner circle thought that an invasion of Japan would be necessary to end the war.[38] Stimson knew in July that diplomacy was competing with war as a way to bring hostilities to a conclusion. More explicitly, he knew that Japanese leaders had been sending out peace feelers since April. It remained true that bitter-end militarists among the Japanese high command nurtured fantasies of suicidal resistance, and defenders of Truman's decision always emphasize that this war party had the upper hand. But the balance was shifting in Tokyo as political factions seeking peace gained in influence. At the center of those, as events would reveal, was Emperor Hirohito.

Much is made by defenders of the Truman decision that most Japanese efforts to obtain surrender terms went through still neutral Moscow and that Stalin simply declined to pass Japanese messages on to Washington, wanting to delay the Pacific war's end until he could enter it for the sake of postwar participation in Asian prizes. But by this time Washington was secretly intercepting and reading Japanese cable traffic and was fully aware that a peace party was coming to the fore in Tokyo. Looking back on that pivotal summer from a vantage sixty years later, after a dozen well-known failures of U.S. intelligence to anticipate an enemy's actions (the Berlin blockade, the Berlin Wall, Soviet missiles into Cuba, the Arab-Israeli wars, Soviet invasions of Hungary and Czechoslovakia and Afghanistan, Vietnamese resistance, the Soviet Union's collapse, Iraq's invasion of Kuwait, the absence of weapons of mass destruction in Iraq), there can be no surprise that American perceptions of Japanese intentions were confused. Still, the assumption that Tokyo was determined to fight on seems flawed.

Some historians argue that the Japanese government made its definitive decision to surrender on June 20, 1945, at a meeting of the Supreme War Direction Council, in the Emperor's presence.[39] Impediments to the actual announcement of surrender included the lack of means of communication with the Allies, uncertainty over what the Allies wanted, and anticipated resistance from suicidal factions in the military. But all of these elements amounted to loose ends that the war council began to tie up, and Washington, with its access to internal Japanese communications, had good reason to know that. In a so-called Magic summary of a top-level Japanese diplomatic intercept dated July 13, for example, Stimson and Truman would have read: "His Majesty the Emperor, mindful of the fact that the present war daily brings greater evil and sacrifice upon the peoples of all belligerent powers, desires from his heart that it may be quickly terminated." On July 17, as the Potsdam conference was getting under way, to take another example, U.S. naval intelligence reports came to Truman and Stimson making explicit that Japan "officially if not publicly" accepted its defeat, and its only remaining concerns were with "reconciling national pride with defeat" and with "finding the best means of salvaging the wreckage of her ambitions."[40] Note that this was the day after the successful test of the atomic bomb at Alamogordo and a week before Truman approved the order to send the 509th Composite Group on its way.

Stimson's awareness of urgent Japanese diplomatic efforts to end the war is implied in his *Harper's* article, but there he makes it seem as if diplomacy had come to an end with the unreasonable Japanese rejection of the Potsdam ultimatum, issued on July 26. "On July 28," Stimson wrote, "the Premier of Japan, Suzuki, rejected the Potsdam ultimatum by announcing it was 'unworthy of public notice.'"[41] Stimson asserts that this Japanese reply gave the United States no choice but to proceed with the atomic bombing. But an American translation of the Japanese word *mokusatsu* as a contemptuous dismissal may have been mistaken. The word can equally be taken as a kind of "no comment," with which the Japanese may have meant only to buy time.

Stimson's account is more nuanced in his memoir *On Active Service in Peace and War*, openly written with Bundy and published a year after the *Harper's* article. In that book, Stimson emphasizes the Japanese objective with their various spring and summer "peace feelers": simple clarification of the precise meaning of "unconditional surrender." Stimson, by his own account and that of others, was one of those who wanted to adjust this demand in ways that might induce a Japanese surrender. At a State-War-Navy meeting on June 19, for example, Joseph C. Grew, the acting secretary of state, urged a large step back from "unconditionality." Secretary of the Navy James Forrestal, writing in his posthumously published diary, offers this account of the discussion:

Surrender Terms: Grew's proposal, in which Stimson most vigorously agrees, that something be done in the very near future to indicate to the Japanese what kind of surrender terms would be imposed on them and particularly to indicate to them that they would be allowed to retain their own form of government and religious institutions . . . Both Stimson and Grew most emphatically asserted that this move ought to be done, and that if it were to be effective at all must be done before any attack was made on the homeland of Japan. Mr. Grew was of the impression that the President had indicated he was not in accord with this point of view. Mr. Stimson said that that was not his understanding.[42]

The primary concern in Tokyo, after the suicide of Hitler and the murder of Mussolini, was the fate of the Emperor. To the Japanese he was a divine being, and it was unthinkable that he be harmed or humiliated. This is true despite current American assessments that Hirohito was a hapless leader surrounded and controlled by fanatical samurai who wanted to fight to the death. That the diehard war party proved nonexistent after the Emperor's surrender, with even the military elites declining to commit "honor suicides," makes the point that this view is overblown.[43]

In 1945, senior American officials knew very well, from a steady stream of Magic intercepts, that Japanese diplomats wanted an assurance that the Emperor's status would be respected. On July 13, for example, the Americans read in a cable that Japanese Foreign Minister Shigenori Togo sent to his ambassador in Moscow, who was urgently seeking an end to the war: "'Unconditional surrender' is the only obstacle to peace."[44]

Even before the June 19 meeting referred to above, Stimson had proposed to General Marshall an abandonment of the term "unconditional surrender" as defining the war's aim. In reply, in a memo dated June 9, Marshall objected that "a deviation at this time would occasion an undesirable amount of questioning and doubt as to the nature of our changed intentions." Marshall instead suggested that "we cease talking about unconditional surrender of Japan and begin to define our true objective in terms of defeat and disarmament."[45] Stimson reports in his memoir that he himself was one of those who "had hoped that a specific assurance on the Emperor might be included in the Potsdam ultimatum."[46] In fact, Stimson wrote a draft of the declaration that included language guaranteeing the continuance of the imperial dynasty. At Potsdam, he was not alone. Another who favored stepping back from unconditional surrender was Winston Churchill.

Recall that the British leader had not been consulted by Roosevelt at Casablanca in 1943, when the president announced the policy at the concluding press conference, and that Churchill only belatedly accepted unconditional surrender as the stated war aim. His fear at Casablanca now seemed to be coming true, as the policy threatened to needlessly prolong the war. On July

18, Churchill broached the question with Truman. He argued against unconditional surrender as a sticking point and urged finding a way to allow the
Japanese "some show of saving their military honor and some assurance of
their national existence." Truman "bluntly" dismissed Churchill's argument.
This enemy had crossed a moral threshold in attacking America, and now
moral mitigation was unthinkable. The Japanese, Truman said, did not have
"any military honor after Pearl Harbor."[47]

Churchill's pragmatic view did not carry, nor did Stimson's. Stimson's
draft of the Potsdam Declaration was mortally altered. In one of the most
fate-laden acts of the war, Truman himself deleted Stimson's paragraph on
the retention of "the present dynasty."[48] The phrase "unconditional surrender" braced the last paragraph of the declaration, where it would stand in
stark relief against a prospect of complete imperial humiliation. To the Japanese this was sacrilege. "Following are our terms," the declaration began. "We
will not deviate from them. There are no alternatives. We shall brook no delay."[49] In striking the language on the Emperor, Truman acted under the express influence of his new secretary of state, James F. Byrnes. The redrafted
ultimatum included a sentence Byrnes composed, a substitution for the language respecting the "present dynasty": "There must be eliminated for all
time the authority and influence of those who have deceived and misled the
people of Japan."[50]

Byrnes, an extroverted Irishman, was a former congressman from South
Carolina, a former Supreme Court justice, and a former senior aide to Roosevelt.[51] He had been Truman's competitor for the 1944 nomination as vice
president, and it is likely that Truman quickly drew him into his circle after
FDR's death as a way to preempt further rivalry. Instead, Byrnes became
Stimson's rival, especially at Potsdam. At that moment, the robust Byrnes
had far more influence with Truman than the aged and by now exhausted
Stimson. The gyre around which their competition would become heated
was the atomic bomb.

Knowing of Byrnes's intimacy with the new president, Stimson had, in
early May 1945, recommended him for the position of liaison between the
White House and the Interim Committee, newly established to oversee the
crucial last phase of the Manhattan Project. On June 30, Byrnes became secretary of state, and by July he had begun to view the bomb as much in relation
to the Soviet Union as to Japan, and that seems to have been the key to his intransigence on the point of unconditional surrender. His attitude calcified
when the bomb became an actuality. The Potsdam conference convened on
July 15. The next day, in an operation code-named Trinity, the bomb was
tested at Alamogordo. Stimson made yet another appeal to Byrnes, more desperate than ever for a way to avoid using the bomb, but Byrnes brushed him

off, invoking Truman. Moscow was in play now, and that mattered more to the new secretary of state than sparing Japanese. Tokyo was yesterday's problem. Moscow was tomorrow's. That defined Potsdam.[52]

The Potsdam Declaration of July 26 rejected all Japanese peace feelers, offered no give on the question of the Emperor, and threatened the total obliteration of Japan. It is important to remember that two days earlier, Truman had already approved the order to drop the atomic bomb on Japanese cities.

3. NOT JAPAN, BUT MOSCOW?

To fully understand the decision Truman made about a weapon he had no part in creating, we must look again at the foundational American assumption of the war, which, however much he may have shared it, Truman had no part in promulgating. Which returns us to that pivotal week in January 1943, when Roosevelt gave rhetorical shape to the determined spirit that was then being (literally) set in concrete in the Pentagon. By defining the Allied war aim as the unconditional surrender of the Axis enemies, Roosevelt put into words a martial absolutism that would animate a building. And not only that. It was in the same period, and reflecting the same spirit, that Roosevelt made another decision that would shape the options with which Truman was presented.

By January 1943, the basic research in preparation for the manufacture of the atomic bomb was virtually complete. Until then, the project had been a collaboration between British- and American-based scientists, but now top U.S. officials, with an eye to the bomb's potential meaning for power relations among nations after the war, proposed restrictions on British access to the project. The president so ordered it. On January 13, 1943, just before Roosevelt headed off to his meeting at Casablanca with Churchill, the British were informed on Roosevelt's authority that henceforth the exchange of nuclear information would be "restricted."[53] Roosevelt would loosen those restrictions somewhat in response to complaints from Churchill, but the point is that FDR, acting in relation to his closest ally, put in place the first pillar of what would become the postwar assumption of American nuclear monopoly. Roosevelt surely felt in part that Europeans had not learned their lesson in World War I, which meant that only the United States could be trusted with this new weapon.

Truman, in tension especially with Stalin, would erect the other pillars, without knowing that in February 1943, in the same fateful weeks, the Soviet Union had launched its own program to build an atomic bomb.[54] (Ironically,

it was also in that same February that American cryptanalysts began intercepting Soviet diplomatic cables to and from espionage agents in the United
States, but they would not break the code — and thus establish that a spy was
already at work in Los Alamos — until years later.)[55]

But Truman's first inheritance was "unconditional surrender." After Roosevelt's death, American leaders lacked his knack for deftly maneuvering
among absolutes of his own making. That they were unable to extricate
themselves in June and July 1945 from the thicket of implications tied to
"unconditionality" connects the use of the atomic bomb directly to FDR's
Casablanca declaration. Casablanca, that is, led to Hiroshima. And recall
again that "unconditional surrender" was not the product of summit delib-
eration, since Churchill had no part in coming to it, but of Roosevelt's unilateral imposition, expressed without Churchill's foreknowledge at a press
conference. The atomic bomb's use, in other words, was a result of the monumental absolutism that had begun to animate the Allied war effort early in
1943, as reflected also in Operation Pointblank, launched just then — and reflected, for that matter, in the monumental Building itself.[56]

Stimson emphasized in his *Harper's* article that the Japanese rejection of
Potsdam made the bomb's use inevitable, but his account drew fire especially
from Joseph Grew, who knew of Stimson's own disappointment with the
final text of the Potsdam Declaration, and with whom Stimson had been allied that summer in pursuing an effective alternative to the horror that fell on
Hiroshima and Nagasaki. Stimson is remembered as having had no ambivalence about the development or use of the bomb, and he is reported to have
been jubilant — he "cut a gay caper"[57] — at the news from New Mexico on
July 16 that the bomb worked. His article, as we have seen, unequivocally asserted that the atomic bombings were tragic but necessary and unavoidable
outcomes of the greater evil that was the war itself. But what Grew had not
forgotten by the time the *Harper's* article appeared was that, in the same period that the Manhattan Project was coming to climax, Stimson was feverishly trying to open another way to end the war than by the bomb's actual
use. Grew's complaint was about this inconsistency, but inconsistency by then
was part of Stimson's method, if not his character. Or was inconsistency inevitable given the complexities?

While Stimson was dead set against shifting the context of the bomb's
significance from Japan to the Soviet Union — Byrnes's impulse — he also
understood how the weight of the bomb was inevitably going to tilt the
scales of global power toward whoever possessed it, an advantage Stimson
was prepared to press. To the extent that he anticipated the postwar situation,
Stimson began as a firm advocate of international controls, but at Potsdam he
did an about-face and argued that the price for breaking the American mo-

nopoly and bringing Moscow into an international nuclear partnership was a democratic restructuring of the Soviet Union that Stalin was certain to reject.[58]

In all of this, in the crucible of world-historic decision-making, Stimson, "a man of strong but inconsistent convictions,"[59] was up against other men — warriors, but statesmen too — who had the advantage of single-mindedness. In contest with them over numerous critical questions, he displayed a political and personal ineffectiveness that may have been compounded by his declining health in old age but was surely tied to an inner ambivalence and perhaps a fatal self-doubt. Most significantly, Stimson continually insisted on the protection of civilians from direct attack, yet he approved the massive bombing of cities before Hiroshima.[60] We will return to that. Like Truman, he claimed to imagine, and for all we know *did* imagine, that the atomic bomb could be used discriminately. Out of professed humanitarian motives, Stimson overruled the target selection committee to spare the ancient Japanese cultural capital of Kyoto on August 6, yet his humanitarian conscience was unmoved by Hiroshima and Nagasaki, neither of which remotely qualified as purely "military targets." Stimson had every reason to know that the bomb would move coercive force into a whole new realm of hyperviolence, yet he failed to grasp the necessity of an equivalent move to a new ethical responsibility. The failure is especially notable in one remembered as the first of the "wise men."[61]

Joseph Grew was therefore annoyed when Stimson's *post facto* account blurred such inconsistencies. Grew knew, in particular, that the *Harper's* piece dodged the crucial issue of Potsdam's insistence on unconditional surrender and the Japanese inability to understand what was meant by it. When Stimson wrote his memoir later that year, he took this point into account, acknowledging there what he had failed to indicate in *Harper's:* "that history might find that the United States, by its delay in stating its position [on the Emperor], had prolonged the war."[62]

But Americans have ignored something even more startling, and that is the fact that not even the two atomic bombs brought about the unconditional surrender of Japan. At 7:33 on the morning of August 10, the day after the bombing of Nagasaki, Washington received a Morse code message from the Japanese leadership body, the Imperial Conference. "The Japanese Government," it said, "is ready to accept the terms enumerated in the joint declaration which was issued at Potsdam with the understanding that said declaration does not compromise any demand which prejudices the prerogatives of His Majesty as a sovereign ruler."[63]

Truman convened his war cabinet at 9 A.M. and asked each of those present if the Japanese message should be taken as an acceptance of the Potsdam

Declaration, despite its clear attachment of a condition. Not surprisingly, Secretary of State Byrnes was adamant in wanting to reject the Japanese offer because acceptance would, as he put it, open the United States "to the criticism that we had receded from the totality and severity of the Potsdam Declaration."[64] Which was, of course, the totality and severity he had himself sponsored. Worse than that, if the United States were now to accept continuance of the Emperor, questions would be raised as to why that condition had not been offered by Washington weeks, even months, before, when it was well known that the Japanese had been seeking it. Byrnes was sensitive on this point, too, because he, as his urging Truman to strike Stimson's language on the subject in the early Potsdam draft indicates, had taken a hard line on the Emperor all along. The scale of suffering inflicted on Hiroshima and Nagasaki could not have been fully grasped on that morning, but Truman's advisers knew that pulling back from the demand for unconditional surrender at that point could well destroy the "no other choice" justification for the use of the atomic bombs which Truman, Byrnes, Stimson, and the others would soon offer.

In the end, the American reply to the Japanese surrender offer finessed the problem by accepting the condition while expanding the context within which the condition stood. "The authority of the Emperor," the reply read, in language effectively the same as that which Truman and Byrnes had eliminated in Potsdam,[65] "shall be subject to the Supreme Commander of the Allied Powers who will take such steps as he deems proper to effectuate the surrender terms . . . The ultimate form of government of Japan will, in accordance with the Potsdam Declaration, be established by the freely expressed will of the Japanese people." Hirohito himself in turn accepted this condition on the Japanese condition, and his will was obeyed even by the diehard military (indicating they were not that diehard). The war was over.

The irony was that there would have been no way to get many — probably most — Japanese soldiers to quit the fight except through the Emperor's authority. By then they were fighting for him, pure and simple. Thus the Allies needed Hirohito in place to end the war. And they respected his role by sparing him the indignity of participating in the surrender ceremony aboard the USS *Missouri*.[66] To have openly acknowledged such intended magnanimity would surely have ended the war with Japan much sooner. Which raises the obvious question: Why did the Americans not do so?

Numerous historians have grappled with such questions,[67] none with more effect than the dean of the revisionists,[68] Gar Alperovitz. His 1965 book *Atomic Diplomacy: Hiroshima and Potsdam* suggests that the atomic bomb was used more to influence the Soviet Union than Japan. In a later book, *The Decision to Use the Atomic Bomb*, which draws on declassified documents,

Alperovitz points out that as early as the first meeting at which the A-bomb was discussed with Truman, on April 25, its impact on "the Russian situation," in General Groves's phrase, was a preoccupation.[69] What if the invasion of an all but defanged Japan was, and remains, a red herring? What if, just as the Nazi threat fell by the wayside, the Japanese threat was not the real issue by the summer of 1945 either? That would explain why Byrnes and Truman, refusing to clarify terms, seemed in no particular hurry to obtain the Japanese surrender. That indifference, embodied in the Potsdam Declaration's return to the language of unconditionality, implies that the overriding purpose of using the atomic bomb was not to end the conflict against Japan but to control the shape of an anticipated conflict with the Soviet Union. What if it were not Emperor Hirohito we were mainly trying to overpower but Premier Stalin? Not a last shot against the Axis but a first shot against the Kremlin, a warning not to act on its clear territorial designs toward Eastern Europe?

In war and politics, there are never one-factor answers to complicated questions. In truth, the atomic bomb was a last shot and a first shot both. The historian Barton Bernstein, for example, argues that the bomb was dropped to hasten the Japanese surrender and also to exert pressure on the Soviet Union.[70] In 2005, the Japanese historian Tsuyoshi Hasegawa, drawing on Japan's own archives, published *Racing the Enemy: Stalin, Truman, and the Surrender of Japan*. Hasegawa argues that Truman used the bomb not to force Japan's surrender (which was coming) but to force it before Moscow entered the war.[71] Learning from such complex historical analysis, one need not argue that Truman was deceptive or cold-blooded enough to order an unnecessary atomic attack. To see a confusion of purposes in wanting to forge a prompt Japanese surrender *and* in wanting to intimidate Moscow is only to acknowledge the dread complexity of the situation in which Truman found himself. The claim to moral and martial clarity and simplicity that he and others made after the fact — that is what deceives.

By July 1945, the bomb was not only a military weapon, it was a political lever. Even before it was operational, the bomb's intended purpose had expanded from straightforward atomic warfare to include what was eventually called "atomic diplomacy." Indeed, it served the latter purpose first, for that is what President Truman engaged in at Potsdam when he slyly told Stalin on July 24 of the successful Alamogordo test (which Stalin already knew about). Truman's gaze was already shifting toward Moscow on the day of his order to use the bomb against Japan. And however the president meant his revelation, Stalin took it as a threat, and that very evening he ordered an escalation of Soviet atomic research,[72] which means the bomb's first use was in fact diplomatic, and it was against Moscow. The nuclear arms race, which would define "atomic diplomacy" for two generations, was on.

But whether American policymakers had already come to the conclusion they would surely have reached not long after the war's end — that the bomb was an anti-Soviet intimidator to be carried, in Stimson's disapproving phrase, "rather ostentatiously on our hip"[73] — it is clear that before using the weapon against Japan, Truman and his inner circle knew that the bomb promised to give the United States dominance in any conceivable postwar world. Such unbridled sway was an irresistible political fantasy, and it undercut, as early as at Potsdam, the nascent American interest in postwar international controls of atomic weaponry.[74] The dream required an expectation of an American atomic monopoly, of course, and in the beginning that was assumed. The prospect of such dominance may have itself been enough to supply the momentum necessary to use the bomb as soon as possible; that prospect trumped every impulse to accept the promising surrender signals from Japan — even if the aim of cementing postwar American preeminence could never be referred to in justifications after the bomb was dropped. Critics of the Hiroshima attack, both before[75] and after, proposed dropping the bomb on an unpopulated area in order to demonstrate its unprecedented lethality. But President Truman decided that the demonstration of American might on hundreds of thousands of Japanese would be more effective, prudent even. However intended, Hiroshima and Nagasaki were exactly that, a double-barreled demonstration, not only — or perhaps not even primarily — to Japan but to the world. "The new age was conceived in secrecy and usurped even before birth by one state," the Nobel laureate Joseph Rotblat has written, "in order to gain political dominance."[76]

4. ATOMIC FORGETFULNESS

Rotblat was one of the original Los Alamos scientists, and he was typical in having signed on to the project of turning nuclear fission into a weapon only out of fear that the Nazis would do so first. We have already noted Philip Morrison's daily rush home at lunch hour, to tune in the BBC to learn if London was still intact. "When it became evident, toward the end of 1944, that the Germans had abandoned their bomb project," Rotblat wrote, "the whole purpose of my being in Los Alamos ceased to be, and I asked for permission to leave and return to Britain."[77] Of the Los Alamos scientists, Rotblat, a physicist who had fled Poland, was the "only one who paused"[78] once the Nazi bomb ceased to threaten. He would go on to be a founder of the Pugwash Conferences on Science and World Affairs, an international movement of scientists working against nuclear weapons, a commitment that earned him (and the Pugwash organization) the 1995 Nobel Peace Prize.

About the time that Rotblat left Los Alamos, another atomic scientist, Leo Szilard, also reacted to the realization that Hitler would not acquire the bomb. Budapest born, at the age of forty-seven Szilard was a key figure in plutonium production at the University of Chicago Metallurgical Laboratory. He had, in the words of Richard Rhodes, "thought longer and harder than anyone else about the consequences of the chain reaction,"[79] and his standing with fellow scientists reflected that. From before America's entry into the war, Szilard, with Albert Einstein, had been instrumental in convincing Roosevelt to embark on the "plutonium weapon" in the first place. Aware that German scientists had discovered fission early in 1939, Szilard, in an October 1939 letter that Einstein also signed, urged the project on FDR.

But by the spring of 1945, Szilard presciently saw that the momentum driving the Manhattan Project threatened not only an unnecessary use of the superweapon against Japan but an eventual nuclear arms race with the Soviet Union. Again with Einstein's help, Szilard arranged a meeting with the president to raise these concerns, but Roosevelt died before it could take place. Seeking a meeting with Truman, Szilard was sent instead to see James Byrnes. They met on May 28 in Spartanburg, South Carolina. This was a month before Byrnes was named secretary of state, but as Truman's liaison to the Interim Committee of the Manhattan Project, he had recently been brought well inside the atomic loop.[80]

To Szilard's amazement, the irascible Byrnes dismissed his worries about an arms race; he saw the bomb as an ace to play against Moscow. "You come from Hungary," Byrnes said to Szilard. "You would not want Russia to stay in Hungary indefinitely."[81] Byrnes added that "Russia might be more manageable if impressed by American military might, and that a demonstration of the bomb might impress Russia." Years later, Szilard wrote, "I shared Byrnes' concern about Russia's throwing her weight around in the post-war period, but I was completely flabbergasted by the assumption that rattling the bomb might make Russia more manageable."[82] Szilard was appalled and frightened by this first display of "atomic diplomacy," by the hubris already accruing to excessive power. He left the meeting more determined than ever to slow the momentum toward use of the bomb. But for Byrnes, who saw that key scientists were mounting a movement to stop the bomb's use, the momentum had just increased.

Unlike Byrnes, Stimson, Truman, and other nonscientists who tended to think of the atomic bomb as a conventional explosive, subject to the same considerations,[83] Szilard and his colleagues realized that a threshold had been crossed and that moral conflagration threatened. They had a vivid sense of the bomb's awesome destructiveness. On the eve of the Trinity test, Enrico Fermi, who had presided over the first chain reaction at Chicago, would offer to take bets as to whether the bomb would ignite the very atmosphere.[84] (We saw that Morrison wondered about this.) By July, Szilard had organized a petition to President Truman expressing grave misgivings about any use of the bomb against Japan: "A nation which sets the precedent of using these newly liberated forces of nature for purposes of destruction may have to bear responsibility of opening the door to an era of devastation on an unimaginable scale."[85] The petition went through several drafts, as Szilard sought to accommodate his more reluctant colleagues. Many of them postponed any consideration of moral or political problems pending the test. Apparently they simply wanted to see whether their scientific assumptions were valid.

Trinity came without delay on July 16. The final form of Szilard's petition was dated July 17, the day after the bomb had proved itself. But even then, few of the hundreds of Szilard's fellow scientists signed. "The accident that we worked out this dreadful thing," Edward Teller said to Szilard, "should not give us the responsibility of having a voice in how it is used."[86] In the end, sixty-nine scientists did sign Szilard's petition, mainly from among his colleagues at Chicago. Many of these men, and some women, were, like Szilard and Einstein, refugees from Hitler's Europe, and as grateful as they were to America, their natural frame of reference was transnational. Their hope for the future of their own work — the future of the bomb and the future of the planet — was that it be subject to international controls and therefore beyond the reach of any one nation's hegemony or narrow ideology. They were particularly concerned to head off a nuclear arms race between the United States and the Soviet Union. More immediately, they feared that the first military use of the new weapon would unnecessarily target a population center. For these reasons, the dissenting scientists wanted to deter a surprise atomic attack against a Japanese city, especially if a demonstration explosion could bring about the end of the war. A demonstration, they believed, would also persuade other nations, including Russia, to participate in a new regime of international cooperation. Thus, in the climactic weeks of the war, with world-historic consequences at stake, the Szilard-led scientists offered what two historians call "the only dynamic and tightly focused effort" to find another way than use of the bomb on Japanese cities.[87]

There were convincing arguments to be made against the premature disclosure of atomic information, above all to the Soviets, and against a mere demonstration. But the Szilard petition specifically addressed the pivotal question of surrender terms being offered to Japan, echoing what Stimson, Grew, and others were saying. On this point the petition could well have figured in the fateful discussions that unfolded in the days between the successful atomic test and the Potsdam ultimatum, but as we shall see, the petition was sidetracked by the man whose job it was to deliver it. Truman did not see the scientists' plea until after the bombs were dropped. Szilard's being shunted aside meant that, in the final and decisive consideration of whether and how to use the atomic bomb, it was forgotten that the project had been launched not against Hirohito or Stalin, but against Hitler.

Forgetfulness would be a permanent feature of the American relationship to nuclear weapons, as was never made plainer than on the fiftieth anniversary of the bombings of Hiroshima and Nagasaki. On that occasion, the Smithsonian Institution mounted a commemorative exhibit built around a display of the *Enola Gay,* the warplane from which the Hiroshima bomb was dropped.[88]

The Smithsonian's Air and Space Museum, on the National Mall, is a festival of aviation, with relics of all the great chapters of flight and aeronautics. Suspended from glistening girders under skylights and enormous glass walls, the Wright brothers' kite-like craft, Lindbergh's *Spirit of St. Louis,* and Chuck Yeager's sound-barrier-breaking jet hover above floor-bound fuselages, space capsules, rockets, and endless streams of tourists. The place is an unashamed celebration of American ingenuity, courage, and virtue. I have gone there many times, and it is impossible to enter the cheery space without a lift of the heart. Until the quite different Holocaust Memorial Museum was constructed a short distance down the Mall, the Air and Space Museum was the most visited site in the capital. And here, in 1995, was an exhibit designed to recall the bombings of Hiroshima and Nagasaki, and to reconsider them.

The museum's curators assembled documents and photographs that intended to give a full picture of the bombings, of the Manhattan Project that led to them, of the valiant air crews that carried them out, and of the consequences on the ground in the two cities where they occurred. The bombings were presented in the context of the war they ended — from Pearl Harbor to Japanese atrocities to the grinding combat in the Pacific. Distorted faces and charred corpses of the bombed were juxtaposed with the grins of the air crew posing by the legendary B-29. To be sure, the real people of Hiroshima and Nagasaki — exposed flesh and bones — compelled more than the aircraft. The solidity of the homes, schools, and temples, and the shadows, literally, of lives obliterated in a flash, spoke of the annihilation that had occurred.

One display of text highlighted passages from the memoirs of Admiral William D. Leahy and of Dwight D. Eisenhower, who had raised an objection to the bomb's use in that July meeting with Stimson. The exhibit also quoted Leahy, who served both Roosevelt and Truman as chief of staff: "It is my opinion that the use of this barbarous weapon at Hiroshima and Nagasaki was of no major assistance in our war against Japan . . . We had adopted an ethical standard common to the barbarians of the Dark Ages. I was not taught to make war in that fashion, and wars cannot be won by destroying women and children."[89]

It was one thing for revisionist historians to question what had come to be called the "Truman orthodoxy" about the inevitable, if tragic, necessity for the atomic attacks, but the citations of Ike and Leahy turned out to be especially inflammatory. Two great military leaders had questioned whether the invasion was necessary, whether an American act of war was humane. Were they now being cited to support the heresy that the United States was an aggressor and Japan a victim? The exhibit, that is, put questions on display as well as answers — as would be expected from a work of history. It attempted to reckon with several of the conundrums that confronted decision makers in the spring and summer of 1945, including questions, such as surrender terms, that we have considered here.

As I hope is true of the present work, the Smithsonian exhibit intended to demonize no one. And, as we do here, it assumed that it is possible to view the past without claiming moral superiority. In the thick of war, people assign rigid places to good and evil, always to the benefit of one's own side. But history allows no such assignation, and at the Smithsonian retrospective, good and evil were not portrayed as having chosen sides. Instead, the exhibit showed a momentous event of the past as ambiguous, complex, and tragic, with multiple meanings for the various people involved — and multiple meanings for *each* person involved. Truman's decision and its consequences, in sum, were presented neither as a simple act of heroic virtue nor as a pact with the devil.

A storm of protest greeted the opening of the exhibit. It was led by veterans' groups, who understandably claim a kind of proprietorship over how the story of World War II is told. The American Legion was joined in its protest, not surprisingly, and less sympathetically, by the Air Force Association, a professional lobbying entity sponsored by the aircraft industry. The association's ongoing commercial stake in the glorious version of strategic air warfare seemed not to undercut its claim to an objective interest in the dispute. Pundits weighed in, editorialists opined, and so did politicians — mounting a tremendous defense of the Truman orthodoxy and a view of American history as celebration without criticism. Such celebration meant deleting from the American memory prickly facts that no longer squared with orthodoxy — for example, that the government's own postwar evaluation of the atomic bombs had concluded almost immediately, as the U.S. Strategic Bombing Survey report put it, that "certainly prior to 31 December 1945, and in all probability prior to 1 November 1945, Japan would have surrendered even if the atomic bombs had not been dropped, even if Russia had not entered the war, and even if no invasion had been planned or contemplated."[90]

It was in the course of this controversy that revisionist historians, who had long been at work reconsidering various elements of the atomic bomb story, became widely reviled. One of them was "disinvited" from a White House commemoration of the anniversary of the war's end,[91] and President Clinton, famous in other contexts for apologizing (he apologized for slavery, he apologized for America's failure to prevent genocide in Rwanda), was moved to say that Truman had made the right decision about bombing Hiroshima and Nagasaki. Clinton, sensing the third-rail character of the question, would not sponsor any reconsideration either.

At the Smithsonian, the director of the Air and Space Museum, Martin Harwit, was forced to resign and the exhibit was canceled, to be replaced by a scaled-down, innocuous commemoration. At the new Holocaust Memorial Museum, visitors were being drawn into a powerful enactment of moral memory in which not only Nazis were faulted for the Final Solution but also some of the great and ongoing institutions of the West, including the Catholic Church and the U.S. State Department. But no such reconsideration was possible regarding the question of the atomic bomb. At the Air and Space Museum, on the fiftieth anniversary of Hiroshima and Nagasaki, a kind of national amnesia[92] was officially instituted, with the blessing of almost all the major media outlets and the highest figures in the Washington establishment. The episode is significant, because it shows that even now Americans have hardly begun to come to terms with what may rank as the most important event in their nation's history.[93]

Hiroshima is locked in the shadows of repressed memory because a reconsideration of the first use of a nuclear weapon would require a reconsideration of Pentagon-centered American power that still depends on nuclear weapons and the lively possibility of a next use. More subtly, the advent of an American nuclear force brought the nation to the threshold less of a spirit of total war — the United States would never actually unleash its full arsenal — than of what might be called a spirit of total victory. America wants its way and, simply by the possession of that arsenal and occasionally flaunting it, America gets its way — which is why the late-twentieth-century, multifactored collapse of the Soviet Union could be perceived as America's having "won" the Cold War, and why the early-twenty-first-century war on terrorism quickly evolved into a global American militarism. The debate over Truman's decision, in that sense, has never been about the past, but about the present and the future.

5. GROVES'S TOBOGGAN

Whether viewed as an ending of World War II or as the staking of a claim to postwar power, or both, is it possible to conclude at this point that those bombs were dropped as a result of a "decision" by Truman? We saw that he approved the order to the 305th Composite Group on July 24, and Truman himself noted the gravity of that date. The plainspoken president's admiring interpreters have always emphasized his damn-the-consequences readiness to make tough choices, and the atomic bombing of Japan ranks at the top of those. "The final decision of where and when to use the atomic bomb was up to me," Truman wrote in his memoir. "Let there be no mistake about it. I regarded the bomb as a military weapon and never had any doubt it should be used."[94] But the triple-phased momentum dating to Roosevelt's decisions in January 1943 — a monopolistic hold on the atomic bomb, unconditionality, and the air war against urban populations — may have been, in fact, unstoppable by the time it swept over Truman, merely carrying him along. To Truman the matter was simple: the war was just, the enemy was evil, the bomb could end the war and punish the enemy. Not incidentally, Truman's political career was made by his ferreting out waste in war-related government expenditures, and he knew that using the bomb decisively was the only way to avoid a politically disastrous postwar confrontation with Congress over the two billion dollars it had cost. That much money, too, carries momentum.

But perhaps the overriding engine driving this process toward its awful climax on August 6 was not rational but emotional. The plainest fact of all was that the atomic bomb, by its sheer overwhelming monumentality, promised to exact a fitting revenge for the deep psychological wound Americans, certainly including Truman, had suffered at Pearl Harbor. Both the policy of unconditional surrender (even if it was not really unconditional) and the actual use of the atomic bombs that it led to could and did satisfy that need, as Truman himself then testified. On the evening of August 9, the day a million Soviet soldiers invaded Manchuria and the day a bomb fell on Nagasaki, Truman said in a radio address to the American people, "Having found the bomb, we have used it. We have used it against those who attacked us without warning at Pearl Harbor, against those who have starved and beaten American prisoners of war, against those who have abandoned all pretense of obeying international laws of warfare. We have used it in order to shorten the agony of war, in order to save the lives of thousands and thousands of young Americans. We shall continue to use it until we completely destroy Japan's power to make war. Only a Japanese surrender will stop us."[95] The language of revenge, which here was offered as the first justification, ahead of shortening the war and ahead of saving American lives, would soon drop out of official explanations of the decision to use the atomic bomb. It remains debatable whether the justification offered last — those young American lives lost in an invasion — was authentic, given questions about the necessity of invasion, but there is no doubt that the first justification, primal vengeance, was true. Truman spoke for himself and the nation.

Truman's biographer David McCullough thus refers to "the decision that was no decision,"[96] and he cites one of the president's intimates: "Truman made no decision because there was no decision to be made. He could no more have stopped it than a train moving down a track . . . It's all well and good to come along later and say the bomb was a horrible thing. The whole goddamn war was a horrible thing."[97] This assessment ignores that, however horrible the war was, American leaders consistently observed basic rules of engagement on the ground (never sanctioning mass rape, for example, as Soviet leaders did in Germany). Here we have interpreters of the Hiroshima event — and defenders of the Truman orthodoxy — wanting to have it both ways. The decision was the right one; or, if it was not right, it was no decision. Truman could not stop the innate rush toward vengeance. Truman could not stem the tide of the largest bureaucratic enterprise in history. He could only appear to influence events that arrived in the wake of all that his predecessor had set in motion.

Some of Truman's critics take this position, too. For example, Barton Bernstein, the revisionist who was disinvited to the White House: "In 1945, American leaders were not seeking to avoid the use of the A-bomb. Its use did not create ethical or political problems for them. Thus, they easily rejected or never considered most of the so-called alternatives to the bomb."[98] Commenting on this, another historian wrote, "Bernstein's approach suggested a conclusion that is, if anything, even harsher than Alperovitz's. So overwhelming was the assumption of use, that use was inevitable. It was not, however, necessary."[99] Indeed, the idea of momentum has another implication, namely that a change in direction is easier to effect when something is well under way than when it is hardly moving. Or, as another historian put it, "While a decision-making process may seem to thunder along like a diesel truck, a firm touch by any one of a number of people can often send it in a different direction. Truman could certainly have applied that touch. Groves could have. Stimson as head of the Interim Committee could have."[100]

Stimson's *Harper's* article first shaped the American memory with its emphasis on the decision, but Stimson concludes, as we saw, and like Truman's intimate just quoted, with a statement about war itself as the driving force. That is a standard human impulse: to deny responsibility for the extreme violence of combat by depicting the battlefield as a place where agency and moral choice no longer apply. This is a way of saying we are still in control because certain things are out of control. It absolves fallibility while admitting fallibility. War is thus experienced as, and then defined as, a usurping force that obliterates personal freedom — and also, therefore, responsibility. Such a force can comfort the conscience of presidents, planners, and officers — as well as looters, rapists, and murderers. (And it treats that force like a god to be appeased in order to urge, with romantic impracticability, the abolition of all war, while ignoring measures needed to keep war on this side of Armageddon.)

A range of factors refutes this deterministic way of thinking about what led to the use of the atomic bomb. Regarding the momentum pushing Truman toward his decision, some historians ask why high military officials were apparently unaffected by it.[101] Were Eisenhower and Leahy not hardened by the rush to vengeance? Stimson and Grew? If the built-in harshness of unconditionality was insurmountable by the summer of 1945, why did all of the senior American officials except Byrnes and Truman want to mitigate it?

The mention of Byrnes takes us beyond impersonal determinism, for a key element of this story is his involvement. We have seen how his intervention before and during Potsdam negotiations proved decisive in deleting the offer of assurances to the Emperor, but that was the lesser of his initiatives. Byrnes's influence on Truman deserves far more emphasis than it has gotten, for before Truman began to ponder his decision, Byrnes had started to shape it. And if human agency is the issue, we would do well to note the influence of the man who was to Byrnes what Byrnes himself was to Truman: the shaper of alternatives, the definer of choice. And that brings us back to the man who built the Building and the bomb both, Leslie R. Groves.

The order that Truman approved on July 24, sending the 509th Composite Group on its way to Hiroshima, was actually signed by General Thomas Handy, in lieu of General Marshall. But the order — "will deliver its first special bomb as soon as weather will permit visual bombing after about 3 August"[102] — was in fact written by General Groves. The order, as we saw, identified four cites as targets (Hiroshima, Kokura, Niigata, and Nagasaki) and instructed the Air Force to deliver "additional bombs . . . as soon as made ready by the project staff." In the order's being presented to Truman in Potsdam, the constitutional provision that the military is subservient to civilian authority was being observed, but the use of nuclear weapons would effectively vitiate the meaning of that provision — beginning then and continuing over the years. This was so because, as Secretary of Defense Robert McNamara and President John Kennedy are seen discovering later in this narrative, civilian authority would always be dependent on the military "guardians"[103] of the nuclear arsenal for operational information, which itself framed or even forced decisions. The commanders of America's strategic arsenal would institutionalize military control of the nuclear option, to the extent of refusing to share strike plans with civilian superiors, but it began with Groves. He told interviewers after the war, "I didn't have to have the President press the button on this affair."[104]

Not only did the order Groves had put before Truman leave the military complete discretion as to timing, kinds of targets (with no stipulations regarding efforts to avoid civilian casualties), and the open-endedness of the bombing; it was not even the only instrument of control. An independent order that Groves also wrote, which he had Marshall approve before leaving for Potsdam, and which Truman never laid eyes on, put Groves atop the chain of command for the dropping of each bomb. The engineer who built the bomb would be the commander who "delivered" it. Normal procedure would have vested this authority in the head of the Strategic Air Force, General Carl Spaatz, to whom the July 25 order was issued. Or the supreme authority of such combat command might have been vested in the chief of staff of the Air Force, General Arnold. But after the war Groves acknowledged that his authority superseded Arnold's.[105] This violation of the sacrosanct chain of command in favor of a uniformed bureaucrat with no combat experience, arranged by the bureaucrat himself,[106] is the most important and least appreciated fact about the atomic bomb by the time it became operational — namely that Groves had more control over the bomb, more dominance over the entire wing of government and science that had been created for and by the bomb, and more influence over those who would participate in the bomb's delivery than any other person.

We referred above to momentum, and a Truman aide referred to the motion of a train. Groves insisted in his 1962 autobiography that "the burden [of decision] fell upon President Truman,"[107] but a year later he implied something else when he described Truman as "a little boy on a toboggan."[108] Though there are those who underplay Groves's role in the A-bomb decision,[109] it seems fair to see Groves himself as that sled carrying the president and others down the hill. Groves said, "Truman did not so much say 'yes' as not say 'no.'" Another time, he offered a different analogy: "The responsibility taken by Mr. Truman was essentially, I think, the responsibility taken by a surgeon who comes in after the patient has been all opened up and the appendix is half cut off and he says, 'yes I think he ought to have out the appendix — that's my decision.'"[110] Groves does not say here that he was the prep surgeon who made the first incision, which made the next inevitable.

How can it be that a relatively junior Army officer accumulated such

power? The answer is simple. Because of its purpose, the scope of his authority as head of the Manhattan Project was without American precedent, before
or since. "General Groves planned the project," a wartime associate said later,
"ran his own construction, his own science, his own army, his own State Department and his own Treasury Department."[111] At the end, he ran his own
Air Force, too.

For the sake of the most tightly held secret in history (although, as the
Klaus Fuchs espionage case showed, not tight enough), the various and complex elements of the Manhattan Project were kept in rigidly separate spheres,
with only one person in a position to know everything: Groves. He was the
administrator in charge of maintaining that security, and no one, including
his superiors, gained access to information unless he wanted them to. He was,
in the words of a contemporary in the War Department, "an absolute dictator, in who[m] his superiors place great faith."[112] Groves described himself as
an "impresario of a two-billion-dollar grand opera with thousands of tem-
peramental stars."[113] Impresario, yes, but he was also the prima donna. He
personally wrote the military order that sent the bomb on its way, and after it
fell, he wrote the press release announcing the fact to the world.[114]

There seems to have been only one instance in which, on something that
mattered to him, Groves's authority did not carry, and that was on the question of target cities. He wanted Kyoto included on the list, but as we saw, Secretary of War Stimson vetoed that on the grounds that Kyoto was the ancient
political and religious capital of Japan. In addition to the fact that Kyoto, with
a million people, was many times larger than the other cities chosen, and
would therefore show off the bomb's destructiveness better, its cultural sanc-
tity was the reason that Groves *wanted* it bombed, for the extra shock to Japanese morale.

For reasons having to do with personal experience (Stimson had been to
Kyoto and loved it) and with a conscience that caused him anguish on the
question of killing civilians, this was a rare point about which the secretary of
war was not ambivalent and would not be cowed. Stimson seems to have convinced himself that the other target cities had military importance in a way
that Kyoto did not. Through June into July, he therefore repeatedly removed
Kyoto from the target list, just as Groves repeatedly put it back on. Groves
later quoted Stimson as heatedly telling him, "This is one time that I'm going
to be the final deciding authority. Nobody's going to tell me what to do on
this. On this matter I am the kingpin."[115]

Eventually, the city itself mattered less to Groves than his authority over
something as central as where his bomb would be used, and he confronted
Stimson on the question "up to a dozen times."[116] Stimson, in this debate with
a lowly brigadier general, turned out not to be the kingpin. On July 22, he had

to go to President Truman to have his order seconded. Kyoto stayed off the list of four cities. It was replaced by Nagasaki. The fact that Groves lost this argument only reinforces its rarity. The system he had created not only successfully produced the atomic bomb but also made him by far the most powerful person in its orbit.

Gar Alperovitz says that Groves played no part in the "real decisions," such as those regarding surrender terms that were not offered to the Japanese, but ever since he began his full-time work on the Manhattan Project in the pivotal month of January 1943, Groves actively manipulated the context within which those decisions had to be made. There was simply no way the war would be ended except by his bomb. The will of Leslie Groves, in other words, *was* the engine of the momentum toward use that would supersede the diplomacy favored by almost every senior American military and political official — not to mention overcoming the conscientious hesitation of scientists who had created the bomb.

Let us return to Szilard's petition of July 1945. We noted that only a minority of Manhattan Project scientists signed it, and those were mostly limited to Szilard's colleagues at Chicago. But there is a reason why the petition's appeal was limited and why it failed to reach Truman, and the reason was Groves. When the petition was being circulated among scientists at the Metallurgical Laboratory in Chicago, Groves was informed of it by one of his counterintelligence agents there. Groves and the scientists were disdainful of each other, although the scientists with large responsibilities on the project, like J. Robert Oppenheimer, "respected his abilities," as Oppenheimer's protégé Philip Morrison told me. Morrison served as a kind of go-between for Oppenheimer and Groves, saw Groves often, and admired him. "Groves was the most apt officer that could have had the job."[117] But even Morrison disagreed with him on the key point that Szilard's petition raised, the question of a demonstration drop of the bomb.[118] That prospect particularly alarmed Groves. He gave absolute importance, as he put it in his autobiography, to "the overwhelming surprise of the bomb. To achieve surprise was one of the reasons we had tried so hard to maintain our security."[119] Thinking of the supreme secrecy that had itself made him supreme, he was not going to surrender surprise through a demonstration because of the ambivalence of scientists.

Groves moved to stop Szilard by challenging the petition as a criminal violation of security. He ordered the scientist to give it to no one whose security clearance was lower than Szilard's own, a tactic eliminating many scientists from merely looking at the petition. Groves was also able to block access to the petition by scientists not based in Chicago. He did so at Los Alamos by getting Oppenheimer to prevent its circulation, and at Oak Ridge by imposing extraordinary security restrictions on it there. If it were not for these moves, more than the sixty-nine Chicago scientists, perhaps many more, would have signed.

When, on July 17, Szilard attempted to have the signed petition delivered to Truman, Groves intercepted it. Recognizing it as "the only dynamic and tightly focused" alternative to his own plans, he held the document until August 1,[120] then sent it "on a low priority basis for delivery to the White House." The scientists' petition may not in any case have altered the decisions that Truman made with Byrnes at Potsdam, but "Groves was not taking any chances."[121]

Byrnes was the key influence on Truman, but it seems likely that the key influence on Byrnes was Groves. When Stimson appointed Byrnes to the Interim Committee in May, it was Groves who briefed Byrnes on the project and its significance. We have already seen how Byrnes shocked Leo Szilard on May 28 at Spartanburg by defining the atomic bomb not as a way to end the war against Japan but as a postwar ace to be played against the Soviet Union. That was exactly the way Groves had come to think of the bomb, too, and in the meeting with Szilard, Byrnes tipped his hand that his thinking was shaped by what Groves had told him. When Byrnes had blithely forecast the American advantage that would flow from the bomb, Szilard, as he later recalled, "spoke of my concern that Russia might become an atomic power, and might become an atomic power soon, if we demonstrated the power of the bomb and if we used it against Japan. His reply was, 'General Groves tells me there is no uranium in Russia.'" It was a ludicrous statement. Richard Rhodes asserts that Szilard was even then being tailed by Groves's agents.[122]

Joseph Rotblat, the scientist who resigned from the Manhattan Project once it became clear that the Germans would not get the bomb, says he came to that decision in part because of "one memorable evening in March 1944." It was a dinner party at the Los Alamos home of a colleague, and Groves was present. Almost offhandedly, "Groves remarked that the real purpose of building the bomb was to subdue the Soviets. This statement at the time was a shock to me. I was later to recall my encounter with Groves." Groves had been thinking that way, in fact, for more than a year.[123]

Because that was his view of the bomb's main importance, the effort to bring the war to a conclusion by means of negotiations with Japan — before the bomb could prove itself and thus establish American dominance — could seem a positive threat to Groves. At the conference table of the senior War Department leaders in the spring of 1945, he was surrounded by men aware both that Japan was all but defeated and that it was showing increasing signs of looking to end the war through negotiation. That changed in May, when Byrnes came to the table as the president's representative, establishing a new momentum away from negotiation that would, as we saw, reach its climax in July at Potsdam, when Byrnes cut off Stimson's appeal for a mitigation of the demand for unconditional surrender. Unconditional surrender had, in fact, become a necessary part of Byrnes's plan. He and Groves simply wanted to get on with the actual use of the atomic bomb in war. The two men knew, as Stimson put it in his memoir, that "the bomb as a merely probable weapon had seemed a weak reed on which to rely, but the bomb as a colossal reality was very different."[124] And in order to be "colossal," the bomb had to be used against cities.

When the Trinity test succeeded on July 16, we saw that Oppenheimer's thoughts went to the Bhagavad Gita, and Morrison thought he saw a second sunrise. But Groves responded to the success of the test by thinking at once of his Building in Arlington, which gave him the true measure of the new weapon's lethality. "I no longer consider the Pentagon a safe shelter from such a bomb," he wrote to Stimson. In a way that perhaps only Stimson could understand, it was the most drastic thing Groves could say. The absolute weapon and the absolute building were joined in Groves's mind, and the link between the two would be permanent. The successful test on July 16 meant that the United States was at last in possession of "the final arbiter of force," in Stimson's phrase.[125] That is the sense in which the bomb is an absolute weapon. Yet its very "finality," in Stimson's word, would ironically — once matched by a counterbalancing Soviet weapon — be made usable as a weapon *not to be used,* and therefore somehow relative again.[126]

But in 1945, the bomb could be seen as changing everything. It was a phenomenon that would in short order transform weaponry, diplomacy, the economy of the United States, its way of presenting itself to and being viewed by the world, and even its understanding of itself. The engine room and icon of that transformation would be the Pentagon.

It is the recognition of world-historic power bestowed by exclusive possession of the atomic bomb that accounts for the glee with which the news of the test was received at Potsdam, by Byrnes and Truman in particular — and the news, defined in code as a successful medical procedure, came from "Dr. Groves," who described himself as "pleased."[127] Groves wrote of a flash that could be seen 250 miles away, so bright a blind woman saw it. When Stimson read aloud the Groves report to Churchill, the British prime minister instantly saw its implication: "Stimson, what was gunpowder?" he exclaimed, so Churchillian. "What was electricity? Meaningless. This atomic bomb is the Second Coming in Wrath!"[128]

To a politician, this was transcendent political power, but to the scientists who made it, the bomb represented another kind of power. "Nuclear explosives have a glitter more seductive than gold to those who play with them," the physicist Freeman Dyson wrote. "To command nature to release in a pint pot the energy that fuels the stars, to lift by pure thought a million tons of rock into the sky, these are exercises of the human will that produce an illusion of illimitable power."[129] Infinite power. Power that, by bringing the ultimate form of death under human control, bestows, as if by magic, redemption from death. That line of the Bhagavad Gita that popped into Oppenheimer's mind at the moment of zero — "Now I am become Death, the destroyer of worlds" — is usually taken as a manifestation of visceral guilt, but it can equally point to the paradoxical exhilaration of undiluted vitality springing from utter destructiveness. Final death, in the mystery of the atomic economy, opens into abundant life. Science inherently pursues immortality, and the control of nuclear energy bestows it. This is why technocratic expertise came to trump moral reasoning. And it is another reason why a mere minority of the Manhattan Project intellectuals signed Szilard's warning petition.

But the appeal of this kind of power reaches beyond the men of the labs, subtly extending the issue from power, however overtly defined, to potency. When Groves sent his coded cable to Potsdam reporting on the Trinity test, it brought news of the birth of a boy. That was because the code word for a failed test — a dud, in the parlance — had been set as "girl." "In light of the imagery of male birth [at Trinity]," the critic Carol Cohn writes, "the extraordinary names given to the bombs that reduced Hiroshima and Nagasaki to ash and rubble — 'Little Boy' and 'Fat Man' — at last become intelligible."[130] Men conceiving and delivering the object that grants them control of Mother Nature: one needn't make more of this gendered undercurrent than to note it as part of what was at play in human consciousness at this moment. The sexual theme, how war valorizes masculinity, was more than implied in the coded message Oppenheimer sent to his wife when the test succeeded: "Tell her she can change the sheets."[131]

So of course the news of the "boy's" birth immediately made Truman feel "tremendously pepped up . . . [with] an entirely new feeling of confidence."[132] And his confidence in relation to Stalin was what counted — a conflict that would be defined by nothing so much as "missile envy."[133] Truman's admiring biographer David McCullough wrote, "Clearly, Truman was fortified by the news. It is hard to imagine that he would not have been. That he and Byrnes felt their hand might be thus strengthened at the bargaining table with the Russians in time to come is also obvious — and perfectly understandable — but by no means was this the primary consideration, as some would later contend."[134]

But how could it not be? Japan was not the real threat at Potsdam. Russia was. Truman would describe the bomb he had just ordered dropped as "the greatest thing in history,"[135] but he was not indulging in mere bloodthirstiness with that reaction. Only a focus on something other than the streets, houses, schools, and temples of Hiroshima kept that remark from being monstrous. It seems reasonable to assume that Truman was not thinking of Japanese casualties but of the power he had claimed for his nation. And it was true, this was power unlike any before in history. It was power with immediate relevance to the emerging rivalry with Stalin. So yes, the atomic bombs, as Truman's defenders insist, were used to end the brutal war with Japan. But that the bombs would be used so precipitously — as soon as they were ready, well ahead of any possible escalation of battle casualties or invasion of Japan, and without pursuing any of the numerous positive diplomatic signals — suggests that they would equally and simultaneously be used to halt Soviet advances in Asia and Eastern Europe. Against the traditionalist-revisionist argument, in other words, the explanation for the bombs is not either-or; it's both.

6. THE SECOND COMING IN WRATH

It says everything about the convergence of the two enterprises over which Groves presided that what might be called the truly decisive event in this entire process took place in a well-appointed, warmly paneled conference room on an upper floor of the Pentagon. It was a two-day meeting of the Interim Committee, presided over by Secretary Stimson and with Groves present throughout. Rhodes calls it a "star chamber."[136] It had grave consequences for the world.

The meeting took place from May 31 to June 1, two days after Byrnes's meeting with Szilard at Spartanburg and a full month before Byrnes was sworn in as secretary of state. In addition to Stimson and Byrnes, the committee members included an undersecretary of the Navy, Ralph A. Bard, two other officials, and four scientists, including Vannevar Bush, James Conant, and J. Robert Oppenheimer. General Marshall was present "by invitation," as was General Groves. The meeting's purpose was vaguely defined by Stimson in his opening remarks: "to assist the Secretary and General Marshall in making recommendations to the President concerning control of this weapon during the war period and organization for post-war control." But Stimson struck a note that indicated the kind of meeting he wanted to have: he hoped, he said, that the committee could approach the subject of the atomic bomb "like statesmen and not . . . merely soldiers anxious to win the war at any cost."[137]

For two days, the committee consulted with various industrialists and scientists, and notes of the meeting suggest an undisciplined and unfocused set of considerations. That was probably a result of the fact that Stimson was distracted, often excused himself, and may have been ill. We saw that Byrnes, six weeks later, would preempt Stimson at Potsdam on the crucial question of assurances to the Emperor, but that maneuvering began here. In Stimson's absences, and even in Stimson's presence, the official log of the meeting suggests that over the two days Byrnes increasingly — "Mr. Byrnes recommended and the Committee agreed . . ." — seized the initiative. This was especially so on the subjects of postwar international controls and wartime use of atomic weapons.[138] Apart from Byrnes, the men present had been considering matters associated with the coming bomb for months, and there is little to suggest that they felt pressure to reach definitive decisions as they opened the meeting.

Secretary Stimson, in his memoir written two years later, said that the Interim Committee's "first and greatest problem" at the meeting was the question of whether the bomb should be used against Japan, and if so, how.[139] But his own opening remarks suggest no such clear purpose; that question was not on the committee's agenda. These men were not yet pressed to decide the matter in relation to Japan, and they expected an open-ended discussion about the various issues raised by the bomb's development. "The fact is," the historian Martin Sherwin writes, "that a discussion of this question [use of the bomb against Japan] was placed on the agenda only after it was raised casually in the course of a conversation during lunch."[140] That would explain why one member, at least, found himself troubled for weeks by what he had impulsively agreed to; it would explain, that is, why that member, Navy Undersecretary Bard, submitted a memorandum of dissent to Stimson a month later, expressly repudiating the momentous recommendation to which he and other committee members had assented.[141]

On the first day of the session, Oppenheimer insisted that some kind of international control of the bomb would be necessary, and General Marshall agreed, both men knowing well that this would require the sharing of atomic information with the Soviet Union. Marshall said he was "certain that we need have no fear that the Russians, if they had knowledge of the project, would disclose this information to the Japanese."[142] But when Byrnes expressed strong reservations about approaching the Russians, even "in general terms," the committee shunted aside the idea of international cooperation. Also on the first day, when the subject of using the bomb against Japan came up, General Marshall expressed the strong opinion that the bomb should be used only "against straight military objectives, such as a large naval installation."[143] Byrnes dismissed this suggestion, too.

On the second day, probably to the surprise of most of the participants, they cut to the quick of the matter. They were forced to it. According to the log, after a remark by General Groves, Byrnes followed with a statement that was clearly made in Stimson's absence: "Mr. Byrnes recommended, and the Committee agreed, that the Secretary of War should be advised that, while recognizing that the final selection of the target was essentially a military decision, the present view of the Committee was that the bomb should be used against Japan as soon as possible; that it be used on a war plant surrounded by workers' homes; and that it be used without prior warning. It was the understanding of the Committee that the small bomb would be used in the test and that the large bomb (gun mechanism) would be used in the first strike over Japan."[144]

With that, the main question that no one had dared to ask before was answered. And with it the three questions that had been tormenting Stimson, Marshall, and the others were resolved: the timing in relation to both negotiations and the slated November invasion; the targeting of workers' homes rather than a "naval installation"; and that there would be no demonstration and no warning. Resolved by Byrnes, according to Groves's own wishes. It is typical of Byrnes's ferocious determination to use the bomb that he went directly from the Pentagon to the White House that very afternoon. "I told the president of the final decision of his Interim Committee," Byrnes later wrote. "Mr. Truman told me he had been giving serious thought to the subject for many days, having been informed as to the investigation of the Committee and the consideration of alternative plans, and that with reluctance he had to agree that he could think of no alternative and found himself in accord with what I told him the Committee was going to recommend." As Richard Rhodes points out, five days would pass before Truman saw Stimson, the committee chair and the man with ultimate responsibility for the bomb. The president then told Stimson, as the latter recalled, "that Byrnes had reported to him already about [the Interim Committee's decision] and that Byrnes seemed to be highly pleased with what had been done."[145] So, apparently, was Truman.

The swagger of Byrnes's self-described position on how to deal with the Soviets was based on his certitude that it would be many years before Moscow had a bomb of its own. Indeed, the "pepped-up" feeling of American leaders in relation to the Soviet Union effectively assumed that Moscow would never possess an atomic weapon. Groves was the first to put into words the harsh corollary of this assumption — namely, the United States had to be prepared to use its nuclear advantage to prevent any enemy from matching it.[146]

The prospect of the Soviet Union's actually accomplishing what the United States had accomplished did not worry Groves. Compared to others, however, he was complacent. The scientists, as Philip Morrison told me, took the opposite view, believing that the Soviets could duplicate the Manhattan Project in four or five years. Byrnes understood the gravity of this question, and when he listened to the experts make their projections, he did not like what he heard. He did his own calculation and doubled that number, pushing the date of a Soviet bomb back to seven to ten years.[147] He was certainly influenced here, too, by Groves, whose own estimate was that it would take the Soviet Union twenty to fifty years to match the achievement over which he had presided.[148] This was a matter of Groves's assessment of primitive Soviet industrial capacity: "Why those people," he said after the war, "can't even make a Jeep."[149] But it was also a matter of overriding vanity, a byproduct of his successes. "He could not imagine," Morrison told me, "that anyone else could do what he had done."[150]

Whether the period projected was ten years or fifty, it was a point off in the indefinite future, a place that did not really exist and from which no real threat could come. An absolutist assumption of an effectively permanent American monopoly of the bomb underwrote the attitudes and behavior of the United States toward the Soviet Union both before Hiroshima and in the crucial year after the end of the war, when an agreement to cooperate was not impossible. Nothing else accounts for America's arrogance. The testimony of scientists who knew better than to underestimate Russian abilities was ignored and soon forgotten.

Byrnes gave impetus and shape to this attitude in the American government, but he depended above all on Groves, who became the all-purpose authority on the durability of American nuclear dominance. In early September 1949, Groves gave a lecture at the National War College in Washington and repeated what he had said many times before. He said it with the certitude of one who knows better than any one else: "The Russians may have scientific know-how, but they don't have the practical skills, the industrial know-how, or the ability to mobilize resources that we do. It'll be ten to twenty years before they make an atomic bomb."[151] Two days before Groves said this, the Soviet Union had secretly detonated its first atomic bomb, as radiation detected in the atmosphere would soon establish. It was not the first time Groves was wrong, but it was the first time he was caught.

The "Second Coming in Wrath" is what it felt like to those on the ground in the two Japanese target cities, but Americans made sure not to take that in. We already noted the impact of John Hersey's "Hiroshima," making the effects of the bomb on human beings real in the American imagination. But that work was published a year after the event and, despite the sensation, did little to prompt a lasting confrontation with what had actually transpired. In that year before the Hersey piece appeared, U.S. scientists had studied the effects of the bombing up close. As a way of determining the altitude of the explosion, they measured the length of the victims' shadows that had been scorched onto walls and pavements.[152] Japanese people had become mere shadows in the American mind, and that was what they would remain.

"Each day," the narrator of *Hiroshima Mon Amour* says, "I resisted with all my might against the horror."[153] The horror of fingers being fused into claws, of eyeballs turning to ash in their sockets at the sight of the blast. "The whole city was gone," a Japanese Catholic priest whose eyes were not vaporized wrote of what he saw in his native Hiroshima.

> It had been there just a few minutes before, but it was absolutely gone. There was fire everywhere. It was all so unreal. For a moment I didn't know if I was alive or if I had died and gone to hell. Then I felt pain and knew that I must be alive . . . Was I dreaming? Then I saw people streaming by. They were fleeing to the riverbank, all horribly burned and in extreme pain. They came from the city center and seemed extremely thirsty, for I saw them slide down the embankment right into the water, where they tried to drink. Their hands were too burned to scoop up the water, so they put their heads into the water and tried to swallow. But the tide was just coming in, and the salt water burned their faces and their lips. Many just slumped in the water and lost consciousness and were covered by the tide. Others jumped in and drowned. Soon the river was filled with hundreds of bodies floating out to sea.[154]

A witness to such horror discerns at once its truest meaning — that a present event like this condemns the very future. This is so even among witnesses whose perceptions were blunted or who later misremembered, and for two generations now Japanese survivors of the atomic bombings have been trying to tell the world what they saw. "Listen to me!" to repeat what the woman in *Hiroshima Mon Amour* cries. "I know it will happen again." The primal fact of Hiroshima and Nagasaki was that such carnage had already happened, but there was no question, for those who were there, of these events growing less terrible with time. The bombs attacked time, too.

We have already seen how President Truman averted his gaze from what took place, which is why he defined the atomic bomb's first targets as "military objectives." Here is more of his diary entry for July 25, the day after he gave the order to the 509th Composite Group: "This weapon is to be used against Japan between now and August 10th. I have told the Sec of War, Mr. Stimson, to use it so that military objectives and soldiers and sailors are the target and not women and children. Even if the Japs are savages, ruthless and merciless and fanatic, we as the leader of the world for the common welfare cannot drop this terrible bomb on the old capital[155] or the new."[156]

Here we see Truman insisting on the military character of the targets, a point on which he would hang his justification for the attack for the rest of his life. Apparently he never pictured that river full of corpses of women and men, children and old people. "Truman never chose, then or later," McGeorge Bundy would write, "to grapple with this self-deception."[157] Even more than his dumb insistence on the military nature of the first atomic targets, however, Truman's statement here that, out of humaneness, Americans could never drop the bomb on Japan's "new capital," Tokyo, reveals the extent of America's denial and moral blindness by that point in the war. Did Truman and the millions of radio listeners who accepted his explanations at face value not know what had already happened in Tokyo? Does our ongoing selective focus on the two bombs dropped in August, in contrast to near-total American ignorance even now of Tokyo's fate before Hiroshima, suggest that we have diminished a far more grievous question about the American war? Is it that the atomic bomb only reinforced a policy of brutality that had already established itself in the national conscience? These questions take us back to the man who, with Groves, did more to shape that conscience than any other: Curtis LeMay.

7. THE HAMBURG THRESHOLD

January 1943. We saw that LeMay led the first American bomber assault against the German homeland. We also saw that he was a technical genius when it came to devising air war strategies; that he led from the front and could inspire airmen to new levels of heroism; that he began with a decided preference for precision bombing, but disavowed any moral implications for that preference; that, indeed, to the question of morality his answer was "Nuts!"[158] Military theorists distinguish between "punishing" attacks that aim to break an adversary's will to fight and "denial" attacks meant to destroy the capability to fight.[159] But to LeMay, the object was to kill and kill and kill until the enemy quit. The justification for that killing would be in the quitting — that was all. And there was no more thinking about the enemy dead than there was about LeMay's own boys. As he said in his memoir, an air commander simply had to refuse to "mope around about the deaths he has caused personally, by deed; or impersonally, in the act of command."[160]

The moping around that LeMay renounced is the brooding introspection by means of which a man of action might come to some moral insight about the larger significance of what he is doing. LeMay rejected such introspection as incompatible with his duty. "You drop a load of bombs and, if you're cursed with any imagination at all, you have at least one quick horrid glimpse of a child lying in bed with a whole ton of masonry tumbling down on top of him; or a three-year-old girl wailing for *Mutter . . . Mutter . . .* because she has been burned. Then you have to turn away from the picture if you intend to retain your sanity. And also if you intend to keep on doing the work your Nation expects of you."[161] LeMay's own daughter, Janie, was four when he began dropping bombs.

Thus, when over the months-long course of Operation Pointblank it became clear that American precision bombing was having no more impact on German warmaking capacity than British area bombing, LeMay's grasp of the significance of that distinction — a grasp defined in utilitarian terms, not moral ones — began to slip. As we saw, the precision was more imagined than real in any case, and among the many techniques that LeMay and other air commanders perfected in that first year was the "turning away from the picture" of what their bombs were doing on the ground. Something like that happened to almost all American Air Forces leaders in 1943 and 1944, a period when the pressures of the air war, in the words of the historian Michael Sherry, "rewarded the pragmatists, the men who maximized the number of trained crews, bombers in the air, targets hit."[162] Men of larger vision, accustomed to maintaining the link between acts and consequences — which is, after all, what we mean by moral consciousness — were increasingly marginalized as the methods of their war were increasingly brutalized.

We saw that Operation Pointblank, the joint British-American air war against Germany, was ordered launched at Casablanca, where "unconditional surrender" was defined as the war's purpose. Roosevelt, as we noted, had begun as one who opposed the bombing of civilian targets from the air, a preference reflected in General Eaker's insistence at Casablanca on AAF precision bombing in daylight — what Hap Arnold had called "our way of making war."[163] But Roosevelt's impulsive demand for total victory, when joined to the reality of air war technology, soon made the protection of civilians a fanciful myth, however much Americans, right on up to Truman, would pay it lip service. Pointblank and unconditional surrender — the two separate decisions worked on each other. It became clear before long that the justification for the mounting savagery of bombing was embedded in the now merciless charter of the war itself. The airmen were the first to discover that "the path to unconditional surrender," in Sherry's words, "lay through unconditional destruction." Rhetoric, that is, constituted reality.[164]

The war that British and American flyers began to wage against Germany after Casablanca became, in effect, a "war of annihilation," in the phrase of W. G. Sebald.[165] That German writer, who was born in 1944, grew up troubled by the vast silence that blanketed the wartime experience of his nation — a silence that was eventually broken after Germans had begun to confront more fully what they themselves had done, especially to Europe's Jews. But Sebald's last book, *On the Natural History of Destruction*, published in 2003, addressed the silence of what had been done *to* Germany. "I had grown up," he wrote, "with the feeling that something was being kept from me: at home, at school, and by the German writers whose books I read hoping to glean more information about the monstrous events in the background of my own life."[166]

One reason for writing my own book is, of course, that those same monstrous events are in the background of my life, too. And if anything, the American silence about them has been equally deafening. If the moral memory of the "greatest generation" and its children has been unable to reexamine the atomic bombings of Hiroshima and Nagasaki, as the Smithsonian controversy of 1995 suggests, that may be the result of an amnesiac veil that still covers what preceded those bombings, first in Germany.

According to a Strategic Bombing Survey study conducted after the war, the Allied bombing campaign against the Third Reich killed 305,000 civilians, while obliterating nearly half of the area of each of the nation's seventy large cities.[167] Later historians have put the number of German air war fatalities at far more than that. Sebald says simply that "about 600,000" German civilians were killed.[168] The vast majority of these deaths occurred in the last months of the war.[169]

But the annihilation can be said to have begun in 1943, less than six months after Casablanca. On July 27, 1943, a massive flight of RAF bombers, with support from the AAF, attacked Hamburg. "The aim of Operation Gomorrah, as it was called, was to destroy the city and reduce it as completely as possible to ashes," Sebald wrote. "Within a few minutes, huge fires were burning all over the target area, which covered some twenty square kilometers, and they merged so rapidly that only a quarter of an hour after the first bombs had dropped the whole airspace was a sea of flames as far as the eye could see."[170] This fire rose in waves to an altitude of more than a mile — four times the height of the Empire State Building. It consumed oxygen so rapidly that gale force winds were produced to draw in more — the first man-made firestorm. Citizens of Hamburg who sought to escape the horror by running to one of the city's many waterways and jumping in were boiled alive. The next day, the corpses not consumed by fire "lay doubled up in pools of their own melted fat."[171]

A series of raids beginning that day and running into early August turned Hamburg into a charnel house. About forty-five thousand civilians died, more than had been killed in the entire, months-long German blitz against England. The bulk of the attacks were carried out at night, with the British using incendiary bombs, deliberately igniting the fires. The Americans, flying in daylight and using explosive bombs, targeted shipyards and factories, but because the fires and smoke made their bombsights useless, the B-17s accomplished little. Afterward, the Americans were less appalled at what the British had accomplished than at what they themselves had not.[172]

Hamburg marked a threshold for both the British and the Americans, if in different ways. For the RAF, all pretense that the purpose of area bombing was "dehousing workers," thus disrupting German industrial output, was dropped. The purpose was indiscriminate destruction, period. Hamburg was a threshold for the AAF because, even if the British carried the initiative, American leaders did not object to the deliberate creation of an exterminating firestorm. Indeed, in Washington, Roosevelt pronounced the Hamburg attack "an impressive demonstration."[173] The American acceptance of this catastrophe was the beginning of the end of the difference between British and American methods and attitudes, which Sherry calls "the collapse of restraints."[174] Methods that would be condemned out of hand if carried out by armies on the ground were becoming routine from the air. After Hamburg, civilian casualties would no longer be seen as "collateral"; they were essential. Even now, American commanders were, as Sherry points out, capable of using the word "murder" to define the deliberate targeting of civilians, but they "then designated it as justifiable homicide."[175]

One of the American commanders who argued, beginning in the late summer of 1943, for a shift in AAF tactics toward area bombing was LeMay, who, you will recall, suffered through the brutal attack on the Messerschmitt factory in Regensburg on August 17. With LeMay as its advocate,[176] the Eighth Air Force launched the first formally acknowledged area bombing raid, against the city center of Münster on October 10, 1943. From the Pentagon, General Arnold made the shift official with a November 1 order decreeing that, whenever precision raids were not possible, area targets should be attacked. Four months later, the AAF launched a massive and indiscriminate raid on Berlin, which might rank as the first full-blown American terror raid in Europe. Average Germans knew now that the war had turned.

Some commanders, like LeMay, indulged no moral qualms about this loosening of restraints. Others took refuge in the casuistry that the British had perfected — the principle of "double effect," for example, according to which a predictable if unintended evil outcome is morally permissible as long as another, separate outcome is the intended objective. Others, in affirming a strategy of bombing central cities, simply accepted the expanded definition of what constituted military infrastructure. Communication and transportation hubs, essentially urban, now joined docks and factories as targets.

But the slippery ethics of these rationalizations were laid bare by other leaders of the Army Air Forces who bought none of it for a minute. In fact, a

fierce argument took place among AAF leaders through the spring and summer of 1944 and lasting into 1945. Sherry characterizes "the intense debate [as
having been] over whether terror attacks would complement the precision
campaign or dilute it, enhance the AAF's reputation or tarnish it, teach Germans a lasting lesson or only embitter them, and inflict righteous revenge or
cause American shame."[177]

One of the staff officers at Eighth Air Force headquarters in London was
Colonel Richard D. Hughes, an expert in picking Allied targets who was also
involved in deciding how they would be bombed. Hughes was older than
most men of his rank, and he had a visible self-assurance. In debates with superiors, he insisted that the principled American refusal to accept area bombing, while perhaps involving a necessary hypocrisy given the technical difficulties of adhering to such a standard, nevertheless "represented in world
thought an urge toward decency and better treatment of man by man."

Brigadier General Charles Pearre Cabell served as leader of Hughes's
unit. Years later, he would be our neighbor on Generals' Row at Bolling, and
his son Ben would be one of the golden older kids who hung around the
Officers' Club swimming pool. Since, like LeMay, Cabell was a figure for
whom I developed a youthful, if distant, admiration, I am relieved to report
that in the crucial 1944 debates over AAF bombing methods, Cabell came
down on the side of those opposed to the shift.[178] Partly because of Cabell's
influence, Eisenhower himself weighed in on the argument, on July 21, 1944,
ordering the Eighth Air Force commander to maintain the strictures of precision bombing. "Let's for God's sake keep our eyes on the ball and use some
sense," he said, rejecting terror tactics of all kinds.[179]

But it would not last. One AAF officer who worked with Hughes in the
day-to-day picking of targets in Germany was Carl Kaysen, to whom I referred earlier. He was a young lieutenant in 1944. We will come back to Kaysen
later when we take up what he did, as an adviser to John F. Kennedy, to negotiate the first arms control treaty with the Soviet Union. Kaysen would be one
of the leading theorists of nuclear war, devoting decades of his life to preventing it. But he began as someone who told bombardiers where to push their
buttons. For the Americans, this was a far more complex matter than studying maps and determining coordinates, and it says much about the seriousness with which the AAF took precision that it relied on people like Kaysen
as target officers. He was a trained economist, and it was his expertise in
what makes for productivity — military productivity — that qualified him for
his role.

Kaysen is now an emeritus professor at MIT. In an interview at his house
in Cambridge in the spring of 2003, Kaysen told me what precision bombing
meant to those who selected the targets, work he did beginning in March 1943

at the Enemy Objectives Unit of the Economic Warfare Division of the American embassy in London. "We were trying to hit industries that mattered. We spent a lot of intellectual effort figuring out which industries mattered, a lot of intellectual effort reading intelligence, and so on. This enterprise, when at its peak, had about a dozen professionals, maybe fifteen. And we were very intense."

So much went into the determination of appropriate targets that Kaysen and his colleagues — "We were smart graduate students and behaved that way" — were given access to the most secret intelligence the British and Americans had. "We read everything, we saw Ultra, we read the POW reports, we looked at the photographs, we looked at old telephone books, we got the back copies of German engineering journals." This was work that would have made no sense to an area bombing campaign, but it, too, with its focus on "production lost" and "systems impact," was carried on at a distance from the flesh-and-blood consequences. The bombardiers could not see what was really happening below them; much less so the target pickers. "We invented a form of poetry called bomb damage assessment," Kaysen told me, "in which we looked at the strike photographs and post-raid reconnaissance. The criterion we used for bombing, let me first express it in very fancy economic terms: we wanted to maximize the value of capital destroyed in post-raid prices, wartime conditions. So if you bombed a furniture factory and destroyed it totally, its value to us would be zero, because in wartime conditions you wouldn't pay anything to repair a furniture factory. We wanted to affect the front-line fighting capacity. So we said steel plants are a bad target because the time from when steel comes out of the rolling mill and it turns up as part of a tank is sixteen months. That doesn't affect things soon enough. On the other hand, if you bomb an oil refinery, especially when Germany was hard up for oil, they will feel it in two weeks." Kaysen told me that his crew focused on "strategic targets" — synthetic-oil plants, tank engine factories, tank transmission factories, a BMW tank factory, electronic industries. "But oil — oil was the best target."

According to a postwar German assessment, this was one aspect of the AAF's strategic bombing campaign that had an impact. As a result of attacks just before and after D-Day, the German production of high-octane fuel — "the heart's blood of the Luftwaffe" — dropped from a normal rate of 316,000 tons a month to 175,000 tons in April, to 30,000 tons in July, to 5,000 tons in September. "The Luftwaffe could not get off the ground because it lacked fuel."[180]

After one particularly effective attack in 1944 on oil works deep inside Germany, Kaysen read Ultra intercepts of a conversation between Hermann Göring and a colleague in which each man explained to the other why it was his — the other's — duty to report the lost oil capacity to Hitler. Kaysen laughed with delight at the memory. And beyond oil, there were bridges. Ahead of D-Day, Kaysen worked on a plan to drop bombs on all of the bridges over the Seine northwest of Paris, and it worked. With evident satisfaction, thinking of a mass of stymied Panzer units, he said, "On D-Day, all the bridges between Paris and the sea were down. Not one was operating."

I asked Kaysen if he and his fellow target pickers were aware of the shift in bombing philosophy that occurred through 1944 into 1945, as the Americans loosened their restraints on targeting, yielding the point on which they had been so insistent at Casablanca. "Yes. And we thought it was terrible." Kaysen was one of the officers who backed Colonel Hughes in his dissent, and now he remembered the man with wistful admiration. "Hughes was a totally free spirit. I remember an occasion on which he was criticizing General Doolittle, who was the bomber force commander, criticizing him for dropping a lot of bombs on targets of no value. And Doolittle said, 'You know, Colonel Hughes, I'm tired of having my balls hauled over a glass-topped fence every time I hit an inappropriate target.' And Hughes said, 'General, we're not here to protect the state of your genitals. We're here to win a war.'"

On another occasion, Hughes demanded of his superiors, "Do we want a Germany virtually de-housed, lacking all public utility services, whose population is little better than a drifting horde of nomads ripe for any political philosophy of despair and almost impossible to administer and reeducate?"[181] Hughes was repulsed by the futility and immorality of terror bombing. To him it was wildly impractical and likely to cause many more problems than it solved.

"There was something called Operation Thunderclap in February of '45," Kaysen said. Thunderclap was the code name for a British Bomber Command plan to deliver a final, crippling blow to the Nazi high command, a blow consisting of the complete destruction, first, of their capital and then, through saturation attacks, of other major cities. The British wanted the Americans involved as equal partners. "Against that," Kaysen said, "Hughes was very outspoken. It involved an experiment as to whether three air forces, the Fifteenth, flying by then from Italy, the Eighth, and the RAF, could obliterate a square mile in Berlin. They picked out a square mile, and they were all going to parade over it and drop their bombs. And Hughes said in the planning meeting that he was here to fight a war, not to kill women and children. There was no target sense in this. It made no military contribution." Hughes, Kaysen, and other target officers had won over General Cabell to their point of view. "We propagandized Cabell," Kaysen told me, "and I guess some of it took."[182]

When Cabell read the plans for Thunderclap, a three-stage campaign against Berlin and cities east of it, he was appalled. "I have just read the great opus, 'Operation Thunderclap,' prepared in the Air Ministry," he wrote to Hughes. "To my mind, which frankly has been greatly influenced by your own thinking, this would be a blot on the history of the Air Forces and of the U.S. We should strongly resist being sucked into any such venture. It gives full rein to the baser elements of our people." Cabell rejected the common rationale for these "baby-killing schemes." They were not intended, as proponents insisted, to bring the war to a quick end or to save the lives of Allied soldiers but rather as simple acts, as he put it, of "retaliation and intimidation for the future."[183]

Eisenhower, who had supported Cabell in July 1944, now saw it differently: "While I have always insisted that U.S. Strategic Forces be directed against precision targets, I am always prepared to take part in anything that gives promise to ending the war quickly."[184] The difference between Eisenhower's July position and his position as the time for Thunderclap approached lay in the fact that, after the shocking Nazi counteroffensive in the Ardennes in December, and with the Red Army well on the way to the million casualties it would suffer that winter and spring, the Allies were beginning to fear deadlock, the static bleeding of the trenches.[185] And so Thunderclap, more commonly referred to by Americans as Operation Clarion, with the British and the Americans flying in tandem, was launched.

8. AFTER DRESDEN

Starting on February 3, the four-phase saturation bombing of Berlin was carried out by the Combined Bomber Offensive. Commanding the Berlin attack, with a force of nine hundred B-17s, was the legendary AAF commander Carl "Tooey" Spaatz, who had made his reputation as one of the few American aces of World War I. The United States had come to center stage in the terror war. The Berlin raids killed twenty-five thousand civilians.[186] But that campaign was only the beginning. Raids were conducted on Leipzig and Chemnitz, cities packed with refugees who had fled from the east, ahead of the advancing Red Army. The resounding boom of Thunderclap came on the night of February 13–14 with the attack on a city about a hundred miles south of Berlin. It was a cultural capital, famous for its art and architecture, its por-

celain factories, and the stained glass windows of its churches. It had no significant war-related industry and had not as yet been bombed. No German
fighting force was stationed there, and it had no antiaircraft or other defenses.
It was the Kyoto of Germany. It was Dresden.

The Americans were supposed to lead that raid in daylight — the official
orders for the Dresden bombing were cut in Eisenhower's headquarters[187] —
but bad weather kept the AAF on the ground. The skies cleared by nightfall,
in time for nearly eight hundred British Lancasters to drop thousands of tons
of incendiary bombs, the deliberate creation of a firestorm that dwarfed what
had happened in Hamburg. Dresden, too, was crowded with refugees, and no
one knows within several thousand how many died. The figure is put as high
as 130,000, as low as 35,000.[188] The firestorm that night could be seen from a
distance of two hundred miles.[189] By the time the AAF arrived over Dresden
in the morning, most of the damage had been inflicted. And though perhaps
the flyers did not see it in the rubble, the great moral threshold of the age had
been crossed.

A Dresden slaughterhouse had been converted into a holding pen for
American POWs, one of whom, Kurt Vonnegut, Jr., would become a well-
known novelist. When the attack began, he and other prisoners were herded
"down two stories under the pavement into a big meat locker. It was cool
there, with cadavers hanging all around. When we came up the city was
gone."[190] Kaysen and his fellow target pickers had helped to destroy many
bridges on the Seine, and one might have expected something similar here. In
Dresden the one target of military significance was a bridge over the Elbe that
the Germans could have used to rush reinforcements to the collapsing eastern
front. After the Allied bombing raids had ended, though, that bridge was still
standing. It did not even make the target roster.[191]

Meanwhile, there were so many dead that the living could not bury
them. Sebald observes that, in the days after the raid, in what was left of
the city's central market square, many thousands of corpses were burned
on open pyres "by an SS detachment that had gained its experience at Treblinka."[192] Eventually, survivors would have to use flamethrowers to dispose
of corpses.[193]

But it wasn't over. As if to match the destruction of the British, the Americans continued the bombing of Dresden — on February 14 and 15, and then
again on March 2, and once more on April 17. Once Thunderclap was
launched, it was hard to stop. "Only the exhaustion of targets and the desire
not to complicate further the task of occupying Germany," Sherry comments,
"brought the campaign against its cities to a halt in mid-April."[194]

The horror of Dresden had been enough to give one of its sponsors
pause: "Are we beasts?" Winston Churchill asked, having registered physical

shock upon viewing a film of the destruction. "Are we taking this too far?"[195] Churchill here seems to have perceived, however dimly, that firebombing was moving him and his minions — and his allies — into another realm, as if he glimpsed what was coming. But his ethical qualm, if that's what it was, passed quickly. The British leader, in a letter to his chiefs of staff, now wrote, "It seems to me that the moment [has come] when the question of so-called 'area bombing' of German cities should be reviewed." But Churchill was not thinking of the moral question, or of the effect of this policy on a civilian population: ". . . reviewed from the point of view of our own interests. If we come into control of an entirely ruined land, there will be a great shortage of accommodation for ourselves and our allies."[196] There had to be standing houses, preferably chateaus, for the officer corps of the occupation.

Among bomber crews, not much was made of the results of Dresden. One veteran bombardier (his bomber was called *Belle of the Brawl*), who was not assigned to the raid but was bunked in the same Quonset hut with a crew that was, told me that the men returned from their bombing run reporting nothing special. He did not learn of what had happened at Dresden for a year.[197]

In America, Dresden drew little notice at the time. On February 22, the raid came up in a press briefing with Secretary of War Stimson, who said, "Our policy has never been to inflict terror bombing on civilian populations. Our efforts still are confined to the attack of enemy military objectives." Apparently this lie was widely believed — perhaps by the troubled Stimson himself — though it was simultaneously clear to anyone reading a newspaper, and certainly to anyone reading the dispatches coming into the Pentagon, that air attacks on German cities were indiscriminate.

This contradiction — military targets, devastated urban centers — was readily accommodated in the American mind. In a propaganda tactic used repeatedly in subsequent wars, much publicity was given to a particular photograph of the ruined city of Cologne — a mass of rubble surrounding the untouched cathedral, with the tallest freestanding spires in Europe. That the cathedral had been spared was taken as proof that AAF bombing was indeed precise and therefore humane. Yet the large residential district surrounding the cathedral could clearly be seen to have disappeared; the spires had in fact been left standing as a landmark for pilots.

By the middle of April, air raids over Germany had eased off, and England-based bomber crews knew what everyone else knew, that Germany was all but defeated. There was little left to attack. Yet early on April 14, the crew of *Belle of the Brawl* were rousted from their Quonset quarters and ordered to suit up for a mission. The plane's bombardier was a young Howard Zinn, who would go on to become a radical historian. Zinn was already a leftist; he had volunteered for the service and pushed for a combat assignment because he wanted to join in the fight against Nazism and fascism. But what he did that day would serve as the ground of his lifelong criticism of war.

Zinn told me the story as we sat in his home in Massachusetts. In April 1945 he was twenty years old. That seems young, but it was a typical age for an American crewman. The commander and pilot of *Belle of the Brawl* was nineteen. That morning the crew was ordered to attack the French seaside town of Royan. Zinn took his position in the plastic nose cone of the B-17.

A *New York Times* dispatch published the next day reported: "The full weight of the United States Eighth Air Force was hurled yesterday against one of Europe's forgotten fronts, the German-held pocket in the Gironde Estuary commanding the great southwestern French port of Bordeaux. The blow by 1,150 Flying Fortresses and Liberators, without fighter escort, preceded a limited land attack by French troops."[198] Years later, Howard Zinn was mystified by the raid of which he had been a part. "The war by then was won. The isolated Germans holed up in Royan were ready to surrender. I was only aware of the twelve bombers in my wing, but when I learned there had been twelve hundred of them, I was astonished. It made no sense."[199] In a written account, Zinn observed, "In a few weeks, the war was over in Europe. The town of Royan, 'liberated,' was totally in ruins."[200]

I asked Zinn what had prompted the raid. "Momentum of the war," he said, shrugging. "Punishing the enemy, although mainly who we hit were French people, not our enemy but our friends." He shook his head. "But there was something else. A new weapon. Why twelve hundred planes to hit such a relatively insignificant target that late in the war? Well, we had a new weapon. I remember when we got the order to go up, and we were briefed. The briefing officer told us that instead of the usual twelve five-hundred-pound demolition bombs, we would be carrying thirty canisters of what he called jellied gasoline. Napalm. It was the first time napalm was used in Europe. I used to think it was the first time napalm was ever used, but then I learned we were already dropping it in Japan. The raid on Royan was the Eighth Air Force refusing to pass up using the new weapon it had been provided. And we flew twelve hundred planes because that was how much napalm we had."[201]

The German experience of the air war of 1945 was enough to traumatize the nation into the generations-long amnesia against which Sebald protests. "The general impression created by the insensate bombing," another German wrote, "was as though the sorcerer's apprentice had been trying his hand and was now unable to stop. It was like an elemental eruption which could no longer be controlled and localized, but which emptied itself over the country like a natural catastrophe."[202] German flyers had killed forty thousand people in air raids on Stalingrad in 1942; Nazis were waging, even at the end, a frenzied war of extermination against Jews; Hitler had been intoxicated with visions of a leveled London in 1940 — and now it was all coming to the cities of the fatherland. On April 20, a final Combined Bomber Offensive raid, involving a thousand bombers, was loosed on Berlin. It was Hitler's last birthday.

In this way, unconditional surrender had become, in Sherry's formulation, unconditional destruction. Another way to put it is that total war had become a push for total victory. We have seen how this policy backfired on the United States in the Pacific theater. In Europe it led to disaster, too. Although an Act of Military Surrender was signed by survivors of a decimated German high command,[203] Germany did not surrender so much as accept its obliteration. Altogether, this martial onslaught, with one side matching the other in ruthlessness, led to the deaths of forty million people. "Total warfare" involved not just the unprecedented size of the conflict but the escalation in brutality made possible by advances in technology, especially by the strategic bomber, the total weapon. "A fire went out from Germany and went around the world in a great arc," the curator of Dresden's City Museum said on the fiftieth anniversary of the bombing, "and [it] came back to Germany."[204]

In the beginning, Franklin Roosevelt had denounced the deliberate bombing of cities as barbaric, and at Casablanca he had supported his air commanders in their insistence on "the American way of bombing." But FDR's surrender policy had set inexorable forces in motion in himself as well, and now he was terror bombing's enthusiastic sponsor. "The German people as a whole must have it driven home to them," he told Stimson in August 1944, "that the whole nation has been engaged in a lawless conspiracy against the decencies of modern civilization."[205] Now those decencies required unbridled attacks on the whole population. And Roosevelt's chief air commander, General Arnold, who had defined "our way of making war" as taking care to protect civilians, with the strategic bomber as "the most humane of all weapons," was by now equally prepared to see city centers reduced to rubble. After Dresden, in response to the anguished Stimson's query as to whether the attack had been as savage as reported, Arnold was harsh: "We must not get soft. War must be destructive and to a certain extent inhuman and ruthless."[206]

The measure of this evolution in the attitude of an entire institution is most dramatically taken in the experience of one man. Freeman Dyson would become a leading nuclear physicist, but as a young statistician he had put himself at the service of the RAF Bomber Command. Here is how he mapped the road along which he then traveled:

At the beginning of the war, I believed fiercely in the brotherhood of man, called myself a follower of Gandhi, and was morally opposed to all violence. After a year of war, I retreated and said, Unfortunately nonviolent resistance against Hitler is impracticable, but I am still morally opposed to bombing. A couple of years later I said, Unfortunately it seems that bombing is necessary to win the war, and so I am willing to work for Bomber Command, but I am still morally opposed to bombing cities indiscriminately. After I arrived at Bomber Command I said, Unfortunately it turns out that we are after all bombing cities indiscriminately, but this is morally justified, as it is helping to win the war. A year later I said, Unfortunately it seems that our bombing is not really helping to win the war, but at least I am morally justified in working to save the lives of the bomber crews. In the last spring of the war I could no longer find any excuses.[207]

9. THE BABE RUTH OF BOMBERS

In Asia the Army Air Forces arrived loaded for bear — but tethered to decision makers thousands of miles away. In Europe the bombing campaign had been run from headquarters in England, but the activities of the AAF in East Asia were run from the Pentagon, by men, especially Arnold, who were determined both to apply the lessons already learned in Germany and to show that air power, which had so far fallen short of being decisive, could win the war against Japan. The larger significance of the fact that this latest — and ultimately most savage — phase of the war would be administered by bureaucrats, depending on new technology far from the places where its effects were felt, lies in the way it defined the Pentagon's place in the postwar world. "Washington waged the air war [against Japan] by remote control," Michael Sherry comments, "thereby reducing a sense of responsibility for the destruction that war entailed."[208]

War as experienced in the flush of close combat was entirely different from war as experienced even a mile from the front line, never mind Washington, D.C. A Marine who made Pacific combat vivid, E. B. Sledge, notes the separation: "We existed in an environment totally incomprehensible to men behind the lines." It wasn't just civilians who could never understand; it was fellow soldiers whose function kept them in the rear echelon, away from the crucible of killing and being killed. Brutality and sadism, inflicted by both sides, were as routine to fighters as they would be forever unimagined by those not fighting. Fighters inured themselves to the horror of what they suffered and what they inflicted by simple denial. "We didn't talk about such things," Sledge writes. "They were too horrible and obscene even for hardened veterans."[209]

Pilots and bombardiers, flying thousands of feet above the results of their handiwork, and confronted with perils from flak or accident that were equally abstract, were already at risk for a morally numbing detachment, but when they returned to their bases in aircraft scorched by the flames they had ignited, both they and their commanders would still be in range of the reality of what their decisions were leading to. But with the transfer to Washington of the minute mechanisms of air war command, this phenomenon of emotional and ethical removal from consequences would be brought to a new level — for the entire institution. It would be a distinguishing mark of the Pentagon from now on, and that mark explains how Pentagon planners could eventually anticipate "victories" that entailed the obliteration of whole cities.

By the time a force of B-29s was ready for deployment to the Pacific theater — planes far more lethal than Europe's B-17s, flying with twice the range against largely undefended targets — much of the move from precision to area bombing that we have been tracking had already occurred. Enemy destruction had replaced enemy surrender as the all but spoken aim of bombardment. Restraints that had made this shift only gradual, and somewhat anguished, in Europe, restraints that had at first inhibited commanders from unleashing the full destructive power of their bombers against cities, did not exist in relation to Japan. "The Germans," as one historian observed, "seemed an enemy only by virtue of transient Nazi rule. The Japanese seemed an enemy by virtue of race."[210] If ever there was an adversary worthy of total war, it was Tokyo.

The Japanese, particularly after Pearl Harbor, were despised in ways the Germans never were, and reports of Japanese atrocities against captured GIs and Marines, from early 1944 on, weighed more heavily in the American imagination than did reports of the Nazi death camps, which started to come at about the same time. Indeed, while the word "extermination" was associated in Europe, negatively, with the Nazi genocide of Jews, it was gleefully claimed in the Pacific as a central purpose by American fighting men who designated the Japanese enemy as rats and rodents, and themselves as their exterminators. "They live like rats, breed like rats, and act like rats," said the governor of Idaho, explaining the rationale for putting Japanese Americans in internment camps.[211] "Rat exterminator" and its equivalent appeared in cartoons painted on the sides of tanks, on the fuselages of warplanes, on shell casings, on helmets.

Americans also presumed that Japanese industrial methods were primitive, involving the allotment of piecework to neighborhoods of laborers, obviating the need to draw fast distinctions between the war economy and the civilian population. That Americans were quicker to define Japanese women and children as legitimate targets of war than they were Germans is reflected in the stark fact that the modest 1942 bomber raid on Tokyo, led by James Doolittle, while making a small pretense that it targeted "war industries," in FDR's phrase,[212] was technically incapable of precision. Its bull's-eye was nothing but the Japanese capital's population center. It was a token attack, involving only sixteen carrier-launched B-25 bombers, its goal being morale-boosting symbolic revenge for Pearl Harbor. But as one historian observes, "Whereas the Japanese attack on Hawaii aimed almost wholly at traditional military objectives, American plans envisaged wholesale attack on civilians" — then and later.[213] Attacks on civilians, openly admitted, would come to define the massive air war over Japan in the spring of 1945, but with Doolittle's raid it was already under way in the spring of 1942 — the period when the newly launched British campaign against German cities was being condemned by Americans. His Tokyo raid, defined by Arnold as "just the dawn of a day of wrath,"[214] made Doolittle a national hero.

The real air war against Japan began with attacks on steel factories in Yawata in June 1944. A first, small-scale incendiary raid, a kind of experiment, was launched by twenty-four B-29s against Nagasaki on August 10, almost a year to the day before the atomic bombing. By the fall, Pentagon leaders, especially Arnold, were pressing for large-scale attacks against urban centers. A September briefing from the Pentagon defined firebombing against Japanese cities, with their paper-and-wood structures and dense populations, as "the golden opportunity of strategic bombardment."[215]

The Pentagon was not happy when the leading air commander in Asia, as if infected by Hughes and Cabell, did not bother to hide his reluctance to embark on a campaign of incendiary-based terror bombing. He was Major General Haywood S. Hansell, the commander of the Twenty-first Bomber Command, based in the Mariana Islands. Hansell had been Arnold's chief of staff and had helped frame the early American argument, against the British, in favor of precision bombing. Hansell had come up through the ranks with Cabell, and the two men thought alike.

For Hansell, the principle of industrial targeting was basic. Civilian targeting was abhorrent. In December, he objected, in a message to Arnold himself, to an order from Washington to begin area bombing. Hansell said that he had "with great difficulty implanted the principle that our mission is the destruction of primary targets by sustained and determined attacks using precision bombing methods both visual and radar."[216] He was moved as much by moral considerations as by practical ones. But his position embodied a point of view away from which, to Hansell's misfortune, Arnold had moved. In January, Arnold replaced him with a man whom Hansell had long outranked, but who had also left behind whatever ambivalence he had had about generalized firebombing. This new man could do that because, for him, the preference for precision was never a matter of principle, only of practical result. He was Curtis LeMay.

By this stage of the war, Arnold had reason to regard LeMay, in a phrase of LeMay's biographer, "as some kind of Messiah."[217] Arnold's own phrase described LeMay as "the Babe Ruth of bombers."[218] LeMay's transfer to the Pacific theater in the latter half of 1944, as commander of the Twentieth Bomber Command, based in China, had been a sure sign of the war's shifting priorities. On December 18 of that year, it had been LeMay's privilege to lead the first full-scale incendiary raid against an Asian city — the Chinese city of Hankow, which was a Japanese base. Thus, just as Hansell was rejecting such tactics, LeMay's B-29s successfully ignited a conflagration that burned for three days.

A few days after LeMay took over for Hansell, combining the Twentieth and Twenty-first Bomber Command, Arnold had his fourth heart attack, which meant that LeMay could run the show as he saw fit. Arnold would have been pleased. A short three days later, LeMay launched his initial area attack against a Japanese city, Nagoya, the first urban target along a corridor that would lead to Tokyo. And a week after that, on the night of February 3, 1945, LeMay's bombers unloaded jellied gasoline on the center of Kobe, population one million, nearly three hundred miles south of Tokyo. Other bombs dropped were mainly incendiary, but some fragmentation bombs were dropped as well, to impede the work of firefighters.[219] It was the first firebombing of a Japanese city, a tremendous success, and, in effect, a rehearsal for what was coming.

LeMay had already learned lessons from the firestorm in Hamburg in 1943, and now in mid-February, two years later, he studied what had just happened in Dresden. He concluded that the B-29s he was working with were too heavy, too burdened with various defensive weapons, and were required to fly at too high an altitude for his purposes. Therefore, as he had done in Europe, LeMay took his problems to statistical analysts. He wanted to jettison everything he did not need: he wanted to be able to fly below the bad weather and the jet stream; he wanted to break his bombers out of the usual rigid formation, which meant they could carry less fuel and more bomb tonnage. All of this, if he could do it, would allow him to load unprecedented ordnance onto his planes, almost all of it napalm or incendiaries. And it would allow him to fly low enough to drop the incendiaries in tight clusters, before wind could disperse their fires.

Early in his command, LeMay came to depend on the guidance of his statistical analysis experts, and as we saw, in England he had relied in particular on a young Harvard statistician named Robert McNamara. It was a measure of his value to LeMay that McNamara now found himself attached to the Twenty-first Bomber Command in the Marianas. Having begun as a captain only two years before, McNamara was already a lieutenant colonel.

Analyzing dozens of factors gleaned from other raids, from wind direction to fuel consumption to flak rates to enemy searchlight use to patterns of the newly discovered jet stream, LeMay's statisticians, including McNamara, gave him what he wanted. LeMay was preparing for nothing less than a jump into a new kind of air war.

In my interview with McNamara in his Washington office in early 2003, he recalled his role with LeMay. "I was advising him on how to plan combat operations." The former secretary of defense paused at his own use of this euphemism. He straightened the fold of the sleeve of his striped button-down shirt. He decided to speak more directly. "I was there in March of '45 when we had the first firebomb raid on Tokyo, and in that night, that single night, we burned to death on the order of a hundred thousand civilians." McNamara fell silent again. He had not been there as a mere observer. I asked him what his role was. He thought for a moment. "I think it was in January of '45 that I wrote a memo to LeMay telling him that this marvelous new weapon, the B-29, was proving ineffective because, although it had been designed to bomb from, say, twenty-four or twenty-five thousand feet, out of fighter aircraft range — a way to assure low casualties — we weren't hitting a damn thing. We couldn't see through the clouds at that level. We weren't accomplishing a damn thing. High-explosive bombs from thirty thousand feet were not accomplishing a damn thing. I'm not suggesting that it was that memo of January, my memo, that led to the decision in March to shift to lower altitudes, seventy-five hundred feet or whatever, and firebomb from there. I just mention it because that is the kind of thing I was doing."

Just after midnight on March 10, 1945, three hundred B-29s approached Tokyo at altitudes of between five thousand and nine thousand feet. The raid was code-named Operation Meetinghouse.[220] Tokyo was a city of about five million people. Navigators carried guidance sheets directing them to fly over the most heavily residential sections of the city. The planned target was an area nearly four miles square, housing about 400,000 people. The official AAF history describes it: "The zone bordered the most important industrial section of Tokyo and included a few individually designated strategic targets. Its main importance lay in its home industries and feeder plants; being closely spaced and predominately of wood-bamboo-plaster construction, these buildings easily kindled."[221]

The first waves of bombers dropped clusters of napalm canisters, which started fires in the rough outline of an X, which then defined the target area for subsequent waves of bombers. The B-29s flew so low that crew members did not need oxygen, but at that altitude the stench of burning flesh was palpable, and they wore their oxygen masks to stifle it.[222] By the time the B-29s were returning to base, the bottoms of their fuselages were singed brown. Not one plane was shot down.

Because of the work of LeMay's statisticians, the warplanes had been reconfigured into flying boxcars whose only load was incendiary bombs. They dropped 1,665 tons of pure fire on the city, the most efficient and deliberate act of arson in history. The consequent firestorm obliterated fifteen square miles, which included both residential and industrial areas. Fires raged for four days.

Official counts put the number of dead at between 80,000 and 100,000. A million people had been rendered homeless. No one could pretend the raid was anything but what it was. The bombing of Tokyo occupies a small back room in the house of the American memory, but it was widely known at the time. In fact, with few exceptions, Americans greeted the news with a special glee. The *New York Times* led its first day of coverage with the headline "300 B-29s Fire 15 Square Miles of Tokyo," and its second with "Center of Tokyo Devastated by Fire Bombs. City's Heart Gone." To define the civilian death toll, the *Times* used the word "holocaust,"[223] a word that would not appear in the *Times* index with reference to the Shoah until 1980.[224] Yet there was nothing of protest in the *Times's* coverage, nothing even of questioning. It was taken for granted at every level of American society that the urban center of the Japanese capital was a proper target.

So much housing disappeared from Tokyo that night that the postwar population of the city was less than half of what it was on March 9. The firestorm effects of both Hamburg and Dresden — the conflagrations generating heat hurricanes that melted cement and boiled rivers — had been flukes, had gone beyond what the bombardiers could control, but LeMay's careful preparations for Tokyo meant he had near-total control over fire conditions. What he achieved went far beyond what had happened in either of the German cities. In Hamburg, as Sebald reports, after the fires subsided, "rats and flies ruled the city . . . flies such as had never been seen before."[225] But in Tokyo, "rats and mice, lice and fleas were destroyed along with other animals."[226] Not even what was necessary for disease had survived the fires LeMay started.

The extraordinarily destructive effects of this bombing — Tokyo's buildings spontaneously igniting not from flames but simply from heat, bomb shelters turned into ovens, the scorched atmosphere itself an exploder of human lungs — were not inevitable, but they were premeditated. The results were deliberate and, in the outcome, a source of not only satisfaction but inspiration. Tokyo would be a model for LeMay's attacks on numerous other Japanese cities, and in ten days he would wreak half the carnage on Japan that had been inflicted on Germany through five years of bombing. In five months, the square footage of destroyed urban centers in Japan would be more than double what was destroyed in five years in Germany.[227]

Although LeMay would not duplicate his success elsewhere, in the weeks after Tokyo his bombers would raze nearly half of the area of sixty-six other cities, killing 900,000 civilians, which surpassed by more than 100,000 the total of Japanese combat deaths. LeMay's campaign would make more than twenty million Japanese homeless.[228] It would stop only when the AAF supply depots ran out of napalm. And how many, in actual terms, is 900,000? Robert Conquest, in writing about Stalin's terror, compared the number of victims to the number of words in his book.[229] For every word in the book you now hold, more than four Japanese women, children, and the elderly were killed by Curtis LeMay's campaign. This paragraph represents five hundred dead.

"The heart of the city is completely gutted by fire," LeMay noted in his diary within a day or two of the Tokyo bombing. "It is the most devastating raid in the history of aerial warfare."[230] The man who led the raid, General Thomas Powers, struck a similar note of macabre triumphalism: the Tokyo raid was "the greatest single disaster incurred by an enemy in military history . . . There were more casualties than in any other military action in the history of the world."[231]

As I listened to McNamara recall his role as one of LeMay's assistants — the author of a memo that had proposed one of the key shifts in strategy that made the conflagration possible — we were both aware that not many years later the power relationship would be reversed, with LeMay an openly resentful subordinate in McNamara's Pentagon. Perhaps thinking of that, McNamara now emphasized his respect for LeMay as "without any question the most outstanding combat commander I ever met. He had only one thought in mind, which was how to achieve his combat objectives."

"Combat objectives?" I asked.

McNamara did not miss a beat. "I was with him when he debriefed the lead crews of the mission that returned from Tokyo and firebombed it. I was sitting next to LeMay. In the middle of the debriefing a captain got up and he said, 'I'd like to know what son of a bitch told us to take this wonderful plane we have down to seventy-five hundred feet. I lost my wing man.' LeMay answered, 'I've lost men, too. But the way to look at it is, his loss meant target destruction. Target destruction is what happens when you go in at seven thousand feet. And that's what to keep your eye on. Target destruction.'"

After McNamara said this, with evident admiration for LeMay and an implied satisfaction that his own role may have been pivotal — wasn't he the selfsame son of a bitch? — I asked, "When did the magnitude of the Tokyo bombing hit you?"

He shook his head, and precision of expression began to fail him. "Well, to some degree, I'm not sure we in command knew, and if we did know, I'm not sure I really understood the magnitude of that bombing. I've since seen photographs." He drifted into another subject. When I later told the historian Howard Zinn, a severe critic of McNamara's during the Vietnam War, that McNamara claimed not to have known what the results of the Tokyo bombing were, Zinn, thinking of his own experience as a bombardier, said, "I believe him. You really don't know the effects of what you are doing. We, the air crews, didn't know. We thought we were hitting 'things.' And the people even farther removed than us didn't know. The whole business was cloaked in denial."[232]

I brought McNamara back by asking the question again, and he asserted with some force, "Certainly the objective of the Fifty-eighth Bomb Wing of the Twentieth Bomber Command was not to kill as many people as we could. It was to weaken the enemy. To go back to LeMay, if you measure effectiveness in terms of destruction to the enemy per unit of U.S. loss, which was his objective, which he achieved, I credit him as the most outstanding officer in combat. He was equally the most dangerous — change the word 'dangerous' — equally the most controversial and, I think, unwise chief senior military officer I ever worked with."

"But that was later," I said.

"Yes."

"And at the time, in 1945, you didn't really appreciate what had happened in Tokyo."

"No. Not then."

"And now? What do you make of it now?"

McNamara's eyes abruptly filled. "Now?"

"Yes."

"Well, it was a war crime." All at once he was on the verge of weeping. "It was one of two war crimes with which I can be charged."[233]

Freeman Dyson, who served the British Bomber Command in a capacity similar to that in which McNamara served LeMay, put the same thought this way, comparing himself to Adolf Eichmann and other managers of the Holocaust: "They had sat in their offices, writing memoranda and calculating how to murder people efficiently, just like me. The main difference was that they were sent to jail or hanged as war criminals, while I went free."[234] It can seem outrageous to equate Allied officers with perpetrators of the anti-Jewish genocide, but the obligation to maintain a moral standard in war is universal, even if the Nazi violation of that standard was unique in its barbarity.

10. BORN IN ORIGINAL SIN

The American air war began with Curtis LeMay in 1943. The AAF's first solo firebombing of a city, Hankow, in 1944, was commanded by LeMay, as was the most destructive single military action in history, against Tokyo. So it will be no surprise that LeMay, as commander of the Twentieth Bomber Command, with its 509th Composite Group, was the man in charge of the airplanes that dropped the atomic bombs on Hiroshima and Nagasaki. In June 1945, he had flown to Washington for his first full briefing on the Manhattan Engineer District. It came from Groves. "This was my first meeting with LeMay," Groves wrote, "and I was highly impressed with him. It was very evident that he was a man of outstanding ability. Our discussion lasted about an hour, and we parted with everything understood."[235] Groves told LeMay that the mission would be under his, LeMay's, control, "subject, of course, to any limitations that might be placed upon him by his instructions."[236] Instructions, that is, from Groves. The two men would control the mission together. It was LeMay who decided that the bomb would be dropped by a lone airplane, flying without escort. But, knowing what he was even then doing to the cities of Japan, he had his doubts as to the atomic bomb's necessity. "I think it was anticlimactic," he would later write, "in that the verdict was already rendered."[237]

While observing that, by August 1945, the use of the bomb as soon as it was ready was taken for granted by Americans in authority, Michael Sherry comments: "Many reasons have been offered (most at the time, but some more in retrospect) for the atomic attacks on Japanese cities: the precedents set by firebombing, the psychological impact of the nuclear bomb, the lives to be saved by quicker termination of the war, the desire for revenge, the assertions of Japanese fanaticism, the need to justify an enormous investment, the technicians' desire to test their creation in the most dramatic way, the alarm that might be felt by the Russians, the supremacy the bomb's use might confer on the United States, and the shock to be given to a war-mad world."[238]

Sherry's litany suggests that these "reasons" coexist in some kind of equilibrium with one another, as if any one of them could have counted as the force that carried the United States and the world across the nuclear threshold. But the history we have been tracking puts "the precedents set by firebombing" on a level above all else. Indeed, this history confirms LeMay's perception, suggesting that the primary shift in American consciousness, the true threshold, was defined by the firebombing of cities. The atomic bombs, instead of establishing a new context, must be seen within that already existing context.

Before the August 6 attack on Hiroshima, and without reference to it, the Weekly Intelligence Review, a communication sent to AAF officers flying daily missions against Japanese cities, defined what the overall goal had become: "We intend to seek out and destroy the enemy wherever he or she is, in the greatest possible numbers, in the shortest possible time. For us, there are no civilians in Japan."[239] LeMay probably had this declaration in mind when, long after the war, he explained the rationale for his campaign by telling Michael Sherry, "There are no innocent civilians. It is their government and you are fighting a people, you are not fighting an armed force anymore. So it doesn't bother me so much to be killing the so-called innocent bystanders."[240]

Because the bulk of Japanese soldiers were mobilized away from Japan, on the Asian mainland and throughout the Pacific, the vast majority of those killed in cities by U.S. firebombs were women, children, and old people. As we have seen, President Truman and other leaders continued to give lip service to the idea that only military objectives were targeted. History might measure the seriousness of Truman's statements to that effect from his declaration, on August 9, that the American bomber force was too humane to drop its devastating weapon on Tokyo. Are we to believe he had not read the *New York Times* back in March? Or does the truth in the insistence on strictly military targeting — Hiroshima as "an important military base" — lie in a meaning of "military objectives" that had been expanded and expanded again, finally to include any living thing that moves. No civilians in Japan, not even in nurseries.

Air warfare had, in effect, redefined war itself, and this is the shift from which Americans turned their gaze, both then and ever since. No longer was military "denial" enough — denial of an enemy's capability to conquer or to hold. No longer was military "coercion" enough — bending of an enemy's will to one's own. Elimination. Extermination. Obliteration. These are the words that began to dominate the martial vocabulary, just as an eliminationist weapon system joined the arsenal. Against every openly stated purpose, the United States embraced a strategy of annihilation from the air, because it could. It was as if the American psyche had itself been occupied by an invading force, one led by the likes of LeMay and Groves, before whose callous certitude the tortuous ambivalence of others had to fall.

Sherry calls this new psychological trait "technological fanaticism" and describes it as an inability to relate means to ends. "At bottom, technological fanaticism was the product of two distinct but related phenomena: one — the will to destroy — ancient and recurrent; the other — the technical means of destruction — modern. Their convergence resulted in the evil of American bombing. But it was a sin of a peculiarly modern kind because it seemed so inadvertent, seemed to involve so little choice."[241] This disorder infected airmen and scientists and the statesmen who directed them. But perhaps the word "fanaticism," defined as "an irrational and often extreme belief,"[242] gives this phenomenon too much credit. Belief? Belief in what, exactly? Better to think of it as nihilism pure and simple.

Men worked hard to accomplish short-term goals — scientists assembling a workable atomic bomb, diplomats maneuvering for advantage, air commanders lowering altitudes to enhance payload — while having abandoned any responsibility for long-term consequences. Mass destruction became its own purpose, its own justification. Only this turn in the underlying psychology of the men making war against Japan in the summer of 1945 accounts for the confusion, myopia, inconsistency, and stubbornness that, as we saw, characterized Leslie Groves, James Byrnes, Harry Truman, and most of those who were advising them. As a result, the warmakers could never evaluate the atomic bomb on its own terms. Despite its distinct destructiveness, after Hamburg, Dresden, Hankow, Tokyo, and sixty other Japanese cities, the bomb had no terms of its own.

Destroy. Destroy. Destroy again. When destruction comes to define the national purpose, annihilation becoming the end product of the best-organized communal effort in history — there is the threshold to remember. By the year 1945, what Americans believed in — judging not from what they said but what they did — was nothing. Where is the surprise, then, that what they would stop at was nothing, too?

It is well understood that the American nation was born in the state of original sin, the mortal sin of slavery — an evil the nation's founders recognized as such, but which they nevertheless affirmed. For decades the nation lived with eyes averted from the rank corruption in which it was conceived, until the day of reckoning came, the wrath of civil war.

The end of World War II marked, for the United States, a kind of second birth, the beginning of a new era of American world power — "the American Century," in Henry Luce's famous phrase. Indulging the narcissism of the writer, I earlier noted the literal birthday — the day of unconditional surrender, Operation Pointblank, the Pentagon dedication, and the jump-start of Los Alamos — as the day of my own birth, January 22, 1943. Better, perhaps, to think of 1943 as the beginning of gestation, ahead of what was delivered in 1945. Proclaimed beautiful at birth — "the greatest thing in history" — that offspring can be fully recognized only now, two generations later, as having been grotesquely deformed, even in the womb: "There are no civilians in Japan."

The epiphany was not in the flash of August 6 but in the smoldering ruins of huge cities on two sides of the world. By 1945, there were no civilians in

Germany, either. The moral conundrum that is usually attached to the atomic bomb clearly precedes it, even if the bomb made the stakes of that conundrum absolute. With atomic weapons, the will to destroy becomes separated from the capability to destroy. With low capability, the will must cross a very high threshold, but if capability is great, as with the atomic bomb, the threshold for will is very low. Atomic weapons are extremely destructive and, as was shown in 1945, easy to use. That combination is what makes the atomic danger extreme — or at least it did so during the period of the American monopoly.

The decisions of scientists to keep working after the Nazi defeat, of Pentagon leaders who forgot about Japanese surrender, of officials whose attention shifted too quickly from an old enemy to a new one, of a president who bent before the rush of what was already coming at him — these decisions came to life only in the context of the hundred million prior decisions made by American citizens to accept annihilation as a national purpose. Total war from the air, culminating in the atomic bombings, required nothing less than the engagement of the whole nation, however much cloaked in denial. "Brutal and bloodthirsty war had long been known, but the depth and impact of air war went much further in striking at the heart of western society both in a physical and psychological manner," observes the British historian John Buckley. "Air Power demanded mass mobilization of economies, industries and scientific establishments to a degree hitherto unknown."[243] Individual Americans put the bombers in the air and cheered them on their way.

I came into my own first awareness when my nation came into its second awareness, understanding itself with grand, postcolonial innocence as a force for good in the world. "We come not as conquerors," Dwight Eisenhower told the vanquished Germans, "but as friends." Actually, Eisenhower was speaking more to himself and to his fellow Americans, an assurance of virtue intended to brace them as they beheld the ruins of what they had done. The Germans knew very well, even if they would never refer to it, and even if they felt they had asked for it, that this would be, at best, a friendship based on death. In synchrony with Germany, Japan, and its own allies, America had made war into something new, total death. Instead of being repulsed by that totality, America redefined itself in its terms.

The self-anointing of postwar American preeminence, moral as much as martial, presumed a refusal to face the fact that America's mid-twentieth-century initiation into world power was as much in the state of mortal sin as its birth in slavery had been. Every notion of a "just war" presumed "proportionality," the idea of consonance between ends and means that we saw in the previous chapter. But proportionality would never apply to nuclear weapons, which even their defenders understood. That was why, from Stimson's

Harper's article to Groves's rejection of the relevance of ethical thought, the aim was to insist on legitimacy by assertion and deception, not by argument or reasoning. Nuclear weapons would never be "proportional," which is, at bottom, why the American embrace of them was wrong. Yet an inhuman weapon and a proven readiness to use it were accompanied by a claim to virtue that made a permanent strategy based on terror seem a positive good. Firebombing, no longer by mere napalm but by nuclear fission, was now the open source of American power — and, hidden, of American identity.

The tortured Henry Stimson saw what this meant for the future of the nation he had served for half a century, and, with a clear mind at last, he would try to stop it. But the man who had, in less than three years, done more than any other to accomplish this basic shift in the meaning of America would go on to make it permanent: my dark hero, Curtis LeMay.

THREE

THE COLD WAR BEGINS

1. TENDERED A COMMISSION

I remember the day I caught my father in front of the bathroom mirror as he practiced his salute. He had come out of my parents' bedroom wearing a tan uniform with a silver star on each shoulder, and I had slipped quietly to the bathroom door to learn why he was dressed that way. It was probably the spring of 1948. I was five years old. My father was thirty-seven. I would not appreciate until much later that his lean good looks and ready smile made him a man of broad appeal, or that his firm will, as familiar to me as it was trustworthy, defined him as a man of authority. To me, he was God. That's all.

I knew what a salute was — my chums and I did it when we were playing war — but Dad's doing it made no sense. He put his board-stiff fingers to his brow, shot them at the mirror, then stopped their forward movement abruptly and brought his hand stiffly down to his side. He did it again. He did not see me because he was staring so intently into his own eyes. He did it again.

I already knew to be proud of my father's status — but as an FBI man. He had been Special Agent in Charge of the field office in Chicago, where I was born, and he was now assigned to FBI headquarters in Washington, where he worked for Mister Hoover. We were living, with my older brother Joe and baby brother Brian, in an apartment in Arlington, Virginia, which I remember most vividly for being near a creek from which Joe drank one day, and then he got polio. I felt guilty for not having drunk from the creek myself, and for not getting sick like him.

If Joe's sudden illness was the cloud over our family, the sun breaking through was Dad's new uniform. As the official Air Force history records it, Joseph F. Carroll had been "tendered and received a commission in the reserves" and was "ordered to active duty in the grade of brigadier general."[1] This is my first memory of photographs being taken: Mom is lining up Dad in the yard outside the apartment building, and Joe and I are on either side, Dad holding Brian in his arms, Mom telling us all to smile, which is unnecessary. Her Brownie makes a hollow click. And then she takes a photo of Dad and me alone, and he holds my hand. It seems appropriate that my mother should be seen as the person behind the camera, outside the picture. I am aware that what has unfolded so far as the story of the Pentagon reads like most historical accounts, a record of the decisions and actions of "great men" with little or no notice of others — not the anonymous throng of men on whom the consequences of those decisions fell, much less women.

My mother, Mary, would have pinned those new silver stars onto my father's epaulettes: "You are the star I steer by," she would have cracked. And there were such women "behind" the other men whom we have been tracking: "Mabel" behind Stimson, "Helen" behind LeMay. In fact, those men came to power at a moment when women had briefly come out from "behind" to play active roles in the victory of World War II. The extraordinary level of female employment in the wartime workforce is a much-noted phenomenon, a tremendous reversal of gender-based norms, but the end of the war changed all that. Voluntarily or not, more than three million women left the workforce within a year of V-J Day. With the war effort over, a new move was on to return to gender norms and integrate soldiers back into society. But it was also as if American men were subtly threatened by the fact that 1945 was the first year in which they were outnumbered in the population by women.[2] Perhaps women were threatened, too, preferring that place behind.

No matter how useful to the war economy "Rosie the Riveter" was, and no matter how influential women like Mary, Mabel, and Helen were behind the scenes — advancing their husbands, for example, by helping to move the considerable levers of power on social circuits — the hard fact is that by far the most notable place occupied by women in the story of World War II was, switching to the Axis nations, as the overwhelming majority of those who were killed by the Army Air Forces bombings. That would have been so because combat-eligible males would have been scarce among urban populations in Germany and Japan by 1945. The male dominance of air power, like the female dominance of air powerlessness, is no mere social construct.

I know from the one photograph I still have from the day of my father's commissioning that I was in uniform, too, wearing my cowboy boots and leather-fringed vest. Because we were outdoors, Dad wore his new hat, which had a shiny brown visor and a yellow braid. I called it an Army hat, and he corrected me, but happily. "Air Force, Jimmy. Air Force."

But what happened to the FBI? Later I would learn that for having arrested a notorious gangland fugitive named Roger Touhy, Dad had been brought into the FBI director's inner circle. In wartime Washington he had developed an expertise in counterespionage. As it came to me, he was in charge of catching spies — first German spies, then Russian. His was an identity my brother Joe and I gloried in as we listened every Tuesday night to our favorite radio program, *The FBI in Peace and War*. Our dad was a G-man. He carried a gun, which I was not allowed to look at, though I had glimpsed it once, in its holster, on his dresser.

But FBI agents wore civilian suits; FBI agents were not soldiers. I knew that much. I have no memory of him catching me as I watched him at the bathroom mirror that day. I have no memory of what followed his pantomime at the mirror. But that first sight of him in the tan uniform — in winter it would be blue — with its silver buttons and pocket flaps, a single star on each shoulder, remains one of the most vivid images I have of him. That moment was a dividing line in time — for me, remarkably enough, as much as for him. Each of us would spend the rest of his life surprised (I am still surprised) that one day, out of the blue — the blue yonder — he was commissioned directly to the rank of brigadier general in the United States Air Force.[3]

An unlikelier candidate for the rank of general in the Air Force than my father would have been hard to find. He grew up poor on the South Side of Chicago, the only one of a brood of siblings to obtain an education, which was a byproduct of a heartfelt urge to serve God. He entered a seminary at the age of twelve. For the next thirteen years he prepared to become a Catholic priest, receiving classical training in philosophy and theology and living according to the rigorous discipline of the late Middle Ages.

He distinguished himself in every way. Excelling at his studies, he was on track to a future in Rome, a career in the Church hierarchy. A superb athlete and happy extrovert, he was prized among his fellows. Genuinely religious, he was a natural contemplative. When he gave practice sermons in the seminary chapel, the faculty showed up to listen to him. Yet on the eve of his ordination he left the seminary and went home to the South Side, as if claws had reached up out of the bog of an Irish past to pull him back. Years later, I asked him why he had not been ordained, hoping for the answer that he had chosen my mother over the Church, but he said simply, "I wasn't worthy."

The Irish term for what he was then, a man who had turned his back on the vocation to which the angels genuflected, was "spoiled priest." He had disgraced his family and angered his religious superiors, one of whom charged him with having stolen his education. But expertise in Thomas Aquinas was a ticket to nowhere in the Depression. My father went to work in the Chicago stockyards, first as a general laborer, up to his ankles in slaughterhouse blood, then as a pipefitter's helper, handing tools into the pit. He began openly seeing my mother, a gum-snapping redhead who had quit school after eighth grade to help support her family, and who was by now a supervisor of telephone operators in the Loop.

Joe Carroll's role in life, after he'd blown his chance with the Church, would be to work at the crummy stockyards job, hope someday to make pipefitter, drink heavily, and fail. But Mary Morrissey saw more in him. At her urging, he enrolled at a streetcar night school in the heart of Chicago. At the end of his shift every day, he would scald himself in the shower to get the stench of the stockyards out of his skin and then ride the el downtown, books under his arm. Six years later, in 1939, he earned a law degree, passed the bar, married Mary, and took a job with the FBI. Eight years after that, he moved into an office in the Pentagon, the youngest general officer in the Air Force, a man who, until then, had done his traveling by train.

In July 1947, Congress passed the National Security Act. This was the climactic response to a pervading insecurity — felt on both sides of the Iron Curtain — that had come in the traumatic wake of the war. Economic, political, cultural, and moral dislocations had reshaped (or misshaped) the world in short order (or disorder). In the United States domestic insecurity would seem paramount, but Red Scare politics, from HUAC to Joe McCarthy, took its energy from what was happening in the world at large.

On one level, the National Security Act was most notable for bringing the Army and the Navy together — on paper — in a unified organization, albeit now with a third service branch, the Air Force. But the act, in also creating the National Security Council and the Central Intelligence Agency, shifted the nation's entire footing in relation to enemies and allies both. Such was the new insecurity, though, that in the Pentagon supposed allies could seem the most threatening of enemies. The act's unification of the services was supposed to solve the problem of interbranch rivalry, which had surfaced again and again during the war, leading to inefficiency and unnecessary fatalities in combat.

We took note of the Navy's acrimonious refusal to move offices into the Pentagon in 1943, in a dispute over square footage, but the alienation had affected the fighting forces' performance in battle and cost lives. We saw how the AAF declined to use its bombers in support of the Navy's anti-U-boat campaign in the Atlantic, but competition between the services in the Pacific was equally fierce. The Army and Navy had undercut each other regularly, especially when it came to competing for budget allotments. Loss of life, ballooning of costs, rejections of joint command, complications in one offensive after another — it could be said that the Army and Navy fought separate wars in the Pacific. And at war's end, General MacArthur was not wild about receiving the Japanese surrender on a battleship; a "Navy trick," as Army leaders called it.[4]

After winning the fight against Nazism and fascism, the U.S. civilian and military establishments fell to fighting among themselves — *about* themselves. The American armed forces had won the war, yet there was, within those forces and outside them, especially in Congress, a sense that the war had laid bare a near-disastrous organizational problem, the solution to which would be a bureaucratic realignment that would amount to "a sort of federal government for the military."[5]

The new unified structure would subsume the Department of War (renamed Department of the Army) and the Department of the Navy under the National Military Establishment, ultimately the Department of Defense — a euphemistic shift of major significance. The Navy was forced at last to move its offices into the Pentagon. Soon enough, the secretaries of war and the Navy were dropped from the president's cabinet, to be replaced there by the secretary of defense, who would preside over the branch secretaries, including that of the new Air Force, and the Joint Chiefs of Staff, formally constituted now. As this legislation was prepared, the secretary of the Navy, James Forrestal, who'd held that position since halfway through the war, had lobbied hard to protect the independence of his service branch. It was Forrestal who had proposed the Japanese surrender ceremony on the battleship, guessing correctly that Truman would love the idea, since the ship was the USS *Missouri*.

As was true of Air Force advocates, Forrestal had been quick to see the usefulness of a Soviet threat in making a case that Navy budgets had to be protected. This dovetailed with his long-standing attitude, for as much as Forrestal loved the Navy, he loathed Communism, had for years. And now that hostility meshed with his parochial resentment of the upstart Air Force. As debates over the new structure of the combined military establishment continued, Forrestal shamelessly protected Navy turf, but he did so by arguing from highflying idealism. Denouncing "autocracy" as undemocratic, he argued that the office of the secretary of defense should have little real power, which implied that the unification would be more symbolic than real. By the time the legislation passed, Forrestal's position was vindicated, and the new law established the autonomy of independent service branches, with the defense secretary as a kind of confederate referee. Having won this bureaucratic dogfight, Forrestal was immediately punished for his success when Truman named him the first SecDef, as the office would soon be known.[6]

The traditional rivalry between the Army and the Navy was simultaneously exacerbated and dwarfed when the 1947 National Security Act also established the Air Force as a separate branch. The Air Force would join the Navy in pressing a budget-and-resources case against the Army, although always under the guise of warnings about Moscow. Yet the fact that Truman, with an eye to the upcoming presidential election, in which he was already the decided underdog, was determined both to demobilize the vast manpower of the land army and to set a zero-sum budget ceiling for the reconstituted Department of Defense meant that the most heated conflict would come down to the Air Force against the Navy.

From the earliest days of the Republic, the Navy had been seen as the ultimate guardian of American security, first as a defensive coastal force, then as a blue-water projection of American power across oceans. But that primacy no longer went without saying. In the new contest, the Air Force claimed the advantage of the atomic bomb, of which bombardiers were self-appointed custodians, and which, in newly developed doctrines of strategic air war, promised absolute power on the relative cheap.[7] The Navy was at a disadvantage here, not only because the planning for bombardment from long-range strategic aircraft excluded Navy capability, but also because in first-round discussions of the atomic bomb, key Navy figures, including Admirals Leahy, King, and Nimitz, had lodged practical and, in the case of Navy Undersecretary Ralph Bard,[8] moral objections. Now, however, the Navy was firmly committed to the idea of the bomb, and insisted that a new generation of so-called supercarriers was its best home.

Even when power was wielded from the Pentagon, air war commanders had enjoyed considerable autonomy in Europe and the Pacific — Marshall rarely queried Arnold on AAF campaigns — and they were not inclined to yield that independence in peacetime. The Air Force would carve out turf and defend it with a fierceness that would make the Army-Navy rivalry seem tame. The new strategic bomber force was the Air Force's priority, and — setting a pattern that would define the American side of the Cold War dynamic — Air Force advocates went for the jugular of their Army and Navy rivals with the blade of the Soviet threat. The darker Moscow's intentions could be shown to be, the brighter were Air Force budget prospects. A defining moment in this contest occurred when the legendary bomber commander Carl "Tooey" Spaatz, Arnold's successor as AAF chief, stunned his interrogators at a congressional hearing. Flashing the image on a screen, he replaced the traditional Mercator projection of the globe, which showed the United States protected by two vast oceans, with a polar projection, which showed a hulking Soviet Union all set to gobble Alaska, and then the rest of the forty-eight states, from across the narrowest of straits. America the vulnerable.

The first secretary of the Air Force was a forty-six-year-old Missouri transplant and Truman protégé named W. Stuart Symington. The son of a college professor and himself a graduate of Yale, Symington had been successful in business. During the war, he'd been president of a St. Louis–based defense contractor that manufactured electric gun turrets for bombers, and he was a fierce advocate of strategic air war as the cornerstone of America's martial future. On one side, he had watched with dismay as demobilization cut the number of combat-ready bomber groups from 218 at the end of the war to fewer than 10 by the end of 1946.[9] On the other, drawing on his own experience, Symington understood better than most what it meant that the American aircraft industry would not survive without a fresh infusion of military orders.[10] And, Symington knew, the only impulse that could spur that was fear of the Soviet Union.

As we saw, the idea behind the 1947 legislation was that the three service branches were to be unified in one government department headquartered at the Pentagon, but just as the Navy was determined to maintain its independence, so the new Air Force, under Symington, fully intended to go its own way, with the atomic bomb the source of *its* power as much as America's. Symington would prove to be Forrestal's nemesis, especially when Air Force budget requests threatened to gut the Navy, reducing it to a function of supply and transport, as if the new Department of Defense would be only about air war.

But Symington's first task, in the fall of 1947, was to break the Air Force free of the Army, which was where my father came in. That the Air Force was now an independent service branch meant, in effect, that everything but its airplanes had to be created from scratch. The Army still "owned" the bases, research facilities, and logistical structures on which the Air Force depended, and the Army wanted them all back. The tension between the services quickly translated into an Air Force determination, where possible, to put distance between itself and every Army institution.

In 1947, the year of the House Un-American Activities Committee, the attorney general's list, the loyalty oath, and the dread of Communist infiltration, nothing loomed larger for Symington than the question of security, a word that had just come into its own. In that season in Washington, approaches to defending national security were either ad hoc or hysterical, but for the Air Force Symington wanted something rational, systematic, dependable. Because he was less worried about "pinks," "fellow travelers," or the supremely inept Communist Party of America than about Soviet espionage, Symington wanted the Air Force to have its own counterintelligence capability. But that was only one concern. To prevent corruption in the allocation of hundreds of millions of dollars in Air Force contracts, he knew he also needed real investigative authority, far beyond the amateurish Army systems that had mushroomed during the war.

Security of air bases, protection against the intrusions of rival service branches (not to mention against penetration by Soviet agents), investigation of corruption in multibillion-dollar defense contracts, and internal controls of the new service branch itself — these requirements exceeded the resources of turf-obsessed and theater-based Army outfits like MI-2, the Criminal Investigation Corps, and the half-dismantled Office of Strategic Services. True to the ethos of the Pentagon, Symington wanted a centralized security operation, subject to the control of a director appointed by him.

What Symington wanted, he realized, was an Air Force version of the Federal Bureau of Investigation, so he asked J. Edgar Hoover for the short-time loan of an FBI expert to develop a proposal for an Air Force organization. Hoover gave him my father. That was in October. By December, Joseph Carroll's description of such an organization was on Symington's desk, complete with laddered charts and a suggested name, the Air Force Office of Special Investigations. The proposal defined an agency that broke all the rules of traditional military organization, with OSI agents operating outside the chain of command, having authority over senior officers, responsible not to local commanders but to an all-powerful director based in the Pentagon. It was exactly what Symington wanted, but when he had my father lay it out for the Air Force's brass hats, they said it couldn't be done, which only meant they refused to do it. To their surprise, and my father's, Symington turned to him, offering the job of setting up the OSI. Dad wasn't sure, but Hoover agreed.

On the Air Force floor of the Pentagon, there were barely muted protests and threats of obstruction, manifestations of the kind of turf protection the OSI would aim to take out, which were enough to make Joseph Carroll want the job. In later years, the Air Force brass, for holding solidly to one position against all outsiders, would be known as the "Blue Curtain,"[11] and that veil was decidedly closed against Joe Carroll. But he was not a man to be intimidated: Roger Touhy had described the G-man who arrested him as terrifyingly cold, ready to shoot. When Symington formally named my father as the OSI's first director, the brass protested that it was illegal for a civilian to exercise line authority over commissioned officers. That was when Symington, using his pull with Truman to sponsor a special bill in Congress, put Carroll in uniform. At thirty-seven, he was instantly appointed the youngest general officer in the Air Force.

In a late-in-life interview with an Air Force historian, my father recounted how, once Symington commissioned him as the head of the OSI, he was cut loose to make his own way through the thickets of Pentagon bureaucracy. He had a two-room suite of offices on the fourth floor of the Building's

E ring, a prestigious location, but otherwise he had to recruit his own staff and find room in the Air Force budget for his organization. For his inner circle he depended on friends he brought over from the FBI. To the other men with stars on the epaulettes of their Air Force uniforms, Carroll was "that cop." But even if they were senior to him, and even if they disdained him as a crypto-civilian, he had the authority to investigate them if they gave him cause. That my father was not one of them was the hinge that made that authority real.

Joe Carroll had mastered his careful salute in front of the bathroom mirror, not understanding that World War II flyboys had prided themselves on the carelessness of their tossed-off hand gesture. Dad's rigid discipline with himself, dating back to the seminary, was reflected now in a self-conscious military demeanor, but the equally rigid men whose company he joined feigned nonchalance. Even the hats of their new Air Force uniforms were crushed already. Not only that. The men Dad passed in the corridors wore tunics that sparkled with the combat ribbons and silver wings they had earned in the flak-ridden skies over Germany and the Pacific, badges of the destruction they had wrought and endured. Operations Pointblank, Thunderclap, Clarion, Little Boy, and Fat Man. The left breast of Joseph Carroll's uniform, where ribbons and a command pilot's wings should have been, was glaringly bare. Nothing, not even for marksmanship (though he was a crack shot). His was the only uniform in the Pentagon like that, and the eyes of all those others always snagged on that absence of ribbons. Among the many experiences my father did not have was participating in the slaughter from the air of one and a half million human beings. So why shouldn't LeMay and the others have disdained him?

2. STIMSON'S SEPTEMBER 11

Of all the people who participated in the decisions that led to that carnage, one in particular had worked to prevent it from happening ever again, Henry Stimson. His vision of the future of American military power thus differed radically from that of the commanders with whom he had worked. At the end of World War II, they readily cast their eyes forward to the next conflict, with a view to prevailing. Stimson understood at once that there would be no prevailing, and he moved to head off that next conflict.

Speaking of himself in the third person, and referring to the late summer of 1945, in the memoir he later wrote with young McGeorge Bundy, Stimson said, "For thirty years Stimson had been a champion of international law and morality. As a soldier and Cabinet officer he had repeatedly argued that war itself must be restrained within the bounds of humanity. As recently as June 1, he had sternly questioned his Air Forces leader, wanting to know whether the apparently indiscriminate bombing of Tokyo were absolutely necessary . . . In the conflagration bombings by massed B-29's he was permitting a kind of total war he had always hated, and in recommending the use of the atomic bomb he was implicitly confessing that there could be no significant limits to the horror of modern war."[12]

Stimson, in fact, had paid little attention to the indiscriminate firebombings in the spring and summer of 1945,[13] but when he did take in their scope, it seemed to him yet another justification for the use of the atomic bomb. Oddly, he and others saw the bomb as a way to end the inhumanity of firebombing — as if incendiary bombing were being carried out by forces other than his own. Stimson's emotions at the end of the war, as we have seen, were a mix of confusion, denial, exhaustion, grief, and guilt. But his troubled conscience, in the end, showed him a way out of the (literal) dead end he had helped to engineer.

Having supervised the construction of the Pentagon, as well as the manufacture of the atomic bomb;[14] having agonized, albeit belatedly, over the expansion of AAF targeting from precision to area bombardment; having approved the shift in AAF ordnance from predominantly explosive to mainly incendiary; having failed to mitigate the harshness of the Potsdam Declaration; having spared Kyoto while insisting against himself that Hiroshima and Nagasaki were somehow military targets; having watched Truman assert a new belligerence toward Moscow; and having been one of the first to appreciate that the atomic bomb changed everything, Stimson took an initiative that was unprecedented even in a career that had begun in the era of the Indian wars.

It was another of those events dated September 11, each one the center of a world in collision with other worlds. The impact of such collisions is our subject. On September 11, 1945, four years to the day after the groundbreaking of the Pentagon, fifty-six years to the day before the Al Qaeda attack on the Pentagon, less than a month after Japan's surrender, and just over a month after the detonation of the Nagasaki bomb, Stimson composed an urgent "Memorandum for the President," which began, "Subject: Proposed Action for Control of Atomic Bombs."

First Stimson told the president what the dawning of the nuclear age meant:

If the atomic bomb were merely another though more devastating military weapon to be assimilated into our pattern of international relations, it would be one thing. We could then follow the old custom of secrecy and nationalistic military superiority relying on international caution to prescribe [sic] the future use of the weapon as we did with gas. But I think the bomb instead constitutes merely a first step in a new control by man over the forces of nature too revolutionary and dangerous to fit into the old concepts. I think it really caps the climax of the race between man's growing technical power for destructiveness and his psychological power of self-control and group-control — his moral power. If so, our method of approach to the Russians is a question of the most vital importance in the evolution of human progress . . . The crux of the problem is Russia.

Stimson already understood that from then on, relations between Moscow and Washington would be "virtually dominated by the problem of the atomic bomb." He had said as much to Truman at their first meeting on the subject the previous April. It was inevitable, he wrote, that the Russians would get the bomb, whether sooner (in three or four years, as scientists argued) or later (in twenty years or more, as General Groves said). That time frame was not nearly as important as avoiding "a secret armament race of a rather desperate character. There is evidence to indicate," he wrote, "that such activity may have already commenced."

"To put the matter concisely," Stimson wrote, he proposed that the United States take immediate steps to "enter into an arrangement with the Russians, the general purpose of which would be to control and limit the use of the atomic bomb." He suggested that by bringing the Soviets into our confidence, they would have reason to believe it when Americans said that "we would stop work on any further improvement in, or manufacture of, the bomb as a military weapon, provided the Russians and the British would do likewise." This meant, and Stimson proposed it, that Washington would "impound what bombs we now have in the United States provided the Russians and the British would agree with us that in no event will they or we use a bomb as an instrument of war unless all three governments agree to that use." Give up the secret. Give up the monopoly. Give up sovereignty over use. Give up control of existing bombs. Stimson, in the cover letter that accompanied this memo, summed up his proposal by using the word "share" twice.[15]

In his very first memo to Truman on the subject of the atomic bomb, the previous April 25, Stimson had already declared that "the question of sharing it with other nations and, if so shared, upon what terms, becomes a primary question of our foreign relations."[16] Now he was proposing to share the atomic bomb with Moscow. "I would make such an approach just as soon as our immediate political considerations make it appropriate."

Stimson was seventy-seven years old, had first been appointed as secretary of war in 1911, and had been secretary of state when the world plunged into the armed chaos of the Depression. As war secretary throughout World War II, he had been anguished by the escalation of air war brutality over which he presided, but he had also done more than anyone to empower the anxiety-free Leslie Groves. Though he'd intervened for Kyoto, he had not flinched from approving the bombing of Hiroshima and its "workers' houses." He had himself set loose the "strapping young giant"[17] of a strategic bomber force. He was at the furthest remove from naïve, but he was worried, as he put it, about "saving civilization not for five or for twenty years, but forever."

So now he warned that relations with Moscow "may be perhaps irretrievably embittered by the way in which we approach the solution of the bomb with Russia. For if we fail to approach them now and merely continue to negotiate with them, having this weapon rather ostentatiously on our hip, their suspicion and their distrust of our purposes and motives will increase." This reference to the atomic bomb "ostentatiously on our hip" is a tipoff that this memo was essentially an argument against fiercely anti-Soviet positions then being taken by Secretary of State Byrnes, who had already proven to be something of a nemesis. Stimson had, the week before, criticized the way Byrnes was preparing for an upcoming meeting of the Council of Foreign Ministers in London: "Byrnes [is] very much against any attempt to cooperate with Stalin. His mind is full of the problems with the coming meeting of the foreign ministers and he looks to having the presence of the bomb in his pocket, so to speak, as a great weapon to get through the thing he has."[18]

Very much against Byrnes, in one of the most remarkable statements ever made by an American statesman, Stimson presumed to assert in his September 11 letter to Truman, "The chief lesson I have learned in a long life is that the only way you can make a man trustworthy is to trust him; and the surest way to make him untrustworthy is to distrust him and show him your distrust."[19]

The man, in this case, was Joseph Stalin. In *On Active Service in Peace and War*, the memoir published nearly three years after this memorandum was written, Stimson averred that Stalin had indeed proven himself to be untrustworthy. Further, in 1948 he called his September 11, 1945, memo "dangerously one-sided," and seemed somewhat embarrassed by it, but that was in the context of the embittered politics and rather desperate arms race of which he had warned, and which by then had indeed made the two nations enemies. In 1948, he even hedged on his poignant and hopeful statement about trusting a man: "But I must add that this does not always apply to a man who is determined to make you his dupe."

In 1945, Stimson was not naïve about Stalin. He had in the past expressed hopes that the Soviet government was capable of liberalization, hopes that proved unfounded, but by the end of the war, having been instructed especially by the U.S. ambassador to Moscow, W. Averell Harriman, he was under no illusions about the Kremlin's recalcitrance.[20] He knew of Stalin's early deal with Hitler, but he also knew the Allies would not have defeated Hitler without Stalin's ruthless offensive from the east. Stimson, as secretary of war, had read the reports from the eastern front, so he knew of Stalin's savagery toward not only Germans but his own soldiers. Stimson had been Herbert Hoover's secretary of state from 1929 to 1933, the years of Stalin's worst crime, and would have read cables detailing it — the terror famine in which anywhere from five to thirty million people died in the breadbasket of Ukraine and other regions as the Soviet leader directed harvests to other parts of his empire. Stimson, in other words, would have known very well what monstrous deeds had been carried out in the name of Stalin's "collectivization."

But in his relations with other great powers, Stalin was nothing if not a realist. Stimson could anticipate that the selfsame Soviet leader, against expansionist pressures in his own establishment, would be responsive to American demands. And events would show Stimson to be right. Moscow is remembered, in the American historical consensus, as only pushing outward during the unsettled postwar period. But in fact the Soviets would withdraw from Iran, leaving Western powers dominant in a nation on Russia's border. They would evacuate Norway, abandon Communists in Greece, Italy, and Finland, and fail to fully support Communists in China. Even in Germany, in pursuit of collective governance, Stalin would support bourgeois elements over Socialists.[21] Likewise Stalin would yield on the question of control over the entrance to the Black Sea, and he would accept, however unhappily, America's refusal to follow through on reparations agreements dating to the Potsdam meeting. If Stimson wanted to approach Stalin in "trust," it was obviously because he knew that the Soviet leader faced severe constraints of his own just then, and knew that the atomic bomb had put Washington in a position of superiority, however pontoon-like in its firmness.

A single death, Stalin famously observed, is a tragedy; a million deaths is a statistic. But Stimson had presided over such fatalities himself, and what weighed on him by now was the vision of many more to come — because of forces he had helped set in motion. To the extent that an exhausted old man could, Stimson felt each of the deaths he had helped to bring about as the death of one person, and then another, and then another, all adding up to a tragic multitude, no statistic at all. "The face of war is the face of death," he wrote in the 1947 Harper's article referred to earlier, an article defending the use of the atomic bomb. But that use, "the least abhorrent choice," had changed everything. Even in defending the atomic bomb, Stimson attacked it.

What he himself had presided over "made it wholly clear that we must never have another war . . . There is no other choice." His perspective in 1947 only reinforced what he had come to understand in 1945. Henry Stimson, on September 11, 1945, in other words, was no Pollyanna, nor some sort of Henry Wallace. If he proposed to make Stalin trustworthy by trusting him, it was not because he hoped Stalin had changed, but because he was certain that, after August 6, the world had. Certainly Stimson had.[22]

Truman, to his credit, made Stimson's radical September 11 proposal the subject of full debate at a cabinet meeting ten days later, on September 21, which happened to be Stimson's seventy-eighth birthday. Stimson, in his 1948 memoir, does not say what occurred, but there is reason to conceive of the meeting as a turning point in the American century. What would remain the basic question of the Cold War was put on that table: Is Soviet foreign policy motivated by an offensive strategy for the sake of ideologically driven global empire or by normal big-power defensiveness, aiming at security? If the former, Stimson's "trust" would be naïve and self-defeating; if the latter, it would be routine statecraft, a search for common self-interest. All too quickly, those suspicious of Moscow's motives would invoke the analogy of Munich, looking to head off a Soviet version of Hitler's aggression. But others, like Stimson, saw less Munich than Mexico, and knew how Washington would react if America's nearest neighbor fell under the control of a hostile power.[23]

After Stimson summarized his proposal, it was supported by Secretary of Labor Lewis Schwellenbach and Postmaster General Robert Hannegan. More to the point was support from Undersecretary of War Robert Patterson. Also in favor was Dean Acheson, undersecretary of state, who was present because Byrnes was in London at the foreign ministers' meeting. Years later, in his memoir, Acheson would backpedal on this support, saying he had spoken "partly out of deference and respect for Colonel Stimson." But as one of Stimson's biographers observes, this was an Acheson who had been bloodied by the McCarthy years and who did not want to appear ever to have been soft on the Soviet Union.[24] Acheson's support of the Stimson proposal would soon lose force in any case, because when Byrnes returned from London a few days later, he firmly opposed it.

Stronger yet than Acheson in favor of Stimson's proposal was Henry A. Wallace, the secretary of commerce and former vice president. Wallace is derided in American memory as a kind of left-wing kook, but he was a scientifically sophisticated man and understood what many did not: that there was no maintaining a monopoly on nuclear physics, no matter what Groves and those he'd convinced, like Byrnes, were saying. So sharing the secret with the Soviet Union amounted only to anticipating what they were surely on the way to acquiring regardless of what Washington did. Sharing, in that sense, could be seen as a realistic way to maintain American influence over the bomb, even as Russia proved capable of producing it. But Wallace was a lightning rod, and his endorsement of Stimson's proposal would alone have been enough to draw opposition from other cabinet members.

No one weighed in more negatively than Secretary of the Navy James Forrestal, who, in his diary, caricatured Wallace as "completely, everlastingly and wholeheartedly in favor of giving [the bomb] to the Russians." Forrestal wrote that the September 21 cabinet meeting "was occupied entirely with a discussion of the atomic bomb." The editor of Forrestal's diary says of the meeting that it "was clearly fundamental in the formulation of this new and dread subject."[25] Wallace, for his part, dismissed Forrestal's as "the most extreme attitude of all . . . a warlike, big-Navy, isolationist approach."[26] Wallace defined the event as "one of the most dramatic of all cabinet meetings in my fourteen years of Washington experience."[27]

Forrestal had become identified as a staunch anti-Communist, and though a lapsed Roman Catholic, he was, for example, associated with Cardinal Francis Spellman's vigorous campaign against Communist influence in the United States.[28] J. Edgar Hoover kept Forrestal apprised of the activities of the Communist Party of America. At Forrestal's direction, his own Office of Naval Intelligence was preoccupied with the search for evidence of Communist subversion, to the extent of monitoring the speeches of his fellow cabinet officer Henry Wallace.[29] All such domestic matters were assumed, of course, to be tied to the international movement centered in Moscow. Thus Forrestal had already taken positions against Stimson on the subject of how to deal with the Soviet Union. The previous April, Forrestal had argued for confronting the Russians over their occupation of Poland, but at that penultimate point in the war Stimson had emphasized all that the Red Army had done and was still doing against Germany.[30] Indeed, Stimson regarded it as unproven that the Russians, in their claims on Poland, were violating the Yalta agreements.[31]

While Roosevelt was alive, Forrestal's anti-Soviet bellicosity could appear as harmless venting. FDR's last official statement was a cable to Churchill, composed only hours before he died, on April 12, and including the line "I would minimize the general Soviet problem."[32] But with Roosevelt's death, Forrestal's intransigence could seem, to an unsure new leader, like much-needed reinforcement. In preparing for a first meeting with a Soviet representative, Truman sought advice. Stimson urged restraint, but Forrestal insisted, "We had better have a showdown with them now than later."[33] The meeting between Truman and Foreign Minister Vyacheslav Molotov took place on April 23, eleven days after Truman became president. Truman echoed Forrestal and other hard-liners, crudely chastising Molotov — an event many call the true beginning of Cold War enmity.[34] The new president's crustiness masked a deep insecurity. The conventional American assessment celebrates Truman's brusque decisiveness, but there is reason to believe it reflected his inability to take in complexity, or to live with it. "If the Russians did not wish to join us," Truman said after the meeting, "they could go to hell."[35]

Now, in response to Stimson's proposal, Forrestal defined the atomic bomb as "the property of the American people," and essentially argued that the administration lacked the authority to give it away. But his forceful characterization of the Soviet Union is what marks Forrestal's statement as yet another pivotal moment. "The Russians, like the Japanese, are essentially Oriental in their thinking, and until we have a longer record of experience with them on the validity of engagements . . . it seems doubtful that we should endeavor to buy their understanding and sympathy." Anticipating a line of argument that would define American foreign policy debates for two generations, Forrestal rejected Stimson's proposal by equating a diplomatic approach to the Soviet Union with Munich: "We tried that once with Hitler . . . There are no returns on appeasement."[36]

Instead of a structure of international control, Forrestal proposed what he called "sole trusteeship," with the United States maintaining complete control over the atomic bomb for the benefit of the United Nations. And with the bomb as a guarantor, the United States, as Forrestal had said two days before in testimony before Congress, "will not tolerate the disorder and the destruction of war being let loose upon the world again."[37] To stop that — here, already, was the permanent conundrum — the United States would have to threaten the ultimate disorder and destruction.

Stimson's biographer Godfrey Hodgson calls the September 21 cabinet meeting "a fork in the road." Regarding Stimson's proposal in hindsight, through the lens of Cold War history, it is easy to dismiss as something Stalin would have spurned or exploited, but that presumes a history of extreme hostility that unfolded after the fact. Had Stimson's view prevailed, according to the historian James Chace, the Cold War "would have been substantially different. Hiroshima would have produced a balance of power rather than a balance of terror. Soviet behavior would likely have been far less confrontational."[38] That Stimson's proposal was not widely perceived as an act of naiveté is indicated by the fact that the Joint Chiefs of Staff, when informed of it, first took Acheson's side, not Forrestal's, and supported the Stimson initiative. The JCS understood that a nuclear arms race leading to war would inevitably tilt against the United States, if only because the less industrialized and less urbanized Soviet Union would be better placed to survive the devastation of atomic warfare, and therefore more inclined to initiate it. The JCS also assumed that the amoral Soviets would be far readier to launch an atomic sneak attack than they.[39] Soon enough, however, the Chiefs would discover how their own interests would be served by Forrestal's more belligerent approach, and they would become firm opponents of any cooperative moves toward Moscow.

Lip service would be paid for a time to the idea of international control of the bomb — the Acheson-Lilienthal report of early 1946, the Baruch Plan later the same year — but these proposals, by requiring sweeping internal inspections, assumed the very thing Stimson had warned against, "the demand by us for an internal change in Russia as a condition of sharing in the atomic weapon."[40] Those proposals also wanted to protect American custody — trusteeship — of at least some atomic bombs while forbidding it to the Soviet Union, a guarantee of Russian rejection. In effect, as one historian observed, America was demanding a certain *quid* from Moscow without making clear what the *quo* would be.[41] Not only that: any nation in violation of the agreement "would be subject to an attack with atomic weapons."[42] The American "peace plan," that is, included a provision for a U.N.-sanctioned atomic war against Moscow.

The road presided over by gun-on-the-hip Secretary of State Byrnes and others who assumed an indefinite nuclear monopoly would open in front of America and the world. The markers on that road are well known, beginning with the Council of Foreign Ministers meeting in London the very week of Stimson's proposal. Soviet Foreign Minister Molotov, perhaps displaying his knowledge of Washington idioms, teased Byrnes by asking him if he had a bomb in his hip pocket. Byrnes replied, "You don't know Southerners. We carry our artillery in our hip pocket. If you don't cut out all this stalling and let us get down to work, I am going to pull an atomic bomb out of my hip pocket and let you have it." Molotov is reported to have laughed.[43]

Franklin Lindsay, a young OSS officer whose wartime service with the partisans in Yugoslavia made him an early expert on the Communists, was present in London as a member of Byrnes's staff. In a meeting with me at his home in Cambridge in 2003, Lindsay described the meeting as "a very abortive seven or eight days." Byrnes and Molotov were at loggerheads. The Americans took their own sphere of influence for granted, and now it extended from the Americas to Western Europe to Japan. But the Soviet claim to a sphere of influence in Eastern Europe was denounced as ideologically driven imperialism. The clash was insoluble. "The first session of the Council of Foreign Ministers," Byrnes said in his official report, "closed in a stalemate."[44] In private, Byrnes equated Stalin with Hitler,[45] an analogy that would soon define American conventional wisdom. "Byrnes didn't understand what the hell was going on," Lindsay told me. "He was in over his head. The meeting broke up in complete disarray. It was a first steppingstone to the Cold War."[46]

Other steppingstones included Stalin's speech in February 1946 in which he was understood as describing conflict between Communism and capitalism as inevitable;[47] Churchill's "Iron Curtain" speech, when he defended "Christian civilization" and English-speaking nations, in Fulton, Missouri, in March;[48] and the Soviet rejection of the Baruch Plan at the United Nations at the end of the year. The Baruch proposal for international control of the atomic bomb, under the United Nations, is lodged in the American memory as a genuine effort at compromise with Moscow, because its provisions for inspections and the exchange of information would have applied equally to both sides. But that, of course, was what made the proposals impossible, since they assumed democratic structures and freedom of information. In the American memory the plan marked Washington's readiness to "give up" the bomb if other nations, particularly Russia, were prepared to forswear its development, but that is not true. The plan took for granted the permanence of an American nuclear monopoly.[49]

Most critically, the Baruch Plan provided that the Soviet Union could not use its U.N. veto on any questions having to do with atomic energy. That veto, however, was the only thing that had allowed Moscow to join the U.N., as was the case with the United States. If Washington was prepared to yield its veto on atomic matters, that was because Washington already possessed the bomb. Moscow's surrendering the veto effectively meant accepting Washington's permanent nuclear dominance. As the historian Melvyn Leffler succinctly comments: "Baruch explicitly designed his plan to perpetuate the U.S. atomic monopoly."[50] Lindsay, who was by then present as an adviser to Baruch, saw all of this. The Baruch proposal "involved such a challenge to Communist control that they would have to reject it," Lindsay told me.

It is a stretch to believe that Stalin would have simply signed on to any plan requiring him to forgo development of his own atomic bomb, if only for its deterrent value, but that does not mean he was blind to the benefits to Moscow of real controls that would have applied to Washington. The point is moot because the American proposals for shared control were not serious.

As the insecurities of James Byrnes led to an obtuse belligerence early in this process, the arrogance of the Wall Street mogul Bernard Baruch led to a premature attitude of take it or leave it. Lindsay told me how he and others, even at the time, opposed Baruch's forcing a vote on the question. Formally presented to the U.N.'s atomic energy body on December 31, 1946, the plan passed by a vote of ten in favor to two abstentions, but since the two were Poland and the Soviet Union, it was a victory that meant nothing. "And so, on the last day of 1946," the historian Daniel Yergin comments, "any genuine effort to head off a nuclear arms race came to an end."[51]

"Bernie likes to get out at the top of the market," Lindsay was told. "So he forced the vote, as if a majority [of U.N. atomic energy representatives] was what counted. All that counted was the Soviet Union, and it was obvious they would say no. Baruch just wanted the vote so that he could claim he had the majority, report to Truman that he had accomplished his mission, and resign. That is what he did."[52] Some market.

But perhaps that outcome should not surprise. One of Baruch's advisers was Leslie Groves, who, confident of an enduring American nuclear monopoly, would have rejoiced at the demise of any impulse to cooperate with the Soviet Union. Lindsay recalls standing with Groves in the Baruch offices, on the sixty-eighth floor of the Empire State Building, one day in the spring of 1946. "I remember Groves well. He was a great big fat man. He was often in the offices with Baruch. I remember standing at the window with Groves, looking down the harbor toward the Narrows. We saw two or three freighters making their way along the Brooklyn shore, which raised the subject of ships entering U.S. ports with nuclear devices. Groves pointed to one ship and said what would happen if it exploded a bomb, gesturing around at the panorama. All that would be destroyed, the docks across to New Jersey, the bridges, the buildings. All destroyed."[53]

What might Groves have been advising Baruch? In that same period, reflecting Groves's impatience even with the thoroughly hedged American effort at international controls, he wrote:

> If we were truly realistic, instead of idealistic, as we appear to be, we would not permit any foreign power with which we are not firmly allied, and in which we do not have absolute confidence, to make or possess atomic weapons. If such a country started to make atomic weapons we would destroy its capacity to make them before it had progressed far enough to threaten us . . . Either we must have a hard-boiled, realistic, enforceable, world-agreement ensuring the outlawing of atomic weapons or we and our dependable allies must have an exclusive supremacy in the field, which means that no other nation can be permitted to have atomic weapons.[54]

Groves already embodied the approach Stimson warned against on September 11, 1945, and Groves, not Stimson, represented the ascendant movement in American thinking. On September 26, five days after the cabinet discussed the Stimson proposal, which noted "indications" that "a rather desperate arms race" had begun, there occurred the first test of an Army WAC Corporal missile at the White Sands Proving Ground in New Mexico. It was the first flight of an American liquid-fueled rocket after the end of the war, the beginning of the missile age.[55] The inexorable momentum of technology had its own force now.

Less than two weeks after the September 21 cabinet meeting, Truman would show himself to have been persuaded by Forrestal, not Stimson, when he publicly affirmed his intention to maintain an American monopoly on the bomb, even if that meant an arms race.[56] In fact, at that point Truman was convinced that Moscow would "never" develop an atomic bomb.[57] As for the cabinet meeting itself, at its end Stimson simply, as he recounts it, "said good-bye to the President and to the Cabinet and hurried away to the Pentagon Building." From there he went to National Airport. "There to my surprise was a huge meeting of apparently all the general officers in Washington, lined up in two rows." These men, for all that had bound them to Stimson, were now cut loose from his vision of the world. The threat of the next war, which terrified the old man, empowered the generals and admirals, who saw their new role as getting ready to fight it. But now, at this turning point, the men with stars on their shoulders, stripes on their sleeves, sang, with great feeling, "Happy Birthday" and "Auld Lang Syne." Stimson boarded his plane. He had resigned.

His last moment of a long life of public service, in one historian's esti-mate, was Stimson's "finest hour."[58] Yet it was also the start of a tradition of powerful men of the Pentagon attempting to reverse the course of events they had themselves set in motion, but they would make their heroic efforts only as, or after, they left the Building. Robert Jay Lifton calls this the "retirement syndrome." The men staying behind, in power, would never see things as they appeared from the exit door.

Whether Stimson liked it or not, his final initiative had given credentials to the man who most fiercely opposed it. The torch was hot to the touch, but it had been passed. Stimson's last day had, in effect, been the first day of the man whose power would only grow until, two years later, he would take over Stimson's Pentagon office, sitting at Pershing's desk — James Forrestal.

3. FORRESTAL AGONISTES

The restless eyes of James Forrestal stare out across the foyer of the River En-trance. Each of the secretaries of defense[59] is remembered in an oil portrait, paintings that line the third-floor corridor leading to the SecDef's office suite, but the head and visage only of Forrestal, the first of their number, is cast in bronze and set on a pedestal near the entrance, a permanent sentry. The irony is that Forrestal, as secretary of the Navy, had refused to move from Navy headquarters on Constitution Avenue near the Mall, and even after Truman named him secretary of defense, only a direct order from the president forced him to move his office across the river.[60] Forrestal detested the Pentagon, and occupied it reluctantly.

To this day, every morning and evening, thousands of Pentagon workers, military and civilian, pass by the Forrestal bust. The face is expressionless but, as with the man himself, a certain fastidiousness is conveyed in the careful ridge of a thin mustache. The lips are set, a signal of determination. Over the years, millions of men and women have rushed through the middle distance in which his eyes have long sought some precarious rest. Forrestal's face, and therefore his personality, thus defines an essential part of the mission around which America's martial legion has organized itself. It is not too much to say that, with this bust evoking his fateful history, both in what he set in motion here and in what that momentum led to for him, James Forrestal haunts the place.

Noting the prominence of the Forrestal memorial's location, the editor of his diaries comments, "But the real memorial is within, in the teeming offices of the vast establishment for defense."[61] The legend inscribed on the plaque beneath the bust reads: "This memorial to James Forrestal, as a spontaneous tribute to his lasting accomplishments in providing for National Security and his selfless devotion to duty, was erected by thousands of his friends and co-workers of all ranks and stations."[62] Just as the stoic mask of the Forrestal bust stamps the Building's entrance with a feeling of barely contained anguish, an emotion rare to bureaucratic expression infuses that inscription, a hint of the shock and grief with which Pentagon employees received the news of Forrestal's end.

He was the favored son of upstate New Yorkers, modest people who harbored high hopes for a gifted child. His father was an immigrant from Ireland, and his mother was Irish American. His mother wanted him to become a priest. At Princeton, Forrestal referred to himself as a "mick" and assumed the air of a self-made man, as if he had clawed his way up to the elite university from poverty. He wasn't so much self-made as, to use a term Arthur Schlesinger, Jr., applied to him, "self-invented."[63] A contemporary at Princeton was F. Scott Fitzgerald, and Forrestal would often be compared to Jay Gatsby[64] — that air of constrained physical power, of longing for acceptance, of something vaguely gangster-like. Indeed, Forrestal was a boxer, and pursued this pastime well into adulthood. He would proudly carry the slightly crooked line of a broken nose. But like Gatsby, his cultivated image was a thin veneer overlaying a rampant insecurity — "the ambitious tightness of the parvenu," as one friend put it.[65] The veneer could work marvels of influence, but it could also be seen for what it was.

In photographs Forrestal had a way of capturing the camera with his eyes, his lips turned slightly up at the corners, the hint of a confident smile. One sees it as a smile like Gatsby's, which "had a quality of eternal reassurance in it, that you may come across four or five times in life." This is the novel's narrator, Nick Carraway. "It faced — or seemed to face — the whole external world for an instant, and then concentrated on *you* with an irresistible prejudice in your favor. It understood you just as far as you wanted to be understood, believed in you as you would like to believe in yourself, and assured you that it had precisely the impression of you that, at your best, you hoped to convey. Precisely at that point it vanished — and I was looking at an elegant young roughneck, a year or two over thirty, whose elaborate formality of speech just missed being absurd."[66] Gatsby was a fake.

Forrestal's Princeton classmates admired him enough to name him Most Likely to Succeed, yet Forrestal mysteriously dropped out of college shortly before his graduation, never to receive his degree. Near the end of World War I, he saw brief service in the Navy, but as an aviator — a forecast of the conflict between air power and the blue-water tradition that would mark his service as secretary of the Navy and then of defense. After the Great War he became a bond salesman, and soon found success on Wall Street. In the midst of the Roaring Twenties, about the time Fitzgerald was publishing *The Great Gatsby*, he was named a vice president of the flourishing investment house of Dillon, Read, and by the end of the 1930s he was its president. He had left his Irish family behind.

Fitzgerald had his Zelda; Gatsby desired Daisy; Forrestal fell for a wildly irrepressible woman named Josephine Ogden, a columnist for *Vogue* and a one-time Ziegfeld Follies girl. In 1926, at the age of thirty-four, he married her. By the time of his ascent to the presidency of Dillon, Read, the beautiful Josephine convincingly carried herself as a patrician. She was the seal of Forrestal's arrival. And she was an alcoholic.

In 1940, Forrestal was made an undersecretary of the Navy, responsible for managing the overnight creation of a mammoth sea power. Josephine pitched in at once by overseeing the design of a uniform for the new women's Navy unit, the WAVES. But in that same year, at the mercy of insecurities of her own, she had a breakdown and was diagnosed with clinical schizophrenia. Curiously, since she was an apolitical socialite, her pathological paranoid fantasy manifested as a dread of Communists. Forrestal's wife was sure that "the Reds" were after her, and after her family.[67] With therapy and medication, Josephine was able to function, although her drinking would worsen and her behavior would make her an item of Washington gossip. In public, Forrestal and his wife mastered the pretense that nothing was wrong, either with her or their relationship. In fact it, too, was hollow, as became apparent to everyone who knew them. The anguish with which they lived, especially as the pressures of war mounted, would be channeled into his "selfless devotion to duty," which kept him at his desk almost every waking hour, and into her late-night, postparty antics. Forrestal and his wife had less and less to do with each other. Eventually, the fear of Communists would define the main bond between them.

In 1944, at the age of fifty-two, Forrestal became secretary of the Navy, a civilian positioned to succeed Henry Stimson, another civilian, as the dominant military figure in Washington. By then Forrestal's drive had come to seem a virtue. Understanding that it was unseemly to spend all of his time at work, he dutifully took up the prevailing pastime of his kind. As his biographers point out, he became famous for record-setting rounds of golf at the Chevy Chase Club. The record he set was not for the lowest score but for the shortest time in which to play eighteen holes — and then back to the office.

Forrestal's initial attraction to the Navy can be understood as a further expression of the relentless social ambition of many of the offspring of immigrants. From colonial times, the Navy embodied the martial ideal of the Anglo-American establishment, much as the sport of yachting defined the rambunctious leisure of the wealthy elite. Just as the officer corps of the Army, with its cavalier ethos, was long dominated by southern gentlemen, so the Navy was the preserve of the upper-class Protestant Northeast. For an Irish-Catholic would-be arriviste, service in the Navy was a way to launch a career, and nothing could mark its pinnacle more dramatically than appointment to the Navy's governing echelon. Forrestal embraced the service with the fierce devotion of a man who knew in some deep part of himself that he was not worthy of it. Having left the chants of the Catholic Church behind, Forrestal would worship to the music of the "Navy Hymn."

The contest between traditional American notions of sea-based national security and the borderless frontiers of air power had been launched with a test off Hampton Roads, Virginia, in 1921, when explosives dropped from General William "Billy" Mitchell's aircraft sank the captured German battleship *Ostfriesland*. By the time Forrestal became secretary of the Navy in 1944, the impingement of the Air Force on Navy prerogatives was clear, just as the AAF was preparing its postwar claim to permanent bases around the world. The global projection of American might was no longer to be a matter of flotillas steaming into distant harbors. Wouldn't multiengine bombers roaring overhead do it better?

What was more unsettling, just as bombing from airplanes had altered the character of coercive force applied against enemies, the kind of security available to a once complacent "fortress America" could be seen to have changed radically, even before the war was over. Forrestal took the lead in arguing for a new naval doctrine, a ship-based strategic force aimed at making war not just against other ships but, in the spirit of total war, against whole societies. This doctrinal shift meant that the new Navy would no longer build itself around the battleship but around the aircraft carrier. As the AAF was arguing for a new strategic bomber force, the Navy, under Forrestal, began demanding investment in a fleet of supercarriers.

When Forrestal opposed Stimson in that pivotal cabinet debate of Stimson's proposal to share the atomic secret, Forrestal's rejection of any conceivable trust of the Soviet Union was based as much on his parochial agenda for the Navy as it was on assessments of the Soviet threat. As we have already seen, the expansionist views of the American military, especially the Air Force and the Navy, were amply served by an expansionist reading of Soviet motives. Forrestal, first as Navy secretary and then as secretary of defense, presided over the introduction of the idea of national security into the postwar debate. Historians of the Cold War argue over the origins of the idea, and over how to measure security impulses against what might be called imperial impulses, applying to the Soviet and American spheres both. We will see more of this debate. Daniel Yergin, who was a prominent revisionist historian in the 1970s, wrote that "the doctrine of national security was a fundamental revision of America's perceived relation to the rest of the world, of what Stimson in 1941 had called 'our basic theory of defense.'" Yergin noted a key postwar transition: "The nation was to be permanently prepared. America's interests and responsibilities were unrestricted and global. National security became a guiding rule, a Commanding Idea. It lay at the heart of a new and sometimes intoxicating vision."[68] And it says everything that the legislation that established the office to which the insecure Forrestal then ascended, with the rising tide of this vision, was called the National Security Act.

In thinking of Forrestal's psychological makeup, one could ask: What kind of security is this? To what extent were apprehensions about Soviet aggressiveness, and aggressive capability, the product of American projections, whether defined psychologically or politically? Historians still debate this, long after the Cold War.[69] Surprisingly, the argument is unresolved, with the scholarship, from revisionist to postrevisionist and back again, in the words of Melvyn Leffler, "open to diverse conclusions."[70] In the postwar period, whatever historians made of it later, emphasis on well-armed Soviet hostility satisfied the need for an enemy who justified the bureaucratic ambitions of the Navy and the Air Force — but also, for that matter, of a labor movement seeking to establish its distance from Communism, of industrialists hungry for the economic stimulus of ongoing military outlays, of universities eager to extend lucrative defense-related research contracts, and of a president looking to shore up support for his uncertain reelection prospects. The birth of the national security state had many midwives.

But there may have been something at work deep in the American psyche, too. After the "crusade" of World War II, to use Eisenhower's word,[71] the nation had come to depend on a negatively perceived Other against whom to define itself positively. With Hitler and Tojo gone, Stalin, the former friend, filled that role nicely. More than that, the bipolar tension could easily be defined moralistically, as if good and evil were in ontological conflict in this political competition.[72] Normal big-power moves to shore up border security and establish areas of influence could be perceived as manifestations of an imperial design — and of an immoral purpose. If the Soviets agreed to terms, they were taken to be deceptive. If they refused terms, they were understood as recalcitrant. Every Soviet move could thus be taken as a mortal, and moral, threat — and, beginning with Forrestal, it was.

The problem comes when the impulse to demonize, arising from considerations that may be largely imagined, leads to a shift in the real that itself becomes threatening. The perception of danger and the danger itself have a way of becoming the same thing. Shadows take on weight. Forrestal's institutional needs as a man justifying, first, Navy expansionism, and then larger military budgets generally, coincided with psychological insecurities that could become precariously exacerbated, especially in times of stress. In Forrestal's case, such stress would be defined by his steady perception that the United States was being forced into military commitments around the globe that its military establishment was unable to keep. As the man in charge of that establishment, as we shall see, Forrestal would be swallowed up in the gap between capability and responsibility. Personal stress and political stress became the same thing. When that happened, there would be no exaggerating either the malice of the enemy or the enemy's capacity to wreak evil — not only far away, but close to home.

4. KENNAN'S MISTAKE

This is the dynamic that underwrote Forrestal's second great act of the Cold War. Having thwarted Henry Stimson's attempt to head off a "desperate" confrontation with Moscow, Forrestal soon thereafter sponsored an obscure diplomat's powerful justification for that confrontation. That diplomat was George F. Kennan, the closest thing in the State Department to an expert on Russian Communism. On February 22, 1946, from his post as a deputy at the American embassy in Moscow, Kennan sent an eight-thousand-word telegram to his superiors in Washington, an elaboration of routine assessments of the postwar outlook as seen from the Russian capital.

As a diplomat, Kennan had been following the development of Stalin's system for two decades, and his fiercely negative reading of it is reflected in his having opposed Roosevelt's 1933 decision to normalize diplomatic relations with Moscow. Throughout the thirties, Kennan regarded the Soviets as far more of a threat than either Hitler's Germany or imperial Japan.[73] He regretted the wartime alliance with Stalin, and now feared him more than ever. The telegram's particular pessimism — Communism is "a malignant parasite that feeds only on diseased tissue"[74] — drew its energy from the recent bellicose speech by Stalin referred to earlier. That Stalin's speech might have been misunderstood in America, as historians would subsequently suggest,[75] seems not to have occurred to Kennan. Indeed, Kennan's reading was the ground on which that misunderstanding became a permanent structure of thought, yet another instance of the unsubstantiated taking on tangible form. Kennan was a worried man.

Technically referred to as Telegram 711, but soon known as the Long Telegram, or simply the LT, the communication rang an alarm in Washington about Soviet intentions. "We have here a political force committed fanatically to the belief that with the U.S. there can be no permanent modus vivendi, that it is desirable and necessary that the internal harmony of our society be disrupted, our traditional way of life destroyed, the international authority of our state be broken if Soviet power is to be secure."[76]

Kennan thus defined an apocalyptic Marxism as the beating heart of the Soviet Union. As the only other nation that had emerged from World War II with its power greatly enhanced, it was not just tactically jousting with Washington for the usual political advantage. Rather, Moscow was ontologically — religiously — opposed to the capital of the capitalist West. Conflict between these two centers of power was inevitable. Compromise was impossible. The eventual end of this conflict would be the total elimination of one system or the other. The USSR was no longer to be understood as having traditional imperial ambitions, much less as an ordinary nation seeking to shore up its own security. The open-ended utopia of romantic revolution — the ultimate dystopia — was Moscow's creed. Therefore existential opposition, irreconcilable and permanent, shaped the only possible future.

Kennan had arrived at this extreme assessment years before, but only now did he find a ready audience for it, and in no one more than James Forrestal. Kennan's telegram, with its Manichaean analysis and air of messianic apocalypse, touched something deep in Forrestal. Admittedly, when one speaks of unconscious motivations, one is moving into the realm of conjecture, but readings of Forrestal's diaries, of his biographers' assessments, and of the public record point to the relevance of such motivation here. Acting on little more than a visceral anti-Communism, it was Forrestal who had instinctively urged (against Stimson) Truman's early confrontation with Molotov; he who had dismissed out of hand the Roosevelt tradition of seeking to ameliorate Soviet behavior through diplomacy; and he who assumed, with Groves, the necessity of an American nuclear monopoly to keep Moscow in check. By early in the postwar period, Forrestal's biographers say, he had "come to believe in the most abstract and theological explanation of Soviet motivation and behavior. The answer seemed to lie somewhere in his Catholic past, in his suspiciousness and insecurity, in his jesuitical fascination with intellectual complexity."[77]

Kennan was no Catholic, but he had attended Princeton a decade after Forrestal and was like him in the secret wound he carried. By then F. Scott Fitzgerald had made his mark, and whereas Forrestal would be compared to Gatsby, Kennan consciously identified with Amory Blaine, the undergraduate hero of *This Side of Paradise*.[78] Kennan came from a middle-class midwestern family, but something in the establishment East touched the nerve of his insecurity. His mother had died shortly after his birth, and his father was aloof. A misfit like Forrestal, Kennan buried his feelings of isolation and resentment in the assumption that the elites who excluded him were superior.[79] He burned with the ambition to be one of them. So had Forrestal, and by the end of the war, the senior man seemed to have succeeded. Through him, Kennan would finally gain, for a time, admittance to the American inner circle.

Kennan's heritage was Scotch-Irish and Presbyterian, and the legacy of John Calvin was in his makeup. Indeed, Kennan identified himself as a Puritan,[80] and that strain of dark moralism intersected with Forrestal's inborn Irish Jansenism. Both men embraced the role of judgmental outsider, continually negotiating envy and scorn. Kennan spurned the Princeton graduation ceremonies; Forrestal, at the last minute, had made himself ineligible for them. Yet both were imbued with the Princeton spirit. As indicated by a lingering identification with its former president Woodrow Wilson, the university was an incubator of American missionary zeal, both political and religious.[81] Although years apart in age and in different ways, Forrestal and Kennan became apostles of an elitist and romantic Americanism, yet each would also claim the anti-Wilsonian mantle of realist. While Forrestal had at once embraced the true faith of business, Kennan embarked on a career in the Foreign Service.

Kennan's attitude was framed by an instinctive anti-Communism, source of a certainty of American salvation worthy of any Presbyterian. From the start, events in Bolshevik Russia appealed to Kennan, but not, as was true of his like-minded colleagues, because of the flawed grandeur of the Marxist idea. The lens through which Kennan saw the works of Lenin, Trotsky, and Stalin was only dark, but his perceptions, proving over time to have been wildly exaggerated, had as much to do with his own need as with what was actually unfolding in the terrorized nation. One again acknowledges a certain psychologizing here, but it nevertheless seems that Soviet Communism became the great negative Other against which Kennan could define himself positively. Such driving opposition, rooted as much in imagination as in anything real, enabled the young Kennan to more clearly define his own identity. His politics, in that sense, were deeply personal. His hated enemy told him who he was, and that he was of the vigilant elect.

In the author of the Long Telegram Forrestal recognized a kindred spirit, and despite its being a classified document, he circulated the text. He ordered hundreds of Navy officials to read it, and even pushed it on those over whom he lacked authority. Because of Forrestal, thousands in the Washington establishment read the telegram and took it seriously. Within two weeks of the telegram's receipt at Foggy Bottom, Winston Churchill echoed its arguments at Fulton, Missouri, giving resonance and solidity to this new and overwhelming dread of Moscow's aims and abilities.[82]

Forrestal met with Kennan, supported the diplomat's wish to return to Washington, and helped him gain employment as an instructor in the ideology of Communism at the newly established National War College, of which Forrestal was a chief sponsor. He asked Kennan to write a fuller exposition of the threat represented by the Soviet Union. With Forrestal as his constant critic and editor through several drafts over the next year, Kennan turned what he called his "telegraphic dissertation"[83] into a full-blown polemic that addressed the most pressing issue of American foreign relations: negotiations with the Soviet Union were pointless "until the internal nature of Soviet power is changed."[84]

This elaboration of the Long Telegram was at first circulated without attribution but with a note that it was expressly prepared for James Forrestal. It was published in the summer of 1947 in the journal *Foreign Affairs* as "The Sources of Soviet Conduct," over the pseudonym "X." This article had an immediate and momentous impact, and it remains perhaps the single most influential American foreign policy declaration ever made by an individual. It was taken to be an elucidation of Russian history and Communism's world-conquering ambition which was both informed and erudite.

It was neither. Scholars and commentators still salute the "X" article without understanding how flawed it was. In failing to discern that normal nationalism — Moscow's as well as Beijing's and Belgrade's — was cloaking itself in Comintern rhetoric, it represented the foundational U.S. mistake of Cold War thinking. Of course normal nationalism would have posed problems, too, with access to markets and raw materials at issue, for example. But that was far different from a transnational adversary working from a malevolent grand design.

The "X" article pessimistically assumed that the fanatically missionary Communists of the Soviet Union could not be uprooted from wherever their doctrine had taken hold, but it could be stopped from spreading. Kennan's writing sharpened American perceptions of a threatening Soviet militarism, and established the myth that "Russia was an enigma that could be interpreted only by specialists such as Kennan."[85] Furthermore, the article defined the only possible response: "long-term, patient but firm and vigilant containment."[86] This idea soon seemed vindicated when, in its name, the Truman administration supported successful resistance movements in Greece and Turkey. With Kennan's "containment" elevated to the status of theology, as in "Truman Doctrine," his telegram and "X" article would remain foundational texts of U.S. foreign policy for two generations.

The significance of Kennan's warning here, however, is its relation to Forrestal, who served as the telegram's megaphone and the article's sponsor. One historian likened Forrestal's response to Kennan to Paul Revere's response to the two lanterns that appeared in the Old North Church[87] — a comparison that has a tragic resonance, as we shall see. Forrestal was at the peak of his influence in Washington, and his endorsement of Kennan's thesis — which the journalist Walter Lippmann criticized as "a strategic monstrosity"[88] — was what gave it credibility. Because of Forrestal, Kennan said, "my reputation was made. My voice now carried."[89] But Forrestal's influence was not only on public discourse but on Kennan personally. Forrestal picked up the thread of apocalyptic analysis in the telegram — that the threat was ephemeral, an "abstract political force"[90] transcending human agency — and urged Kennan to make it the dominant motif of the article, which Kennan did.

As the extreme and worrisome analysis took hold of Washington's thinking, it solidified Forrestal's influence as much as Kennan's, laying the groundwork for the shift in the center of power away from Foggy Bottom to what had once been known as Hell's Bottom. With the world-historic threat from Moscow now defined as absolute and inevitable, power would even move away from the White House, with Truman only the first of the presidents to discover that his authority over the Pentagon was more theoretical than real. Kennan's article would be used to pressure Truman on the lifting of budget ceilings for the major military buildup Forrestal wanted, as well as for the decidedly nonmilitary, but equally anti-Soviet, Marshall Plan. What might be called the Kennan paradigm, however, would have its most far-reaching consequences in underwriting the arms race, establishing an essentially unsupervised nuclear priesthood and, sooner and later both, spawning disastrous American misadventures in Asia.

Kennan would later claim to have been misunderstood, insisting that he had intended the American response to Soviet messianism to be more political than military. Indeed, in the original telegram he had, after all the alarms, recorded his conviction that "the problem is within our power to solve — and that without recourse to any military conflict."[91] Embedded in Kennan's distinction between the political and the military is the essential argument over the origins of the Cold War. The differences between the United States and the Soviet Union were real and serious, but they were political in nature. The differences derived, arguably on both sides but certainly on the Soviet side, from deep insecurity in the face of huge changes brought on by the war and its aftermath. But it was the United States, more than the Soviet Union, that militarized that political conflict, making it far more dangerous and costly than it needed to be.

This development began to unfold first in the mind of James Forrestal. In his perception, at a time of massive demobilization, the urgent military need was paramount, and the article by "X" was read to support that. The strictly *political* challenges in a Europe on the verge of collapse — with, for example, French and Italian electorates ready to go Communist — would take second place to worries over armed aggression. To understand the magnitude of this mistake, it helps to recall the potency of Communism's appeal at the time, and the widespread assumption that capitalism was bankrupt. It was not just France and Italy. Between 1940 and 1945, Communist Party membership throughout Europe had grown steadily, and then had soared at war's end. In Czechoslovakia, membership had gone from 28,000 in May 1945 to 750,000 by the following September — well before the Russians turned to coercion.[92]

Yet containment soon meant, above all, *military* containment, a strategy that would be headquartered not in the State Department but in the Pentagon, which is why Forrestal's biographers call him "the godfather of containment."[93] On this point Kennan acknowledged Forrestal's hand in the work that was published in *Foreign Affairs;* he had written the article to provide, he said, "what I felt to be Mr. Forrestal's needs at the time when I prepared the original paper for him."[94]

That time was pivotal. We have noted it before. The Long Telegram was sent in February 1946. Churchill gave his "Iron Curtain" speech in March. In June, Bernard Baruch, whose speechwriter was then coining the term "Cold War,"[95] presented his obviously doomed plan at the United Nations. In that same month, demonstrating a determination to go promptly ahead with atomic development, the United States openly conducted its second set of atomic bomb tests in the Pacific. (Although Forrestal traveled to the Bikini atoll test site with General Curtis LeMay, now the deputy chief of air staff for research and development, as his expert adviser, the Navy had sufficiently outmaneuvered the Air Force to take operational control of the test. Signifying the competition, the test consisted of one bomb dropped from a B-29 and another exploded from beneath the sea. The Navy and the Air Force were now locked in conflict over who would control the bomb. LeMay was less Forrestal's escort than his monitor.[96])

By that September, a rift had opened in the Truman administration as Secretary of State Byrnes, remembering the Roosevelt approach, pushed back against Forrestal and Kennan. Byrnes, as we saw, had made Stimson nervous, with the bomb "rather ostentatiously on his hip" and with his bullying early approach to Molotov. Byrnes had been among the first to recognize grave political differences with Moscow, but he did not believe they foreordained a global conflict. And he had soon seen where the ideologically driven bullying tactics were leading.

So he tried to change them. In a speech written by a young John Kenneth Galbraith and delivered in September in Stuttgart, Germany, Byrnes repudiated the idea that military conflict with the Soviet Union was inevitable, and he reasserted American faith in diplomacy as a way to resolve conflict.[97] Byrnes's effort to restore moderation was complicated a week later, however, when, in Madison Square Garden, the increasingly marginalized secretary of commerce Henry Wallace denounced the Forrestal approach. "The tougher we get," Wallace said, "the tougher the Russians will get."[98] Wallace was regarded as such a loose cannon that he could discredit a position simply by embracing it. Byrnes knew it had happened when Wallace agreed with Stimson on sharing the bomb the year before, and now it happened to him. The Wallace speech touched off a furious reaction. To reassert his own control, and signaling, once again, his acceptance of Forrestal's view, Truman fired Wallace before the end of September.

Truman then circulated among his top officials a 100,000-word statement of his own thinking, composed by his most trusted aide, Clark Clifford, and a colleague. Called "American Relations with the Soviet Union," and drawing directly on the Long Telegram, the document showed that the Forrestal thesis was now policy: "The language of military power politics is the only language which the disciples of power [in Moscow] understand . . . Therefore, in order to maintain our strength at a level which will be effective in restraining the Soviet Union, the United States must be prepared to wage atomic and biological warfare."[99]

None of this is to argue that there were not reasons to worry about Soviet intentions in 1946, but the worry, especially in light of what would come later from Moscow, seems overblown at this early date. According to the judgment of historians, Clifford's memo summarizing Soviet aims and abilities was simply wrong.[100] Secretary of State Byrnes knew it at the time, and saw the anguish the memo caused as unnecessary. He rejected the subordination of the political to the military, but he was by now without influence. He submitted his resignation in December, although with a warning to Truman that "nations, like individuals, must respect one another's differences."

That Byrnes would be replaced as secretary of state by Army Chief of Staff George Marshall is emblematic of the Pentagon's having trumped the State Department. General Marshall, a moderate and diplomatic figure, nevertheless embodied the arrival in America of a new class of martial (no pun intended) thinkers, whether civilian or uniformed. The circle of Forrestal's influence would be complete when his protégé Kennan was quickly elevated by Marshall. As director of the newly formed Policy Planning Staff, with an office next door to Marshall's own, Kennan would dominate American foreign policy for the following crucial three years.

Before leaving, Byrnes made one last plea for "a sympathetic understanding between the United States and the Soviet Union."[101] It was too late. A few days after Byrnes's resignation, Americans forced the fateful vote on the Baruch Plan at the United Nations, sealing the U.S.-Soviet alienation with nuclear competition. But now, in this fuller context, we see why the Baruch dance with the Soviet Union to the music of shared international controls was only a going through the motions. Kennan was just introducing the idea of containment — he first used the word in a War College lecture in October[102] — and the key to containment was an open-ended American monopoly on the atomic bomb.[103] When the "X" article was translated for Stalin, the word "containment" was rendered as "strangulation."[104]

These developments in the last part of 1946 marked the end of the debate between those who, attuned to political differences, nevertheless wanted to seek cooperative arrangements with the Soviet Union, based on mutual self-interest, and those who wanted confrontation, based on mutual suspicion and with the conflict defined militarily. There were two ways to see the Soviet Union; the negative had now won out. "American leaders," as Daniel Yergin explains in a lucid summary of the debate that went on for a generation, "might have seen themselves confronted by a cruel, clumsy, bureaucratized, fear-ridden despotism, preoccupied with reconstructing a vast war-torn land. Instead, the Americans were convinced that they faced a cunning, sure-footed enemy, engaged in a never-ending drive for world hegemony." A tenuous international network that would be riven with ideological inconsistencies? A hollow military culture that would always be cannibalizing itself to meet

American challenges? An inefficient system that would eventually collapse of its own corruption? Would a military challenge from the West play to Soviet strengths or weaknesses? Given Russia's history as a nation repeatedly traumatized by invasions from the West, would Washington's demonizing opposition postpone Russian liberalization, or even collapse? Or hasten it? Alas, these questions were not asked in the crucial period. An answer to a different, dreamland question supplied itself. A fantasy Kremlin, entirely unrelated to the actualities of Moscow as it existed, was taken in the American imagination to be the absolute enemy. In Yergin's succinct phrase, "The basic ideological outlook was settled."[105]

Calvinism, Jansenism, Wilsonianism, Puritanism, Manichaeism, the wound of ambition, the curse of personal insecurity — it may seem a stretch to emphasize such sources of American decision-making, but Forrestal and Kennan themselves invoked equivalent emotional contexts in reaching conclusions about the Soviet Union. Kennan's famous "X" article, in an early draft still under Forrestal's control, was titled "Psychological Background of Soviet Foreign Policy." When Forrestal sent a copy of that draft to his former boss at Dillon, Read, Clarence Dillon, he included a note that said, "Nothing about Russia can be understood without also understanding the implacable and unchanging direction of Lenin's religion-philosophy."[106]

Forrestal and Kennan, for all their touted participation in the emerging postwar, "vital center" consensus of a "realism" that would reject formulas of abstract idealism in favor of hard-nosed, world-as-it-is perceptions, were in fact themselves driven by abstractions, albeit ones that came disguised. The most important of these, implied in Forrestal's attribution of "religion-philosophy" to Lenin, had to do with a universalist reading of the character of totalitarianism, one that took hold of American perceptions just then, springing not from analysis of what Soviet Communism was actually like, but from an imagined Totalitarianism that would always be spelled with an uppercase T. Even in the name of realism, that is, one faith was being proselytized to confront another.

Arthur Schlesinger, Jr., was an early theorist of the pragmatic realists, but he recalls as their big mistake the embrace of this "mystical theory of Totalitarianism." In conversation with me, he said, "We came to the conclusion rather quickly that Stalin's personality, which was totalitarian, was reflected in the state. We looked at Stalin and we assumed that this was what we were dealing with. But it was more complicated than that."[107] Here is how Kennan himself, writing in his memoir some years later, defined that obsession:

> When I used the term "Soviet Power" in the X-Article, I had in view, of course, the system of power organized, dominated, and inspired by Joseph

Stalin. This was a monolithic power structure reaching through the network of highly disciplined Communist parties into practically every country in the world. In these circumstances, any success of a local Communist party, any advance of Communist power anywhere, had to be regarded as an extension in reality of the political orbit, or at least the dominant influence, of the Kremlin. Precisely because Stalin maintained so jealous, so humiliating a control over foreign Communists, all of the latter had, at that time, to be regarded as the vehicles of his will, not their own. His was the only center of authority in the Communist world; and it was a vigilant, exacting, and imperious headquarters, prepared to brook no opposition.[108]

But it was indeed more complicated than that.

Schlesinger pointed out that the prophets of mystical totalitarianism, just then coming into vogue, were George Orwell and Hannah Arendt. "Orwell carried the inner logic of Nazism and Stalinism to the end of night," Schlesinger wrote more than fifty years later. "In so doing, he encouraged the theory of totalitarianism as unitary and irreversible, obliterating all autonomous institutions in society and reconstructing the human personality itself . . . Arendt claimed as historical actuality what Orwell conceived as admonitory fantasy."[109]

Such a perception of an enemy is truly something to fear, and increasingly Americans constructed their nightmares around this political anguish. Arendt in particular would encourage the equation of Hitler's totalitarianism and Stalin's, and that equivalence became part of the American consensus, as if the late 1940s were the early 1930s. However much such an analogy distorted the intentions and the capabilities of the Soviet Union, it missed the crucial difference: that the United States, having been toothless when Hitler came to power, was by now the most heavily armed nation in the world.

In fact, the Soviet Union and the "world Communism" of its rhetoric were far less unitary and universalist than the "Totalitarian school" believed — a mistake that would lead Washington to miss the significance of Stalin's excommunication of Tito in 1948 at the beginning of the Cold War, of Ho Chi Minh's nationalism in the middle of it, and of Lech Walesa's nonviolent resistance movement toward the end. But beginning in early 1947, the monolithic view of Soviet world power dominated American policy, and it came with a fateful corollary that Forrestal was among the first to articulate: war with the Soviet Union was inevitable.[110] The former banker was the beau ideal of capitalism, and his economic outlook — wanting rapid reconstruction of European markets, built around a viable and sturdy Germany, and easy access to Middle East oil — required a belligerent pushback against Moscow. Still, not even the interests of the world of high finance from which he'd emerged were paramount in Forrestal's forecast. He came to his expectation of certain war not through pragmatic assessments of what the Kremlin leaders were actually doing or capable of doing, but through "the most abstract and theological explanation of Soviet motivation and behavior."[111]

5. FOUNDATIONAL PARANOIA

The effect of all this on Forrestal's state of mind is reflected in a comment he made about his new digs at the Pentagon when he moved in as the new secretary of defense in 1947: "This office will probably be the greatest cemetery for dead cats in history."[112] His immediate effort to reverse the fact and spirit of demobilization called for a campaign against postwar American complacency. To generate support for the increases in the military budget that the new Navy and new Air Force required, Forrestal would have to, as Senator Arthur H. Vandenberg, his main ally on Capitol Hill, put it, "scare the hell out of the American people."[113] It seems not to have occurred to Americans embarked on such a course that the rhetoric and actions designed to instill fear in the United States would equally do so in Russia. Here is a great irony: by portraying Stalin and his system as warmongering monsters, Kennan and his sponsors helped push the Kremlin in that direction. Kennan had begun by defining the Soviet leaders as being at the mercy of paranoid hallucinations about threats from the West, but soon those threats were not hallucinatory. Kennan had argued that only fear of an outside enemy would enable Stalin to retain power, and then Kennan sponsored exactly that fear.

Fear was growing inside James Forrestal, too. He may have reached the pinnacle of success through passage of the National Security Act, but personal security was not his strong suit. The massive bureaucracy for which he assumed full responsibility in September 1947 was itself geared to reward worries about enemies. But not all of what Forrestal confronted was irrational. He was responsible for the consonance between military ends and means, and the ends of a newly fashioned global commitment were far outstripping the means. It was as if he alone of the men in Washington saw the gap opening "between commitments and capabilities," and to Forrestal that gap began to look like an abyss.[114]

Paranoia is defined as a "psychiatric disorder involving systematized delusion, usually of persecution."[115] The Pentagon was the very heart of such systematization, with money, influence, promotion, and prestige flowing to those who were most convincing in warning of threats. And if the threats were grave enough, it would not matter whether they were delusional or not.

The bureaucratic jargon spoke of "worst-case" planning, and the new idea of national security demanded it. Imagining weird scenarios was a requirement.

Paranoid thinking consists of a twin dynamic: fear of an enemy outside is accompanied by fear of an enemy inside. This pattern was firmly implanted in Western consciousness during the Crusades, when Christendom mobilized against the Islamic infidel in possession of the Holy Land. But no sooner was the First Crusade launched against the Muslim enemy outside, with Pope Urban II's cry "God wills it!" in 1095, than crusaders attacked, in the spring of 1096, the infidel inside: the Jews living in cities along the Rhine. This was Europe's first pogrom. Nearby Jews were not physically at risk until faraway Muslims were attacked. In the Christian mind, fear of the enemy outside became fear of the enemy inside.

The same dynamic came into play in the United States, where a subliminal "paranoid streak" had long had its effect.[116] The extreme suspicion of American residents with ties to enemies abroad had shown up as early as 1789 with the Alien and Sedition Acts and as recently as the Palmer Raids after World War I, and it was back. The perception of the Soviet Union as America's mortal enemy was publicly enshrined with the speech President Truman gave to a joint session of Congress on March 12, 1947, the articulation of the Truman Doctrine: "At the present moment in world history nearly every nation must choose between alternative ways of life." The "paranoid style," to use Richard Hofstadter's phrase, took on a new edge when applied to Communism because now the threat was global. Here begins the American bipolar definition of world polity. This artificial distinction was rooted not in the way the peoples of the world were actually organizing themselves but in the Manichaean theology of the Totalitarian school. From now on, Washington would perceive nations as "for us or against us," with little capacity to accept nonalignment.

"I believe that it must be the policy of the United States," Truman declared, "to support free peoples who are resisting attempted subjugation by armed minorities or by outside pressures."[117] Again: to be sure, there were real threats from Soviet-supported movements in Greece and elsewhere, but at that early point, historians now mostly agree, they were overwhelmingly political rather than military in character. As the historian Walter LaFeber points out, the Soviet Union "had been less aggressive in the months before the President's pronouncement than at any time in the post-war period."[118] In obtaining $400 million for support of armed resistance in Greece and Turkey, Truman began the era of militarized containment of the Soviet threat — "strangulation."

Even the Marshall Plan, announced in a speech by Secretary of State George Marshall less than three months later and held dear in the American memory as an act of altruism, was a handmaiden to this brand of containment. Marshall movingly said that American largesse was "not directed against any country or doctrine, but against hunger, poverty, desperation, and chaos."[119] Compassion played a role in the plan, but more vital was the role played by containment ideology. Marshall extended the offer of help to the Soviet Union, but the strings attached, especially regarding disclosure of closely held economic data, as Marshall knew, made Moscow's participation in it impossible. This unprecedented humanitarian and economic aid — $10 billion, worth ten times that much in today's dollars — was intended to convert Western Europe into an anti-Soviet bulwark. The program, as much as any Iron Curtain, was the defining division of Europe into East and West. Truman himself said it: the Truman Doctrine and the Marshall Plan "are two halves of the same walnut."[120]

The prospect of a Red Army move against central and Western Europe "scared the hell out of the American people," as Vandenberg had suggested was necessary. But the Truman Doctrine speech scared some of Truman's advisers, too. His new secretary of state, George Marshall, understanding that Moscow had been less aggressive in recent months than at any time since the war, and at that moment on his way to meetings there, was "somewhat startled to see the extent to which the anti-Communist element of the speech was stressed." He sent Truman a message, cautioning him that he "was overstating the case a bit."[121] Perhaps aware of the way such crusading impulses had been turned against Jews in the past, Bernard Baruch had a stronger reaction. Although no friend of Moscow, as we have seen, Baruch criticized the speech as "tantamount to a declaration of . . . an ideological or religious war."[122]

Too late. Global opposition to Communism was now a pillar of American policy. The twin pillar of this dynamic — identifying the enemy outside — soon led to its domestic equivalent: paranoia at home. One week and two days after the Truman Doctrine speech, the president issued an executive order (number 9835) designed to root out Communists in America, the Federal Employee Loyalty Program. After a set of WHEREASES and a NOW THEREFORE, the first provision read, "There shall be a loyalty investigation of every person entering the civilian employment of any department or agency of the executive branch of the Federal Government."[123] The House Un-American Activities Committee had been established in 1938 as part of a Republican campaign to undermine the New Deal, but with Truman's executive order making loyalty an absolute value, HUAC came into its own. It was unremarkable that conservative Republicans would show unbridled enthusiasm for what would grow into an outright anti-Communist witch-hunt, but for Democratic liberals to enlist in the new campaign was another matter. As Godfrey Hodgson points out, an obscure Communist candidate for president fifteen years before had been openly endorsed by such figures as Ernest Hemingway, John Dos Passos, Edmund Wilson, and Katherine Anne Porter, but now virtually no one spoke up against the demonizing of that same party.[124] The search for Communists inside America would be as intense as opposition to Communists outside. The paranoid mindset was now operational.

6. WAR INSIDE THE PENTAGON

James Forrestal was paranoia's impresario. Soon after proof of loyalty was established as a criterion for federal employment, he sought to require that all reporters assigned to cover the Pentagon pass a loyalty test. He presided with a passion over loyalty checks among the thousands of Pentagon employees. Now policy disagreements could be made to seem like disloyalty, and a chill settled over internal debate. The chief obstacle to Forrestal's program of a revived military capable of meeting new commitments was the postwar American impulse to disarm, rooted less in budget constraints, however compelling, than in the nation's oldest sense of itself. But now Forrestal explicitly branded Communists as sponsors of the postwar disarmament movement.[125]

As secretary of defense, Forrestal would in fact find himself surrounded by enemies, but they were the furthest thing from Communists and had no qualms about voicing dissent, despite the new atmosphere. They were the service chiefs. Having protected the Navy, during debates preceding the National Security Act, by insisting that the secretary of defense should have little real power, Forrestal was now as much at the mercy of his old Navy allies as of the Army and Air Force. Their rivalry was the bureaucratic equivalent of battlefield combat, but one condition all three service branches soon shared was conflict with the secretary of defense, who was fruitlessly trying to rein in that rivalry.

Rivalry is built into the military ethos. Paratroopers believe they are the most important element in the fighting force — they have to, in order to overcome a natural fear of jumping out of an airplane. Submariners and frogmen, fighter pilots and Marines, engineers and bombardiers — every fighting man, to be effective, must be convinced of the central significance of his role. When the Pentagon won out, in just such a rivalry writ large with the State Department, as the locus of projected American power, it was inevitable that the service branches would fall to squabbling over dominance. Across time, military officers would, in general, be less inclined than civilians, whether at Defense or State, to advocate military intervention "on the periphery," in Third World conflicts. But the brass would powerfully and consistently argue for force levels aimed at countering the main Soviet threat — whether strategically or tactically. Each service would have its separate priority.[126] But squabbling, in each case, would be based on the most fiercely and sincerely held conviction.

The only possible solution to such competition would have been for the secretary of defense to operate as a strong referee, but again, Forrestal himself had helped make that impossible. The secretary's role is defined in the National Security Act as "the principal assistant to the President in all matters relating to the National Security." But with the newly empowered juggernaut of the Pentagon bureaucracy gaining momentum, the president was no longer in control of this process. Truman was riding a tiger. On the one hand, he encouraged, for reasons of his own political struggle and with insufficient critical analysis, the growing sense of danger from Moscow.[127] On the other hand, the more alarming that danger appeared, the more power shifted to the tribal chiefs of the military.

At an early meeting of the service secretaries and chiefs of staff in the fall of 1947, Forrestal told them he intended to convene such gatherings regularly, with a view to interservice amity. Eisenhower, present as Army chief of staff, averred that if he happened to be unavailable, he would send his aide to such meetings. Forrestal did not challenge him. In the same context, Forrestal told the secretaries and chiefs that he wanted all three branches to adopt a common uniform, a signal of the unification that would ultimately make rivalry unnecessary. But immediately Forrestal's own Navy refused to consider such a move, on grounds of morale. "The Air Force then countered, with tongue in cheek," according to one account, "that it had reason to believe a great many Navy enlisted men would welcome any uniform other than the one they were wearing (bell-bottom trousers with a thirteen-button flap in front). The proposal quickly degenerated into a name-calling hassle, and Forrestal gave it up. At that point, the Air Force announced that if a distinctive uniform was so important to morale, it wanted one, too."[128]

Uniforms were the least of it. At the end of World War II, the Army Air Forces was made up of 2.25 million men; less than two years later it numbered barely more than 300,000.[129] Once the Air Force was established as a separate service by the National Security Act, urgent rebuilding was its agenda, and it did not hurt that one of its senior leaders, and soon to be its chief of staff, was General Hoyt S. Vandenberg. He was, not incidentally, the favorite nephew of Senator Arthur Vandenberg, the Republican kingpin whose cooperation Truman and Forrestal desperately needed. The Air Force, in its drive to secure the main part of the military budget, and especially to make permanent its control of the atomic bomb, saw no need to compromise.

The Army, meanwhile, was more than 100,000 men below its authorized level of 669,000, and more men were still being discharged every day than were enlisting. It had tremendous manpower requirements for the occupation of Japan, Germany, and peripheral nations. The Navy was a full 200,000 men short of approved levels.[130] The Army and Navy were clamoring for funds to reverse these trends. But what really alarmed the Air Force was the Navy's demand for the new supercarrier that would be large enough to handle B-29 bombers. At the same time, as General Leslie Groves approached retirement as chief of the so-called Special Weapons Group, the Navy was maneuvering to have him replaced with an admiral. Vandenberg, by now the Air Force chief of staff, moved to head this off with the appointment, in February 1948, of another Army officer to replace Groves.[131] Air Force and Navy wrangling over atomic control would continue.

While the service chiefs vied with one another in the Pentagon during that first fall of unification, anxieties were fed by developments abroad. In November 1947, the Communists paralyzed France with a series of general strikes. In December, the government of Romania was taken over by a Soviet puppet regime. The Communist insurgency in China was scoring victory after victory over Chiang Kai-shek's Nationalist army. Communists in Italy seemed poised to score a takeover through elections. Early in the new year of 1948, Czechoslovakia installed a cabinet friendly to Moscow. For Forrestal, the inability of his service chiefs to come to terms was becoming a source of weakness as threats from the Communist enemy mounted — all taken to be orchestrated from the Kremlin.

By the start of March, Forrestal was desperate. Events in Czechoslovakia[132] were being defined in Washington as a coup by Soviet agents, and on March 5 Forrestal was shown a secret cable that had come to Army intelligence from General Lucius D. Clay, the American proconsul in Berlin. "For many months, based on logical analysis, I have felt and held that war was unlikely for at least ten years. Within the last few weeks, I have felt a subtle change in Soviet attitude which I cannot define but which now gives me a feeling it may come with dramatic suddenness . . . My feeling is real. You may advise the chief of staff of this for whatever it may be worth."[133] What made this communication doubly alarming was the fact that Clay had been one of the staunchest supporters of negotiation with and accommodation of the Soviet Union. In Berlin he had complained more about French noncooperation than Soviet. He believed in the possibility of Soviet-American rapprochement.[134] An alarm from him was bound to carry weight, and it did. Clay's cable marked the start of a two-week panic in Washington that would come to be called the "spring war scare."

With a newfound urgency, Forrestal now forced the service chiefs and secretaries to meet with him away from the Pentagon, convening at President Truman's favored retreat at Key West, which happened to be a naval installation. He told them that for the sake of the nation they had to come to some kind of cooperative agreement over roles and missions. And they had to agree on a budget proposal that he could take to Congress. But the very day that the meeting began in Key West, March 10, news came that the last Czech opponent of Communism, Foreign Minister Jan Masaryk, had died, either murdered or, as the official Czech announcement said, a suicide. The mysterious death — the man either jumped or was thrown from a window — sparked talk of war from Europe to America, but in Key West it stunned Forrestal. According to one of his biographers, Forrestal "referred to it often, both in public and in private, as a key turning point in the Cold War. The frequency of reference, however, suggests that Masaryk's death may have had for him a more personal meaning."[135]

The Key West meeting in that anxious week did lead to the appearance of cooperation among the service leaders. Most crucially, the Air Force agreed to a Navy air component that would support tactical missions, while the Navy agreed not to pursue a strategic air force of its own. Moved by the incipient "war scare," the service leaders were unanimous in calling for new budget ceilings, an immediate restoration of the draft, and the transfer of total control of atomic weapons from the civilian Atomic Energy Commission to the military services. Forrestal went from Key West to a meeting with the president in Washington, and in reporting these conclusions to Truman, he added, on his own authority, according to notes in his diary, that "the Navy [would] not be denied use of the A-bomb [and] the Navy [was] to proceed with development of 80,000-ton carrier and development of HA [high altitude] aircraft to carry heavy missiles therefrom."[136] Forrestal's readiness to carry these two buckets for the Navy to the White House would backfire on him when the Air Force learned of it.

The next day, Forrestal noted, the newspapers were "full of rumors and portents of war." In a note to himself, he observed that "it is inconceivable that even the gang who run Russia would be willing to take on war, but one always has to remember that there seemed no reason in 1939 for Hitler to start war, and yet he did."[137] On March 17, President Truman, before yet another joint session of Congress, made the most of the war scare and seemed ready to issue a new call to arms. "Truman Will Ask Vast War Preparation" was the banner headline on the *Washington Times-Herald*.[138] Truman did talk of war: the Soviet Union had "destroyed the independence and democratic character of a whole series of nations in eastern and central Europe."[139] It was time to stop it. In response to events in Czechoslovakia, Truman had said that "moral, god-fearing peoples . . . must save the world from Atheism and totalitarianism."[140] And now he showed what that meant. He called for universal military training and a restoration of conscription, but what he emphasized over new arms outlays was quick passage of the European Recovery Program, the Marshall Plan.

On March 30, the newly established Central Intelligence Agency debunked General Clay's agitated cable from Berlin, finding "no reliable evidence" that the Soviet Union "intends" to launch a war "within the next sixty days."[141] It was still a grim assessment, but one that might have defused the war scare. Historians now agree that the panic about imminent war amounted to little more than "yet another exercise in crisis politics by the Truman administration,"[142] courtesy, largely, of Forrestal.

By late March, however, Truman's embrace of the alarmist rhetoric had made the threat of war real in Washington — and also in Moscow. On March 31, Congress passed the Marshall Plan. On the same day, Soviet soldiers raised the first barriers on roads leading into Berlin, a move that would harden three months later into the Berlin blockade.

As Congress took up the challenge to gird for war and reestablish the nation's military might, Pentagon leaders were called to testify before various committees. Forrestal had left Key West with the impression that the service chiefs had come to some accommodation. Before the Senate Armed Services Committee he appeared confident that he was speaking for the entire military establishment. The secretary of the Navy, John L. Sullivan, testified that Russian submarines had been spotted near American shores, hyping the importance of the Navy to the nation's security, to Forrestal's satisfaction. But when Secretary of the Air Force Stuart Symington went before the committee, Forrestal felt blindsided. Contradicting the secretary of defense, who had placed requested Air Force personnel levels at 400,000 men and 55 strategic bomber groups, Symington testified that the Air Force could not possibly perform its mission with fewer than 500,000 men and 70 bomber groups. In fact, Symington's position had hardened since Key West, after he had learned that the Navy, with Forrestal, was still pressing for the supercarrier, which could only mean it still aimed for a strategic bomber force of its own.

In April, both Senate and House Armed Services committees voted for Symington's 70 groups, which for budgetary reasons made it inevitable that the committees would reject universal military training, which Truman himself had requested. Forrestal's humiliation was complete when he went to Truman for support against the Air Force secretary. Although the president publicly rebuked Symington for his proposal's exceeding White House budget limits, Truman also made clear that he was not going to buck Symington, his fellow Missourian. Worried about his election prospects, Truman refused Forrestal's plea for an increased budget ceiling, which alone might have eased interservice sabotage. Forrestal's mantra was "a balance of forces," but

Symington, for his part, was not shy about arguing that the Air Force had to be in balance not with the Army or Navy but with the aggressive forces of the Soviet Union. Symington knew that the public, still enthralled by the romance of air power, was with him.

After that April, Symington and Forrestal were enemies. This was particularly painful for Forrestal. Having gotten Symington his prewar job as head of Emerson Electric, when Dillon, Read controlled an interest in the company, Forrestal had considered him something of a protégé. But Symington was of the Missouri establishment, Clark Clifford was a friend of his from St. Louis, and if anyone was his mentor, it was Truman. Add to that Truman's need of Senator Vandenberg's cooperation, and Vandenberg's attachment to his Air Force general nephew. In that company of rivals, Forrestal didn't have a chance. It was then that he began manifesting signs of what colleagues took as fatigue.

7. BLOCKADE AND THE BIRTH OF THE AIR FORCE

The Soviet blockade of roads and railways leading to Berlin began in earnest in June. Stalin was claiming the sole right to govern the city, since it was well inside the Soviet occupation zone. The United States and its allies were equally insistent that the four powers together had jurisdiction of Berlin, and therefore all had the right of free access. But the conflict was subtler and more fraught than that. The Soviet move followed a decision by the United States, France, and Britain to introduce a separate currency for the West's occupation zones in Germany, including the West's zones in Berlin, and the Russians were seeking to protect their own zone from the inflationary intrusion of an economic engine over which they had no control.

The first Soviet attempts to impede entrance to Berlin were simply searches for the unauthorized currency, searches to which the French, British, and Americans refused to submit. The blockade thus originated less in Moscow's lust for territory than in uncoordinated monetary policies, which condemned the excluded Soviet sector to economic stagnation. The new Western currency, following on the Marshall Plan, guaranteed Soviet economic isolation. That would have burdensome consequences for the USSR, as Washington surely understood, but "priorities were priorities," as Melvyn Leffler put it, in summarizing the American decision to freeze Moscow out of the economic benefits of Western European recovery. "And there was no more important priority than reviving the production of western Germany."[143] From now on, more from Washington's choices than Moscow's, the west was West and the east was East. The perfect symbols of this new situation were, first, the currency dispute, and, second, coming in train, the blockade.

In any case, once the road barriers went up, the line was drawn, and the enemy could be perceived only in the worst of terms. After the fact, many revisionists have wondered how Washington could have missed the mono- lith-breaking significance of Stalin's expelling Tito and Yugoslavia from the Cominform, but it says everything about this event that it occurred just then, in June 1948, as the Berlin blockade got serious. The blockade, in a sense, rein- forced univocal perceptions of the Eastern "bloc." Given events in Yugoslavia, American analysts might have begun to disentangle nationalism from Com- munism at this point, but alarms over Berlin were ringing so loudly as to drown out any other signals coming from the Soviet sphere.

For both sides, Berlin was a *casus belli*. General Clay was ready to start shooting to guarantee his forces the right of access to the city, but he also put in a phone call to the Air Force's European headquarters in Wiesbaden to ask if the flyboys could bring up some coal.

The Air Force recognized the potential for a major, and perfectly timed, public relations coup, and they seized it — down to the name, Operation Vittles. Not just coal. The Air Force commandeered every available C-47 and C-54, stripped them of seats, and outfitted them to carry everything from raw coal to chicken feed. Pilots from all over the European theater were rushed to Rhine-Main Air Force Base near Frankfurt, which would be the staging area for the largest air transport operation in history.[144] Beleaguered Berlin would be supplied all its needs by air, an end run around the Russian provocation and a demonstration of the apparently limitless capacity of air power to pro- tect America's security. More commonly known as the Berlin airlift, the as- tounding operation continued for more than a year, with flights around the clock hauling thousands of tons of supplies every day. Finally, in September 1949 — after having put chips on a different square, as we shall see — the Sovi- ets would yield, allowing road and rail traffic into Berlin to resume.

As it happened, the man who was Air Force chief in Europe just then, and who took Clay's phone call at headquarters in Wiesbaden, where I would go to H. H. Arnold High School a decade later, was Major General Curtis LeMay.[145] How much coal do you want? LeMay asked. How much can you carry? Clay replied. Soon all the cargo planes in Europe, and many others fer- ried in from the States, were hauling fuel and food. As the planes swooped low in their approaches to Tempelhof, Gatow, and Tegel airfields in West Berlin, the crews opened hatches to toss out candy bars that had been tied to tiny handkerchief parachutes. To a generation of Berlin children, the American flyers were the "chocolate bombardiers." The airlift was quickly dubbed "the LeMay Coal and Feed Company."

LeMay had led the first American bombing raid against Germany; he had commanded the raid on Tokyo; and he had authority over the bombing of Hiroshima and Nagasaki. This was different. "A lot of us folks who worked hard on the Lift," he later wrote, "found a kind of tonic in the enterprise. We had knocked the place down; had battered it, burned it, slain or mutilated many of the inhabitants. Now we were doing just the opposite. We were feeding and healing."[146]

LeMay also stood ready to destroy. He proposed a plan to General Clay to send an armed column up the autobahn to challenge the blockade, and if the Soviets tried to stop it, he would unleash his Air Force. "We planned to enfilade their radar positions so that we could hit the airdromes in Germany where all the Russian [planes] were lined up wing tip to wing tip," he told an interviewer in 1971. "We probably could have done a good job of cleaning out their air force with one blow with what we had, using the B-29's as well as the fighters." LeMay's war plan was code-named Halfmoon.[147] Clay said no.

But the B-29s remained LeMay's ace in the hole. Before the airlift they were not stationed in Europe. LeMay seized the occasion of the blockade to bring the long-range bombers forward to the European theater for the first time. Those planes were well known as the carriers of the atomic bomb, and until now they had been restricted to the United States. Exploiting pressures tied to Berlin, LeMay managed to get twenty-eight B-29s assigned to his command. Their posting in August, first to Munich, then to England, where they would be safer from Soviet attack, was an implicit but clear threat that Soviet aggression, including interference with the cargo planes flying in and out of Berlin, would be met with atomic retaliation, aimed not at Soviet armed forces but at Russian cities. LeMay's way of doing business.

In fact, the planes were not configured to carry the bomb; the Atomic Energy Commission, not the Air Force, controlled atomic weapons; and the move was a bluff. For the bluff to be taken seriously, it did not hurt that LeMay was in command of the B-29s. Forrestal strongly endorsed the move, having argued for extending the protection of America's nuclear capability to Europe as a way of influencing Soviet behavior. Forrestal had written in his diary some months before: "The only balance that we have against the overwhelming manpower of the Russians, and therefore the chief deterrent to war, is the threat of immediate retaliation with the atomic bomb."[148]

As the Berlin crisis unfolded, Forrestal succeeded in getting Truman's assurance that "as much as he hated to do it, he would approve the use of atomic weapons if circumstances warranted it." At the Pentagon, this assur-

ance — and no other authorization — marked the beginning of institutionalized strategic planning built around atomic air attack.[149] The Berlin airlift, in
other words, was more than a celebration of humanitarian air power. It was
the start of the new doctrine of "extended deterrence," the idea that an attack on American allies would be treated as an attack on the United States,
coupled with an expressed willingness to inflict massive casualties on Soviet
civilians as a way of influencing the behavior of the USSR's leaders vis-à-vis
Europe.

Emphasizing this prospect, the airlift also prompted the leaders of France
and Belgium to allow the first American air bases to be built in those countries, a move LeMay supervised. It was the start of the U.S. strike force, aimed
at Moscow. That fall, President Truman made LeMay's bluffing initiative real,
and his subsequent creation of new bases relevant, when he authorized the
use of atomic bombs against Russia if Europe was attacked. The principle
would be made public in April 1949, with the airlift still on, at the signing of
the North Atlantic Treaty. The founding of NATO, especially in that context,
made permanent the military, as opposed to political, character of the Western standoff.[150] Weapons — not coal, and not feed either — would define the
competition between East and West.

From now on, Washington would expect only the worst from Moscow,
and would be prepared to respond with the worst. The Soviet Union had
erected its Iron Curtain; the United States had replied with a nuclear curtain.
LeMay's initiative led to the European-based nuclear strike force that remains
to this day. And before the airlift was over, LeMay was transferred back to the
States to get the nascent Strategic Air Command[151] ready to carry out the
threat that was all at once the basis of American power.

8. THE RUSSIANS ARE COMING

With the crisis in Berlin at full heat, the tight ball of string inside Forrestal
was steadily unraveling. At his request, George Kennan issued an analysis of
what the Soviet blockade of Berlin meant. Published in late November 1948
and adopted by Truman as a policy statement, Kennan's paper baldly stated,
"Communist ideology and Soviet behavior clearly demonstrate that the ultimate objective of the leaders of the USSR is the domination of the world."[152]
Stalin had thus emerged as a nightmare figure in Forrestal's imagination, a
man of unlimited evil reach. But the daily challenge to Forrestal, and the
more wearing one, came from his former friend Stuart Symington.

In May 1948, defying what had been the Air Force's understanding at Key

West, Congress approved funds for the Navy's supercarrier. The Navy crowed and began laying plans for construction at once. The Air Force took the supercarrier as a sign of the Navy's dogged determination to build a strategic bomber force of its own and to control the atomic bomb. The Air Force had to retaliate. In July, Symington gave a much-publicized speech in which he criticized Forrestal's administration of the military establishment as putting American security at risk. Forrestal reprinted in his *Diaries* the message he immediately sent to Symington: "If the account of your speech in Los Angeles on Friday evening, as reported by Gladwin Hill in today's *New York Times*, is accurate, it was an act of official disobedience and personal disloyalty. I shall await your explanation." The diary goes on to note that he also called the president to tell him he would ask for Symington's resignation as "the only possible course. The President agreed."[153] But Forrestal had no stomach for the confrontation with Symington. When the Air Force secretary dissembled in response to Forrestal's complaint, Forrestal knew he was lying, but he made nothing more of it. Forrestal's biographers comment: "A bolder, more self-confident man would have acted on the facts and accepted the consequences; indeed, a man who understood the dynamics of power and authority would have seen the necessity to act in his own interest. Symington's insubordination in July was not an isolated incident . . . To permit it to continue, unchallenged and unpunished, was to accept a further erosion of Forrestal's own authority. And that is what happened."[154]

Over the succeeding months, Forrestal was helpless as the Navy–Air Force dispute worsened, descending to deceit, rumormongering, and outright defiance by both sides of budgetary guidelines, security regulations, congressional protocols, even the president's authority. When Truman won election in November, he ceased to care much about the issues involved, since he no longer had to fear voter rejection of his spending requests. In the event, the Navy and Air Force escalated their demands, and each cultivated allies on Capitol Hill as assiduously as they ignored Forrestal and Truman.

Like a shark smelling blood in the water, the press zeroed in on the hapless Forrestal. Obsessed with the Pentagon's voracious need for Middle East oil, he had opposed Truman's support of Israel, for which he was condemned as an anti-Semite. His eccentric family life — Josephine, his unstable wife, was mostly traveling in Europe — left him vulnerable and alone. His diary shows that, through the autumn of 1948, he was obsessed with his responsibility for the atomic bomb. No one imagined yet that the Berlin airlift could supply the city indefinitely, and that crisis always seemed within days of an apocalyptic climax. He continued to badger General Marshall and the president about whether he was actually to plan for the bomb's use in the expected war, and when they seemed to say yes, he escalated the old campaign to have custody of atomic weapons transferred from the Atomic Energy Commission to sole military authority. He began worrisome contacts with the British on the subject. LeMay now headed the Strategic Air Command, and the B-29s he had based in England would conduct the nuclear attack on the Soviet homeland.

Forrestal was consoled by the American atomic monopoly and noted that "the Russians cannot possibly have the industrial competence to produce the atomic bomb," but he also dreaded that the American atomic threat "by itself will not be a deterrent to their making war."[155] The sheer vastness of Soviet territory and the leadership's indifference to the suffering of its own people could make Russia undeterrable. Nevertheless, he returned from a November trip to Berlin convinced that the atomic bomb was America's only hope, which in turn made him see the importance of the Air Force's strategic bomber force with new clarity. He finally cut the Navy loose from his first loyalty, but it was only dread of an imminent war that made him do it.[156] After the election, he pleaded with Truman, at long last, to raise the military budget ceiling to accommodate all that the Joint Chiefs were telling him they needed. Again Truman refused.[157]

Early in 1949, after the resignation of George Marshall as secretary of state, rumors began to circulate that Forrestal, too, would be removed. Newspaper columnists attacked and ridiculed him. Though he was exhausted and emotionally spent, the thought of ending his tenure at Defense filled Forrestal with panic. In the same week, Symington published his annual report as secretary of the Air Force, once again contradicting Forrestal to emphasize the need for more bombers. By now aware of the bombers' crucial role in the standoff with Russia, Forrestal wasn't sure he disagreed with Symington. When reporters asked Forrestal if he expected to remain in office, he snapped, "I am a victim of the Washington scene."[158] At the White House, aides noticed that he had so compulsively rubbed a particular patch of his hair that raw scalp showed through. Eisenhower commented on how "badly" he looked: "He gives his mind no rest, and he works hours that would kill a horse."[159] Through February, Truman refused to confirm his intentions about Forrestal's future one way or the other. Forrestal told associates that he had decided to resign, but when Truman abruptly asked for his resignation on March 1, he was "shattered."[160]

Forrestal submitted his letter of resignation the next day, effective later in the month. Truman announced as his replacement Louis Johnson, a lawyer known mainly as an effective fundraiser for the president's surprisingly victorious election campaign. Forrestal's retirement ceremony was scheduled for noon, March 28, at the Pentagon. That morning he called Truman to ask if he really wanted him to resign. "Yes, Jim, that's the way I want it."[161] The ceremony went ahead as planned, and that afternoon at the White House, Truman presented the Distinguished Service Medal to Forrestal, who was so overcome with feeling that he could not respond.

The next day, at similar ceremonies, Forrestal was honored by senators and congressmen at the Capitol. As he was leaving to return to the Pentagon, where he had been assigned a small temporary office, Stuart Symington approached him. Forrestal was about to get into his car. Symington said, "There is something I would like to talk to you about." The two men rode back to the Pentagon alone, and no one knows what was said between them. Forrestal went directly from the car to his office. A short while later, he was found sitting at the desk in that office, hat on his head, staring at the wall. An aide approached him. Forrestal said, "You are a loyal fellow." He repeated that sentence again and again.[162]

Forrestal had cracked. He was taken from the Pentagon in a borrowed car. The next day, to avoid publicity and to get him some rest, he was flown to Florida, where Josephine was visiting Robert Lovett, who had recently resigned as undersecretary of state and who would himself be appointed as secretary of defense a couple of years later. Upon arrival, Forrestal told his host, "Bob, they're after me." It wasn't clear who "they" were at first. Forrestal had sometimes spoken of Jews and "Zionist agents" stalking him,[163] but in the end he was undone by fears of his great enemy. Years before, when Josephine had become delusional, "they" were "the Reds," and now Forrestal, too, vented his anxiety that the Communists were after him. On the beach he saw umbrella stands as microphones set to record his every word. He believed that Communists had infiltrated the White House, which accounted for his dismissal, and he was sure that Communists were going to kill him for all he had done to urge his countrymen to oppose them.

When Truman was told what Forrestal was saying, he ordered the Secret Service to investigate. They reported back that the fear was without foundation. Forrestal, the Secret Service assessment said, had suffered "a slight nervous breakdown."[164] Rumors flew around Washington. One radio report had it that Forrestal was found in his pajamas a few blocks from Lovett's house, and he was calling out, "The Russians are coming!"[165]

In response to alarms first raised by George Kennan, Forrestal had been described, as noted earlier, as resembling Paul Revere, jolted into action by the sight of two lanterns hanging in the Old North Church. In telling Forrestal's story to its conclusion, however, biographers deemphasize the political aspect of his mental state. They seem to prefer the image of the spoiled priest, speculating that Forrestal's psychosis was rooted in his failed Catholicism. Indeed, he was reported to have confessed near the end that he was being punished for being "a bad Catholic."[166] Military psychiatrists would seize on such a reading of his troubled life, repeatedly forbidding a Catholic priest from visiting him at Bethesda, for example, as if Forrestal's careening anxiety was pushed over the limit by the ghost of that rigid, moralizing mother.[167] And killer angels in a tortured mind evoke fewer public questions than "the Reds," who would, in fact, be driving many Americans around the bend before long. More than a few would believe it was true that Forrestal had been targeted by Moscow, and Senator Joseph McCarthy would soon claim that among the "names of Communists" he flourished, beginning on February 9, 1950, some had been personally supplied to him by James Forrestal.[168]

One needn't credit such conspiracy theories to see Forrestal's demise as much in political terms as psychological ones. The image of the colonial silversmith galloping along the Boston–Lexington road alerting his fellow Americans to the imminent arrival of the British enemy is an apt one for Forrestal. "The Russians are coming! The Russians are coming!" The news accounts saying he did just such a thing at the end in Florida were unreliable, yet they captured something crucial to his mental illness. "The Russians are coming!" was the message he'd proclaimed from his high horse of power at the Pentagon. From his places as secretary of the Navy and secretary of defense, beginning with his abrupt deflection of Henry Stimson's proposal to make the Soviets trustworthy by trusting them, Forrestal did more to establish the ethos of national security than any other person. Beginning in 1945, he consistently exaggerated the dangers posed by the Soviet Union, and this exaggeration required two others — the regular overestimation of what Moscow's military force could actually do, and the equivalent underestimation of American capabilities. This pattern would be repeated in 1950, with the secret review of Soviet purposes called NSC-68; in 1957, with the Gaither Report, which demanded an urgent U.S. buildup; in 1960, with the "missile gap" crisis; in 1969, with warnings of a Soviet "first strike"; in the 1970s, with opposition to the Strategic Arms Limitation Talks; and in the 1980s, with the Committee on the Present Danger, which prompted the Reagan buildup. We will see more of each later. The pattern begins with Forrestal.

By calibrating the Soviet "threat" against the demands of domestic politics and the self-interest of American military fiefdoms, without testing that threat against disciplined and authenticated intelligence, Forrestal set a precedent that would serve as the Pentagon's organizing principle from then on. Because of this, the bronze bust memorializing Forrestal is where it belongs, at the entrance to the Building. The public consequences of his actions were momentous. But so were the private ones. Forrestal set this national security juggernaut moving at the expense of his own security. For him the political and the personal became the same thing, and something like that was about to happen to America. Forrestal's anguish over the threat posed by Stalin's Soviet Union passed over into clinical paranoia, but not before he had put in place political and military structures that abetted the rise of what might be called public paranoia. Forrestal was among the first for whom fear of Russia and fear of nuclear war became the same thing, too.

"The nation's danger had become his danger," as his biographers say; "the nation's failure, his failure."[169] Perhaps. But it could equally be suggested that his deep insecurity had become the nation's. For his part, George Kennan, who did so much to reinforce the worst fears of Forrestal's mind, later saw that such an obsession with security in an insecure world would lead to madness. Especially once nuclear weapons were introduced into it. Instead of going insane, Kennan changed his mind. He became, as his biographer called him, "a Cold War iconoclast," a lifelong dissenter from the Totalitarian-school consensus that he had himself founded.[170] Perhaps seeing Forrestal's fate helped Kennan to do so.

After a few days in Florida, Forrestal was brought quietly back to Washington, where he was admitted to Bethesda Naval Hospital. He was in the safe bosom of his beloved Navy. Forrestal was described as suffering from "operational fatigue," a military diagnosis.[171] To keep his true condition secret, hospital officials decided not to commit him to the psychiatric ward on the hospital's locked-down first floor. Instead he was put in the VIP suite on the sixteenth floor, rooms that had been luxuriously appointed for President Roosevelt. Orderlies were there to bring him juice, not watch over him. The suite's windows were unlocked.

On May 22, Forrestal's body was found thirteen floors below, on the roof of a corridor-bridge joining two wings of the building. "Mr. James Forrestal took his own life at the United States Naval Hospital, Bethesda, Maryland, at 2:00 A.M.," the official announcement read in part, "by climbing out of a window."[172]

Forrestal's funeral was held at the Memorial Amphitheater at Arlington Cemetery three days later. Senator Arthur Vandenberg, the Senate's chief backer of Forrestal's Cold War alarms, wrote in his diary, "The Navy band played Handel's 'Largo' — and of course that put me wholly out of commission. The Air Force band played 'Lead Kindly Light.' And then as they slowly marched from the Amphitheater to the high hillside where Jimmy finds his peace at last, the big Army band played 'Onward Christian Soldiers' — and I thought I would expire. There was something about it all which was so intimately tragic and yet so spiritually exalted. I am sure Jimmy did not die in vain."[173] Among the mourners that day, who surely contributed to the "spontaneous" fund that erected the bronze bust at the entrance to the Pentagon, were my mother and father.

9. NAVY VERSUS AIR FORCE

Forrestal's death was a blow to the Navy, but not the most grievous one. His successor as secretary of defense, Louis Johnson, had moved right after taking office to cancel the supercarrier that Forrestal had approved. The keel of the *United States* had been laid with great fanfare on April 18, 1949; on April 23, less than one week later, Johnson ordered the construction halted, the project canceled. The Navy had projected that the ship, the first of twelve they wanted, would cost $186 million, but the Air Force chief of staff (and Senator Vandenberg's nephew), Hoyt Vandenberg, had put the cost at closer to $500 million.[174] Johnson's mandate from Truman was to gain control of the Defense Department's budget, but as one official put it, he made "two enemies for every dollar he saved."[175]

For Vandenberg, the budget issue was a smokescreen, since the Air Force saw the carrier as the Navy's bid for a strategic air force and dominance of atomic warfare. The long-range bomber was an alternative to the supercarrier, which is why the Air Force opposed the new ship. It is a measure of how thoroughly the atomic bomb as a strategic weapon dominated Air Force thinking by this point that Vandenberg should have taken the lead in this dispute. During World War II, as commander of the Ninth Air Force in Europe, his planes had served mainly as tactical support for Eisenhower's armies. He was instinctively unsympathetic to the bombing of cities.[176] Before becoming chief of staff, he had served in Air Force intelligence and, for a time, as head of Central Intelligence. But since Hiroshima, atomic bombing of cities had become central to the Air Force's purpose, and with atomic weapons, targets were defined not by factories or rail yards but by square miles. To be chief of the postwar Air Force was to embrace such a mission, and Vandenberg had. He was one of the first to argue that the overwhelming manpower of the Red Army massed on the edge of central Europe could be balanced only by strategic bombing, aimed at Russia itself.[177] Vandenberg had become like LeMay.[178]

So the cancellation of the *United States* was a great Air Force victory, coming as it did at the climax of the Air Force triumph of the Berlin airlift. But to the Navy, the cancellation of the supercarrier meant war — with the Air Force. The Navy's objection to Air Force strategic planning is often characterized as just a matter of rivalry for control of the atomic bomb, but there was a serious point of criticism in the Navy argument. Instead of attacking Soviet cities, the Navy urged tactical assaults on the Red Army's infrastructure, designed to stop the Soviet force east of the Rhine. Strategic bombing of urban centers was militarily useless, in the Navy view. It was a key point, touching on the absurd assumption that would forever undergird nuclear doctrine.[179]

After Johnson's cancellation of the *United States,* the Navy secretary, John Sullivan, resigned in protest, and the howl of the Navy brass would soon be called "the revolt of the admirals." That questions were raised by Navy men about Forrestal's last ride to the Pentagon, when Symington had arranged to be alone with him — What had Symington said? Was Symington responsible for the beloved Forrestal's crack-up? — only intensified hostility toward the Air Force and its leaders.

The Navy lost no time in striking back. On May 25, the day of Forrestal's funeral, a fiercely partisan Navy supporter in Congress, James E. Van Zandt of Pennsylvania, made a motion to investigate allegations of corruption in the Air Force's acquisition of the new B-36 bomber, together with allegations that the B-36 was dangerously flawed. Van Zandt was himself a captain in the Navy Reserve, and he barely concealed his allegiance to the Navy in its conflict with the Air Force. The next day, in a speech on the floor of Congress urging the adoption of his motion, Van Zandt, citing rumors "I have heard from sources I cannot disregard,"[180] leveled shocking accusations at Symington, Vandenberg, Defense Secretary Johnson, and other Air Force leaders, including LeMay.

The B-36, dubbed the Peacemaker,[181] was the first true intercontinental bomber, and tensions over Berlin made its deployment an Air Force priority. By May 1949, the Strategic Air Command, of which, since March, Curtis LeMay had been chief, was commissioning the plane by the dozen as it rolled off the assembly line of the Consolidated-Vultee Corporation (soon to be renamed Convair). With the B-36, the United States finally had the capacity to launch a major attack against the Soviet Union, and SAC had a plan for doing so. The 1949 Operation Dropshot foresaw the destruction with three hundred atom bombs of one hundred Soviet cities — an equivalent, with the improved bombs, of more than eight hundred Hiroshimas.[182]

That LeMay presided over such a strategy, and was rapidly assembling the force to carry it out, prompted the hostile admirals to resuscitate the Navy's moral objection to atomic warfare, first articulated by Admiral Leahy in 1945. The official Air Force history calls this a "somewhat specious argument,"[183] as if the Navy did not by then have its own nuclear ambitions. But the Navy's issue, however disingenuous it might have appeared, was not nuclear use as such, but massive urban bombardment. "Must we translate the historical mistake of the Second World War," the admirals asked, "into a permanent concept merely to avoid clouding the prestige of those who led us down the wrong road in the past?"[184]

LeMay's SAC battle plan was secret at the time, of course, as were the operational statistics of the B-36, and so Van Zandt's public charge that the B-36 was an inferior plane was not easily refuted. But his most sensational accusations were against Symington and Vandenberg. The former, Van Zandt said, had approved the B-36 despite its flaws because the head of Convair, Floyd Odlum, offered him money and a position to head Convair in the future. Vandenberg's interest allegedly involved an adulterous affair with Odlum's wife, the famous aviatrix Jackie Cochran. There was even an implication that Symington, Vandenberg, and Cochran had engaged in a ménage à trois.[185] For all of these scurrilous accusations, Van Zandt offered only the corroboration of an anonymous letter, a document that seemed fully credible but that came to him, he said, from a source he did not know.

The letter, several thousand words in length and containing fifty-five separate charges against the Air Force and its leaders, was admitted into the *Congressional Record*. Within days, the House Armed Services Committee, under the chairmanship of Georgia's Carl Vinson, formerly the chairman of the now defunct Naval Affairs Committee and another Navy partisan, voted to undertake "Thorough Studies and Investigations Relating to Matters Involving the B-36 Bombers." If the supercarrier *United States* could be canceled, so could the Peacemaker.

10. THAT COP

A year earlier, as we noted, Stuart Symington had overseen the creation of the Air Force's own investigative agency, the Office of Special Investigations. By now, the OSI, my father's operation, had established something of a beachhead in the inhospitable culture of the Pentagon. The unproven new agency, headed by an outsider with no influence, was assumed to be a career killer, and only Air Force officers who had actual contact with the young general were drawn in. My father had the Irish charm, and with a passionate commitment to his mission, he promoted the OSI effectively, if slowly. Over time, officers had accepted transfer to the upstart operation from the offices of the inspector general, the air provost marshal, and air intelligence. They joined a select group of FBI men who had worked with Joe Carroll and who'd been happy to come over to the Pentagon, joining the OSI as civilians. The men who worked for Joe Carroll became fervently attached to him.[186]

But my father was far from being accepted by the men with whom he worked only at arm's length in the Pentagon. His tunic was still without medal ribbons, the only senior officer of whom that was true in the entire armed services. He was still in his two-room suite of offices on the fourth floor of E ring, a kind of pariah to all but those who knew him. Years later, as recounted in official Air Force records, he described the "skirmishes" with Air Force veterans who regarded him as an interloper. He knew that to gain the confidence of those who disdained him as "that cop," he needed, as he put it, an important case, "a *solved*" important case. "And one came along," he said, referring to Van Zandt's anonymous document. "It attacked the integrity, patriotism, and morality of Symington and General Vandenberg. Well, that erupted like an A-Bomb, and the OSI had its case."[187]

Or, as the Air Force history puts it, "Stunned by the sudden, incredible charges, Symington and Vandenberg immediately called on Carroll for assistance . . . 'They asked me to personally investigate this matter and to find out, if possible, who wrote the letter,' Carroll later recalled."[188] If the flyboys despised him for being a cop, still, he thought like one. He obtained a photostatic copy of the original letter, and he asked J. Edgar Hoover to place the FBI laboratory at his disposal for typewriter comparisons. "Carroll's agents prowled the Pentagon halls at night," the Air Force history says, "taking typewriting specimens from a number of offices." The offices of interest, of course, were those of the chief of naval operations and the secretary of the Navy. The OSI men, in what was almost certainly a violation of the law, broke into the Navy offices in the middle of one night after another. One of my father's close associates at the time, Colonel Keefe O'Keefe, told me in the mid-1980s that my father, drawing on skills he'd honed tracking German spies in Washington during the war, had himself picked the locks of the Navy secretary's office and led his small team through the shadowy rooms, collecting typewriter samples.

"Lo and behold," my father is quoted in the Air Force history as reporting, "we got an unequivocal, positive identification from the Bureau."[189] One of the pages of typescript taken from a Navy office had a font the FBI technicians had matched to that of the accusatory document. As had been repeatedly established in court, such a match carried the certainty of fingerprints. The OSI had found the typewriter that had produced Van Zandt's "anonymous" letter, sitting on a desk in the offices of the secretary of the Navy.

Symington was called to testify before the Vinson committee, one of whose members was Congressman Van Zandt. Slowly and dramatically, in his long opening statement, Symington took up seventeen separate charges made against him and Vandenberg in the letter, including the innuendo-laden charge that the two of them had repeatedly spent weekends with Jackie Cochran at her Palms Springs ranch. To each charge, Symington said, "That is not true," and he produced evidence to back up his statement. The letter implied that Curtis LeMay had been named SAC commander in March because he was also involved in the conspiracy to buy the inferior bomber, and

Symington rebutted that, too. And then, in a stirring conclusion, Symington rebuked the committee for its dependence on a "document for which so far no one has desired to assume paternity." He challenged Vinson and the other congressmen to take the trouble to learn not only who the anonymous author was, but "also the organization which employs him, and the cause which he serves."[190]

In the *Congressional Record,* Symington's conclusion reads, "An effort has been made to show that the Air Force, and I personally, have done wrong in the purchase of the B-36. It is not true. We hope the basic and greatest result of these hearings will be freeing air power once and for all from the shackles of the past — so that it can take its place as a true member of the joint defense team of land, sea, and air, with its mission clear. In accordance with your own agenda I hope you will determine who is responsible for accusing the Air Force command of such mass conspiracy against the best interest of the country."[191]

But Vinson and Van Zandt, the Navy partisans, were emphatic in saying there was no way to learn who the accuser was. No way, therefore, to finally discredit him. But at the crucial moment, Melvin Price, a congressman from Illinois, leaned to his microphone and asked Symington, "Do you know who may have started these rumors against the Air Force and against you personally?"

Symington answered, "Yes, I know who wrote the anonymous document."

There was a stir in the hearing room. The *Congressional Record* reflects it in noting that Chairman Vinson, who had been fussing with his cigar, said he didn't hear Symington's answer. Symington repeated it. Vinson, stunned, asked Symington to furnish him and the committee counsel, Joseph B. Keenan, with the anonymous author's name, to which Symington said, "I already have, to Mr. Keenan, Sir."[192]

In the commotion, it became clear that Keenan had not read whatever document Symington was referring to, and the committee adjourned in disarray. In a subsequent session, the record shows that "General Carroll, the Air Force Investigator" had delivered his report — "a compendium of information, investigation, and leads" — to the committee counsel's office the day before Symington's testimony.[193] The report identified the typewriter that had produced the anonymous document, the location of the typewriter in the office of the undersecretary of the Navy for air, Dan A. Kimball, at the desk normally used by Secretary Kimball's special assistant, Cedric Worth. Referring to his own report, General Carroll's text concluded, "This is a document of the Air Force Office of Special Investigations, and it is *not* anonymous. It was prepared by Brigadier General Joseph F. Carroll, the Director of OSI, and it was approved by W. Stuart Symington, the Secretary of the Air Force, and General Hoyt S. Vandenberg, the Chief of Staff of the United States Air Force."[194]

Cedric Worth, now a civilian but formerly a Navy commander, was immediately subpoenaed to appear before Vinson's committee. At first he denied being the letter's author, but faced with Joseph Keenan's stern cross-examination, drawing on the OSI report, Worth admitted that he wrote the letter, and that it was all lies. He denied that his superiors were involved in his charges, and in later sworn testimony they would say the same thing. Worth would be fired. Few believed that he had acted without authorization. Over subsequent weeks, the committee subpoenaed other witnesses. Testimony consistently backed up what Symington had said and what the OSI investigation had revealed. *Newsweek*'s comment about the way Worth was exposed was "If the Air Force fights with the B-36 the way it fights *for* it, heaven help America's enemies."[195]

"Are you aware of the heartache you have caused with this anonymous document?" Keenan asked at the end of Worth's testimony. "Yes," Worth replied. But Keenan by now was furious, for to the committee's lawyer the whole miserable business had gone far beyond allegations of mere corruption. "In this crucial period of our history," he said, the most damaging question raised had been about the integrity of America's responsible custody of the atom bomb.[196] It was that sacred trust that Worth had violated, seducing Congress itself into nearly doing so.

Did Worth realize, an angry Keenan asked, that "the United States Government is fortunate in having forthright and honorable men in charge of its procurement of aircraft and in the operation of the air force?" Worth answered simply, "Yes."

But Keenan wasn't finished. "And aren't you yourself proud of them?" To which Worth said, "Quite."

In summary remarks, as he adjourned the special hearings for good, Chairman Vinson, the one-time Navy champion, made the meaning of the "studies and investigations" of the formerly beleaguered B-36 crystal clear: "The Air Force selected this bomber, procured this bomber, solely on the ground that this is the best aircraft for its purpose available to the Nation today. At this time, I feel that the Nation should know that the Secretary of Air, Mr. Symington, and the leaders of the Air Force . . . have come through this inquiry without the slightest blemish."[197]

The B-36 was a go. The Navy would not challenge Air Force dominance for a decade.[198] LeMay's Strategic Air Command would be the main custodian of the atomic bomb. Strategic bombing of cities would define American defense doctrine. In Symington's formulation, "air power would be freed from the shackles of the past." Symington himself would soon go on to a distinguished career as a U.S. senator from Missouri. And, as the Air Force history cites my father saying, "from that moment on, OSI could do no wrong."[199]

Little more than a month after Stuart Symington had turned to my father for help in disproving the Van Zandt charges, in the company of General Hoyt Vandenberg and J. Edgar Hoover he presented my father with his first medal, the Legion of Merit, one of the most distinguished ribbons an officer can wear. My father's tunic would no longer be bare. The photograph taken that day has long been one of my prized possessions, but it was only after having learned the full story recounted here that I understood why the four men are smiling so.

The final session of the B-36 hearings of the House Armed Services Committee took place on August 25, 1949. The Air Force, in my father's words, "was jubilant and vindicated."[200] Not for long.

President Truman would not announce the fact for nearly a month; the now retired general Leslie Groves was still predicting it would not happen for decades; the CIA was saying years.[201] Even scientists had convinced themselves of a "longer time" before it could happen.[202] Nevertheless, four days after the hearings closed, on August 29, the Soviet Union, at a secret test site at the Semipalatinsk range in Kazakhstan, exploded its first atomic bomb.

FOUR

SELF-FULFILLING PARANOIA

1. STALIN'S TEETH

James Forrestal committed suicide in a fit of clinical paranoia. As secretary of defense he had presided over the construction of an American fear of a Soviet Communist conspiracy that went beyond what Moscow actually threatened at the time, amounting to a kind of public paranoia. "Mind-forged manacles," in William Blake's phrase, closed on the man and his nation both. The person on whom Forrestal most depended for this was George Kennan, who with his Long Telegram and "X" article personally erected one of the pillars of the American Cold War imagination — which was, not incidentally, a definition of the Russian outlook itself as paranoid. "At bottom of Kremlin's neurotic view of world affairs is traditional and instinctive Russian sense of insecurity," Kennan wrote in his 1946 telegram. "Russian rulers have invariably sensed that their rule was relatively archaic in form, fragile and artificial in its psychological foundation, unable to stand comparison or contact with political systems of Western countries. For this reason they have always feared foreign penetration."[1]

To those who held this view, the Soviets were dangerous, in large part, because they continued a long-established Russian tradition of projecting a fantasy enemy onto the West and then of taking drastic measures, internally and externally, to blunt anticipated onslaughts, no matter how improbable such attacks might appear to those living far from Red Square. The United States had no choice, in this view, but to prepare for conflict with Moscow because Soviet neurotics, for no apparent reason, anticipated such conflict. Out of deep Russian psychosis, Kremlin leaders, to repeat Kennan's line, "have always feared foreign penetration." Now they feared it from the United States.

If a deluded Forrestal was reported to have been crying "The Russians are coming!" not long before his suicide, Russian leaders were imagined, equally deluded, to be steadily crying "The Westerners are coming!" Or, as the historian Marshall T. Poe puts it, "For them [the Russians], the Europeans were always coming, even though a neutral observer would think otherwise." But Poe goes on, "Yet the paranoia theory hardly seems credible (and indeed seems somewhat deluded itself), given the cold, hard historical facts of Russian-European relations."[2] Those relations were marked for centuries by assaults on Russia from, precisely, the West.

Between 1654 and 1667, Polish armies invaded Russia in territorial conflicts over what is now Ukraine; in the 1670s the invaders were from the Ottoman Empire; at the end of that century they were Swedes, who came again a decade later, as did the Ottomans. The Austrians, too, came, in the eighteenth century. In 1812 the French invaded, followed by the British in 1853 — and, again, by the Ottomans later in the century.[3] In the twentieth century the Germans came twice, with devastating effects both times. Paranoia? "No nation on earth," Poe says, "has faced such continuous and deadly military pressure."[4] That pressure, as much as any wound in the Russian psyche or premise in Communist purpose, accounts for the suspicion that Moscow brought to encounters with former allies at the end of World War II.

In American assessments of the origins of the Cold War, emphasis is almost always given to the diabolical character of Joseph Stalin, who ruled the USSR with an iron fist from 1924 until his death in 1953.[5] Stalin's record makes it impossible for even the most thoroughgoing revisionist to assert any kind of moral equivalence between the Soviet Union and the United States.[6] Stalin so embodied American fears that I remember thinking, as a boy of ten that year of his death, that with him gone the tension with the USSR was bound to ease soon. Stalin was dead; that meant our side had won, no?

We knew that Stalin's name meant "steel," and I for one would not have been surprised to learn that inside his unsmiling mouth were two rows of steel teeth. Franklin Roosevelt had called him Uncle Joe, but by the end of the 1940s he was America's nightmare figure — that blood-red tide (even in black-and-white newsreels) spilling over Europe and Asia on those Movietone globes. In my case, the nightmare was sometimes literal because of the radio shows my brothers and I listened to before going to sleep. "Who knows what evil lurks in the hearts of men? The Shadow knows." The program we never missed was *The FBI in Peace and War.* I can still hear the thunderous bass of its theme song, one of the default tunes I find myself humming to this day. That melodrama, which supplied my brothers and me with fantasies of our G-man father before his Air Force commissioning, often referred to Stalin as the evil genius whose spies were everywhere. *He* was the Shadow, and his henchmen were, as we learned to call them, spooks. They were Masters of Deceit, a phrase J. Edgar Hoover used as the title of an anti-Communist diatribe. Indeed, Stalin was Hoover's nemesis, which brought the contest close, since in those early years Dad was one of Hoover's own. If anyone could thwart Stalin, the wily and virtuous agents of the FBI could. As a child — this was *my* cowboys and Indians — I felt personally invested in the world-historic duel.

As if a cloak-and-dagger political contest for the planet were not enough, Stalin was a figure of my religion, too. We Catholics of the old school defined who we were by whom we hated, and if Stalin was Hoover's mortal enemy,[7] he was equally the pope's. As Eugenio Pacelli, a Vatican diplomat in Munich in the 1920s, the pope himself had been roughed up by German Bolsheviks, and as Pius XII, his ferocious hatred of Communism was quite personal. My parents were not overly pious Catholics, yet attachment to His Holiness, perhaps especially for Irish Americans in the generation before John Kennedy, was a mark of identity. Pius XII's photograph — that ascetic profile, showing one glinting lens of his rimless spectacles — hung inside the front door of our house, and the monthly magazine *The Pope Speaks* was always on the coffee table. "The Pope! How many divisions has *he* got?" Stalin sneered when Roosevelt proposed including the Vatican in talks, but Pius XII put firmly in place the Church's stark, and ultimately powerful, opposition to Soviet Communism. The pope defined the Church's contest with Communism as "one of the most dangerous persecutions she has ever known."[8] Every Catholic Mass in the world ended with a special prayer for the conversion of Russia. In 1949, the pope excommunicated, with a flourish of his signature on a decretal, every Communist on earth — something he had never done to Nazis, nor even to Hitler.[9]

As if in retaliation, Stalin's puppets arrested bishops and cardinals throughout the Communist world — Warsaw, Zagreb, Beijing. Priests were martyred and churches were seized. The cardinal archbishop of Hungary, József Mindszenty, was charged with treason and imprisoned for life. About Mindszenty in particular Catholics were staggered, and the cardinal became, in a way, a member of every Catholic family around the globe, including ours. (Mindszenty would escape his Communist prison during the short-lived Hungarian uprising in 1956 and take refuge in the American embassy in Budapest, where he remained until 1971.) The only comic books my brothers and I were allowed to have in the house, produced by the Knights of Columbus, featured tales of Eastern European Catholic resistance to Stalin. I remember the cartoon drawings of "brainwashed" children whom "commissars" had convinced to report on the clandestine Masses their parents attended.

Communism began as a utopian dream, aiming at a classless society, property owned by all, the state withered away, full equality for the first time in history. Otherworldly religion, with its rejection of "this" world and every utopia claimed for it, was Communism's taunting foe. And both sides knew it. In Russia, Lenin's face had replaced the iconic face of the Byzantine Jesus, but to Catholics, Stalin's face — those anthracite eyes, that cockroach of a mustache[10] — had the bloodthirsty look of evil. He was a devil figure pure and simple, an enemy worthy of the name. And he was my enemy.

Stalin was from Georgia, not Russia. The son of an alcoholic cobbler, he was a seminarian until he was twenty years old, when he embraced Bolshevism with religious zeal. In succeeding Lenin as party head, Stalin cunningly and ruthlessly eliminated his rivals and secured a firm grip on power. He was every bit the autocrat the czars had been, but he brought political terror, Red terror, to a new level. Whole provinces were turned into prisons. During the war, Soviet soldiers captured by the Germans were *ipso facto* regarded as "traitors to the motherland." Upon release after the war, tens of thousands were ordered executed by their own leaders just for having been POWs. Political cadres and the Red Army officer corps were repeatedly purged through the years. Stalin's overhaul of agriculture, known as collectivization because it corralled privately owned farms into state-owned collectives, pitted peasants against farm owners (called kulaks), resulting in the state-sponsored slaughter of an entire class of landowners. The ensuing deaths of so many of its own citizens prompted the regime to nationalize the mortuaries. The foul odor of dead bodies blanketed the Russian countryside.[11]

The horror of the terror-famine in Ukraine (1928–1932) stands out even among the crimes Stalin committed. That breadbasket region was notable for its many independent farmers, who had good reason to forcefully resist collectivization — resistance that was not to be tolerated. While a million children were murdered by the Nazis in the Holocaust, three times that number of children died in the government-sponsored murder campaign in Ukraine.[12] The era of Stalin's reign informally came to be referred to, in the Soviet Union and elsewhere, as the time of the "twenty million" — the estimated number of those who were murdered by the state.

Murder was not all of it, however. There were what one historian calls "the psychological horrors of mass falsification."[13] Stalin was altering not only political and physical reality, but psychological reality as well. Deceptions of all kinds blunted perception, distorted memory, diluted certainty. Five Year Plans, for example, were declared successes — sometimes after three or four years — regardless of the economic facts of industry and agriculture. Broken-down factories were said to be efficient, dysfunctional organizations were praised as exemplary, functionaries were labeled as heroes of the revolution, creative citizens were condemned as nonconformists, photographs were doctored, history books were rewritten, journalism became a mode of fiction. The people of the Soviet Union, feeling they had no choice, bowed under such crass manipulation of the real. Looking back from a post-1989 vantage, Václav Havel would call it "living within the lie."[14]

Regarding Stalin, his biographer Robert Conquest, also the author of *The Harvest of Sorrow,* the major work on the terror-famine, says, "An ideology which may itself be regarded as paranoid was incarnated in one of the most purely paranoid leaders in modern history."[15] So the theme of paranoia appears yet again. But there is reason to believe that, toward the end of World War II, not even Stalin was firmly anticipating conflict between his nation and the West. Documents released after the opening of Soviet archives in 1991 indicate that, as late as 1944, he did anticipate something like the Cold War, but he expected that the main conflict would be between Great Britain, protecting its empire, and the United States, seeking to extend its economic and political dominance. Sensing many more strains with Churchill than with Roosevelt, Moscow expected a postwar continuation of its own alliance with Washington.[16]

Conducting an American review of the archival material, Melvyn Leffler has shown that the Soviets did not consciously set out to make satellites of Eastern European nations, to make alliances with Communists in China, or to support a Communist war in Korea.[17] A post-Soviet Eastern assessment, also drawing on opened Moscow archives, equally contradicts the prevailing early assumption of Western historians: "Nowhere beyond what Moscow considered the Soviet borders did its policies foresee the establishment of Communist regimes."[18] The Red Army, after the war, rapidly demobilized, dropping from more than eleven million troops in 1945 to less than three million in 1947. Moscow did not begin as the rapacious bear Americans imagined.[19]

Instead of feeling paranoid late in the war, Stalin had reason to feel more confident than ever. True, Russia had suffered millions of casualties, but its armies were on the march.[20] The Red Army's taking of Berlin and its anticipated conquest of Manchuria established the superiority of Soviet military might as never before. But in August 1945, Stalin's "sense of invulnerability" was shockingly and abruptly shattered. This was yet another way in which Hiroshima changed everything. "Then plump," as a British diplomat put it, "came the atomic bomb."[21]

*   *   *

Here is how W. Averell Harriman, writing from Moscow in November 1945, assessed the shift. He was trying to explain to Washington why the Soviets, with their moves that autumn in Bulgaria, Romania, Turkey, Iran, and Manchuria, had embarked on a "unilateral expansionist policy." Harriman wrote: "With victory came confidence in the power of the Red Army and in their control at home, giving them for the first time a sense of security. Suddenly the bomb appeared. This must have revived their old feeling of insecurity . . . As a result, it would seem that they have returned to their tactics of obtaining their objectives through aggressiveness and intrigue."

Viewing Russia through a lens like Kennan's, Harriman saw a resurgence of paranoia, only now it was in relation not to Europe but to the United States, which, as if out of the blue, posed a grave threat to the Red Army and the motherland. This is not to argue that Soviet expansionism was sparked only by America's use of the atomic bomb — the Red Army was in Poland before the bomb — but rather that the insecurity that led Moscow to seek protective zones to the west was significantly exacerbated by the recognition of what a hostile America could do. Moscow was afraid again, channeling its insecurity into expansive belligerence, a reaction Harriman called "the psychological effect of the atomic bomb on the behavior of Soviet leaders."[22]

Truman had mentioned the bomb to Stalin at Potsdam, but obliquely. Hiroshima was something else. The light of that fireball made two things irrevocably apparent to the Soviet leader: first, that the United States possessed a weapon of unprecedented destructive power and the means to deliver it, not only against the Red Army in Europe but, from European bases, into the Russian heartland; and second, that the United States would not hesitate to use it. Nagasaki only confirmed the perception. It did not take a paranoid personality, or nation, to be alarmed at this development.

Soviet scientists had begun the effort to build an atomic bomb on February 11, 1943 — at almost the same time the Manhattan Project began in earnest, with Leslie Groves's appointment of J. Robert Oppenheimer to head up Los Alamos. As the historian David Holloway and others point out, the Soviets would successfully piggyback on the secrets of the American bomb project, especially through the Los Alamos spy Klaus Fuchs, but their atomic science was actually well advanced before the war, and at least some Russian scientists discounted what they learned of the Americans' methods.[23] The industrial aspect of constructing a bomb would prove a daunting obstacle while the war raged on the eastern front.

Stalin, like Roosevelt, was motivated by the dread of Hitler's obtaining the bomb first. As the war went on, Soviet intelligence concluded that the German "uranium project" was not making headway, and Stalin stopped allocating increasingly scarce resources to his own nuclear program.[24] But on

August 7, 1945, less than twenty-four hours after Hiroshima, Stalin put his fellow Georgian Lavrenti Beria in charge of an urgently renewed atomic bomb project.

Beria was the head of the NKVD, the secret police. During the purges of the 1930s, he had ordered countless executions and carried out many himself. In 1940, Beria was the force behind Stalin's notorious execution of twenty-five thousand Polish prisoners. As the most ruthless member of the regime, Beria had perfected the use of murder as a method of efficient administration, and it is a measure of Stalin's interest in acquiring the bomb that he put this killer-manager in charge.

Before Beria's assembled scientists, chief of whom was the renowned Russian physicist Igor Kurchatov, Stalin said that August, "A single demand of you, Comrades. Provide us with atomic weapons in the shortest possible time. You know that Hiroshima has shaken the whole world. The equilibrium has been destroyed. Provide the bomb — it will remove a great danger from us."[25] When the scientists succeeded, those in charge were named Heroes of Socialist Labor; their assistants received the Order of Lenin. If they had failed, as Beria's presence made clear from the start, the latter would have been imprisoned; the former would have been shot.[26]

In the year after Hiroshima, as we saw, there was much public discussion from Washington about internationalizing the atomic bomb. We saw how the American impulse to intentionally burden the proposals doomed their chances for success. It wasn't only that American schemes, culminating in the Baruch Plan, were ambiguous and predicated on patently unacceptable demands on the Soviet Union, but that, in Stalin's view, whether he would have welcomed them or not, the proposals themselves were insincere, mere attempts to deter him from going forward with his own atomic project.

We will never know what success a different approach from Washington would have yielded, but as it was, Stalin found ample reason for skepticism.[27] On November 5, 1945, for example, while Dean Acheson and David Lilienthal were still publicly discussing some version of Stimson's idea of sharing the bomb, Stalin heard from two of his British spies, Donald Maclean and Kim Philby, that London had firm assurances from Washington that the United States was going to protect its atomic monopoly indefinitely.[28] Acheson and Lilienthal were talking of taking up the problem of nuclear controls directly with Moscow, as Stimson had proposed. However, Stalin knew, also in November, that Truman had told the British prime minister that the issue would be put before the United Nations.[29] There would be no one-on-one diplomacy with Moscow on the matter. Stalin, that is, had secret intelligence that the first U.S. initiatives toward cooperation were duplicitous.

Stalin took the American talk of internationalization no more seriously than he took the Soviet propaganda line, put forth at the United Nations by Andrei Gromyko beginning in 1946, in favor of an outright ban of the bomb. The Soviets would repeatedly call for total nuclear disarmament over the years, always as a way of scoring points in the propaganda war. But however much Stalin found reason to dismiss as a lie the expressed American wish to avoid "an arms race of a rather desperate character," the maneuvering that made him suspicious was not the whole story. Beginning with Stimson, there *was* an American wish to find a modus vivendi with Moscow, but it was always the wish of a marginal minority in the U.S. government. The dream of internationalization would in all likelihood have come to nothing no matter what Stalin did.

Indeed, Stalin knew that Washington was already in a debate with itself over the lengths it would go to protect its atomic monopoly. In particular, he knew that some, like General Groves, openly advocated preemptive attacks on any discovered Soviet atomic research facilities.[30] Nor was Stalin unaffected by the alarmist, sometimes hysterical rhetoric coming from America. Forrestal's paranoia, Kennan's grim warnings, Symington's wild exaggeration of the Soviet threat, Truman's doctrine, Washington's war footing — it all, in the contemporaneous words of Walter Lippmann, "furnished the Soviet Union with reasons, with pretexts, for an iron rule behind the iron curtain, and with the ground for believing what Russians are conditioned to believe: that a coalition is being organized to destroy them."[31]

Once Stalin had embarked on the bomb-building project, and then once his scientists had actually achieved a first nuclear chain reaction — an event that took place on Christmas Day, 1946 — he imposed an even more brutal regime of secrecy and control not only on the remote research areas and supersecret industrial sites, but on his whole society. It is impossible to know what Stalin would have done absent the American atomic bomb, but its presence as a factor in Moscow's calculations guaranteed the worst.

As had been true of the Manhattan Project in the United States, building an atomic bomb required an abrupt and complete militarization of the Soviet scientific establishment, a reordering of the mining industry, and the channeling of a huge percentage of industrial capacity toward atomic manufacturing. The far larger wartime American economy had proved able to absorb such dislocation with relative ease, but that would not be true in the still staggered Soviet economy. Whatever chance there might have been for a gradual liberalization of the USSR after its victories in World War II, the necessities of a vast clandestine activity like the atomic bomb project, and the fears associated with it, imagined and real, pushed Stalin in the opposite direction. More purges and an expansion of the gulag — where more than one hundred thousand slave laborers would work in uranium mines — marked this period, followed by a gradually escalating campaign against Jews. As one historian commented, the price of Moscow's ticket into the atomic age was to turn the Soviet Union "into a super-secret 'black box.'"[32]

In August 1949, to Stalin at least, it seemed worth it. He did not announce the successful Soviet atomic explosion for a full month, some weeks after Truman's announcement, precisely because, ever afraid of an American strike against his nuclear facilities, he wanted his scientists to have made more than one or two bombs. His very announcement was intended as an implicit and initial act of deterrence: You wouldn't dare attack us now.

Yet Stalin was not imagining worrisome scenarios. War seemed to be close on both sides of the divide. The previous April, with the signing of the North Atlantic Treaty that established NATO, the threat to Moscow moved from the mainly political realm to the mainly military. In May 1949, Truman ordered the construction of a guided missile test range at Cape Canaveral, Florida, under the authority of the Strategic Air Command. SAC had, in the same period, in relation to the then unfolding crisis over Berlin, already begun to plan its attack of Soviet targets, and Stalin knew it. Three months into the blockade, in September 1948, Truman's National Security Council issued a policy statement (NSC-30), "United States Policy on Atomic Warfare," which ordered SAC to be "ready to utilize promptly and effectively all appropriate means available, including atomic weapons, in the interest of national security . . . [and to] plan accordingly."[33] Authority to order atomic strikes was reserved to the president, but Truman assured the Air Force commanders he would not hesitate to exercise it. His claim to authority here must be understood in the full context of what limited him. Though Truman had established the structure of sole presidential control over the use of nuclear weapons with the Atomic Energy Act of 1946, he actually exercised little control. For example, he was not kept informed of the size of the nuclear stockpile.[34]

As we saw, LeMay, as Air Force commander in Europe when the Berlin crisis began, had moved B-29 Superfortresses to forward bases in England — the first time A-bomb-capable warplanes had crossed the Atlantic, even if they were not bomb-laden yet. And when LeMay himself was transferred to head up the Strategic Air Command, NCS-30's order to "plan accordingly" was being implemented in the clearest way. And if Stalin ever doubted the American bombers' ability to reach all the way to Moscow with the atomic bomb, SAC had, in March 1949, flown a modified B-29 (designated B-50) nonstop around the world, using the revolutionary technique of in-air refueling. As if that weren't enough, SAC's new B-36 could fly nearly ten thousand miles without refueling.[35]

The record suggests that through the various war scares Truman never seriously considered using nuclear weapons against the Soviet Union, but the full weight of such a decision, in the actuality of Pentagon "controls and communications" inherent in that phrase "plan accordingly," may not have been exclusively his. Ensconced at SAC, first at Andrews Air Force Base in Maryland, then in the more secure (in the atomic age) Offutt Air Force Base in Nebraska, Curtis LeMay would act again and again in the coming years as if bomb-use authority were his. And if anyone could make Stalin's paranoia real, it was LeMay. The 1948 air offensive he had planned against Russia was called Broiler.[36]

But now the Soviet bomb made Russia safe. Stalin had perfectly enacted his part in a drama that experts have dubbed "the security dilemma": whatever one party to conflict does to make itself safer inevitably undercuts the perceived safety of the other. The dynamic is mutually self-defeating, yet it can provide a kind of temporary consolation. Thinking of the danger he had escaped, but not the one he had created, Stalin could be pleased. With unfeigned gratitude, he told his scientists after their successful test, "If we had been late with the atomic bomb by a year or a year and a half, then we perhaps would have had it 'tested' on ourselves."[37]

2. No to the Hydrogen Bomb

The cycle of threat-counterthreat was under way. Worst-case readings of enemy intentions, exaggerations of enemy capabilities, the impulse to threaten, joined to the instinct to keep hidden from the adversary the fear that being threatened in return naturally caused — all of these elements of what came to be known as deterrence were put in place as components of the Soviet-U.S. standoff. Deterrence would be credited as the source of a strange stability, but first it generated a lethally dangerous arms race. It did so here, at the very start, with Moscow's dramatic matching of American atomic capability, provoking precisely the response in the United States that Soviet leaders dreaded.[38]

If Stalin felt safe because he now had the bomb, Americans' fears inflated with the trauma of a Pearl Harbor looming once more in the nation's psyche.[39] Within weeks of Truman's announcement of the Soviet atomic test, on October 1, 1949, Mao Zedong, in a red-flag-festooned Tiananmen Square, formally declared the birth of the People's Republic of China. A Sino-Soviet alliance was assumed.

Communists were taking over the world. The Soviet Union lacked an intercontinental bomber force, the means to deliver the bomb, yet serious people in Washington regarded as imminent the prospect of a Soviet assault. That same fall, the chief of staff of the Air Force, General Vandenberg, warned, "There are strong reasons to believe that a sudden surprise attack by Soviet atom bombers would result in not only inflicting unthinkable mortalities on our people and our industry, but also might cripple our strategic air forces, thereby denying us the means to redress the balance through retaliation." Vandenberg's warning became specific: "Almost any number of Soviet bombers could cross our borders and fly to most of the targets in the United States without a shot being fired at them, and without being challenged in any way."[40] These words addressed a theoretical threat that assumed maximal performance of Soviet medium-range bombers being flown on suicide missions, because the range involved in such an attack precluded return. In reality, the situation Vandenberg conjured up for the readers of his memo would not be "operational" for five years, when, in 1954, the Soviet Union finally deployed a fleet of long-range bombers — yet even those would barely reach the U.S. mainland. Nevertheless, it seems clear that Vandenberg spoke from deep conviction, displaying a tendency that was becoming habitual in the national security establishment: to so exaggerate the extremity of the threat posed by the USSR that the one doing so inevitably internalized it, believed it, argued for it, acted on it.

Immediately after the news of the Soviet A-bomb, Truman ordered a crash program to increase the U.S. atomic arsenal, which grew from about fifty to three hundred bombs by June 1950.[41] But the most fateful step taken in response involved another decision by Harry Truman, one with consequences potentially more ominous even than Hiroshima's.[42] In the American mind, it was the bombs used against Japan that ushered in the cosmos-threatening nuclear age, but the difference in destructive potential and ease of manufacture between the A-bomb and what came next cries out to be noted as equally decisive. What came next, of course, was the H-bomb, yet individuals who had thought longest and hardest about the "Super," as it was called, were determined that the United States not develop it.

The atomic bomb is a fission bomb, "fission" meaning to split into parts. The bomb draws its destructive power from a splitting of the nucleus of the atoms of heavy elements (either uranium or plutonium). The division itself is produced by bombarding the nucleus with neutrons that are set moving in a rapid chain reaction. The elements produced by this splitting weigh less than the original atoms, with the difference having been transformed into energy. Explosive energy.

I remember the principle being illustrated on a fifties television show (was it *Watch Mr. Wizard?*) by a stunt involving a veritable carpet of mousetraps — it must have been several hundred — lined up to cover the entire floor of a large enclosed room. The traps were loaded to spring. Delicately balanced on each trap's trigger was a ping-pong ball. When a single ping-pong ball was tossed into the room, landing randomly on a set trap, an instant chain reaction of explosions was triggered. In less time than it took to say "mousetrap," every trap in the room went off, the hundreds of balls releasing one another and colliding in the air, a force of energy I could actually see.

The hydrogen bomb takes an event like that and uses *it* as the trigger. It is a fusion bomb, the word "fusion" meaning to combine. The energy set loose by the splitting of the atom's nucleus, in this case, is used to generate heat and pressure sufficient to combine, rather than split, the nuclei of a light element (hydrogen) with the new nuclei of a heavy element (helium). The crucial role of fission-generated heat, measured in millions of degrees centigrade, as a triggering event is why this device is called thermonuclear. When fusion occurs, a byproduct loss of mass again takes place, as the physical matter of a near-infinite number of nuclei is transformed once more into energy. But the scale is different. A fusion bomb unleashes explosive power far surpassing that of a fission device. A single H-bomb generates destructive energy one hundred to one thousand times the yield of the A-bomb dropped on Hiroshima.

It is as if Mr. Wizard's room were one of thousands of rooms in, say, the Pentagon; and as if all the Pentagon's rooms were themselves full of triggered ping-pong balls, each room set off nearly simultaneously by every other, each room acting in the larger reaction as each ball had acted in the smaller. Not one room blowing up, but the largest building in the world. Instant mass destruction.

Scientists working on the Manhattan Project saw the potential of a fusion bomb early in their work, but under Oppenheimer's direction they concentrated in their urgency on the easier-to-accomplish fission bomb. Even at that early stage, however, some of them were alarmed by the uncontrollable destructive potential of the Super. Although work on the hydrogen bomb was given the lowest priority at Los Alamos, one young physicist continued research on it through 1944 and 1945. His name was Edward Teller. He had emigrated from Hungary only in 1941. His devotion to developing a fusion bomb would prove to be unyielding, and after the successful Soviet A-bomb test in 1949, he began to advocate for an H-bomb project.

But by 1949, the men who had been Teller's superiors at Los Alamos did not concur. Oppenheimer chaired the standing General Advisory Committee of the Atomic Energy Commission, and after the Soviet test the committee took up the question of how the United States should meet the challenge of the Soviet A-bomb. Before October was out, the committee submitted its report to David Lilienthal, the chairman of the AEC. The committee, whose eight members included key veterans of the Manhattan Project — Enrico Fermi, I. I. Rabi, James B. Conant, and Oppenheimer himself — was unanimous in opposing the development of the H-bomb: "There is no limit to the explosive power of the bomb except that imposed by the requirements of delivery . . . The weapon would have an explosive effect some hundreds of times that of present fission bombs . . . It is clear that the use of this weapon would bring about the destruction of innumerable lives; it is not a weapon which can be used exclusively for the destruction of material installations of military or semi-military purposes. Its use therefore carries much further than the atomic bomb itself the policy of exterminating civilian populations."

Additional statements by these scientists — hardly shrinking violets, since they had themselves initiated the nuclear age — are notable for their urgency:

> We believe a super bomb should never be produced. Mankind would be far better off not to have a demonstration of the feasibility of such a weapon, until the present climate of world opinion changes . . . To the argument that the Russians may succeed in developing this weapon, we would reply that our undertaking it will not prove a deterrent to them. Should they use the weapon against us, reprisals by our large stock of atomic bombs would be comparably effective to the use of a super.
>
> In determining not to proceed to develop the super bomb, we see a unique opportunity of providing by example some limitations on the totality of war and thus of limiting the fear and arousing the hopes of mankind.

Rabi and Fermi added an "annex" to this statement, giving a nearly apocalyptic warning. Such a weapon, they said, "enters the range of very great natural catastrophes. By its very nature it cannot be confined to a military objective but becomes a weapon which in practical effect is almost one of genocide." In the American memory, little attention is paid to the difference between the coming of the fusion weapon and the coming of the fission weapon. The insistence by two of the most distinguished physicists of the age that the difference is of ultimate importance has been all but forgotten. Rabi and Fermi's rejection of the H-bomb could not have been firmer. "The fact that no limits exist to the destructiveness of this weapon makes its very existence and the knowledge of its construction a danger to humanity as a whole. It is necessarily an evil thing considered in any light." Rabi and Fermi also argued that any decision about the H-Bomb must be made in the context of an urgent "consideration of broad national policy."[43]

The full five-member Atomic Energy Commission took its own vote and, three to two, seconded Oppenheimer's committee. *No.* Lilienthal himself voted against the H-bomb. When he had worked for the Tennessee Valley Authority, he had harnessed natural energy for society's benefit, and perhaps that experience informed him now. "We keep saying," he wrote, "'We have no other course!' What we should be saying is, 'We are not bright enough to see any other course!'"[44] Lilienthal was determined to find another course. He wrote his own report agreeing with the General Advisory Committee: no H-bomb. He gave both reports to Truman at the end of the first week of November, both negative.

In discussing Truman's 1945 decision to drop the A-bomb, we noted the "toboggan" factor, with the president at the mercy of an irresistible momentum toward use. But the momentum here ran in the opposite direction. To the question of whether Truman could have defied his experts on the A-bomb, an answer is suggested by the fact that he did just that on the H-bomb.

Seeking another recommendation — perhaps the one he wanted — Truman formed a special three-member committee of the National Security Council consisting of Secretary of State Dean Acheson, Secretary of Defense Louis Johnson, and Lilienthal. They were referred to as the Z Committee. At once, advocates of the H-bomb, led by Teller among the scientists and Vandenberg among the Joint Chiefs, began to lobby the committee. Whereas Harvard's president, James Conant, had urged against, MIT's president, Karl T. Compton, argued in favor. The debate was an open secret in Washington. Great figures like General Marshall and Eleanor Roosevelt weighed in — in favor of the new weapon.

Secretary of Defense Johnson required no lobbying. Seeing things more drastically than the Joint Chiefs of Staff, he was resolutely in favor of going ahead with the H-bomb. Indeed, he wanted a crash program to develop it. He and Lilienthal were polar opposites, and during the committee's rare formal deliberations they clashed. The decision was going to fall, in effect, to Acheson.[45]

Recall Acheson's position in 1945. When outgoing Secretary of War Stimson proposed to "enter into an arrangement with the Russians" regarding some kind of "sharing" of the atomic bomb, in order to avoid an arms race "of a rather desperate character," Acheson, then assistant secretary of state to James Byrnes, offered the strongest possible second to Stimson's idea. In a separate memo to Truman, Acheson deplored "the policy of exclusion [of the USSR from atomic weapons] in an atmosphere of suspicion and hostility, thereby exacerbating every present difficulty between us."[46] But by the autumn of 1949, relations between the United States and the Soviet Union were different, and so was Acheson. In the intervening years, he had been among those overestimating the Soviet danger, and by now the exaggerations had assumed the character of his own convictions.

Personal issues affected Acheson's position as much as political ones. Or rather, with Acheson the political had become the personal, for just as he was presiding over the H-bomb deliberations, the Hiss controversy was approaching its climax, throwing a particular shadow over the secretary of state.

Alger Hiss was one of FDR's brilliant young New Deal lawyers. He had accompanied Roosevelt to Yalta, was present for the founding meetings of the United Nations, and served as president of the Carnegie Endowment for International Peace. The year before, when Hiss was accused of having been a Communist by Whittaker Chambers, Acheson had said he "wouldn't turn his back" on the former State Department official. Now Hiss was on trial for perjury, and would soon be found guilty. Acheson was paying for his association with Hiss: he himself was accused of being soft on Communism. Acheson's future depended on a firm refutation of that perception, and the H-bomb debate gave him the opportunity to demonstrate his anti-Soviet toughness.

It was in this context of mounting Red Scare hysteria that Acheson renounced his earlier support of the Stimson proposal, saying he had spoken well of it mainly out of respect for the old statesman. By the fall of 1949, after the Soviet atomic bomb and the Chinese Communist victory, Acheson had convinced himself of the danger of the Communist threat. "The conversion of Dean Acheson to a hard-line stance on dealings with the Soviets," his biographers wrote, "was perhaps the most dramatic and significant of any postwar American statesman."[47] Acheson's conversion, that military force should supersede diplomatic response as the core of U.S. foreign policy, would reverberate across generations.

Acheson had long depended for advice and analysis on George Kennan, the former Forrestal protégé who had done much to sound early alarms about the Soviet danger. Kennan was now the head of State Department policy planning, and his office in Foggy Bottom was a short distance from Acheson's. But as Acheson's ideology had evolved in one direction, Kennan's, as we saw, had gone in the other. However much it was justified by appeals to his own previous writings, Kennan regarded the armed belligerence of American responses to the Soviets as a mistake, and he was particularly apprehensive about what the Super would lead to. He saw the decision on the hydrogen bomb as momentous, likely to end forever any chance of finding a way out of the dead end of nuclear confrontation. Kennan regarded nuclear weapons "as instruments of genocide and suicide,"[48] and he did not hesitate to say so to Acheson. Instead of the crash program to build the Super that the Pentagon wanted, Kennan proposed an immediate, urgent — and finally authentic — effort to come to terms with Moscow on the old question of international controls. "We had done lip service, when we spoke in international forums," Kennan told Acheson, "to a desire to see atomic weapons abolished . . . [but]

it was perfectly clear . . . that we were basing our defense posture on such weapons, and were intending to make first use of them, regardless of whether they had been or might be used against us, in any major military encounter."[49] Kennan here proposed a policy of "no first use," which would become an endlessly and fruitlessly repeated plea over the years. Kennan was among the first to see that the very possibility of an H-bomb made it plain that the time to change all this had come.

Whereas formerly Acheson had depended on Kennan's perspective, now he was dismissive of it. "If that is your view," Acheson told him, "you ought to resign from the Foreign Service and go out and preach your Quaker gospel, but don't do it within the department."[50] Kennan was crushed. And then gone, soon dispatched on a meaningless mission to Latin America. Acheson lost no time in replacing him, and he did so with a man who was eager to tell the secretary of state what he wanted to hear — another former Forrestal protégé, a more faithful one, named Paul H. Nitze.[51]

3. NITZE TO THE RESCUE

Nitze was forty-three years old in 1949. Unlike Kennan, he was a man whose patrician style — fine suits, debonair manner, fabulously wealthy wife[52] — was real, and he knew nothing of Kennan's insecurities. That is probably why the more deeply insecure Forrestal had been so drawn to Nitze from the start. Forrestal had hired him at the investment firm of Dillon, Read in 1929 and then brought him to Washington in 1940. Nitze's far more complacent perspective on the H-bomb was rooted in his idiosyncratic experience with the Strategic Bombing Survey after World War II. We took note of this presidentially established commission earlier, and its postwar mission to evaluate the effects of U.S. bombing. Nitze was a senior administrator of the survey in both Germany and Japan.

In 2003, I met with one of Nitze's colleagues on the survey, the man in charge of determining the bombing's overall economic effects, John Kenneth Galbraith. This distinguished statesman, author, and professor was in his nineties when I spoke with him, and he told me that his work on the survey represented "the most important months of my life." As was true of Nitze, Galbraith's lifelong attitude toward air warfare was shaped by his survey experience, yet his conclusions were the opposite of Nitze's.

Galbraith, too, conducted investigations in Germany and Japan, and it fell to him, along with George Ball, to summarize the survey's conclusions. We noted the key findings earlier: after U.S. bombing began, German production went up, not down; the desperate state of the Japanese economy in the summer of 1945 meant that neither the atom bomb nor the much-dreaded invasion it supposedly replaced were necessary to force surrender on Tokyo. These findings represented a direct rebuttal, in particular, of the arguments being made in favor of the formation of a separate air force, built around the "triumph" of strategic bombing. The reaction to the summary of findings was fierce. "'Us-buzz,' it was called," Galbraith said. His work on the survey, Galbraith told me, involved him in "the bitterest conflict I've ever been associated with."[53]

Nitze was the man who had first hired Galbraith for the Strategic Bombing Survey, but by the end Nitze was chief among those rebutting the Galbraith view. He defended the conventional wisdom, despite the survey's data, that strategic bombing had been decisive in both theaters. They had begun as friends, but the survey put Nitze and Galbraith on opposite sides of a debate, and an approach, that would continue for the rest of their long lives.

I interviewed Galbraith in the living room of his home in Cambridge as darkness fell. It was Halloween, but on Francis Avenue, a street where a number of senior Harvard professors lived, no children were out. I brought up Nitze, who was still alive at the time, living in Maryland. Galbraith nodded, clearly recalling all that had set them apart. "Paul," he said softly. "Paul."

Nitze repudiated Galbraith's debunking of the bomber generals' claims, and he cooperated with a successful Air Force campaign to marginalize the survey results as summarized by Galbraith and Ball. The Air Force issued its own survey, trumpeting the bombing as decisive. I asked Galbraith about a statement he had once made about Nitze — he called Nitze "a Teutonic martinet"[54] — and he repeated the words now, but ruefully rather than combatively. Nitze had brought a spirit of cold rigidity to the work of the survey. Unlike other members of that team, Nitze took a strictly mechanistic approach to the grim task of measuring the effect of Allied strategic bombing. With regard to Hiroshima in particular, he spoke of himself as applying "calipers" to the dead.[55]

Instead of viewing what he found in the devastated Japanese city as evidence of what Bernard Brodie was soon to call "the absolute weapon," Nitze saw the A-bomb as a version of the incendiary devices that had been used elsewhere. His somewhat mathematical grasp of the horror of what had been done to Tokyo and dozens of other Japanese cities — one history credits him as a rare man "who faced the truth of what had already been happening"[56] — apparently dulled his capacity to perceive the threshold that had been crossed when the A-bomb fell from the *Enola Gay*. Not even a visit to the radioactive wasteland around ground zero helped him see the difference. With a proper system of air raid shelters, he concluded, the citizens of Hiroshima and Naga-saki would not have fared too badly — an opinion that inclined Nitze to view the weapon in relative terms (and ever after make him a proponent of bomb shelters).

Galbraith's full description of Nitze had defined him as "a Teutonic martinet happiest in a military hierarchy." To Galbraith, he epitomized the civilian who, not having been tested or credentialed by combat, rushed to outdo the warriors in bellicosity, a phenomenon Galbraith derided as "Penta-gonania."[57] After the war, Nitze served as State Department liaison with the Pentagon, a position he loved. This was at a time when the War Department, having been supreme under Roosevelt for the obvious reason that a war was on, was solidifying its bureaucratic advantage over Foggy Bottom, seeking to make it permanent now that peace had come. Fear of the Soviet Union, as we saw, was the Pentagon's power lever, and Nitze helped to lift it. Even as a State Department functionary, he accepted the open-ended necessity of military dominance.

The Pentagonania syndrome affected individuals, but it also affected in-stitutions. In this period, a new phenomenon appeared in America, with Nitze its avatar. This was the militarization of the State Department — Ache-son's conversion writ large — with diplomacy, as a tool of American influence abroad, downgraded in Foggy Bottom. Civilians were more warlike than sol-diers, State more so than Defense.[58] (Interestingly, no such transformation had happened when General of the Army George Marshall, architect of the World War II victory, had served as secretary of state from 1947 to 1949. His program for Europe was decidedly unmilitary. Nor was Marshall able to re-verse this trend when he served briefly as secretary of defense in 1950 and 1951. The old general's tenure as civilian head of the Pentagon was frustrated, even during Korea, precisely because the energetic center of the nation's hot war against the Communists remained across the river, at the State Department, where it had ignited.)

In 1950, Dean Acheson, the secretary of state, was by far the most power-ful figure in Truman's cabinet, and his influence was felt in nothing so much as the advancing of a narrowly military view of America's place in the world. The irony here is that Acheson, operating from State, promoted the Penta-gon's agenda far more effectively than did Louis Johnson, Marshall's prede-cessor as secretary of defense. In fact, the top Pentagon leadership was weak in this period, at the mercy not only of the striped-pants crowd across the river but also, as was about to become clear in Korea, of freelancing com-manders like Douglas MacArthur. (LeMay was another commander who op-erated with little regard for the authority of his civilian superiors, but unlike

MacArthur, he would not get his comeuppance until he had done his worst. Or best, depending on your view of the mushrooming nuclear arsenal.)

This tradition of the State Department as the center of America's militarist impulses would continue during the tenure of John Foster Dulles in the 1950s and right through to President Kennedy's appointment of Robert McNamara as secretary of defense. (Perhaps mostly through the force of his personality, in contrast to the self-effacing, if hawkish, secretary of state, Dean Rusk, McNamara would finally bring martial dominance back to the Pentagon.) The point here is that Paul Nitze, as Acheson's agent, and as the one who put the new reality of a militarized State Department into words, was the leading edge of this change. He did more to blur the distinctions between State and Defense than anyone. He felt at home in the Building, and he instinctively shared the perceptions of the men in uniform. He became a strident Air Force advocate, a defender of strategic bombing. Most notably, he accepted the Air Force position that the A-bomb was just another explosive device, requiring neither political nor moral scruples, much less oversight, that might hinder the rapid construction — and use — of an Air Force nuclear arsenal. In that way, Nitze was the one who set LeMay loose, as we shall see.

If Nitze did not see the difference between conventional bombs and the atomic bomb, he was unlikely to see the difference between the atomic bomb and the Super. That became even more true when he fell under the influence of Edward Teller, who would be a kind of permanent instructor of Nitze, shaping his perceptions of weapons and their possibilities from the 1940s through the 1980s. Truman's decision to go ahead with the H-bomb had empowered Teller, who oversaw its development, work that was concentrated at Los Alamos.[59] Teller owed a large debt to Nitze, who, as its executive director, had organized the considerations of the three-man committee that finally gave Truman the justification he needed to order the H-bomb, and who then articulated the rationale for a crash program to build an H-bomb arsenal. Teller and Nitze would, in effect, be a tag team for two generations, with the former insisting on the scientific possibility of ever more powerful weapons, and the latter providing the political justification for them.

No real difference between the A-bomb and the Super? Fermi, Rabi, and the other physicists made the point that the difference in destructive potential was almost unlimited. But it was more than that. The H-bomb, while achieving far greater energy yields and explosive power, required less fissionable material, like plutonium, in its manufacture than the A-bomb. This made a rapid buildup far cheaper and easier to accomplish.[60] Against the likes of Nitze and the bomber generals, the difference between fission and fusion weapons would later be eloquently articulated by Winston Churchill: "There is an immense gulf between the atomic and the hydrogen bomb. The atomic bomb, with all its terrors, did not carry us outside the scope of human control or manageable events in thought or action, in peace or war. But [with the H-bomb] the entire foundation of human affairs was revolutionized, and mankind placed in a situation both measureless and laden with doom."[61] The momentum set loose by the American decision to build the Super would, in a few decades, lead to the accumulation of tens of thousands of hydrogen bombs, equivalent to more than a million Hiroshimas. Eventually, the world arsenal of thermonuclear weapons would top 70,000, with the total of all kinds of nuclear weapons surpassing 100,000.[62]

But in 1950, advocates of the H-bomb either could not imagine such a prospect or, if they could, did not view it with alarm. Certainly Nitze didn't. And since Nitze was Acheson's new head of policy planning and the executive director of the three-man committee that had to make the final recommendation on whether to go ahead with the Super, his influence would be decisive. With Acheson and Johnson in agreement, and Nitze in charge of drafting a statement, "the committee's conclusion was forgone."[63] Lilienthal's skepticism about the fusion weapon — "extremely unwise"[64] — was overridden.

In opposing the H-bomb, as the scientists' committee had, Lilienthal argued that before making such a decision the government should embark, as he put it, on a thorough "re-examination of our objectives in peace and war."[65] This was Lilienthal picking up on the recommendation of Fermi and Rabi for a "consideration of broad national policy." As a kind of sop to his old friend, Acheson agreed to that aspect of Lilienthal's position. On January 31, 1950 — ten days after Alger Hiss was found guilty — the three committee members went to the White House to report to Truman. Build the H-bomb, they said. As Acheson began to present their reasoning, Truman cut him off. "We'll go ahead," he said, and dismissed the committee. He had what he wanted. A new toboggan was heading down the hill. The meeting had lasted seven minutes. The next day, a *New York Times* headline read, "Truman Orders Hydrogen Bomb Built."[66] Albert Einstein greeted the news with the tart comment "General annihilation beckons."[67]

Acheson, meanwhile, took steps to initiate the broad review of American military policy in light of the new weapon, as Lilienthal proposed, although Lilienthal's point had been that such a consideration should be undertaken *before* the H-bomb decision, not after it. American hysteria mounted now as the British physicist and Los Alamos veteran Klaus Fuchs was exposed as a Soviet spy. A newly Communist China signed a "friendship treaty" with the Soviet Union. And just now Senator Joseph McCarthy began his crusade against Communists in the State Department, throwing Acheson and his circle more on the defensive than ever. In this climate, what proved to be a momentous reexamination of U.S. strategic thinking would proceed — under the guidance of Paul Nitze.

4. FORRESTAL'S GHOST: NSC-68

The most important aspect to note about Paul Nitze's long career is the way in which it carried forward the spirit of James Forrestal. Nitze loved Forrestal, who gave him his start. At their first meeting, in the offices of Dillon, Read in 1929, Nitze had been smitten. In a letter written at the time, he described Forrestal as "being very keen and forceful. A much finer specimen than anything I have seen for a long time."[68] More than ten years later, in 1940, their friendship had ripened to the point that it was to Nitze that Forrestal turned for advice about whether to take a position as an assistant to President Roosevelt. When he took the job, Forrestal soon sent a summoning telegram to Nitze: "Be in Washington Monday morning." When Nitze obeyed, he moved in with Forrestal, sharing his house on Woodland Road in a tony section of northwest Washington. Thus began Nitze's lifelong career at the seat of government.[69]

Paul Nitze would serve every president, in one capacity or another, from Franklin Roosevelt to Ronald Reagan. It may not be too much to say that he did more to shape American attitudes toward military power, and nuclear weapons in particular, than any other figure. Over four decades, especially with the Committee on the Present Danger, founded in the early fifties and revived in the seventies, he would be unrelenting in raising his anti-Soviet warnings.[70] Nitze delighted in the derivation of his name, tracing it to Nike, the Greek goddess of victory. A spirit of absolute victory, uncompromising and single-minded, defined his personal and political ambition. Nitze would reach the pinnacle of his influence as Ronald Reagan's chief arms control negotiator, a story to which we will return later.

The shadowy thrust of his influence was apparent early. After the war, it had been Nitze who first brought to Forrestal's attention the belligerent speech Stalin delivered in February 1946. Nitze called it "a delayed declaration of war against us." Forrestal agreed and went to work on a declaration of his own.[71] Nitze and Forrestal, with George Kennan at first, formed an alliance to raise concern in Washington about the Soviet threat. One of those whom they had to convince was Dean Acheson, who, as we saw, was inclined to downplay dangers from Moscow, as indicated by his support of Stimson against Forrestal. The early divergence of Acheson and Nitze anticipated the permanent argument between those who emphasized the inherent aggressiveness of Soviet ideology and those who saw Moscow as a traditional nation intent on shoring up a security zone for itself. In 1946, Acheson dismissed Nitze's hawkish warnings: "Paul, you see hobgoblins under the bed. They aren't there. Forget it."[72]

But by 1950, after Forrestal's suicide, after the Soviet A-bomb, after the Red Scare had begun, and after Kennan's marked turn away from the creatures under the bed, Acheson valued Nitze precisely for his faith that the hobgoblins were still there. All of this informed Nitze's first great work of statecraft: the "re-examination of our objectives in peace and war" that produced the Cold War's defining statement of American martial purpose. On April 7, 1950, little more than two months after Truman gave the go-ahead for the H-bomb, the president was presented with a document titled "United States Objectives and Programs for National Security." Referred to ever after as NSC-68, it was Nitze's ponderous reiteration of the alarmist view he had inherited from Forrestal.[73] Only now, the slightly hysterical themes of a man who, owing to his patent emotional distress, had remained on the national margin suddenly found expression in the ordained center of the establishment. What had been the much-debated implications of the Truman Doctrine — amplified by the ad hoc maneuverings, service rivalries, and war scares of the late 1940s — were now schematically spelled out as the coherent consensus on which policy decisions would depend in the future. In fact, Nitze's statement read like nothing so much as the *ex post facto* justification for the most important policy decision of the era, the one Truman had made in ordering the development of the hydrogen bomb. Given that *a priori* decision, the Nitze document had to be extreme, and it was.

NSC-68 saw the world as divided between two mutually hostile systems of belief and politics, with one having the unabashed ambition ("dynamic extension") of replacing ("ultimate elimination") the other. The Manichaean theology of America's postwar political doctrine was here explicit and complete:

> The Kremlin regards the United States as the only major threat to the achievement of its fundamental design. There is a basic conflict between the idea of freedom under a government of laws and the idea of slavery under the grim oligarchy of the Kremlin . . . The idea of freedom, moreover, is peculiarly and intolerably subversive of the idea of slavery. But the opposite is not true. The implacable purpose of the slave state to eliminate the challenge of freedom has placed the two great powers at opposite poles . . . The Soviet Union, unlike previous aspirants to hegemony, is animated by a new fanatic faith, anti-

thetical to our own, and seeks to impose its absolute authority over the rest of the world.[74]

Us against them. A fight to the death. NSC-68 anticipated that, once it could, Moscow would launch a surprise nuclear attack on the United States, but in the meantime its assault would come on many fronts. The Soviet Union and world Communism were identical, and with such antagonistic forces there could be no compromise, no negotiating, nothing but resistance. The very existence of a capitalist economy and of democracy, of everything valued in America, was at risk. And it was at risk not just within national boundaries on the North American continent, but globally.

Every threat to something called freedom, anywhere in the world, was a mortal threat to the United States. "The assault on free institutions is world-wide now, and in the context of the present polarization of world power, a defeat of free institutions anywhere is a defeat everywhere."[75] This assumption that "free institutions" had to be defended at all points on the globe would lead, first, to the American establishment of an effectively imperialist system of dispersed air and naval bases, and, second, to an overextension of American forces. But perhaps more damaging, it would lead to an obliteration of a proper hierarchy of interests, with the United States as committed to the defense of distant oligarchies with unpronounceable names as to nations in the heart of Europe.

The stark bipolarity of NSC-68 would be one stout pillar of America's Cold War perceptions. It was set firmly in the foundation of unconscious assumptions that had long organized the perceptions of the West and that had now come to dominate the mindset of, for example, Nitze's sponsor Dean Acheson. "The threat to Western Europe," he wrote in his memoir, regarding his view in 1950, "seemed to me singularly like that which Islam had posed centuries before, with its combination of ideological zeal and fighting power." Recalling the Crusades and bringing its lessons of strategic alliance forward, Acheson added, "Then it had taken the same combination to meet it: Germanic power in the east and Frankish in Spain. This time it would need the added power and energy of America, for the drama was now played on a world stage."[76]

Western civilization had come into its own by defining itself in opposition to an enemy in the East. The Russian imagination might drift back to those seventeenth-century invasions, but the inner clock of Western Europe, and its American offspring, had been set running in the eleventh century. The anti-Islamic wars of resistance and *reconquista*, dominating politics and culture for nearly three centuries, depended on messianic mysticism, apocalyptic fervor, and millennial dread. The crusading world was divided between good and evil, the faithful and the infidel, with the pope himself consecrating the "War of the Cross." The alliance with God was certain. For the first time in the history of Christendom, violence was there defined as a sacred act, and anyone who took up the fight was promised salvation: "God wills it!" Instead of Urban II and the rallying sermon in Clermont, the American crusade had Paul Nitze and NSC-68.[77]

If the medieval Crusades had monks and priests as their preachers, the American crusade had a young evangelical minister, Billy Graham. Within days of the Truman announcement that the Soviets had exploded an atomic bomb, Graham had pitched a big tent in Los Angeles for a traditional revival, but it drew huge crowds, eventually numbering in the hundreds of thousands. "God is giving us a desperate choice," Graham preached, "a choice of either revival or judgment. There is no alternative . . . The world is divided into two camps. On one side we see Communism . . . [which] has declared war against God, against Christ, against the Bible, and against all religion . . . Unless the Western world has an old-fashioned revival, we cannot last."[78] It is not incidental to this history that Graham, whose mission took off in a climate of transcendent fear, from then on called his revivals "crusades."

Today, on the other side of the threshold of the third millennium, when the defined threat is Islam once again and the ominous relevance of the Crusades has fully shown itself, it seems obvious that the hidden psychological power of such a culture-forming legacy was a key factor in the anxious readiness of Americans to see the Soviet threat in apocalyptic terms. One indication of renewed American millennialism in the late twentieth century was the resuscitation of the rhetoric of evil in politics. "Ronald Reagan, calling the Soviet Union 'the evil empire' in March 1983 was, probably unconsciously, repeating the thought, if not the words, of Paul Nitze more than thirty years earlier." This is Carl Kaysen's assessment. "The apocalyptic tone of the first dozen pages of NSC-68 sounds more like the prose of John Bunyan than [of] . . . Washington bureaucrats."[79]

Nitze was not himself an apocalyptic prophet. A lifelong member of the realist school, he would have acknowledged none of the psychohistorical elements beneath the view he had articulated with such force. But the contrast with the other supreme realist of the time, George Kennan, is striking. At least since repudiating the martial impact of his "X" article, Kennan had, in one historian's summary, "called for selective, discriminatory resistance to Soviet expansion, relying minimally on military threats and hardly at all on explicit or implicit threats to use nuclear weapons." Nitze, in NSC-68, called for "resistance everywhere and anywhere, with military force and the nuclear threat in the forefront."[80] Obviously, one target of this rhetoric was Congress, which would have to fund such an enterprise, but NSC-68 also took firm hold of the mainstream establishment's imagination. It is significant that it did so just as the "total" weapon, the H-bomb, was embraced by that same establishment.

Nitze himself, after the Reagan years, would argue that the view outlined in NSC-68 not only had been vindicated but had "won" the Cold War.[81] (We will return to this debate.) Nitze's statement assumes, of course, that the resolution of that conflict in favor of the United States resulted only from the actions of the "good" in America against the "evil" actions of men like Mikhail Gorbachev (and, presumably, others who supported him in *glasnost, perestroika,* and the rejection of violence as a way of coping with the Soviet collapse). And NSC-68 put in place the foundation of anti-Soviet Totalitarian-school orthodoxy, justifying a permanent garrison economy — namely, that war with this recalcitrant enemy was inevitable.

But NSC-68, in its expectation of the worst from Moscow, went far beyond rhetorical flourish. As soon as Moscow believed it could prevail in an armed conflict with the United States, it would attack. Projecting from current trends, the year 1954, by which time the Soviets could be expected to have at least one hundred atomic bombs, was tagged "the year of maximum danger" for a surprise nuclear assault launched by Moscow.[82] Robert Lovett, soon to be named secretary of defense (and the man from whose house Forrestal had reportedly run, crying "The Russians are coming!"), served as a consultant to the NSC-68 group. Lovett aptly captured the document's spirit. It was time, he told Nitze and his committee, to "start acting exactly as though we were under fire from an invading army. In the war in which we are presently engaged, we should fight with no holds barred. We should find every weak spot in the enemy's armor, both on the periphery and at the center, and hit him with anything that comes to hand. Anything we do short of an all-out effort is inexcusable."[83]

The document's lasting significance lay in its specific military recommendations for meeting the threat, a "policy of calculated and gradual coercion." In this Nitze was the Pentagon's dream advocate, as he pushed for both the rapid buildup of a nuclear arsenal, based on the coming hydrogen bomb, and the expansion of conventional forces. The battle would have to be taken to the enemy, a kind of *reconquista* strategy that would be called "rollback." Indeed, NSC-68 brought new meaning to that fraught word: U.S. policy must be "to check and to roll back the Kremlin's drive for world domination."[84]

For the United States and its allies to achieve this would require a major escalation of defense spending, which assumed in turn a dramatic growth in the level of taxes, as well as a fundamental shift in America's understanding of itself. The nation, in the face of such a historic danger, would have to become a kind of garrison state, and it would have to solidify its political and economic dominance of other nations in the "free bloc" as well. Never mind that the meaning of freedom itself — both at home and among our allies, who would be expected to submit to Washington's notions of international order — would have to be adjusted. Likewise American attitudes toward morality in politics, for NSC-68 sanctioned any and all measures "overt or covert, violent or non-violent, which serve the purposes of frustrating the Kremlin design." This sweeping embrace of an ends-justify-the-means ethic prompted John Lewis Gaddis to define NSC-68 as "the most morally self-conscious state paper of the era — but one that would end up justifying . . . amoral policies."[85]

When Truman read the document that was handed to him on April 7, he was appalled. In its assessment of the Soviet threat and how to deal with it, it gave expression to his own mindset, an insecure belligerence he had manifested again and again, most recently in his H-bomb decision. Even its assertion of ends justifying means felt familiar, given the decisions he'd had to make. But the bald statement of last-ditch military confrontation, and its meaning for the tight budget he was still parsimoniously defending, spelled doom for all that he hoped to achieve as president. Aware that NSC-68's urgent warning would lead to political pressures he could not resist, and perhaps also frightened of what it would spark in Moscow if Stalin learned of it, Truman ordered all copies of the document brought to him at once, and he locked them up in the safe in his office.

Copies were nevertheless leaked to the press (NSC-68 would not be declassified until an order by Henry Kissinger in 1975), and its alarms were widely heard. Truman, desperate to protect his budget, might have continued to oppose NSC-68 and all that it implied, but then, as Dean Acheson put it with such sublime understatement, "Korea saved us."[86] Or as one history of the Strategic Air Command put it, the outbreak of hostilities on the Korean peninsula in June 1950 was "a fortuitous turn of events."[87]

5. KOREA SAVED US

In September 1950, with the Korean War in its third month, Truman ordered NSC-68 "to be taken as a statement of policy."[88] In fact, the two taken together — Communist aggression in East Asia and a paranoid American mindset prepared to both misread it and overblow it — led to the transformation of American society called for in NSC-68. Beyond mere mobilization, what occurred was nothing less than culture-wide militarization, and it was reflected, first, in the collapse of Truman's budget restraints. The defense budget in 1951 was $13.5 billion; in 1953 it was more than $50 billion.[89]

That quadrupling of federal outlays meant, to focus only on the Strategic Air Command, a doubling of the number of active bomber units in the same period. And it meant that a hurried program brought on line the first completely jet-powered bomber, the B-47 Stratojet.[90] Such massive increases in defense spending in so short a time sparked the fifties economic boom that changed America. What few citizens would notice, as their living standards shot skyward, was that the boom assumed, in the memorable phrase of a soon-to-be secretary of defense, a "permanent war economy."[91]

"As a distillation of what became the dominant American attitude toward the Soviet Union for the whole period of the Cold War," Carl Kaysen wrote, "NSC-68 is exemplary."[92] Historians differ on the question of whether NSC-68 caused the policies that were implemented in its name or merely reflected the underlying assumptions that would have led to such policies in any case. But ironically, what followed from NSC-68 in the United States can be seen to have caused a reaction in the Soviet Union that led exactly to the thing to fear. NSC-68 was dead wrong in its central assessment of the Soviet threat in 1950. The dreaded Russian bear was, at that point, relatively toothless,[93] certainly in comparison to what it would become. But once the U.S. buildup began that year, with an overt intention of preparing for war with the Soviet Union, Moscow had no choice but to follow suit. The USSR did indeed embark on a new aggressiveness, with easily detected preparations for war, but these were reactive moves. As Kennan and others had warned,[94] paranoid fears of Soviet capacities and intentions proved to be self-fulfilling prophecies.

In nothing is this more true than in the matter of the hydrogen bomb, which had spawned NSC-68 in the first place. As Truman prepared and issued his order for the production of the Super, the men in the Pentagon, spurred by the vision being articulated by Nitze, pressed for a crash increase in the nuclear arsenal — A-bombs as well as, when ready, H-bombs. And President Truman gave it to them. The stockpile that he had already expanded went from those 300 bombs in 1950 to well over 1,300 by late 1953.[95] Truman approved such massive construction of nuclear reactors and production facilities — plutonium reactors increased from 5 to 13; U-235 gaseous diffusion plants from 2 to 12[96] — that "no president after Truman needed to order more."[97] Within about three years, the megatonnage of America's nuclear arsenal would increase 150-fold, with no limit in sight.[98] A new generation of smaller, more "usable" atomic bombs was quickly developed, making fighter aircraft, such as the F-84, atomic capable. At the same time, U.S. missile technology was progressing, preparing the transformation of nuclear delivery systems. In 1950, for example, the modified V-2 gave way to the Corporal, the first American rocket capable of carrying a nuclear weapon. By Truman's order, the Air Force was given operational responsibility for surface-to-surface missiles, a major extension of LeMay's Strategic Air Command.[99] Vastly more nukes married to a hugely expanded SAC: this was the single most fateful dynamic of this crucial period; it led to an increase in the nuclear stockpile from the 300 weapons early in 1950 to well over 18,000 by 1960.[100]

And yet, having loosed, and now greatly empowered, the nuclear genie, President Truman would again be suddenly faced with the question of whether to actually release it. The theoretical schema outlined in NSC-68 looked very different when the nation was at war; and war came, as it were, out of nowhere. Almost as a matter of course, according to the universal insistence of Truman's commanders, especially of the Air Force, the atomic arsenal had to be readied for use, and it was. Atomic bombs were armed and brought forward to bases in Asia, their legal custody transferred from the Atomic Energy Commission to the Air Force. The president alone remained responsible for actually ordering the use of atomic weapons, but exactly how he was to do this in wartime was unclear. It had been unclear in 1945, and the structures of command, control, communication, and intelligence — the so-called C³I systems — were vaguer now than then. What would happen when American soldiers were at risk and the infamous fog of war rolled in? No one really could say.

The Korean War took America by surprise. It is sometimes called the forgotten war, and its veterans were made to feel invisible. The story, for our purposes, can be briefly summarized. That the first great armed conflict between Communism and capitalism should have happened on that peninsula was unpredicted. Unlike Berlin, which was divided between the Soviets and the Allies in 1945, neither American nor Soviet military leaders attached any strategic importance to Korea. Mutually antagonistic occupation zones were nevertheless soon established, divided by the 38th parallel. Syngman Rhee, an old man of seventy-five (who had studied at Harvard and Princeton), became leader of the South, and Kim Il Sung, a thirty-five-year-old veteran of the Chinese Communist resistance to the Japanese, became leader of the North. Soviet occupation troops withdrew from Korea in 1948. By 1949, all American forces had been withdrawn as well. In a soon-to-be-infamous speech in January 1950 — the "Press Club speech" — Dean Acheson declared that Korea was outside the "defense perimeter" of American security concerns.

On June 25, 1950, perhaps misled by that speech into thinking that the United States would not respond,[101] North Korean troops crossed the 38th parallel, sweeping into Seoul and farther south. That Stalin, heretofore indifferent to North Korea's lust for territory, gave Kim his head in this way is probably related to his alarm at the aggressive American posturing embodied in NSC-68. But Stalin was not the impetus behind the North Korean move. At most, historians now conclude, he was permissive, not instrumental. Stalin "was very skeptical about North Korean aggression, and only consented to it" — Arthur Schlesinger, Jr., summarized the consensus view for me in a conversation we had in the spring of 2003 — "because of an assurance from Kim Il Sung that it would be wrapped up quickly, and the U.S. would not have time to intervene."[102]

At that time, regarding Stalin, Washington's window on the world was clouded by paranoia, and the instant consensus in 1950 was that Kim Il Sung was a puppet whose every move was orchestrated by string pullers in Moscow. But what to do about it? The first reactions to the news from Korea, even within the anti-Soviet consensus, were quite divided. It was not clear that a military response to the aggression was inevitable. Korea wasn't Germany, and it wasn't even clear that the two Koreas weren't one nation embarked on civil war, and civil wars were not America's business.

At that crucial moment, who was to speak for diplomacy? Who was to draw distinctions of international politics and economy, genuine national interest, and alternatives to bloodshed that might have raised the cloud of paranoia? What about America's "national security perimeter" anyway?

In a continuation of the slant that had led to NSC-68 in the first place, Foggy Bottom was truer to its origins as the site of the original War Department than to its current role as seat of the State Department. Among decision makers in Washington, Acheson and his circle, especially Nitze, were the main advocates of war, while Secretary of Defense Louis Johnson and the Joint Chiefs at the Pentagon — including, notably, JCS Chairman Omar Bradley — were opposed to committing American ground troops so far away, and in a conflict of only tangential significance to the United States. State won out over Defense, Acheson won out over Johnson and the Chiefs, and Truman ordered a military response. This instance of the State Department's central involvement in military matters would become the pattern from now on, with the secretary of state spending far more time on questions of defense than of diplomacy.

At the U.N. Security Council, boycotted by the Soviets, the Americans won approval for a "police action" to repulse the aggression and restore the integrity of the border at the 38th parallel. Thousands of American soldiers were dispatched to the peninsula, but all they could do was slow, not stop, the advancing Communist forces.

Douglas MacArthur was the commanding general. In September, just as Truman was formally adopting NSC-68, which was already serving as the ideological underpinning of the American decision to go to war, MacArthur pulled off the greatest tactical triumph of his long career. Indeed, on the beaches of dozens of islands across the Pacific six years earlier, MacArthur's forces had rehearsed for it. Braving thirty-foot tides, a bold amphibious landing of eighty thousand Marines at Inchon, a port city some twenty miles west of Seoul, hundreds of miles behind enemy lines, totally surprised the North Koreans. This began the great American counteroffensive, which succeeded in pushing the Communists back across the 38th parallel.

The U.N. mandate was fulfilled, but MacArthur was not satisfied. He wanted to reunite the entire peninsula, under the American client Syngman Rhee. In October, he ordered his armies to cross the 38th parallel as well, in pursuit of the enemy and its territory. The story is often told as if, in this move beyond what the Security Council had sanctioned, MacArthur were acting without authorization from Washington — MacArthur's "provocation," McGeorge Bundy would call it[103] — but in fact, again in the spirit of NSC-68, the general's moves reflected exactly what the Nitze core of the administration wanted. Indeed, the National Security Council now issued the directive (NSC-81) that explicitly used the term "rollback." George Marshall, who had replaced Johnson as secretary of defense, cabled MacArthur ("eyes only") that he could feel "unhampered . . . north of the 38th parallel."[104] But MacArthur was also instructed not to refer publicly to this directive from Washington. "Rollback" would be secret.

Air Force bombers were brought into the fray, taking out targets all over North Korea. The Air Force commander bragged that his bombers could "flatten" China as well. The bombers flew interdiction missions, hitting bridges and supply routes, for example, not strategic missions. Strategic targets, in this war, were in China, north of the Yalu River, which marked the border with North Korea. In the beginning, China was off-limits to the bombers, but would it remain so? The Strategic Air Command, under Curtis LeMay in Omaha, Nebraska, moved two B-29 groups to Japan, an echo of the provocative basing of the "atomic bomber" in England during the Berlin crisis. Meanwhile, the real atomic weapon capability was based on Guam, a wing of "B-50A's, atomic capable." These planes would regularly rehearse their nuclear bomb runs, dropping iron bombs for practice. In an official Air Force history, SAC records that it could have dropped atomic bombs on preselected targets in Korea and China within sixteen hours of the order.[105]

SAC's assumption had to be that, once an atomic strike was launched against China, war with the Soviet Union would shortly follow. Operation Shakedown was the name of SAC's all-out war plan, and it assumed atomic attacks against Soviet cities, more than a hundred atomic bombs[106] to be dropped in simultaneous waves from bombers flying from bases in Maine, Labrador, the Azores, Guam, and the United Kingdom. Officials at the White House and the Pentagon had little idea of SAC's intentions, what it would do once the bombers were airborne, or how it would do it. Of the SAC war plan at the time of Korea, LeMay told an Air Force historian in 1984, "It was ours. There wasn't anything that came out of Washington."[107] Until the Korean War, LeMay had been required to clear his "Basic War Plan" with the Pentagon and the AEC, but that changed now. "With incredible chutzpah," one military historian notes, "LeMay claimed that submitting the plan for approval would jeopardize its security — that, in short, the Joint Chiefs (meaning the Army and the Navy) were not to be trusted. Not only was neither the President nor his Secretary of Defense kept apprised of operational nuclear plans; even the highest ranking military officials apparently were in the dark."[108]

By late November, MacArthur's offensive was approaching the Yalu River. Whether that near intrusion on Chinese territory was the cause, or whether Mao Zedong had already determined to defend the regime of Kim Il Sung, he ordered his powerful army into the fray. "A phantom, which casts no shadow" is how the military historian S.L.A. Marshall described Mao's force, and certainly MacArthur did not see its pounce coming.[109] On November 24, hundreds of thousands of Chinese soldiers stormed down onto MacArthur's forces. The front was three hundred miles wide. "We face an entirely new war," MacArthur cabled Washington.[110]

But in fact the Americans were not facing it. They were overwhelmed by the onslaught of "Chicoms," and they ran. The panic spread all the way to Washington. The Pentagon rushed to plan for a Dunkirk-like evacuation of the entire U.N. force from Korea. Dean Acheson described what was happening in South Korea as the worst defeat of U.S. forces since the Battle of Bull Run. Nothing like this humiliation had occurred in either World War I or World War II.

6. TRUMAN'S OTHER DECISION

On November 30 at a Washington press conference, with the mortifying rout still under way, Truman said that the Korean conflict, even with the Chinese intervention, was the result of Russian Communist aggression, the source of a new world crisis. Moscow was the enemy. Korea was only Moscow's forward line. The president declared his intention to hold that line, "to halt this aggression in Korea." He promised to take "whatever steps are necessary." Did that include the atomic bomb? a reporter asked. "That includes every weapon we have," Truman answered, and then added, about the bomb, "There has always been active consideration of its use." When a reporter pressed, Truman cut him off, saying, "It's a matter that the military people will have to decide. I'm not a military authority that passes on those things . . . The military commander in the field will have charge of the use of the weapons, as he always has."[111]

There it was. Nitze's view fully vindicated. The atomic bomb just another weapon in the arsenal. The atomic bomb, therefore, under MacArthur's authority, not the president's. That afternoon, headlines screamed that the bomb was being readied for use against the Chinese. A headline in the next day's *Times of India* read, "No No No!"[112] Also on that day, reports came to Washington that half a million Soviet soldiers were mobilizing in Siberia, with Soviet bombers being moved to within range of Korea. But while Truman was laying the blame for the Korean debacle on Moscow, Stalin, as post–Cold War Soviet archives reveal, *did not want* an American defeat in Korea. He was even prepared to accept U.S. dominance of the peninsula — "Let the United States of America be our neighbors in the Far East," one former KGB official quotes him as having said in the fall of 1950 — because he was sure an imminent American defeat would trigger global war. Stalin knew what Truman said at his press conference, and he knew what SAC was preparing to do.

MacArthur wanted to bring the war to China with bombing and blockades. Acheson reports in his memoir that the retreating MacArthur's alarms to Washington included the threat that, unless he could use atomic weapons, he would have to evacuate his force from the peninsula.[113] To MacArthur, the collapse of his army promised the opportunity of a massive expansion of the war. As his biographer notes, to him the idea of a limited war was like limited pregnancy.[114] MacArthur lives in the American memory as the avatar of unthinking — and unauthorized — aggression, but it is important to acknowledge that in his thinking here, he was reflecting only the full spirit of NSC-68, a geopolitical framework that embodied an establishment consensus and that Truman had already approved. The crisis in Korea was merely the occasion for learning what NSC-68 looked like in reality. And acting in that spirit had clearly brought Truman and the world to the brink. While he brandished the atomic bomb at his November 30 press conference, he made an additional remark to reporters, putting into words the full horror of what he had just threatened: "It is a terrible weapon and it should not be used on innocent men, women, and children who have nothing whatever to do with this military aggression. That happens when it is used."[115]

This warning seems to have represented Truman's second thought even as he was having it. Truman was the only man who had ever ordered the use of the atomic bomb, and beneath the veneer of his permanent insistence on its necessity against Japan, he remained haunted by what he had done. That may be conjecture, but it seems reasonable in the light of his actions now, when the cold shadow of the bomb fell on him again. His press secretary soon issued a "clarifying" statement, that the atomic bomb remained under the president's sole authority and that no decision to use it had been made. Whatever his commanders thought, and whatever the belligerent advisers in Acheson's circle were recommending, Truman seems to have come to a decision of his own: no atomic bombs for MacArthur, no matter what he threatened. Truman allowed the grave crisis of America's worst military defeat to pass without recourse to the use of a weapon that would surely have moved the war into a whole new realm. What would a President Dewey[116] have done? That is, what would a president for whom the consequences of such a decision were only abstract have done?

Such consequences were not abstract to Truman. No wider war, he decided. No atomic war. Over the following weeks, he repeatedly defied the urging of some of his closest advisers, who wanted an atomic bomb to be used immediately against China. The division among senior State and Defense officials was not over whether a wider war was inevitable or desirable, but over when it should be fought — and against whom. Some thought the United States was ill prepared for a global war and should wait for the NSC-68 buildup to take effect. Others thought the sooner the better — and against Russia, not China.[117]

Stuart Symington, who as secretary of the Air Force had done so much to empower LeMay and SAC (and my father), was now the chairman of the National Security Resources Board, an adjunct to the National Security Council. Symington was Truman's Missouri friend, and it was he who, in early January 1951, presented NSC-100, which recommended sending LeMay's atomic bombers against China, with a simultaneous warning to the Soviet Union that it would be attacked, too, for any "aggression."[118] Again Truman said no. Later, in writing of this period, he described what prompted his refusal to seriously consider what some of his senior military advisers were urging on him: "I could not bring myself to order the slaughter of 25,000,000 noncombatants . . . I just could not make the order for a Third World War."[119]

What Truman was manifesting here, of course, was the White House version of the transformation that had taken place in the State Department. From then on, the president of the United States would be occupied more with military matters than with anything else. Indeed, White House organization would soon reflect that, with a National Security Council becoming the primary mode of executive action. Beginning with Korea and running right up to the administration of George W. Bush, "real decision making al-

ways involved aides who managed the NSC for the president."[120] The ethos of
the Pentagon had overtaken the State Department, and now it overtook the
White House. It was not that the Pentagon would be forever in the loop, but
rather that the Pentagon would *be* the loop. The Pentagon's business would
be the only business that would get the government's full attention.

In the event, the American forces in Korea were able to dig in and hold on to
positions on the peninsula. No Dunkirk. No MacArthur even. Truman fired
him on April 11, 1951. One key, if little noted, factor in MacArthur's arrogant
defiance of Truman is the fact that those in his chain of command, certainly
including George Marshall, were unable to exert proper authority over him
because the energetic center of the war was never in the Pentagon. It was in
the State Department, with Acheson wielding the influence. This seems to
contradict the point just made about Pentagon influence, but it actually extends it. While the ethos of State and Defense was the same — a warrior ethos
— the bureaucracies remained separate. Acheson simply had no way of extending *his* authority to MacArthur, and MacArthur took advantage of that
until Truman stopped him. It should also be noted, as Ernest May points out,
that while the removal of MacArthur firmed up the principle of civilian control over the military, those most appalled by MacArthur's behavior were military leaders (Marshall, Bradley, Eisenhower), and in firing MacArthur, Truman, with the public and Congress that supported him, "followed one set of
military leaders instead of another."[121]

Right-wing America, rallying to MacArthur, saw his removal as an abandonment of "rollback."[122] But in fact the main source of friction between Truman and the supremely arrogant MacArthur was Truman's refusal to order
an all-out atomic war. Instead, Truman settled for a demoralizing and bloody
stalemate. GIs and Marines would claw their way back up to the 38th parallel,
grateful to have gotten that far. Rather than victory, the American forces in
Korea found themselves in a replay of the trenches of Flanders, a no-win impasse that went on for the rest of Truman's term and that continues, vesti-
gially, to this day.[123]

Right The point is that, just as Truman changed the course of history by deciding to use the atomic bomb in 1945, he changed the course of history again by
deciding not to use it in 1950 — perhaps "the most important point," in one
historian's assessment, "at which the action of an individual changed the
course of nuclear history."[124] Truman's decision here put in place three pillars
on which the rest of U.S. policy in the Cold War stood. Two of those pillars
still thankfully undergird the fragile world. First, in a century defined by total
war, Truman established the precedent of limited war.[125] Some things are not
worth the cost of victory. Second, Truman, having first loosed the atomic

bomb, now established a taboo against its use ever again. American leaders, including Truman himself later in the war, might threaten nuclear use, but they would again and again stop short of ordering it. If Truman had allowed his commanders any use of atomic weapons whatsoever, even if as an act of successful prevention, even if somehow restricted to the battlefield, or even if, by some fluke, concentrated primarily on military targets — there is no doubt that subsequent presidents and other leaders of nuclear powers would have followed suit. It was the desperate character of the unprecedented American defeat on the battlefields of Korea in November 1950 that made this real. If the United States, under the president who had ordered the atomic bombing of Hiroshima, would not use the bomb in response to *that,* then the bomb — Nitze notwithstanding — would never again be considered just another weapon in the nation's arsenal. Or any nation's. The return of the absolute weapon.

The third pillar of U.S. policy put in place here stood until the administration of George W. Bush. In vetoing an expansion of the Korean conflict into a preemption of the Soviet Union, Truman rejected the then much-touted idea of preventive war — the idea that, as one of his advisers put it, America should become an "aggressor for peace."[126] In particular, Truman rejected a recommendation from Air Force Chief of Staff Hoyt Vandenberg, offered in December 1950, for an all-out atomic attack — Operation Shakedown after all — against the Soviet Union. "He did not say so specifically," noted a State Department official of Vandenberg's proposal, "but the implication was that it would be better for us to precipitate hostilities at an early date in order to prevent further USSR atomic build-up."[127]

Given that no such course was ever followed, it seems impossible after the fact to credit such proposals with anything like rationality, much less prudence. MacArthur is remembered as a kind of loose cannon, and so, for that matter, is LeMay. But Vandenberg, Symington, and others (including such intellectuals as Bertrand Russell, William L. Laurence, and John von Neumann[128]) who promoted the idea of a preemptive nuclear attack were taken to be exemplars of moderation at the time. Even Oppenheimer, who had valiantly opposed the buildup of the arsenal he had created, embraced the logic of nuclear attack as a way of heading off a full-blown nuclear war.[129] Early in the atomic age, a preventive war was taken to be preferable to an arms race that would inevitably culminate in war. Better to have the war while the United States still had superiority of force.

And the notion of preventive war is back in the center of American geopolitical orthodoxy. That the United States in the twenty-first century has embraced prevention as a defining strategy, based on the same rationale offered by Vandenberg, only suggests how easily it could have done so in 1950, before it was vulnerable to Soviet retaliation. George W. Bush has not used nuclear weapons for prevention, but the principle is identical. What made Truman's threefold decision against total war, against atomic war, and against preventive war so historic is the fact that he made it just as the destructive power of nuclear arsenals was about to escalate toward infinity with the coming of the thermonuclear bomb. Truman's decision, that is, took actual use of the weapon off the table at the point when it became powerful enough to destroy the table and the house and the neighborhood and the world.

7. THE TEST

If only that were the last momentous decision by Truman on which this story turns, but there was one more, and it went the other way. Work on the hydrogen bomb, under the direction of Edward Teller, proceeded quickly at Los Alamos. As Truman's term drew to a close in 1952, the scientists were confident that they had indeed succeeded in creating the fusion device, the Super. The time came to test it.

At that point, the leading nuclear physicists once again tried to slow, if not head off, the upward-spiraling arms race. They believed that preventive war was not the only alternative to a disastrous, open-ended nuclear competition. Agreement was an alternative, too. What the scientists proposed was an indefinite postponement of the H-bomb test. The Soviet Union was assumed to be moving toward its own thermonuclear weapon; in fact, the young Russian physicist Andrei Sakharov had been leading a team at work on a Soviet Super since 1949.[130] The American physicists were proposing that the test be postponed, that the Soviets be informed of the postponement, and that they be invited to do likewise — both states to refrain from moving toward the final stages of fusion development. Such a mutual restriction on testing would be easy to monitor, since radioactive fallout from any thermonuclear test would be readily detected. If one side tested, the other could follow suit. This proposal anticipated what would be agreed to in the 1963 Partial Test Ban Treaty, but if it could be enacted now, the threshold into infinitely greater levels of destruction would not be crossed. Because the United States achieved the capacity to test first — the Soviets would not be ready until August 1953 — the initiative belonged to Washington.[131]

In the summer of 1952, before the election of Dwight Eisenhower, Vannevar Bush approached Secretary of State Acheson. Bush, the former chairman of the wartime New Weapons Committee, which oversaw the Manhattan Project, was then president of the Carnegie Institution in Washington.

In testimony before the Atomic Energy Commission, when it investigated "the matter of J. Robert Oppenheimer" in 1954, Bush recounted what he had done two years earlier, during his visit to Foggy Bottom. He said that, speaking on behalf of the most distinguished atomic scientists, he proposed the test postponement to Acheson. "I felt strongly that the test ended the possibility of the only type of agreement that I thought was possible with Russia at the time, namely an agreement to make no more tests. For that kind of agreement would have been self-policing in the sense that if it was violated, the violation would be immediately known. I still think we made a grave error in conducting that test at that time . . . I think history will show that was a turning point."[132]

Philip Morrison, one of Bush's colleagues on the Manhattan Project, told me that Bush's prestige in both science and government at that time was such that a proposal from him had to be taken seriously. He was in effect picking up where Fermi and Rabi had left off two years before with their attempt to head off what they had called the genocide weapon. But the earlier proposal for a complete rejection of H-bomb development was far less likely to have been reciprocated on the Soviet side than Bush's. Hans Bethe, another Manhattan Project veteran and a Nobel laureate, wrote in 1990 that the Bush proposal could well have been matched in Moscow, especially in light of Stalin's death, which had occurred just then. Bush's proposal, Bethe wrote, "might have saved the world from a thousand-fold escalation of the explosive power of the atomic bomb."[133]

"Bush almost did it," Morrison told me. In addition to his meeting with Acheson, Bush made the proposal in writing to Truman, who put it before his secretary of defense, Robert Lovett (Forrestal's intimate friend). Acheson rebuffed Bush. So did Lovett. And then so did Truman. As he had in ordering the development of the H-bomb, Truman disregarded the scientists' advice on testing. "A missed opportunity, right there," Morrison said, "absolutely."[134]

Truman's decision to use the A-bomb in 1945 and his decision to go forward with the H-bomb in 1950 reflected the ever-present military and bureaucratic appetites, as well as pressures born of technological opportunity, and so would the choice he made here. Yet this decision was different. By now Truman knew both what nuclear weapons could really do and that presidents would forever be surrounded by men who wanted to use them. But if he went ahead with the H-bomb test, it wasn't out of callowness. Once again, univocally dark perceptions of Kremlin recalcitrance dominated thinking. Acheson and Truman dismissed the possibility that any humane gesture from the American side would be matched by the Soviets. Nevertheless, post–Cold War history suggests that Americans might have appealed to principled parties in Stalin's establishment. Indeed, the unfolding of Andrei Sakharov's career suggests that even then the American physicists were not alone in their concern.

Sakharov believed in the deterrence value of his project, but he was still haunted by the disastrous potential of the weapon he had created. At a banquet celebrating the first successful test of the Soviet H-bomb, Sakharov proposed a toast: "May all our devices explode as successfully as today's, but always over test sites and never over cities." He later recalled that his stunned colleagues reacted "as if I had said something indecent."[135] Sakharov became an objector to his own project's consequences as early as the mid-1950s. In 1961, he boldly challenged Premier Nikita Khrushchev to his face on the resumption of nuclear testing, yet he survived as Russia's leading nuclear physicist for some years more. And the fact that the outspoken Sakharov was repeatedly rescued from imprisonment by powerful patrons in the Kremlin suggests that government figures matched the scientists in their concern. Perhaps the most revealing fact in this connection is that, in Sakharov, the Soviet H-bomb project was presided over by a man who would consistently criticize his own government's belligerence (condemning the Soviet invasion of Afghanistan, for example) and then win the Nobel Peace Prize, while his counterpart in the United States, Edward Teller, would always be a warmonger, an advocate of nuclear expansion and escalation until the day he died.[136] The American physicist with moral qualms, J. Robert Oppenheimer, was disgraced for those qualms, becoming, in one estimate, "an American Dreyfus";[137] Sakharov's beliefs would eventually make him a national hero. He was an apostle of détente and played an important role, on the Soviet side, in the acceptance of the Partial Test Ban Treaty. In other words, the Soviets were not the monolithic devils U.S. policymakers took them for.

Whatever his personal assessment of the scientists' proposal for a thermonuclear test postponement, Truman was by then a lame-duck president. He could have left the fateful decision to his successor. Instead, in one of his last acts as president, he ordered the world's first thermonuclear device tested. The explosion of the 10.4-megaton "Mike," as it was dubbed, occurred on October 31, 1952, at the Eniwetok atoll in the Pacific, four days before the presidential election. As scientists predicted, the explosion was five hundred times more destructive than the Hiroshima bomb. Not only the target structure disappeared; so did the entire island of Elugelab on which it stood, replaced by a vast underwater crater. The thermonuclear age had begun.

Vannevar Bush, in his testimony before the AEC two years later, said, "I still think that we made a grave error in conducting that test at that time, and not attempting to make that type of simple agreement with Russia. I think history will show it was a turning point that when we entered into the grim world that we are entering right now, that those who pushed that thing

through to a conclusion without making that effort have a great deal to answer for."[138]

8. DUCK AND COVER

The day of Eisenhower's inauguration was clear and cold. I was there. It was
two days before my tenth birthday. My brother Joe and I had taken the bus
from Alexandria, Virginia, to stand on Pennsylvania Avenue and watch the
parade. I remember the oil-drum fires, the souvenir stands, the hotdog ven-
dors with steam coming from their mouths.

And I remember feeling confused. Mom and Dad were Democrats, pretty
much in the way they were Catholics. More than that, they were Chicagoans,
from the same state as Adlai Stevenson, whom Eisenhower had defeated. My
family's affiliation with the Democratic Party was more than ideological, ethnic, or religious. Dad's father had worked as a janitor in a Democratic ward
house on the South Side, a job that required him to deliver a dozen votes in
every election — votes the party machine would carefully count. At the beginning of their marriage, two of those votes had been Joe and Mary Carroll's.
They hadn't been able to move out of the neighborhood until they'd replaced
themselves on the ward lists with reliable votes that could be credited to
Grampa.

Carrying on the South Side spirit, Mom had worked for Stevenson's campaign in northern Virginia. When she got the monsignor of our parish to pay
the poll tax for the nuns, Mom did not hesitate to tell the sisters whom to vote
for. She was appalled when, coming from the voting booth, one nun after another proudly announced having voted for Ike. Stevenson, after all, had been
divorced. My parents' devotion to him, despite the Church's disapproval, was
an early lesson in how to be a Catholic without complete surrender. All of this
meant, however, that we were a disappointed family when, for the first time in
twenty years, a Republican was taking office as president.

And yet Eisenhower was everybody's hero. Certainly he was mine. Out of
family loyalty I couldn't bring myself to wear an "I Like Ike" button, but I
found a vendor who sold me an acceptable alternative: "I Like Everybody." It
was around then that I was treating the Pentagon as my personal Saturday
playland, and I was acutely conscious of my father's status as a general officer.
I sensed that Ike's status as the greatest general of all (five stars to Dad's
two) had blurred the political loyalties of my staunchly Democratic family.
Looking back on it now, knowing more of the air of barely concealed panic
that defined the culture of government, I wouldn't be surprised to learn that
my father had actually voted for Ike.[139] After all, at the Office of Special Inves-

tigations General Carroll's overriding preoccupations were with Soviet espionage, sabotage, and infiltration. There was the enemy abroad and the enemy at home, unrelenting threats both, and as a boy I knew it. Dad was at the center of the effort to counter what was perceived as an all-pervasive danger of conspiracy and betrayal directed from the selfsame Moscow that, through its Asian proxy, had emasculated the American military in Korea, forcing it first into stalemate and then into truce talks that were as pointless as they were unending. Ike promised to halt all this: he was going to Korea. America didn't need a politician, it needed a commander in chief. How could a general, even an unrated one like Dad, not vote for him? My father would never have told my mother, of course.

As for me, Ike had made a more compelling impression than Stevenson had. Because the early days of television made steady use of wartime film footage — *Victory at Sea,* and its Richard Rodgers theme song "Beneath the Southern Cross" (also known as "No Other Love") — the triumphs of D-Day were vivid, and so was Eisenhower's role. Just as I was becoming fully conscious of the larger world, the Korean War had seized the popular culture, and I understand now that it had done so because of the deep frustration it had left Americans feeling. War movies were everywhere, and the related motif of cowboys and Indians ("redskins") was a thinly veiled transference. The Commie Reds were demonized in comic books, and that my brothers and I were not allowed to read them only made us more attuned. We became expert at slow browsing at newsstands.

The Red Chinese, we knew, were beasts. They did not care for the lives of their own children; they imprisoned priests, as Bishop Fulton J. Sheen warned on Tuesday nights, and "violated" nuns; they brainwashed what POWs they hadn't murdered; they attacked in hordes, with more soldiers than GIs had bullets; they wanted California. So why shouldn't an American boy have been deliciously frightened? Slant-eyed, bucktoothed, an all-purpose caricature that had begun with "Japs" — the Chicoms were the demons my brothers and I conjured in our endless games of war. Outfitted with the Army-surplus gear that was then ubiquitous — olive-drab knapsacks, cartridge belts, helmet liners, canteens, bayonet sheaths (but not the blades), canvas leggings — we peered up out of our foxholes (tree wells) primed for sneak attacks, tumbled down hills into machine-gun nests (bushes), crawled on our bellies and elbows across minefields (vacant lots), tossed hand grenades (crab apples) into bunkers (sewer openings). I loved playing war. If anything, I felt slightly disloyal to my father for being a leatherneck instead of a bomber pilot.

The thought of bomber pilots conjured the other peril — what I tried not to think about, but which haunted me. What I most dreaded as a child was the close danger of the atomic bomb. In my forays in the Pentagon, I had discovered its inner courtyard and recognized it as ground zero. An upbeat *Movietone News* report on a mock A-bomb raid on Washington intended to be reassuring by showing that the president would be safe in a White House bomb shelter, but nobody said what would happen to the rest of us.

The bomb, far from unthinkable, was everywhere in my childhood world.[140] In a way that can only seem perverse now, the bomb, and nuclear science generally, had been embraced as a Madison Avenue marketing tool, as an emblem of progress, entrepreneurship, hope. The gleaming chrome bumpers of automobiles were shaped like warheads. Westinghouse sold household appliances by bragging about its contracts to build atomic reactors. Breakfast cereals promised to start the day off with "atomic energy." Sending off Kix box tops, Joe and I, as noted earlier, waited for our "genuine" atomic bomb rings to arrive in the mail. The bullet-shaped crown of the ring swiveled back to reveal a secret chamber in which, when held close to the eye, the "actual splitting of the atom" could be seen. No one explained whether that mystery sparkle — a bit of mica? — was radioactive, but when Joe then needed glasses, I wondered.

The x-ray machines at the Red Goose shoe stores *were* radioactive, but we didn't know it. When, using "atomic science," we peered into the dark to compare the bone structure of our feet with the fit of our shoes, we were poisoning ourselves. *Popular Mechanics* published the blueprints for a bomb shelter, and I wanted one. The *Saturday Evening Post* ran an article, "How You Can Survive an A-Bomb Blast," that served only to make clear (". . . prone position in a ditch or gutter . . .") that you couldn't.[141] Real-estate ads for houses and lots outside cities offered "good bomb immunity." RCA introduced a flashlight-size "atomic battery," capable of keeping electrical devices going for twenty years. At the local post office, citizens could pick up a pamphlet with instructions on mail delivery following a nuclear attack. One of the forbidden comic books of the day was called *Atomic Warfare,* which I fingered at the newsstand as if it were pornography.

The men in the Pentagon suffered from one kind of delusion. We, the people, suffered from another, but an inch below the surface of it all was a feeling of pure dread, rooted in nothing less than political despair. "Better dead than Red" came into its own as a slogan of heroic resistance to Communism, but what it really represented was an inhuman emptying out of hope and moral values. In the new age, that preference for martyrdom meant an embrace of not only individual death but civilizational, even global, death. On country roads, young American males began playing the game of chicken, gunning their hot rods at each other at full throttle — a replication of what was passing for foreign policy. Death was everywhere in the driver's seat. In the middle of the night, when I would wake up cold with what I now know were the first intimations of mortality — my parents are going to die? — it was the mushroom cloud with which I associated the feeling.

On January 12, 1951 — the day after NSC-100 was presented to Truman by Stuart Symington, recommending a preemptive nuclear attack against China and, perhaps, the Soviet Union — the president established the Federal Civil Defense Administration. The agency was to sound the clarion call to the population at large, preparing it for the catastrophe that seemed increasingly likely.[142] The dangers of nuclear war and, especially, ways of surviving it were to be the subjects of a massive educational effort. Industrial dispersal, bomb shelters, television shows, radio alerts ("This is a test"), movies, pamphlets, and posters — all of the FCDA's activities paled in comparison with one nationwide elementary school program that stamped the nightmares of a generation: Duck and Cover!

At St. Mary's School in Alexandria that spring I was in third grade. My teacher was the unforgettable Sister Miriam Teresa. Behind her back we called her M.T., as in "empty," but she was anything but. A stern woman, she was not to be ignored or disobeyed. One afternoon, she lowered the blinds of the large classroom windows and dimmed the overhead lights to show us a movie. Whir of the projector, motes dancing in its gray cone. What leapt onto the screen was a cartoon, but it was not funny. An animated character named Bert the Turtle told us what to do. Our desks would be our turtle shells, and by pulling in our heads, like Bert's, we would be all right. *Duck and Cover!*

At the end of the cartoon, still in the shadows, the nun drilled us, reciting the mantra: Under your desks, head down to your knees, arms over your ears, eyes closed tight. *There will be a blinding light, don't look!* The flash was made to seem the scary part. We knew from the cartoon that there would be flying glass, fire, heat, a slow-motion collapse of walls and ceilings, and then a giant mushroom cloud. But all of that would pale beside the light, brighter than a thousand suns. If we opened our eyes and peered toward the window, we would instantly go blind. If people living in Baltimore looked toward the fireball exploding over Washington, or citizens of Milwaukee toward the fireball over Chicago — all blind.[143] The rules of Duck and Cover were printed on little wallet-size cards, which Sister Miriam Teresa passed out, like communion. And then we waited in the dark, in silence. When some kid giggled, Sister snapped her clicker, once.

We did not know that the drill was coordinated throughout the school. At a certain point a siren went off, one we had never heard before — but we would hear it again and again as the Duck and Cover air-raid drill was repeated several times a month. The sound was frightening, because it was in the world with us and not part of the cartoon. The nun's voice rose above the siren: "Now!" We scrambled under the desks, not clear anymore what was real and what wasn't. The classroom lights were still dimmed. I remember the stunned silence amid those shadows once everyone was settled. No giggles.

Then a shock of light burst into the room. It was only the nun rolling up the window shades, not the atomic bomb. I heard the swish of the rosary beads hanging from her belt. I turned my head toward the sound. From my place under my desk, I could see only her stout-heeled black shoes striding as she moved along the row of windows. And then it hit me. Without meaning to, I had broken the rule. My eyes were open. The bright light of the afternoon stung, and for a minute there, yes, I *was* blind.

This was what Eisenhower would save me from. Even as a child, I understood why America had elected him. On inauguration day, I shinnied partway up one of Pennsylvania Avenue's light poles. I saw the marching bands, the mounted police, plumes of steam rising out of the horses' nostrils. I saw squads of soldiers in drill formation and girls waving from a decorated flatbed truck. Then the president's open car approached. I saw his homburg and his white silk scarf. He looked my way and waved. I cheered Eisenhower with relief.

9. MASSIVE RETALIATION

When, the previous November, Truman had sent word to the president-elect that a hydrogen device had been successfully tested in the Pacific, Eisenhower was on the golf course in Augusta, Georgia. He took the briefing about "Mike" in the club manager's office. But the affable Ike was far from casual about nuclear weapons. He had opposed the bombing of Hiroshima as unnecessary, and the man he chose for his secretary of state, John Foster Dulles, had denounced the atomic attacks on Japan as immoral. But by the time they took office, Eisenhower regarded the atomic bomb as something to "be used just exactly as you would use a bullet,"[144] and Dulles had applied the word "immoral" to Truman's policy of anti-Soviet containment because it did not use the atomic threat robustly enough.[145] To track the danger of nuclear war, the *Bulletin of the Atomic Scientists* had established a "Doomsday Clock" in 1947, when it put the time at seven minutes to midnight. In 1949, with the explosion of the Soviet A-bomb, it moved the clock to three minutes before midnight, and now, in 1953, moved it to two — the closest it would ever be.[146]

Eisenhower's first priority on assuming office was to end the conflict in Korea, and in the way the story is told in America, he had a simple plan for doing so. Breaking with the ambivalence and hesitancy that had marked Truman's approach to the atomic bomb, Ike was going to make sure that Moscow, Beijing, and Pyongyang all understood that he would use the weapon, and soon. A historical narrative that emphasizes Eisenhower's readiness to use the ultimate weapon to end the war as decisive must disregard dangerous and repeated moves toward atomic use that occurred under Truman. More than once the president was presented with serious recommendations for such action.[147]

Nevertheless, in Eisenhower's mind, it seems that he took office ready to widen the war if the Communists did not cooperate in ending it. It is no surprise that he should have had more confidence in his own ability than in Truman's to make such intent and will real to the enemy. As chairman of the Joint Chiefs of Staff in 1949, Eisenhower had supervised strategic planning for an atomic assault on the Soviet Union — before it had a bomb of its own — so the thought of actual use was not new to him. Much is made of the fact that, at a meeting of the National Security Council within weeks of his taking office, Eisenhower said, according to the official record, "that we should consider the use of tactical atomic weapons on the Kaesong area, which provided a good target for this type of weapon."[148] In fact, a new atomic artillery piece was soon test-fired, and its production was speeded up. In his memoir written later, Ike says that his public determination to use any means necessary to end the conflict was decisive. He would proceed, he said, "without inhibition in our use of weapons." That clearly included the atomic bomb.[149]

It seems that John Foster Dulles saw to it that a blunt summary of the new president's NSC remarks, together with threats that the war would soon be spread to Manchuria, were forwarded to Indian Prime Minister Jawaharlal Nehru, who could be relied on to send them along to the leaders in Beijing. As early as March 1953, the Chinese began to relent in the stalled truce negotiations at Panmunjom, and in June an armistice was agreed to. Also in June, Eisenhower authorized a major transfer of atomic weapons from the AEC to the sole custody of the military.[150] The fighting ended in July.

Dulles and Eisenhower were satisfied that their willingness to, in Dulles's famous word, move to the "brink" had brought about the change in Communist attitudes. Brinkmanship would define the Eisenhower-Dulles mode from then on, and Dulles would flamboyantly claim that during his time in office, the United States had gone "to the brink of total war" three times to thwart Communist aggression (the other two were over Vietnam and Formosa).[151] That does not count the Lebanon landing in 1958, when both the Soviet Union and the United States threatened nuclear war.

That the mild-mannered, "likable" Eisenhower chose John Foster Dulles as his secretary of state (not to mention Dulles's brother Allen as director of the CIA) was the largest single indication that a radical change in the rhetoric of American policy, if not its substance, was coming fast. Dulles had written the most warmongering planks of the Republican platform, denouncing, for example, "the negative, futile, and immoral policy of 'containment,' which abandons countless human beings to despotism and Godless Communism."[152] Ike knew very well what he was getting when he picked his secretary of state (as when he picked his Red-baiting vice president, Richard Nixon). The importance of Dulles as a shaper of America's Cold War nuclear bellicosity cannot be overemphasized. Ensconced in Foggy Bottom, he was happy to carry forward Dean Acheson's militarization of the State Department, and he recognized, incidentally, an ally in Paul Nitze, the nemesis of George Kennan, the father of containment. Instead of firing Nitze with the rest of Acheson's staffers, Dulles restored him to his role as an intermediary between State and Defense.[153]

But where Acheson had merely militarized American foreign policy, Dulles nuclearized it. In 1952, as a way of criticizing President Truman's temerity in Korea, for example, Dulles had published an article in *Life*, "A Policy of Boldness." He wrote that the only way to deal with Communist challenges "is for the free world to develop the will and organize the means to retaliate instantly against open aggression led by Red armies, so that, if it occurred anywhere, we could and would strike back where it hurts, by means of our choosing."[154] In the Dulles view, the wily Russians had succeeded in making atomic weapons seem somehow more immoral than other weapons. He not only wanted "to break down this false distinction,"[155] but also to make clear American readiness to use the weapon. This stance, for which Korea would be claimed as a victory, would become known as "massive retaliation," and Dulles would formalize it as American policy in a much-noted speech at the Council on Foreign Relations in January 1954.[156]

One important result of the early Eisenhower assumption that the threatened unleashing of America's nuclear arsenal was an efficient mode of anti-Communist coercion was to reinforce the massive expansion of that arsenal just as it began to be built. If an atomic threat could have such an effect, think of what a thermonuclear one would do. And the new, relatively cheaper fusion weapons offered a solution to another of Eisenhower's problems, which was how in the world to get budget-busting defense expenditures under control. If atomic weapons were an inexpensive alternative to a Red Army–matching conventional force, hydrogen weapons would be cheaper yet. Eisenhower understood that the prodigious militarization of America implied by NSC-68 was incompatible with a free economy, but, more urgently, he wanted to balance the budget.

As the most admired military figure in the world, he was unburdened by an insecurity like Truman's, and did not hesitate to act on his own instincts.

National security over the long term required fiscal restraint; it was that simple. Massive retaliation, with decreases in conventional forces and increases in strategic nuclear capacity, promised to enable that. Massive retaliation meant "maximum protection at bearable costs."[157] It also meant a broad scaling back of the military establishment, with the brunt of the cuts sustained by the Army and the Navy. Instead of competing services each having its war plan — conventional war like Korea, peripheral war mounted from ships — there would be one war plan, which essentially involved nuclear attacks against the cities of the USSR and China. The Air Force would be supreme.

Dulles and Eisenhower understood as well as anyone the importance of avoiding war in the age of the hydrogen bomb. Critics of their new policy — the "New Look," as the press named it — objected to the idea of massive response to even minimal provocation, but Eisenhower had concluded that the United States simply could not compete with the conventional power of the Soviet Union. Certainly there was no stopping an invading Red Army in Europe, so the mere threat of massive retaliation was intended to deter that invasion. But the conviction, rooted in Korea, that the credible threat of total nuclear war was the way to bend the will of an otherwise recalcitrant enemy required the nation, more energetically than ever, to prepare for it. Keep those nuclear weapons coming. And if the New Look involved a scaling back of the Army's ground forces, it also meant a crash program to replace the firepower of that scaled-back force with tactical nuclear weapons.

But was it true that the Chinese and North Koreans yielded at Panmunjom, in the spring of 1953, out of fear of American atomic weapons? Washington's conviction that this was the case would indefinitely reinforce a dependence on the nuclear threat and a reluctance to show any sign that might be perceived as weakness. Negotiation was equated with appeasement. But domestic political realities shaped this perception as much as foreign policy ones did, and Washington cultivated nuclear brinkmanship as a political style with as much attention to responses inside the United States as to responses outside.[158] So in the early months of Eisenhower's administration, for domestic political reasons more than for authentic foreign policy purposes, the new president wanted to establish himself as far tougher on the Communist enemy than Truman had been.

Despite John Foster Dulles's rhetoric, Ike was no more enthused about a policy of rollback than his predecessor had been,[159] but an extroverted brandishing of the atomic bomb could distract from that. Even after Korea, Eisenhower continued the lifting of Truman's restriction on atomic control, putting more and more nuclear bombs into military custody, allowing deployment on bases and ships. By the end of his administration, only one tenth of the arsenal remained under the control of civilians.[160] The bomb was another weapon, period. And Ike wanted that known.

It served none of Eisenhower's purposes, in other words, to look for an opening from military responses into diplomacy. That is why he seems barely to have noted the event that just then changed everything on the other side of the Iron Curtain — in nothing more, we know now, than in relation to the stalemate in Korea. That event has been recognized since the late 1980s as having had more influence on the willingness of the Soviets and the Chinese to end the Korean War than any nuclear threats:[161] the death of Joseph Stalin.

10. THE MISSED OPPORTUNITY

When Stalin died, on March 5, 1953, tectonic shifts occurred in the Communist world — his trusted henchman Lavrenti Beria would soon be shot, for example — but Eisenhower and Dulles, viewing that world monolithically, missed them. New Soviet leaders promptly issued a statement calling for the resolution of conflict "on the basis of mutual understanding."[162] The CIA, headed by Allen Dulles, within a week reported numerous "peaceful or friendly gestures by the Soviet Union since Stalin died."[163] Yet in those same post-Stalin days, Eisenhower and John Foster Dulles approved a proposal to establish a top-secret Volunteer Freedom Corps, mobilizing Eastern European refugees to infiltrate behind the Iron Curtain. Rollback after all. In Eastern Europe and Russia, the tactic would come to nothing,[164] but it marked the beginning of the CIA's "black" operations in the Middle East, South America, and Southeast Asia, where they would stir up much trouble.

Arthur Schlesinger told me that the main difference to history that Eisenhower, not Stevenson, was elected in 1952 was that at Stalin's death, Stevenson would surely have tried to establish a new modus vivendi with the Soviet Union. Eisenhower, in the throes of domestically inspired toughness, did not. We know from post–Cold War Soviet archives that such a hope for improvement in relations with the West animated many in the Kremlin, and that hope would be central to the power struggle that ensued among members of the Politburo elite.[165] But the first issue on which such men agreed was to end the conflict in Korea. Clear, encouraging signals were sent from Moscow to Beijing and Pyongyang.

Meanwhile, Winston Churchill, who was once again British prime minister, was equally energetic in moving toward a lessening of tensions with Moscow; what would later be called détente he called "easement." Churchill had been the first to define the East-West conflict in ontological terms — and, celebrating the "English-speaking races," in ethnic terms — but he was also one of the first, as we saw, to appreciate how the nuclear arms competition, and especially the coming of the Super, made the defusing of that conflict urgent. Because of the hydrogen bomb, as one historian put it, Churchill "repudiated the views of a lifetime."[166] Almost immediately after Stalin's death — on March 11 — Churchill proposed a three-way summit meeting with Eisenhower, the new Soviet leader, Georgi Malenkov, and himself. With Stalin gone, surely new understandings would be possible.

Eisenhower was skeptical. He had no need to reiterate, as he put it to an aide, "just plain indictments of the Soviet regime,"[167] but he wasn't going to follow Churchill's lead into wishful diplomacy. To him, the seventy-eight-year-old British leader was no longer reliable, and Malenkov was just another Communist. Eisenhower may have been less susceptible than Churchill had been to a prior demonizing of the Soviets (Churchill saw Jewish conspiracy behind much revolutionary ferment in the interwar period), but Ike could never forget the shock he felt in 1945 when he had learned from Soviet Field Marshal Zhukov, in Berlin, that when he needed to clear a minefield, he did so in the most efficient way, by ordering his own soldiers to march through it.[168] The Soviets were brutes, pure and simple. And Stalin had stooped to ever-greater brutalities, his last years marked by purges of "rootless cosmopolitans," anti-Semitic assaults, and vast expansions of the gulag. "De-Stalinization" would soon be a Soviet watchword. But Washington was watching for nothing that would mitigate its Manichaean view. (The famous Twentieth Party Congress speech in 1956, in which Khrushchev denounced the legacy of Stalin, would take the CIA completely by surprise.) No sooner had Ike received Churchill's proposal than, on the same March 11, he cabled back an answer: No.[169]

One month later, on April 16, 1953, before the American Society of Newspaper Editors, Eisenhower gave what would become famous as his "Chance for Peace" speech, taken to be a heartfelt expression of longing for another way. "The world knows that an era ended with the death of Joseph Stalin . . . Now, a new leadership has assumed power in the Soviet Union. Its links to the past, however strong, cannot bind it completely. Its future is, in great part, its own to make." Eisenhower spoke eloquently about the costs of the conflict that had been put in place in the Stalin era: "Every gun that is made, every warship launched, every rocket fired signifies, in the final sense, a theft from those who hunger and are not fed, those who are cold and not clothed."

But as Moscow had to read that speech, it was only a reformulation of the old demand that, for improved relations with America, the Soviet Union had to yield its most basic notions of ideology and social organization. It was the Baruch Plan all over again. The Soviet Union would have to cede control of its neighbors, allow the reunion of Germany, agree to limitations on the size of its armed forces and the prohibition of atomic weapons, and, of course, open its society to "a practical system of inspection under the United Nations."[170] Eisenhower's biographer writes, "It was a lot to ask — too much, in fact."[171] Ike spoke of peace, but what he wanted was surrender.

When, at the end of that year, on December 8, 1953, Eisenhower gave an equally heartfelt speech before the United Nations, called "Atoms for Peace," his plea was even more eloquent: "The United States pledges before you — and therefore before the world — its determination to help solve the fearful atomic dilemma — to devote its entire heart and mind to find the way by which the miraculous inventiveness of man shall not be dedicated to his death, but consecrated to his life."[172] At some level, Eisenhower's sincerity here cannot be doubted, but his "pledge," in fact, was contradicted both by the absence of any meaningful follow-up with practical diplomatic initiatives and by contrary military policies that were actively under way. And the Soviets knew it. Exactly one month after this speech, on January 8, 1954, Eisenhower's National Security Council officially resolved to use nuclear weapons if the shaky Korean armistice collapsed.[173] Eisenhower did not have to give the order, but he was prepared to. A few days later, Dulles proclaimed the massive-retaliation doctrine. And only three months later, in April, Eisenhower proposed to the French the use of atomic bombs at Dien Bien Phu. Eisenhower's entire strategy, outlined in the "Atoms for Peace" speech, of promoting the peaceful use of nuclear reactors, led to the proliferation of nuclear technology — and weapons.

Eisenhower earnestly sought to dispel the atomic threat. But he made it worse. In a phrase one historian has applied to Dulles, Eisenhower suffered from "nuclear schizophrenia."[174] And his peaceful rhetoric, combined with a ferocious nuclearization of diplomatic style and military force, served his purposes. As McGeorge Bundy later characterized it, the huge growth of the American nuclear arsenal under Eisenhower, with a crash program to infuse it with hydrogen bombs, matched by a simultaneous expansion of the Strategic Air Command under Curtis LeMay (both continuations of Truman policies), were "sheltered in part by the very profession of peaceable purpose that stirred the General Assembly"[175] in the "Atoms for Peace" speech. And when, not long after the speech, the United States openly repeated its massive-retaliation threats — "to engage in whatever operations may be required" — over Vietnam and Formosa,[176] the main results were that the post-Stalin Soviet Union began working to double and triple its own nuclear capacity, and Mao ordered the development of a nuclear bomb for China.[177]

11. Defense Intellectuals

The operative word in the phrase "massive retaliation" is retaliation. To retaliate, the dictionary says, is "to return like for like, especially evil for evil." The explicit assumption of the Eisenhower-Dulles policy was that the United States would not be the one to initiate hostilities. There was a deliberate ambiguity in whether a nuclear strike would be made in response to conventional moves by the Soviet Union or its surrogates (for example, against Berlin),[178] but the burden of the declared strategy was that America's enemy would be overwhelmingly punished for any and all acts of hostility.

Corollary to massive retaliation was a rejection of the concept of preventive war. As we have seen, there had been advocates of a preemptive strike against targets in the Soviet Union since the early postwar period. Before 1949 and the Soviet A-bomb, even figures associated with peace had argued for unprovoked attacks on nuclear facilities in the USSR — the way to avoid the "arms race of a rather desperate character" — and among the Pentagon brass, especially in the Air Force, calls for surprise assaults on Soviet targets had been common. "A-Day" was the designation given to the point in time when the United States would lose its nuclear advantage; the time, that is, when American forces could no longer take out Soviet atomic facilities without significant risk of a reply in kind. The National Security Council under Eisenhower seriously considered such preemptive attacks, but before long — the Soviets tested an H-bomb in 1953 and began stockpiling the weapon — scenarios that featured relatively precise use of atomic bombs were made obsolete by the nearly unlimited power of the newly fused hydrogen bombs. Instead of imagining attacks that cost hundreds of thousands of enemy lives, or even a few million, the H-bomb moved projected rates of death into the hundreds of millions.[179] A-Day came and went, and with it, at the official level, any notion of preventive war. The thought of a preemptive American attack, Eisenhower said, is "an impossibility today . . . Frankly, I wouldn't even listen to anyone seriously that came in and talked about such a thing."[180]

But the logical inconsistencies in strategic theory — the way to peace is preparation for all-out war — soon began to push policymakers, and the new class of defense intellectuals on whom they depended, into a kind of wonderland. Once the two powers had nuclear weapons systems that were both deliverable and somewhat capable of surviving attack, the idea of actually going to war became, in a word that found its way into use now, unthinkable. But thinking, in fact, came hard and fast. "Think" was the motto of the IBM Corporation, whose machines did the computations on which military planners now relied.

Bernard Brodie, as early as 1946, had called the atomic bomb the "absolute weapon."[181] It could seem so until the hydrogen bomb. Thermonuclear weapons, with their capacity to destroy whole civilizations, if not all life on the planet, led to what theorists called the "thermonuclear revolution"[182] in strategic theory. "Stability doctrine," "controlled counterpopulation warfare," "counterforce targets," "game theory," "deterrence" — such words entered the lexicon not only of professors now, but of blue-uniformed officers who employed the professors. After World War II, Air Force leaders had established a kind of in-house think tank to sharpen strategic theory — arguments for air war, "global force projection," and so on — as part of the campaign to move a strategic bomber capability to the center of American defense. Theoretical arguments for the "revolution in warfare" were useful against the Army and Navy in the interservice dogfight over a zero-sum budget. To that end, the Air Force established an internal research-and-development project that evolved into RAND, at first a division of Douglas Aircraft under AAF contract and then, in 1948, an independent research entity based in southern California.

"Thermonuclear Jesuits"[183] like Bernard Brodie, Herman Kahn, Albert J. Wohlstetter, and William Kaufmann — and later, Thomas Schelling, Henry Kissinger, Daniel Ellsberg, James Schlesinger, and others — applied their brilliance to paradoxical questions that were impossible to answer definitively. How to imagine a "controlled" use of fusion weapons; how to anticipate an enemy's rational behavior in an irrational situation; how a "spasm attack" might be stopped short of total war. The absurdity of the legend "Peace is our profession," stenciled on the fuselages of SAC bombers, had its equivalent in the intellectual exercises of some of the greatest thinkers in America. One historian has noted the ironies such policies involved: "The basic axioms of the nuclear age, therefore, were soon identified: the impossibility of defense; the hopeless vulnerability of the world's major cities; the attraction of a sudden attack; and the necessity of a capability for retaliation. There were inklings of the debates that were to dominate strategists in the coming decades: the danger of a successful first strike against nuclear forces, the impossibility of deterring madmen, and the paradox of intensive defensive preparations taking on the appearance of a provocative act."[184]

What is most important to remember about the invention of the new intellectual discipline of "air power theory," despite its academic pretensions, is its origin as a wholly owned subsidiary of the U.S. Air Force. (The codependence of the scholar, Dr. Strangelove, and the general, Jack D. Ripper, would be perfectly spoofed in the 1964 film *Dr. Strangelove, or: How I Learned to Stop Worrying and Love the Bomb.*)[185] The physicists at Los Alamos and the engineers at MIT embodied hard science at the service of the Defense Department; the political philosophers and economists at RAND embodied social science in the same martial rank — all of it a new phenomenon, the academic equivalent of the manufacturing investments of the new defense industries. Universities, academic disciplines, businesses, research institutions, the great corporations, national and local legislative bodies — America reinventing itself as a garrison state. When, at the end of his time as president, Eisenhower famously warned of the "military-industrial complex,"[186] he did so as if he had not presided over its flowering. And he could have made that duo a trio by adding "-academic."

The philosophizing of the defense intellectuals in the early nuclear age, through the Eisenhower years and into the Kennedy period, gave a kind of ethical underpinning to what was, after all, an outbreak of moral chaos. A few of these thinkers criticized the illogic of threat-mongering — warning of self-fulfilling prophecies, unintended consequences, and the like — but mostly the professors, whether as dupes or as knowing supporters, served as intellectual legitimizers of Pentagon predispositions.[187] Their "thinking," in fact, was proof that nothing in that fraught period was really unthinkable. Again and again, as we have seen, U.S. civilian and military leaders forcefully advocated using nuclear and thermonuclear bombs, coming close enough to be terrifying — and they did so with theoreticians backing them up. Marc Trachtenberg, a historian of this phenomenon, looking back from 1991, wrote:

> We as a society suffer today from what can only be called an extraordinary case of collective nuclear amnesia. A picture of the past has taken shape that has very little to do with what our nuclear past was really like. It is now often taken for granted that even in the 1950s nuclear war was simply "unthinkable" as an instrument of policy; that nuclear forces were never "usable" and served only to "deter their use by others"; and that the threat of "massive retaliation" was at bottom just pure bluff, because the United States would never be the first to launch a nuclear strike. This picture has taken shape because it serves important political purposes of both the left and the right, but one cannot immerse oneself in the sources for this period without coming to the conclusion that something very basic has been forgotten.[188]

What has been forgotten is that the American military establishment not only was prepared to launch a nuclear strike, but on occasion was eager to, with the collusion and active support of its civilian overseers and of the "theologians" on whom it depended for intellectual and, if only implicitly, moral guidance.

As indicated by their active service in a succession of Pentagon regimes, and despite many claims to objectivity, the defense intellectuals' primary function was to justify the endless upward spiral of the arms race and its interruption at any point by an act of nuclear war. They did this especially by reinforcing a mindset that expected the worst from enemies — and the rest of the world as well. The "paranoid style," when adopted by the defense intellectuals, was not only justified but made to seem the height of rationality, able to be articulated even in the formulas of hard science. In the Eisenhower years, the strategists tended to view the massive-retaliation doctrine skeptically, as leaving, for example, the United States no options between all-out war and capitulation. Later they would develop arguments for the "selective" use of nuclear weapons, which in the real world would nevertheless be "massive."

But varied and sometimes contrasting theories about nuclear war, expressed over many years, rarely translated into real adjustments in actual war-fighting plans, which remained mostly constant.[189] LeMay's initial vision of the strategic force as a destroyer of cities would be the ground in which the enterprise remained firmly planted. Finely calibrated notions like "strategic balance," "sufficiency," "flexible response," and, ultimately, "mutual assured destruction" would not slow the accumulation of bombs, warheads, and ever more esoteric means to deliver them. The intellectuals eventually helped invent the "arms control and disarmament" track of U.S.-Soviet relations, but there, too, as we shall see, every arcane agreement in arms limitation seemed to lead to explosive growth in those areas to which agreed limits did not apply. That is why, whenever serious "arms control and disarmament" negotiations took off, so did new escalations of nuclear weapons. That was so because, of course, the arms control enterprise assumed the importance of maintaining U.S. nuclear dominance. Across the decades, the professors never forgot for whom they worked: the bomber generals.

The ultimate bomber general remained Curtis LeMay, and it is significant that he was, in fact, RAND's progenitor, having been named in 1945 to the new Air Force position of deputy chief of staff for research and development, from which the enterprise grew.[190] Though all of the "absolute weapon" abstraction, through its several iterations, was ultimately at the service of SAC's agenda, LeMay never gave a hoot about theory. What he had wanted to do when he began the R&D project was to get new "instrumentalities" — weapons. But here the story gets personal again. A decade after starting RAND, when he was commander in chief of the Strategic Air Command and at the peak of his power, what he was trying to do was stop my father.

12. OPERATION TOP HAT

From FBI agent to Air Force security and counterintelligence chief, Joe
Carroll by the mid-1950s had established himself as a Pentagon general. My
mother, the former telephone operator, had reinvented herself as the general's
wife. This was when we still lived in a modest house south of Alexandria, well
before Dad had rank enough for Generals' Row. We lived in Hollin Hills, a
tract development that featured modern, split-level homes for free-spirited,
liberal young lawyers and Capitol Hill staffers — an unlikely place for the Air
Force family we had so unexpectedly become.

My buddies were the sons of journalists and civil servants. On our street,
I would learn many years later, lived the historian Bernard Fall, who, while I
was probably delivering the morning newspaper to him, was writing *Street
Without Joy*, what would become a definitive alternative history of Vietnam, a
foundational text of the antiwar movement, when it was published most of a
decade later. My memories of Hollin Hills — the gravel pit, the creek, the
stone wall in the woods, the tree house — feature my brothers and mother
more than Dad, who was always at work. Now I understand that a nagging
guilt at that absence might have been what prompted him to take me to the
Pentagon on those occasional Saturdays.

The Office of Special Investigations, in that Red Scare era, was at the
heart of American threat-obsessiveness. For all the anxiety expressed about
Communist spies in the fifties, it is noteworthy that out of the few hundred
thousand people, at most, who had joined the Communist Party from the
1930s through the 1950s, only a few hundred were named by the U.S. government as being under suspicion of espionage, and of those only a handful were
ever identified as real threats to national security. In general, there was more
subversive reporting to Moscow about farms and farm policy than about industry. Yet the American dread of Communist infiltration underwrote one of
the most repressive ideological assaults in the nation's history, with the right
wing effectively eliminating from the nation's political discourse appeals to
the Socialist idealism that was, in the same period, reinvigorating politics in
Europe. Because of Red Scare anxieties, Americans would uncritically accept
the maturing of an economic system that, in its effect if not its structure, condemned most of the world to crushing impoverishment. The humane aspects
of Marx's critique of capitalism would not be reckoned with in the United
States, with dangerous consequences that define the ever more polarized
twenty-first century.

That can be seen in hindsight. At the time, however, political anxiety was not taken to be a matter of left versus right, and it was so all-encompassing that we children felt it too. The panic was tied, above all, to one thing Americans were sure of — that the atomic bomb, the most closely guarded secret in the nation's history, had been stolen. Whether Soviet scientists needed access to the secrets of Los Alamos or not, we knew that they had had it. We took little note of the fact that the access was mainly through London. Beginning in the early 1950s, that is, the likes of Alger Hiss were far from the only issue. The names Klaus Fuchs, David Greenglass, and Ethel and Julius Rosenberg amounted to the starting roster of the next level of American irrationality, and that was where the Air Force OSI came in.

My father's agency was responsible for catching spies and for protecting secret installations like Los Alamos from infiltrators and saboteurs. In our minds, the distinction between actual agents of the Soviet Union and members of the Communist Party blurred. Vigilance against all of them was the order of the day. AFOSI, in the argot of a later motto, was "the eyes of the eagle." Mission protection. Mission support. But by 1954, owing to alarms set off by Senator Joseph McCarthy and others, every agency in government was under pressure, including the Army. Infiltrators, saboteurs, conspirators — weren't they everywhere? And who was investigating the investigators?

OSI was one of the agencies whose methods were reviewed by a special, government-wide committee on intelligence, chaired by the retired Air Force hero James Doolittle. That may have been the start of my father's friendship with him. On one of my visits to the Pentagon, Dad introduced me to Doolittle, and I was struck by the evident affection between them. I was also struck by Doolittle's small stature, which I attached to his name. Doolittle was bald and elfin, but his personality sparkled, and I remember thinking he was a nice man. But what really struck me was the physical contrast between the famous bomber pilot and my dad, one of the first times I noticed my father's imposing presence, his charisma even. It didn't hurt that Doolittle was in civilian clothes, my father in uniform. Next to the hero, Dad held his own.

Doolittle, of course, had commanded the first air raid on Tokyo, in 1942 — the first deliberate act of area bombing by the Army Air Forces, without pretense that civilians were to be spared. An act of revenge for Pearl Harbor. Doolittle had been awarded the Congressional Medal of Honor for it. Before that he had been a Rhodes scholar, and he held a Ph.D. in aeronautical engineering from MIT. After the war, he was an executive at Shell, but in 1954 he had taken on this special task for Eisenhower.

"It is now clear," Doolittle reported as chairman of the presidential committee on intelligence, "that we are facing an implacable enemy whose avowed objective is world domination by whatever means and whatever cost. There are no rules in such a game. Hitherto acceptable norms of human conduct do not apply. If the United States is to survive, long-standing concepts of 'fair play' must be reconsidered. We must develop effective espionage and counter-espionage services, and must learn to subvert, sabotage, and destroy our enemies by more clever, more sophisticated, and more effective methods than those used against us. It may be necessary that the American people be made acquainted with, understand, and support this fundamentally repugnant philosophy."[191]

It was as if my father took Doolittle's challenge personally. Doolittle wanted effective counterespionage operations, and my father gave him one in the supersecret OSI project that was code-named Top Hat. It would succeed in ways beyond what anyone would have wanted. This was a "Vulnerability Test Program" in which American OSI agents committed acts of low-tech sabotage against facilities of the Strategic Air Command, to expose the chinks in its armor. This was an activity of which I never heard my father speak, and I learned of it only in researching this book. Of all the secrets my father held, perhaps, for a time, the gravest was that America's mighty strategic force, so overwhelming, so feared, constructed at such enormous cost, was liable to be disabled by commando-style raids that amounted to not much more than frat-boy tricks.

By the mid-1950s, the Strategic Air Command's operational assets were vast, by far the most lethal assemblage of weaponry in the history of the world. There were well over a thousand B-47 bombers, and a new fleet of B-52s would grow into the hundreds. To enable these warplanes to reach their targets anywhere on the globe, SAC possessed more than seven hundred KC-97 tankers.[192] Despite all the fears of Soviet power, this arsenal would never be matched by America's enemy. But that did not mean it could not be fatally attacked — from behind.

That was what my father did. Speaking decades later, he described the origins of Operation Top Hat for an Air Force oral history, the rough transcript of which I found, yet further decades later, in a file drawer at the office of the OSI historian at Andrews Air Force Base. "In thinking about our counter-sabotage responsibilities," he told the interviewer, "the thought occurred to me that, in conjunction with a surprise bombing attack, and to prevent our unleashing our strategic retaliation, the Soviet Union did not have to undertake the magnitudiness [sic] and difficult effort to accomplish the task of actually destroying our bombers on the ground. They could achieve the same result by holding our bombers on the ground by preventing them from taking off for only two hours. I say two hours because this was the amount of warning that we would receive from our DEW Line, the Distant Early Warning alert line in the north."[193]

And so my father, acting with a small band of OSI agents, began, on his own authority, a campaign of faux sabotage against SAC bases, with the aim of measuring SAC's ability to thwart enemy actions to disable the strike force on the ground. Soon the OSI's aim became to make plain to SAC commanders that they were in no way prepared for such offbeat and unpredicted assaults.

At first the "sabotage" was simple — attaching simulated explosives to the spans that separated atomic bomb storage facilities from the flight line, showing how easy it would be to prevent the timely loading of weapons onto bombers. Or OSI agents would sneak into the supposedly secure area where bombers stood ready and attach fake explosives to the undercarriage of the mammoth planes. Instead of "Kilroy was here," they might scrawl, "One dead bird."

The first OSI test of this sort was conducted at a SAC base in Japan, and as OSI's official history has it, the leader of the clandestine team going in at night was my father. I recall his trips to Japan in the fifties. He called them inspection trips, and I always imagined him striding before lines of troops in rigid formation, as if his job were to be sure their shoes were properly shined. Now I adjust the memory, and picture my father in commando clothes: black turtleneck, black stocking cap, black grease on his face. He was an athletic man, and this was when he was well into his forties. He told the Air Force oral historian, "I do have a personal recollection of starting these tests overseas in Japan. As I recall, in a way it was a mistake on my part because in Japan indigenous Japanese guards were being used, and that night I was challenged so pre-emptorially [*sic*] by a Japanese guard that I almost lost my life."

Soon the importance of such testing was apparent even to SAC Commander Curtis LeMay. "The project took on an air of good-natured rivalry between the two men," the official history recounts, "with LeMay touting the effectiveness of his Air Policemen and Carroll confident of his agents' abilities to confound their efforts . . . There was an aspect of real danger . . . because armed APs would be unaware that the intruders were OSI agents . . . If apprehended, agents were sometimes in for rough treatment by resentful APs. If successful, they were likewise heaped with abuse for causing difficulties at a base or jeopardizing operations."[194]

Operation Top Hat came to a climax on July 17, 1957. That night, with LeMay's cooperation, OSI sabotage teams simultaneously struck at thirteen SAC bases in the continental United States — the "Zone of the Interior." Each test began with an agent delivering a letter to the base commander from LeMay. It informed the commander that a Red Alert test was under way, simulating an incoming Soviet attack, and that he himself had just been "killed" by the agent. From then on, the hapless general officer was to observe the test, with the OSI agent at his side as a kind of referee, to see how his command performed.

LeMay was standing by, with General Carroll, at SAC headquarters in Omaha to take telephone calls from any commander who did not believe the letter. Then, to cite one sabotage technique carried out that night, OSI agents in small planes made unauthorized, lights-out landings on the runways of various SAC bases. The planes rolled down the length of each tarmac while agents in the body of the planes tossed out dozens of three-pronged steel spikes, littering the runway, making it impossible for fleets of otherwise invincible B-52s to take off. In the time it would take to clear the runways, the Soviet strike would have already hit them. Such incidents occurred across the country. One hundred OSI agents, within a few hours, demonstrated again that the sophisticated SAC bomber force could be delayed, if not disabled, by nothing more than oversize jacks.[195]

The Eisenhower-Dulles strategy of massive retaliation presumed a level of SAC invulnerability that did not exist, and, if only because of Operation Top Hat, LeMay knew it. His superiors in Washington, with faith in the overwhelmingly destructive nuclear arsenal, could imagine the United States deterring hostile actions from Moscow indefinitely, but such deterrence depended on Moscow's assumption, too, that a retaliatory strike would be inevitable. But it wasn't. The SAC bomber force, simply by being delayed, could be destroyed on the ground. That is to say, LeMay knew that a strategy based on retaliation would not work. If the Soviet Union claimed the advantage of being the first to strike, LeMay could not be certain of getting his bombers off the ground in time.

I don't know the precise connection, but a month after Top Hat, in August 1957, my father was transferred from OSI in Washington to Germany, his one tour of duty away from the Pentagon. He was appointed chief of staff of the Air Force in Europe, headquartered in Wiesbaden. This was a line position that an unrated officer like him should not have held. In Air Force terms, it was an extraordinary promotion for a man who was not a pilot and who had not served in a combat wing. It seems that Top Hat capped a successful run as OSI director, the position Joe Carroll had held since Symington brought him over from the FBI a decade earlier. On the other hand, it is hard to imagine that LeMay was grateful to General Carroll for having shown him up, but perhaps in the end what Top Hat did was convince LeMay more than ever that instead of retaliation, he had to think preemption. He simply had to get his planes off the ground not before a Soviet nuclear armada crossed the DEW line but before the Soviet planes themselves left the ground.

LeMay took two steps to overcome SAC's vulnerability. A new jet tanker, the KC-135, a modified version of Boeing's civilian 707 jetliner, made it theoretically possible, through air refueling, to keep one third of the B-47 and B-52 fleets in the air at all times. LeMay began to test the idea in the weeks after Top Hat, a program he called Operation Reflex Action. Before long, it became standard procedure, with dozens of SAC bombers, from Britain, Spain, North Africa, and Alaska, airborne at all times. And, more significant, in that summer of 1957 LeMay succeeded in getting the first of his own U-2 planes. The high-flying spy plane had been developed by the CIA, which had been reluctant to share it, but soon SAC had a fleet of twelve.[196] LeMay started conducting his own overflight surveillance of Soviet bomber bases. Intelligence gained in this way would not be instantly available — film had to be developed, photos analyzed — but with his own reconnaissance flights, LeMay could harbor the illusion of omniscience. In his mind, he would know before anyone else when Soviet pilots so much as thought of taking off.

13. THE GAITHER REPORT: NITZE AGAIN

LeMay's private insecurities were matched at the time by a growing uneasiness among defense experts about the general state of U.S. military readiness. The Eisenhower-Dulles strategy, in the beginning, had depended on the clear perception that the American nuclear arsenal was vastly larger than Moscow's, but by 1957 there were reasons to assume that the Soviet thermonuclear force was itself vast, and Moscow's new jet bomber fleet was ready to deliver it. Soviet capability and the willingness to use that capability were synonymous in the minds of many American leaders. If it was not unthinkable that that force, in combination with a Top Hat–style sabotage, could destroy SAC on the ground, it was not unthinkable that the Soviets would do it. Eisenhower may have gotten his budget under control — with defense reductions amounting to 20 percent between 1953 and 1955, and with a budget surplus in 1956 — but at what cost?

Around this time, the Navy warned emphatically that the Soviet Union had mobilized a huge submarine fleet that threatened more than Germany's ever had during World War II. The Army made its objections to the New Look even plainer. Cutbacks had been made in its budget, battle order, and personnel levels — and in its very mission as the centerpiece of national defense. In 1955, the Army chief of staff, Matthew Ridgway, resigned in protest, and a year later he published *Soldier,* a memoir and stinging critique of Eisenhower's military policies, especially his abandonment of the conventional fighting force in favor of SAC-based massive retaliation. Ridgway's successor as chief, Maxwell Taylor, would do the same thing, and his 1960 book, *The Uncertain Trumpet*, would make the issue a national controversy.

But even the Air Force had its complaints. The Soviet Union had spent the 1950s assembling its own powerful strategic force, and the U.S. Air Force, for all of its dominance of defense budgets, was not happy to see its huge advantage over the enemy gradually shrink away. Yet that shrinkage was more apparent than real. Air Force intelligence began to warn that the Soviets were outproducing America in strategic bombers. It was a fantasy, but it took hold in the Pentagon, a danger that would soon become known as the "bomber gap."[197]

SAC complained, for example, that while it added whole new fleets of B-47s and B-52s, its total operational assets were in decline. SAC lodged that complaint without explaining that the decline resulted from the retirement of obsolete B-29s, B-36s, and B-50s, and also of thousands of tactical aircraft and fighter planes that had served as escorts for the old sitting-duck bombers. The new jet bombers did not require swarms of fighter escorts, so an entire generation of warplanes did not need to be replaced. But in the Pentagon a habit of mind had become entrenched that took for granted ever-skyrocketing weapons investment and a need for permanent "superiority" over the Soviet Union. And always there was a self-justifying, if paranoid, tendency to greatly overestimate what the Soviet threat amounted to. That paranoia by now inhered as much in the weaponry as in the enemy. As a former Pentagon intelligence analyst told me, recapitulating the "bomber gap" mindset: "Take ten Soviet copies of the B-50, load each one with a ten-megaton nuclear bomb, and have them fly against the U.S. Even if only three make it, there go Boston, New York City, and Washington, D.C."[198]

The "bomber gap" was a later version of General Hoyt Vandenberg's hysterical warning in 1949 that "almost any number of Soviet bombers could cross our borders." At that time, the effective capacity of the Soviet air force had been zero, but was that the case by the mid-1950s? Who knew?

The Pentagon mindset and the Eisenhower approach were in conflict from the beginning, but it became public when administration spokesmen began using the word "sufficiency." On the matter of bombers, for example, Eisenhower rejected what he called "the numbers racket." He told reporters in 1956, "I say it is vital to get what we believe we need. That does not necessarily mean more than anybody else does . . . There comes a time . . . when the destructiveness of weapons is so great as to be beyond imagination, when enough is certainly plenty, and you do no good, as I see it, by increasing these numbers."[199]

As it happened, after he was comfortably reelected, Eisenhower responded to the pressures of his various critics by establishing a special commission in May 1957. It was called the Gaither Committee,[200] after its chairman, H. Rowan Gaither of the RAND Corporation and the Ford Foundation, and its original mandate was to consider only the question of whether the United States should embark on a large-scale bomb shelter program. Gaither was soon taken ill and was replaced by Robert C. Sprague, the chairman of an electrical equipment company. The committee brought in numerous consultants, none with more experience — or stronger convictions — on national security questions than Paul Nitze.

After having left the Eisenhower administration in 1953, Nitze had become one of the critics of the New Look. Eisenhower's budget-balancing program, with its narrow focus on air power, was an effective repudiation of the far more comprehensive militarization laid out in NSC-68. Nitze, the consistent echo of his mentor James Forrestal, had been roundly warning of the mounting threat from Moscow, and the Gaither Committee gave him a microphone. Dominating the committee "by force of mind and personality,"[201] Nitze persuaded the members to expand their brief from the narrow question of bomb shelters to the entire matter of national security policy. Having been the main author of the alarmist NSC-68 in 1950, Nitze now seized the initiative with the Gaither Committee.

Another of its members was Franklin Lindsay, whom we noted early on as a consultant to both James Byrnes and Bernard Baruch. Lindsay told me that one of the committee's first areas of inquiry was into the ability of the Strategic Air Command to carry out its mission. Lindsay, together with fellow member Jerome Wiesner, traveled to SAC headquarters in Nebraska. This would have been in the same period that Operation Top Hat was putting SAC's fallibility on display — inside SAC. It is easy to imagine how contemptuous and defensive LeMay would have been with these civilian interlopers, especially since the OSI was exposing SAC's Achilles' heel. LeMay would not have wanted these bureaucrats to know of that, and indeed, as Lindsay said of that first visit, "We were given the bum's rush . . . and it so infuriated Sprague, and I guess the rest of the group, that they went to Eisenhower, and Eisenhower sent word through the channels, 'The Gaither Committee is my committee, and you tell them what they want to know.'"

So the committee had its formal meeting with LeMay. It took place in the Pentagon office of the secretary of the Air Force. "LeMay was there," Lindsay recalled, "and a bunch of colonels sitting around the border of the room. The Air Force chief of staff, Tommy White, was there." One of the members put the crucial question to LeMay: "'General, you have only tactical warning,' which meant," Lindsay explained, "Soviet bombers crossing the DEW line into Canada. 'How many of your aircraft can you launch, bombed up and fueled, getting into the air, before you're hit on the ground? We've got reports that the Russian air force is crossing Canada, headed for you. How many of your aircraft can you launch in retaliation?'

"LeMay said, 'None.' It was really a dramatic moment." In recounting this, Lindsay paused for emphasis. "The secretary of the Air Force said, 'General, did you hear the question?' He rephrased it and asked it again. LeMay again said, 'None.'"

Lindsay shook his head at the memory. He was an old man now, and in his youth, as a guerilla fighter with the partisans in the Balkans, as a high-level aide in post–World War II negotiations, and as a senior CIA operative, he had seen and experienced many extraordinary events. But this memory of LeMay ranked with the most extraordinary of them. "Essentially," Lindsay continued, "LeMay had built an air force that could only get off the ground for a first strike."

That was why LeMay wanted his own U-2s, just then being deployed — to see for himself evidence of Soviet preparations. Lindsay reported that he and the others understood at once that LeMay, by that point in 1957, had left the notion of retaliation behind. He would rely on SAC reconnaissance instead of the too late warning of the DEW line. He was going to make his own assessment of Soviet bomber activity on the ground, watching for remote moves toward launch. We are talking of LeMay's fantasy of how such events would unfold. Once U-2 photos showed him evidence of a bomber force preparing for a strike (after the laborious process of film development and photo analysis), he would hit them first. "If I see that the Russians are amassing their planes for an attack," LeMay said on another occasion to Robert Sprague, according to a historian's account, "I'm going to knock the shit out of them before they take off the ground."

"But General LeMay," Sprague objected, "that's not national policy."

"I don't care," LeMay replied. "It's my policy. That's what I'm going to do."

Sprague was astonished by LeMay's acknowledgment of his rogue strategy, but he also accepted its necessity. He resolved not to make an issue of it.[202]

Whether LeMay had the authority for taking such action seemed not to be a problem. In response to a question on that point, Lindsay recalled, LeMay suggested that such authority was implicit by saying, "I cannot believe that the president of the United States would fail to order the first strike before being hit on the ground."[203] Shocking as this open assertion of a first-strike strategy was to Lindsay, Sprague, and other committee members, it was nothing but a manifestation of the inevitable tension between prevention (which Eisenhower, like Truman before him, had ruled out) and preemption (which no military leader could responsibly renounce). LeMay had a pre-emption plan that was separate from the war plans that the JCS and the president knew of and approved. Indeed, beginning in 1951, he had never submitted SAC's Basic War Plan to the Joint Chiefs, much less to their civilian superiors.[204] The problem for the American system, with its principle of civilian oversight, was that assessments of a situation calling for preemption, and knowledge of the pressures for timely action, belonged to the "guardians of the arsenal."[205]

In his confrontations with the Gaither Committee, LeMay was showing how, in the nuclear age, civilian oversight of American military policy had become largely mythical. He was also showing that, with the massive-retaliation deterrent force much more vulnerable than imagined, the nuclear weapon was already cocked and on a hair trigger. The instant it looked as though the Soviets might be moving, even in preliminary ways, toward assault, the United States was going to order a nuclear attack. With a bombs-away commander like LeMay in charge of the crucial judgment, the world was far closer to the nuclear horror than anyone had thought.

Whatever alarm the Gaither Committee's members took away from the interview about LeMay's claim to dominant authority over the decision to launch a nuclear war, the committee's alarm about the state of American preparedness became general. That was especially so once Nitze made his full influence felt. The committee began writing the final draft of its report in the beginning of October 1957,[206] and as Nitze had jacked up concerns over national security seven years before, he was doing it again. The Gaither Report was titled "Deterrence and Survival in the Nuclear Age." America's deterrence capability was weak, it said. America's survival was at risk.

Moving well beyond the starting point of bomb shelters, the report asserted that no defensive measures could offer adequate protection. The Soviets were more determined than ever to overrun the free world, and the bulwark designed to thwart that prospect, the Strategic Air Command, was fatally flawed. "The current vulnerability of SAC to surprise attack," the report warned, "and the threat posed to SAC by the prospects of an early Russian ICBM capability, call for prompt remedial action."[207] The Gaither Report insisted on the urgent need for large increases in the strategic arsenal, a major escalation of the U.S. ballistic missile program, and a full restoration of conventional military strength, at levels envisioned in NSC-68. Tens of billions of dollars would have to be spent on defense, and fast.

It is hard to know what impact this drastic assessment of American vulnerability would have had in the absence of what occurred just then, but in the event, on October 4, 1957, the context in which such questions were considered changed radically. On that day, the Soviet Union launched *Sputnik,* a word that can be translated as "fellow traveler" — as if to tweak the nose of Senator Joseph McCarthy, who had used the phrase to demonize opponents. The first space satellite, *Sputnik* was a gleaming, basketball-size object that orbited the earth every hour and a half. At night, like a twinkling star, it was visible to the naked eye. *Sputnik* started the space age. But Americans perceived that it had been boosted out of the earth's atmosphere by a rocket that could equally well deliver a nuclear warhead from Moscow to Washington. Edward Teller defined *Sputnik* on television as a defeat "more important and greater than Pearl Harbor."[208]

As Nitze's vision had been legitimized in 1950 by North Korea's invasion of the South, so his vision now, with staggering and instant proof of Soviet missile superiority, was made the absolute truth of a new American consensus. And because of Nitze's insistence on the essential evil of the Communist system and its Soviet leaders, the dread was reinforced that Moscow would not hesitate to launch an assault that would kill hundreds of millions of innocent people. Meanwhile, a contrasting American virtue that would allow no such thing was taken for granted — as American war plans, especially including SAC's, prepared for just this kind of assault against Soviet and Chinese populations. The logic of nuclear horror, in other words, was the same on both sides, but Nitze and others always insisted on a difference: U.S. motives were pure while Soviet motives were malign, even if the eventual outcome of action was the same. Nitze was bringing forward the Manichaean vision with which he had been stamped a decade earlier by James Forrestal.

As early as 1954, not long after leaving the Eisenhower administration, Nitze had disapproved of the president's policies. Trashing government decisions he had no role in shaping would in fact be a lifelong habit. He wrote in that year to the journalist Joseph Alsop, "As you know, I generally felt the last administration [Truman's] was doing too little too late. The trouble is this administration [Eisenhower's] is doing less and less beyond issuing empty and misleading statements."[209] To Nitze, the emptiest statements had to do with Dulles's massive retaliation, for he regarded the strategy, in the words of his biographer, as "inadequate if not dangerous, foolish if not wicked."[210] Even without access to Operation Top Hat's assessments, Nitze knew America's strategic bomber force was vulnerable, and *Sputnik* underlined the point. Thus the Gaither Committee emphasized that America's bomber force would soon be overtaken by Soviet intercontinental ballistic missiles. The report said that within a year the USSR would have twelve ICBMs ready for use. The Russians were two to three years ahead of the United States. As if to prove the truth of this dire warning, the first American attempt to launch a space satellite, atop a Vanguard "launch vehicle" on the following December 6, blew up on the launch pad.

Within days of that, Nitze's Gaither Report was leaked to the press. "The Russians are coming!" was given more credence than ever, only now the Russians had a new weapon. "The still top-secret Gaither Report portrays a United States in the gravest danger in its history," a story in the *Washington Post* declared. "It pictures the Nation moving in frightening course to the status of a second-class power. It shows an America exposed to an almost immediate threat from the missile-bristling Soviet Union."[211]

Missiles! Before the smoke cleared from the disastrous humiliation of the Vanguard explosion, the "missile gap" was born.[212]

Nitze is one Forrestal-inspired figure whose impact on this story is felt again and again. Another is Stuart Symington, my father's first mentor. We last saw him as a National Security Council official urging nuclear use on Truman in 1951, and before that as secretary of the Air Force, in a limousine with Forrestal just before Forrestal's breakdown and suicide in 1949. By 1957, Symington was a U.S. senator from Missouri who had become the Senate's leading advocate of air power, and he was quick to pick up on the Gaither Report.

A decade earlier, Symington had perfected the game of projecting worst-case readings of Soviet capabilities and intentions as a way of winning political and budgetary battles. That pattern reached a climax of sorts in 1956 when, as chairman of a major Senate hearing, he had helped create the broad public perception of a bomber gap. A parade of Air Force generals, including LeMay, testified that the Soviets were on the verge of surpassing the United States in both the number and quality of medium- and long-range bombers. It was a complete fantasy, but it worked, and the Air Force got the increases it wanted.[213]

In those years, Symington had been fighting for the supremacy of the Air Force, but now he was planning to run for president in 1960, and the fight was for himself. The Gaither Report gave him the opening he had been preparing for. The bomber gap was his dress rehearsal, and now his Russians-are-coming focus shifted from intercontinental warplanes to ICBMs. Dread and warnings over the perceived missile gap became central to his campaign for the White House. Symington put the soon-to-come Soviet ICBM force at three thousand.[214] In fact, at the start of 1960 the number of operational Soviet ICBMs was four, based on two launch pads.[215]

Such exaggeration might have worked for Symington were he not outdone in near-hysterical rhetoric by his younger rival, John Kennedy. Despite its Republican cast, numerous members of the Gaither Committee served as advisers to the Kennedy campaign, and Nitze in particular influenced JFK's understanding of the Soviet threat.[216] The missile gap would be the wedge JFK used most pointedly against Eisenhower. "The fact of the matter," Kennedy declared on the Senate floor in 1958, "is that during that period when emphasis was laid upon our economic strength instead of our military strength, we were losing the decisive years when we could have maintained a lead against the Soviet Union in our missile capability." And to Kennedy the meaning of this deficit was as frightening as it was obvious. Every American could see the threat in the night sky, the swiftly moving man-made star that offered twinkling proof of what the enemy could do.

With the steady cadence of a tribune bearing terrible news, Kennedy began to strike the theme from every platform. "Missile lag," he sometimes called it, but soon the more common word "gap" defined the alarms he sounded. "[Russian] missile power will be the shield from behind which they will slowly, but surely advance — through Sputnik diplomacy, limited brush-fire wars, indirect non-overt aggression, intimidation, and subversion, internal revolution, increased prestige or influence, and the vicious blackmail of our allies." In John Kennedy, Forrestal had his most eloquent heir. "The periphery of the Free World will slowly be nibbled away," Kennedy said. It was a battle we were already losing. We were the most prosperous people in history, in the throes of an economic boom. We were the most heavily armed nation the world had ever seen, yet on every side our rival and his surrogates stood ready to pounce: the whole great American dream was a house of cards about to fall. Kennedy made catastrophe seem imminent and, without some major changes (and without him), inevitable. "The balance of power," he decreed, "will gradually shift against us."[217]

Kennedy is remembered as having been elected president because he made Americans feel young and hopeful again. I remember it that way myself. But it is equally the case that he was elected president because he made us afraid again.

FIVE

THE TURNING POINT

1. LIFE OF THE PENTAGON

I was sitting at the wheel of my father's Lincoln. It was late at night. My eyes went restlessly from the scene through one of the car's windows to the scene through another. To one side of me, the reflection of the illuminated obelisk of the Washington Monument shimmered in the black sheen of the Potomac like a stack of gold coins, Neptune's treasure. On the other side, like a looming canyon wall, was the becolumned façade of the River Entrance of the Pentagon. Just above me were the grand windows of the office of the secretary of defense, Robert McNamara, and to their right, only a few rooms removed, were the twin windows of my father's office.[1] I knew what the view from the secretary's four large windows was, because I had seen it: the shallow dome of the Jefferson Memorial, the needle of the Washington Monument, and, far off, the sharp dome of the Capitol, all glimpsed above a rounded hedge of mature trees.

I checked my watch. During the weeks of that summer of 1961, Dad had consistently worked late. Some evenings, like tonight, a few hours ago, Miss Ginsberg, his secretary, would call the house on Generals' Row to say that he would dismiss his driver early if I would come pick him up. Dad's motive here, a thoughtful releasing of his driver so the man could be home with his family, was more about his aide than me, yet I always jumped at it. I loved the rare chance to drive the Lincoln, with its telephone mounted on the hump of the drive shaft; I loved the rare time alone with him.

I was eighteen years old. I had just completed my freshman year at

Georgetown University, and through the windshield of the Lincoln I could see the dark outline of the gothic spire of Healy Hall in the far distance, the building that held the musty library reading room where I went not to read so much as to be alone. Georgetown had been an unexpected place of unhappiness. In the fall, I had been thrilled to be John F. Kennedy's neighbor, and his election as president — an Irish Catholic! one of us! — had been my rite of initiation into the complex realm of political concerns, where anxiety is the other side of hope. At Georgetown I was an Air Force ROTC cadet, wearing a uniform like Dad's, shoehorning myself into a dream of being a B-52 pilot. Indeed, on "Rotsee" days I literally shoehorned my feet into my father's spare shoes because they had been spit-shined by his orderly, an instant credit for me. When, at morning inspection, the cadet colonel put the tip of his shoe next to mine, a moment of comparison the other cadets dreaded, my heart leapt because the colonel could see the passing clouds reflected in the gleam of my toe. My father's toe, actually, although I never said so.

I used that cadet uniform, and Dad's status on base, which was subtly flaunted by three stars on the bumper even of the Volkswagen, to bring dates to the Officers' Club at Bolling, where the dance-band musicians were all sergeants. I could impress girls with the simple act of driving on base and returning the air policeman's salute at the gate, then swinging by LeMay's house (girls had also heard of LeMay) and letting them get a look at my house, next door, only slightly smaller.

Debutante balls, tea dances, mixers, the Young Democrats, stuffing envelopes for JFK. At the inauguration, I stood amid the freezing throng listening to a speech, really listening, for the first time in my life. How far I'd come from the day I'd shinnied up a pole on Pennsylvania Avenue to watch Ike ride by with Truman. When I now looked up at the glamorous young president, whose hair was feathered by the cold wind — no homburg for him — it was a version not of myself that I saw, but of the self I longed to be. That the torch of freedom had been passed to a new generation meant, exactly, that it had been passed to me. Kennedy justified the secret feelings I already had, and his eloquence made me want to speak of them, but I did not know how.

So I defined myself by the swirl of being a college kid in the most exciting city in the world, a Hoya in my blue blazer and khakis, penny loafers and a crewneck sweater. Georgetown was an all-male college in those days, but there were sister schools all over town — Visitation, Trinity, Marymount, Goucher in Baltimore — and I organized my peripheral vision around girls in pleated skirts and sweater sets and uplift bras. And understanding something new about the warrior ethos, I traded in the blazer as often as possible, like Clark Kent, for that blue uniform with its silver insignia of my future. Off we go into the wild blue yonder, and one reason we do so, I suddenly knew, is for the effect it has on the women we leave behind. For all anyone knew who looked at me, I might have been Curtis LeMay's son instead of my own conflicted father's.

That Dad was conflicted was not, of course, something I was conscious of then. Only recently, in writing a memoir and this book, did I begin to fully see what he was dealing with inside the Building, from his time as a postwar gumshoe general to the 1960s, when the pins were removed from the scaffolding of his hard-won image. To cross the threshold into adulthood is to take the world as it is for granted, but in looking back I understand that the world as it was could and should have been different. Only now do I sense how the weight of the events tracked here impinged upon my father. Only now do I see that when I carried myself like a Washington prince while secretly feeling like an impostor, I was just like him.

One morning at inspection, the cadet colonel, unable any longer to tolerate how my shoes outshone his, brought his stout heel down on my toe, crushing the thick veneer of polish it had taken my dad's orderly a year to fashion. Oedipus wreck.[2] I would submit to my father's will in that season — as my father, together with the most independent-minded Kennedy men, fulfilling Roosevelt's fear and Eisenhower's warning, would submit to the impersonal will of the very Building looming in the night beside me.

As time haunts my perceptions now, so it did then, in the summer of 1961. I couldn't shake a sick feeling that went back to our family's sojourn in Germany, where Dad had been transferred in 1957. If you recall, before that we had lived in a tract house in a suburb south of Alexandria. Those couple of years at Wiesbaden were the first time our family lived in the Air Force culture, and what Dad had learned to take for granted at the Pentagon came to me as something of a shock. In my childhood romps up and down the broad ramps of the Building, I had had only bare glimpses of life inside the brave new world that was being constructed in the 1950s, from NSC-68 to the Gaither Report, from the New Look to the missile gap. The military establishment, built around a pulsing nuclear arsenal, was a nation within a nation. But when we moved into Air Force housing, my brothers and I attending Air Force schools, my family worshiping at Air Force churches, shopping at Air Force food stores, eating at Air Force snack bars, playing golf on Air Force courses, going to the movies at Air Force theaters, all on the edge of flight lines near earth-covered bunkers in which ordnance was stored — it was like being kidnapped by gypsies, only to learn that your father was the gypsy king. Sure, I loved it, especially the intimate brush with the power of his rank. Overnight, I had become what I remain, however paradoxically, to this day — a general's son.

But being brought so far inside what I would much later think of as the garrison state also left me feeling, right from the start, unsettled and secretly out of place. As I indicated earlier, the high school I attended was named for H. H. Arnold, the bomber general who had set LeMay loose first in Germany, then in the Pacific. Arnold's portrait hung in the school lobby, and the five stars on his epaulettes were what rank-conscious kids were bound to notice first. But when you stood in front of the painting, the general's gray eyes seemed forever lost in a middle distance above your head. I knew he was called Hap, but from the stern look of him in that picture, he was not a man I wanted to be like. "We must not get soft" — his words to Stimson regarding Dresden. "War must be destructive and to a certain extent inhuman and ruthless." Those were words I did not know, and I would not have known what to make of them if I did, but Arnold's was a portrait I stopped looking at. "I had grown up with the feeling that something was being kept from me," the German writer W. G. Sebald recalled, "at home, at school, and by the German writers whose books I read hoping to glean more information about the monstrous events in the background of my own life."[3] Sebald and I were alike, although we grew up on opposite sides of the secret.

The kids I met in Wiesbaden — "Army brats," but of the Air Force — took for granted what struck me as an astonishing familiarity with their fathers' work and concerns. They knew, for example, what had never occurred to me: the American forces in Germany and their families were there not to serve as a real military front line but as the mere tripwire that would compel the United States to keep its pledge to defend Europe against a Red Army offensive — defend it with the all-out nuclear strike of massive retaliation. There were 250,000 American troops stationed on that front line, but there were an equal number of dependents. When the Red Army offensive came, as everyone assumed it eventually would, we sons, daughters, and wives would instantly be dead. So, of course, would our dads. Lambs of God, sacrificial offerings. But our deaths, acting as the very trigger of Armageddon, as my new friends explained to me, would have a patriotic meaning, unlike the consequent deaths of those other hundreds of millions, poor devils. Our deaths, sparking the great American killing machine, would mean something.

Picking up clues from the other kids, I compensated for my hidden whim-whams with a martial assertiveness, as if the wild blue yonder were the only place for me. When I had first learned that the Wiesbaden high school sports teams were called "Warriors," I redoubled my newcomer's determination to go out for football, even if I'd never tackled anybody before. I discovered you could tackle a runner just by falling down in front of him at the last moment, a technique I mastered. I made the team, and soon I could imitate the gladiator swagger that was the only way to walk onto the field in all that padding. Warrior indeed. In a world full of secrets. But already with a secret of my own.

What might have been the normal insecurities of a shy high school kid pretending to be outgoing were compounded, in my case, by an acute awareness that we were not that far from the Iron Curtain, which obsessed me in those years. The welling ocean in my chest that I could still associate with the cool feel of the linoleum tiles on the floor of Sister Miriam Teresa's classroom at St. Mary's School now became a function of my new geography. The once abstract enemy was just across the Taunus Mountains, which I could see from my bedroom window. Some nights I went to sleep afraid. Not that you'd have read my nervousness in the ease with which I tossed around, with the coolest of my classmates, the flyboy jargon that defined our fathers' world: words like "fast mover," "strat wing," and "airborne alert," but also "deterrence," "provocation," and "survivability," abstractions I hardly understood. The name Forrestal meant little or nothing to me, but I realize now that I was doing as a boy what he had done as a man — channeling a deep personal insecurity into a show of brusque readiness for war. I was coming of age having internalized — without knowing it and only to a point — the grim spirit that had begun, in fact, the day I was born.

So, of course, what better place and time to have approached the threshold of manhood than there and then? Throughout our "tour" in Germany, Eisenhower and Khrushchev had sparred over Berlin, with various crises along the way. While it was true that the occupation army was the tripwire, the air base at Wiesbaden was the tip of the first spear that would be thrown, and SAC had an untouted strat wing of B-47s there that were always on alert, intermediate-range bombers whose navigational gyroscopes were programmed not for Red Army positions in East Germany but for Moscow. At the Base Operations building — "Base-Ops" — was a snack bar that was open around the clock, and some of us high school kids went there late at night for Cokes and fries, and just to hang around while the fighter pilots came and went in their olive-drab flight suits, helmets under their arms, oxygen hookups dangling. We boys all claimed to want to be one of them, and soon enough I had convinced myself it was true.

But late in my senior year, like a replay of *Sputnik*, the Russians landed a blow that knocked us all back, Eisenhower especially. On May 1, 1960, they shot down a U-2, a black bird operated by the CIA. When the official explanation from Washington said it was an off-course weather plane, I believed it — and had an argument with one of my classmates, who insisted that it was a spy plane, and that it was secretly based at Wiesbaden. (Years later, when I understood that SAC and the CIA were both flying the U-2 in Soviet airspace, its being based at Wiesbaden made sense.) And then I guessed that the boy's father was a flight-line mechanic who worked on the spy plane. Just because my father had told me nothing did not mean other fathers had kept their sons in the dark. That, too, was unthinkable to me then. I told the kid he was full of shit; President Eisenhower would not lie. But Khrushchev produced the U-2 pilot, Francis Gary Powers, to show that Ike had presided over the construction of a tower of deceit.

Later I would learn that the president was angry that Powers hadn't committed suicide, as captured CIA agents were supposed to do. Lies? Suicide? What the hell was going on? The Reds were liars, not us. And suicide was a mortal sin. The Reds believed the ends justified the means, not us. In my mind, such profound ethical differences were what the Cold War fight was all about. Around that time, I tried to talk to my father about the sick feeling I couldn't shake, the ocean in my chest. *If a mechanic NCO can talk to his kid, why can't you talk to me, Dad?* But I made the mistake of starting with the U-2, so he brushed me off: "You know I can't discuss that."

By the time I graduated from H. H. Arnold, my father had been transferred back to the Pentagon with a big promotion. He wore three stars on his shoulders now, having surpassed in rank most of the World War II bomber generals who had disdained him a decade earlier. He was now the Air Force inspector general, a position on the Air Staff, which brought with it the house at Bolling, orderlies to cook and serve our meals and shine those shoes. There was the limo for Dad, and my mother's place, with Helen LeMay, in the generals' wives' power circle. At Bolling, which sat on the Maryland side of the Potomac, at the southern edge of the District of Columbia, about three miles downriver from the Pentagon, we were no longer at the tip of the spear, but it was the worldwide command headquarters for the whole Air Force, and as such, to apply the phrase I would hear years later, we were in the heart of the beast.

At Georgetown, I tried to stifle what was by now my familiar uneasiness, channeling it into all that young-prince-of-Washington ardor. Jazz with Charlie Byrd at the Showboat Lounge, double dates to hear Count Basie at the Carter Baron Amphitheater, jitterbug contests, which somehow I often won. And, always, my snappy salute coming through the gate at Bolling. But on some nights, sleep still took me down the well of an anguish I did not understand. I threw myself more than ever into ROTC, signing up for flight training, finding myself at the stick of a small plane with an instructor in the next seat. Probably because of my father's rank, if not his shoes, I would be named outstanding cadet of the year, having fooled, apparently, everyone but myself. When I was alone, in that reading room in Georgetown's Healy library, say, my gaze would drift out the window, floating above the iconic Washington skyline, and I would admit that something was wrong.

I have mentioned my unhappiness, and here it was. The more my flyboy dream came true, the more it felt like anyone's but mine. Something was wrong. I did not know what. Georgetown is a Jesuit school, and I went to see a black-robed counselor a few times, not with an impulse to confess, but to ask for help. I could not put into words what I was feeling, and I remember long silences during which I stared at the pattern of the threadbare rug in the priest's office. At one point, he suggested that perhaps I was receiving a signal from the Lord, that I wasn't meant for worldly things, that God was choosing me for Himself.

That I should be a priest was a wish, I knew, that my parents had harbored since I was a child, but I had long since hoped they'd gotten over it. I deflected the priest's observation, but not before he put a pamphlet into my hands. "Many are called, but few are chosen." Nothing in me wanted to be a priest, but every Irish-Catholic boy of my generation had been spiritually vaccinated in infancy with the idea of "vocation," and it was impossible for me to walk away from the Jesuit residence that day without a dim but awed intimation of a different future. Pray for the grace of vocation, the pamphlet said. Right. Many are cold, but few are frozen.

Picturing that mystified and unhappy lad now, my younger self, I wish I could reach back through time and touch his shoulder sympathetically. It was not his older self with whom he longed to be in conversation, nor some Jesuit, but his father. Still, I would tell him what I have learned the hard way, over a lifetime. That Jesuit priest misunderstood him, and nudged him toward what would prove, years later, to be the cul-de-sac of triumphalist religion. The oceanic feeling in his chest was not of God, but of war. War, too, in the thermonuclear age, is a source of transcendent fear and trembling. A perfect creature of his era, young Jim had built an inner life around the outer dread of what was coming, and though political rhetoric — including, above all, Kennedy's — both created that dread and exploited it, Jim was like every American in not being able to speak of its impact. In relation to this mystery he felt utterly alone, but in that he was like everyone. His deepest feelings were already hostage to the larger world around him, and, yes indeed, in that world there were things to be afraid of, and there was much to be unhappy about.

Those unsettled, alienating, and frightened feelings of yours, I would explain to young Jim if I could, *just prove that you are paying attention to what is going on around you. You never heard of NSC-68 or the Gaither Report. You may not know who Forrestal was, or who Nitze is, or why LeMay obsesses you, but your father has their infection, and you are catching it, even now, from him. The human race has been led to the edge of an abyss by the very ones you are trying to imitate, so why shouldn't you be anxious? You will spend the next forty years trying to put words on the inchoate emotion that already defines you. You*

*will someday write a book, not about God but about what followed from the day
you and the Pentagon were born. That book will be your long-delayed conversation with your father.*

If the Pentagon and I were born in the same week, we came of age together,
too. I am not speaking of the mere Building, of course, or of the Defense Department bureaucracy with its inbuilt systems and forces and requirements,
but of something larger, with an unprecedented power of its own. This book
is the biography of that something larger. The Building was the center of an
agency, but it also came to *possess* agency — the capacity to act in ways that
transcended the wills and purposes of the people who claimed responsibility
for the Defense Department at any given time. The Pentagon, that is, was
coming into its own as a kind of metapersonal creature, with its own beliefs
and desires that could seem independent of the beliefs and desires of the men
passing through its offices.[4] So much money, so much power, so much cultural energy had been invested in the Pentagon that it was by now taking on a
life of its own. That life is my subject.

To an extent unimagined then, the American boom time of the 1950s was
driven by contracts written in the offices of the Pentagon, as the percentage of
federal dollars spent on defense grew and grew. Like industry, cultural institutions, notably the university, and the labor movement and the fourth estate
were transformed by their conscription into the Cold War enterprise of national security.

Tensions among the power centers in the Pentagon, particularly those of
the interservice rivalries, generated a force field of expansion that no one
foresaw and no one controlled. Every American military entity organized itself against two enemies: the Communist monolith and every other American military entity. Actions taken to shore up budgets and turf by the various
Pentagon fiefdoms were always justified by appeals to the ever-worsening
threat posed by the hostile Soviet Union, but in fact many of those actions
were not aimed at Moscow but at rivals down the corridor. Every self-protec-
tive move by one service branch produced equal or greater moves by the others, leading to an action-reaction dynamic that began to resemble the released energy of fission.

The metaphor is apt, since at the heart of this dynamic was the new phenomenon of a militarized scientific establishment. The disgrace of J. Robert
Oppenheimer in the mid-1950s — the hearings that removed his security
clearance — had taught scientists what the price of resisting scientific militarism would be, and, more positively, the billions of defense dollars pouring
into research of all kinds generated Cold War fervor at laboratories around
the country. Where once scientists sought prestigious fellowships as the high-

est recognition, as one of them pointed out to me years later,[5] now they longed to be chosen for one of the burgeoning "science advisory panels" that dotted the military and governmental landscape. The pattern had been set at Los Alamos during World War II, when the most brilliant thinkers in the world chose to define themselves as deferential subordinates of a simple-minded military elite, all in the name of national unity in the war effort. The flow of power was all in one direction, and that power multiplied. A kind of critical mass took hold, as this bureaucratic machine fed itself in the concentrated chamber of the Pentagon. The Building, in terms of energy generated in the national economy, the academy, the press, and the political culture, became its own nuclear reactor.

Likewise, anxieties attached to the steady expectation of the absolute worst from the Soviet Union led to irrational impulses that always outran the normal checks and balances of government. The perception nurtured among the American public that the Pentagon alone stood between the nation and obliteration reversed the Pentagon's relationship with the political sphere. With Congress in its thrall and presidents at its mercy, the Pentagon *defined* politics. It is not without significance that Senator McCarthy's scare campaign ran unchecked, emasculating the State Department, Congress, the White House, and the press, until he foolhardily took on the Army. The Army destroyed him.[6] The Pentagon was invincible. Eventually, as we saw, a secretary of defense would define himself as Ahab lashed to the back of a thrashing, wild, unchecked Moby Dick, unable to rein in the monster.[7] The Pentagon's character as a transcending center of mind, conviction, and will, able to thwart the agency of its putative masters, was fully established.

Roosevelt had been afraid of something like this when he expressed reservations about the concentration of masses of people, money, and power in one huge place set apart. That was why he intended that the Pentagon be a temporary building, to be dismantled after the emergency of the war. Instead, it became the holy of holies of government, receiving incense from the White House and Capitol Hill both. It was Truman who, first by legitimizing nuclear weapons with their use, and then by yielding to the panic after the explosion of the Soviet atomic bomb in 1949 and the pressures of North Korean aggression in 1950 to embrace thermonuclear weapons, had set the great white whale loose. And it was Eisenhower who, three days before he left office, in confessing his disappointment that the world had not moved toward "disarmament, with mutual honor and confidence," clearly identified the main obstacle to this goal for which the world longed — and the obstacle was not merely the Soviet Union.

Eisenhower pointed to the phenomenon of which the Pentagon was headquarters, the "conjunction," as he called it, "of an immense military establishment and a large arms industry." This was, he said, "new in the American experience." He understood exactly how the thing had happened; indeed, he had enabled it. "We recognize the need for this development. Yet we must not fail to comprehend its grave implications . . . In the councils of government we must guard against the acquisition of unwarranted influence, whether sought or unsought, by the military-industrial complex. The potential for the disastrous rise of misplaced power exists and will persist."[8]

It was not a coup by a man on horseback that Eisenhower was warning of, as many mistakenly and therefore dismissively thought, but the impersonal workings of a frenzied cycle in which money feeds on fear which feeds on power which feeds on violence which feeds on a skewed idea of honor which feeds on demonization of an enemy which feeds on more fear which feeds on ever more money. Something new. Something unstoppable. Something dangerous. An entire world within a world, built around the harsh fact of what Eisenhower had presided over: the construction of a stockpile in excess of eighteen thousand nuclear warheads.[9] This world came with its own rules, its own economy, its own self-protection.

When Ike's old comrades had to choose between him and this new behemoth, the brass did not hesitate: "Never has a general been so hated," he confided not long before his term ended, "as I am now in the Pentagon."[10] Without quite naming the threat — the nuclear arsenal itself — the old general gave his country fair warning of its danger. In doing so, Ike followed Henry Stimson into the netherworld of career regret, another government leader denouncing Pentagon assumptions, but only upon surrendering the power to influence them. Over the years, many holding power in and over the Pentagon would do this. "Retirement syndrome," to note Robert Jay Lifton's phrase again.

Three days after Eisenhower's farewell address, John F. Kennedy replaced him as president. JFK seemed ready to meet any challenge, but like the earlier Ike and Truman before him, he thought his only enemy was in front of him. He did not know it yet, but he was replacing Eisenhower not only as president but as Ahab.

2. A LARK IN BERLIN

That spring, the high of Kennedy's inauguration had been replaced, first, by the shock of the Soviet Union's putting the first human in space. On April 12, 1961, Yuri Gagarin blasted into orbit, circled the globe once in a ride that lasted one hour and forty-eight minutes, and returned safely to earth, landing in a field. The awe Americans felt about Gagarin's flight, in common with people everywhere, was confounded by a new blast of the old fear, for the cosmonaut's feat proved once more how much better at building missiles our enemy was. This was the kind of setback we had come to associate with the infirm and complacent Eisenhower, not Kennedy. It was *Sputnik* all over again. Gagarin's *Vostok 1* could well have been a thermonuclear bomb on Washington. The Russians are coming!

But one week later came the second shock — Kennedy's misadventure at Bahía de Cochinos, the Bay of Pigs. On April 17, 1,500 American-sponsored Cuban exiles landed on the south side of the island of Cuba. They were immediately betrayed not only by the Cuban population, which declined to rise up as the CIA plan assumed it would, but also by what was widely perceived as Kennedy's own failure of nerve, for at the last minute he had called off the air support that was supposed to have enabled the invaders to succeed. The man who was going to protect us from the very danger he had made so palpable suddenly seemed unsteady. That appearance, however, belied a deeper reality — that Kennedy showed enormous courage in accepting defeat at the Bay of Pigs. But few saw it that way.[11]

Fidel Castro, the Cuban leader, thought he had taken Kennedy's measure, but so, more alarmingly, did Nikita Khrushchev. In June, at a summit meeting in Vienna, the Soviet leader openly badgered Kennedy, who looked visibly intimidated. The point of contention was Berlin again, but this time a swaggering Khrushchev made his threat of war explicit. "I want peace," he said, banging the table, "but if you want war, that is your problem." He may well have been referring to the fact that, as a free-swinging presidential candidate in 1959, Kennedy had declared that maintaining America's presence in Berlin was fully worth war, even nuclear war.[12] It was one thing to say this on the stump, another to contemplate it in the teeth of Soviet bluster. Kennedy came away from Vienna, as British Prime Minister Harold Macmillan observed, "rather stunned — baffled would perhaps be fairer."[13]

Such were the events I brooded over while waiting for my father outside the Pentagon that night in the summer of 1961.[14] As I had the summer before and would again a year later, I was working as a clerk at the FBI, a job I had because of my father's lasting connection to J. Edgar Hoover. The word "clerk" does not catch the weight of what I was doing, of how I was being drawn deeper into the melodrama of the time. I was a cryptanalyst's aide in the FBI's cryptanalysis/translation section, which had its offices in a deliberately nondescript and anonymous building that passed as a garage about four blocks from the Capitol. "Cryptanalyst's aide" was a phrase I was forbidden to use away from the office. That the FBI had a code-breaking operation at all was a secret, and it thrilled me to have been brought into the clandestine realm where my father was royalty.

My work at the Bureau could not have been more mind-numbingly mundane: I spent each day poring over computer printouts, page after page filled with digits. The numbers were grouped in fives, with perhaps twenty groups to a line, fifty lines to a page, each job consisting of hundreds of pages. My boss the cryptanalyst, a math-whiz FBI agent, would instruct me in what to look for — counting certain digits in each line, say, and noting the number in the margin. Some other clerk would duplicate my work, and someone else might feed our fresh numbers back into the computer. Eventually, the boss would review the marginal notations and new computer calculations himself, looking for patterns that might, to a genius like him, reveal the meaning of the numbers. What made this work exciting was the fact that the digits were cryptograms, intercepted cable traffic between the Washington embassies of various nations. The cryptanalysis section was said to have cracked a Japanese code during the war, but by 1961, with enemy computers capable of putting together nearly purely random ciphers, cracking any of the cryptograms we were working on was practically impossible. We told each other otherwise, of course.

I always knew which nation's secret I was working on, because one word of "plaintext" appeared in each intercept, in the upper right-hand margin of the first page. That word identified the city in which the message had originated. "Moscow," I might read, or "Prague," and I could never see a Communist capital so identified on the page without feeling a brief rush of vertigo — my own role at last in the great contest. The task gave me a channel into which to force my fear, controlling it. Every morning, despite my utter incomprehension of the numbers in front of me and of the meaning of what I was to do with them, I arrived at my desk with renewed fervor, a determination to make a perfect count, to give my boss what he needed to unravel the secret, which might be just the thing to enable us to win. The first surprise I had as a teenage would-be code breaker, incidentally, was when I came to work one morning and saw the word "London" in the corner of the top page of the stack of printouts. London! I understood without having it explained to me that we were in the business of intercepting the encoded messages of not just our enemies but our friends.

Only a few weeks before driving to the Pentagon that night, I had spent several days working on cryptograms that had been sent to the Soviet embassy on 16th Street, four blocks north of the White House. My boss, in his excitement, and no doubt violating the rule of need-to-know, explained the significance of those particular pages to me. The plaintext word was "Vienna," because the messages were being sent from the site of the momentous Kennedy-Khrushchev summit meeting then under way. In my very own hands I held the secrets of what the Russians were saying to each other about the encounter while it was going on.

Berlin. I knew from the newspapers that Berlin was the big subject at Vienna, so it stood to reason that that word was buried in the pages in front of me. A key! Berlin. It had to be there somewhere.

"Berlin," Khrushchev once said, "is the testicles of the West . . . Every time I want to make the West scream, I squeeze on Berlin."[15] But despite such flamboyant machismo, Berlin was a source of insecurity for the Soviet leader, because by the late 1950s, he had reason to fear that the Russian nightmare — West Germany in control of its own nuclear weapons — was coming to pass. *That* was what all of Khrushchev's posturing on Berlin was about, and his concern was, in fact, not only real but reasonable. The West German defense minister, a right-wing politician named Franz Josef Strauss, openly advocated arming the Bundeswehr, the German armed forces, with atomic weapons, and President Eisenhower encouraged the idea of sharing the U.S. nuclear arsenal with Bonn. "For God's sake," he said, "let's not be stingy with an ally."[16]

When Berlin reemerged as an East-West flashpoint in the late 1950s, the only story Americans were told was the old one of the imperialist reach of the Russian bear. No hint was given that Moscow might actually be addressing a legitimate concern, and certainly no one explained that Khrushchev, in "squeezing," was responding to a rebuff from Eisenhower of an unusual and highly reasonable Soviet offer. In March 1958, the Soviets had proposed that the stationing of nuclear weapons in central Europe be prohibited, effectively making a nuclear-free zone of Poland, Czechoslovakia, and East and West Germany. Obviously the aim here was to prevent Bonn from having access to or authority over nuclear forces of any kind, but in return Moscow was prepared to restrict its own nuclear deployments and break its own ironclad rule against inspections, because the proposal would mean nothing without an unprecedented Soviet readiness to submit to regular inspections, if only in its satellite nations. When Ike refused this offer, as it had to appear in Moscow, the Soviets found reason to conclude that NATO intended to turn West Germany into a nuclear power — and that, for very good reasons, Moscow could not tolerate.[17]

By 1961, it was not only that Berlin was useful to Khrushchev as a point of pressure. It had also become his biggest problem. The divided city had long been an open sore for the Communists. Through the fifties, driven by the "miracle" of West Germany's Marshall Plan–induced economic boom, the western half of the city had become a prosperous capitalist showcase, in stark contrast with the devastated eastern sector, where bomb rubble still stood in accidental pyramids from which tree-size weeds had sprouted. But worse than that for the Soviets, the postwar agreements among the four occupying powers provided for free movement about the entire city, which meant easterners could easily go west and, through West Berlin, out of the Soviet zone altogether. Throughout 1959 and 1960, the more Khrushchev threatened to close off the city, the more people of the East packed up and fled it.

I had felt the tension over Berlin myself, only the year before, when, as a high school student, traveling from the air base at Wiesbaden, I had gone with chums to the divided city. To us, with its gleaming new stores on one side, its bombed-out shells of buildings on the other, the place was a kind of crazy wonderland, and over a long weekend we crisscrossed the city on the grimy, Communist-run elevated trains. It was an adventure in bipolarity, an initiation into the Manichaean global contest. Berlin embodied the division over which world wars had been fought and on which the coming world war would turn. Yet the place put us in a larky mood.

Feeling bold, we bought red neckerchiefs of the Young Communist movement at a war memorial in East Berlin and wore them as headscarves, babushkas, as if we were "mustache women," the Communist hags who watched over every turnstile and elevator bank. We delighted in our open display of contempt, even as soldiers with red stars on their caps glared at us. They were hardly older than we, but with cigarettes hooked in their lips and machine guns cradled in their arms, they were an intimidating sight, which made us, in our nervous exuberance, all the more impudent. We waved at them, tugged at our red scarves, wagged our hips, and ran, heading for the stairs up to the S-Bahn. That easily, we were safe. Counting the trains and numerous streets, there were ninety crossing points between the two halves of the city, and over the weekend we treated them like the escape routes of Chutes and Ladders. When I later read about the exodus of East Germans, who left everything to flee west using those same crossings, I thought of the frightened-looking people on that dingy commuter line and felt ashamed to have treated it all like a game.

But our lark was not over. Returning to West Germany at the end of the weekend, we took the U.S. Army train, the way we'd come, and we were feeling our oats. Our fellow passengers were Americans like us — young GIs on leave, dependent wives and children, on rotation home. We were the only unsupervised teenagers, a status we exulted in. This time, as we approached the East-West border near Helmstedt — the actual Iron Curtain! — we were not intimidated, since we had traveled the other way three days before. As the train slowed, American military policemen went from compartment to compartment, ordering passengers to lower the window curtains. Strictly defined regulations, worked out by four-party treaties, governed procedures at the border, and one of them required that all of the curtains on this special American train be closed. This was probably because the Soviets did not want photographs taken of their heavily armed military units, including a tank battalion on station nearby. Indeed, the passengers — decidedly including us — had been forbidden to take any photographs inside East Germany at all.

At the border, the train engine shut down. Long minutes passed. In our shadowy compartment, my buddies and I began daring each other to raise the curtain, and I was the one to put the lens of my eight-millimeter movie camera — my father's camera, actually — between the curtain and the glass. Through the crack, I peeked out and saw the nearby tanks, each with its large red star, the snout of its turret gun pointed right at us. I pressed the camera button, and it began to whir. My friends stifled whoops, and I felt a dangerous thrill of defiance, as if I were sticking it to old Joe Stalin himself.

My movie camera was still running when the compartment door was thrown back with a loud slam, and a knot of uniformed men burst in on us, all with guns drawn. I saw the blue uniform of the East German *Volkspolizei*, the brown uniform of a Soviet officer, and the tans of two white-helmeted American MPs. There were shouts in a language I did not recognize, not German — Russian! One of the Americans, a large Negro, grabbed my camera and in a flash had it open. He deftly unspooled the film and turned to demonstrate to the others that he had done so, the ribbon of celluloid draping from his hands like an offering. The exposed film was useless now, which, I saw, was his point. *No pictures here — leave the kids alone.*

The East German and Soviet soldiers were angry and agitated, but eventually they yielded to the American's authority. It was his train. They left. Then the MP sullenly checked our dependents' ID cards. When he saw mine, registering my father's rank, he shook his head. Ordinarily he would write us up, with the complaint, in the case of a dependent, going to the father's commanding officer, guaranteeing the child's rebuke. In my case, that was further up the chain of command than the MP cared to go. He brusquely gave my ID card back to me, saying, "You should be ashamed of yourself." As he turned to leave, he hesitated at the door. "Some damn fool like you," he said, glaring right at me, "is going to start World War Three."[18]

When Khrushchev squeezed on Berlin at Vienna in June 1961, it was because by then thousands of East Germans, and citizens of Poland and Czechoslovakia and other Communist satellites, too, motivated by *Torschluss-panik* (gate-closing panic), were escaping to the West every week through Berlin.[19] Even the knowledge that the relatives they left behind would be severely punished did not stop the exodus. Losing the best educated and most skilled of the Communist-dominated population, the Soviet Union and its East German puppet regime could not allow this to continue. The simplest solution was to cut off Allied access to West Berlin altogether, claiming the entire city for East Germany. At the June summit meeting in Vienna, that is exactly what Khrushchev threatened to do. He announced that the USSR would sign a separate peace treaty with East Germany, ending the postwar occupation zones, deeding the whole city to the Communists. If the blustery Soviet leader carried through on his threat to unilaterally overrule British, American, and French claims to Berlin, Kennedy would have no choice but to defy him, which Khrushchev would define as a violation of East German sovereignty and a cause for war. "If the U.S. wants to start a war over Germany," Khrushchev told Kennedy, "let it be so." And then the Soviet leader added, "This is what the Pentagon has been wanting."[20]

3. THERE WILL BE WAR

But war over Berlin in 1961 would not be what it might have been a decade earlier. In that reading room in Healy Hall at Georgetown, I had read a book that everyone was talking about that year, *On Thermonuclear War* by Herman Kahn. Kahn was an overweight, owl-eyed RAND analyst who had become the unlikeliest of pop celebrities. Noted in magazines like *Life, Look,* and the *Saturday Evening Post,* Kahn's highly technical work represented a first breakout to a broad audience of the arcane theorizing of the new breed of defense intellectuals. The book was as overweight as its author, chock-full of every theory that had been floated at RAND. Kahn presented himself, one sees now, with a certain PR flair, a self-proclaimed prophet who would dare think aloud about what, until then, had been stamped unthinkable.[21] Nuclear theology, yet it was like reading pornography. Kahn did not so much publish his theories as inflict them, and in receiving them with fervid interest, the public was responding somewhat like a masochistic victim would to his well-paid sadist.

The undercurrent of prurience in Kahn's appeal picked up where *On the Beach,* the Stanley Kramer film of the previous year, left off. The movie, adapted from a book by the pseudonymous Nevil Shute, told the story of a nuclear war's last survivors — small-town people in Australia, waiting for the arrival of the radioactive cloud. Gregory Peck and Ava Gardner had never made such love before. And moviegoers in America, including me, had never before left theaters so in the grip of aftermath *tristesse.* By the late 1950s, Americans were beginning to confront the new meaning of mortality: not just the death of individuals but, conceivably, the slaughter of humanity.

With jarring equanimity, Kahn's book offered specific and staggering descriptions of what an actual nuclear exchange would entail: the immediate

deaths of hundreds of millions and a widespread genetic deformity of the human race reaching far into the future. "Will the survivors envy the dead?" one
chapter title asked. The answer seemed to be, Not really. The survivors, Kahn
insisted, will be fine. Kahn's imaginative fatalism was such that he made the
particular suffering of the victims of a coming nuclear exchange seem, if not
acceptable, then not unimaginable. "Japan, after all, not only survived," an
arms control expert would write during the most frenzied period of nuclear
buildup, justifying it, "but flourished after the nuclear attack."[22]

And yet. However limited, and therefore "thinkable," the nuclear theorists tried to make the effects of the coming war seem, the uninitiated like me,
still at the mercy of wholly unpictured horrors, were far closer to what was
real. The experts who gave intellectual and moral blessing to the accumulation of thousands of nuclear weapons had a vested interest in downplaying
the damage of atomic warfare — if only because a vivid grasp of that damage
would have led people to question the entire enterprise.

Years later, scientists outside the government would repudiate the Pentagon's estimates of the effects of nuclear use as massively underestimating the
catastrophe that would result. A full-blown nuclear exchange would not only
destroy whole societies, to cite only one concern, but result in a dramatic de-
pletion of the ozone layer, leading to a dangerous increase in ultraviolet radiation in the atmosphere, which would act as a death ray aimed at every living
thing. At the same time, dust and ash spewed into the air as a result of the
many nuclear detonations would result in an all-enveloping stratospheric
cloud, blocking the light and heat of the sun, plunging the planet into a "nuclear winter."[23] Nuclear war would obliterate the environment's capacity to
support human life as we know it.

Even shy of a full nuclear exchange, military planners contemplating the
limited use of nuclear weapons as a way, for example, to "coerce compliance"
over this issue or that did not take into account the inexorable pressure any
such use would exert toward full — unlimited — nuclear use. Such pressure
was a matter of built-in mechanisms of escalation,[24] but it also involved the
experts' failure to understand what nuclear weapons would actually do.

Experts calculated damage according to a narrow scale of "blast effects,"
but blast, however damaging, would not be the worst of the effects of the attack. Firestorm damage vastly exceeded blast damage in the World War II
bombings of Hamburg, Dresden, Tokyo, Hiroshima, and Nagasaki, yet projections of fire figured precious little in the calculations of analysts at SAC,
the Joint Chiefs, and RAND as they anticipated future bombardments. One
scientist, at work early in the twenty-first century, made the astounding discovery that, throughout the Cold War and after, Pentagon planners never
took serious measure of the predictable effects of the massive fires that nu-

clear detonations would set off. "War plans are the government's main means for envisioning what would happen were nuclear weapons used, and they deeply influence the views of the military officers and others who would act in a crisis." This is the assessment of the Stanford scholar Lynn Eden, writing in 2004. "Because fire damage has been ignored for the past half century, high-level U.S. decision makers have been poorly informed, if informed at all, about the damage that nuclear weapons would cause. As a result, any U.S. decision to use nuclear weapons — for example, a political decision to employ a 'limited' option to signal 'restraint' — almost certainly would have been predicated on insufficient and misleading information. If nuclear weapons had been used, the physical, social, and political effects would have been far more devastating than anticipated."[25]

Yet even as an uninformed teenager anticipated it, this war was devastating enough to plunge him into frightened sadness. It was upon reading the appallingly complacent reflections of Herman Kahn in Healy Hall that my eyes would lift from the page, to look out at the D.C. skyline to see if it was aflame yet. Kahn's one positive proposal was for a large-scale, immediate project of shelter construction, so that casualties might be counted in the mere tens of millions instead of the hundreds of millions. Fallout shelters along the Mall, below the crenelated towers of the Smithsonian Institution, and in the tunnels of the Capitol. Fallout shelters in every basement! Even I could sense that Kahn's concrete theorizing about mass violence and how to survive it was making the prospect of the actual use of nuclear weapons, whose horrors he could both conjure and dismiss, more likely, not less. Kahn was putting into words what the world I took for granted had assumed. He was, that is, "Up we go" made flesh. Suddenly I was a passenger in a train compartment again, looking out the window at the blurred landscape rushing past, with a black man's voice saying, "You damn fool."

The old tradition of perceiving the Soviet threat in more drastic terms than it actually warranted was obsolete by now, if only because the Soviet Union was certain to have assembled a large thermonuclear arsenal and the means to deliver it. That was as clear as *Sputnik*, as clear as Yuri Gagarin. On a Tuesday night in late July that summer, President Kennedy went on national television to prepare the country for the possibility of war over Berlin. "Good evening," he began. I watched him in the TV room of the house on Generals' Row, a converted sunroom off the parlor. Through the window behind the TV set, I could see the lit windows of General LeMay's house.

In Kennedy's first sentence, he got to the point:

Seven weeks ago tonight I returned from Europe to report on my meeting with Premier Khrushchev and the others. His grim warnings about the future of the world, his aide-mémoire on Berlin, his subsequent speeches and threats which he and his agents have launched, and the increase in the Soviet military budget that he has announced, have all prompted a series of decisions by the Administration and a series of consultations with the members of the NATO organization. In Berlin, as you recall, he intends to bring to an end, through a stroke of the pen, first our legal rights to be in West Berlin — and second our ability to make good on our commitment to the two million free people of that city. That we cannot permit.

The resolute Kennedy did not refer to what, in the first shaken hours after the Vienna meeting, he had said of Khrushchev: "He just beat the hell out of me."[26]

On television, Kennedy then turned to a map of Germany, with free West Germany in white, naturally, and the East in black but for the white island of Berlin. Listening to the president, I pictured the city through which I had so gleefully run, red bandanna fluttering at my neck. West Berlin, he said, "is the great testing place of Western courage and will . . . We cannot separate its safety from our own. I hear it said that West Berlin is militarily untenable." I picture Kennedy leaning toward the camera. "And so was Bastogne. And so, in fact, was Stalingrad. Any dangerous spot is tenable if men — brave men — will make it so.

"Accordingly . . . ," Kennedy announced, "I am now taking the following steps." He announced that he was immediately tripling the draft call, adding hundreds of thousands to the Army and Navy; that he was increasing planned levels of the SAC bomber force, 50 percent of which had only recently been put on fifteen-minute alert; and that he was putting before Congress the next day an emergency appropriation for the addition of more than three billion dollars for defense. We knew that Kennedy was dead serious because (in stark contrast to a later era, when a president waged war while cutting taxes) he told us all of this would mean sharply increased taxes. There would also be cuts in federal programs, interruptions in the normal lives of many citizens, and other "burdens which must be borne if freedom is to be defended. Americans have willingly borne them before, and they will not flinch from the task now." The highflying rhetoric of "bear any burden," which had so uplifted those who heard the inaugural address in January, was now frighteningly concrete.

"We have another sober responsibility," he added gravely. Every American, he said, needed to have a well-stocked hole under the house in which to hide, and he was asking for emergency funds to pay for it. "In the event of an attack, the lives of those families which are not hit in a nuclear blast and fire can still be saved — if they can be warned to take shelter and if that shelter is available." It was Duck and Cover all over again, only now it would be a massive and expensive project of the whole government. He would request more than two hundred million dollars of Congress the next day. Fallout shelters instead of desks. The nation must be prepared to live underground.[27] "To sum it all up," he said, nearing his conclusion, "we seek peace, but we shall not surrender. That is the central meaning of this crisis, and the meaning of your government's policy." War was the central meaning. It was coming.

We saw as much in our young president's anguished face that night. We did not know it, but he had come to the Oval Office for that speech on crutches. Back pain, since Vienna, had made him virtually a cripple, a condition he hid from the public through heavy drug use and stoic will. Yet his suffering that night was palpable. I remember that tears came to my eyes when, altering his tone of voice, Kennedy said, "I would like to close with a personal word." I think that television viewers all over America, as I did, drew closer to their sets just then, closer to him. "When I ran for the presidency of the United States, I knew that this country faced serious challenges, but I could not realize — nor could any man realize who does not bear the burdens of this office — how heavy and constant would be those burdens." The image of the burdened, solitary president goes back to Lincoln, but in Kennedy, at that moment, perhaps, it seared the American mind as never before, and began the nation's obsession with the man and the office.

There is an irony here, one rarely spoken of but one widely perceived even at the time. What made Kennedy's responsibility so devastatingly solitary was the foundational fact of the nuclear age — that he alone bore the ultimate weight of any decision to use nuclear weapons in defense of Berlin. But the solitary burden lay not in his decision to order a nuclear strike, since he would reliably be surrounded by men counseling just such a course, but in the possibility of his refusal to take their recommendations. In any given crisis, the president might decide not to order a nuclear attack, but he could never admit that.[28]

Misjudgments of men in power, he said then, had led to three devastating wars in his lifetime. "Now, in the thermonuclear age, any misjudgment on either side about the intentions of the other could rain more devastation in several hours than has been wrought in all the wars of human history." When Kennedy closed by asking "in these days" for "your good will, and your support, and above all your prayers,"[29] no one could doubt the depth of his need. That, too, confirmed the all but explicit message of the speech: we were on the edge of a nuclear war. At the end of the Vienna summit, Kennedy had been quoted as having told Khrushchev, "It will be a cold winter," but the full text of what he said in response to the Soviet ultimatum went unreported: "Then, Mr. Chairman, there will be war. It will be a cold winter."[30] On television,

Kennedy's conviction that war was coming could be seen in his eyes. Americans have largely forgotten the nuclear dread of that summer, partly because, in memory, events of the Cuban Missile Crisis, fourteen months later, outweigh it. But it was real at the time, when we, in the poet Robert Lowell's phrase, "talked our extinction to death."[31]

4. HEAD TO RICHMOND

And now, a few days later, there I was, waiting for Dad to come out of the Pentagon. At last he appeared, striding for the car in his tan uniform, the silhouette of his hat sharp against the lights of the River Entrance. As he reached the car, he tossed his cigarette aside and got in next to me. He lit up again. I sensed his preoccupation at once, and assumed he would have nothing much to say. I was wrong.

What followed was a moment I have written about before. I used to think it established a bond of feeling between my father and me, but now I understand that what happened merely acknowledged the bond already in place. The few words he spoke as I drove the car across Washington, heading for Bolling, remain the point around which my consciousness still pivots. Here is how I recounted it in my memoir, *An American Requiem:*

> Tonight Dad is in a somber mood . . . He is smoking, flicking ashes out the window. He has said nothing. Finally, he crushes the cigarette in the dashboard ashtray and turns to me. "Son, I want to say something to you. I'm only going to say it once, and I don't want you asking me any questions. Okay?
>
> "You read the papers. You know what's going on. Berlin. The bomber they shot down last week. I may not come home one of these nights. I might have to go somewhere else. The whole Air Staff would go. If that happens, I'm going to depend on you to take my place with Mom and the boys."
>
> "What do you mean?"
>
> "Mom will know. But you should know too. I'll want you to get everybody in the car. I'll want you to drive south. Get on Route One. Head to Richmond. Go as far as you can before you stop." He didn't say anything else. As I remember it, neither did I.[32]

I knew at once what my father had just done: a version of what Kennedy had done on television, which was simply to display his fear. He was displaying it *to me.* Now I see the connection between Kennedy's speech and my father's statement. Each was the source of what I would call a nuclear bond. "No president," the historian Michael Beschloss has commented, "had ever spoken so directly about the possibility of a nuclear attack."[33] For a decade, Americans had lived with the subliminal dread of a world-ending holocaust — sublimating it, especially during the McCarthy-driven Red Scare — but that summer the horror of nuclear war was experienced not as an abstraction, a danger hovering at a distance, but as an imminent event, not "someday," but tomorrow perhaps. That consciously experienced fear trumped politics and partisanship, and, even including Republicans and the press, it established a new bond between the American people and their president.

And so too, on an intimate level, between my father and me. I thought for a long time after that night that he must have known of a specific danger unfolding just then, but now I understand that the danger that season was general, not specific. "There was never a particular day on which it seemed likely that direct conflict would break out," McGeorge Bundy recalled of the time, "but there was hardly a week in which there were not nagging questions about what would happen if . . ." Bundy defined it as "a time of sustained and draining anxiety."[34] My father was privy to the actual planning that was taking place inside the Pentagon — and no, he was not Herman Kahn, a man who could contemplate Armageddon with complacent detachment. His anxiety was sustained and draining, and he let me glimpse it. He could not contemplate what Kennedy had called that rain of devastation as if it were without consequence *for him.*

The consequence for me was that at last I could openly acknowledge the oceanic feeling I had long been carrying in my chest as what, in fact, it was. Fear, pure and simple. In my memoir I wrote that I became afraid that night, and would remain afraid for a long time, but now I see that I had already been afraid. *Some damn fool like you is going to start World War Three.* On that night I could acknowledge my fear because, in his roundabout way, that was what Dad had done.

The trip down Route 1 that my father ordered was no more realistic — no more a matter of real action — than Kennedy's grand bomb shelter plan was. I have no memory of seriously contemplating such a drive. I didn't check maps or keep the car gassed up. Nor did I obsessively hang around the house to see if Dad came home. At some level, I knew that if the nuclear strike, of which he was palpably afraid, and from which, presumably, he wanted us to escape, did occur, the thought of driving to Richmond was absurd.

Absurdity abounded. On the cover of the September 15, 1961, *Life,* an issue devoted to fallout shelters, the headline read, "Survive Fallout: 97 out of 100 People Can Be Saved. Detailed Plans for Building Shelters." The article was a fairy tale, suggesting that life after a nuclear war would be just like life before, only the American dream-dwelling — "a simple room in the basement built with concrete blocks" — would be a well-appointed, carpeted cave. Drawings showed attractive mothers making up beds for Dick and Jane, but inside "a big pipe in the back yard under three feet of earth." Families were pictured living happily, "snug" in the protected "clubhouse." A foreword written by Kennedy himself recommended the article. "My fellow Americans," he wrote, "nuclear weapons and the possibility of nuclear war are facts of life we cannot ignore today . . . I urge you to read and consider seriously the contents of this issue of Life."

That autumn and winter, the nation's low-grade war hysteria took the form of a bizarre unreality in which Americans blithely anticipated the postwar world of fallout shelters, with food and water supplies uninterrupted, electricity still working to power fans and lights, all with the assumption that after a few days or weeks, citizens would reemerge to some version of the world as it had been. Kennedy and his administration encouraged this nonsense. In him, as in the public at large, the fixation on shelters served as a mental block, holding back the true horror of what might be coming.

And so with my dad's commissioning me to get "Mom and the boys in the car." And go to what? That night, coming from some heated planning session or other in the "Tank," or with the Joint Chiefs, or perhaps in LeMay's office, Dad would have been thinking about the effects on Washington of even a single thermonuclear bomb, aimed, say, at the ground zero of the courtyard inside the Pentagon. He would have been thinking of the expanding fireball consuming the air, its heat four times the heat of the sun; of the instantaneous shock wave that would send this superheated air out over many square miles, sucking cooler air back to the unquenchable fireball, which would create winds of many hundreds of miles an hour — a hurricane squared, but instead of lashing the earth with rain, this one would simply scorch. Within seconds, the shock and heat would engulf all structures, people, and natural features in the city, certainly downriver as far as Bolling Air Force Base. The Potomac would be set to boiling. Combustible material, from human clothing to human flesh, would burst into flame. Steel would melt. Every living thing in the open face of this thermal blast wave would disintegrate, disappear. All of this in the first few dozen seconds after detonation. All of this before the even more devastating second stage, the full and independent firestorm, began. "Within tens of minutes," one expert on the subject (not Herman Kahn) wrote, of one nuclear device exploding in that one place, "the entire area, approximately 40 to 65 square miles — everything within 3.5 or 4.6 miles of the Pentagon — would be engulfed in a mass fire. The fire would extinguish all life and destroy almost everything else."[35]

And where did Dad think Route 1 would carry his beloved family? Even if Richmond survived the dozens, if not hundreds,[36] of bombs that the Soviets were prepared to rain down on Washington (and the description above is of the effects of one bomb), that river city to the south would have also come within range of the massive attack against major naval facilities at Norfolk and Newport News, Virginia. And so with every city of any size on the eastern seaboard — all within the zone of near-instant destruction. If we somehow managed to get past Richmond, we would have found ourselves in a post-holocaust netherworld without food, clean water, and medical services, a world overrun with fugitives suffering from radiation sickness, the environment poisoned by fallout, the survivors unruled and unorganized, alike in the agonies of mass despair at what had befallen the race and at the slow, miserable disintegration of the objects of value that had not been destroyed at once. I knew all this. I knew better than to think seriously of heading to Richmond, as I never gave a thought to a bomb shelter, nor wondered why Dad didn't either.

In the car with me one night in August 1961, riding from the site of ground zero, my father showed me his fear, that was all. He showed me his love for us and his confidence in me. In doing so, he gave me permission to acknowledge my own fear and to feel my full and permanent love for him. As a result of that night, I felt my bond with my father as the only trustworthy thing in my life. As Kennedy had made us afraid — even unconsciously — as a way of making us love him, so had Dad — equally unconsciously — done some such thing to me. But my father's revelation did something more. He hinted at the radical limits of the profession he had chosen, the one on the edge of which I was poised, and in part because I saw those limits, and in part to please him, I would choose a different path — the Catholic priesthood, which ironically would lead me to break the bond with him. But that is another story.

5. LET BOTH SIDES

It was not for his being a cold warrior that so many of my generation loved John Kennedy. He did two things at once. He made us afraid of nuclear war with the Soviet Union, and he aggressively pushed back at Moscow in ways that made the prospect of such a war entirely real. And while he exacerbated the nuclear danger, he made clear his determination to lead the world away from it. While Kennedy made us afraid, that is, he also gave us hope of being released from fear.

It was in his inaugural address that we saw both aspects of Kennedy's charisma. I remember it — I wore my ROTC uniform that day and listened to him from an anonymous place in the freezing throng on the east apron of the

Capitol. The speech is most often recalled as a Cold War call to arms, with its ringing "pay any price, bear any burden, meet any hardship, support any friend, oppose any foe to assure the survival and success of liberty." But far more emphasis was given to a different vision — not of threat but of reconciliation. "To those nations that would make themselves our adversary, we offer not a pledge but a request: that both sides begin anew the quest for peace, before the dark powers of destruction unleashed by science engulf all humanity in planned or accidental self-destruction." In Kennedy's mind the issue was clear: how in the nuclear age war readiness aimed at its own eventual elimination. "We dare not tempt them with weakness. For only when our arms are sufficient beyond doubt can we be certain beyond doubt that they will never be employed. But neither can two great and powerful groups of nations take comfort from our present course — both sides overburdened by the cost of modern weapons, both rightly alarmed by the steady spread of the deadly atom, yet both racing to alter that uncertain balance of terror[37] that stays the hand of mankind's final war."

After the sweeping rhetoric calling on both sides to achieve new things, he became specific: "Let both sides, for the first time, formulate serious and precise proposals for the inspection and control of arms — and bring the absolute power to destroy other nations under the absolute control of all nations." Kennedy here could be heard as echoing the futile old Baruch approach, giving emphasis at the outset to inspections and controls the Soviets would never abide. But he was making his administration's priorities clear — and also the source of the bond we felt with him at once, for at the center of the inaugural address was a compelling awareness of the bomb. He evoked it six times in those brief moments, speaking directly to our almost completely unarticulated dread, telling us how much he wanted to move away from dependence on nuclear weapons as a source of national security, precisely because there was no security there. The summoning trumpet, he declared, was not a call to arms, and the "burden of a long twilight struggle" was not a reference, as subsequently misremembered, to rollback wars on the contained margins of Communism, but to "a struggle against the common enemies of man: tyranny, poverty, disease, and war itself."[38]

From the beginning of his career as a congressman from Massachusetts (1947–1953), Kennedy had been a proponent of strong defense. Upon first coming to Washington, he firmly backed Harry Truman in his demonizing of the Soviet Union, in his embrace of NSC-68, and in the expansion of the nuclear arsenal. But Kennedy was an early skeptic of Eisenhower's policy of massive retaliation. He agreed with those, like Maxwell Taylor, who saw an overreliance on nuclear threats as encouraging sly Communist maneuvers below the range of what would draw an American nuclear response, and he watched the startling nuclear buildup in the early Eisenhower years with alarm. Kennedy faulted massive retaliation for the way it condemned an American president to choose between holocaust and humiliation.[39]

After *Sputnik,* with Khrushchev boasting that he was turning out ICBMs "like sausages," Kennedy was, as we saw, one of the shrillest critics of the socalled missile gap. Indeed, pulling away from his Democratic rival Stuart Symington, he drew energy enough from the issue of Eisenhower's failure to keep pace with Soviet nuclear capacity, particularly missile and rocket production, to defeat Richard Nixon in 1960. This was so despite the fact that Eisenhower, himself at the mercy of arms procurement pressures he would denounce, had ordered a huge buildup of American strategic missiles.[40] America was much more the sausage maker than the USSR.

But while Kennedy faulted his Republican opponents for having "fallen behind" the Soviets, making America vulnerable to nuclear blackmail if not outright nuclear attack, he also lambasted Eisenhower for having done far too little to slow the arms race. As one historian observed, "This one-two punch was certainly clever politically, for it offered the broadest possible appeal. And yet Kennedy, true to his earlier views, saw no contradiction between the two approaches: only military strength permitted arms control, and both were essential to security."[41]

Arms control was not an empty mantra to Kennedy; it was an urgent priority. Unlike Symington and other hawks, and to the horror of men inside the Pentagon, Kennedy was capable of using the word "disarmament" and advocating it.[42] His proposals for increased military strength were regularly linked with calls for negotiations with the Soviet Union and mutual accommodation based on the mitigation of jointly held fears. Kennedy made Americans see Eisenhower as having been far too complacent about both preparing for the worst and finding ways to avoid it. By contrast, there was nothing complacent about Kennedy. In relation to bolstering the arsenal and defusing it, his perceptions were shaped by the horrors of nuclear war. Those of us who had felt those horrors, if only subliminally, since crouching under desks in grade school, heard Kennedy's words as aimed directly at us.[43]

In fact, Kennedy's heated campaign rhetoric, and the policies of escalation to which it committed him as president, fueled the arms race and prompted new levels of defensive Soviet belligerence that again brought the Berlin crisis to a boil in the summer of 1961. What Khrushchev had failed to understand was that Kennedy, as an unproven and untested leader, was far more vulnerable to his bluster than Eisenhower, the great general, had been. It had happened before. Roosevelt could remain calm in the face of Stalin's bullying; Truman panicked. Eisenhower refused to be drawn into a crisis by Khrushchev's demands; Kennedy's short presidency was defined by crises, made steadily worse by his own anguish.[44]

When Kennedy gave that frightening war-footing speech in July, including the announcements of new SAC alerts, draft calls, and the bomb shelter program, Moscow reacted with the construction of the Berlin Wall in August and, on the last day of that month, the resumption of nuclear tests, which would include the open-air detonation of a fifty-megaton device, the largest thermonuclear explosion ever. With that, a bilateral two-year moratorium on testing was over,[45] and the United States followed suit with its own test, although underground, two weeks later. Hopes for a nuclear test ban treaty were dashed.

In the longer term, Kennedy's perceived readiness for war, and his touted determination to establish and maintain a gross American superiority in strategic forces — the first successful test of a new ICBM, the Minuteman, occurred ten days after Kennedy took office, and he immediately ordered its deployment — prompted the Soviet Union's counterbalancing movement of missiles into Cuba, which would precipitate the next near disaster a year later. Simultaneously, pressure mounted on Kennedy that summer and fall of 1961 to find ways of proving his toughness to Khrushchev. His gaze shifted from Berlin to Indochina, where Communist insurgents were boldly challenging American allies. Only five weeks before Vienna, on April 29, Kennedy had ordered a first deployment of U.S. combat soldiers — albeit designated "advisers" — to the area. "Now we have a problem in trying to make our power credible," he said to James Reston of the *New York Times*, "and Vietnam looks like the place."[46] In the heat of Berlin, in the autumn, Kennedy authorized U.S. soldiers to engage in combat in Vietnam. The war's first American mortality would come on December 22, 1961.

All of this began with candidate Kennedy's exploitation of the perceived missile gap, which originated, after *Sputnik,* in Air Force intelligence exaggerations, pushed especially by Symington and legitimized in the Gaither Report, which was mainly written, as we saw, by Paul Nitze. The Kennedy-Khrushchev dynamic lays bare the built-in contradiction of the deterrence structure that was fully mature by then: how the blustering threat of one side prompted in the other precisely the behavior the threat was intended to preempt. Nitze, on the American side, was the high priest of this misperceived urge to intimidate. He became one of Kennedy's campaign advisers and a source of Kennedy's declamations. As is well known by now, there was a missile gap in 1960, but it overwhelmingly favored the United States. Whether Kennedy knew it or not, his missile gap pronouncements were another in the long line of phony — and ultimately deadly — American warnings that the Russians were coming.[47]

This story never seems to get very far from the figure of James Forrestal, Nitze's mentor. Kennedy himself served for a time as an aide to Forrestal, accompanying him to Potsdam in July 1945. That was a position young Kennedy had gotten through his father's connections, and the favor would be returned when Kennedy appointed Forrestal's son, Michael, to a staff position on the National Security Council.[48] When Kennedy won the election in 1960, the man to whom he first offered the position of secretary of defense was Robert Lovett, who had served as defense secretary under Truman and who had formerly been an acolyte of Forrestal's. For our purposes, the point to note is that it was from Lovett's Florida estate that Forrestal had reportedly run crying "The Russians are coming! The Russians are coming!" Lovett did not want the top Pentagon job in 1960, and he might have recommended Nitze for it, since they had worked together in drafting NSC-68, the Truman-era document that had promulgated Forrestal's fears as policy. Instead, probably unaware of the connection to this history, Lovett recommended the recently appointed president of the Ford Motor Company, Robert Strange McNamara. Kennedy knew that Nitze would be disappointed, and he promised Nitze that he would become McNamara's deputy.

McNamara, as we saw, had honed his statistical-analysis skills as an AAF officer on Curtis LeMay's staff during World War II, helping, among other responsibilities, to maximize the destructiveness of the B-29 firebombing of Japanese cities. The application of strict rationality to problems of war had prepared McNamara to transfer that approach to problems of business when he joined Ford, and it worked. McNamara was key to a phenomenal turnaround at the automobile manufacturer, and the success of his rigidly applied method had taken him to the top of the company in just over a decade. He arrived at the Pentagon determined to rationalize its culture, too. But Nitze was a living link to the Forrestal tradition, and it is as if McNamara wanted to keep his distance from the ghost of paranoid alarms. McNamara had a nose for irrational assumptions, and the Pentagon reeked of them. If warning flags were to be raised from his Department of Defense, it would be because cool intellectual analysis, fact-based conclusions reasonably arrived at, called for them.

McNamara could not know it in the first days of his tenure in the sweeping office above the River Entrance, but his innate impulses as a manager and thinker would put him in direct conflict with the now well-established — mythologized even — culture of the Building. He was Ahab, setting out from New Bedford.

6. THE NEED FOR NEW INTELLIGENCE

One sees an accidental symbol of the new course McNamara hoped to set in his decision about Nitze. Despite Kennedy's promise to Nitze, McNamara refused to appoint him as deputy secretary. Nitze settled for the lesser post in which he had briefly served in the Eisenhower administration, assistant secretary of defense for international security affairs.[49] Nitze had by now proven adept at ingratiating himself with superiors and adapting to the shifting moods of the defense culture, but he would be less than successful in the Kennedy administration. Despite his already extensive experience and his eighteen-karat social connections, Nitze would never join Kennedy's inner circle.

Coming off the Gaither Committee, though, Nitze had begun as an important influence on Kennedy the candidate — in nothing more than on the subject of the missile gap. Nitze was a fervent believer in it,[50] and Kennedy depended on his assessment. But here, too, McNamara's instincts took him in another direction. He told me, in the interview I conducted with him in his Washington office in 2003, that the very first thing he did on becoming secretary was to take up that question with Pentagon intelligence analysts.

Since Kennedy's own election campaign had made the missile gap the nation's burning question, McNamara knew he had to deal with it at once. If the Soviet Union was far ahead of the United States in rocket manufacture and deployment, the kind of turnaround McNamara would have to orchestrate in the Pentagon was clear. If, as some hold, Kennedy was disingenuous in warning of the missile gap,[51] McNamara would establish that, too. He had to know what the facts were and how they were arrived at. "So I went up to the Air Force on that first day," he said.

He had no reason to know that the day he was referring to was the one I had come to regard as the Pentagon's eighteenth birthday. "I went to A-2 [the chief of air intelligence]. I can't think of his name. He was a major general, very nice guy. I said I want to see the basis of your study, the underlying data. So he got out photographs and everything. Well, the photographs were U-2 photographs and were very, very limited, in the sense that you couldn't be sure — at least I couldn't be sure — what the hell we were looking at. The A-2 seemed to be quite certain, but as it turned out, he was looking at them through Air Force glasses."[52]

McNamara compared the U-2 photographs with those from the new reconnaissance satellite *Discoverer*,[53] and what he found was not only that the missile gap charge was false — Arthur Schlesinger, not an uninterested observer, later wrote that it was "in good faith overstated"[54] — but that the intelligence system on which he and the president had to depend was a shambles.

Each of the five services had its own intelligence operation. When McNamara asked the Army for its estimate of deployed and ready Soviet missiles as of January 1961, he was told ten; the Navy put the number at less than half that. The Air Force set the figure at more than fifty, and perhaps as high as two hundred. Within the Air Force, the Strategic Air Command had yet another, independent intelligence operation, and it insisted on higher numbers yet. And there were equivalent disparities on projections of the gap in the future. The Air Force had been the main source of all missile gap alerts, beginning in 1957 with the Gaither Committee's and including Stuart Symington's warning that the Soviet Union by the early 1960s would have three thousand ICBMs. When McNamara demanded that Air Force intelligence officers justify their estimates in light of the *Discoverer* photographs, they could not. "Even Air Force analysts were embarrassed by the pictures," the historian Fred Kaplan wrote. "The images starkly rebutted the estimates of Air Force intelligence."[55] Soon it would be "discovered" that the actual number of deployed Soviet ICBMs was four.

McNamara saw what was happening, what had by then become a regular feature of Pentagon information gathering. Of the Air Force intelligence chief, McNamara said to me, "I'm absolutely certain he was not trying to mislead anybody — the Air Force chief of staff, the president, or the secretary of state, or anybody." In fact, it was worse than mere deception. As we have seen again and again, each service branch assessed enemy capacities based less on objective readings of Soviet arsenals than on the branch's own procurement wishes. Thus what Navy intelligence emphasized were sonar soundings that showed a dangerous growth in the Soviet submarine force. The Army saw the Red Army's drastic expansion of conventional divisions and tank brigades on the edge of Europe and the prospect of Communist aggression in brushfire wars in the Third World. And the Air Force saw everything through the lens of its plans for the new B-70 bomber and for the ten thousand Minuteman missiles a worst-case reading of missile gap required.

As McNamara indicates, none of this is to indict intelligence agencies for outright dishonesty.[56] Intelligence assessments moving up a chain of command have a way of confirming presuppositions at the top. We saw how, during World War II, Allied bomber generals wanted to believe an air war against cities would destroy enemy morale, and British intelligence assessments (disputed by some Americans) said it would be so. In the late 1940s, Harry Truman wanted to believe in a long-term American nuclear monopoly so that he could berate Moscow — and Leslie Groves and then the CIA assured him it would be so. The same pattern would be repeated when Lyndon

Johnson was told what he wanted to hear about Vietnam, and when Ronald Reagan's obsession with the "evil empire" drew support from intelligence that missed the significance of nonviolent democracy movements — the opposite of "evil" — behind the Iron Curtain.

What McNamara was seeing was the third-generation effect of intelligence entities whose missions were defined so emphatically by the individual services that their ability to serve a broader national interest was almost entirely destroyed. He was confronted with a deeply embedded organizational corruption, the kind of morass that would drive an exacting manager like him crazy. As a man already obsessed with his responsibility to oversee the national security, he knew he would not tolerate such chaotic (as he had to think of it) information management. The worst offender by far was the Air Force — reflected, of course, in that branch's overwhelming dominance of the Pentagon budget and the nation's defense posture. The result of such narrow loyalty was a grievous and dangerous misreading of the true nature of the enemy America confronted, even if the misreading in this case was in America's favor. Almost as troubling was the prospect of significant embarrassment that would surely come when President Kennedy had to acknowledge that a central claim of his election campaign was (as Eisenhower had insisted) false. It was McNamara's first encounter with the great white whale of Pentagon culture, and he moved immediately to harpoon it, as if he were back at Ford, killing off the Edsel.

"I concluded that we just had to get rid of five independent intelligence services," McNamara said to me. Intelligence was the pulse of the Pentagon's heart, the ultimate source of bureaucratic power, and within days of his being sworn in as secretary of defense, McNamara moved to take control of it. "It wasn't that I didn't want differences of opinion, but I wanted the differences of opinion sorted out rather than giving the president five different views, or giving the secretary five different views. So I conceived of forming the Defense Intelligence Agency, with a commitment to gathering and evaluating information based on a higher loyalty than to any one service." McNamara paused. Then he added, "It was an issue of civilian control over the military." His control.[57]

That spring, McNamara moved to replace the fiefdoms of the various intelligence agencies, each reporting to its own service chief, with one unified agency, reporting not only to the Joint Chiefs as a group but directly to him. The move was unheard of, the first real act of service unification to occur since the three main service branches had resoundingly beaten back attempts at unification in the early postwar period. McNamara had arrived at the Pentagon with the idea that he would reorganize it according to "mission categories," which would lump Air Force Minuteman missiles, for example, with the

Navy's Polaris missiles, as if in a new service branch called "Strategic Attack Force," or some such. But he soon saw that the existence of service branches and the rivalry among them were as much a part of the department's culture as ramps in the Building itself.

Still — and knowing that if he could not rely on the basic data about and interpretation of enemy capacity and intention, all else was meaningless — he remained determined to take control of such information. Over the next several years, McNamara would introduce other kinds of interservice streamlining, combining procurement and commissary enterprises, for example, but intelligence gathering was the most jealously guarded activity in the military. Everything from mission to budget to battle order began and ended with the assessments of J-2, A-2, and ONI, and no service chief was going to willingly surrender an inch of that turf. McNamara was a shrewd enough manager to see a fight coming, but it soon became a test for him — not so much of his own authority but of the constitutional principle of civilian control. By taking control of information and its interpretation, he would bring the Pentagon behemoth to heel.

Constitutional principle or not, by 1961 the inbuilt Pentagon opposition to such change could well have been insurmountable, but as it happened, something else occurred in the same period to make the shift as much a priority for President Kennedy as for McNamara — the Bay of Pigs. In the same first week of the new administration that McNamara was discovering there was no missile gap, Kennedy was being presented with an up-or-down decision on La Brigada. Allen Dulles, the CIA director (together with his deputy, General Charles Pearre Cabell, whom we saw earlier as an Eighth Air Force targeting officer who objected to indiscriminate bombing of German cities), told Kennedy that he had the power, with one command, to free Cuba from Communism. An act of real rollback at last. Dulles was firm in saying that CIA intelligence indicated that the plan for the island's invasion would work. The Cuban people would rise up against the dictator Castro. Kennedy was not sure, but there was no one to question what the CIA chief was saying. Arthur Schlesinger later expressed the belief "that if one senior advisor had spoken out against the expedition, it would have been cancelled."[58] The president felt he had no choice, given the operation's origins under the war-seasoned Eisenhower, but to go with what the CIA was telling him. Dulles did not mention Eisenhower's ambivalence about the plan.

That plan was full of holes. The CIA had missed the big picture: the Cuban people had no inclination to overthrow Castro. And it had botched the smallest of details: invasion air support was ill-timed because CIA pilots forgot to set their watches to a different time zone. The operation, of course, was a catastrophe. Kennedy took full responsibility for the debacle — "I am the responsible officer of the government"[59] — but he also quietly determined to fire Dulles (and Cabell), and he resolved never to be dependent on a single, unquestioned source of intelligence again. He was prepared to back up McNamara's quick-strike attack on military intelligence, unfolding just then, mainly because a new, powerful, McNamara-dominated Defense Intelligence Agency would counterbalance a CIA he had every reason not to trust.

By July 1961, as the Pentagon was braced, with President Kennedy, for the possibility of war over Berlin, McNamara had completed his preparations for the new, consolidated intelligence operation under his control. A few weeks later, soldiers of the German Democratic Republic and the Soviet Union startled the West by throwing up the Berlin Wall, a development the CIA had utterly failed to anticipate. A few days after that, McNamara crossed the Pentagon's internal Rubicon by announcing that the Defense Intelligence Agency was open for business.

To the surprise of some, given the past problems and the prospect of heated struggle ahead, he named as its first director a general officer from the Air Force. One historian noted that the appointment of an Air Force officer muted the resistance of the Blue Curtain,[60] but that would prove to be temporary. This man was not a bomber general. He was not even a pilot. He had defined his relationship with the Air Force's elite Strategic Air Command by literal acts of trespass. He lived next door to Curtis LeMay, but he was known for having challenged him. As head of a multiservice intelligence corps, there would never be any question of his loyalty, and eventually, in relations with his own service branch and with a future secretary of defense, that transcending loyalty would destroy him. By McNamara's recommendation and President Kennedy's appointment, the first, and ultimately the longest-serving, director of the Defense Intelligence Agency was Lieutenant General Joseph F. Carroll.

My father's appointment was announced around the time that he got into the Lincoln beside me that night. What little I grasped about his new job, I read in the papers. In *U.S. News & World Report* I read an article headlined "'Spy' Chief at Pentagon: Air Force's General Carroll." It said, "General Carroll, 51, is a former FBI agent. In his new position, he will direct a joint staff of some 1,500 intelligence personnel, drawn from the Army, Navy and Air Force. The agency's assignment: 'to obtain greater unity of effort among all components of the Department in developing military intelligence.' Pentagon spokesmen said there was no direct relation between creation of the joint military-intelligence unit and the proposals to reorganize the civilian Central Intelligence Agency."[61] Two days after this article appeared, on August 30, 1961, the Soviet Union resumed nuclear testing, taking the CIA, and therefore Kennedy, by surprise. The president was even more enraged at the CIA, and the nascent DIA's independent and competing mission seemed more important than ever.

When I had arrived at McNamara's office in 2003, he promptly told me that the only reason he agreed to give me an interview was out of regard for the memory of my father. I remember from my own visits to the Pentagon how close my father's office was to that of the secretary of defense — only a few office suites away. As a start-up agency not yet a year old, the DIA, trumping the Central Intelligence Agency, would be the first to find hard evidence of the Soviet missile buildup in Cuba in October 1962.[62] My father then requested expanded air surveillance of Cuba, and he briefed McNamara throughout the crisis.[63] During the Vietnam War, it would be DIA analysis that convinced McNamara, notwithstanding the Air Force's evidence, that the bombing campaign against North Vietnam was not working, leading him to call for the bombing halt that helped cost him his job in 1968.[64]

In 1996, I had published a book about my father, and a year later, when I interviewed McNamara by telephone for a magazine article, he told me he had read it. "Your book is very moving. I knew your father well. I trusted him. He was one I could trust. Your book moved me to tears. It is moving me to tears right now." Together, as secretary of defense and head of the DIA, they had come to a position that the Pentagon hated. Now McNamara, in that phone interview, struggling to regain his composure, summarized that position: "In view of Hanoi's total commitment to achieving victory at any cost, there was never a chance for a U.S. victory at a price we were willing to pay. Never. Never. Never. Never." The notes I took during the interview end with the words "He sobs, and hangs up."[65]

7. MCNAMARA AND LEMAY

Before peaceniks loathed McNamara, the generals and admirals did. He was a man on a mission of control, and by 1961 control was not a part of the culture of the Pentagon. Ever since the struggle between Truman's budget cutters and advocates of a massive strategic force had been resolved in favor of open-ended nuclear escalation, the guardians of the arsenal had been free agents. After NSC-68 and the Soviet H-bomb, the Air Force, and to a lesser extent the Navy, had put the pedal of weapons development and deployment to the floor; and after *Sputnik*, they had kept it there. Always with the assistance of key supporters on Capitol Hill. Eisenhower and then Kennedy might speak of arms control, but the Pentagon's guiding principle was not control but growth. This unalterable condition of America's military establishment, despite its being challenged in 1961 by Kennedy and McNamara, was, in effect, the true hell's bottom on which the Pentagon stood.

The upward movement of arms acquisition proved to be unrelenting, and Pentagon planners could hear the talk of opposing politicians only as lip service made necessary by the electorate's naïve wish for a sweeter world. Anyone who took seriously the idea of arms control, much less disarmament, was in danger of being labeled subversive. Over time, the main result of this hard fact of strategic life would be to drive the USSR to match levels of U.S. nuclear escalation. A truth of the Cold War, in other words, would be that one engine could drive both escalations, Soviet and American, and the engine room was, more often than not, in the bowels of the building on the Potomac River.

Whatever competition with the USSR amounted to, the spark plug of this engine of endless arms development and accumulation, as we have seen repeatedly, was the competition among the armed services of the United States and the competition of each service with itself.[66] McNamara might speak of civilian control, and he would staff the Pentagon with young, civilian "defense intellectuals,"[67] but the military ethos that so dominated the impersonal mind of the Building made the distinction between uniform and business suit irrelevant.

Actually, the distinction that mattered most, by the time of McNamara's arrival, was between the blue uniforms of the Air Force and Navy, on one side, and the brown of the Army on the other — exactly because the Army was marginal to a program of national security built around intercontinental strategic attack. Implementing Kennedy's idea of flexible response meant rescuing the Army from the limbo to which it had been condemned by the concept of massive retaliation. That rescue would, first, involve the resurrection of men who had lost the interservice debates under Eisenhower, especially Maxwell Taylor, and, second, lead to the crucifixion of Vietnam, a defeat that, ironically, remains the monument to the Army's one victory in the war inside the Pentagon.[68]

As the intelligence struggle, sparked by the missile gap, demonstrated, if McNamara was going to gain control of the Pentagon, he would have to take on his old service branch, the Air Force. Curtis LeMay was vice chief of staff when McNamara took office, and he was very much the heir apparent to General Thomas White, whose term as chief of staff would end in the late spring. McNamara had been a relatively junior officer on LeMay's staff during World War II, but we saw what a critical contribution the "stat control" genius had made to LeMay's firebombing missions. If LeMay imagined that McNamara would defer to him now, he was wrong.

LeMay vigorously fought the Kennedy-sponsored resurgence of the

Army. When Kennedy brought Taylor out of retirement to serve as his military adviser, then to take over the Joint Chiefs, LeMay recognized the appointment as an assault on Air Force superiority. Taylor, in fact, questioned the very premises of strategic air power. "LeMay, your airplanes are no good," Taylor presumed to declare. And then he threw the gauntlet down: "We've got these new missiles coming along, handheld by infantrymen. An infantryman will shoot you down." LeMay retaliated by challenging the idea that Taylor's reconstituted Army, built around a new Air Cavalry, should even be allowed to fly helicopters, since the air belonged to the Air Force. The Taylor-LeMay disputes were so intense, LeMay later recalled, that "it took a lot of will power to keep from letting him have one."[69]

As if made to order for McNamara, an opportunity to impose his method and personality on the culture of the Pentagon awaited him in the expensive matter of a new warplane. Or, rather, two new warplanes. Both the Air Force and the Navy had next-generation tactical jet fighters under development. The Air Force's was the F-105, and the Navy's was the F-4H. Distinctions that mattered enormously to the men who would fly these planes — Navy aviators screeching down onto the decks of sea-tossed aircraft carriers needed heavier planes with beefed-up landing gear and a tailhook assembly, but the extra weight came at the expense of power; Air Force flyboys wheeling up in dogfights needed lighter machines and more power — meant little or nothing to McNamara and his analysts. One of his first decisions as secretary, coming right out of the mold that made him the hero of Ford, was to overrule the Air Force and the Navy both, ordering the development of one new plane — the TFX, eventually designated the F-111 — that the two services would share.[70] When Navy and Air Force designers could not agree on technical specifications for a common plane, McNamara simply declared, in that case, he would design it himself.[71]

He had not hesitated to step into the Pentagon's kill zone, the conflict between the Navy and Air Force that had, among so much else, contributed to the suicide of his predecessor James Forrestal. In one stroke, McNamara reversed a pattern of deference to the two services that had begun with Forrestal, and with that stroke he achieved the impossible, which was to make the Air Force and the Navy allies. They were joined now in their resentment of him, and it would be transcendent. The death of every Navy and Air Force pilot while flying the F-111 would somehow be blamed on the secretary of defense. He would be the first American official held personally liable for casualties, and with Vietnam, the phenomenon of such warrior rage would be magnified a thousandfold.

If LeMay fought McNamara on the TFX, that was a mere warm-up for their battle over the Air Force's far more sacred program: the development of a new long-range strategic bomber to replace the purportedly aging B-52. The first contracts for the B-70 had been awarded the manufacturer in 1957, but another of McNamara's early efficiency moves was to order the program cut back. Instead of looking forward to a full-complement wing of forty-five bombers, the Air Force was told to expect three prototype aircraft, redesigned as reconnaissance planes, not bombers. In McNamara's view the new Minuteman ICBM, just coming on line, made the new strategic bomber redundant. The battle over the B-70 would be waged for years, and the Air Force, in the end, would lose.[72] The strongest argument in favor of the new manned bomber was that the B-52, already a decade old in the early 1960s, was on the verge of obsolescence. The B-52 is still flying today.

McNamara, in his interview with me, went out of his way to praise LeMay, and he refused to be drawn into any reminiscence of their conflict. But the record shows that no one fought the new secretary on a range of fronts more vigorously than his former commander. "I ask you," LeMay said to his Air Force colleagues, "would things be much worse if Khrushchev were Secretary of Defense?"[73] The battle between LeMay and McNamara had "monumental significance," one defense expert told me, a significance "that the country doesn't really understand." LeMay, convinced of his own notions of what American survival required, wanted nothing less than full control of the nation's capacity to wage nuclear war. McNamara defeated LeMay, preserving the constitutional principle of civilian control, especially of the nuclear arsenal. "Whatever else he did, McNamara deserves a lot of credit for that."[74]

Yet through those first stormy months of their contest in the Pentagon — one might say, *over* the Pentagon — there must have been some residue of obeisance left in McNamara from those early years, because in the middle of ferocious bureaucratic warfare in which LeMay was McNamara's main antagonist, the secretary of defense forwarded the general's nomination as Air Force chief of staff to Kennedy. The Kennedy administration could not have welcomed the idea of a dismissed LeMay's biting criticism once he left the service, but the retirement list of the Pentagon had produced other such critics. McNamara could have simply sent LeMay on his way; he defied the Army brass in just that way by bringing Maxwell Taylor out of retirement to be the new chairman of the Joint Chiefs. But he did nothing of the kind with LeMay, who was sworn in as Air Force chief, the top dog at last, on June 30, 1961.

I wondered about that when I interviewed McNamara. Why had he promoted the man? But every time I brought the discussion back to LeMay, McNamara praised him. In the haze of memory, McNamara seemed to believe that he had wanted LeMay, but the record of their disputes makes that unlikely. The explanation is obvious: LeMay had real power. He was to the

Pentagon what J. Edgar Hoover was to the Justice Department, and just as Attorney General Robert F. Kennedy had to live with his nemesis, so did McNamara.[75]

But McNamara did not have to like it. LeMay's swearing-in ceremony took place at the White House. The gathering was small. In addition to President Kennedy, Senator Symington, LeMay's bomber gap coconspirator, was there. So was Vice President Lyndon B. Johnson, for whom LeMay had bent regulations to provide a special, permanent "airlift" (Air Force transportation), including construction of an airstrip on Johnson's Texas ranch. The secretary of defense, however, was not present. His absence was not explained.[76]

McNamara's struggles to unify military intelligence and tame the beast of unchecked weapons procurement pale beside his effort to seize control of war planning and to "rationalize" the strategic theory on which it was based. In nothing was his effort more Herculean, in nothing more dangerous, and in nothing more confounded. And Curtis LeMay was more his nemesis there than anywhere else.

The missile gap problem opened directly into the problem of strategic theory. If it was true, as LeMay's successor at SAC had contended in 1960, that Soviet missiles "could virtually wipe out our entire nuclear strike capability within a span of thirty minutes,"[77] it was as important for McNamara to understand the actual American capability as that of the Soviets. What he found was that meaningful information about the extent of American nuclear capability, and especially nuclear planning, was about as hard to come by as for a defense minister in Moscow. When he first inquired of the brass about nuclear war planning, he was told, astoundingly, that that subject was secret. Too secret for him, as defense secretary, to be brought into it.[78]

The question of what an American nuclear strike would involve was far from abstract in the early weeks of the Kennedy administration. Apart from Cuba, the first foreign policy conundrum with which JFK was presented was in Laos, a small nation that abutted Vietnam. Communist and non-Communist factions were struggling for dominance, and Cold War geopolitics required that the contest be defined as one between the USSR and the United States. Even before Kennedy took office, at a transition briefing with the Joint Chiefs of Staff on January 13, 1961, his people were confronted with a proposal, according to a *Chicago Sun-Times* report three weeks later, "that the U.S. launch a preventive atomic attack to stop Communist infiltration of Laos."[79] As the newspaper reported another three weeks later, the proposal came from LeMay.[80]

LeMay was not the only one advocating a preemptive use of nuclear weapons in Laos. Through that first spring, the Communist threat there continued to dominate discussions between Kennedy and his military advisers, and not long after the Bay of Pigs debacle in April, the chairman of the Joint Chiefs, Lyman Lemnitzer, also asked for authorization to use the atomic bomb in the Southeast Asian nation. But by then Kennedy was appalled, and he regarded the advice as ludicrous. He complained to his confidant McGeorge Bundy that while his State Department advisers "don't seem to have *cojones,* the Defense Department looks as if that's all they've got. They haven't any brains." On Laos, Kennedy ignored his military chiefs and cobbled together a diplomatic agreement with Moscow, both sides backing away from confrontation.[81]

The experience of that first, quick rush toward nuclear use left Kennedy with a deep disdain for LeMay, which only compounds the mystery of why he had approved McNamara's promotion of the bomber general to the position of Air Force chief that spring. For the president, too, LeMay was simply untouchable. Kennedy avoided him, but on the occasions when he did have to deal with him, he was always left feeling "choleric."[82] The contempt was mutual, and would reach a climax during the Cuban Missile Crisis in 1962, with LeMay openly defiant of the president's refusal to order an all-out assault against Soviet bases in Cuba. LeMay was insubordinate during those tense deliberations, calling Kennedy's chosen strategy of blockade instead of attack "almost as bad as appeasement at Munich." In reply, Kennedy coldly asked, "What did you say?"[83] Afterward, Kennedy said to his aide Kenneth O'Donnell, "Can you imagine LeMay saying a thing like that? These Brass Hats have one great advantage in their favor. If we listen to them, and do what they want us to do, none of us will be alive later to tell them that they were wrong."[84]

8. ALL-OUT SPASM ATTACK

Upon taking office, McNamara soon grasped the essential problem, one that had been put in place under Truman and maintained throughout the Eisenhower years. All the civilian control in the world meant nothing as long as the generals' strategic planning — how, when, and at what a nuclear strike would be launched — was not subject to oversight, much less criticism. Statesmen of every age have rarely understood what is actually involved in the actions of their militaries, especially once hostilities break out, but in the nuclear age that distance is exacerbated.

Kennedy, like Eisenhower before him, was accompanied everywhere by a stoic-faced warrant officer carrying the "football," a briefcase holding the codes with which a nuclear attack could be launched. In theory, the authority to act belonged solely to the president, but McNamara soon grasped the fact that such authority was hemmed in by the military's dominance of command, control, communication, and intelligence, the so-called C³I systems. The men in uniform not only conveyed to, but shaped for, their civilian masters information regarding everything from "operational nuclear planning" to "distant early warning" to "targeting requirements." Authority that is so dependent on subordinate structures is not authority in any meaningful sense. Neither Truman nor Eisenhower had expressed any interest in the technicalities of nuclear war, and SAC took presidential detachment as an ironclad precedent for its permanent "guardianship," to use Janne Nolan's word. But McNamara saw that the technicalities counted for everything, and that his most urgent task was to make the president's authority over the "button" real.

McNamara soon learned of the existence of a Joint Strategic Capabilities Plan — in the argot, the J-SCAP. "I learned very, very early, in January of '61," he told me, "that Eisenhower had implanted what I think was called the Joint Evaluation Subcommittee,[85] which consisted of four-star officers, examining the use of nuclear weapons. They prepared a report, and I said, 'I want a copy of that,' and they said, 'No, there's only one copy of that . . .' I said, 'Well, get it. I'm going to read it.'"[86]

Beginning in 1951, LeMay had refused to submit what was then called the Basic War Plan to any authority outside SAC. Not even the Joint Chiefs were in a position to evaluate what the plan called for. Under Eisenhower, attempts were made to wrest control of nuclear planning from SAC, but they failed.[87] The bomber generals shared with their superiors only what they chose to, and by 1961 no one was in a position to know which of several planning documents was in fact operative. The White House was given the Single Integrated Operational Plan, or the SIOP, which purported to coordinate Air Force and Navy strategic targeting. But the J-SCAP was something separate, a more detailed and complete plan, which no civilian had ever read.

The first person to do so was Daniel Ellsberg, a RAND analyst, who had served as a Pentagon consultant in the waning days of the Eisenhower administration and was now part of a group loosely defined as McNamara's "whiz kids." Through midlevel colonels whom he befriended, Ellsberg gained access to the J-SCAP, and what he found appalled and "terrified"[88] him. The war "plan" was no plan at all. It simply called for an all-out strike on every city in the Soviet Union, its satellite nations, and China, and assumed enemy mortalities in excess of four hundred million. This spasm of world-ending violence could be set off by any and all Soviet provocations. The plan involved, in Ellsberg's words, "no intermediate steps, no flexibility, and no warnings."[89]

Early in February, within weeks of becoming secretary, in an unprecedented exercise of civilian authority, McNamara demanded and got a complete briefing on the SAC war plan — J-SCAP, SIOP, everything. He traveled to SAC headquarters in Omaha to get it. General Thomas Power, the SAC commander, briefed him. He was the general who had said that if, after a nuclear exchange, two Americans are left, to one Russian, "we win." Now he laid out plans that called for the instant launching of around two thousand strategic bombers and ICBMs, with a total of well over three thousand nuclear weapons, against more than a thousand targets, both military and civilian. The entire "Sino-Soviet bloc" would be hit. Cities the size of Hiroshima would be bombed with fifty times the megatonnage of 1945. No distinction was made among the various Communist nations. They would all be obliterated, with hundreds of millions of casualties. The plan Power outlined did not calculate what the radioactive fallout of such a holocaust would do. All of this would follow in the wake of vaguely defined provocations by the Soviets, mostly imagined as distant "incursions" or "aggressions" far away, offenses well short of any attack on the United States itself. The most likely such provocation would be the movement of a few tank divisions across the Elbe River separating East and West Germany.

McNamara was shocked and disgusted by the briefing, and said so.[90] The entire enterprise, with its unimagined scale of destruction, seemed a nightmare to him, but SAC's callousness was less infuriating to him than its incompetence. Its estimates seemed wildly inaccurate, and its ranking of targets was ad hoc, completely lacking in distinctions and gradations. Nothing angered McNamara so much as shallow thinking, but he grasped at once that this systemic failure to match action and consequence served a purpose. His critique went to the heart of what had driven nuclear escalation for a decade. The Pentagon's logic was absurd, but it held a guiding principle: an infinite number of targets requires an unlimited offensive force.

Mistaking a systemic dynamic for personal venality, McNamara charged SAC's generals with grossly and deliberately underestimating the destruction they contemplated, but only "to justify continued additions to the strategic arsenal."[91] A military command's greatest responsibility is for war planning that reflects the actualities of an anticipated battlefield, but SAC was engaged in planning for its own bureaucratic and budgetary self-interest. A SIOP that called for indiscriminate and total destruction of every conceivable enemy target required an open-ended and limitless accumulation of nuclear weapons and the means to deliver them — and that was its point. The grave mistake that had been enshrined in the Pentagon under Forrestal — war planning for the sake of bureaucratic advantage — was finally being named. McNamara left Omaha with a new understanding of his primary responsibility as secretary of defense. He had been put in charge of a monster. His job was to take control of it and tame it.

In the succeeding weeks and months, McNamara would demand alternatives to the all-out spasm attack that seemed the beginning and end of SAC's purposes. He wanted "flexible response" and "controlled escalation" and "intermediate steps" that would give the president "options" if the Cold War turned hot. But he wanted more than that. Curiously, given his history as LeMay's accomplice in what McNamara himself now describes as the "war crime" of the firebombing of Tokyo, he also wanted a more "humane" plan of assault. By 1961, McNamara had become a moralist who was deeply offended by the notion that the United States would embark on a war that consisted only of attacking the enemy's civilian population centers. Soon, moving toward a "counterforce" strategy that would mainly target the enemy's military bases, he would adopt for a time a "no-cities" strategy, aiming to spare civilian centers entirely, as if in penance for Tokyo.[92]

McNamara, who so prided himself on rationality and analysis, seemed not to understand that the effect of thousands, or just hundreds, of thermonuclear explosions centered on bases throughout the targeted nation or nations would still result in devastated cities, whether by blast or fallout. That the idea of a "humane" nuclear war plan is folly does not detract from the poignancy of the purpose McNamara set for himself from that first experience at SAC headquarters. He simply wanted to reconcile nuclear war with some kind of moral impulse. For the most part, his predecessors had not bothered to try.

In one of the supreme ironies of this whole history, McNamara's determination to mitigate the moral horror of massive retaliation by targeting the enemy's military positions instead of its cities[93] seemed to make nuclear war more likely. His doctrine would not only fail, it would lead to a major acceleration of the arms race and the dangers confronting the world. That is so because taking out cities requires many fewer warheads than taking out individual military positions. In attempting to move away from massive retaliation, he handed the generals and admirals another stick with which to beat the drums of escalation, drums that were always heard in Moscow.[94]

In another irony, the move toward a counterforce would also be taken by Moscow as evidence that the United States was preparing for a preemptive attack, which is why Pravda denounced the no-cities doctrine as "monstrous."[95] It presaged a first strike that would destroy the Soviet ability to retaliate. The fact that counterforce rhetoric entered the American strategic lexicon when Washington was pushing a new civil defense and bomb shelter program had to compound Moscow's anxiety, because such citizen-protecting steps could be a further signal that a first strike was in the offing.

McNamara might have insisted that preemptive strikes were nowhere on his agenda of strategic reform, but he was bringing about this shift in strategic thinking just as he was discovering — as the Soviets may well have done — how firmly the idea of preemptive nuclear attack was embedded in the war plans that LeMay and SAC had put at the center of American military purpose. At that first February briefing at SAC headquarters, as he described it to me, McNamara fervently recalled that he felt he was being ambushed on this very point, a replay, in effect, of what had happened — in secret — when Gaither Committee members had gone to Omaha four years earlier. "I went through the whole thing with General Power," McNamara told me, speaking of the J-SCAP and SIOP, the plans for general war. "There were four options: one, two, three, four — all retaliatory. But there was four-A as well, and that called for a first strike. Right away I went to see the president, and I told him that 'U.S. strategy calls for the U.S. initiation of the use of nuclear weapons under certain circumstances, and I want to tell you, that's wrong.'"[96]

Kennedy and McNamara had to know that Eisenhower had been prepared to "push [the] whole stack of chips into the pot" in a showdown over Berlin, and they may well have known that Eisenhower had instructed his National Security Council to be prepared for a preemptive nuclear strike during that crisis.[97] McNamara's conviction, stated in 2003, that "the initiation of the use of nuclear weapons" would be "wrong" does not mean that he did not understand that "initiation" can be reduced to a fine point when split seconds separate the gunfighters' draw; nor does it mean he did not seriously contemplate such initiating use himself when his own clock turned to high noon. He recalls telling the president in February 1961 that a first strike would be wrong, but by the fateful Berlin summer of that year, several events had transpired to complicate McNamara's moral view.

We have taken note of some of them: Kennedy's Vienna confrontation with Khrushchev in June, followed by Kennedy's mass mobilization order in early July, a prelude to his war-alarm speech in late July, with its call for fallout shelters. We now know that the men in the Kremlin were frightened by Kennedy's speech. Within days, Khrushchev gave speeches of his own that were heard in the West as only belligerent.[98] But there was an agitated plea from the Soviet leader as well: "The flywheel of war preparations may have acquired such speed and momentum that even those who had set it revolving will be unable to stop it."[99] Then he ordered the erection of the Berlin Wall.

Active American dread of Soviet intentions in Berlin was put in an entirely different context by a discovery made in the same period. We noted that it was already apparent in the winter of 1961 that the so-called missile gap favored the United States, but in the spring, Defense Department analysts, with data from the new *Discoverer* spy satellite, concluded that the Soviet Union's nuclear force was in fact far smaller and far more vulnerable than ever imagined. For the first time since Forrestal's breakdown, the United States had hard data on the basis of which to accurately assess the Soviet threat. And it was not that grave.

The CIA concluded that there were only four operational ICBMs, all on low alert, at a single, easily targeted site called Plesetsk, in Russia. Soviet radar was poor. Air defenses were inadequate. At Soviet air bases there were only about two hundred operational bombers, and they were lined up like ducks in a row, easy to hit; their nuclear bombs were stored far away from the planes, making a quick launch impossible. The Soviets had deployed several dozen relatively short-range missiles on submarines, but the subs were usually kept in port, easily targeted.

But don't relax. The discovery of the Soviet Union's radical strategic inferiority brought with it a new kind of threat, because an enemy that knows of its relative weakness has all the more reason to strike first, especially once its weakness becomes known to the other side. Having spent a decade terrified by self-projected images of Soviet superiority, American strategists found an opposite reason for terror, a first lesson in the fact that parity, not superiority, is what leads to the possibility of stable relations between two nuclear superpowers. "The delicate balance of terror," in Albert Wohlstetter's definitive phrase,[100] was upset by what the spy satellite had revealed. Thus America's recognition of Soviet weakness made the fear of imminent war worse, not better.

As tensions over Berlin simultaneously sharpened, Kennedy grew increasingly frustrated with the general-war scenarios he was getting from the brass. At one briefing, he asked JCS Chief Lemnitzer, "Why do we hit all those targets in China, General?" China had no nuclear weapons, had nothing to do with Berlin. The general replied, "It's in the plan, Mister President."[101] During one briefing, on July 18, 1961, Kennedy "got up and walked right out in the middle of it."[102] McNamara and his civilian advisers were desperate for a war plan that involved something less than the SIOP's all-out spasm attack against hundreds of cities behind the Iron Curtain, with hundreds of millions of mortalities.

But the new intelligence on Soviet vulnerability suddenly made another way possible, and it involved the counterforce strategy McNamara was ready to embrace. What if it were possible for a limited, pinpointed nuclear strike to take out the Soviet strategic force while it was still on the ground? Such a strategy, if successful, would spare the United States the horror of the full-blown nuclear exchange that had come that summer to seem ever more likely. It would end the "desperate arms race" of which Stimson had warned in 1945.

Kennedy and McNamara were not going to depend on LeMay, Power,

SAC, the JCS, or anyone in the Pentagon, for that matter, to draw up the detailed plan of a limited counterforce strike, to see if an alternative to a globe-destroying SIOP was in fact reasonable. At issue was more than the question of what the United States would actually do if it came to war. The way plans defined the use of nuclear weapons *before* war broke out was decisive to the political pressures that a president could bring to bear against an adversary ahead of violent conflict, and such plans also, over the longer term, would determine the way strategic forces were constructed and deployed.[103] So it was not only the use of weapons that was at stake; it was also their deterrence value and as a source of diplomatic influence. But before anything else, "use" had to be defined and carefully imagined. Kennedy gave the responsibility for this to his national security adviser, McGeorge Bundy,[104] who gave it to his deputy, Carl Kaysen.

9. THE KAYSEN MEMOS

We saw Kaysen earlier, as an Army Air Forces targeting officer during World War II, working (at age twenty-three) out of an office in London, choosing what Eighth Air Force bombardiers would aim at. It is an odd note of this history to recall that Kaysen, McGeorge Bundy, his brother William, and Robert McNamara, all part of the Kennedy-era inner circle, were young officers working within a few miles of each other, on similar projects, in England during the war.

That someone with Kaysen's background as a trained economist was given responsibility for target selection, we saw, was an indication of the seriousness with which the Americans took precision bombing. Kaysen worked in those years to guide the destruction of oil refineries and transportation facilities, intending to hobble Germany's war machine. He not only guided bombers but, using aerial photography, evaluated their missions after the fact. "We invented a form of poetry called bomb damage assessment," he told me when I interviewed him in 2003. It might seem a strange claim, poetry linked to bomb damage, yet young Kaysen was working to limit that damage.[105]

When Kaysen had become aware of the shift away from precision toward area bombing, as represented by Operation Thunderclap — the 1944 attempt, as he put it to me, "to create the effect of a nuclear weapon, so to speak, [to] obliterate one square mile of Berlin" — he was appalled: "Operation Thunder*crap*, we called it."[106] Kaysen worked for, and admired deeply, the Eighth Air Force's hero of the opposition to anticivilian area bombing, Colonel Richard D. Hughes. With Hughes, young Kaysen had learned, in effect, to ask: Accepting damage as a given, how can one make it effective yet also limit it? That question had now come back, unimaginably magnified.

In a way, the assignment Kaysen was given in 1961 was a version of his first mission, for devising an alternative to the SIOP general-war plan was an exercise in target selection. But now the context was completely different, and bombing had moved into another realm. It was a realm in which for years no one had, in fact, asked the most basic questions. When Kaysen went to SAC headquarters in Omaha to more fully inform himself on the SIOP, his questions to the generals were greeted with bristling responses. "None of your goddamn business" is how Kaysen described their attitude toward him. At SAC he got the impression that he would "be thrown in the brig and never heard from again." But this civilian was inquiring on behalf of the president, and soon enough SAC's generals gave him what he needed.

Kaysen and his colleagues[107] undertook a task that flew in the face of nuclear-age conventional wisdom — that the atomic bomb was, in a phrase of the early theorist Bernard Brodie, "inevitably a weapon of indiscriminate destruction."[108] This should have made obsolete the role of an economist in maximizing the application of force against the enemy. But as he had done in 1944, Kaysen set out precisely, in 1961, to discriminate.

Kaysen characterized his task as a "back-of-the-envelope" project, "to show that we could have a successful, clean first strike."[109] What he came up with, completing his top-secret report on September 5, was a contingency plan that did in fact envision an American nuclear assault targeting the strategic forces of the Soviet Union. The plan was called "Strategic Air Planning and Berlin," and in it Kaysen suggested, against prevailing Pentagon assumptions, that a Soviet move against West Berlin need not ignite an all-out nuclear apocalypse.

Kaysen took for granted that the U.S. response would have to be nuclear, but he argued that it "should seek the smallest possible list of targets, focusing on the long-range striking capacity of the Soviets, and avoiding, as much as possible, casualties and damage in Soviet civil society." The response Kaysen had in mind would be, relative to Pentagon doctrine, limited, involving about fifty SAC bombers instead of many hundreds; it would include no missiles. The plan was detailed enough to take up questions of navigation and specific targeting. Instead of the more than one thousand targets cited in the SIOP, Kaysen's plan proposed attacking eighty-eight. It is unclear what effect such projections actually had on Air Force planning, and it may be that the Air Force never developed the capacity to launch such a limited strike.[110]

Kaysen's report concluded, nevertheless, that the attack was feasible:

"While a wide range of outcomes is possible, we have a fair probability of achieving a substantial measure of success." The odds of this success, defined as hitting the enemy's bombers and missiles on the ground, were something like nine in ten. Compared to the Strategic Air Command's SIOP, there would be vastly fewer Russian casualties — but, showing what a moral wasteland the geography of nuclear planning had already become, the Kaysen plan still assumed that "mortalities from the initial raid might be less than 1,000,000 and probably not much more than 500,000."[111] It likewise assumed some chance of a minimal Soviet retaliatory strike, which, however small, would involve significant American casualties. Kaysen put the best case at near zero casualties, the worst case at something like three quarters of the nation's population. What circle of hell had men come to, that such numbers could seem, on any scale, benign?

No one knows to this day what President Kennedy's full reaction was to all of this. His attitude at this point is probably best described as profoundly ambivalent. He took the Kaysen proposal seriously enough to follow it up with a meeting with the JCS chief and the SAC commander two weeks later, on September 20. At that meeting SAC's General Power dismissed the idea of a limited nuclear strike, and insisted, according to declassified minutes of the meeting, that "the time of our greatest danger of a Soviet surprise attack is now." At last a SAC general was standing in the Oval Office and putting it to the president: "If a general atomic war is inevitable, the U.S. should strike first."[112]

Strike with everything. From spasm to Armageddon. Three days after this White House meeting, on September 23, the first attempted "silo-lift" launch of a Titan I ICBM was carried out successfully at Vandenberg Air Force Base in California,[113] evidence of what so filled the SAC commander with hubris. But his arrogant self-confidence backfired, perhaps in the way that U.S. strategic superiority would. General Power, like LeMay, antagonized Kennedy in the extreme, and that very extremity had the effect, in the president's mind, of underscoring the barbarity even of the minimal attack under consideration. The ease with which the general made the leap across that "if," positing inevitability, is what separated him from the president at that moment. Embedded in that "if" was the future of the earth.

That Power and Kennedy had different sensibilities and intuitions did not remove the questions, and they had become sharp: Under what circumstances should the United States initiate a nuclear war? Does the president's order of *any* nuclear use necessarily trigger the Strategic Air Command's SIOP/J-SCAP holocaust? Key State and Defense Department figures took up the questions at a White House meeting on October 10. No consensus was reached, although Paul Nitze was there arguing, as Power had, for a nuclear first strike. "This, I believed," he recorded in his memoir, "could assure us victory in at least a military sense in a series of nuclear exchanges, while we might well lose if we allowed the Soviets to strike first."[114]

A further meeting was to discuss the questions on October 20. In preparation for that meeting, Bundy sent a memo to Kennedy: "The issue, bluntly, is whether we can and should have nuclear strikes short of the massive strategic attack which is the current basic plan for general war . . . Again you may wish to press for continued analysis." When the memo was declassified, to be found in Kennedy's papers years later, it could be seen that Bundy had scrawled a message in its margin: "McNamara has just called to say they are not prepared on this for today."[115]

Disputes have arisen about what Kaysen's intentions really were with "Strategic Air Planning and Berlin." Some have assumed that, since he saw it as feasible, he was recommending such a first strike. There are reports that some of Kaysen's colleagues at the time, upon learning of his memo, vigorously attacked him. Kennedy's aide Theodore C. Sorensen, in one widely cited anecdote, confronted Kaysen in a White House corridor, crying, "You're crazy! We shouldn't let guys like you around here."[116] I interviewed Sorensen in 2003, and I asked him about the incident. He denied having said such a thing to Kaysen, telling me he had no impression that Kaysen ever promoted the idea of a first strike. Kai Bird, the biographer of McGeorge Bundy, observes that there is a fine line between "contingency" and concrete "planning."[117] To contemplate a course of action is to take a first step along it. Yet the Kaysen document makes clear that his concern, given the broad assumption that the danger of a coming nuclear war was real, was overwhelmingly to find an alternative to the massive-retaliation straitjacket of the SIOP.

After Fred Kaplan published a summary of "Strategic Air Planning and Berlin" in the *Atlantic Monthly* in October 2001, Kaysen wrote a letter to the editor, published in the January 2002 issue, in which he said that the article "may leave your readers with the impression that I *was recommending* a nuclear strike in the Soviet Union. The document makes plain that I made no such recommendation." In fact, Kaysen made "two recommendations for action" in the document, both aiming to lessen the likelihood of nuclear use, not increase it. The recommendations were, first, to require the commander of SAC "in the appropriate fashion to examine the impact of false alarm," and, second, to require SAC, the Joint Chiefs, and the Strategic Target Planning Staff "in the appropriate fashion to consider the preparation of alternatives to SIOP-62 for the use of our strategic striking power in the context of Berlin contingency planning."[118]

All these men took for granted that the danger of nuclear war was real. They were responsible for dealing with that danger, where possible to mitigate it, but where necessary to somehow anticipate it. Historians can never know what those men would have done in extremis because they did not know themselves.[119] Any decades-later attempt to apply a moral standard to their enterprise would be off the point without a vivid sense of the dominating context, which was the real and present danger of some kind of nuclear conflagration. Twenty-first-century Americans, in the grip of "nuclear amnesia," in the historian Marc Trachtenberg's phrase, may be incapable of conjuring such a sense. There is a big difference between looking at the sea from a tranquil beach and being out on it in a storm and feeling its swelling rage. And the sea, in this case, was not the worst part. Kaysen, my father, and the others call to mind nothing so much as a clutch of men in storm-tossed whaleboats, banging up against a thrashing white whale, futilely tossing harpoons, trying to subdue a primal force with lashes, each man secretly hoping the thing gets away before it kills him. Without their knowing it, a similar clutch of desperate whalers are on the monster's other side, doing the same. The Soviets. How did the thing look to them?

If Kaysen was the American who looked the monster of an apparently inevitable nuclear war most directly in the eye, it is not quite true to say that he refrained from blinking. We noted that his first-strike memo was dated September 5, 1961. While he was contemplating an actual plan of nuclear assault, he was also thinking of a way to avoid such an outcome. What about simply steering the boats away from the leviathan? Even better, what about rowing around to the other side and seeing things from the other point of view?

Two weeks before submitting "Strategic Air Planning and Berlin," Kaysen had sent another memo to McGeorge Bundy, dated August 22. He outlined "my instinctive reactions to the Berlin situation." Kaysen suggested a major revision of the West-East argument over the beleaguered city, beginning with a new proposal to the Soviet Union. The United States, Kaysen argued, against present policy, should accept Soviet definitions of the East German boundary; should recognize the sovereignty of East Germany; should leave the question of eventual unification to the German states themselves; and — accepting the demand that Eisenhower had repudiated in 1958, which sparked the Berlin crisis to begin with — should establish "a nuclear-free zone in Germany." In return for all of this, the United States should insist only on the protected freedom of West Berlin. In accommodating the main, long-stated requirements of the Soviet Union, Kaysen was advocating a shift away from mutual belligerence, with Berlin as the flashpoint, to what he called "peaceful coexistence."[120] The historian Kai Bird calls the Kaysen memo "a seminal document of the Cold War," and argues that if Kennedy had acted on it, "the Cold War might have ended much earlier than 1989."[121]

In effect, Kaysen was inviting a moral reckoning with how Berlin had come to be an East-West flashpoint in the first place. A short review may be instructive. Toward the end of World War II, the Allies agreed that once they occupied Germany, they would issue a common occupation currency, tied in value to the Reichsmark and required for all monetary transactions by civilians and occupiers alike. The problem came when three million American GIs were paid in the occupation Reichsmarks. They were able to redeem them for dollars, but the millions of Russian soldiers, paid in the same currency, were not able to redeem theirs for rubles, because the Soviet economy was a shambles. This made the Reichsmarks relatively valueless for Russian soldiers, although they could exchange them with GIs. This disparity soon led to a dangerously destabilizing black market, and it also meant that the United States, when converting Russian-issued Reichsmarks into dollars, was paying costs of the occupation that properly belonged to Moscow. To stop that, the U.S. government decreed that it would no longer redeem Russian-issued Reichsmarks for dollars. This immediately impoverished the Soviet soldiers, and it caused the first real breach in the alliance that had defeated Hitler. There were other points of contention, such as reparations and four-party authority, but the currency dispute came to symbolize them all.

Soon, though, the impossibly compromised Reichsmark was replaced by something that had real value to Americans and Russians both — the cigarette. A cigarette economy came into being, but cigarettes can be as dangerous to the health of social systems as they are to the body. American soldiers could buy a carton of cigarettes at the PX for a dollar. That same carton, on the black market, would bring the GI as much as a thousand Reichsmarks, at a time when a German's wage for a week's work was about eighty Reichsmarks. But even more destabilizing, the cigarette, like the dollar, was made in the USA, guaranteeing American dominance. Soviet resistance to that dominance, in the beginning, was all about currency. Disputes over the currencies in the two zones of Germany led directly to the Berlin airlift in 1948, and indirectly to the construction of the Berlin Wall in 1961.

Here was a reality to which Americans hardly ever attended — that, perhaps more than in the great ideological differences between East and West, the conflict that bled into the Cold War had its source in unforeseen, and probably preventable, inequities in financial exchange and value. The tragedy, of course, is that the largest difference between Russia and America in 1945 was that the former's economy had been destroyed by the war against Hitler, while the latter's had been rescued by it. Could Americans see the past in such terms — that is, in terms that took seriously the Soviet side of the story? This, in effect, was the question Carl Kaysen was asking after the Berlin Wall went up.

In the event, Kennedy seems to have entertained Kaysen's proposal — McGeorge Bundy seconded it — but he did not act on it. Over the coming weeks, as we have seen, the president was more focused on the prospect of nuclear war with the Soviet Union than on finding ways of defusing what made it seem so likely. The war of nerves that had begun in Vienna required toughness, not a friendly reach across armed borders — a conclusion Kennedy would have drawn as much from political realities in the United States as from the threat from abroad.[122] Kennedy's perceptions of positive possibilities with the Soviets had to have been considerably narrowed by the air of war emergency that dominated Washington that autumn; it was in September, recall, that Kennedy, writing in *Life*, urged Americans to dig fallout shelters. Once the standoff was overwhelmingly cast in military terms — at its outset, in April, Dean Acheson had defined Berlin as "the touchstone of American resolve and honor . . . [requiring] all-out force"[123] — the president found himself in the familiar box labeled "credibility." Or, as Bird succinctly puts it, "After the Bay of Pigs he could not afford to look feeble."[124]

Thus when the Soviets resumed nuclear testing on August 30, to be followed by fifty more tests that autumn — every test more a political shot than a scientific one — Kennedy knew that he would have to follow suit, just to avoid appearing soft. (The word "soft" was to the early sixties what "appeasement" was to the late thirties.) Kennedy was supported in his impulse to resume testing by, among others, Paul Nitze, from his position as assistant secretary of defense. Nitze advanced the Pentagon line that tests were absolutely necessary, and that warnings of health hazards from radioactive fallout were exaggerated.[125] Carl Kaysen disagreed with Nitze, as he would on many other occasions.[126] Kaysen opposed matching the Soviet move. When he told the president that the world would think better of America if it refrained from testing, Kennedy brusquely called him a "peacenik."[127] Toughness, or rather its appearance, was all.

Even so, the Americans and the Soviets navigated the troughs and swells of that period without going to war. Khrushchev solved one of his two large problems by building the Berlin Wall, and Kennedy quietly defused the other Soviet concern over Berlin, reversing Eisenhower, by making it clear that West Germany was not going to become a nuclear power in any sense. Indeed, under Kennedy it became understood that the United States accepted the "two Germanies" as a Cold War given.[128] As Kennedy eventually found it possible to reject any move toward a nuclear strike, so did Khrushchev, presumably deflecting on his side the dangerous contingency plans of his rational advisers and the mad urges of his bomber generals. The difference is that the United States, knowing of its rank superiority for the first time, might actually have convinced itself of the logic of attack — a case of the whiz kids joining the generals. Moscow had to know that any initial use of nuclear weapons was total and complete suicide; in Washington it could seem otherwise. Indeed, in an extreme form of perverse logic, restraint in the face of Soviet vulnerability could itself be taken as suicidal.

That season was the first and last, in the thermonuclear age, in which one side understood itself as having the opportunity, with reasonable certitude and relatively little likelihood of damage to itself, to eliminate the other side's nuclear threat once and for all. It was an option put before Kennedy by Carl Kaysen, and, seeing the matter clearly for the first time — the point of Kaysen's exercise — Kennedy refused.[129] That he also failed to seize an opposite opportunity, to take further steps that might have defused the Cold War — also put before him by Kaysen — is profoundly regrettable but, in the scale of history, as it ran, weighs less.

10. EDGE OF THE ABYSS

The Cuban Missile Crisis, unfolding one year later, dominates America's Cold War memory, although I remain one of those for whom the word "Berlin" carries as cold a breeze on the neck as "Cuba."[130] The two are linked, of course, because Khrushchev's deployment of missiles in Cuba was an attempt to overcome the strategic imbalance that the Berlin confrontation had made plain — at least in Moscow. Thus one historian suggests that the Cuban Missile Crisis be regarded as "the final phase of the Berlin Crisis: it was only after that episode that Berlin appears to have faded away as an issue."[131] Together, Berlin and Cuba — in not having led to war — mark a great turning point.

Perhaps I compulsively seek out personal connections to this history, but it has always struck me that the missile crisis began when a Defense Intelligence Agency photo analyst noticed certain trapezoidal markings on the ground at Cuban military installations, recognizing a pattern he knew from missile bases in the Soviet Union. The analyst reported this to my father, who immediately requested reconnaissance overflights — the initiating order of the melodrama.[132]

The Cuban Missile Crisis resulted from the Soviet Union's perception that the United States had the ability to deliver a first-strike knockout blow. Because missiles in Cuba would counter that, they were put there to protect the very survival of the USSR. We now know that in 1962 the Soviet ICBM force, consisting of about thirty launchers, was one tenth the size of the American force.[133] The great intelligence success, that the DIA discovered the Soviet deployment before it became operational, went hand in hand with a monumental intelligence failure, that Washington did not anticipate the Soviet reaction to its strategic disadvantage.

The dangers of those tense thirteen days in October 1962 are well known, and the more classified information about the confrontation is revealed, the greater the dangers appear to have been.[134] For example, McNamara makes the point now that, unknown to the Americans at the time, the Soviets had placed more than one hundred tactical nuclear warheads at the disposal of their forces in Cuba, an arsenal that, if used, would almost certainly have led to conflagration. A review of the transcripts of tapes that recorded the crisis deliberations of the president and his advisers — the ExComm, or Executive Committee — leaves one with the overwhelming impression of John F. Kennedy's distance from the instinctive, as well as the considered, responses of the men on whom he had to depend. Kennedy at first reacted like the others, declaring at an initial meeting of the ExComm his intention, "certainly," to "take out" the Soviet missiles.[135] But very soon Kennedy moderated his position and his tone. He settled into a mood and mode of his own.[136]

Dean Acheson was at the table as an admired senior statesman, legendary for "wisdom." Yet his advice to Kennedy would almost surely have led to a nuclear war. So, too, with Paul Nitze, assistant secretary of defense. True to his origins as the protégé of Forrestal and Acheson, and to his contributions to NSC-68 and the Gaither Report, he was among the "toughest" of the advisers. "Paul Nitze was leading the charge of the hawks," Undersecretary of State George Ball recalled. "I didn't believe the president would consent to an air strike on the missile bases in Cuba, but I was scared to death that Nitze . . . would wear the president down."[137]

Curtis LeMay was Nitze's cheerleader. In the ExComm deliberations, as we saw, the general called John Kennedy's position "appeasement," while later Nitze used the same loaded word to characterize Robert Kennedy's caution.[138] In conversation with a journalist years after the event, Nitze dismissed much of the ExComm's anguished discussion as "sophomoric — lots of morality issues raised."[139] Kennedy himself picked up on such condescension. Nitze's "tone in the meetings," his biographer observed, "was that of a stern elder, stiffening the backbone of the young president."[140] After the crisis passed, Nitze's influence in the Kennedy administration, such as it had been, was seriously eroded.

In the ExComm deliberations, Kennedy not only defied what at one point was the majority's urge for assault, but insisted that his chosen approach, primarily a sealing off of the island nation, be called a "quarantine," because "blockade" can be taken as an act of war. Such concern to avoid even the appearance of provocation is what LeMay dismissed as appeasement, the most fraught accusation that can be made against an American or British statesman and one that carried special insult for the son of Joseph P. Kennedy, whose public career was destroyed by that word. LeMay's use of it was a crossing of the swords.

For twenty years, LeMay's career had embodied the thrusting aggressiveness of a new kind of American power. Civilians like Kennedy (notwithstanding his war-hero status) could privately sneer at the crude belligerence of the bomber generals, but they had come to represent the exact measure of the nation's self-reinvention. The missile crisis was an illuminating moment, and in LeMay's performance Kennedy had to see the truth laid bare. Through technology and the horrors of history, the meaning of war had been transformed. War, in turn, had transformed America, recasting its idea of itself, its economy, its politics, its culture. In all those years, neither LeMay nor the fire-breathing forces he represented had been effectively opposed. By the time Kennedy became president, the nuclear priesthood had turned the Pentagon into its holy of holies. Finally, over Cuba, with the issue joined, Kennedy said no to LeMay.[141] He said no because the crisis revealed that what would be called "mutual assured destruction" (MAD) was already a fact, but he also said no because he saw what had already happened to America.

The president was able to do this only because of what he had been through the year before, over Berlin. The nation had "had the experience," in a line of T. S. Eliot's, "but missed the meaning."[142] Kennedy, in contrast, saw the meaning of the nuclear brink quite clearly. He went into the Cuban Missile Crisis having already come to terms with his constitutional responsibility as the man in charge of America's nuclear arsenal. Kennedy had, in effect, already decided that what LeMay represented was insane; that the insanity went beyond the personal eccentricities of the bomber generals to the entire system that empowered them; that there was no sane "alternative" use of nuclear weapons; that LeMay was simply not going to take the world across the nuclear threshold, no matter what.

As it was learned only years later, Kennedy made a solitary decision to resolve the crisis by proposing what was anathema to almost all of his advisers: a trade of the fifteen U.S. Jupiter missiles in Turkey for the Soviet missiles in Cuba. The Jupiters were outmoded anyway, but Nitze called the idea "absolutely anathema . . . as a matter of prestige and politics."[143] But Kennedy knew that prestige and politics were issues as much for Khrushchev as for him. The missile swap was a face-saving arrangement that Khrushchev accepted.

The conventional story, probably originating with Robert Kennedy, is that President Kennedy insisted on absolute secrecy for this deal, showing a strong commitment to the appearance of hard unyieldingness.[144] But there is good reason to think that was not so. As Dean Rusk revealed in a letter to a meeting of ExComm veterans in 1987 in the Florida Keys, Kennedy was prepared to yield the point if the Soviet leader refused to enact such a deal in secret. Indeed, anticipating that, Kennedy had taken steps to use the offices of U Thant, the secretary-general of the United Nations, to openly propose the Jupiter swap if Khrushchev insisted on its being public. What Rusk revealed in 1987 was that Kennedy was, in effect, prepared to relinquish the "toughness" card. If the trade needed to be made public, and it was taken as JFK's "blink," so be it.[145]

After the Cuban Missile Crisis, American and Soviet leaders alike wanted to back away from confrontation. "Recognition that the level of nuclear danger reached in October 1962 was unacceptably high for all mankind," Kennedy's national security adviser, McGeorge Bundy, wrote later, "may be the most important single legacy of the Cuban missile crisis."[146] By the end of 1962, McNamara had begun to repudiate his misbegotten counterforce strategy. His mistakes in strategic thinking had helped ignite the nuclear fuse, empowering the very bomber generals he had set out to rein in. Throughout the Pentagon bureaucracy, with the one telling exception of the Defense Intelligence Agency, his grand plans for managerial reform were coming to nothing. The wall he'd built between himself and the brass would imprison him when the war in Vietnam began. The so-called "education of Robert McNamara"[147] had begun. Even in 1963, the strains of it were evident. Kennedy was warned that his secretary of defense was behaving as Forrestal had just before his suicide.[148]

Emblematically, the man who embodied the Forrestal approach to national security, and who carried the personal legacy as Forrestal's protégé, hit a wall in this period, too. Failing to grasp how he had alienated Kennedy, Paul Nitze had convinced himself that he would soon be promoted to the Pentagon's number-two job. Sure enough, it opened up, but Kennedy named Nitze instead to the post of secretary of the Navy, a position on the margins of policymaking, a clear demotion. Humiliated, Nitze complained to the president, who essentially told him to take it or leave it. Nitze accepted the appointment.

And then an odd thing happened. The Senate confirmation of the nomination should have been routine, but a conservative young Republican congressman from Illinois, looking to make a mark by embarrassing the Kennedy administration, attacked Nitze from out of nowhere. The congressman charged him with having attended a National Council of Churches meeting years before, an event at which disarmament had been advocated by some in attendance. Disarmament! Showing his ignorance, the congressman charged the author of NSC-68 and the Gaither Report, two of the most hawkish statements ever to come out of Washington, with being "soft." The proponent of a first strike over Berlin and an all-out air assault on Cuba was a disarmer! It was a ludicrous charge and hardly honest. Even if the young congressman was ignorant of Nitze's militant history going back to the Strategic Bombing Survey, he had to have known that John Foster Dulles, secretary of state at the time of the Council of Churches meeting, had also attended, had even given the keynote speech. It was hardly a gathering of pinkos. And Nitze had, in any case, publicly argued against disarmament positions. But the attack was launched, and others in Congress picked it up, a club with which to hit the Democrats. Nitze's nomination to a job he did not want was nearly defeated. The wound of the insult would never quite heal. The first-term congressman who slandered him was named Donald Rumsfeld.[149]

Meanwhile, the culture of the Pentagon was hardly unaffected by events of the tumultuous Kennedy years. McNamara would carry forward a mistaken lesson from Berlin and Cuba, that the exercise of military power is basically a bargaining process — game theory, as they called it at RAND — an idea that would sink him when a pajama-clad revolutionary army rejected the bargain, refused to play the game.[150] SAC might go on dreaming of its all-out spasm attack, and indeed the SIOP war plans would remain largely unchanged, with the brass positing an ever-expanding target list, and consequently an ever-expanding arsenal. LeMay would recover some of his influence with a new president, Lyndon Johnson, who, appointing him to a second term as Air Force chief, used him as a shield against the right wing — and liked him for having been disliked by the Kennedys. But the Defense Department as such, with few exceptions, would no longer devote energy to imagining a nuclear war that might be "managed." The taboo against nuclear use was reinforced, a development that would be effectively enshrined as policy when the supremely survivable Minuteman and Polaris missiles, and their Soviet equivalents, were deployed.

The practical possibility of a first strike that would trump retaliation was about to disappear.[151] Even as this allowed a new level of nuclear stability, it meant that the fantasy of controlled nuclear violence was punctured. What the pioneering theorist Bernard Brodie had declared in 1946 was back: the atomic bomb was "inevitably a weapon of indiscriminate destruction."[152] The mutual recognition of that is the ground of "balance." That humane condition assumes a surrender to the barbaric. The doomsday deterrence strategy that had formed the core of Eisenhower's "massive retaliation" would soon go by the name of "mutual assured destruction," but while the former was a policy, the latter was (and remains) an existential condition. Second-strike capability was mutual, and so therefore was radical vulnerability. Cities were the target again. All cities. Everyone's.

But how to slow, if not reverse, the momentum toward such a conflagration, which had nearly overtaken planners and leaders on both sides twice in a year and a half? Before the crisis over Berlin, the richest promise of a Cold War thaw had been embodied in the hope of an agreement to halt nuclear testing. Such an agreed cessation of the air-polluting and arms-escalating test regime had been near the top of Eisenhower's agenda beginning in 1958, and it was to have been the subject of the 1960 Paris summit, which was sabotaged after the Soviets shot down Francis Gary Powers's U-2. Tensions over Berlin and Cuba had made chances of a test ban agreement seem more remote than ever, but then the terrifying events of October 1962 made everything seem different yet again. Indeed, in his crisis-ending communication to Kennedy on October 28, Khrushchev suggested that the Soviet Union "should like to continue the exchange of views on the prohibition of atomic and thermonuclear weapons, on general disarmament and other problems relating to the relaxation of international tension." Kennedy promptly affirmed the same hope: "Perhaps now, as we step back from danger, we can make some real progress in this vital field."[153]

But it was not so simple. Any move toward a test ban was opposed in Washington by the Pentagon and the Atomic Energy Commission. The Pentagon's dream weapon, then and now, was an antiballistic missile system, and it could not be developed without extensive testing. New generations of tactical nuclear weapons for the battlefield required open-ended testing, as did the unchecked impulse to continue expanding the strategic arsenal. The Army, Navy, and Air Force were united in decrying any sort of ban. Likewise, key figures in the Senate remained as skeptical as ever. On the Kremlin's side, a test ban would make Soviet nuclear inferiority permanent — the United States had thousands more strategic weapons than the Soviets — and that alone prompted Moscow's military establishment to oppose it. For the Soviets, the question of on-site inspections remained a sticking point, and though advances in seismic detection technology made it conceivable that on-site inspections would no longer be necessary, Kennedy would never be able to find political support for a comprehensive test ban that did not include inspections. But Khrushchev made an extraordinary break with the Soviet past, and put his own position on the line, by sending word to Kennedy before the end of 1962 that he would accept inspections after all — two or three a year. This offer was rejected by the Americans, who wanted eight. The negotiations went nowhere.

Kennedy predicted that future historians would look back on 1962 as the year when the tide began to turn.[154] But if that were to be so, he knew that he would have to somehow take control of the flow. Kennedy described himself as haunted by the prospect of the spread of nuclear weapons to ten or twenty other nations, and he knew that the upward momentum of the nuclear arms race between the United States and the Soviet Union, generated nowhere more powerfully than in his own Department of Defense, had to be checked if the world was to survive. He made crucial decisions that kept that momentum going, ordering the development of a thousand Minuteman missiles, for example, which, while thousands fewer than SAC wanted, was still hundreds more than some of his own experts told him was necessary. Where Eisenhower had authorized the deployment of nineteen Polaris submarines, under Kennedy that was increased to forty-one subs.[155] Defense spending was $41 billion in 1960; it would be $50 billion by 1965.[156] Kennedy approved such plans knowing full well they were responsive more to Pentagon turf pressures and demands from Capitol Hill (he was more afraid of Senator Richard Russell than of LeMay *or* Khrushchev) than to any strategic requirements arising from foreseeable Soviet threats.

Kennedy, in other words, had to stanch the flow that he himself had kept moving. In the beginning, his bluster had forced Khrushchev into reckless adventurism, and then their shared high-wire act above the nuclear precipice had prompted them both to reach out in negotiation, but the Soviet leader's reach went further than Kennedy could match. Khrushchev was the perceived loser in confrontation and conciliation both, and his position in the Kremlin was far less certain than Kennedy's in Washington.

If a new political hope was to be rekindled, Kennedy would have to find a way to do it. In order for that to happen, the political climate of fear and paranoia that he had himself encouraged would have to change. Kennedy, that is, would have to change. And how the world perceived him would have to change. But none of this was likely. "I am not hopeful," he said in May 1963.[157]

11. AT AMERICAN UNIVERSITY

When it came to imagining a new future, Kennedy knew that the inertia of his own government was as much an obstacle as the inbuilt recalcitrance of Kremlin leaders. That is why he took his next major foreign policy initiative in secret, without consulting Foggy Bottom, much less Hell's Bottom across the river.

By this time in his presidency, he understood the limits of his office; he knew how swiftly the power centers in Washington could be mobilized to thwart him. Despite all the prerogatives guaranteed him by the Constitution, he had only one true source of power: the ability to change the minds and hearts of the public through the use of language. The debasement of political rhetoric is so thoroughly taken for granted in the early twenty-first century that it is hard to remember a time when a mere speech could alter a political situation, accomplishing a kind of social alchemy, transforming the weary anguish of a nation into an unexpected political hope. On June 10, in the commencement address at American University in Washington, Kennedy set out to give such a speech.

He said that he chose "this time and place to discuss a topic on which ignorance too often abounds and the truth is too rarely perceived — yet it is the most important topic on earth: world peace." Almost immediately, everyone listening to him grasped the meaning of his declaration. He was a man cutting to the quick of his own experience, describing all that he had learned in the terrible two years since his disastrous meeting with Khrushchev in Vienna. This speech was the answer to the war-alarm speech he had given after that meeting, when he had single-handedly made America afraid. After two years of fear, it was time for something else. "What kind of peace do I mean? What kind of peace do we seek? Not a Pax Americana enforced on the world by American weapons of war. Not the peace of the grave or the security of the slave. I am talking about genuine peace, the kind of peace that makes life on earth worth living, the kind that enables men and nations to grow and to hope and to build a better life for their children — not merely peace in our time, but peace for all time."

Kennedy's listeners were not just the university graduates, not just the large American broadcast audience. Khrushchev listened to what his young nemesis said that day, and he would permit the rebroadcast of Kennedy's entire speech throughout the Soviet Union — a first. Everyone who heard Kennedy, or later read what he had said, knew that the president's words were informed by what he and Khrushchev had learned together. "I speak of peace because of the new face of war.[158] Total war makes no sense in an age when great powers can maintain large and relatively invulnerable nuclear forces . . . It makes no sense in an age when a single nuclear weapon contains almost ten times the explosive force delivered by all of the allied air forces in the Second World War. It makes no sense in an age when the deadly poisons produced by a nuclear exchange would be carried by wind and water and soil and seed to the far corners of the globe and to generations yet unborn."

The language of peace was "soft." Kennedy himself had never been given to it. This was the first time in any major public utterance of his that no attempt was made to be rhetorically tough. That was why he had prepared this text in isolation from the power centers over which he presided — and by which, until now, he had been imprisoned.[159] But no more. "I realize that the pursuit of peace is not as dramatic as the pursuit of war — and frequently the words of the pursuer fall on deaf ears. But we have no more urgent task."

And then, in the most extraordinary passage, the president made a declaration that was unprecedented in the Cold War. Nothing like it had been heard since Henry Stimson addressed Truman's cabinet in September 1945. "Some say that it is useless to speak of world peace or world law or world disarmament — and that it will be useless until the leaders of the Soviet Union adopt a more enlightened attitude. I hope they do. I believe we can help them do it. But I also believe that we must examine our own attitude — as individuals and as a nation — for our attitude is as essential as theirs." As essential to the Cold War conflict, that is. "And every graduate of this school, every thoughtful citizen who despairs of war and wishes to bring peace, should begin by looking inward — by examining his own attitude toward the possibilities of peace, toward the Soviet Union, toward the course of the Cold War, and toward freedom and peace here at home." An American president declaring the need for self-criticism. Suggesting that the problem belonged as much to Washington as to Moscow. That the United States, too, had the duty to "adopt a more enlightened attitude."

"First: Let us examine our attitude toward peace itself. Too many of us think it is impossible. Too many think it is unreal. But that is a dangerous, defeatist belief. It leads to the conclusion that war is inevitable — that mankind is doomed — that we are gripped by forces we cannot control."

Kennedy warned against a kind of utopian dream of peace, which invites discouragement by never coming. "Let us focus instead," he said, "on a more practical, more attainable peace — based not on a sudden revolution in human nature but on a gradual evolution in human institutions — on a series of concrete actions and effective agreements which are in the interest of all concerned." Later in the speech, Kennedy enumerated such specific steps — from a grand hope for new structures of international law to a proposed hot line between Moscow and Washington; from renewed negotiations toward general disarmament to a first move in that direction, with work toward a treaty to outlaw all nuclear tests.

"There is no single, simple key to this peace — no grand or magic formula to be adopted by one or two powers. Genuine peace must be the product of many nations, the sum of many acts. It must be dynamic, not static, changing to meet the challenge of each new generation. For peace is a process — a way of solving problems."

Kennedy bemoaned the misperceptions that prevailed in both the Soviet Union and the United States: how each side had "a distorted and desperate view of the other," which meant conflict was seen "as inevitable, accommodation as impossible, and communication as nothing more than an exchange of threats." Here was an American president repudiating at last the paranoia that had poisoned Washington's attitude since the time of Forrestal. And, equally significant, here was an American president rejecting the Manichaean de-monizing of Communist Russia, which had formed the spine of policy since the Truman Doctrine. "No government or social system," Kennedy declared, "is so evil that its people must be considered as lacking in virtue." Americans and Russians, he was boldly saying, are actually alike. "Among the many traits the peoples of our two countries have in common, none is stronger than our mutual abhorrence of war." But there was the tragedy, because of how war threatened now. And Kennedy accepted responsibility for the mutual night-mare, defining it exactly. "We are not here distributing blame or pointing the finger of judgment . . . We are both caught up in a vicious and dangerous cy-cle in which suspicion on one side breeds suspicion on the other, and new weapons beget counterweapons."

And then, in the most succinct statement of his presidency, and perhaps the most important, Kennedy told the nation and the world — and the people behind the Iron Curtain — what must happen now, and why. "In short, both the United States and its allies, and the Soviet Union and its allies, have a mu-tually deep interest in a just and genuine peace and in halting the arms race. Agreements to this end are in the interests of the Soviet Union as well as ours — and even the most hostile nations can be relied upon to accept and keep those treaty obligations which are in their own interest. So, let us not be blind to our differences — but let us also direct our attention to our common inter-ests and to the means by which those differences can be resolved. And if we cannot end now our differences, at least we can help make the world safe for diversity. For in the final analysis, our most basic common link is that we all inhabit this small planet. We all breathe the same air. We all cherish our chil-dren's future. And we are all mortal."[160]

It was unlike anything any U.S. president had said since the Cold War be-gan. In a sense, he had completed the thought he had begun with his inaugu-ral address — how the human condition had been changed by universal dread of nuclear weapons — by saying that, however changed we were, we all re-mained mortal. And human beings under the threat of nuclear annihilation were in touch with that mortality in an unprecedented way. Mortality was what bound us.

Politicians in the United States were unsure what to make of what Ken-nedy had said. His own State Department, as one official put it, was caught "flat-footed."[161] But Khrushchev knew at once that it was, as he said, "the greatest speech [given] by an American president since Roosevelt."[162] It changed everything. Six weeks later, on July 26, 1963, Kennedy went on television to announce that "yesterday a shaft of light cut into the darkness. Negotiations were concluded in Moscow on a treaty to ban nuclear tests in the atmosphere, in outer space, and under water. For the first time, an agreement has been reached on bringing the forces of nuclear destruction under international control — a goal first sought in 1946."[163]

To Kennedy, this treaty was the turn in the tide he had been looking for, and he announced it almost two years to the day after he had issued his momentous war alarm. To reverse that warning had surely become his urgent personal goal, felt most deeply when he had sat at his desk alone, at night, poring over war plans, including those provided him, so chillingly, by Carl Kaysen during the Berlin crisis. But now, for the first time, nuclear war did not look inevitable. That Kennedy had dispatched Kaysen to Moscow as his personal representative[164] at the test ban negotiations was an act of punctuation, ending a sentence that two years before had been allowed to trail off.

That the Partial Test Ban Treaty was indeed partial, did not apply to underground tests, broke the hearts of some disarmament advocates. One negotiator who wanted to hold out for a "comprehensive" ban wept at the compromise.[165] At the other extreme, sponsors of the arms race, including Edward Teller, and beneficiaries of it, such as the leading defense contractors, denounced the agreement as a betrayal of national security. If the American people supported the treaty, it was probably due as much to fear of radioactive fallout as to any softening toward the Soviet Union. Even the limited treaty was stoutly opposed by the Pentagon, with SAC Commander Thomas Power, in a not untypical act of insubordination, publicly condemning it. The Joint Chiefs' support was essential to getting the treaty ratified by the Senate. Under intense pressure from McNamara — and the Joint Chiefs' leader, Kennedy's friend Maxwell Taylor — they grudgingly backed it, with Air Force Chief Curtis LeMay making his resentment crystal clear.[166]

The Chiefs, in fact, were bribed for their support with promises of unfettered underground testing, and hawkish senators were bribed with promises of lavish defense increases down the road. Such maneuvering produced one ironic result: a quickening of nuclear development, not a lessening. There would be no letup in the rapid accumulation of nukes and the steady increase in their lethality. An arms control pattern was thus set at the start; it would be repeated in 1972, when the Nixon administration had to buy off the Chiefs and skeptical senators to get SALT I, the first Strategic Arms Limitation Talks treaty, ratified. The phenomenon was compared with squeezing a balloon: compressing one part expands another. When one method of nuclear development was limited by a treaty, permitted methods not controlled by the treaty would always grow exponentially. Arms control in one area resulted in escalation in another. The Pentagon behemoth would continue to find chutes down which to run unchecked.

Kennedy staked his political future on getting quick ratification from the Senate, launching an extensive public campaign. In September, the Partial Test Ban Treaty was overwhelmingly approved. After 336 explosions in the atmosphere over thirteen years, the nuclear powers agreed to stop. Kennedy saw this as the beginning of something, not the end. Not long after the treaty's approval, continuing the impulse, Kennedy undertook a secret initiative with Fidel Castro, seeking accommodation through, as he put it, "a sweet approach." He was determined to lay to rest the problem that had most vexed his presidency, and most threatened the world.[167]

But there wasn't time. Two months after the Partial Test Ban Treaty was ratified, in his last speech, on November 22, 1963, he said, "Our chances for peace are better than they have been in the past."[168] At American University, he had based his plea for a new way on the simple fact that "we are all mortal." When the president's own mortality was so traumatically laid bare, his plea for peace, notwithstanding all it contradicted in his career, became the pulse that would beat on without him.

12. WHY WE LOVE HIM

I wrote earlier of standing in the inaugural throng on the Capitol's east plaza, listening to Kennedy's address, watching a version of the man I longed to be. I was an eighteen-year-old freshman at Georgetown, in northwest Washington. On Sunday, November 24, 1963, I returned to that plaza, to stand in a slow-moving line that snaked its way to the Capitol, up the steps, into the great rotunda. By then I was nearly twenty-one, and I was enrolled in a Catholic seminary in northeast Washington. On that weekend, 250,000 people stood in that line to pay their respects by walking past the slain president's coffin. It was draped with an American flag, and at each corner stood a uniformed honor guard, one from each service branch — a kind of interservice unity at last. I remember best the stark silence of the crowd outside, and how, for the few moments it took to pass through the templar hall, no one seemed to breathe. There was weeping, but it was soundless.

The next day, I went across town to stand, again amid thousands, on the curb across the street from the Cathedral of St. Matthew, where Kennedy's Requiem was sung. I craned now to glimpse my mother and father entering the church, in a procession made up of the most powerful people in the world, led by Charles de Gaulle. My parents, I knew, were as bereft as I was, and that sadness was a fresh point of connection between my father and me. People of my generation regarded the young president as having uniquely addressed us, but Kennedy, through McNamara, had tapped my father for special work. As a young FBI agent, transplanted from the South Side of Chicago to Washington in wartime, and then as an upstart Air Force general, literally ill suited in blue, my father had been a man apart. Only with Kennedy had he come into his own. McNamara's independence had licensed Joe Carroll's, and Kennedy was the source of authority for both of them. That affirmation had been the ground of my father's affection for the president, but there were other reasons. The Irishness. The Catholicism. The unbridled joy of outsiders having arrived.

And one other thing. By the autumn of 1963, Kennedy had addressed my father's nuclear anguish. He had led a band of men from one edge of hell to the other, and my father was desperately proud to have been one of its minor members. What he had entrusted me with that night in the Lincoln, driving from the Pentagon to Bolling in the season of Kennedy's war panic, had in some measure been resolved, and in a small way my father had helped resolve it. In the contest between LeMay and Kennedy, my father, despite his uniform, had thrown in solidly with the president, because of whom, finally, there was no longer any question of getting the boys in the car and driving to Richmond.

That Dad had come to believe in Kennedy, even to love him, had been made clear to me the night before the state funeral. In distress, I went to see my parents at the house on Generals' Row. When I came through the door my father was there, his blue shirt open at the collar, the knot of his blue tie loosened. In a gesture that would become a cliché of the next generation, but which then was unusual and, between us, unprecedented, he took me into his arms, a firm embrace. His grief and mine were the same. It would be a bond between us for the rest of our lives, one of the few that would not break. When my parents were buried at Arlington National Cemetery — my father twenty-eight years after the president, my mother thirty — the gravesite seemed sacred to each of them, I know, because it was up the hill from the ever-burning flame of John Kennedy's.

Much has been written about Kennedy's death, and speculation about its impact on the national — no, world — psyche has been endless. His youth, his glamour, his class, his inspiring rhetoric are always emphasized. An aura of political idealism surrounds the Kennedy myth, as if he were a civil rights prophet, which he was not; as if he accomplished great acts of social reform, which he did not. It is as if the fierce, nearly universal attachment to his image is rooted in a kind of political infatuation. He was elected president by the narrowest of margins, but when he died a sizable majority of voters recalled having cast ballots for him. In the decades since, revelations about his health, his promiscuity, his ruthless pragmatism have done nothing to dull the glowing esteem in which he is held. If anything, the American attachment to the memory of John Fitzgerald Kennedy is firmer now than ever.

Why is that? When he was murdered, his widow instinctively understood that the funeral rituals should be modeled not, as officials assumed, on Franklin Roosevelt's but on Abraham Lincoln's. Hence the military procession, the muffled drums, the caisson, the riderless horse with the boot reversed in its stirrup. It was on a replica of Lincoln's catafalque that Kennedy's casket rested in the Capitol rotunda.[169] Jacqueline Kennedy grasped the essence of the trauma through which Americans had moved under their leader. The wartime ordeal through which Roosevelt had led the nation was severe, but the emotional bond with him had more to do with the Great Depression than World War II. The Depression had wounded the citizenry in ways the war had not. The love that the people had for Roosevelt was like the love of dependent children for a father.

Lincoln, on the other hand, had been the moral and political stillpoint of the catastrophe of the Civil War, and Americans in the North felt that their anguish was his. They felt that their survival as a people was due to him. It was not love for a father but for a courageous compatriot with and by whom survival had been forged. Something like that was true of Americans' feeling for Kennedy, but compared to Lincoln, it remained implicit, because the anguish through which he had led us had been more a grave threat than an actual outbreak. Lincoln had offered a way to make sense of, and deal with, the intense physical suffering that racked the nation, but catastrophe in prospect is traumatic, too. In the early sixties, America's suffering was the more intense for being emotional and psychological, pure terror at what was coming.

That the dreaded thing did not come is part of why it has been mostly deleted from the nation's memory, but also it has been willfully forgotten because the thing was so awful. The horror of nuclear war was experienced not as an abstraction, a danger hovering at a distance, but as an imminent and certain event, not "someday" or "far away" but tomorrow and here. Americans of the Kennedy generation look back on the Cuban Missile Crisis as if that two-week period encompassed the duration of fear, but in fact it was the climax of a terror that had been building in us since we'd first been ordered, by a turtle named Bert, to crouch under our desks. During the Eisenhower years, an accumulating dread of nuclear war with the Soviet Union was sublimated in the unbridled paranoia of the Red Scare, and then in a small elite's esoteric and apparently absurd "thinking of the unthinkable," but by 1961, nuclear fear came into the open as a practical possibility. That is the permanent significance of Kennedy's July 30 television speech, when he asked us to pray for him. When we did.

The president told us he would protect us, and we believed him. The consciously experienced fear of nuclear war trumped politics and partisanship. It established a powerful bond between the young leader and the American people. For two years, with palpable and — as we now know — flawed humanity, he met his responsibility. We watched obsessively, fully aware of what was at stake. For many of us, his promise of peace at the end — the American University speech, the Partial Test Ban Treaty — was the start of a feeling of our having been right to trust him. When Kennedy was murdered before our eyes, the feeling of relief was cut short, and we were returned to our previous dread. The forgotten monster of transcendent violence reared its frightening head for a moment, and we remembered. In this narrative, the image of the thrashing, uncontrollable beast has been applied to the impersonal forces that push toward a world-historic disaster, but on a November afternoon it concentrated itself more narrowly, on just one man.

Below the surface of American rationality, the fearful summer of Berlin, 1961, and the terrible autumn of Cuba, 1962, came crashing back in late 1963, as if all that we dreaded had come to pass, even if the real devastation befell only him. Instead of the fireball destroying the planet, a muzzled flash of it destroyed the planet's best, which was enough. We were blinded after all, oh Bert. On that Friday afternoon in November, we were left with unfinished business, from which, in our dazed state, we hid. We turned away from conscious considerations of nuclear war, equally from responsibility for it, leaving the commissioned few to their own unchecked pursuit of the unleashed monster. They pursue it today.

The nation never resolved all that John Kennedy had come to mean to us. It never resolved the task we set ourselves with him. Until we do, his name will have its incomparable power. One need not imagine him, had he lived, immune to the pressures of the ongoing Cold War to realize what still sets him apart among American presidents. Kennedy allowed us to experience our nuclear fear for what it was, and more, to see a way out of that fear, even if only in a glimpse. Even if, to this day, we have not taken it.

SIX

THE EXORCISM

1. PRESENT AT THE DESTRUCTION

"October 21, 1967, Washington, D.C., USA, Planet Earth," the proclamation read. "We Freemen of all colors of the spectrum, in the name of God, Ra, Jehovah, Anubis . . ." I have no memory of having been handed a copy of this crudely mimeographed page, but I was there. The words feel familiar to me, and I might have recited them with all the others. I might have taken the page when a braless hippie proffered it, surely would have. Though the day was traumatic for me, my memory of it is hazy. This was my initiation into whacked-out peace demonstrations, but there would be dozens of others, two or three of them at the very place, the Pentagon. If memory is the place in which a thing happens for the second time, what of the things that had happened already again and again?

I do remember, on that first day, waif-like young women in Indian print dresses that were somehow both loose-fitting and revealing, their breasts on display, the nipples that seemed ready to kiss you. Here was the moral anarchy, conservatives would surely say, that always followed defiance of authority. Robert McNamara would remember them from this demonstration as having exposed their bralessness to his vulnerable young soldiers,[1] although no one I ever spoke to saw such a thing. I was still a Catholic seminarian, which may be why the image of girls — free*women* of all colors — preempts other associations when I recall the day of the March on the Pentagon. In the American memory, it was the day the peace movement became a mass phenomenon, but for me it was the day my relationship to the Building changed forever.

That morning a hundred thousand people had gathered east of the river, at the Lincoln Memorial, for songs and speeches against the war in Vietnam. And then around half[2] of them writhed and roiled like a primeval sea snake[3] across Memorial Bridge, aiming to violate the precincts of the war's high temple. In previous antiwar demonstrations in Washington, the procession had taken protesters along the Mall to the Capitol, a ritual of petition to legislative leaders. But this move in the opposite direction was to be confrontation, not petition, a challenge by "the people" to the "warmakers" themselves. This gathering was to be, as the organizers stated, "resistance," an escalation of protest, which is why half of those who had attended the rally at the Lincoln Memorial had chosen to remain on the D.C. side of the river — and why I had gone downtown from the seminary that morning with tremors of ambivalence.[4]

In order to approach the Pentagon, the protesters had to cross, unknowingly, the acreage of the original site of the War Department building, the site Roosevelt had rejected because he did not want a huge new edifice, a war building at that, to break the axis of national reconciliation that ran from the Lee mansion on the ridge of Arlington to the Lincoln Memorial. But what was national reconciliation now? I was afraid of what we were doing. Confrontation, as I might have said, was not my thing.

But what if that was not our actual purpose? The mimeographed sheet suggested another one: "In the name of God, Ra, Jehovah, Anubis, Great Spirit, Dionysus, Yahweh . . ." No, not confront the Pentagon but drive the evil spirits from it — which was the point of the sheet that had been passed through the crowd of demonstrators, with rubrics for an act of exorcism. The text rolled on: ". . . Thor, Bacchus, Isis, Jesus Christ, Maitreya, Buddha, Rama, [we] do exorcise and cast out the EVIL which has walled and captured the pentacle of power and perverted its use to the need of the total machine and its child the hydrogen bomb."

What could such a litany have meant to me? I was in the last phase of training for the priesthood in a seminary on the far side of Washington, and I was not liable to be moved by a fake exorcism. If I had already begun to timidly claim my distance from the ferocious militarism that had caused the deaths of fifteen thousand American boys in Vietnam (one of those shot-down pilots should have been me), not to mention the dropping of well over a million tons of bombs on the country, North and South — still, I was no drug-addled pantheist. This was hippie voodoo.

"By the reading of this paper, you are engaged in the Holy Ritual of Exorcism. To further participate, focus your thought on the casting out of evil through the grace of GOD which is all [ours]. A billion stars in a billion galaxies of space and time is the form of your power, and limitless is your name."[5]

My memories of the demonstration are vague, somewhat generic, yet I know for sure that my thoughts would have been focused only on my father, from whose office window in the "pentacle of power" I never took my eye. If I had joined the protest at all, it was only because, surrounded by thousands, I was sure he would never see me. Dad was in the fifth year of his tenure as director of the Defense Intelligence Agency, a position that, more than most in the vast military establishment, put him in the crosshairs of both the wars then under way: the war in Vietnam and the war inside the Pentagon. Beginning with the self-immolation at the Pentagon of the Quaker Norman Morrison two years before, the Vietnam War had increasingly become an obstacle between my father and me. I was soon to have my last holiday meal at the house on Generals' Row; he and I were to sink below the surface of a common silence, which would be mostly what we shared from then on.[6]

But in the autumn of 1967, I knew nothing about my father's struggle inside the Building — not that he knew anything of the transformation I was undergoing. Mine, I see now, was the larger ignorance. He had his reasons for not speaking of his experience to me: national security. What were mine for not speaking to him?

Over time, I have come to wonder if he was as alienated in his world as I was in mine, but such a question was unthinkable then. It had been years since I'd gone to the Pentagon to visit him, much less to play there. Now, upon my return, if that's what this was, I felt a bolt of shame. Like my arrival here, I was coming reluctantly — and, regarding him, secretly — to what would forever be a marginal place in the peace movement. At first it was the coming I was ashamed of; later it would be the reluctance, the marginality.

Ironically, it was because I had entered the Church, which pleased my father so, that I had begun to move away from him. John F. Kennedy, in that speech at American University in 1963, had put the word "peace" at the center of a new patriotic ideal. "Peace itself," he said. "Too many of us think it is impossible."[7] But an entire movement of Kennedy's children had sprung up, insisting it was not impossible. Of those, none had been more powerfully summoned than we Catholics, called first by Pope John XXIII's 1963 encyclical *Pacem in Terris*, which defined the new longing for peace as a sign of the times, boldly rejecting the idea that nuclear weapons could ever be used as instruments of justice.[8] The first Catholic to reject the escalating war in Vietnam as such, when it was only months old, was Pope John's successor, Paul VI, who went before the United Nations in 1965 and declared, "War no more! War never again!" In that unforgotten speech, the pope had defied Lyndon Johnson by citing President Kennedy, "a great man now departed": "Mankind must put an end to war, or war will put an end to mankind."[9] Wasn't that the unassailable logic that had come out of not only 1945 but the crises of 1961 and 1962? And wasn't that why the loss of November 22, 1963, was still felt? Only days before this demonstration, I had learned that Father Daniel Berrigan, a Jesuit poet, known to be one of the Kennedys' priests, was going to join it, marching all the way to the Pentagon. How, then, could I not?

Yet here I was, surrounded by puppeteers and drummers; girls jangling bell-studded leather straps; tambourine-slapping boys in paisley shirts, headbands and Army field jackets, mustaches and filthy hair — all reeking of incense and self-righteousness. The "people" were self-consciously leaderless, yet the voices began to rise as one. The recitation of the litany of gods culminated in the chant "Out demons! Out! Out demons! Out!"

We had been allowed to go only as far as the north parking lot, and the Building — my father's window — loomed in the far distance, yet the frenzy gathered force, moving beyond its bacchanalian esprit. Someone with a bull horn chanted, "Back to darkness, ye servants of Satan," and the crowd roared its appointed antiphon, "Out demons! Out!" Fists were raised and shaken, and lines of battle-dressed soldiers stared mutely back. One observer defined the demonstration as "each side coming face to face with its conception of the devil."[10]

And there was my problem. Whatever the men in the Pentagon were to me by then, they were not demons. This rough and shallow gathering was insulting the very Building, and to my chagrin I still possessed my old affection for the place. Those ramps, the concourse with its drugstore, the huge map of the world that covered the wall of my dad's office, the leather couch by his secretary's desk, where I had curled up to do my homework. I had an urge to cry out "Silence!" I had come here not to demonize but to grieve. The exorcism text opposed EVIL and GOD, identifying the first with the "pentacle" and the second with the puerile mob assaulting it. But what did they know? What were the ramps and rings to them, the heroes in paintings on the walls, the clusters of battle flags, the clock room, with its timepieces showing the hour in every world capital, including Moscow? Yes, time. The Pentagon and I were born together, and if one of us was the evil twin, it had to be me.

If I knew that the denounced generals, even as they presided over the great mistake of Vietnam, were not demons, it was because one of them was Dad. If, unlike everyone around me, I could not hate Robert McNamara, it was because regard for him, support for his purposes, remained the core of my patrimony. His purposes may have been thwarted, but they were not evil. And so with the place over which he presided. I never accepted the Manichaean assumptions of the peace movement. I never made a move of my own as part of it, therefore, without an overriding sense of my complicity. The world was awash in good intentions. Ours, theirs, everyone's. Still, terrible things had come to pass. "Out demons! Out!"

What went wrong? Weren't we all betraying the sacred moments that had bound us as a people — that weekend of Kennedy's death when Americans were united in feelings too deep for words? That communal tie, forged in the new liturgy of television, had seemed transcendent, and permanent. The sadness was intensely personal, yet it was essentially political as well. That weekend was when the dread we'd felt over Berlin and over Cuba had befallen one of us instead of all.

It has been an assumption of this work that an unarticulated nuclear dread formed the spine of my generation's character, if not the nation's. It may be my narcissism to say so, since it obviously formed the spine of mine — the dread that had moved Dad to commission me for a trip to Richmond and beyond. A trip that I never set out on, yet a trip from which I have not yet returned. Nuclear dread was the ground on which our misery stood when the man who had begun to show us a way through it was violently murdered. How had we gone from the heartbroken intimacy of 1963 to the anguished alienation of 1967? It was America's question as well as mine.

2. LeMay to the Absurd

Looking back on those watershed years, and having considered the records and testimony of the men whose choices shaped the time and whose lives were destroyed by it, I recognize a spark of wisdom in the hippie impulse to understand the horrors then being sponsored by the Pentagon in terms of the mystery of evil. Not evil as the Manichaeans and Puritans saw it, assuming that the demons reside in the hearts of those who see the world differently; not evil in the way of any cosmic dualism that divides the world between good and bad, as if the Pentagon were surrounded on that October day by forces of pure virtue, as if the men inside were not themselves torn, struggling, desperate to do what was right, more devoted to the ideal of peace — willing to bear the suffering involved in its pursuit — than any weekend larkhead in paisley.

Even someone like Curtis LeMay. By October 1967, my former neighbor had become a figure of the absurd in the United States, mocked in movies as a trigger-happy general in the grip of a demonic lust for the sheer destruction of the planet. Within months of the Pentagon demonstration, he would be a candidate for the vice presidency of the United States, running on the American Independence Party ticket with the racist Alabama demagogue George C. Wallace. The sight of the two short, chubby men in ill-fitting brown suits, holding each other's arm aloft, was enough to make the gods of the Good War weep — such was the hollowness of the heroic ideal around which America had constructed its Cold War self. LeMay's pronouncements on Vietnam had made him the poster boy of the "baby burners." He wanted to bomb the enemy "back to the Stone Age."[11] He wanted to unleash the whole arsenal, including nukes. He derided the air war against Vietnam, as conducted by McNamara, as if it were effete, timid, reluctant — when in fact more bomb tonnage had already, by late 1967, been dropped on the rice paddies, jungle trails, river deltas, and hamlets of the impoverished nation than the Allies had dropped on Germany in World War II. And World War II makes the point, for the demonized LeMay advocated for Vietnam only a version of what the sainted FDR had ordered for Germany and Japan.[12]

LeMay had been a civilian for a year and a half. His retirement ceremony was held in February 1965 at Andrews Air Force Base, in a giant hangar from which *Air Force One* had been temporarily removed to make way for the party. I was there with my mother and father — a final ritual of my own belonging, although I did not know that yet. Feeling shy in my black seminarian's suit and narrow black tie, I knew full well, in that sea of blue uniforms, that I looked like an undertaker, and I hung at my father's elbow. I was still young enough to be gratified that I was as tall as he, and, as I always did in his presence, I stood up straight. The three stars on his epaulettes marked him as one of the senior figures present, and I burned with pride, but also envy. Secretly I longed for a blue uniform of my own, from my ROTC days, but Dad could not have been more pleased to present to his friends his lean, earnest son who was going to be a priest. He introduced me to Tooey Spaatz, Ira Eaker, and Rosie O'Donnell,[13] legends of the Army Air Forces, and their evident affection for my father made me swell. I also met the movie star Jimmy Stewart, who was there in the uniform of an Air Force brigadier general, his rank in the Reserves.[14] Stewart addressed my father as "sir." Dad introduced me to the even more glamorous-looking Senator Stuart Symington, a tall, silver-haired patrician who, when he greeted my mother, put a hand on each of her shoulders and kissed her cheek with what seemed a special warmth. She teased him knowingly, and then she and my father shared a laugh with the senator that put an old affection on display, and I remembered that Dad had begun at the Pentagon as his protégé.

But I was a connoisseur of emotional weather, and I noticed something else. I did not know what to make of it at the time, but LeMay never came near my father, and once, as he passed nearby, my father made no move to greet him — or remind him of who I was. I recognized a snub, but it seemed mutual. To my own surprise, I myself had no wish to greet the general.

The stage-set accoutrements of the LeMay festivities in the hangar included one of the B-17s he'd piloted in Germany as well as a huge B-52 on the apron outside. The two planes represented a bracketing of LeMay's achievements as the man who, practically by himself — leading the first air raid against Germany proper in 1943, then heading up SAC in the 1950s and solidifying its dominance in the first half of the 1960s — had pushed the foundation blocks of America's world supremacy into place.

The month before LeMay's retirement, Lyndon Johnson had once more been sworn in as president, having vanquished Barry Goldwater, the Arizona senator whom Johnson had successfully portrayed as a warmonger. At the end of the infamous television commercial that showed a young girl plucking daisy petals as a lugubrious narrator counted down to a nuclear detonation, Johnson's voice could be heard saying, "These are the stakes. To make a world in which all God's children can live . . . We must either love each other, or we must die."[15] We had a president elected on the promise of peace. So why should the "Peace is our profession" legend painted on the fuselage of the B-52 not have seemed like an honest wish to me?[16] Never mind that Senator Goldwater was present for LeMay's ceremony, wearing his uniform, like Jimmy Stewart, as a general officer in the Air Force Reserve.[17]

I knew so little, as did everyone else. The very week of LeMay's retirement, President Johnson ordered the commencement of Operation Rolling Thunder, the air war against North and South Vietnam, which began — in secret from the American public — when warplanes struck a target defined as an ammunition dump,[18] but which would develop into the most comprehensive sequence of air assaults ever conducted.[19] Even so, as events would show, Rolling Thunder would not be LeMay's idea of a bombing campaign, which would define both its failure and its tragic virtue. The bombing of South Vietnam would be notable for its unrestrained destruction, an obliteration of the country we had gone to war to defend. But in the North, out of fear of bringing the Soviets or Chinese in, restraints would be imposed: bombs would not be dropped on harbors in which Russian ships sat, nor too close to the Chinese border. Instead of bombing to destroy and win, the air war in North Vietnam, from the outset, would embody the "bargaining" and "game theory" of the nuclear philosophers whom LeMay disdained. By now they returned his disdain with contempt. That many defense intellectuals were associated with RAND, the California think tank that LeMay himself had helped to found, only underscored his bitterness.[20]

Vietnam was a showcase of the intellectual exercise, force applied to coerce a political settlement rather than to destroy the enemy. "Gradual escalation" was supposed to compel by inflicting intolerable pain while preserving the "hostage value" of what had yet to be destroyed. What the new breed of theorists did not imagine, as their highly rational campaign was launched, was that for this enemy, the only possible settlement presumed its own utter destruction. The Vietnamese Communists, who could not be coerced but only killed, never lost sight of the basic human truth from which the Pentagon "humanists" were in flight — that war, once begun, is the opposite of rational.

That Rolling Thunder, as conducted against North Vietnam, aimed at "compellence" rather than obliteration was a measure of the distance traveled since 1945, yet that distance was revealed, through the brutality of carpet bombing and napalm and free-fire zones in the South, to be a mirage. I could not know, as I joined in the celebration of Curtis LeMay, how he would disapprove of the "restrained" Rolling Thunder campaign in the North, or how, from an opposite side, its "limited" purpose — eventually involving hyperviolence in Cambodia and Laos, too — would come to appall even me. No more could I have grasped the large hint of trouble coming — a hint of the fatal, undermining ambivalence — in the fact that just as Robert McNamara had not found it possible to attend LeMay's swearing-in as Air Force chief of staff in 1961, the secretary of defense had not found it possible to attend the retirement ceremony.

3. ERRORS OF THE MIND

What were such complexities to that mob of exorcists in October 1967? Nothing at all. LeMay, McNamara, Eaker, Spaatz, Carroll — demons, all the same. "Out demons! Out!" But it was not so, not remotely so. As endless testimonies and declassifications would make clear over the next generation — David Halberstam's book, the Pentagon Papers, the Westmoreland libel trial, Neil Sheehan's book, Stanley Karnow's television series *Vietnam*, McNamara's own memoir — the Pentagon, before it was at war in Southeast Asia, was at war with itself, in the rings, ramps, corridors, "tanks," messes, and conference rooms of the largest building in the world. Standing against a global Communism it took to be monolithic, the Pentagon wanted to be taken as a monolith, and, alas, so it was. But it was not true.

And to accomplish any mature reckoning of the time and its agonies, account would have to be taken not just of divisions *between* the men in the Pentagon, divisions of which peaceniks were universally ignorant — LeMay against McNamara — but also of divisions *within* the men in the Pentagon — McNamara against himself, my father against himself. Peaceniks, in the thrall of Oedipal projection, as abstract to the mob as it was personal to me, could not imagine it.

Yet in such blurred complexities reside the only possible meanings by which to measure evil. What is evil anyway? By this point in a chronicle that began, in January 1943, with a self-righteous demand for unconditional surrender, along with the decision to launch the Pointblank bombing campaign (albeit with Eaker's rejection of area bombing), followed by the commissioning of the Los Alamos enterprise, a set of questions presents itself.

Does the accumulating force of primal choices that lead to consequences that lead to new, graver choices result in consequences that, had they been foreseen at the start, might have forced a different decision to begin with? What was Franklin Roosevelt afraid of when he expressed his qualms about the huge new War Department headquarters, when the first plans were put before him? What, for that matter, did President Truman make of the nuclear "toboggan" onto which he was invited to leap, even after it was careening downhill? Did Roosevelt harbor some intuition about the metapersonal accumulation of power that comes when individual choices set events moving, when management of those events requires the expertise of teams, of staff, of service branches — ultimately of an impersonal bureaucracy that soon exists not for the sake of fulfilling the purposes of any individual decision maker, or of any single presidential administration, but for its own sake? Did Truman, who had reason to know better than anyone that his decision to bomb Hiroshima had been made even before he heard about it, draw conclusions about the turbines that had already been set spinning in the bowels of the Pentagon? And what was the effect on the future of decisions that had been made for shallow or mistaken reasons? The poet Rosanna Warren, quoting Max Beckmann, defines the human condition as a dragging along, "strapped to you, the corpse of all your errors."[21]

Norman Mailer stumbled onto a passing reflection on this mystery while he cavorted with the hippie exorcists. Drawing a line from Hiroshima to Vietnam, he wrote, in *The Armies of the Night*: "The history of the past was being exploded right into the present . . . Mailer was haunted by the nightmare that the evils of the present not only exploited the present, but consumed the past, and gave every promise of demolishing whole territories of the future."[22] The prankish impulse to invoke exorcism, in other words, was a serious attempt, despite itself, to deal with an outbreak to which only the word "evil" could apply — evil for which, as Mailer and the hippies showed quite clearly, we moderns have no satisfactory language. The demonstrators who remained at the Pentagon long after darkness fell that night, and after Mailer and other resisters had been carted off to jail, were reduced to a wistful nostalgia for something holy, softly singing the sweet refrain, though it was October, of "Silent Night."[23]

The bureaucracy created for the War Department and then the Defense Department would have characteristics peculiar to a system in which the supervisory class of political appointees — "ins and outs" — rotated every few years, as uniformed military functionaries came and went even more frequently, leaving as the relatively permanent order the professional bureaucrats of a civil service whose ideological and political commitments would remain hidden. Eventually, theorists attempting to understand what I am calling the metapersonal dynamics of the Pentagon would explore the "grooved thinking" of the bureaucracy itself, with ideology and organizational loyalties and history trumping the most acute present analysis. Theorists speak of the Pentagon's institutional culture, a part of which is the military culture, indicating that "culture," too, can be understood as having some kind of agency. Such impersonal forces, impossible to pin down or hold accountable, can have an overriding impact on the range of any one person's possible choices, or on the efficacy with which choices are made.

One classic study examined decision-making during the Cuban Missile Crisis, where distinctions could be drawn among the "rational actor," the "organizational process," and "bureaucratic politics."[24] This and other theoretical inquiries focused (whether academic studies invoke the language or not) on the mysterious relationship between the responsible, free agency of individuals and the malevolent impersonality of forces they cannot control.

The missile crisis is in fact not the best case study for this broad dynamic because it was an instance in which a single "rational actor," President Kennedy, was able to decisively overcome dangerous impulses rooted in organizational process (the Navy's way, for example, of enforcing a blockade) and bureaucratic politics (the Joint Chiefs and the civilian "Wise Men" in favor of invasion). But over the arc of events we are tracing in this book, defined by Henry Stimson as "an armaments race of a rather desperate character," rational actors, whether presidents, military leaders, or cabinet secretaries, are rarely capable of deflecting, much less controlling, the bureaucratic, procedural, political, and economic forces that do so much to shape policy. That was the point of Eisenhower's swan-song lament in 1961, but the pattern was well established by then. Not long after Stimson issued his warning in 1945, George Kennan, who had just ridden a wave of such factors to power — lending prestige to Stimson's nemesis, James Forrestal — leapt off the wave to warn of its undercurrents: "I am convinced," he wrote in his memoirs, "it is the shadows rather than the substance of things that move the hearts, and sway the deeds, of statesmen."[25]

There is nothing new in any of this — from Plato to Rousseau, thinkers have asserted the corrupting link between individual choice and social context — except for how the question of the length and chill of those shadows changed with the advent of the atomic bomb. Indeed, the introduction of nuclear weapons transformed military theory by accommodating a "structural dissonance"[26] in expressly nuclear planning that would once have been dismissed as illogical, even absurd. When that happened, the errors of the past took on a new kind of weight — atomic weight. In the nuclear age, the past would forever impinge on the present. "I am oppressed by an error of mind," Montaigne observed four hundred years ago. "I try to correct it, but I cannot root it out."[27]

But what happens when the "error of mind" is attached to the ultimate fuse? The ever-upward momentum of warhead accumulation, say, and the tendency to attribute to a nuclear-armed enemy the worst motivations are instances of what theorists call "path-driven" responses; decision-making is guided in large part by decisions made in the past. No decision adds more weight to action than the decision to use violence, especially in the new age. "Wars generate their own momentum and follow the law of unanticipated consequences," the chastened McNamara observed in his memoir. He could have been speaking for Roosevelt, Truman, and Eisenhower. Then he added with poignant understatement, "Vietnam proved no exception."[28]

Would the men (especially Forrestal) who disdained Stimson's warning about desperate days ahead have been quite so dismissive if they could have foreseen the eventual accumulation (when Forrestal's paranoia became policy), between the Soviet Union and the United States, of something approaching a hundred thousand nuclear warheads? When Eisenhower warned of the military-industrial complex, was he looking for language to describe a new, overpowering thing that had come into existence without his permission, that had taken on a life of its own, that drew energy from the narrow ambitions of parts of the bureaucracy, but that when taken together gathered a momentum that outran any one faction's purpose or intention? When Kennedy drew potent political advantage from warnings of a nonexistent missile gap, whatever he knew or did not know of its actuality, could he have imagined how his successors, remembering his political victory, would be haunted by the fear of being perceived as weak in relation to a Soviet Union that was, in fact, forever scrambling to keep up with American advances?

Momentous decisions had been made, and we have looked at them in succession, in 1943, 1945, 1949, 1952, 1957, 1961, 1962, 1963, and 1965. Had each of these discrete choices — concerning the use of bombs, the methods of their delivery, their megatonnage, always their legitimacy — combined in a chain of choice-and-consequence / new-choice-and-graver-consequence amount-ing to an unanticipated whole that transcended any one part or anyone's imagined expectation of what such a sum of parts could be? And what if that whole began to show itself as an action, no matter what its intention, capa-ble of moving in directions that no one would have wanted, an action that, once set in motion, cannot be stopped? What language to use for such a phe-nomenon?

On the eve of World War I, Henry James saw just such a thing under way, and he compared it with a current or "tide," in his word, carrying humanity like a leaf, like a twig, toward the "Niagara" of August 1914.[29] Earlier, we saw how, at the height of the Berlin crisis, Nikita Khrushchev, with an atheist's knack for the apt machine metaphor, reported the same feeling of being at the mercy of the metapersonal, perhaps the metahistorical, by warning that the "flywheel of war preparations have acquired such speed and momentum that even those who had set it revolving will be unable to stop it."[30]

John Kennedy, in that momentous American University address, de-nounced the "dangerous, defeatist belief . . . the conclusion that war is inevi-table — that mankind is doomed — that we are gripped by forces we cannot control." Kennedy, with Khrushchev, turned back the flywheel momentum of which his Soviet counterpart warned, and together they set a new direction for the Cold War with the Partial Test Ban Treaty.[31] During the Cuban Missile Crisis, as Graham Allison recounts it, Kennedy did discover himself as the "rational actor" who could move events, and that showed in the rest of his presidency. But this broad history, and the experience of the Kennedy admin-istration itself, as it was tragically transformed into the Johnson administra-tion, keeps the question of "forces that cannot be controlled" — of Kennan's "shadows" — at the center of any attempt to tell the story of the Building out of which unthinking hippies sought to drive the devil.

4. GREAT WHITE WHALE

In the seminary, in that same period, I had moved away from any childish no-tion of Satan as a personal being to be taken literally, as if humans were wit-nesses to, or victims of, a cosmic battle between otherworldly armies led by Lucifer and Saint Michael the archangel. In my religious education, literary notions had replaced pious ones, perhaps, but there was still the problem of human affairs being at the mercy — Ngo Dinh Diem's assassination leading to John F. Kennedy's, much as, later, Martin Luther King's murder would seem linked with Robert Kennedy's — of transcendent malevolence.

I had not yet heard the Pentagon compared, as I would years later, to Moby Dick, but the analogy would have been instructive in 1967. Wasn't the great Building "the ship of the soul" of America? Weren't those of us gathered there like the "many races, many peoples, many nations, under the Stars and Stripes"? D. H. Lawrence, in his *Studies in Classic American Literature*, describes us as "beaten with many stripes, seeing stars sometimes. And in a mad ship, under a mad captain, in a mad fanatic's hunt. For what? For Moby Dick, the great White Whale."[32] By 1967, Johnson was the mad captain, or perhaps McNamara was, but the whale was surely that Building, its unbounded energy, its pure ill will. Those in pursuit always ended up lashed to the monster's back. The point of the comparison, as those who made it hardly ever averred, was that the great white whale was Melville's figure of fundamental evil:

> The White Whale swam before him as the monomaniac incarnation of all those malicious agencies which some deep men feel eating in them, till they are left living on half a heart and half a lung. The intangible malignity which has been from the beginning: to whose dominion even the modern Christians ascribe one-half of the worlds; which the ancient Ophites of the east reverenced in their statue devil; — Ahab did not fall down and worship it like them; but deliriously transferring its idea to the abhorred white whale, he pitted himself, all mutilated, against it. All that most maddens and torments; all that stirs up the lees of things; all truth with malice in it; all that cracks the sinews and cakes the brain; all the subtle demonisms of life and thought; all evil, to crazy Ahab, were visibly personified, and made practically assailable in Moby Dick. He piled upon the whale's white hump the sum of all the general rage and hate felt by his whole race from Adam down; and then, as if his chest had been a mortar, he burst his hot heart's shell upon it.[33]

If Ahab went after Moby Dick with "a wild vindictiveness," so did the crowd massing on the Pentagon. But driving out demons was not as simple as a bunch of hippies thought. Whatever I made of Melville, I was learning my Scripture in the seminary, and I knew from Genesis, which is a meditation on the sources of evil in the world, that the beast in the Garden of Eden — not a whale but a serpent — was a bit player in the drama of creation until Adam and Eve took it seriously. Genesis implicates human choice as a source of evil, but the point is that the consequences of such choice far outweigh any imagined anticipation. The price of a bite of an apple, after all, was the loss of paradise, not just for the primal couple but for all their descendants. This "error of the mind," strapped like a corpse to the living body of the present, is called, in the Catholic tradition, "original sin," and its consequences, accumulating

over time — from Cain and Abel to the Tower of Babel — assume the metapersonal, metahistorical force of what is called evil. Momentum, Niagara,
flywheel, tide, shadows, the corpse of the past: "I try to correct it, but I cannot
root it out." Or, as Karl Marx put it, "The traditions of all dead generations
weigh like a nightmare on the minds of the living."[34]

One official who witnessed such a process up close in the early days of
the Vietnam War described the unfolding, within the "institutional culture,"
this way: "They begin by lying to Congress and the public, all for the best of
reasons; in this case the felt necessity of 'containing' communism in South
Vietnam. Next they lie to each other, concealing information and even private
opinions that might introduce a note of discordant doubt. And finally, they
lie to themselves — having become so profoundly, psychically committed to
the wisdom of their actions, having raised the stakes so high, that any admission of error would be a failure of unacceptable dimensions."[35]

The poet laureate of this phenomenon was Saint Paul, whose esoteric
language, had any of the hippies known of it, would have trumped their
chest-thumping, monosyllabic self-assertions. Paul knew that demons — "the
wiles of the devil," as he put it — were the least of it, which is why he gave far
more emphasis, in defining evil, to the encrusted forms that result from just
such progressions of ignorance, compromise, and deceit, small venalities that
grow into something huge. Paul's metaphors for this phenomenon are overwhelmingly institutional, not personal, and as such he pointed to exactly the
kind of problem Truman, Eisenhower, Kennedy, and McNamara both faced
and exacerbated. "For we are not contending against flesh and blood," Paul
wrote in his Letter to the Ephesians (6:10–12), "but against the principalities,
against the powers, against the world rulers of this present darkness." These
are not fallen angels, and they are not individual villains. They are "sovereignties," in his word, and the thing to understand about them is that they are
constitutionally hostile to human beings. Paul is here using the language of
politics and of human organization. Scholars tell us he is surely thinking of
the Roman tyrants and the crushing force of an uncaring imperial bureaucracy, but he is pointing to something about the human condition.

"Totalitarianism" is a contemporary word that carries some of the grave
implications of the archaic-sounding "principality," and Americans would
have no trouble, along with the philosopher Hannah Arendt or the early
George Kennan or, for that matter, the Reagan-era diplomat Jeanne Kirkpatrick, in recognizing totalitarianism as a source of "present darkness." But
can we imagine that what we constructed to oppose it involved us in the same
dark mystery? They did not know it, but that was the question the hippies
and Norman Mailer had come to the Pentagon to ask. Human organization
itself, the "grooved thinking" through which the past institutionalizes itself in

TOP: Under construction, 1942. Ground was broken for the Pentagon on September 11, 1941.

LEFT: Sixty years later, almost to the minute, American Airlines flight 77 hit the Building, killing 125 people inside as well as the plane's passengers and crew.

The site chosen for the Pentagon, once a swamp, was originally known as Hell's Bottom. It was the largest office building in the world until the early 1970s, when the World Trade Center surpassed it. On 9/11, the Pentagon resumed its place as the biggest office building.

After the 9/11 attacks, the repair of the Pentagon was completed in exactly one year. The original construction took only eighteen months from start to finish.

TOP: The week the Pentagon formally opened, in January 1943, Operation Pointblank was launched, sending B-17s against German cities for the first time. At the start of the war, President Roosevelt had opposed the bombing of cities.

LEFT: The lead pilot of the first B-17 raid into Germany was Colonel Curtis LeMay, who went on to command the bombing of Tokyo, the dropping of atomic bombs on Japan, the Berlin airlift, and the Strategic Air Command. In the early 1960s, he lived next door to the Carroll family.

TOP: On March 10, 1945, American B-29s firebombed Tokyo, killing between 80,000 and 100,000 people. LeMay called it "the most devastating raid in the history of aerial warfare."

LEFT: J. Robert Oppenheimer and General Leslie Groves examine the results of the first A-bomb test, in July 1945. Before heading up the Manhattan Project, Groves had supervised the construction of the Pentagon.

BELOW: Hiroshima, 1945. President Truman defined Hiroshima as "an important military base." American bombing of Japanese cities in the last six months of the war killed more than 900,000 civilians.

TED POLUMBAUM/THE NEWSEUM

At left, General George Patton; at right, Secretary of War Henry Stimson; Harvey Bundy, Stimson's aide, is in the center. Stimson was in charge of the War Department throughout World War II, overseeing the building of the Pentagon and the creation of the atomic bomb.

On September 11, 1945, Stimson (left) proposed to "share" the atomic bomb with Moscow to head off a "desperate armaments race." He was opposed by Secretary of the Navy James Forrestal (right), who carried the argument, setting off that arms race. In 1947, Truman appointed Forrestal as the first secretary of defense.

Forrestal (right) was unable to tame the Pentagon's interservice rivalry, and in 1949 Truman forced him out. Forrestal later had a psychological breakdown, and he committed suicide while undergoing treatment. His personal paranoia shaped America's Cold War paranoia.

Forrestal's nemesis was Secretary of the Air Force Stuart Symington (second from left). Here, in the company of J. Edgar Hoover and Air Force Chief of Staff Hoyt Vandenberg, Symington awards a medal to General Carroll.

LEFT: In 1947, my father, Joseph Carroll, went from the FBI to the newly created Air Force as founder of the Office of Special Investigations. He entered the service as a general officer, to the chagrin of the Pentagon brass.

BELOW: The two-star general, 1950. After serving as founding director of the Air Force's OSI for a decade, Carroll spent most of another decade as founding director of the Defense Intelligence Agency. The DIA's mandate was to rein in intelligence abuses by individual services and to act as a check on the CIA. This put Carroll in conflict with his own Air Force, which had sounded alarms about a "missile gap." There was indeed a missile gap — hugely in America's favor.

The B-52 was at the heart of the Strategic Air Command, which flourished under Curtis LeMay. In 1950, there were about 200 atomic bombs in the U.S. arsenal. By 1960, that figure had grown to nearly 20,000, most of them hydrogen bombs. The B-52 is still flying.

Herman Kahn was a leading "nuclear Jesuit," one of the new breed of defense intellectuals who made "thinking the unthinkable" into a science. Their calculations served to justify the steady growth of the nuclear arsenal.

MRBM FIELD LAUNCH SITE
Sagua la Grande No. 2
17 OCTOBER 1962

MOTOR POOL

TENT AREA

MOTOR POOL

ERECTORS

LAUNCH PADS

3 MISSILE READY BLDGS AND
MISSILE CONTAINER 63 LONG

LAUNCH PADS
WITH ERECTORS

The world came closest to nuclear disaster during the Cuban Missile Crisis in 1962. This intelligence photo shows the deployment of Soviet missiles in Cuba. A photo like it led General Carroll's DIA to discover the presence of the missiles. Around the same time, my father revealed to me his fear of a nuclear holocaust, which changed my life.

In June 1963, President Kennedy gave the commencement address at American University. It was a plea for peace unlike any other given by an American president before or since. Khrushchev allowed it to be broadcast in the Soviet Union—a first. Shortly after the speech, the two nations agreed to the Partial Test Ban Treaty, the beginning of arms control.

TOP: General Carroll reviews troops of the Army of the Republic of Vietnam, South Vietnam, 1962. The war in Vietnam killed millions of Vietnamese and more than fifty thousand Americans.

MIDDLE: In 1967, Secretary of Defense Robert McNamara (at left, with Secretary of State Dean Rusk) turned against the war he had begun, in part because DIA analysis showed that the U.S. air war was not working.

BOTTOM: Left to right: General Carroll, CIA Director Richard Helms, General Marshall Carter, head of the National Security Agency, and General John Davis of the Army dedicate a new NSA building in 1966. The DIA and the CIA were rivals, but in the debate over antiballistic missiles in the late 1960s, Helms and Carroll were in agreement, which put them both in conflict with the secretary of defense.

LEFT: Vietnam protesters rally behind the flag, and John Kerry, a veteran, speaks out against the war.

BELOW: In 1967, Philip Berrigan developed a new kind of anti-war protest: acts of civil disobedience intended to symbolize resistance and impede warmaking. With his brother, Daniel, and other Catholics he began with raids on draft boards, and over the next thirty years conducted Plowshares actions against military bases and weapons manufacturers. By the time of his death in 2002, Philip had spent eleven years in prison for acts of conscience.

Miners in Chile rally to support their president, Salvador Allende, who was killed in a U.S.-sponsored coup on September 11, 1973. Throughout the twentieth century, ordinary people found ways to resist the oppressive power and violence of the state. Ultimately their actions, to the surprise of "realists," changed the course of the Cold War.

President Gerald Ford's chief of staff was Donald Rumsfeld (left), and Richard Cheney (right) was his deputy. Rumsfeld would become secretary of defense under Ford, and Cheney would fill the post under George H. W. Bush. Together, Rumsfeld and Cheney would prepare the Pentagon to weather its greatest challenge: the end of the Cold War.

Ronald Reagan and Pope John Paul II shared an opposition to Communism, and both survived assassination attempts. And while Reagan obsessed about imagined Soviet aggression in Central America, the pope supported nonviolent democratic movements behind the Iron Curtain, especially in his native Poland.

In 1980, Randall Forsberg, an MIT graduate student, issued "A Call to Halt the Nuclear Arms Race," sparking the Freeze campaign. A million supporters gathered in Central Park in 1982, American Catholic bishops backed the Freeze, and eventually so did Congress. Reagan resisted the idea at first, but he would come to heed it too. Forsberg's Freeze decisively altered America's Cold War climate.

LEFT: Red Square, 1988. When Reagan was asked about his labeling of the Soviet Union as an "evil empire," he pointed at Gorbachev and replied that it was evil until this good man came along "and made all the difference." Reagan responded positively to Gorbachev's initiatives for ending the arms race and the Cold War.

BELOW: President George H. W. Bush and Solidarity leader Lech Walesa of Poland. The American government missed the significance of the nonviolent Solidarity movement, which the realists in Washington dismissed as irresponsible idealism.

The Pentagon's "apostolic succession" was embodied in Paul Nitze (right), seen here with Secretary of Defense William Cohen during the Clinton administration. Nitze began as a young aide to James Forrestal in 1940 and went on to serve in eight administrations. He did more than any other figure to justify the ever-growing nuclear arsenal, but he ended, in 1999, by advocating unilateral nuclear disarmament.

After the end of the Cold War, Bill Clinton had the chance to transform the Pentagon. But the military men did not respect him, and they thwarted him. Hawks dominated foreign policy, and Cold War spending was maintained. Yet despite its status as the lone superpower, America proved impotent in the face of genocides abroad.

In 2001, Donald Rumsfeld became secretary of defense for the second time, chosen on President George W. Bush's behalf by another former secretary of defense, Richard Cheney. U.S. military spending soon surpassed that of all other nations combined; a new generation of nuclear weapons was ordered; a doctrine of preventive war was embraced; and a war was launched against Iraq.

Only reluctantly had President Roosevelt approved the Pentagon's construction on the far side of the Potomac; he did not want the military establishment isolated from the seat of government. Across more than sixty years, the Pentagon's isolation became dominance, as the executive and legislative branches submitted to the pressures of the Department of Defense.

the present, transcending the intention of any one organizer, can be the carrier of evil.

This understanding shifts attention, if only momentarily, away from the moral agency of a single person, including LeMay, to something larger. LeMay, too, was at the mercy of an "error of the mind," multiplied over time, that preceded him. We use the word "evil" to get at this "something larger," if only to indicate the almost irresistible magnitude of what we poor banished children of Eve are up against. This is a far more dangerous reality than anything the half-stoned flower children imagined on that October day, not least because it implicated them as much as the stoic GIs whom they taunted with the suggestive writhings of their musk-scented bodies.

Yet far from excusing individuals or downplaying the moral significance of any one person's choices, this understanding emphasizes the ultimate consequences of every human choice, even banal ones. If John Kennedy rides to the White House warning of a nonexistent missile gap (depending on skewed Air Force intelligence fed to him by Stuart Symington), how does that weigh on Lyndon Johnson's fear of being charged with an "ABM gap" eight years later, or Jimmy Carter's of being charged with softness twenty years later? Equally, the idea of "sovereignties" coming into being through an accumulation of missteps and errors over time assumes the moral complexity of every choice, too, showing how apparently justified choices — the decision, say, to bomb a factory that is surrounded by workers' houses — can bleed into obviously problematic choices, like the decision to bomb those houses. The point is that human choices set in motion forces that, driven ever more dynamically along a chain of consequences, can be overpowering — "forces we cannot control," in Kennedy's phrase. But even the one liable to be overpowered, whether by principalities, institutional culture, the military-industrial complex, the bureaucracy, the Building, or merely by the toboggan's momentum, remains responsible. That Kennedy insisted on that near the end, teaching us that choices for good set their consequences moving, too, is why we love him.[36]

5. McNamara's Endgame

"Out demons! Out!" The Pentagon may not have been possessed in the autumn of 1967, but it was surely haunted. On the wall opposite Robert McNamara's desk — General Pershing's desk — was a portrait of the first secretary of defense, James Forrestal. In McNamara's time, implications of Forrestal's fate had begun to hang in the air of that office, like motes of poisonous dust, in the middle distance of Forrestal's two dead eyes. At least once, McNamara stopped in the midst of computations of ammunition requirements for Vietnam, stared into his predecessor's painted eyes, and burst into tears, shocking a subordinate.[37] In early 1965, around the same time that McNamara had found a reason not to attend LeMay's retirement ceremony, his most urgent purpose, according to a close aide, was to convince Lyndon Johnson to launch the bombing campaign against Vietnam.[38]

McNamara liked to describe himself as a businessman who, upon being appointed as defense secretary, had had to bring himself up to speed on military matters, but his faith in the efficacy of strategic bombing harks back to his formative experience as LeMay's stat control officer during the firebombing of Tokyo. Hadn't the Air Force brought the Japanese to heel? If nuclear terror — the SIOP and J-SCAP procedures — had become a point of contention between LeMay and McNamara, and if the former believed that the goal of bombing was destruction, while the latter believed in "compellence," still, in 1965 they shared an absolute faith in bombing. LeMay, stuck in the mode of massive retaliation, had come to strike many as insane, but McNamara, having invented the concept of flexible response, was bombing's intellectual apostle. He had devoted himself to finding an alternative to Armageddon, a way for America to exercise its military power rationally, and Operation Rolling Thunder would be it — a coercive war conducted from the air, aiming, just as Operation Pointblank had, to break the enemy's morale.

McNamara's fervent faith in this kind of bombing was infectious, and his first convert was the untested president. But then, even before the great October 1967 demonstration, that faith had turned to ashes in McNamara's mouth, while Johnson remained a true believer. It would be the stalwart president who, when he mistook the secretary's moral collapse for a merely emotional one, feared he had another Forrestal on his hands.

"Everything he believed in was being knocked on its ass in Vietnam," a White House aide said of McNamara. This witness saw the secretary regularly in the spring and summer of 1967, as he came to and went from meetings with the president. "Here was a guy who really believed that the truth is what you get out of the machine when you ask for it. You know, what will we do about x? and here comes the answer, the organizational truth. It just wasn't working. The heat was terrific. He was, I think, a very disturbed guy, and I think the president was aware of this also."[39]

Sizing up his tormented secretary of defense, Johnson said at one point, "We just can't afford to have another Forrestal."[40] But in truth, by the fall of 1967, regarding emotional stability, the president had one. That was so even if its manifestation, a disillusionment with violence, was opposite what the ever-bellicose Forrestal's had been.

McNamara watched the October demonstration from an ad hoc command post on the roof of the Pentagon. What he saw disgusted him, but it frightened him, too. He admitted to being afraid that the demonstrators would breach the line of young soldiers whose rifles, by his order, were not loaded.[41] He was afraid someone would get hurt. McNamara had been known to visibly tremble, but the fear that most held him in its grip was hidden. McNamara by then was already lashed to the back of a monster whom no one had done more to set thrashing than he. The previous May, in "an act of abundant moral courage,"[42] he had written a secret memo to President Johnson warning him that the war in Vietnam was unwinnable and that the best course was to pursue "minimum objectives," a negotiated settlement, not victory, although that would inevitably imply defeat. "All want the war ended," he wrote, "and expect their president to end it."[43] That memo, drafted with his closest aide, John McNaughton, represents McNamara's attempt to halt the insane momentum he had himself set going. Johnson ignored the memo.

A few weeks later — cursed indeed — McNaughton was killed in a civilian plane crash in North Carolina. A few weeks after that, on August 25, 1967, McNamara went public with his true feelings about the war, feelings that were convoluted, confused, overwhelmingly despairing. He did this before the Preparedness Investigating Subcommittee of the Senate Armed Services Committee, chaired by Senator John Stennis. The subject of the hearing was the air war, which McNamara no longer believed in. Eight hawkish senators sat on the subcommittee, but by far the dominant figure, McNamara's antagonist, cycling us back to the first circle of Hell's Bottom, was W. Stuart Symington, who, on that mysterious automobile ride from Capitol Hill to the Pentagon, had administered some kind of coup de grâce to Forrestal.

Before McNamara testified, a parade of generals and admirals had laid out the case for an expanded air war, with detailed lists of targets that, until then, had been off-limits. They wanted, as the now retired Curtis LeMay had put it, to "stop swatting flies, and go after the manure pile." Enough of the RAND-inspired bullshit about morale bombing and compellence. It was time to take the gloves off, time to bring the other fist out from behind the back, time to destroy the enemy pure and simple. The subcommittee hearings had built up tremendous public pressure, to which Lyndon Johnson had been yielding, approving more and more targets. Finally the senators called the secretary of defense. "We intended all along to have you," Stennis told him as he was sworn in.

Then McNamara opened fire with a withering eight-page statement. "McNamara Doubts Bombing in North Can End the War," the next day's *New York Times* trumpeted.[44] He firmly repudiated the Joint Chiefs' proposed new target list and ridiculed the idea that more bombs dropped from airplanes would do any more to undercut the fighting spirit of the Communists than eighteen months of savage assaults had already done. Citing intelligence analysis from the Defense Intelligence Agency — briefings from my father that amounted to betrayals of his blue uniform, which LeMay would have hated my father for — McNamara insisted that the bombing campaign was not moving the enemy closer to negotiations, much less to yielding. There was little reason to believe the bombing was seriously inhibiting the enemy's capacity to wage war.[45] "I submit to you, I am secretary of defense and I am responsible for lives and I am not about to recommend the loss of American lives in relation to those targets . . . The destruction of all of them would not make any material difference in the war, and that is my only point."[46]

It was Symington who cut to the quick of McNamara's testimony. During the lunch break of the hearing, the senator went right to the reporters in the corridor. He said that if the secretary of defense was right in contradicting the Joint Chiefs, then the war was lost, and the United States should get out of Vietnam "at the earliest possible time."[47] This meant defeat and disgrace. In fact, it was a fair characterization of McNamara's true position, but it was not one to which the secretary was remotely ready to admit. Symington was simply throwing the gauntlet down, knowing that no matter how McNamara responded, he was done for.

When reporters confronted McNamara with what the senator had said, he responded with stammers: "Symington . . . is completely wrong. My policies don't differ with those of the Joint Chiefs, and I think they would be the first to say it." McNamara, when challenged, lied. He renounced the very positions he had, with such fierce energy, just taken in the hearing room. He added, pathetically, "I think there is some misunderstanding as to the basis of the argument over the bombing campaign in the North." But that was false. There was no misunderstanding. McNamara was opposed, period. Even if he could not say so with consistency. When the Chiefs heard of McNamara's weasling — denouncing the bombing, then affirming it — they almost resigned en masse to protest his bad faith.[48]

At that hearing, McNamara had finished himself with the president. By the October demonstration, six weeks later, the hatred with which the protesters denounced him outside the Pentagon was matched by the contempt with which he was regarded inside. Two weeks after that, Johnson announced McNamara's appointment to the World Bank. At his last meeting with fellow cabinet members and other of the president's senior advisers, held at the State Department in Foggy Bottom, the building that Roosevelt had intended as the War Department headquarters, McNamara fell apart. Johnson's close adviser Harry McPherson was there, and he described how McNamara got up "and with such fury and passion and tears he's lashing out at the whole war, his voice rising and cracking and the room swelling with all of it; 'the goddamned bombing campaign, it's been worth nothing, it's done nothing, they've dropped more bombs than in all of Europe in all of World War Two, and it hasn't done a fucking thing!'"[49]

There it was, McNamara's endgame, but not the war's. What is evil if not the tide that runs on even after humans have named it and turned against it? Forrestal had set something moving, and McNamara, in his time, saw how dangerous it was. Trying to turn the Pentagon away from its worship of massive retaliation, he led the way into a limited war, which seemed at first a humane alternative. Faced with the prospect of a world insanely destroyed by unchecked strategic bombing, in other words, he found a rational way to apply the force of bombing. He invented a new role for the B-52. He set a generation of bomber pilots loose. All done with the best of intentions. All disastrously misconceived. What is evil but the inability to stop the evil thing one has begun, even after recognizing it as such? Principalities and powers indeed. McNamara, as he fell mute in the face of what he'd beheld, making no further attempt to stop it, considered himself the first to see these awful truths. But he was wrong.

6. FROM DISARMAMENT TO ARMS CONTROL

The unruly mob below his window, whom McNamara (and I) held in such contempt, saw through the cloud of illusions long before he did. Realists take for granted the foolishness of the idealists who want another way than war, yet that movement is part of the Pentagon's story, too. By the fall of 1967, the struggle inside the Building — embodied in the conflict between McNamara, who opposed further escalations in Vietnam, and the Joint Chiefs of Staff, who strongly advocated escalations — had reached a stalemate. Equally, the struggle in Vietnam itself had reached a stalemate, with the United States winning militarily and the Communists winning politically. Against the expectations of every military theorist, both forms of impasse were broken by "the change of heart [of] yet another player in the game . . ." Neither the geniuses at RAND, who were still churning out their strategies of coercive force, nor the uniformed functionaries who were toting up computerized comparisons of enemy battle orders and body counts, nor the brass hats, nor the despairing secretary of defense himself, none of them knew that the game had another player. Yet one day in October, changing every calculation, there we were, taking over the field: ". . . the American public."[50]

When I think back on my own ambivalent participation in that massive demonstration, which would be followed within months by McNamara's resignation, the Tet Offensive, Lyndon Johnson's decision against bombing, his renunciation of the goal of victory, and his decision not to run for reelection, I wish I had buried something of value in the ground on which we protesters trod. I would return there now, dig the thing up, and use it as an object of meditation. How little we knew; how little we know now. The greatest military force in history was turned from its self-destructive course — its potentially world-destructive course — by a scraggly bunch of nobodies who, in the American system, could not be ignored in gathering to confront the Building. It is true that the Vietnam War, continued by Richard Nixon and Henry Kissinger and their vain quest for "peace with honor," would continue for another seven years, but its open-ended escalation was stopped cold in that autumn of 1967, and the perception of the war as a terrible mistake began to be openly acknowledged by and before the public at large. The story of America's overpowering post–World War II martial impulse, enshrined in the Pentagon, cannot be told, that is, without a respectful nod to what opposed it from the start.

In the beginning, as we saw, there was Stimson, warning of "an armaments race of a rather desperate character." If that warning was ignored by James Forrestal and his successors, it was being sounded by the mob that gathered under McNamara's window in 1967. Most observers missed the obvious significance of the fact that the demonstrators were overwhelmingly young, having come to the Pentagon to protest not only against Vietnam but against the horror they had been made to contemplate since crouching under their desks in second grade. "Not only is ours the first generation to live with the possibility of world-wide cataclysm," declared the Port Huron Statement, composed by the Students for a Democratic Society in 1962 and widely circulated on campuses throughout the 1960s, "it is the first to experience the actual social preparation for cataclysm, the general militarization of American society." The statement used the atomic bomb as a kind of centerpiece. In the students' consciousness, in the words of one historian, the bomb "reigned supreme."[51] They were sick of watching as "the world tumbles toward the final war."

The student movement was much maligned, and had taken tumbles of its own toward anarchic mischief-making, but student criticism of "military-industrial politics" could also be surprisingly shrewd — young radicals talking back to the geniuses of RAND. The Port Huron Statement includes sophisticated analysis of the "permanent war economy," a dissection of the way interservice rivalry was driving the arms race, a clear statement of the moral absurdity of deterrence theory ("Unless we . . . can convince Russia that we are willing to commit the most heinous action in history, we will be forced to commit it"), a naming of "paranoia" as the factor behind American attitudes toward the Soviet Union, and a rebuttal of McNamara's counterforce strategy on precisely the grounds that were soon to lead McNamara himself to abandon it. Although the great majority of American students kept their distance from the confrontational tactics of the Students for a Democratic Society, the original SDS declaration continued to speak for the generation because it captured the spirit of desperate longing for another way. "If we appear to seek the unattainable," it concluded, "then let it be known that we do so to avoid the unimaginable."[52]

Tom Hayden, main author of the Port Huron Statement, was in the crowd outside the Pentagon, and so were Dave Dellinger, Abbie Hoffman, and others already made famous by antics of the antiwar movement. But I think of Daniel Berrigan, the dignified Jesuit priest whose presence at the demonstration that day sanctioned mine. A man of high reputation, an award-winning poet, the author of books I carried with me to chapel for morning meditation, Berrigan was a role model to me. Training to be a priest, I was already presuming to think of myself as a poet. Like him, I would eschew the Roman collar in favor of black turtleneck sweaters, clerical suits in favor of black chinos. That Berrigan was an intimate of the Kennedys also endeared him to me. At the Kennedy compound in Hyannis Port, he had confronted McNamara over the war in 1966.[53] Still, he was no radical, and my identification with him, as his opposition to the government intensified, would be the key to a door opening into a whole new identity.

Berrigan was arrested that day at the Pentagon, his first act of civil disobedience. "I had no intention of getting arrested," he told me years later, "but I saw the brutality with which the protesters were rounded up."[54] Berrigan was in jail for a week. Upon his release, he called his mother, who said to him, "You're out of jail, but Phil is in."[55] Unknown to Daniel, on October 27 his brother Philip, also a Catholic priest, had led a group into the Selective Service offices at the Custom House in Baltimore, where they poured blood on draft files — a first act of Catholic antiwar civil disobedience. There would be dozens more.[56]

Just as McNamara's decisions were made along a chain of choice-and-consequence going back years, so were the Berrigans'. Daniel was a protégé of the Catholic activist Dorothy Day, the founder of the Catholic Worker movement. She had drawn notice for a series of arrests, beginning in the mid-1950s, for "noncompliance" with laws requiring citizens to participate in civil defense drills for nuclear attack.[57] Through the fifties, Day's *Catholic Worker* newspaper was an American proponent of the worldwide Ban the Bomb movement. After World War II, the disarmament movement, discredited by the "realism" of a Cold War consensus, was nevertheless continued by international pacifist organizations like War Resisters' International and the Fellowship of Reconciliation. After Korea and the advent of the hydrogen bomb, it was widely recognized that history had become, in H. G. Wells's phrase, "a race between education and catastrophe."[58] But the disarmament proposals that followed World War II, including David Lilienthal's and Bernard Baruch's, had come to naught. The United Nations, like the League of Nations before it, had been intended at its birth as an alternative to war, but that dream was quickly dispelled in the chill of the Cold War. While world leaders gave lip service to the idea of eliminating nuclear weapons, the United States and the Soviet Union were hell-bent on stockpiling them — our subject up to now.

Yet resignation in the face of that dark impulse was not universal. In the late forties and early fifties, Communists in Europe openly sponsored various peace conferences and organizations, obviously concerned that the United States would use the bomb against the Soviet Union. But soon calls for disarmament came from religious and scientific groups, as well as nonaligned nations. In 1953, the *Bulletin of the Atomic Scientists*'s Doomsday Clock showed the time as two minutes before midnight. Indeed, scientists would be in the forefront of the movement to oppose the normalization of nuclear weapons. In 1955, Bertrand Russell and Albert Einstein issued a manifesto alerting the world to the danger of thermonuclear weapons and called on scientists in particular to raise their voices. In 1957 the Pugwash Conferences on Science and World Affairs was founded by scientists opposed to nuclear weapons,[59] and in the same year a group of middle-class American professionals established the National Committee for a Sane Nuclear Policy (SANE).[60] In many countries, ordinary citizens took to the streets to protest the legitimization of the bomb, although in the United States, a nation traumatized by the McCarthy-driven Red Scare, the disarmament movement continued to be associated by many with Communism, a Soviet plot to defang the West from within. Even Dr. Benjamin Spock, once he became associated with SANE, would be regarded with suspicion by many who had depended on his child-rearing advice.

In the Pentagon, the repudiation of any ideal of disarmament was a triumph of the realists, a replay of the old contest between Stimson and Forrestal. Those who expressed concern about the "desperate" accumulation of nuclear arms were regarded as naïve. After the USSR acquired an atomic bomb in 1949, a hardnosed Washington forgot that its wisest and most powerful figures had once taken disarmament as a policy goal for granted.[61] President Eisenhower's attitude toward the enterprise may be indicated by the fact that he appointed as his "special assistant for disarmament" the buffoonish perennial presidential candidate Harold Stassen, and that he allowed Stassen to be controlled by John Foster Dulles, who had no interest in disarmament. In 1955, Stassen proposed that the word "disarmament" be dropped in favor of the far different "arms control," a move that those who still hoped to eliminate nuclear weapons derided. The Swedish diplomat Alva Myrdal, for example, proposed "a boycott against the use of 'arms control' as an overall term. It is nothing but a euphemism, serving regrettably to lead thinking and action towards the acceptance as 'arms control measures' of compromises with scant or nil effect."[62]

Myrdal took an active part in the worldwide demand for another way, work for which she would win the Nobel Peace Prize in 1982. What she saw in the 1950s was that "control" of nuclear weapons meant acceptance. That alone explains why the military enthusiastically embraced arms control; why such prophets of the atomic era as Herman Kahn and Edward Teller comfortably participated in the arms control conversation;[63] and why that most military-minded civilian Paul Nitze would become, first under Richard Nixon and then under Ronald Reagan, a leading arms control negotiator.

While the agenda for arms control was mostly determined by strategic interest, it is important to acknowledge that some regulation of nuclear growth was better than none. Although legitimizing nuclear arsenals, arms control did become the basis of a negotiations regime that, while checking weapons growth in a few instances, also bought time for the U.S.-Soviet stalemate to end without calamitous war. Still, the arms control agenda was largely turned to the interest of the nuclear priesthood. The course of the arms race showed how Alva Myrdal's warning was to the point. Arms control was indeed a betrayal of disarmament.[64] As the growth that occurred after this shift in terminology demonstrates (from a few hundred weapons to tens of thousands), the control of one source of nuclear escalation inevitably translated into the uncontrolled escalation of other sources.

We have taken note of the effect on John F. Kennedy of the traumatic war threat of the summer of 1961, which eventually led to his plea for peace at the American University commencement in 1963. But a more immediate signal of his having measured the nuclear abyss is a speech he gave at the United Nations on September 25, 1961, as the shaken Soviet Union and United States were resuming the mad practice of nuclear testing.[65] In the midst of the tension, the much-admired U.N. secretary-general, Dag Hammarskjöld, on a peace mission to the Congo, was killed in a plane crash, which prompted Kennedy's decision to strike a tone before the General Assembly, and the world, that was radically different from both his war alarm speech of July 25 and the blustery exchanges between the two superpowers in the weeks since.

"We meet in an hour of grief," Kennedy began, and as it would be later, human mortality was his bracing context. Then he put forward the first comprehensive plan for complete nuclear disarmament since the Baruch Plan had called for international control of atomic energy in 1946. In doing this, Kennedy rejected the advice of those who regarded even a rhetorical commitment to the ideal of disarmament as irresponsibly utopian. Against the realists, who were inclined to settle for the incremental and the achievable, Kennedy proposed, "for the first time," a full American repudiation of nuclear arms development.

It was as if he already understood that control of this demonic momentum would prove to be the ultimate illusion. "Men no longer debate whether armaments are a symptom or a cause of tension. The mere existence of modern weapons — ten million times more powerful than any that the world has ever seen, and only minutes away from any target on earth — is a source of horror, and discord, and distrust. Men no longer maintain that disarmament must await the settlement of all disputes, for disarmament must be a part of any permanent settlement. And men no longer pretend that the quest for disarmament is a sign of weakness — for in a spiraling arms race, a nation's security may well be shrinking even as its arms increase."

Kennedy proposed an end to the production of nuclear weapons; the prevention of their transfer to nonnuclear powers; the outlawing of nuclear weapons in outer space; the gradual destruction of all existing nuclear weapons; the immediate end to construction of strategic bombers and missiles and the destruction of existing ones; and the establishment of a permanent U.N. peacekeeping force. He also suggested new approaches to international control of armaments and called for an immediate agreement to end nuclear testing, independent of all other arms negotiations. "The risks inherent in disarmament pale in comparison to the risks in an unlimited arms race." As if he could see ahead to the terrible escalation over Cuba, Kennedy said, in conclusion, "The events and decisions of the next ten months may well decide the fate of man for the next ten thousand years . . . Ladies and Gentlemen of this Assembly, the decision is ours. Never have the nations of the world had so much to lose, or so much to gain. Together we shall save our planet, or together we shall perish in its flames."[66]

In those same weeks of 1961, to make real his stated wish for negotiations, Kennedy created a new government agency whose responsibility would be to push this agenda. The bureaucracy wanted it to be called the Arms Control Agency, but, as if Kennedy had taken Alva Myrdal's point literally, he insisted on the political and rhetorical rescue of the crucial word "disarmament." He ordered it inserted in the name: the Arms Control and Disarmament Agency.[67] Although the House of Representatives deleted the despised word from the establishing legislation, Kennedy had it restored.[68] One congressional opponent said, after the law's enactment, that maybe the new agency wasn't such a bad idea, since "all the nuts could be kept in one place where we can keep an eye on them."[69] The head of the ACDA would have his office at the State Department in Foggy Bottom, in the very room that Henry Stimson had used before moving to the Pentagon,[70] but the ACDA director would, unlike Stassen, report directly to the president.

Kennedy, with his desperate rhetoric and his executive action, was already — before Cuba — looking for an alternative to the course he himself had helped set going. In the short term, his efforts would seem to come to nothing, as the Soviet Union and the United States continued, over the next full year, to march to the edge of the abyss. "Such was the implacable surge, the remorseless trend of events," one historian said of that metahistorical tide of which we have taken note. "Man was being steadily driven along the path that could lead only to his own destruction, and where all conscience and all common sense bade him halt, he plodded steadily and fatalistically forward."[71] But Kennedy had flagged the problem: the prospect of the "planet a flaming funeral pyre."[72] In the vision he articulated and sought to institutionalize — against the tide — the president laid out an agenda that would define the antinuclear peace movement for a generation. This purpose would be central to no one more than Daniel and Philip Berrigan.

7. THE BERRIGAN BROTHERS

Three months after the demonstration at the Pentagon, American peace movement leaders accepted an invitation from the Communist government of North Vietnam to send "responsible representatives" to Hanoi for the purpose of receiving three freed U.S. prisoners of war. POWs in the North were almost all downed Air Force and Navy flyers. (Lieutenant — later Senator — John McCain, USN, had been shot down and captured in October, on the same day that Philip Berrigan poured blood on draft files in Baltimore.) This would be the first release of captured pilots, a symbolic gesture of goodwill (with an obvious propaganda aspect) in observance of Tet, the New Year holiday. Daniel Berrigan was asked if he would go, and he agreed. He left so hastily that he forgot the small New Testament that he carried with him everywhere. His companion on this mission was Howard Zinn, whom we saw earlier as a B-17 bombardier dropping bombs on civilians in France in 1945, and who was by now a history professor at Boston University and a leading critic of the Vietnam War.[73]

Priest and former bombardier left for Hanoi on January 31, 1968, but just then the Communists launched massive attacks, the Tet Offensive, in which eighty thousand North Vietnamese soldiers poured out of the jungle, assaulting cities throughout South Vietnam.[74] Civil air traffic in the entire region was paralyzed, and the two Americans were delayed in Vientiane, Laos. They arrived in Hanoi a week late and spent their first night in an underground shelter as U.S. bombs fell on the city — "under the rain of fire," in Berrigan's words.[75] "It was a new experience for me," Zinn wrote later, "a bombardier on the receiving end of bombs from the air force I had been a part of. I had that taut feeling in my belly that I remembered from my World War Two missions — fear. I thought, I guess I deserve this."[76] Berrigan, for his part, experienced that and subsequent nights of bombing as an initiation. Night after night, he huddled with children, who remained with him as the main image of the war's real sufferers. He wrote a poem about them, "Children in the Shelter":

> Imagine; three of them.
>
> As though survival
> were a rat's word,
> and a rat's death
> waited there at the end
>
> and I must have
> in the century's boneyard
> heft of flesh and bone in my arms
>
> I picked up the littlest
> a boy, his face
> breaded with rice (his sister calmly feeding him
> as we climbed down)
>
> In my arms fathered
> in a moment's grace, the messiah
> of all my tears. I bore, reborn
>
> a Hiroshima child from hell.[77]

Five days later, Berrigan and Zinn were taken to a prison, where three American flyers were handed over to them. *What's your hometown? How are you fellows doing?* The five made an awkward group. They were put on a plane to Vientiane, where American officials were waiting. The officials brushed the two peace movement escorts aside and took charge of the pilots. Zinn and Berrigan never saw them again.[78] Both returned to the United States more committed to the antiwar movement than ever. Of Berrigan, his biographers write, "By the time he returned home, he was a changed man, angrier, less forgiving."[79]

Those were days — the U.S. military "victory" at Tet announcing the Pentagon's political defeat — that changed America. The news that Lyndon Johnson was rejecting escalation, curtailing the bombing, and renouncing his own political ambition appeared in the newspapers on the morning of April 1, April Fools' Day. When Americans realized it was no joke, many felt exhilarated, but that hopefulness was short-lived. Three days later, Martin Luther King, Jr., was murdered. Within weeks, chaos reigned in the streets of Prague and Paris, and students took over buildings at Columbia University in New York. In the Soviet Union, Andrei Sakharov, the father of the H-bomb, started his open resistance. That same spring, Aleksandr Solzhenitsyn published his devastating novel *Cancer Ward,* a rare critique of the Soviet system. The war in Vietnam showed no signs of having turned a corner, unless it was the one into Laos, where a savage U.S. bombing campaign was begun. And in May, the Berrigan brothers struck again, this time together.

On May 17, 1968, Daniel, Philip, and seven others[80] entered draft board offices in Catonsville, Maryland. They removed files from drawers and took them outside to a parking lot, where they ignited the papers with homemade napalm, concocted of gasoline and Ivory Flakes. Thinking of the children with whom he had huddled underground in Hanoi, Daniel wrote a statement for the group: "Our apologies, good friends, for the fracture of good order, the burning of paper instead of children . . . We could not, so help us God, do otherwise. For we are sick at heart, our hearts give us no rest for thinking of the Land of Burning Children." Then came the lines that tore through people like me: "We ask our fellow Christians to consider in their hearts a question that has tortured us, night and day since the war began. How many must die before our voices are heard, how many must be tortured, dislocated, starved, maddened? . . . When, at what point will you say no to this war?"[81]

The Berrigans seized the conscience of a certain wing of the American Catholic Church. Their liturgical approach to war resistance struck a chord, and over the next several years, dozens of Catholic priests, sisters, and laypeople would enact versions of the Berrigans' anti-draft-board civil disobedience. When Catonsville happened, I was in the last year of my interminable training for the priesthood. I was ambivalent about the life I was about to embrace, but the radical priests redefined my ambition. It was an extreme time, with assassinations and riots, an air of unleashed violence, and the mounting disillusionment of a generation. The Berrigans' responses seemed to demonstrate the acute relevance of an expressly Catholic sensibility, and their willingness to take great risks for peace was an unexpected justification for a lifelong vow of celibacy. The traditional images of piety and devotion that were supposed to motivate a young priest left me cold, but the Gospel-based boldness of a life built around "peace and justice," as we'd begun to say, seemed irresistible.

The trial of the Catonsville Nine took place in the fall of 1968, opening in the same week that George Wallace named Curtis LeMay as his running mate. The candidates would be dismissed as the "bombsy twins."[82] Any ambivalence I might still have been feeling about the Berrigans' witness evaporated when my former neighbor explained his position on the nuclear bomb at a press conference: "I think most military men think it's just another weapon in the arsenal . . . I think there are many times when it would be most efficient to use nuclear weapons . . . I don't believe the world would end if we exploded a nuclear weapon." A world of mine ended that day.

In the intensely private way I experienced it, the Catonsville trial, which I followed obsessively from the seminary in Washington, was like an initiation rite and a funeral rite both. When the defendants were found guilty, Daniel Berrigan described the verdict as coming on the "happiest day of our lives," yet it seemed a crushing injustice to me. My passionate attachment to these antiwar priests galvanized my decision to be ordained a few months later. Having let go of the ideal of one kind of father, inside the Pentagon, I embraced another, the one I'd encountered outside.

Over the next two years, as I modeled my priesthood after the Berrigan brothers, especially Daniel, the Catonsville Nine appealed their sentences of two to three years in prison; their appeals were denied at every level, and were finally exhausted. Then, continuing their war resistance, the brothers and their codefendants went underground rather than turn themselves in — yet another shock, which seemed wrong to me at first, then exactly right. Most of the Nine were quickly captured, but Daniel remained a fugitive through the spring and summer of 1970.[83] Surfacing at antiwar rallies, he taunted the FBI, infuriating J. Edgar Hoover, who was still a hero in my family's house — my kid brother Brian was a newly commissioned FBI agent.

I was by then a chaplain at Boston University, where, unknown to me, the former bombardier and now professor Howard Zinn was one of those helping to hide the priest. If they had asked for my help, I would have given it. My opposition to the war, compared to the draft board raiders, was timid, but by then it was complete. Enough, certainly, to infuriate my father, beginning the end of my relationship with him. Then Brian, carrying the badge that had once been Dad's, was assigned to the expanding squad of agents trying to track down Daniel Berrigan and arrest him. Brian's superiors at the Bureau ordered him to infiltrate the Catholic peace movement through me, although he knew very well it was unthinkable that I would, in any way, cooperate. My die, such as it was, had been cast, and Brian knew it. But that is another story.[84]

8. ENTER THE ABM, REENTER NITZE

The inexorable current running toward Niagara and carrying all with it would flow on in Vietnam for another seven years. Millions more people would tumble over the falls to their deaths, including tens of thousands of Americans — despite every effort, in 1968, by the secretary of defense, the president, and the American voters to rechannel it.

And what of the deeper current, flowing toward the edge of the nuclear abyss? One month before the October 1967 Pentagon demonstration, which, amid so much else, launched Daniel Berrigan and me on our separate, unexpected courses, Robert McNamara had made one last attempt to turn that tide, too. Whether he succeeded in overcoming his own inbred ambivalence remains in question, but the event represented the kind of effort toward peace that the Pentagon demonstrators, myself included, never imagined could take place inside the Building.

The occasion was a speech McNamara delivered to newspaper editors in San Francisco on September 18. In remarks titled "The Dynamics of Nuclear Strategy," the secretary painstakingly showed how the arms race had brought less security, not more, to both the United States and the Soviet Union; how a mutual paranoia had stimulated excessive arms manufacture on both sides; how moving to the next stage would be extremely dangerous and self-defeating. And McNamara said what that next stage was: the antiballistic missile system, which Moscow was preparing to embark upon, and for which the Congress, led especially by the Republican hard-liner Melvin Laird of Wisconsin,[85] was clamoring.

In 2003, McNamara described his remarks from that day thirty-six years before as "the first speech against the ABM that had ever been given."[86] That may not be quite true: President Johnson had proposed "slowing down the arms race" with a ban on "defenses" against ballistic missiles in his State of the Union speech in 1967.[87] But the purpose of McNamara's address, coming weeks after he had argued before Congress against escalation of the Vietnam War, was to lay out a full argument against the ABM. "Were we to deploy a heavy ABM system throughout the United States," he said, "the Soviets would clearly be strongly motivated so to increase their offensive capability as to cancel out our defensive advantage. It is futile for each of us to spend $4 billion, $40 billion, or $400 billion — and at the end of all the spending, and at the end of all the deployment, and at the end of all the effort, to be relatively at the same point of balance on the security scale that we are now . . . The arms race would rush hopelessly on to no sensible purpose on either side."[88]

McNamara had come to the big paradox of the nuclear age — that defense and offense had reversed polarities, taken on opposite meanings. He saw, in particular, how an American ABM system would be destabilizing. Since such a defense would not be able to withstand a full-blown Soviet attack, Moscow could conclude that its real purpose would be to catch what was left of Soviet retaliatory forces after a bolt-from-the-blue U.S. first strike. By implying that the United States was building such a first-strike capacity, the defensive ABM system would give Moscow an incentive to preempt it, launching a first strike of its own.

In parsing all of this, McNamara had, in effect, descended to the engine room of the Pentagon and was now defining what made the turbines of the arms race turn: to build up defensive capacity was inevitably to stimulate offensive capacity. Any defensive system, he said with utter logic, "can rather obviously be defeated by an enemy simply sending more offensive warheads, or dummy warheads, than there are defensive missiles capable of disposing of them." It was obvious, perhaps, but it was nevertheless a counterintuitive conclusion to have reached — that defense was dangerous and should be avoided — and it would be a hard idea to sell.

Indeed, McNamara had tried to convince the Soviet premier, Aleksei Kosygin, of the action-reaction logic at a summit meeting in Glassboro, New Jersey, the previous June. "He was a fairly squat man. He had a huge neck," McNamara told me. "As I was talking, the blood was rising to his head. His neck was bulging and he pounded the table and he said, 'Defense is moral, but offense is immoral.' They didn't understand at all."[89] The Soviets seemed determined to proceed with an ABM system of their own. To head that off, forestalling yet more pressure on the Pentagon's engines, McNamara would try to persuade Americans. Not even his own staff agreed with him. And here we return to the haunted figure of Forrestal, father of American paranoia, progenitor of the arms race, whose protégé Paul Nitze reenters the story.

Nitze, you will recall, was an author of the two main arms race manifestoes, NSC-68 and the Gaither Report. We last saw him when he was the secretary of the Navy designate, being pilloried as, of all things, an "accommodationist"[90] by, among others, Congressman Donald Rumsfeld. Nitze was confirmed for that position in the aftermath of the Kennedy assassination, and he served as Navy secretary from 1963 to 1967.[91] Not long before McNamara's anti-ABM speech, his deputy secretary of defense, Cyrus Vance, resigned because of health problems. Nitze had first expected to be named to the Pentagon's number-two position in 1961, and now, finally, in July 1967, he was. He would run the day-to-day operations of the Defense Department while McNamara dealt with Vietnam. Vance had agreed with McNamara about the ABM, but Nitze did not. In one of his first duties as McNamara's deputy, he participated in the drafting of the September speech, which may account for the reversal that put the speech's astounding last paragraphs in conflict with all that McNamara had just said.[92]

Having testified against the bombing of Vietnam in August, McNamara, when challenged by Stuart Symington, had immediately repudiated his own position, claiming he agreed with the Joint Chiefs. Now he did the equivalent. Three decades later, in boasting to me that he had made the first-ever speech against the ABM, he had felt compelled to add, "with the exception of about one paragraph, or half a page."[93] Some half a page. Having articulated the most eloquent case against the arms race and the ABM ever made by a Pentagon insider, he concluded his remarks by announcing the upcoming deployment of the Sentinel ABM system — one designed, he said, to protect against China, not Russia! Clearly, McNamara was remembering the line of argument he had used with Kosygin the previous spring, hoping to head off a Soviet ABM. Here, with rank disingenuousness, McNamara was pretending that an American ABM would not threaten Moscow. The final decision, he said, was "to go forward with this Chinese-oriented ABM deployment; and we will begin actual production of such a system at the end of this year."[94]

The Chinese had exploded an H-bomb the year before,[95] and now McNamara claimed that a Chinese ICBM might be tested within weeks. (It would actually be eleven full years before the Chinese had a workable ICBM.)[96] The idea that the United States needed an ABM defense against China was ludicrous, and just as the Joint Chiefs had, only weeks before, publicly dismissed McNamara's inconsistent positions on bombing in Vietnam, they now testified that, no matter what the secretary of defense said, the new ABM system would be aimed at Russia, not China.[97] To reinforce the impression that the system to be deployed was no threat to the Soviet Union, McNamara had described it as "small," yet it was larger than the nascent system the Soviets had begun deploying.[98]

Here McNamara can be seen knuckling under to the pressure to do something he opposed, pressure from the Chiefs, from Republicans in Congress, led by Melvin Laird — the ABM was "Congress-oriented, not China-oriented," he later admitted[99] — and pressure from his own staff, embodied in Paul Nitze, the man whose very name honored the Greek god of victory. The push to victory, however abstractly conceived, remained the greatest Cold War pressure of all.

And then there were the inexorable pressures of the bureaucracy, where researchers and officers charged with envisioning and preparing to implement an ABM system became convinced of the urgency to deploy as fully and as quickly as possible. And pressures, always, were political. As Lyndon Johnson looked forward to the presidential election campaign, he had to feel the pressure of the strategy that had elected Kennedy and him in 1960, knowing how the Republicans could exploit an "ABM gap" against him in 1968. That is why it was almost certainly the president who required McNamara to announce the deployment of an ABM system, even while arguing against it. In fact, this inconsistency served McNamara's deeper purposes, for it enabled him to separate the ABM, in the words of one historian, "from both the Soviet threat and any politically popular promises for population defense, thereby setting in motion what was to become the architecture for negotiated, mutual arms restraint."[100]

One might have expected a president to feel undermined by a defense secretary's blatantly displaying the contradiction at the heart of policy, yet not so. Johnson was susceptible to the side of McNamara that wanted to find a way to bring a halt to all nuclear arms escalation — to, in a phrase of McGeorge Bundy's, "cap the volcano."[101] As we saw, Johnson had himself proposed a limit on "defenses," and he had taken delight in announcing in March 1967 that the United States and the Soviet Union had agreed to begin discussions to limit offensive and defensive weapons systems, what would become known as the SALT talks.

If anything, Johnson was more burdened than Kennedy by his nuclear responsibility, although he lacked Kennedy's gift for expressing its effect on him. Johnson, for example, reported a recurrent dream in which, as recalled by one of his aides, "he would wake up in the night, pick up his red telephone, and say, 'Secretary of Defense, you there? Joint Chiefs, you there? CinC-SAC, you there? This is your Pres-i-dent. I've been tossing and turning, and I've decided that we've got to hit the Russians with all our A-bombs and H-bombs. So I'm putting my thumb on the button. I'm mashing it down.' Johnson would then stop and say, 'And do you know what they say to me? They say, 'Fuck you, Mr. Pres-i-dent.'"[102]

There was the dilemma: absolute dread of a coming nuclear war and absolute requirements to prepare for it. As the collapse into buffoonery of bomber-turned-political-candidate LeMay showed, the contradictory pressures were breaking men right and left. All of this amounts to the powerful pressure exerted on its leadership by an American population, which since 1945 had been conditioned to expect the worst from an omnipotent Kremlin, in response to which the only security was an ever-upward escalation of American arms. Nitze had preserved in a kind of bureaucratic amber the paranoid mindset that originated with his mentor Forrestal, and that had been vigorously inflicted on the national consciousness for a decade. "It's a we/they world," Nitze told Pentagon colleagues after he had been named deputy secretary of defense. "It's us against the Soviets. Either we get them first, or they get us first."[103]

As if to prove his point that improved defense translates into escalated offense, McNamara in this same period — while looking to slow, if not halt, the arms race — approved the most fateful escalation of American offensive weapons since the H-bomb. Eleven days after his September 18 speech against the ABM, he elaborated his argument against an anti-Soviet ABM system, even in the face of evidence that the Soviets were deploying an ABM, by announcing that the United States would deploy multiple independently targeted reentry vehicles (MIRVs). This meant that each Minuteman missile could be armed with four, five, or up to fourteen warheads, instead of one. Such an increase in the number of offensive weapons — the multiplied number of targets each single missile could hit — would overwhelm any conceivable Soviet defense, neutralizing whatever advantage the Soviets' ABMs gave them. But it also meant a huge, rapid expansion of the U.S. nuclear arsenal, which meant, in turn, a crash program in the Soviet Union to keep up.[104] For this reason, again, McNamara explicitly opposed the program, even as he was ordering it. "MIRV potentially is even more destabilizing than the ABM," he argued. "It means very large numbers of separately targetable warheads, and could arouse concern on the other side that the adversary is seeking a first-strike capability."[105]

McNamara's order here is nothing if not a rank demonstration of the impersonal upward pressure of nuclear escalation, pressure strong enough to override even a powerful man's contrary impulse. Within months, both the United States and the Soviet Union would begin testing multiwarhead missiles, crossing yet another threshold.[106] This development would prove to be a particular American nightmare, only realized later, because Soviet ICBMs were far bigger than the Minuteman and could carry many more warheads. *The Russians are coming!*

With Nitze at his side, and all the while sounding alarms against what he was himself ordering, McNamara thus ended his term as secretary of defense very much in the mad spirit of James Forrestal, though he was Forrestal's conceptual opposite. Like Stimson after Hiroshima, McNamara instinctively grasped that nuclear weapons could never form part of any rational plan of use, and that even the threat of use was inherently irrational under any circumstances. Yet McNamara presided over a system based on the threat of nuclear use and on the readiness to carry out that threat. Forrestal became unhinged because of his paranoid fears about the Russians. McNamara became unhinged because he was responsible not for a paradox but for a contradiction. Vietnam offered a different instance of the same dilemma, McNamara having become the personal embodiment of the goal of saving the country by destroying it.[107]

McNamara would always insist that he was not suicidal at the end. He described his last months in the Pentagon to me as merely "the most difficult of my life." So not suicidal, perhaps, but he was self-destructive. He saw that the only way out of the nuclear madness, as out of Vietnam, was through negotiated settlements, yet with every step he took toward negotiations, he found a way to step back. Instead of killing himself, in other words, he simply undercut himself. And then he set out on a career that, while it seemed exemplary for many years (at the World Bank, then on to a wealthy retirement beginning in 1981), aimed ultimately at self-ruin, which was the only possible outcome after what he had done as secretary of defense. Having sponsored the Vietnam War, he had finally enabled a halt to its ground-force escalations, but he would not utter a word of public criticism as Nixon savagely expanded the bombing,[108] with the war grinding on for another seven years. McNamara had laid the groundwork for breakthrough arms control treaties (the Outer Space Treaty of 1967, the Nuclear Non-Proliferation Treaty of 1968,[109] and the Antiballistic Missile Treaty in 1972), but he had set in motion forces for nuclear growth that would run on for twenty years, making the arms control process a cruel hoax.

As an old man far removed from power, McNamara became an apostle of nuclear disarmament and a guilt-ridden apologizer for his "war crimes" in Japan and Vietnam.[110] His fixation on numbers became an object of ridicule, even when displayed in self-criticism. "Three million six hundred thousand Vietnamese were killed," he told me when I interviewed him in 1997, "the equivalent in U.S. population of twenty-seven million."[111] He was a lonely pariah, forever ready to weep, a figure more of pathos than of tragedy. Always he was at war with what he had done, with who he was. Not only defeated by the monster he had come to tame, he had discovered it inside himself.

"But at last in his untraceable evolutions, the White Whale so crossed and recrossed, and in a thousand ways entangled the slack of the three lines now fast to him, that they foreshortened, and, of themselves, warped the devoted boats toward the planted irons in him."[112] Ahab and Moby Dick drew ever closer together until, in the end, they were one.

Nitze outlasted McNamara in the Pentagon, and his warnings went steadily in the opposite direction. He was, in his biographer's word, a Cassandra,[113] forever afraid of Moscow, constantly asserting the nation's need for ABMs and MIRVs. And when, after the election of Richard Nixon, Nitze left the administration, he carved out a new role for himself as an advocate of escalation outside the government. McNamara's warning against the ABM, despite his own ambivalence, resonated among Democrats, and antinuclear scientists suddenly found their expertise newly relevant. A powerful movement against the ABM was born in the late 1960s, and McNamara had made their best argument for them. "The whole anti-ABM crowd," Nitze would later complain, "was caught up in a perfectly asinine line of thought — the sort of half-baked thinking that had gotten us into trouble before and would do so again."[114]

Nitze, not content to have helped undermine McNamara's opposition from inside the Defense Department, made countering the opposition to the ABM his own first priority after he left the Pentagon. With his NSC-68 mentor Dean Acheson, Nitze organized a group, in 1969, to warn the nation against the disarmers. "Virtually nothing had changed since NSC-68," his biographer observes; only in 1952, Nitze was warning about "the year of maximum danger" as 1954, and now he was saying it would be 1974.[115] Nitze's new group was called the Committee to Maintain a Prudent Defense Policy, and one of its chief results was the rescue of his government career, for this anti-Soviet Cassandra was the Nixon administration's idea of an arms control negotiator — arms control always at the service of checking Soviet advantages; arms control, that is, as another weapon in the Cold War. (In exactly this way, surviving as an insider-outsider-insider, Nitze would eventually serve under six presidents.)

In November 1969, Nixon appointed Nitze to the Strategic Arms Limitation Talks (SALT I) delegation, whose work eventually led to a 1972 agreement theoretically capping the number of strategic missile launchers, although it did nothing to limit ICBMs already being developed and offered nothing reasonable to prevent the use of MIRVs.[116] McGeorge Bundy defined SALT I and the ABM Treaty, which were signed together at the Nixon-Brezhnev summit in Moscow, as the largest arms control agreements "achieved in the nuclear age," powerful symbols of a hoped-for détente, but Bundy could also point out that these arrangements left existing forces and new programs "essentially unconstrained."[117] Even Henry Kissinger would soon regret that he had not "thought through the implications of a MIRVed world more thoughtfully in 1969 and 1970 than I did."[118] An aide to Kissinger later wrote that "the refusal to ban MIRV's was the key decision in the entire history of SALT."[119]

Having Paul Nitze as an arms negotiator was like hiring the district attorney as your defense lawyer. The thing to note here, however, is that the Committee to Maintain a Prudent Defense Policy, which catapulted Nitze back into government, was staffed by two brilliant young graduate students whose work for this committee amounted to a baptism in defense policy — Richard Perle and Paul Wolfowitz. That simply, the dead hand of James Forrestal extended its reach into the near and distant future.[120]

9. NIXON AND LAIRD

On January 20, 1969, a Republican replaced a Democrat in the White House. Nothing symbolized the difference between the incoming administration and its predecessor more dramatically than the appointment of Melvin Laird as secretary of defense. As we have noted, he was a leading hawk in Congress and had made his mark as a proponent of the antiballistic missile system. With his arrival at the Pentagon, the days of ABM ambivalence were over.

Laird and Nixon, renaming the Sentinel as the Safeguard, announced early on that the "limited" system McNamara had ordered would be expanded. The issue had become thoroughly politicized, with opposition to the ABM drawing energy from the broader antiwar movement. The Safeguard soon emerged as an issue on which Democrats in the Senate began to fight the Nixon administration, and the ABM suddenly appeared to be vulnerable to an appropriations cutoff. Laird offered a shocking justification for the proposed expansion of the small "anti-Chinese" system into a full-blown anti-Soviet system — that the Soviet Union had recently changed its entire strategic aim, and the United States was facing a grave new level of threat that the previous administration had overlooked.

The first National Intelligence Estimate, assessing long-range Soviet strategy for the new Nixon administration, according to Paul Nitze, "made the outright judgment that the Soviets were interested only in parity, and that once they had attained parity, they would be satisfied and they would stop. They would understand there was no point in their trying to reach a position of superiority."[121] The Johnson administration, under McNamara and his successor, Clark Clifford, had concluded that the quest for nuclear dominance was a dangerous illusion, and they had found what the intelligence community regarded as hard evidence that the Soviets had come to the same conclusion. There was a hope for stability in a mutual acceptance of "sufficiency," and even for a leveling off of the frenzied arms race.

Nitze was sure that any such assessment of Soviet acceptance of parity was wrong, had said so under McNamara, and now took his case to Laird, who was easily convinced. Nitze argued that the intelligence experts were as misguided as the "soft" Johnson elite had been. If Nitze was right, and the Soviets were still pursuing superiority, the United States would have to pursue it as well. And, not incidentally, it was the Soviet push toward superiority that made the ABM essential.

Thus, just as McNamara had begun his tenure as secretary of defense in conflict with the Pentagon's intelligence reports (the missile gap) — a problem with which he turned to my father, to start up the Defense Intelligence Agency — so now one of Laird's first battles (if hidden from public view) would be with his own intelligence chief, who had helped prepare the estimate that asserted there was no looming "superiority gap" at all. That chief, the DIA director, was still my father. He would hold that position longer than any other of the agency's directors, to this day.

As the Pentagon Papers would show, when they were published in the *New York Times* and other newspapers in mid-June 1970,[122] the intelligence community generally had been critical of the waging of the Vietnam War from its earliest days, and consistent notes of dissent had been given, in particular, by the Pentagon's own Defense Intelligence Agency. The conduct of the war would be marked by disputes over estimates of enemy strength, for example, with military commanders in Vietnam usually optimistic and Washington-based analysts (at the CIA as well as the DIA) pessimistic.

By the pivotal years of 1968 and 1969, my father was in his prime, self-assured and professionally powerful. Or so it seemed. His hair was silver by then. He was as tall as ever, and as lean, and as weathered by dawn hours on the golf course several times a week, his only relaxation. Among the men on Generals' Row, he had long since become a figure of authority, thoroughly at ease with his three stars, the lightning bolts on the visor of his hat. He was greeted with deference when he entered the Officers' Club, a far cry from the dismissive glances that had been tossed his way when he was "that cop" transplanted from the FBI. Now he was the man theoretically in charge of information on which every aspect of military power depended.

I never knew, during the Vietnam War, what particular stresses my father was under, but after the war I came to understand that he was embroiled in its very crucible. From the beginning of McNamara's tenure, Dad was married to the Kennedy administration's reform agenda in the Pentagon, and to the extent that reforms had worked, my father was identified with his own service branch's strongest enemy (hence LeMay's coldness at that retirement party). To the extent that reforms had not worked (the DIA would never get complete control of military intelligence), my father was McNamara's partner in failure. In regard to the nuclear arms race, I knew from my own experience ("Head to Richmond") that Dad was as haunted by the dangers of nuclear war as Kennedy and McNamara were, and as opposed to the itchy carelessness of the bomber generals, who beat back McNamara's attempt to take over SIOP war planning. In regard to Vietnam, my father's problem, as I would learn, was more immediate, since his job constantly required him to report information up the chain of command, and especially to the secretary of defense, that his can-do military superiors did not want to hear — and certainly did not want to have reported. For example, as laid out in the Pentagon Papers, a DIA report, "An Appraisal of the Bombing of North Vietnam Through 12 September 1966," had defied the expectations and wishes of both the Air Force and the Joint Chiefs by finding "no evidence" that the air war had inhibited the movement of North Vietnamese troops and supplies or affected "popular morale."[123] In sum, he was telling his Air Force colleagues and the Chiefs, in relation to the war as it was being fought, including eighteen months of savage air bombardment: No can do. And, when proven right, instead of being vindicated, he was, like his civilian superior, undermined as a man.

No can do. He was telling me a version of the same thing as I finished my training for the priesthood, was ordained, and took my uneasy place, as chaplain at Boston University, on the so-called Catholic Left. Why shouldn't he have been, as I remember him from the time and in contrast with his Officers' Club image, unusually edgy, narrow-eyed, quick to take a drink alone in the living room? He and I had grown estranged, as I had fallen more and more under the influence of the Berrigans and their ilk. What did not occur to me then was that my father had grown equally estranged from those with whom he worked in the Building, especially after losing McNamara as his sponsor, protector, and partner in the twofold anguish of undeflected truth and ineffectual ambivalence.

The most basic responsibility of military intelligence is to count the enemy, an effort that, in Vietnam, General William Westmoreland described as like "trying to estimate roaches in your kitchen."[124] The Tet Offensive, claimed as an American victory, had laid bare the harsh fact that the United States had undercounted the enemy it faced in South Vietnam by 100 percent, showing that the war, before it was anything else, was a huge intelligence failure. The war, that is, was my father's own failure, as he experienced it. But his particular struggle, beginning with Rolling Thunder in 1965, had been in relation to the Air Force, whose blue uniform he wore. He found himself consistently signing intelligence assessments of the effects of the air war, North and South, that contradicted solemn Air Force claims. When McNamara concluded that the bombing was stiffening Communist resolve, while doing little to impede the flow of supplies and reinforcements to enemy battle units — conclusions that led to his break with the war in the summer of 1967 — he was drawing on DIA reports.[125]

What my father faced over Vietnam, he faced more acutely in the debate over the intentions of the Soviet Union. Only, on that front, history would show, he was not wrong. When Secretary McNamara testified before Congress, in February 1968, that it was "extremely unlikely"[126] that the Soviet Union would seek to develop a first-strike capability, he was drawing on DIA assessments. A year later, Melvin Laird, in one of his first acts as secretary of defense, contradicted his predecessor. On March 21, sworn before the Senate Foreign Relations Committee, he baldly asserted about the Soviets, "They are going for our missiles, and they are going for a first-strike capability." He leaned into the microphone for emphasis. "There is no question about that."[127]

10. KNOCKOUT BLOW

Laird was forty-six years old, a longtime politician who, as a young veteran, had been elected to his father's seat in the Wisconsin legislature. In Washington he had emerged as a "better dead than Red" hard-liner, always ready to use the issue of softness on defense against the Democrats. In 1962, he had published a book that served as a Republican manifesto, *A House Divided: America's Strategy Gap.* Laird was a Pentagon acolyte who had made a regular point of rebutting the famous warning of Dwight Eisenhower. "The military-industrial-labor team," he said in speeches before veterans' groups — no "complex" for him — "is a tremendous asset to our nation and a fundamental source of our national strength."[128] As defense secretary, Laird would move to undo McNamara's centralizing reforms, restoring the prerogatives of the brass in budgeting and planning, reinstating coveted weapons systems, like a new bomber for the Air Force, and pushing for a major expansion of the ABM for the Army. Regarding the war in Vietnam, it was Laird who coined the word "Vietnamization," and he would preside over the tradeoff that combined a phased withdrawal of U.S. ground forces with a massive expansion of bombing in pursuit of "peace with honor."[129]

We have seen that Representative Laird was a leading advocate of the antiballistic missile, and when McNamara admitted that the Sentinel system he ordered was aimed less at China than at Congress, he was thinking of the pressure exerted, above all, by Laird. On March 14, 1969, President Nixon, depending on advice from Laird and National Security Adviser Henry Kissinger, announced his decision to deploy an ABM system. This was around the time Kissinger announced the administration's intention to "prevail" in Vietnam. Nixon's Safeguard ABMs would be aimed at Russia, not China. This was how the Joint Chiefs had wanted the ABM defined all along, but the plan flatly contradicted the Johnson administration's stated assessment, going back to McNamara.

The justification for that major shift was the startling "discovery" to which Laird testified a week after Nixon's announcement: the frightening new conclusion that Moscow had abandoned the nuclear balance of deterrence in favor of a strategy aimed at wiping out the U.S. retaliatory capability with a surprise ("first strike") attack, a "knockout blow."[130] When asked to explain how the new administration had reached this conclusion about Soviet intentions, Laird said, "The key information was gathered by our intelligence sources during the month of December." During Johnson's last full month in office, that is. "It became known to me after I became Secretary of Defense."[131]

But there was a problem. The National Intelligence Estimate titled "Soviet Strategic Attack Forces," which was then being prepared by the U.S. Intelligence Board,[132] chaired by CIA Director Richard Helms and including DIA Director Joseph Carroll, said, "We believe that the Soviets recognize the enormous difficulties of any attempt to achieve strategic superiority of such order as to significantly alter the strategic balance. Consequently, we consider it highly unlikely that they will attempt within the period of this estimate to achieve a first-strike capability."[133]

This was a consensus finding of the USIB, but the estimate process allowed for agencies in dissent to register objections. Air Force intelligence had offered such dissent,[134] reinforcing, as always, that service's demand for more ICBMs of its own. Insiders would recognize such special pleading, but the Air Force position showed that disagreement with the consensus was possible, which only drew attention to the fact that the Pentagon's overall intelligence agency was firmly part of the USIB's consensus. The DIA was on record, that is, as rejecting a Soviet first strike. But Secretary Laird, the DIA's superior, was now saying just the contrary, under oath. The fact that Laird had flatly contradicted his "intelligence sources," including the Pentagon's own agency, while claiming to base his assessment on those sources, became known to the Senate committee, and opponents of the ABM seized on the discrepancy.

A furor ensued in Washington that spring, with Democrats using the issue against the new Republican administration, and with advocates of arms control desperately trying to block what seemed to be a major new escalation of the arms race. "I consider a statement such as you made of extreme importance," the Foreign Relations Committee's chairman, J. William Fulbright, told Laird in a subsequent hearing. "Not only regarding what our own plans are, but because of its effect upon the Russians and other people. It is a matter of great importance, and I want to know what your statement was based upon."[135]

Laird was learning a lesson about the difference between being a shoot-from-the-hip politician and the secretary of defense, the difference, as *Time* put it, between "talk of the kind a Congressman can easily get away with, but a Defense Secretary cannot."[136] The Democrats and ABM opponents pressed the advantage Laird had given them. "Your statement made to this committee on March 21," Fulbright charged, "was not based upon a finding of the Intelligence Board . . . that the Soviets were going for a first strike . . . It is clear your statement was not based on a conclusion by the intelligence community."

"My statement," Laird replied, "was based upon the information given to me by the intelligence community."[137]

Richard Helms was called to testify before the Senate committee in a closed hearing, and after he did so, Fulbright said of Helms's testimony, "It sure didn't sound like what the Secretary of Defense has been saying."[138] In fact, in the week before the Fulbright-Laird confrontation, on June 12, 1969, the USIB (with Helms and Carroll concurring in a "consensus judgment") approved a memo to the National Security Council that declared that the Soviets had neither the ability nor the intention of moving to first strike.[139] Then, on June 29, 1969, the USIB issued yet another memo — with the CIA and the DIA concurring again — which asserted, "Our judgment of the doctrines and goals which govern Soviet strategic programs remain as we stated them in NIE 11-8-68."[140] Remain, that is, as understood during the Johnson administration, when no one spoke of a Soviet shift to a first strike.

When Kissinger learned that the CIA director had contradicted the secretary of defense, jeopardizing the ABM, he reportedly wanted President Nixon to fire Helms.[141] But the senators were alerted to the issue, and the cashiering of Helms would have been inflammatory. Because the controversy was out in the open, Helms was safe. Indeed, a Senate committee later looked into the question of whether the CIA director had been unduly pressured in this instance. That committee found that "during the summer and fall of 1969, the White House and then the Secretary of Defense indirectly pressured the DCI [director of Central Intelligence] to modify his judgments."[142] In June, the report says, Kissinger demanded to see Helms in his White House office, where Kissinger, in the words of Helms's biographer, "demanded that the Board of National Estimates revise its paper."[143]

But the National Intelligence Estimate represented the conclusion of the DIA, too, and in subsequent congressional hearings, that became a source of acute embarrassment to Laird. "The DOD people have the authority to make their own estimate," Fulbright challenged Laird, "based upon your own intelligence. That is correct, is it not?" What Fulbright knew was that the DIA agreed with the estimate in question and had helped write it: "Soviet first strike . . . highly unlikely," as opposed to Laird's "No question about that." Laird deflected the thrust, but Fulbright pressed him: "It seems to me that it is quite possible, not necessarily illegal or beyond its jurisdiction, for the Department of Defense to arrive at a different conclusion on such a question as has been under consideration here."

Now Laird did respond: "We have not done that, Mr. Chairman. I want to make that very clear. We have not arrived at a different position from the intelligence estimates in this whole matter . . . I have not overstated the case at any point. I have always used the intelligence estimate, the agreed upon estimate." To which Fulbright replied, "I am not trying to level an accusation."[144]

But he was. The intelligence estimate had made the clear assertion that the Soviet Union's going for a first strike was "highly unlikely." The Defense Intelligence Agency concurred in that conclusion, and had reiterated it at least twice during June alone. Laird was hoist on his own petard, and by the summer, with the Senate split and the issue roundly politicized, the ABM system was in jeopardy. Nixon and Kissinger were on Laird's back; he was blowing it. Then a strange thing happened. Helms was not fired, but an adjustment was made in the National Intelligence Estimate. In an "updating" of the estimate of Soviet ICBM capability, the key sentences that were causing Laird such problems disappeared, and when the update was published, the offending words were gone.[145]

Richard Helms had too high a profile and too influential a political constituency to be fired by Nixon in the midst of this dispute, and he was also a man who knew when to yield a point. "After an assistant to Secretary of Defense Laird informed Helms," in the words of the Senate investigation, "that the statement contradicted the public position of the Secretary," Helms ordered the deletion.[146] "A willingness to compromise," his biographer comments in relation to this incident, "was both Helms's strength and his weakness . . . To get along, he often had to go along."[147] Helms himself later said that when the CIA chief "clashes with the Secretary of Defense, he isn't a big enough fellow on the block."[148]

But General Carroll, the less powerful and deliberately anonymous agency chief deep inside the Pentagon, was something else. If one thing had distinguished his career, it was an inbred inability to go along. For years, his main constituency had been Robert McNamara, as together they tried to transcend the parochialism of interservice rivalry, but Carroll had no constituency now. His primary loyalty had been not to the Joint Chiefs, not to his own Air Force, but to McNamara's demand for uncorrupted intelligence. The newspapers were full of the dramatic push and pull between Laird and Fulbright's committee, including leaked reports about the contradictory secret testimony of "intelligence chiefs." Whatever testimony my father offered in the matter did not become public. At the time, I asked my mother about it, and she told me that Dad had been called to testify. Later, I asked my father, and he demurred. When I pressed him, he told me that his assessment had been and continued to be the same as Helms's: there was no evidence of a

Soviet intention to go for a first strike. "Dick Helms and I agreed on that," he said.

Within days of Secretary Laird's having testified before Fulbright's committee that his Pentagon intelligence sources were in complete accord with the soon to be adjusted USIB estimate on Soviet intentions, my father was removed as head of the DIA. The crucial deletion of text, to which Helms agreed, eliminating evidence of Laird's contradiction of his own intelligence service, did not occur until after my father's termination.[149] I am left to speculate about the exact nature of my father's demise, but my conclusion, first reached thirty years ago, seems reasonable. In 2003, I spoke to a former DIA analyst who worked for my father at the time, and he remembered the end of General Carroll's tenure vividly, and how it was tied to the ABM debate as it approached a climax on Capitol Hill. "We were all aware of it. I am sure they said something to him like, 'Now, Joe, can't you give us a break on the ABM?' To which he would have said, 'Don't make an argument for a weapon system based on corrupted intelligence.'"[150]

In 2005, on the other hand, I spoke to the official historian of the Defense Intelligence Agency. He had no knowledge of the dispute, but he did recall that General Carroll had clashed with Laird over "organizational issues."[151]

General Carroll never made public any point of contention between himself and Secretary Laird, which was consistent with his long-standing commitment to maintain the lowest of profiles. The DIA historian's impression was that my father could have continued as director "into the 1970s," but I know from my mother that that is not true. In July 1969 my father was abruptly told that he was being transferred to a new job. I recall my mother telling me that the position was at an Air Force base in Texas. This assignment, to a slot tied to the rank of major general, entailed a demotion, a loss of the third star my father had worn for a decade. My mother was crushed by the news, and indicated that my father was as well. In a classic instance of psychosomatic reaction, his back "went out" just then.

Stress is opportunistic, physicians tell us, and it finds the body's weak point. My father's chronic problem with a slipped disk suddenly became acute, nearly paralyzing him, and his doctor urged an operation. Within days of having been told of his transfer, he was admitted to the hospital at Andrews Air Force Base, and I went at once to Washington. I did not know of it, but military medicine had its own diagnosis for the condition my father was suffering: "hysterical conversion symptoms," a kind of behind-the-lines shell shock. For a decade, day in and day out, he had been facing impossible challenges, with little or no support, under orders to create an enterprise that the very institution he served was determined to defeat. In the end, defeat came.

My father would have been the last person to compare his condition to what GIs were suffering in Vietnam, but his physical collapse mimicked that of men brought down on the battlefield. Even then, as I heard from Mom, yet knowing nothing, I had a vague sense of him as a casualty of the war.

I was six months into my priesthood. Daniel Berrigan's conviction was on appeal, and I was helping to organize rallies for his support. My father and I no longer discussed anything having to do with the war — our affectionate ease with each other was a casualty for sure — but when I arrived at the hospital the night before his scheduled operation, my mother was relieved. When she saw me in the corridor outside my father's room, her eyes filled. I took her into my arms, and it was then, in an indiscreet rush, that she told me of my father's having been "fired," as she put it. When I asked why, she said, "Because he testified against Secretary Laird."

I knew of the Senate hearings, and assumed my father had been called before the Fulbright committee, which may be the case. Because of what my mother told me, I remembered it that way.[152] My father's "testimony" may have been at a hearing of the U.S. Intelligence Board, whose recently declassified records do underscore DIA contradictions of Laird in the crucial period. Beyond that, I don't know. Nothing I have learned in the further investigation I did for this book makes me alter the conclusion I long ago came to, that my father defied his superior and was punished for it.

His removal cleared the way for the subsequent adjustment in the intelligence estimate. My mother did not discuss the matter with me again. My father would never have discussed it with me, except that the Laird-ABM dispute became a subject of public discussion five years later, when the Church committee, a Senate investigation into "foreign and military intelligence," took up questions of the intelligence community's conduct. It was then that my father told me he had agreed with Helms on the key question of Soviet intentions — no evidence that Moscow was going for a first strike.

To see my father stretched out in a hospital bed, practically paralyzed, was a far cry from that day in 1947 when I had first seen him in his general's uniform. He was my first god, laid low. As I entered the dusky room, he looked over at me, and I saw a kind of helpless relief come into his eyes. I had never seen him looking weak before, and I did not know what to say. A casualty indeed. Generals far from the front lines are broken by warfare, too. Wellington, after Waterloo, wept uncontrollably.[153] My father solved the problem of my hesitancy by reaching a hand toward me. Instead of weeping, he said with simple purity, "Would you give me your blessing, Father?"

It seemed a joke. I had offered a priestly blessing over both my parents on the day of my ordination, but not since. At first, I could not imagine that he was serious, but then I realized that he was. I glimpsed a vulnerability in him that I would not understand until years later — until now. And only now do I appreciate what an act of generosity, given all that was already wrong between us, it was for him to let me see his need. A need, apparently, for a word of consolation.

We made awkward small talk for a few minutes, and then, only because I knew he wanted me to, I caressed his head with my left hand, in the priestly way. I was struck by the softness of his silver hair. He closed his eyes. With my right hand I made the sign of the cross over him and prayed. "May the blessing of God, Father, Son, and Holy Spirit, descend on you and remain with you forever." I pressed my fingers into his scalp instead of kissing him, which, to my shame, I did not know how to do.

A few weeks later, on August 9, Nixon, Kissinger, and Laird got their ABM. The Senate was evenly divided on the question. The authorization was approved when Vice President Spiro Agnew broke the tie.[154] And a few weeks after that, in September, my father, at a small, brief ceremony at the Pentagon, retired from the Air Force.[155] For his eight years of service as the director of the Defense Intelligence Agency, he was presented with the Distinguished Service Medal. If Robert McNamara, who remained respectful of my father's memory thirty-five years later, was Ahab, my father was Starbuck, and both went down, leaving small birds "screaming over the yet yawning gulf . . . all collapsed, and the great shroud of the sea rolled on as it rolled five thousand years ago."[156]

11. BOMBING THE PENTAGON?

Taking off from peacenik evocations of evil at the Pentagon, I earlier cited the image Henry James applied to the movement of the world toward catastrophe — a current or tide, in his word, carrying humanity, like a leaf, like a twig, toward the Niagara of August 1914. Jonathan Schell adapted the image of Niagara to define the twentieth century's bondage to war and the ominous prospect for the human race if that bondage is not broken.[157] In 1970, the Federal Bureau of Prisons sent a psychiatrist to interview Philip Berrigan, imprisoned at the penitentiary at Lewisburg, Pennsylvania. The doctor's purpose was to try to learn from Philip where his fugitive brother, Daniel, might be hiding. In the course of the interview, the psychiatrist said, with exquisite condescension, "You people are like salmon, trying to jump Niagara Falls."[158]

Was that so? In the early peace movement days, the Berrigans and their circle were motivated by pristine conscience, certain of the moral economy in which they moved. In the three years after the 1968 Catonsville raid, mainly Catholic resisters conducted similar draft board raids in Milwaukee, Boston, Rochester, New York, Los Angeles, Providence, Evanston, Camden, and other cities. They burgled FBI offices in New York and Pennsylvania, and they attacked Dow Chemical offices in Washington. Dozens of people were involved, many of them priests and nuns. The terrible escalations of the spring of 1970 — the war into Cambodia, the deaths of American students at Kent State and Jackson State — brought more into the movement. One group styled itself the East Coast Conspiracy to Save Lives.

I was tangentially connected to all of this, knew many of the raiders and admired them, although my inbuilt caution, and concern for my father, prevented me from enlisting in the ranks of the outlaws. But in Boston I turned over my campus ministry offices to the antidraft conspirators, and eventually I would testify for them at various trials.[159] The loosely affiliated network referred to itself as the "action community," but outsiders dubbed the activists the Catholic Left. Accustomed to offering religious justifications for their actions, they took their own virtue for granted. Others were not so sure, even within the broader peace movement. The Catholic brand of symbolic war resistance, built around burglaries and property destruction, involved at least implicit threats of force. "I believe in revolution," Philip Berrigan wrote in 1967, "and I hope to continue making a nonviolent contribution to it."[160] It was a sincere statement; neither Berrigan nor any of those who flocked to him would have deliberately hurt anyone, and it was their abhorrence of the rampant killing in Southeast Asia that drove them. But broken doors, poured blood, ignited papers, intimidated clerks, the risk of police using force — the raiders' intentions aside, there *was* an air of violence around these actions. I accepted it at the time, and still regard the tactics as proportionate, given the violence of the war.

And then, on November 27, 1970, J. Edgar Hoover, in testimony before Congress, accused the Catholic Left of planning kidnapping and sabotage of major government facilities in Washington. He identified the plotters as "an anarchist group" led by the Berrigan brothers. He named the East Coast Conspiracy to Save Lives, and said it planned to "kidnap a high government official." Soon eight people were indicted for conspiracy to kidnap Henry Kissinger and to blow up heating tunnels under Washington buildings.[161] The scheme, it seemed, was to hold "someone like Henry Kissinger"[162] hostage, releasing him only when B-52 raids were halted. The tunnels to be blown up included those under the Pentagon — a direct attempt to impede the war effort. Philip Berrigan was one of the eight who were charged. His brother was named as an unindicted coconspirator.[163] If the military could escalate, so, apparently, could the peace movement. Or was escalation built into the nature of things by now, that tide, that metahistorical force?

The Pentagon! I remember thinking when I heard of the accusation. *What the hell is this?* Of course I was thinking, *My Pentagon!* And then I realized that I did not want my movement friends to know how I had loved that place. Nor did I want them to know, thinking of the brutal end my father had come to not long before, the reasons that *I* had for hating it.

I was relieved to find that everyone I knew in the movement reacted to Hoover's charges with mocking incredulity. Hoover was out of his mind — the "Hoover Vacuum Conspiracy."[164] But when the government presented its case as the trial of the Harrisburg Eight opened the following year, it turned out that a government informant had served as a courier between the imprisoned Philip Berrigan and a Catholic nun named Elizabeth McAlister. She was a tall, lovely woman whom I had met at various meetings. I knew her as soft-spoken and gentle, but the indictment painted a quite different portrait. Like many others, I instinctively knew that the charges would be proven wrong.

Philip and Elizabeth had exchanged many letters through the informant, and now they were made public, to staggering effect. The letters did seem to detail the kidnapping and sabotage plots, with discussions of the violence that could ensue.[165] But the conceived actions outlined in the letters were all so much bluster, as anyone who knew the priest and the nun understood at once. They were incapable of hurting anyone. McAlister had encouraged the imprisoned Berrigan with reports of such "planning," she explained, as a way of cheering him up.[166] The airy talk might have been indiscreet, foolish perhaps, but it was not malicious. Nevertheless, outside our circle of sympathizers, the pristine virtue of the Catholic movement was pierced by such reports, however misconstrued they were.

And then it turned out, as letters made clear, that Philip and Elizabeth had become intimate friends. Such a development might not seem momentous — hundreds of priests and nuns were falling in love with each other in those years — but Berrigan, in addition to all else, had stood for a new justification for religious celibacy. The vowed life, independent of family ties and devoted to a higher cause, was a necessary part, as he had put it, of a "revolutionary lifestyle." For me and countless other young priests and nuns of the Catholic Left, he had supplied a heroic rationale for our constrained state of life. The old pieties about chastity as a "better way" had lost their meaning, but celibacy as a signal, and in support, of radical devotion to peace and justice had replaced them. Berrigan's personal witness seemed indispensable to the life we were trying to maintain. The discovery that he and Elizabeth were discreetly moving away from such notions was a disillusionment. In retrospect, I see their discovery of each other as a healthy coming to terms with what is real, an authentic affirmation of love. My disappointment then had more to do with my illusions than their relationship.

As for the legal case — plots to bomb the Pentagon? kidnap Henry Kissinger? — it ended in a mistrial, with the jury unable to reach a verdict. The charges against the Harrisburg Eight were ludicrous. The Justice Department and the FBI looked foolish as well as sinister. But a judgment was passed on the Catholic Left, too. The press coverage of the trial made the movement seem all too human. As with politics, so with religion. The life of dedicated virtue for the sake of a higher cause was made to seem a sham.

Daniel Berrigan remained faithful to his brother and to his own Jesuit priesthood. His antiwar witness maintained its moral edge. Philip Berrigan and Elizabeth McAlister started a new life of antinuclear resistance, based at a commune called Jonah House, in Baltimore. Their activism, and eventually that of their three children, was marked by dozens of courageous acts of witness, at the cost of yet more prison sentences. They fulfilled the political as well as personal promise of their marriage. A relatively small circle of Catholics and peace activists remained Berrigan admirers — certainly including me — but the larger society took little notice of their activities.

The arc from Catonsville to Harrisburg was the Catholic equivalent of the progression from the Port Huron Statement to the siege of Chicago, from Woodstock to Altamont. As an influence both inside and outside the Church, the Catholic Left simply dispersed, with many priests and nuns walking away from both their religious vocations and the movement.[167] I myself left the priesthood in 1974, a year after Phil was released from prison.

In the case of the SDS, the disillusioned remnant did, in fact, go on to bomb making and terrorism. Some went through the door to murder. Tom Hayden, the principal author of the Port Huron Statement and Daniel Berrigan's predecessor in Hanoi, looked back from the Reagan years: "I used to reject Reinhold Niebuhr's philosophy that there was a flaw in the human condition, that perfectibility was unattainable," he said. "I now think that there's quite a bit of truth to that, for individuals, for revolutions, for nations."[168]

This was a far cry from the sharp Manichaeism of the Pentagon march of 1967 — *Out demons! Out!* — when Norman Mailer could see a clear divide between the military on one side and "the unnamed saints on the other."[169] Just as the Vietnam War was the occasion for the puncturing of American armed innocence — a movement from Forrestal to McNamara — so, too, with America's antiwar critics. *Who is the slayer? Who the victim? Speak!* Protesters had gathered at the Pentagon to cast out evil, and then pacifists were taken to be thinking of using bombs against the Pentagon as a way of stopping the bombing. Whatever evil was, it had had its way with all of us, with the Pentagon its totemic center from start to finish.

12. NOT WITH A BANG

I had my own, decidedly Oedipal part in all this, culminating in my version of the war's madness in late 1972. I was one of that benighted minority who actually believed that George McGovern would defeat Richard Nixon in that year's presidential election. McGovern ran on the single issue of antiwar outrage. He embodied the full circle America had come, having served as a B-24 pilot in bombing raids over Europe, the very start of the nation's high-tech belligerence. By the year of his candidacy, most U.S. troops had been pulled back from combat and Vietnamization was well under way. The Paris peace talks were in their fourth fruitless year. Nixon, with the collusive support of the press, had convinced the American people that the peace talks were the story, not the war — this despite the fact that the bombing campaign in Vietnam, Laos, and Cambodia was more savage than ever.[170] When the nation voted overwhelmingly for Nixon, as if the war were over, I was startled by a rush of despair.

And then came the Christmas bombing of Hanoi. The peace talks were stalled far more by the recalcitrance of America's ally in Saigon than by the Communists, but in the name of breaking the impasse, Nixon ordered the most violent bombing attack since World War II, a campaign that ran from December 18 to December 30.[171] Hanoi, Haiphong, and other cities in North Vietnam were hit, and for the first time ever, B-52s were used against urban populations. "Hanoi was bombed," Kissinger's biographer wrote, "in order to force changes in a treaty that the U.S. had already seen fit to accept. The modifications for which these lives were lost were so minor that neither Nixon nor Kissinger would adequately remember what they were."[172]

The giant B-52 had been a personal icon of mine, and I was acutely aware of it when, after America's losing only one throughout the course of the war, 15 of them, out of 120 in the campaign, were shot down in those two weeks. It was then that something in me finally snapped. Having resisted being drawn into anything more than the passive resistance of trespass demonstrations — at Air Force bases and at the U.S. Capitol — I was moved, during the Christmas bombing, to an escalation of my own. With a group of about a dozen Catholic peaceniks, I planned an "action" designed to symbolically, and perhaps for a brief time actually, shut down the Pentagon. We could not read of the bombing of Hanoi and other cities and do nothing.

The scheme we concocted was bizarre. We would rent four large dump trucks, fill them with concrete debris, and, at the start of rush hour, drive to the four main access ramps to the Pentagon's River Entrance and unload the concrete in the middle of the road. The idea was to block the ramps long enough to seriously snarl the rush-hour traffic. There were too many ramps and roadways around the Building, and bus tunnels beneath it, to imagine really preventing large numbers of workers from getting through, but if we could clog the River Entrance for an hour or two, the secretary of defense would be stopped, and so, we thought, would the top brass. I was central to the planning, because I knew that the men who rated limousines arrived by that entrance. Reporters would show up, and cameras, and for a time the world would hear that someone's shoe had tripped up the war machine.

The plan called for us to masquerade as construction workers. At the appointed moment, we would hop out of the trucks with red flags, halt the traffic, keep the cars clear of the dump site, and ensure no one was hurt. I remember one planning meeting in the Paulist seminary in Washington. Those who were on the scene proceeded with the scheme, pooling money for the rentals, finding a demolition site where we could get the debris, buying hardhats, making practice runs in cars. We set the action for the fourth week in January. I commuted back and forth between Boston and Washington in the weeks before the agreed date, never telling my parents, who had retired from Generals' Row to their old house in Alexandria, that I was in town. I was both terrified and exhilarated as the date approached. I moved to Washington, ready.

On January 20, I and my fellow conspirators stood in the crowd on Pennsylvania Avenue to jeer and curse Nixon as he went by in his second inaugural parade. How dare that bastard flash the peace sign at us — even if, to him, it meant only victory. How far I'd come from Eisenhower's parade in 1953, when my button read "I Like Everybody." Ever since my mother had carried me in her arms as an infant to the last inauguration of Roosevelt, I had attended these parades as liturgies of my intense love of country, but at this inauguration there was no love in my heart. What I felt for Nixon and those who honored him was only hate. My hatred for Nixon poisoned me.

Then on January 22, just before our D-Day (for "Debris"), came the news that the peace talks had finally borne fruit. An agreement was reached, the Agreement on Ending the War and Restoring the Peace in Vietnam. It was to be initialed by Kissinger in Paris the next day. Nixon announced the cessation of American combat activities in Vietnam as of that date. All American troops would be withdrawn from South Vietnam within sixty days, and all American prisoners of war would be released and returned to the United

States. The relief I felt was deeply personal, because I knew at once that I would not have to conduct my "raid" on the building I still thought of as my father's house. I would not have to go to jail. I would not have to betray the most precious moments of my life. January 22, 1973, was my thirtieth birthday. As I alone knew, that week also marked the thirtieth anniversary of the day the Pentagon was dedicated.[173]

Not all of my friends had such reasons for relief. To them, the peace accord changed nothing. Nixon was a liar. Saigon was still waging war with U.S. backing. But our troops are out, I and others argued. This is it! The disagreement over the meaning of the Paris Accords and over our plan was fierce enough that friendships cooled. Four or five of the group were determined, in the end, to go ahead with the Pentagon action, even though it would mean manning one truck instead of four. There would no longer be any question of closing off all access to the River Entrance, much less the whole Building. Contemptuous of me and the others who dropped out, the remnant went ahead with the rental, the debris, the dumping on the roadway. Despite hurling bundles of flyers into the air, declaring their intent to shut down the military, their act of protest had no effect on anything. The dumping of debris was assumed to be the accident of inept construction workers. Cars, including limousines, were able to easily circle past the pile of concrete chunks. The Pentagon wasn't shut down. Its work was hindered not at all. The press ignored the action. In fact, no one knew an action had taken place.

I was relieved not to have participated in a deed of such insignificance, but also humiliated by having failed to do so. My friends who carried it out were true heroes of intention, which sometimes is enough. But I was something else.

My Pentagon. I never told my father. My fucking Pentagon. This is the way the war ends, not with a bang but a whimper. How pleased Forrestal would have been by this reduction to the absurd of all that he, had he lived to see it, would have despised. Everything that came within range of the gaze of his bronzed eyes, it seemed, fell under the curse that had ruined him. America had said no to the war in Vietnam in 1968, yet the war raged on for seven more years. Even to oppose the war, it turned out, was to be implicated in it. In its malevolence. In its absurdity. A stupid war. An inconsequential last act of war resistance. Yet even in 1973 the war did not end. Despite the truce, American bombs kept falling. Two more years of carnage. My friends who carried out the dump truck action were right. I was wrong.

And after our "peace," didn't we Americans, by the thousands, find other things with which to concern ourselves? By the time Saigon fell two years later, it could seem a surprise that there were any U.S. personnel still there.

That the last of them were chased out of the country, clambering onto helicopters, was the perfect emblem of the war's disgrace. The shame was so complete that America would live in denial of it for the rest of the century.

The Pentagon, meanwhile, would go on adding to its massive nuclear arsenal. As always, it did this, it said, to prevent the use of the massive nuclear arsenal. Arms control justified the next phase of the arms race. The spirit of Forrestal unleashed. Madness. Paranoia. The demonic. The nation at the mercy of currents rushing toward Niagara. A few salmon swimming upstream, but futilely. A chastened Philip Berrigan looked back on the final disarray of the peace movement and he, too, confessed what the war had done to him. A true prophet, he was often taken to be self-righteous, but he wasn't, not for a moment. "We didn't work the evil and hatred out of ourselves."[174]

....

SEVEN

UPSTREAM

1. NUCLEAR PRIESTHOOD

With the coming of Richard Nixon, the narrative shifts from MAD to madman. Americans are accustomed to looking back on the early seventies as a time when the nation drew perilously close to a brink. In government, a constitutional breakdown was narrowly averted. In the culture at large, extremes became the norm. The outlandish became the ordinary. Confrontation defined encounters between young and old. The civil rights movement reinvented itself as Black Power. The rhetoric of revolution trumped the language of peace. The feeling was, we had lost our way. The world seemed newly fraught with risk. In the sixties, the dangers — Berlin, Cuba, assassinations — had been palpable. Now, however, we were afraid without knowing what, exactly, threatened us. More than anything else, as history begins to show, the thing to fear in those years was the crazy man in the White House and those whom he empowered in the Pentagon.

The story that we have tracked took its fateful turn when the paranoia of James Forrestal found political expression in the military competition between the Soviet Union and the United States — each imagining the worst of the other and preparing to defend against it. By 1970, the standoff between the two enemies was most dramatic along a thousand-mile frontier in Europe, where close to two million men aimed ten thousand tactical nuclear weapons at each other.[1] But it was competition in strategic weapons, above all, that had come to define the "armaments race of a rather desperate character" of which Henry Stimson had warned on September 11, 1945. Well back from the bristling frontier in the heart of Europe stood two nuclear behemoths, poised to hurl at one another — at the earth itself — a total of something like fifty thousand nuclear bombs and warheads, most of which represented Hiroshima many times over.[2]

On the American side, through Republican and Democratic administrations alike, that arms race had overpowered every attempt to curb it, with the result that the United States accumulated a combined strike force of long-range bombers, land-based missiles, and nuclear-armed submarines so insanely in excess of any rational purpose that national security was reduced to a mythical obsession. The Soviets, for their part, with their versions of Forrestal, LeMay, and Nitze, saw no alternative to the project of trying to match this escalation. To Washington's permanent surprise, year in and year out, Moscow proved capable of doing so, even if it meant cannibalizing its civilian economy. A decade after Kennedy had warned of the spurious missile gap, the Soviet Union had acquired hundreds more ICBMs than the United States.

Arms control, despite its being used as a trumping alternative to disarmament, had become the most feverishly held wish of the much-derided doves in Washington,[3] but the militant realists had successfully exploited it as a way of curbing Soviet nuclear growth. The Arms Control and Disarmament Agency migrated over the years, its center of influence, and its preoccupation, shifting from the State Department to the Pentagon. Especially under Nixon, wily arms control negotiators, like Paul Nitze, were less concerned with defusing the nuclear confrontation than with obtaining Soviet concessions that would preserve an American edge in that confrontation. The great arms control breakthrough came, as we saw, on May 26, 1972, when the SALT I agreement and the Antiballistic Missile Treaty were signed by President Nixon and General Secretary Brezhnev at a summit meeting in Moscow. With the ABM Treaty, each superpower agreed to forgo any attempt to defend itself against the strategic forces of the other.[4] Moscow and Washington had their separate reasons for wanting such an agreement, and the détente it symbolized, but the enormous cost of an ABM system was persuasive to both.

This agreement banning defensive systems could satisfy the purposes of a strong ABM proponent like Nitze (recall that he had tapped the young duo Richard Perle and Paul Wolfowitz to argue *for* the ABM in 1969) because it protected the U.S. advantage in the next round of *offensive* weapons development. The Joint Chiefs could support the ABM ban because neither the Air Force nor the Navy was institutionally invested in the antiballistic missile, and the Army, sinking in Vietnam, was equally wounded in the bureaucratic struggle. Despite all this, the ABM Treaty carried forward the counter-weapons momentum that had begun with the Partial Test Ban Treaty in 1963, followed by the Nuclear Non-Proliferation Treaty of 1968. The ABM Treaty, which would remain in force until George W. Bush repudiated it in 2001, was long celebrated as "the backbone of the arms control regime,"[5] and as such, despite the mixed motives of its sponsors, it represented a triumph of nonviolence from within the heart of the war machine.

But ironically, the ABM Treaty also stimulated the deadly next phase of strategic arms growth, and as such it remains a good illustration of the perverse dynamic that turned arms control against itself. While Soviet and American SALT negotiators focused on stopping an antiballistic missile system that was never going to be technically feasible in any case, the Pentagon pursued what came to be called "arms control sweeteners,"[6] the sort of bribes that would ensure military support for SALT I and the ABM Treaty. The Air Force would get a new bomber (the B-1), the Navy a new submarine (the Trident), and the Army a new tank (the Abrams).[7] Paul Nitze was a self-appointed dispenser of such sweeteners. To him, arms control was just another way of channeling arms development.

Ever since Robert McNamara had abandoned a counterforce capability in favor of mutual assured destruction — making any use of nuclear weapons truly "unthinkable" — military planners had been looking for ways to return to targeting the enemy's strike force as such. They wanted to find a way to make the use of nuclear weapons thinkable again, and the idea of attacking the Soviets' nukes, hitting their missile silos and air bases instead of their cities, offered it. And the new, highly accurate technology of multiple warheads, MIRVs, seemed the key. So while arms controllers restrained the ABM, the Pentagon went wild with MIRVs, accumulating warheads — mounting two, three, eventually ten on each missile — to compensate for the perceived Soviet edge in the missiles themselves. MIRVs were more dangerous and more destabilizing than a workable ABM would have been, and it was inevitable that the Soviets would embrace MIRVs, too. Their deployment by both sides over the decade of the 1970s — after détente and arms control breakthroughs — meant a staggering further growth in nukes: the 1,700 strategic missile warheads in the American arsenal (ICBMs and SLBMs, submarine-launched ballistic missiles) quickly grew, approaching 15,000, a figure the Soviets matched.[8] Worse, the deployment of such classic counterforce weapons meant pursuing what amounted to an American first-strike capacity after all, which could be perceived as a shift away from the doctrine of deterrence, to which the Soviets had no choice but to respond.

The Nixon administration, under Melvin Laird (1969–1973) and then James Schlesinger (1973–1975) as secretaries of defense, and especially under Henry Kissinger, the national security adviser (1969–1973) and then secretary of state (1973–1977), set about, in other words, to reverse McNamara.[9] At the most obvious level, McNamara was reversed when the center of gravity in Washington shifted back across the Potomac, Kissinger picking up where John Foster Dulles had left off as the preeminent wielder of American power, in Washington and around the world. This is not to say that the Pentagon lost its dominance — Kissinger, like Dulles before him, shared the Pentagon worldview — but that its dominance, remaining total, transcended the power of its titular head. The Pentagon, which directed the Vietnam War, was responsible for America's greatest mistake in the 1970s, yet it more than ever defined the heart of the American government. This was so for the simple reason that the Pentagon had become, in effect, the nation's nuclear reactor — nuclear power being the source of national power.

James Schlesinger and Henry Kissinger understood the link between the two kinds of power in ways that few others in government had, and they both wanted to secure nuclear-based dominance to foster America's recovery from Vietnam. They sought nothing less than a triumphant return to the position of preeminence the United States had enjoyed after World War II. Experts on nuclear weaponry, Schlesinger and Kissinger were its apostles. They wanted to make nukes usable, and they wanted to make nuclear war winnable. Not that they proposed, exactly, to fight such a war. The idea was that the perceived ability and willingness to fight and win a nuclear war would pay off in power that no nation could resist. Here was the reversal of McNamara, who had renounced any such hope. The question of what "win" meant, of course, would be forever fudged. Corollary to this was the pursuit of a "limited" nuclear capacity — the ability to strike the as yet elusive balance between nuclear attack that would halt Soviet adventurism and the massive strike that would spark all-out nuclear war.

Schlesinger and Kissinger had been Harvard classmates,[10] and though they were bureaucratic rivals and would eventually disagree bitterly over the wisdom of arms control, they shared a basic disposition on the question of nuclear weapons. Kissinger had made his reputation as a nuclear theorist, first with an influential 1955 *Foreign Affairs* article in which he argued for limited nuclear war, and then with his 1957 book *Nuclear Weapons and Foreign Policy,* a foundational text for the doctrine that the mere possession of nukes translates into world-historic power. Not incidentally, both works depended heavily on the influence of Paul Nitze,[11] but unlike Nitze and most other defense intellectuals, Kissinger, like Herman Kahn, found a broad audience for his theorizing. His hyperrational arguments against the Eisenhower era's "unthinkable" doctrine of massive retaliation spawned an image of him (with Kahn) as the prototypical Doctor Strangelove.

Schlesinger, in contrast, was a tweedy pipe smoker, blandly professorial, a far less sensational figure. He began as a RAND theorist, one of the clique that

consistently attempted to rationalize nuclear war, devising an endless succession of fantastic attack scenarios and forever advocating the weapons systems
that might make them plausible. Recall that RAND had begun as an Air Force
research operation founded by Curtis LeMay. Yet during the 1950s LeMay and
other bomber generals famously disdained the civilian intellectuals for what
the generals saw as efforts to rein in their orgiastic approach to strategic planning. LeMay's readiness to launch a nuclear war at the first signs of enemy
mobilization did, in fact, depend on not actually thinking about it too much.
Hence SAC's firm devotion to the all-out — and quite irrational — SIOP targeting plan.

Yet when theorists argued for "flexible response" and "limited strikes"
and "modulated assault," they were effectively making the absolute weapon a
relative one. Ironically, this had the effect of strengthening the bomber generals' hand — and adding to the necessary panoply of nuclear weaponry. Plans
for limited nuclear war always required a much more elaborate strategic force
than the Armageddon scenario. Robert McNamara, depending especially on
the young RAND analyst Daniel Ellsberg, had also attempted to make the nuclear dilemma rational, trying to take control of the SIOP — yet the profound-
est manifestation of the inexorable "Niagara," which has emerged as our subject, came when McNamara's rigorous efforts at control ended by loosening
the nuclear restraints even further (denouncing the ABM while ordering its
development, approving the first step toward MIRV), fixing a Cold War pattern. When Schlesinger replaced Laird as Nixon's secretary of defense in July
1973, joining Kissinger at the pinnacle of power, it was as if the priests of nuclear theology had finally been named its demigods.

2. THE MADMAN THEORY

Any attempt to find a coolly rational way to use nuclear weapons, whether for
their threat value in coercive diplomacy or in an actual war, however limited,
presumed that the people in charge of such use were themselves rational.
With Nixon, that presumption, in short order, was shown to be a problem, as
insiders like Kissinger and Schlesinger were in a position to see. As the late-
twentieth-century release of classified documents and tape transcripts of the
Nixon era make clear, we are talking here about a personality disorder beyond
the merely eccentric. The issue was neither Nixon's brooding self-pity nor his
contemptuous disregard for those who disagreed with him. The publication
of various records of Nixon's taped conversations and rants have put on full
display his vulgarity, pettiness, and prejudice, and his regular drunkenness.[12]

But with the ongoing release of transcripts of secret White House recordings, what has generated insufficient alarm — and scandalously little reflection by nuclear theorists — are the revelations of Nixon's insane flirtation with the actual use of nuclear weapons.

The fact that the world survived the decades-long nuclear standoff of the Cold War has led to the complacent assumption that nuclear war just wasn't fated to happen. Most historians and political scientists have defined deterrence as a doctrine that "worked," with the Soviet Union and the United States having cooperated to erect a reliable structure of mutual stability.[13] But a close look at the erratic way Nixon exercised his responsibility as the man in charge of America's arsenal suggests that "stability" is a fantasy of hindsight.

Given how he behaved during a period in which relatively eased superpower tensions gave rise to the term "détente," it is hard not to conclude that Richard Nixon, if he had been challenged, say, as Kennedy was over Berlin or Cuba, would have ignited the holocaust. As it was, Nixon repeatedly ordered his military forces, including the nation's strategic nuclear forces, to a level of alert one step short of nuclear war.[14] Except for Kennedy during the Cuban Missile Crisis, no other president has done this even once, and it is instructive to note that the Soviet Union never ordered its nuclear forces to such a state of alert.[15] Under Nixon, U.S. strategic forces were brought to a war footing at least three times,[16] and his closest advisers worried that, for his own insane purposes, he would do it even more.

"I call it the madman theory, Bob," Nixon told his aide H. R. Haldeman. "I want the North Vietnamese to believe that I've reached the point that I might do anything to stop the war. We'll just slip the word to them that 'for God's sake, you know Nixon is obsessed about Communism. We can't restrain him when he's angry — and he has his hand on the nuclear button' — and Ho Chi Minh himself will be in Paris in two days begging for peace."[17] Six months into his presidency, Nixon's frustration with Hanoi's refusal to budge in its demands at the Paris peace talks was extreme, and he put his madman ploy in gear. For this account, I depend on the political scientists Scott D. Sagan and Jeremi Suri.

From October 10, 1969, to the end of the month, the U.S. military was ordered to full global war readiness alert without any provocation, and with no explanation given to commanders regarding the alert's purpose. Nuclear-armed fighter planes were sent to civilian airports, missile countdown procedures were initiated, missile-bearing submarines were dispersed, long-range bombers were launched, siop targeting was begun. On October 27, in the climactic action designed to make it seem the madman was loose, the Strategic Air Command was ordered to dispatch B-52s loaded with thermonuclear weapons toward the Soviet Union. Eighteen of the bombers took off from bases in the United States in an operation named Giant Lance. "The bombers crossed Alaska," Sagan and Suri write, "were refueled in midair by KC-135 tanker aircraft, and then flew in oval patterns toward the Soviet Union and back, on eighteen-hour 'vigils' over the northern polar ice cap."[18] The ominous flight of these H-bombers to, and then at, the edge of Soviet territory continued for three days. This was all done in total secrecy — not kept secret from the Soviets, of course, since they knew quite well what was happening, but from the American people.[19]

Nixon's purpose, apparently, was to intimidate the North Vietnamese and their Soviet sponsor into thinking he might use nuclear weapons against them. He was under the impression that Eisenhower's threat to use the atomic bomb against North Korea in 1953 had been decisive in Moscow's pressuring its Asian ally to come to terms in that conflict, and he wanted a replay of that strategy. Nixon's feigned throwing of the nuclear punch, however, was far less subtle, and less manageable, than any threat Eisenhower might have made. In assuming that such a bluff had worked before, Nixon was almost surely mistaken, since, as we saw, the Communist decision to accept the Korean truce had far more to do with moderates taking over in the Kremlin after the death of Stalin than any nuclear fear. There was an echo of this timing in Nixon's move, since the North Vietnamese leader, Ho Chi Minh, had died only weeks before, in September.[20] But Nixon sought no more of an opening in Ho's death than Eisenhower had in Stalin's. Ironically, Nixon was moving the world toward global Armageddon because American antiwar politics made it impossible for him to launch the massive, but far less drastic, conventional bombing campaign against North Vietnam that he preferred.

As it unfolded, his secret nuclear alert seemed to threaten Moscow far more than Hanoi. The military commanders who were implementing Nixon's madman ploy may not have known what was behind it, but Secretary of Defense Laird did know, and he vigorously opposed the alert as wildly dangerous. Nevertheless, it was carried out, mainly because Nixon's key adviser, Henry Kissinger, in the words of his biographer, "bought into the madman theory."[21] Kissinger, who made an art of sycophantic manipulation of Nixon, praised him in the midst of this adventure for having "the guts of a riverboat gambler."[22] The unclassified transcripts of private conversations between Kissinger and Nixon show them to have been far more cavalier about nuclear weapons than any of Nixon's predecessors had been: "I'd rather use the nuclear bomb," Nixon said at one point. "The nuclear bomb. Does that bother you? I just want you to think big, Henry, for Christ's sake."[23]

The madman gamble was perilous beyond anything Nixon and Kissinger imagined. For one thing, their assumption that the president could actually control the nuclear force once it was brought to the edge of war was false.

Most obviously, the SIOP procedures for the delivery, arming, and firing of nuclear weapons, which had been put in place by Curtis LeMay in the early 1950s, were still in force (despite McNamara), giving military officers far more responsibility for nukes than the politicians could have realized. That meant the president was risking his own irrelevance to the process he had set in motion. Beyond that, the command, control, communication, and intelligence systems on which Nixon depended for his sense of mastery over the alert were subject to breakdowns, of which he remained mostly ignorant.

For example, the general in charge of the Strategic Air Command, on his own authority, without informing Washington and without complete knowledge of the alert's purpose, ordered the B-52 squadrons based on Guam not to participate in the nuclear alert. This contradicted what Nixon and Kissinger thought was happening. Unlike SAC bombers everywhere else, these Pacific-based warplanes were not loaded with nuclear bombs, and they were not poised to deliver them. The SAC commander decided this because the Guam crews, unlike B-52 pilots elsewhere, were actively at war, carpet-bombing Southeast Asia. They were already stressed to the breaking point by the round-the-clock missions they had been flying over Vietnam. Furthermore, SAC had vigorously complained that those tactical missions undercut the Guam B-52s' ability, if called upon, to perform their strategic role, so SAC was not about to show Washington that they could carry out such a mission now. The general's order both reflected a combat limit and sought to make a bureaucratic point. Yet that order, unknown to Nixon, was fraught with an unintended implication, unknown to the general, which could have sent up the balloon.

The Soviets, depending on agents on Guam and electronic surveillance of various kinds, had to be aware that those particular B-52s, alone of SAC's entire fleet, were not brought to nuclear readiness, yet the madman signal Nixon wanted to send — a threatened attack against North Vietnam — would have required the nuclear arming first and foremost of those very planes. When the SAC commander exempted them from the alert, the Soviets could have reasonably concluded only that the coming nuclear assault was global, not regional, and that it was aimed at their own homeland, not the nation in Southeast Asia.[24]

More extraordinary, and making the ploy even more dangerous than Laird and others thought, was Nixon and Kissinger's apparent failure to take into account that in those same weeks a border dispute was simmering between China and the Soviet Union.[25] The two Communist rivals were themselves approaching war footing, and Moscow already had reasons to be wary of America's tilt toward Beijing. Thus, when the Soviets picked up signals of an American nuclear countdown, they would have had every reason to assume that the United States was preparing to attack in support of Beijing, perhaps launching a preemption of Moscow's own contemplated attack against China. This other circumstance, that is, meant the Soviets could have seen the American threat not as irrational, as Nixon intended, but as consistent with a reasonable strategic purpose.

As if such accidental complications were not unsettling enough, as Sagan and Suri point out, the whole madman theory of coercion was flawed in its essence, depending as it did on twisted logic that assumed an adversary would respond to a calculated show of irrationality with something other than irrationality of its own.[26] Presumably, Nixon wanted a frightened Moscow to persuade a frightened Hanoi to change its behavior in Paris as a way of heading off Washington's insanity. Rational Russians would save the world from crazy Americans. Come again?

The history of U.S. edginess in relation to threats from the Soviet Union and the permanent fact of the hair trigger on which Curtis LeMay had put the Strategic Air Command suggest that if the Soviets ever sent their bomber force over the North Pole, in its own version of Giant Lance, thousands of nuclear bombs and warheads would have been hurled at once from silos in the Dakotas, from missile launchers on submarines around the world, and from SAC bases throughout the Western Hemisphere. In other words, if Brezhnev and Gromyko behaved as Nixon and Kissinger did in October 1969, the world would almost certainly have been plunged into nuclear horror. Ever since Forrestal, the American military establishment had assumed (and would continue to assume) that virtuous America was too humane ever to start a nuclear war, while also taking for granted that the demon Kremlin, seeing an advantage, would not hesitate to do so. That contradiction, too, informed Nixon's riverboat gamble.

In the event, the Soviet Union did not respond irrationally to the madman ploy. The North Vietnamese ignored it. The secrecy of both regimes has made it impossible to know for sure what they made of the American alert.

One thing suggests, however, that the Soviets understood with new urgency the importance of getting the nuclear madness under control. On October 25, in the midst of Nixon's alert, in a move worthy of a Russian chess master, Moscow proposed a date and a place for the start of arms reduction negotiations — November 17, barely three weeks later, in Helsinki. The United States accepted, and the long-delayed SALT talks began.[27]

That process led to Nixon's triumph at the Moscow summit in May 1972. We already saw that both sides agreed to the ABM Treaty, to head off the huge expense of missile defenses, but Nixon's political purpose just then was also served by the arms control breakthrough. His reelection campaign was heating up, and Democrats were challenging him on the still flaming war. The

SALT agreements deflected the challenge, reinforcing the myth of Nixon as a peacemaker,[28] and the following November Nixon trounced George McGovern, the antiwar candidate.[29] But the Watergate burglary, just weeks after the Moscow summit, had set in train events that again brought the United States to the nuclear edge. Only this time the madman bit was no ploy.

The dangerous climax of the Yom Kippur War, in October 1973, coincided with the collapse of Nixon's authority as president, when, during the Watergate crisis, the infamous "Saturday night massacre" took place, as Attorney General Elliot Richardson and his deputy resigned rather than carry out Nixon's order to fire special prosecutor Archibald Cox. At 7:05 P.M. on the night of October 24, Henry Kissinger received a phone call from Ambassador Anatoly Dobrynin, who delivered an ultimatum from the Soviet leadership: if the United States did not join forces with the Soviet Union for a peacekeeping intervention in Egypt, to separate the Israeli and Egyptian armies, the Soviets would intervene alone.

In one of his memoirs, Kissinger reports that he had to interrupt the Dobrynin call to take a call from his "drunken friend." Kissinger, being discreet, does not refer in his memoir to the extent of Nixon's early evening inebriation, but he describes him, in that phone call, as being "as agitated and emotional as I had ever heard him." The memoir goes on: "Talk of his possible impeachment increased daily. He expressed the hope that at a briefing scheduled for the next morning I would tell the Congressional leadership about his central, indispensable role in managing the Mideast crisis. He had already urged me to call some Senators to make this pitch — a symptom of the extremity in which this proud man felt himself. He spoke of his political end, even his physical demise: 'They are doing it because of their desire to kill the President. And they may succeed. I may physically die.'"[30] In 1949, the secretary of defense had declined into a state of clinical paranoia; now it was the president.

Kissinger abruptly told Nixon of Dobrynin's call, and in his memoir makes no pretense that Nixon had any role in shaping a response to "the gravest foreign policy crisis of the Nixon presidency." Telling the president of the Soviet move, Kissinger reports, "I said curtly that we would veto it."[31] That night, Nixon continued to drink. Kissinger, on his own authority, assembled the National Security Council in the White House Situation Room, although without the president or vice president — "the statutory membership of the National Security Council minus these two men."[32] So it was that without any input from, much less the control by, the nation's elected leaders, Kissinger and the others decided how to respond to the Soviet ultimatum. What they did — "playing chicken," as Kissinger put it[33] — was to order America's worldwide military forces to yet another nuclear alert. If Kissinger felt entitled to take his turn to play the riverboat gambler, it was because Nixon had already sanctioned such nuclear gamesmanship.

Again the alert was intended to be secret, not from Moscow but from the American people. The nuclear alert — the start of SIOP targeting — was meant to put the Soviets on notice that if they carried out their threat to intervene in Egypt, they were risking all-out nuclear war with the United States. The point should be emphasized that the demonized Soviet Union never, ever rolled the dice with the future of the planet like this. When British Prime Minister Edward Heath learned of this American move to the brink, he called the White House to protest, but Kissinger refused to put him through to the president because Nixon was drunk.[34]

3. THE SCHLESINGER DOCTRINE

One of those at the Situation Room table, sharing in Kissinger's assumption of authority, was Secretary of Defense James Schlesinger. In his mind, this must have been the precedent for the extraordinary step he took later in the Watergate crisis, as Nixon's last days and hours as president were running out. With his enemies closing in on him, the desperate Nixon unburdened himself to aides in the privacy of the Oval Office, and published transcripts show how emotionally unhinged he became. His aides regarded him as psychologically unbalanced. Nixon's power over the nation's nuclear arsenal seemed, dangerously, a particular preoccupation both of the president and those around him. Nuclear authority seemed personal to him, and it was something he felt free to flaunt even outside his inner circle. The historian Janne Nolan, for example, tells of Nixon's bragging to Senator Alan Cranston, "Why, I can go into my office and pick up the telephone and in twenty-five minutes seventy million people will be dead."[35] This is just the opposite of Lyndon Johnson's fantasy, that if he ever ordered a nuclear attack, his subordinates would reply, "Fuck you, Mister President."

Nixon might have thought he had the power to create such a catastrophe, but in his waning time as president it was not true. Meeting at the Pentagon with General George S. Brown of the Air Force, the chairman of the Joint Chiefs of Staff, in July, a few weeks before Nixon's resignation, Schlesinger issued the directive that "any emergency order coming from the president" be first shown to him, the secretary of defense, before any action was taken.

Schlesinger did not make his directive more explicit. He could have been cautioning against a Nixon attempt to use the military to support him in defiance of the Supreme Court or the Congress — a military coup. But Nixon's ultimate authority over the nuclear chain of command was certainly at issue, too, especially once his mental stability had come into question. It seems reasonable to infer that Schlesinger was prepared to thwart Nixon's constitutional authority as commander in chief. And it seems reasonable to think that Schlesinger was also ready to insert himself between Henry Kissinger and the nation's military, if Kissinger tried again to exercise authority of the kind Schlesinger had seen him assume in October 1973.

Immediately after his meeting with Schlesinger, General Brown summoned his fellow Chiefs. "I've just had the strangest conversation with the Secretary of Defense," he reported.[36]

Schlesinger, in other words, moved smoothly into the power vacuum created by Watergate in the last days of Nixon's administration — and in the early days of Gerald Ford's, he sought to stay there. Even though he was, as secretary of defense, bound to support the president's policies, Schlesinger, in the summer of Nixon's demise, did not hesitate to openly oppose the SALT process in which Nixon and Kissinger were investing hopes for a rescue of Nixon's reputation. The Pentagon objected to SALT by then because it seemed to aim at nuclear parity with the Soviet Union instead of maintaining superiority. American Cold War orthodoxy had as its foundational doctrine Winston Churchill's rejection, in his 1946 "Iron Curtain" speech, of "balance" of power in favor of "preponderance,"[37] and the credentialed statesmen of Washington had sought to give at least lip service to this purpose ever since.

Was Kissinger, in sponsoring SALT, guilty of heresy? When challenged on this by reporters, he blurted, "What, in the name of God, is strategic superiority? What is the significance of it, politically, militarily, operationally, at these levels of numbers? What do you do with it?"[38] Kissinger had finally arrived at his version of the Stimson position, acknowledging that in the nuclear age the idea of superiority is meaningless, and decrying an absurd, open-ended arms race to which the Pentagon remained addicted. In Schlesinger, who was still devoted to the old orthodoxy, Kissinger had a true nemesis.

Schlesinger was supported in all this by Paul Nitze, who resigned from Nixon's SALT delegation in June 1974 because he thought Nixon was pursuing an unfavorable deal with the Soviets for his own Watergate-related purposes. Nitze and Schlesinger teamed up to oppose any SALT agreement. More ambitiously, Schlesinger, untainted by the Watergate turmoil that was paralyzing the White House, saw an opportunity to revise the nation's nuclear doctrine at last. Paradoxically, while taking steps designed to prevent the actual use of nuclear weapons in a period of crisis — his order countering the White

House — Schlesinger wanted to loosen the restraints on nuclear use during times of normalcy.

It is another manifestation of the odd mystical energy attached to the date 9/11 to note that on September 11, 1974, just a month after Nixon was forced from office on August 9, James Schlesinger, in testimony before the Senate Armed Services Committee, put forward a major new rationale for limited nuclear war. In speeches prior to this appearance, he had outlined the "Schlesinger doctrine," arguing for first-strike capability, for a revised SIOP that aimed at fighting and prevailing in nuclear war, and for the reduction of "inhibitions on the use of nuclear weapons for the resolution of political conflicts." The senators had to be shocked to find themselves confronted with a secretary of defense, as Janne Nolan put it in describing Schlesinger's position, "discussing holocaust in cold-blooded terms."[39]

One of the ironies of this long narrative is that the senator who most vigorously challenged Schlesinger on this occasion was Stuart Symington of Missouri, who, as secretary of the Air Force in the late 1940s, had done so much to put in place the massive-retaliation doctrine, which had led to the idea that nuclear weapons were not to be used — a doctrine that Schlesinger now wanted to leave behind. Symington, who began as an ardent Cold War militant, ended his career, without having changed his attitudes at all, being dismissed as soft.

4. ENTER RUMSFELD AND CHENEY

If Symington, a ghostly figure from the beginning, passes from the scene with the coming of Gerald Ford, two new figures enter it with power. Ford had been the House minority leader, a politician with no significant experience in foreign policy. His insecurities as the nation's first unelected president were legion, and they were not helped by his having to depend on two figures, Kissinger and Schlesinger, who were alike in their condescension toward Ford. Kissinger's knack for coating his superiority with servile ingratiation served him better with the new president than did Schlesinger's unvarnished hubris.

At first Ford felt he had no choice but to pursue Nixon's unfinished détente agenda with the Soviet Union. Following Kissinger's lead, he met with Brezhnev at Vladivostok on November 23, 1974, less than three months after becoming president. There, the American and Soviet leaders agreed on the basic principle that would inform a SALT II accord: equal levels of strategic weapons.[40] Each side would still have thousands of nukes and delivery systems — "arms control" once again legitimizing sky-high numbers — but this was considered "parity." Any such retreat from nuclear superiority remained anathema to hawks in the Senate, especially Senator Henry Jackson of Washington and his protégé Richard Perle; to the Pentagon and the Joint Chiefs; and to the secretary of defense. To all such SALT opponents, anything Moscow would agree to was for that very reason suspect; the negotiations were a sucker's game pure and simple. Cold War doctrine, in place since Truman, took Soviet dishonesty for granted. Commies would lie, they would cheat, they would blow up the world for no good reason. America, so the doctrine said, was different.

To Jackson, Perle, Nitze, and their ilk, the Soviets were obviously trying to get America to settle for parity while secretly plowing ahead toward superiority of their own. The old paranoia, it seemed, was still fueling the debate. Bowing to such pressures, as Ford eyed his own unsteady political future (and saw the anti-détente polemicist Ronald Reagan fixing his sights on him), he distanced himself from his own Vladivostok position.

The man on whom Ford depended as he sought to navigate between the Scylla and Charybdis of Kissinger and Schlesinger was his White House chief of staff, a former fellow congressman named Donald Rumsfeld. As a conservative Republican from an affluent Illinois district, Rumsfeld had routinely voted against legislative vestiges of the War on Poverty, federal programs designed to help the poor, but that had not prevented Nixon from naming him director of the Office of Economic Opportunity, the antipoverty agency. Rumsfeld's job was to gut it. This was the beginning of the right-wing Republican campaign to roll back the "big government" bequeathed by Lyndon Johnson's Great Society, a movement that would gain great success under Ronald Reagan. Rumsfeld's two young deputies there were Richard Cheney and Frank Carlucci. Rumsfeld had left OEO to serve in the Nixon White House. He was spared the poison draught of Watergate by having been named ambassador to NATO at the end of 1972. When Ford succeeded Nixon, he immediately turned to his trusted ally Rumsfeld for help. And Rumsfeld, appointed chief of staff, once again named Cheney as his deputy.

At Ford's elbow, Rumsfeld outmaneuvered Henry Kissinger, undercutting the uncertain new president's faith in the entire project of détente. (Its opponents loved to point out that the French word meant both "relaxed tension" and "trigger.")[41] Rumsfeld was one of the first to resuscitate, from its Truman-era iterations, the moral argument against the Nixon-Kissinger realpolitik project of making big-power deals with the wicked Communists, an appeal to which Ford, the moralistic midwesterner, was susceptible. It was not only that the Soviets were not to be trusted, but the link between arms control concessions and Soviet behavior on human rights, in particular emigration policies and the repressive treatment of dissidents, had to be reestablished. Détente was taken to be a form of incipient ethical relativism, a signal of the Vietnam-induced rot of American character.

Rumsfeld had a hard-liner's sympathy with Schlesinger, but the arrogant secretary of defense had impossibly alienated his insecure superior, and Ford wanted to escape his shadow even more than Kissinger's. In the fall of 1975 — a "Halloween massacre" — Ford's chief of staff made his move. Now thoroughly under Rumsfeld's sway, the president fired Schlesinger outright,[42] removed Kissinger from his position as national security adviser, banishing him to the relative harmlessness of Foggy Bottom, and replaced William Colby at the CIA with George H. W. Bush. (Rumsfeld saw Bush as his own main rival to become Ford's vice president in 1976, and the intelligence post removed him from contention.) In the most dramatic move of all, Rumsfeld had Ford appoint as Schlesinger's replacement at the Pentagon none other than himself.[43]

These maneuvers were misunderstood at the time as a victory for Kissinger (he was replaced as national security adviser by his own deputy, Brent Scowcroft), and the firing of the anti-Soviet extremist Schlesinger dismayed those who always worried about America's going soft. No one was more dismayed, however, than the old Cold Warrior Paul Nitze, who took Schlesinger's dismissal, after the Vladivostok capitulation, as the occasion to revive his Committee on the Present Danger. The committee warned again, as Nitze's group first had in the early 1950s, of a Soviet push toward superiority, the opening of yet another "window of vulnerability."[44] But now the warning, even more drastic, was that the Soviet Union was quite willing to launch a nuclear attack through that window, no matter the cost in human life. The Soviets — here was the consistent theme — were ontologically and morally different from us.

Nitze, of course, emphasized present U.S. weakness by regretting the loss of former strength, though in former times he had always emphasized weakness. And no one ever seemed to call Nitze on the simple fact that every window of vulnerability of which he warned (1952, 1957, 1962) had closed without a problem. There was surely a personal element in Nitze's readiness to fault Ford's new secretary of defense, no matter how hawkish, because as a congressman Rumsfeld had, as we saw, humiliated Nitze during congressional hearings in 1963.

It is hard to believe that observers could have taken Rumsfeld's maneuvers as anything but a triumph of traditional anti-Soviet ideology, given what they put in place. Rumsfeld immediately sought major increases in defense spending, reversing the dramatic downturn in the percentage of the gross national product that had been spent on the military under Nixon.[45] Rumsfeld's move to the Pentagon marked the definitive end of détente, destroyed any chances for SALT under Ford, and laid the groundwork for a post-Vietnam generational shift that would aim at, and ultimately accomplish, the restoration of America's overwhelming military dominance, a supremacy unapologetically based on nuclear weapons.

Among those empowered by Rumsfeld were his acolyte Cheney[46] and his factotum Carlucci, each of whom would follow him as secretary of defense, together with Richard Perle and Paul Wolfowitz, who would, from within the government and outside it, be permanent Pentagon tribunes of American hegemony. They would be joined by the likes of Colin Powell, Richard Armitage, and Condoleezza Rice. The group Rumsfeld put in place, shaping policy through the Reagan years and then coming fully into their own when Rumsfeld returned to the E-ring office over the River Entrance in the early twenty-first century, would eventually become known as the Vulcans, a name James Mann used as the title of his book on the group. What they all had in common was a hunger for martial dominance that was born of the failure of Vietnam.

Ford came into office at the final humiliating moments of the Southeast Asian war. Nineteen seventy-four was the year in which the South Vietnamese resistance to the Communists began to collapse. In order to gain South Vietnamese President Nguyen Van Thieu's agreement to the 1973 Paris Accords, which enabled the United States to withdraw its combat forces, Nixon, manipulated by Kissinger, had signed a secret letter guaranteeing "my assurance of continued assistance . . . We will respond with full force should the settlement be violated by North Vietnam." Kissinger had publicly denied in 1973 that there was any such private assurance, but Thieu had it, and when his forces fell in 1974, he called on Ford to fulfill it. Ford wanted to, and so did his crew at the Pentagon, but by then Congress had cut off funds for any resumption of U.S. combat activity in Vietnam. Rumsfeld, Cheney, Perle, Wolfowitz, Armitage, Powell, and Rice all took the American reneging quite personally. They came into real power, as it were, powerlessly.[47]

Never again. They deliberately engineered an act of global revenge for the disgrace of Vietnam, a war that would be remembered, astoundingly, as an instance of American victimization. To overcome it, the Vulcans aimed at achieving nothing less than a fulfillment of the post–World War II dream of unchallenged American supremacy. Forrestal triumphant after all. Rumsfeld led the charge. And like Forrestal, he not only saw enemies that did not exist, he took their invisibility as proof of their existence.[48]

In a foreshadowing of the hard-edged belligerence that would define this group when they took full control of the Pentagon in the early twenty-first century, the first thing they did under Gerald Ford was to shape, in violation of America's obligations under the Paris Accords, a punitive embargo of Vietnam that would choke its economy for twenty years. As the Vulcans' chronicler James Mann points out, whereas their predecessors, the "Wise Men" and "the best and the brightest," were spawned in the nurturing waters of Wall Street and Harvard, respectively, Rumsfeld's circle of true believers emerged from the culture, ideology, and moralism of the Pentagon itself.[49] The Building, it would seem, was coming at last into its own.

Its triumph, however, would not come easily. In the first post-Vietnam instance of military challenge, within weeks of the fall of Saigon, Ford's team would stumble badly — and an ominous shadow would fall over the future. A U.S. cargo ship, the SS *Mayagüez,* was raided by a Cambodian naval force in May 1975. Another of the Kissinger legacies in the region had been the fall of Cambodia, a month before, to the Khmer Rouge, and the new Communist regime was flexing its muscles. The ship's thirty-eight American crew members were taken prisoner. Rumsfeld, with Kissinger's concurrence, persuaded Ford to bypass diplomacy and display his toughness, first by bombing the port city of Kompong Som and then by ordering an operation aimed at rescuing the crew. Ford denounced "an act of piracy," and U.S. Marines, like swashbucklers, swung aboard the captured ship (the first such hostile boarding at sea since 1826), only to find it abandoned. In another foreshadowing, the Rumsfeld circle had based its action on ridiculously flawed intelligence. Hundreds of other Marines invaded an island where the captured crewmen were thought to be. In the battle there, forty Americans were killed — for nothing. It was then discovered that the *Mayagüez* crew had been released unharmed shortly after being captured, set adrift in a Thai fishing vessel.[50] Despite vast differences in scale and intention, the incompetent rescue attempt was a kind of overture, complete with the music of bombing, for the war Rumsfeld would orchestrate against Iraq beginning in 2003. The *Mayagüez* action was overwhelmingly popular with Americans, lethal to young U.S. soldiers — and it was unnecessary.

5. JIMMY CARTER'S QUESTION

Jimmy Carter was a southern boy who'd followed a beaten path to a military academy, in his case Annapolis. He was commissioned a naval officer just after the end of World War II and assigned to the elite submarine service. The first generation of nuclear subs was under development then, and Carter always counted himself a protégé of Admiral Hyman Rickover, the father of the nuclear Navy. Carter should therefore have been a friend to all things nuclear. Yet his naval career was interrupted by the death of his father, and in 1953 he returned to Georgia and a life of farming and small-town politics. By the time he was president, he had set himself more firmly against nuclear weapons than any major figure in government since Henry Stimson. Then, despite himself, Carter turned out in the end to be the monster's next sponsor. Ahab all over again.

It began even before his inauguration in January 1977. Carter had run for president with a promise, "I will never lie to you," but in some dark way he lied to himself. As an openly religious moralist, he set himself not only against the chicanery of Richard Nixon but also, implicitly, against the un-principled realpolitik of Henry Kissinger. In that, Carter echoed the extremist Republicans who undercut Ford from the right. Yet there was a split in Carter, and eventually it would lead to a fatal inconsistency and a final failure of his most important effort. The split could be seen early on. As a candidate, he took advice (and money) from Paul Nitze and the fervent anti-Soviet scholar Zbigniew Brzezinski, as well as from more moderate figures like Cyrus Vance, Harold Brown, Paul Warnke, and Leslie Gelb. These moderates, although veterans of significant Pentagon experience, were, in the words of Fred Kaplan, "all doves, men who had opposed counterforce, who thought nuclear weapons had little utility beyond deterring war, who held a more sanguine view toward the Soviets than [hard-liners] felt was responsible." Such doves were offered positions in the new administration, as was the hawkish Brzezinski, but not Nitze, whom Carter dismissed as "arrogant."[51]

Carter claimed to want to rescue détente, was emphatically in favor of the SALT process, and had ridiculed Gerald Ford for backing away from the agreement he had reached with the Soviets at Vladivostok. That Ford took Rumsfeld's advice on these same questions made him vulnerable to Carter's critique from the left, and probably cost him the election. But Carter was also a supreme moralizer, a vigorous critic of Moscow's ruthless suppression of dissidence, and a linker of arms control and human rights — all of which, in the end, helped doom him to follow Ford into electoral humiliation.

Carter's emphasis on human rights — he said his devotion to the principle was "absolute"[52] — is often understood as having come at the expense of attempts to engage the Kremlin in the arms control process, and looked at solely from the American side, it is true that demands tied to human rights undermined détente. But looked at from the other side, the entire human rights movement, which had gained strength in the mid-1970s, had a slow but undermining effect on Soviet tyranny. Beginning with the Helsinki Agreement in 1975,[53] dissidents behind the Iron Curtain had a charter and a commission, and eventually their efforts, in the name of human rights, would bring about a far greater change in the Soviet system than anything the Pentagon did.

But Carter took nuclear weapons as absolute, too. As if he had been privy to Nixon's dangerous, but at the time unknown, mismanagement of the nuclear arsenal, Carter came into office determined to save the world from the threat that Nixon had done so much to exacerbate. When a new president gets his first briefing on the nuclear enterprise over which he has sole authority, the experience, in one historian's image, is like "taking a drink of water from a fire hose."[54] But Carter, as a young naval officer at the other end of the SIOP, had come to know the nuclear monster firsthand, and now he wanted, above all, to break it.

It is a measure of the rigidity of American Cold War assumptions that his attempt to alter the Cold War dynamic is remembered by hawks and doves alike, on both sides of the Iron Curtain, as wrong-headed. Carter's fellow son of the South, Robert E. Lee, in an oft-quoted remark, said, "It is well that war is so terrible, or we should grow too fond of it."[55] Judging by how "fond" the various players in the Cold War drama were by the time of Carter's ascendancy — fondness measured by an across-the-board refusal to alter the status quo at his invitation — a cold war was not terrible enough.

On January 12, 1977, a week before his inauguration, Carter summoned the Joint Chiefs of Staff to a meeting at Blair House, across the street from the White House. The president-elect sat through a detailed briefing in which, with charts, maps, and pointers, he was told how seriously outgunned the United States was by the Soviet Union in almost every category of weapons, from nuclear warheads to tanks. Carter thanked the Chiefs for the briefing, then stunned them when, brushing past the expected discussion of budget requirements and security needs, he asked them the one question he had brought to the meeting: "How long would it take to reduce the number of nuclear weapons currently in our arsenal?"

What? The chairman, General George Brown, did not understand what Carter meant. The Chiefs exchanged looks. The president-elect asked again, "How could we cut the number of missiles? What would it take to get the number down to a few hundred?"[56] Down to two hundred, say. Even with a cut of thousands of warheads, such an earth-destroying arsenal would still be enough to deter the Soviets, no? Carter was asking a question, but it was clear to everyone in the room that he was putting an agenda item on the table, his first one. However much he had supported SALT, Carter was attuned to its built-in contradiction, understanding how arms control was serving as a cover for the ongoing expansion of nuclear arms. He surely knew, for example, that since SALT had been agreed to in 1972, less than five years before, the number of warheads on the MIRVed missile force had doubled. At that moment, the number of atomic and hydrogen bombs on the earth, stockpiled as well as deployed, had topped one hundred thousand, with each side holding approximately half.[57]

Carter's implicit proposal to the Chiefs, to get the number of strategic weapons down to two hundred, more than enough to obliterate the Soviet Union, would, in fact, become a common one only a few years later, with such reputable figures as Robert McNamara, George Kennan, and McGeorge Bundy calling for "deep cuts" in the strategic arsenal.[58] But in 1977, such an application of common sense to the nuclear project, involving not just a cap on the escalating accumulation of nukes but a drastic cut in the arsenal, even if achieved through bilateral negotiations, was beyond the pale. Nixon was not insane, Carter was. This was not arms control, it was disarmament.

Carter's question was met with mortifying silence. "You could hear a pin drop," said one participant later.[59] Brzezinski, present because he was by then Carter's chief foreign policy adviser, was humiliated. It was as if Carter had gathered America's corporate chieftains to tell them that he intended "to solve the problem of poverty by dissolving their corporations and distributing their assets to the poor."[60]

What Carter's critics, ever since, seemed not to understand is that he was instinctively trying to undo not just an institutional mindset but a mystical construct. Carter would be maligned for his attention to other unspoken American assumptions — how, during the energy crisis of the late 1970s, for example, he presumed to speak of U.S. "self-indulgence and consumption."[61] Against the Joint Chiefs, he was daring to challenge nothing less than the "invention," in Margaret Mead's word,[62] of the Cold War itself, a system of competition in armaments that was a substitute for the hot battle of actual war.

The Cold War arms race, despite its risks and ever more exorbitant costs, had served as its own source of order, and even of control. Carter grasped, as if alone, that the initiative in the arms race had more or less consistently belonged to the United States: the Soviet buildups in the late 1940s, the early 1950s, the early to mid-1960s, and the 1970s had followed, respectively, Hiroshima, NSC-68, the missile gap escalation, and the Nixon-Laird embrace of MIRV. America deployed its atomic bomb in 1945; Moscow did it in 1949. America's intercontinental bomber came in 1948, Moscow's in 1955. America's hydrogen bomb in 1952, Moscow's in 1955. America's submarine-launched ballistic missile in 1960, Moscow's in 1968. America's multiple-warhead missile in 1964, Moscow's in 1973. America's MIRV in 1970, Moscow's in 1975. And now America was ahead on the long-range cruise missile.[63]

If America could take the lead on the way up the arms ladder, why not on the way down? This impulse was given symbolic importance when Carter

put forward the name of Theodore Sorensen for the position of CIA director, since Sorensen was the main author of Kennedy's American University
speech, which sought the same thing.[64] Carter grasped, in other words, that
there was nothing eternal about the arms race, nothing absolute. And he understood that most of the responsibility for the inexorable escalation belonged to Washington. Men had launched it, Pentagon men. Men could stop
it, Pentagon men. But not the Pentagon men he was talking to.

When the Chiefs returned to the Building across the river, their open ridicule of the incoming commander in chief would be called the "revolt of the
generals," a sequel, decades later, to the "revolt of the admirals," which had
marked the initiation of the strategic arsenal when the Air Force had been
given its keys. Indeed, Carter's idea threatened to open that old wound, since
he assumed that the two hundred missiles to which the American force could
be reduced would be based on submarines. But not even the Navy took his
idea seriously.[65]

If Brzezinski sought to temper the idealistic hopes of his new boss, he
had not succeeded a week later, when Carter stood before the nation as its
new president. An inaugural address is an occasion for high-flown rhetoric,
but when Carter spoke, his heartfelt expression could seem to signal the true
end of what Gerald Ford had called "our long national nightmare."

"The American dream endures," Carter said. "We must once again have
faith in our country — and in one another." I had been present to see every
president since Roosevelt inaugurated, but in 1977 I was far away in every
sense. The years of Nixon and the shameful last chapters of the war in Vietnam over which Ford had presided had destroyed my easy affection for
America. My whole life had been upended. An early worshiper of the FBI, I
had only contempt for what Hoover's men had done to friends and heroes of
mine, although my brother Brian remained an FBI agent. Yet some of those
same friends and heroes had matched their fiercest critics in self-righteousness, leaving me behind. I had resigned from the priesthood, a repudiation of
the tradition in which I had been raised. That completed my alienation from
my father, who was in the early stages of the Alzheimer's disease that would
eventually kill him.

The grief I felt for the premature loss of my father was the same as the
grief I felt for the loss of my country. As a young college student I had
glimpsed a terrible future in the fear I saw in the eyes of my father when he
turned to me one night. The content of that future — "Head to Richmond.
Go as far as you can" — had turned out not to be what I dreaded, yet it was
still terrible. War had already cost me everything I loved, and I had not even
been in combat. I was lucky, war being what it is, that all I'd had amputated

was my sense of larger virtue. Determined to make a life as a writer, I had withdrawn from social activism. I wasn't trying to make the Church better, or the world, just the sentences on a page.

I was living alone in a small apartment north of Boston. I had no particular feeling for the Southern Baptist being sworn in as president that day. In his campaign he had seemed smugly certain of his own righteousness, and that alone had made him an alien figure to me. As an ex-priest, a defeated peacenik, I had no sense of virtue of my own. But on that January 20, I found it impossible to completely forgo my old habit, and I tuned in the inaugural proceedings on television. I remember drawing closer to the screen as I heard what Carter was saying: "Let our recent mistakes bring a resurgent commitment to the basic principles of our nation, for we know that if we despise our own government, we have no future."

In that one sentence, Carter caught me, for it was true, although I had not admitted it before. I did despise our government, and I despised the thing in myself that made that possible. "Our recent mistakes" surely included the 1972 reelection of the guileful Nixon over McGovern, but did they not also include, as Philip Berrigan had suggested, our failure to beware the guilefulness of self-righteousness? Jimmy Carter's earnest goodwill was on full display, and to my surprise I found myself drawn to him. I found myself believing him. "Our commitment to human rights must be absolute, our laws fair, our national beauty preserved; the powerful must not persecute the weak, and human dignity must be enhanced." I did not know what Carter had said to the Joint Chiefs the week before. I sensed his turn of mind, though, aiming toward a thought I had never expected to hear expressed by an American president again. I recalled standing in the throng when John Kennedy spoke unabashedly of peace, a public hope I regarded by now as dashed forever. Yet this new president was saying, "We pledge perseverance and wisdom in our efforts to limit the world's armaments to those necessary for each nation's own domestic safety. And we will move this year a step toward our ultimate goal — the elimination of all nuclear weapons from this earth. We urge all other people to join us, for success can mean life instead of death."

How could I not have believed him? This unlikely figure was inviting me back into what I had long experienced as the first communion of my own identity. Nuclear dread was the spine of my consciousness. Or rather, more potently, the spine of my unconscious. My generation had been stamped in childhood by the nightmare of the mushroom cloud, and in our youth, over Berlin and over Cuba, we had felt its hot breath on our necks. With Kennedy's death we pushed an asbestos lid down on that combustible fear, but it was still burning within us, all through what Daniel Berrigan called "our years of the Bomb."[66] The Cold War had radioactive heat at its core. That Carter, four-teen years after the seasons of mortal East-West confrontation, had called the fear by its name — nuclear weapons on the earth — was to us what it had been for the generation of the Somme and Verdun: to have language applied to the horror at last. From the start of the Great War, a similar interval of fourteen years had passed when Robert Graves and Erich Maria Remarque and Ernest Hemingway and Siegfried Sassoon all published their master-pieces.[67]

Jimmy Carter, for a moment, seemed a political masterpiece, a man in charge of the world, determined to push the world's most pressing problem back on itself. In truth, as we would learn, Carter's listeners brought more to that moment than he did. In his inaugural address he was invoking the Amer-ican dream; Ford, in his first remarks as president, had referred to the Nixon collapse as the national nightmare, but the two words meant something dif-ferent to people my age. The nightmare of our childhood spawned the dream of our youth, but now weren't we being invited to glimpse the vision of our maturity? "When my time as your president has ended," Carter said, "I would hope that the nations of the world might say that we had built a lasting peace, built not on weapons of war but on international policies which reflect our own most precious values."[68]

After that speech, Jimmy and Rosalynn Carter got into their limousine for the traditional drive down Pennsylvania Avenue to the White House, ahead of the great parade, the parade I had taken such delight in, except for the one time I cursed Nixon. But the president's motorcade stopped at the foot of Capitol Hill, just as it entered the broad avenue. The couple got out of the car and began to walk. They held hands. They waved at the people lining the street. It was a version of the gesture that had set the hatless Kennedy apart from the homburged Eisenhower.[69] Carter was hatless, too, but for the first time since Kennedy's assassination, an American president, having stepped out of his bulletproof bubble, was entirely exposed, utterly vulnera-ble, as if the decade of assassinations and curses had never happened. The simple act of their walking the one mile from the Capitol to the White House seemed a signal that a new beginning was possible after all. Spectators cheered and wept. Cameras picked up tears on Carter's cheeks. A simple, good man.

For a few moments, I sensed the relief of the nation. What had he just promised? Perseverance and wisdom? That in the coming year he would lead the world in taking "a step toward our ultimate goal — the elimination of nu-clear weapons from this earth." The steps he was taking now, incredibly, made it seem possible.

6. THE FROZEN SMILE

Carter's inaugural wish for "a lasting peace, based not on weapons of war" was not to be. In addition to the "generals' revolt," there was a more momentous civilian revolt. Paul Nitze, as we saw, had received no appointment in the Carter administration. When he heard of the Blair House meeting at which Carter had broached the subject of cutting the nuclear arsenal to a few hundred, when he heard the inaugural goal of "elimination" of those weapons, the insult he already felt changed to rage and, as always, alarm. Nitze regarded the administration with a contempt that was as personal as it was strident, and his hatred fueled his worry. The danger had never seemed more present, his committee never more necessary.[70]

Over the next four years, Nitze drove the opposition to Carter's foreign policy. He was joined in this by Republicans, who used the defense debate to advance the usual partisan agenda, and even by arms control advocates, who, out of office, turned against their own project, Henry Kissinger among them. Having commissioned the SALT process, Kissinger testified in Congress against Carter's SALT II in 1979 in exactly the way Nitze had argued against SALT I. It was true that the Soviet nuclear arsenal expanded hugely between 1965 and 1975, but the question was whether Moscow intended to outstrip the U.S. expansion or more or less match it. Invoking the specter of Soviet superiority was the conservatives' way, in fact, of advancing American superiority. More than that, they promulgated the dubious thesis that the Soviets really believed there could be such a thing as victory in a nuclear war involving tens of millions of dead on both sides. This had been the self-serving paranoid fantasy of arms advocates since Forrestal, and Nitze kept it current. It was never true.[71]

By the late seventies, Carter saw the SALT process as the way to bring the arms buildup under control, whatever it aimed for. But by now SALT was radioactive. Nitze not only deflected Carter's every impulse toward disarmament, but, exploiting Carter's bureaucratic ineptitude, he succeeded in turning the president's agenda against itself, making nuclear arms *control* the thing to fear, not nuclear arms. Carter was vulnerable to such wily opposition. A brilliant engineer, he had little feel for the human, which crippled him as an advocate and a defender of turf.[72] Carter had promised "wisdom and perseverance," but he delivered only one of them, and perseverance without wisdom is not worth much in politics. Nitze could have had him for lunch, but Carter, in effect, devoured himself.

He failed to see, as we noted before, how his emphatic, "absolute" commitment to human rights would work against his "ultimate goal" of major nuclear arms reduction, for what the Kremlin heard from Jimmy Carter was scolding moralism more than antinuclear partnership. After his inaugural, he scorned the Soviets for their mistreatment of dissidents. He wrote a letter of support to Andrei Sakharov, who had gone from being revered as the father of the Soviet H-bomb to being the USSR's leading internal critic. In that January letter Carter expressed sympathy for "prisoners of conscience," to which the Soviets responded, in early February, by arresting prominent dissidents and charging them with espionage.[73] The Soviets seemed intent on teaching the new president a thing or two, but here also he was slow to learn. It was only when Moscow pushed back that Carter seemed to realize he had himself pushed first.[74]

When Carter dispatched Secretary of State Cyrus Vance to Moscow in March, he sent with him a proposal for mutual cuts in nuclear arsenals that went far beyond the agreement reached by Ford and Brezhnev at Vladivostok. The Soviets found the proposal impossible to take seriously, and they were insulted that the Vladivostok achievement could have been so cavalierly tossed aside. Ernest May and Richard Neustadt helped me to understand how Carter's proposal here backfired. The president, in effect, made the same mistake with the Soviet leadership that he had with the Joint Chiefs: he failed to understand how their Cold War mission, dangerous as it was, gave them an identity and a purpose. He failed to understand in both cases how the appearance of discontinuity with what had gone before would guarantee opposition and, in the case of the Soviets, would undercut their fragile confidence in the predictability of America as a negotiating partner. In sum, Carter was foolish to think that, however self-evident the virtue of a reduction of nuclear forces seemed to him, his own military or his enemy — or the military's supporters in Congress — would abruptly abandon their long-held purposes.

Leonid Brezhnev was presiding over a system that had, since the death of Stalin more than twenty years before, achieved only one success: its ability to match and perhaps overtake the United States in military production. With the Soviet economy and society groaning under the deprivations of scarcity that resulted from the buildup of missiles and long-range bombers marked with the red star, how could Carter have imagined Brezhnev suddenly repudiating the course on which he and his predecessors had set the USSR at such cost to the average citizen? Carter, presiding over a booming American economy, seemed blind to what his proposal would mean to his Soviet counterpart. Brezhnev had grown fond of matching the Pentagon, so why should he not have begun to harbor the hope of surpassing it?[75]

Similarly, by seeming to denigrate the Ford-Kissinger achievement at Vladivostok, Carter misread what his initiative would mean to his political opposition at home. As a result, he deprived himself from then on of the support of key Republicans in his arms control campaign. Carter seemed oblivious of a basic fact of Washington life, that while negotiating with Brezhnev, he was also bound to negotiate, on the same track, with Senator Henry Jackson and his tiger mascot, Richard Perle. To Carter's domestic critics and the Soviets both, he seemed to have ridden into the complexities of arms control on a moral high horse, blind to the realities of a deeply ambiguous enterprise.

For example, the across-the-board cuts based on absolute numbers of warheads that Carter proposed that March ignored the subtlety that cuts should be made in *types* of weapons first, not in numbers of them. The arms control process had already taken aim, that is, at weapons that could be used in "out-of-the-blue" attacks. Until first-strike weapons were reduced, other reductions would be destabilizing and therefore dangerous. Carter seemed not to know that.[76] Nor did he seem sensitive to the fact that once he publicly put deep cuts on the negotiating table, anything short of that — which would previously have been regarded as real progress — would seem a setback.

For all these reasons, the Vance mission to Moscow led nowhere. But then news reports characterized what had happened as the Soviets' rejecting Carter's proposal for deep cuts in strategic weapons, which left Kremlin leaders feeling that they had been set up for a propaganda trick. They said so. "A cheap and shady maneuver," Foreign Minister Andrei Gromyko complained.[77] The *New York Times* quoted the veteran diplomat George Kennan as blasting Carter for having been "too sudden, too public, too narrow and even too discourteous." The *Washington Post* described the Vance delegation's return as the "most disorderly retreat from Moscow since Napoleon's."[78] Historians have since concluded that the most damaging outcome of the Carter-Vance initiative was in setting the bar so high on arms control negotiations that later, "realistic" achievements seemed insignificant.[79]

When Carter exercised his prerogative as commander in chief to pursue his arms reduction agenda, that backfired, too. For example, in June 1977, less than six months after taking office, he unilaterally canceled the long-in-development B-1 bomber, which Gerald Ford had defined as essential in his farewell address.[80] Naturally, this made Carter the Air Force's sworn enemy, and the hawks in Congress lined up against him as a true disarmer. But doves and arms controllers objected, too, since the B-1 could have been traded for a similar concession from the Soviet Union. Furthermore, the B-1, unlike the MIRVed Polaris, Trident, and Minuteman missiles, could not be used as a surprise-attack weapon against the Soviet Union. A "slow mover," it was decidedly a second-strike weapon, and many arms controllers preferred it to the new Trident submarine system as a possible step back from the uncertain edge to which MIRVed missiles had brought the superpower standoff. The irony deepened when, to replace the B-1 in America's next-generation arsenal, Carter opted for the long-range cruise missile, the Tomahawk, which, as a cheap, low-flying, base-anywhere, hard-to-detect, impossible-to-count strategic weapon, would be as destabilizing as MIRV had been. Despite the fact that the cruise missile was relatively low-tech, Moscow saw the move as an escalation of the arms race.[81]

In May of that first year, Carter had ordered the withdrawal of all U.S. combat forces from South Korea, only to find that Congress could block his order. In July, Carter's much-announced wish to lower the threat of nuclear war seemed reduced to the absurd when he said he was considering the deployment in Europe of the newly developed neutron bomb, a weapon that destroys people but not property. In all of this Carter was showing that goodwill, high ideals, and executive authority are beside the point if they are not braced by a full appreciation of the power of the "Niagara" current on which the arms race runs. For all his experience as a Navy man, he was like a sailor steering a ship with his eye only on the wind, paying no heed to the fact that the tide was running against him. A tide, in Carter's case, that had been picking up momentum for three decades.

As Carter left office, four years after his bold declaration at Blair House, the SALT II Treaty, signed by Brezhnev and Carter in 1979, would settle for far less drastic reductions than those Vance had proposed in Moscow in 1977. In the "arms control sweetener" tradition, Carter would approve, one month after the SALT II agreement was announced, the highly accurate MX missile system: whereas the Minuteman III was MIRVed with three warheads, each MX missile would be MIRVed with twelve. Inevitably perceived in Moscow as a first-strike weapon, the MX marked yet another upward turn of the arms race.[82] Even so, the SALT II agreement was firmly in the sights of Paul Nitze and company. They attacked it as appeasement. SALT II would never be ratified by the Senate.

On November 4, 1979, sixty-six Americans were taken hostage in Iran.[83] On December 12, NATO announced its decision to deploy 108 Pershing II launchers and 464 ground-launched cruise missiles on European soil, which Moscow denounced as a major escalation. On December 25, Soviet forces invaded Afghanistan, and Carter ordered the financing of resistance to the Soviet puppets in Kabul (eventually spawning the group called Al Qaeda). On January 3, 1980, Carter withdrew the SALT II Treaty from the Senate.

Most momentously, on January 23, 1980, in his State of the Union speech, the president announced what would be called the Carter Doctrine, according to which the United States demanded permanent access to Persian Gulf oil, which it would protect by "any means necessary, including military force."

Where before the United States had sought to protect its access to Middle East oil through surrogates, from now on its claim would be direct. Jimmy Carter had begun by calling for reductions in U.S. imports of foreign (mainly Persian Gulf) oil, then the source of more than a third of America's oil needs. But if the nation could not shake off that addiction, now the U.S. military would protect it. The consequences of this shift ordered by Carter would be played out in 1991, with the Gulf War, and in 2003, with the war against Iraq. By then, oil imports (still mainly from the Persian Gulf) had risen to more than half of the U.S. supply.[84]

On April 28, 1980, the U.S. military was humiliated when, with helicopters choking on sand, it failed in a desert rescue attempt of hostages in Iran. "Carter reluctantly called on the military," an Army general would later explain, "and the military reluctantly answered. And it ended in disaster."[85] America had never seemed so weak. The nation had become thoroughly disillusioned with a president whose smugness was impervious even to clear instances of his own incompetence. Indeed, Carter's failures seemed epochal: "Our nation's situation is much more dangerous today," a gloating Donald Rumsfeld told Congress, "than it has been at any time since Neville Chamberlain left Munich."[86] Americans at the time had no knowledge of Carter's 1977 Blair House meeting with the Joint Chiefs, but the citizenry across the political spectrum had arrived, three years later, at the same place as the military leaders. Pure contempt.

When Senator Edward Kennedy declared his intention to oppose Carter for the Democratic Party's presidential nomination, I, like many other Democrats, welcomed it, without apparently registering the significance of the odd fact that the strident Senate hawk Henry Jackson (Richard Perle's sponsor, Nitze's ally) was backing Kennedy, too.

From the right, the (to us) feckless Ronald Reagan opposed Carter for having put the United States at the mercy of a rearmed and reignited Soviet Union. (Although it was Carter, not Reagan, who began the major arms buildup of which Reagan boosters would crow. Even Reagan's Strategic Defense Initiative, called Star Wars, was prepared for by Carter's authorizing an expansion of research into antisatellite weapons systems, a violation of the decades-old Soviet-American intention to protect outer space as a realm of peace.)[87] One 1980 poll of military officers found that a mere 1 percent planned to vote for Carter's reelection.[88] Yet in a final retreat from his own first impulse, Carter signed Presidential Directive 59, which greatly expanded the SIOP, the list of targets to be hit in the Soviet Union in the event of nuclear war, from 1,700 in 1970 to 7,000 in 1980.[89]

The Carter directive ordered the Pentagon to prepare to fight a "protracted" nuclear war, which was a long-sought victory for those who wanted such a prospect to be "thinkable" — an ultimate reversal of Robert McNamara. Just as the Carter Doctrine was a direct descendant of the Truman Doctrine, PD-59 was the son of NSC-68. "The nation's policy," in one historian's summary, "was taking a turn back to 1950."[90] War with the Soviet Union seemed more possible than at any time since the early 1960s. By the summer of 1980, the nuclear monster was riding higher than ever.

Through all of this, Paul Nitze, America's Cassandra, sought the added role of Carter's Nemesis. But needlessly. Carter was his own Nemesis. His failure, however, belongs as much to those of us who had responded to his brisk idealism at the outset as to him. We are obligated to take the lessons of his self-destruction seriously. Since leaving office, Carter has proven himself in the roles of diplomat, moral exemplar, and elder statesman — also carpenter. But the historic question goes to the way Carter used power while he had it.

His four years as president, coming as the United States approached the great post-Vietnam crossroads, represented a grace period in which the illusions of warmaking power had been dramatically laid bare. Military force can do only so much in the world, and overreliance on it, as a source of influence or identity, can be suicidal. That surely was the lesson of Vietnam. Carter grasped that more clearly than almost anyone else of his time, and he moved to seize the moment, aiming to drastically reduce the role of the Pentagon in the nation's life and to reverse the course of the "desperate armaments race" that had defined politics and economics for a generation.

But good intentions are not enough. Ideals are not enough. And the warning here is that when ideals are thwarted, they can readily betray themselves. Those of us who bathe in the soothing water of virtuous intentions, eschewing the gritty challenges of political struggle and bureaucratic infighting, imagining that the call for peace is enough to bring it, must acknowledge Carter as our character ideal. His achievements — "or more precisely," as John Lewis Gaddis puts it, "the absence of them" — stand as our rebuke.[91]

The man who entered office strolling down Pennsylvania Avenue, willingly exposed, benignly smiling, was transformed by the world's refusal — Russia's refusal, the Senate's refusal, the Pentagon's refusal — to bend to his better will. Carter had wanted to end the Cold War, the arms race, the "balance of terror." To his humiliation, he learned that the government elites on both sides of the Iron Curtain had no interest in his program. From their "mutual" if distinct points of view, the Cold War worked: it enabled each superpower to be dominant in its sphere. It provided, then protected, tremendous levels of influence, wealth, and prestige to whole segments of each society — the military brass, but also the bureaucrats of national security, the manufacturers of weapons, the workers they employed, the political leaders whose scope of action was always wider when the governed were afraid. Carter's own Democratic Party had made good use of the Cold War, as an excuse not to pursue truly progressive solutions. Why begin now? Carter had come into office focused on the potential horrors to which all of this might lead. He ended his term as imprisoned in the Cold War system as those he'd foolishly sought to free from it.

The smile became a frozen mask, the open-avenue vulnerability became a retreat into the presidential mansion, and the benign goodwill became the seething anger of a moralist spurned for his morality. In the end, Carter's frustration made him vindictive. Having pointed the way to ultimate peace, he punished those who refused to take it by pushing them more than ever back toward ultimate war. He began by telling the Pentagon men that their twilight time had come; he ended with the Pentagon men celebrating,[92] more than anyone else, morning in America.

7. THE PEOPLE ARE HEARD

A million people gathered in a field in Kraków, Poland, on June 10, 1979, and while claiming no such thing, they pulled one of the two linchpins from the wheels of the Cold War. Nearly a million people gathered in a field in the heart of New York City on June 12, 1982, removing the other pin, although pundits would deny they had done any such thing. In each case, individuals who had considered themselves lonely dissenters found themselves in the midst of a vast throng — not alone, but members of a new kind of majority. In Poland obviously, and in New York more implicitly, new revolutionary movements were empowered just by acts of massive gathering. The long arms-race narrative that began with the impasse between Henry Stimson and James Forrestal on September 11, 1945, and continued with the open-ended stalemate of mutual paranoia — mutual assured destruction — between Moscow and Washington, took an unexpected turn when people on both sides of the Iron Curtain lifted their voices in such volume that they could no longer be denied, voices crying *No!*

On September 11, 1907, as we saw, Mohandas Gandhi, in an act of resistance to racist laws in Johannesburg had begun the great countermovement of nonviolence, which would roll mostly unnoticed against the Niagara current of twentieth-century politics. Gandhi-style resistance to the forces of oppression was dismissed by realists because, as it was often said, the Indian fakir was opposed by the relatively benign British colonial system, not a brutal totalitarian regime.[93] And Gandhi had known nothing of the dangers or complexities of nuclear stalemate. The realists would be the last to see what was coming, but beginning with those two gatherings in Kraków and New York, the countermovement of people power showed itself as something to be reckoned with, in relation to the totalitarian monolith of Soviet imperialism and to the nuclear arms race. The "great man" theory of history would once again be called into question, as masses of anonymous men and women did what Stimson, Eisenhower, Khrushchev, Kennedy, Nixon, Kissinger, and Carter had proven unable to do: decisively alter the course of the ever-escalating nuclear competition between the Soviet Union and the United States. Against the orders of the command society in the East, and against the predictions of the Pentagon-sponsored experts of the Totalitarian school in the West, who saw no other outcome to the Cold War but violent paroxysm, such people, starting with an unknown electrician in Gdańsk, Poland, and a female graduate student in Cambridge, Massachusetts, rejected the basic assumptions of Cold War ideology.

When Ronald Reagan died in June 2004, as respected a historian as Michael Beschloss could assert that this one man had "seized the day and ended [the] epic global struggle" of the Cold War. Indeed, the obsequies repeatedly gave the departed Reagan such credit.[94] "The Great Liberator," the cover of the *Weekly Standard* proclaimed. But that is fancy worthy of the man who imagined that the world conformed to his idea of it, and not the other way around. Reagan was a reactor to events in the last stage of the Cold War, not an initiator of them. Margaret Thatcher said of him after his death, "Ronald Reagan had a higher claim than any other leader to have won the Cold War for liberty."[95]

But there's the point. The leaders received the unexpected gift of an opening to the Cold War endgame, a gift that came from the streets of cities on both sides of the great divide. Led initially by the electrician Lech Walesa east of the Iron Curtain, and west of it by a young woman named Randall Forsberg, the originator of the nuclear freeze movement, a groundswell of ordinary people brought the Cold War to a head. To connect Walesa and Forsberg is not to equate the oppressions to which they were responding, as if Soviet totalitarianism were not uniquely brutal. But the Cold War had imposed a kind of ruthless autocracy on both sides, the autocracy of the bomb. Twin revolutions, against the Kremlin and the Pentagon, each reflecting different circumstances of arms race authoritarianism, developed simultaneously. As unlike as their experiences of oppression were, Forsberg's movement and Walesa's necessarily had the same ultimate goal, which was nothing less than the end of the Cold War. Their instruments in ending it were Pope John Paul II, Mikhail Gorbachev, and, only despite himself, Ronald Reagan.

The Cold War was based on fear. On the American side, a paranoid dread of Communism, given foundational expression by the suicide of the terrified James Forrestal, had underwritten the apparently open-ended expansion of the nuclear arsenal. The national security state was deeply insecure, although its institutions (the Pentagon, but also the FBI, the CIA, the academic think tanks, the defense industry, the militant Congress) thrived. Year in and year out, every U.S. leader had expressed his view of the world in what came to be known as "the standard threat speech"[96] — the unimpeachable idea that the Russians were coming. No matter what happened — Tito's dissent, Stalin's death, Khrushchev's retreat, China's break with Moscow, détente, arms control agreements, joint ventures in space exploration — Washington was afraid of Moscow.

And, unequivocally, vice versa. After the Second World War, the devastated people of the Soviet Union were vulnerable to paranoid perceptions of their own, and they saw America as a mortal enemy, too. Absolutely so, when the threat of nuclear war was felt. Historians (establishment and revisionist, of the West and of the East) have devoted a library's worth of books to laying blame for the Cold War, but its unfolding suggests that blame is beside the point.[97] Ideological conflict, geopolitical pressures, the obliterations of war — both peoples were driven more than slightly mad by the fear of nothing less than history itself.

8. BE NOT AFRAID

"Be not afraid!" was the theme of the new pope's first address, in 1977,[98] and as his pontificate unfolded, the repudiation of fear was John Paul II's constant message. To no one was it more powerfully addressed than to those millions living under the hammer of Soviet repression, who instantly recognized the Polish pope as theirs. If fear fueled the arms race, it was also used by the Soviet regime to ruthlessly maintain control of its empire. When John Paul II made a triumphant return to his native Poland in 1979, he boldly addressed such fear as the first thing that had to be overcome, and he did not shy away from the political implications of his message. "The Polish pope," he said, "comes here to speak . . . before Europe and the world of those often forgotten nations and peoples. He comes here to cry with a loud voice." And then, acknowledging that the movement for which he cried could belong only to the people themselves, he declared, "The future of Poland will depend on how many people are mature enough to be non-conformist."[99] The pope issued this call in a realm where, until then, nonconformity had often been regarded as a capital crime.

In that same period, President Carter was surrendering to fear — his own, the Pentagon's, the nation's. The Soviet Union, with its invasion of Afghanistan, seemed newly belligerent. American impotence was on display in Iran. The U.S. economy, with double-digit interest and inflation rates and high unemployment, threatened to go into free fall. Carter responded as his predecessors had, with anguish and threats.

But in Kraków on that day in June, a different sort of voice rolled out over the huge crowd that had, against the will of the government, come to listen and behold. "You must be strong, dearest brothers and sisters! . . . There is no need to be afraid. The frontiers must be opened. There is no imperialism in the Church, only service."[100] And its main service now would be to support the nascent will of the Polish people, and the peoples of all the Soviet satellites, to be free. The pope would do this by asserting the truth, again and again. The truth of unacceptable conditions of life in the Soviet empire, and the truth of the individual's ability to alter those conditions by what Václav Havel called the "singular, explosive, incalculable political power of living within the truth." Gandhi had called this "truth force." In the Soviet Union, Solzhenitsyn had called it the refusal to live by the lie. Such was the moral hope that John Paul II was steadfastly evoking — a simultaneous renunciation of violence and a claim to power. From one end of the century (Gandhi) to the other (Berrigan) a vision came fully into its own. "Be not afraid!"

Within weeks of the pope's visit, the nascent Polish impulse toward nonconformity, having been embodied in the millions who had poured into the fields and streets, began to take visible form. Barely more than a year later, at the Lenin shipyard in Gdańsk, Lech Walesa, using a souvenir pen from the pope's visit, put his name to what might have been his death sentence, but which was instead the founding declaration of the trade union Solidarity.[101] In the grit of antitotalitarian resistance, Václav Havel in Czechoslovakia, as a leader of the human rights group Charter 77, promptly joined Walesa as one of this vision's new tribunes.[102] They renounced violence while claiming power, moral power.

John Paul II is often paired with Ronald Reagan. A potent and widely accepted myth has it that they formed a "holy alliance"[103] against the Soviet Union. This seems to square with the absolutism of the Vatican's long-standing antagonism toward Bolshevism and Communism, an opposition that was embodied in Pius XII's having excommunicated every Communist in the world (this from the pope who never excommunicated Nazis, or even Hitler, who died with his name on the rolls of the Catholic Church). I am of the generation of Catholics whose first political attitude — contempt for and fear of Communists — was inculcated by the Church. The Polish pope was perceived at first as an avatar of this tradition. After all, he had spent his priesthood as an open critic of the Communist regime in his native land, and he had more reason to demonize the Soviet Union than Reagan did. Yet his attitude was not so simple.

John Paul II proved in many ways to be an ultraconservative pope, particularly regarding internal matters of Church doctrine and discipline. But the pope and Reagan were not allies. On the questions that mattered most to each of them — economics and military power — they were polar opposites. Both were lifelong opponents of Communism, but in very different ways. Reagan came into the presidency flaunting a moralism that prompted him, at his first press conference, to denounce Communists as innate liars, cheaters, and criminals — the kind of rhetoric that had not come from Washington since early in the Cold War.[104] In contrast, one of the first initiatives John Paul II took as pope was to reach out with unexpected warmth to the mayor of Rome, the first Communist mayor in the city's history.[105] In relation to Italian Communists, John Paul II continued the Vatican's version of détente that had begun with John XXIII, and if he used his office to press Moscow, and its puppet regime in Warsaw, it was with a view to influence and change, not merely to condemn.

While John Paul II was embracing the trade union Solidarity and decrying the injustices of free market capitalism (in, for example, his 1981 encyclical *Laborem Exercens*, "On Human Work"), Reagan was proving himself a union-buster by firing eleven thousand air traffic controllers in the name of that selfsame free market. The denunciation of unions was a regular Reagan theme — this from a former union president. Under Reagan, American capitalism would show itself to be more indifferent to the social consequences of corporate policy than ever. At the same time, the Catholic Church would be American capitalism's fiercest critic. While Reagan was using Communist moves against Solidarity as an excuse to reject arms control negotiations with the Soviet Union, the pope was denouncing both sides of the arms race[106] and promoting bishops who were the fiercest critics of America's part in it.[107]

It was Reagan's obsession with military power and military solutions that blinded him to the significance of Solidarity, a movement that resolutely renounced violence. Reagan would embrace the savage, death-squad-dominated Contra movement in Central America in the name of opposition to Communism, but he and his administration ignored the far more significant, and ultimately triumphant, Solidarity movement because they could not imagine nonviolent resistance as powerful. Every institution in Washington — the Pentagon certainly, but also the CIA, the Congress, the political press, and the White House — missed the meaning of the entire democracy movement behind the Iron Curtain because the orthodoxies of the Totalitarian school gave no credit to the political power of peaceful protest. Thus, after a generation of right-wing calls for a rollback, when the real rollback began, the American right wing was blind to it.[108]

The pope, in contrast, grasped the meaning of nonviolent struggle at once: it was the only kind for him. Therefore he boldly supported Solidarity. Indeed, the noun "solidarity" became a staple of his rhetoric on every subject, an unsubtle signal to the people behind the Iron Curtain and their leaders. The pope openly gave moral support to the nonviolent resistance in his native land, understanding that moral suasion was the key. Nor was it just the Roman Catholics in Poland to whom the pope appealed. His affirmation of the significance and promise of a nonviolent but direct challenge to the Soviet system was a tremendous boost to those in other Eastern European nations, in the Soviet republics, and in Russia itself who were daring to "live within the truth."

Aleksandr Solzhenitsyn had begun doing so in 1962, with his *One Day in the Life of Ivan Denisovich,* a book Soviet authorities tolerated because it jibed with their anti-Stalin campaign. In the seventies, he was still at it, especially with *The Gulag Archipelago,* which marked the true beginning of open dissent in the USSR.[109] By the early 1980s, Andrei Sakharov, his wife, Yelena Bonner, the dissident scientist Yuri Orlov, and champions of Soviet Jewry like Natan Sharansky recognized John Paul II's voice as addressed to the broader world for them.[110]

By the time John Paul II returned to Poland, in June 1983, Solidarity had been outlawed and Lech Walesa was persona non grata, but the pope demanded to be allowed to meet with him. Because the pope made a public issue of it, the government had no choice, the meeting was arranged, the attention of the world was fixed, and just like that Walesa was restored as a national leader. Everywhere the pope went on that visit, people gathered by the hundreds of thousands to cheer him. Again and again, when riot troops pressed them and police helicopters blasted orders to go home, the people refused to disperse. Instead, picking up on the pope's spirit, they chanted at the overlords, *"Przebaczamy!"* — "We forgive you."

Only days later, in July, the Polish regime lifted martial law and released political prisoners, including many of those associated with Solidarity. Among eastern bloc nations, this was an unprecedented surrender by a totalitarian regime to the popular will. What began as a trade union, as one leader observed, had become "a nonviolent national resurrection."[111] This lifting of martial law in response to the will of the Polish people, a will made powerful by the pope's direct encouragement, marks July 1983 as an important turning point in the Cold War, the point from which the rapid loosening of the brutal Soviet grip followed, the point from which the end of Soviet Communism itself followed.

Reagan was simply unaware of the meaning of it all, which is why it is foolish to credit him with the lead role in ending the Cold War. These events and what they led to contradicted everything the Reagan administration had ever believed about the implacability of the Soviet system. The assumptions of American anti-Communism proved to be irrelevant to the way Communism finally unraveled. Reagan, in adhering to those assumptions, was a man with no self-doubt and less self-reflection, and though he would often change (inconsistency would seem a virtue when, as we shall see, he abandoned his moralistic belligerence in relation to the Soviet Union), he would never acknowledge a mistake — not his own and not America's.

The pope, for his part, would put moral self-criticism at the center of his pontificate, and called on the Church to do likewise. When he visited Auschwitz on his first trip to Poland, he knelt at the death camp to recite the words of the Catholic confession and audibly emphasized its climactic phrase, *"mea culpa, mea culpa, mea maxima culpa!"*[112] It never occurred to the pope to declare himself the winner of the Cold War, because for him there was no question that that tragic history could open into something properly regarded as victory.

The appearance of a moral partnership with the Vatican served the purposes of Reagan's right-wing inner circle, some of whom were Catholics (Secretary of State Alexander Haig, CIA Director William Casey, U.N. Ambassador Jeanne Kirkpatrick, and National Security Council officials John Poindexter and Robert McFarlane). But Reagan's exacerbation of American paranoia about Soviet intentions, and his immediate moves to launch the biggest peacetime military expansion in history,[113] countered the pope's emphatic rejection of fear as life's organizing principle. The pope would be a steady critic of the Reagan buildup, and when the Strategic Defense Initiative was unveiled, John Paul II would condemn it for attempting to move weapons into space.[114]

Political fear was the predominant note of Reagan's public life, but as events showed, he was unlike Forrestal in being free of personal fear. This became clear to all on March 30, 1981, when he was shot by a crazed would-be assassin. "Honey, I forgot to duck," he said to his wife before undergoing surgery. Unlike Alexander Haig, who shocked a worldwide television audience with the barely concealed panic with which he declared, "As of now, I am in control here,"[115] Reagan went through the trauma of almost being murdered with courage, grace, and equanimity. An actor by trade, Reagan displayed a depth of character that was impossible to fake, and the heart of the nation opened to him. Only a month after being seriously wounded, he addressed a joint session of Congress with an esprit of which America no longer believed itself capable. "Reagan's gallantry, and the brio he brought to his recovery," as the *Boston Globe's* John A. Farrell assessed it, "moved his 'revolution' to a higher plane. The country had endured almost two decades of assassinations, scandal, social turmoil, economic stagnation and unhappy presidencies. Now the old movie star, in the best Hollywood tradition, had taken a bullet, shrugged it off, and risen more determined than ever."[116]

It was because Reagan had been put so dramatically to the test, and had passed that test, that he forged his powerful bond with John Paul II, because less than two months later, the same thing happened to the pope. On May 13, an Islamic radical shot him at close range in St. Peter's Square.[117] There was no wife waiting for his spontaneous joke as he regained consciousness; the pontiff's first words were of forgiveness toward his assailant. John Paul II was as valiant in his recovery as Reagan had been, and the moral stature of both men was enhanced around the globe. As they embarked on their separate campaigns for change, their having been spared lent a messianic edge to their purposes — and there did seem to be a twinning of the charismatic heroes.

It was then that Reagan's minions began to claim their "holy alliance," but the Vatican kept its distance, ever wary of a presidential administration whose belligerent public agenda remained all about fear. Reagan's sense of his own mission took on a quasi-religious aspect, which struck the leaders of the Catholic Church as oddball. This was not only a matter of Reagan's mystical sense of having been tapped by God for an epoch-making purpose — he told the pope as much when they met at the Vatican on June 7, 1982[118] — but also of his susceptibility to the endtime mythology of Armageddon[119] as a context for understanding East-West conflict. The Vatican, given far more to realpolitik than to political mysticism, understood the dangers of such a view as a basis for policy. But the more certain Reagan became of his mission, and the more convinced of his righteousness, the more shocked he was when his approach began to backfire.

9. WE WIN, YOU LOSE, SIGN HERE

Ronald Reagan, a longtime connoisseur of the Soviet threat and a tribune of warning, all at once and to his dismay found that, among many of his countrymen, he himself had become the thing to fear. Whether his unbridled and ever more messianic militarism sparked horror in the Soviet enemy or not, great numbers of his own people grew afraid of Reagan. This occurred despite the admiration most felt for the way he had come through the assassination attempt. The fear was partly due to the extremists who came into office with him, figures later characterized by George H. W. Bush as "marginal intellectual thugs."[120] Richard Nixon had warned Leonid Brezhnev in 1974 that "if détente unravels in America, the hawks will take over."[121] It had happened, and it was so. But they were not just hawks.

It was Jimmy Carter, that moralistic liberal, who had paved the way for equally moralistic right-wingers, who deplored the tradition of Republican realists in foreign affairs (Nixon and Kissinger) as much as they hated the softness of Democrats. But there was an economic aspect to this ideological arrival, for with the entry of the Reagan team into government, the prospect that Eisenhower had warned of — the corruption of American defense policy by its identification with an economic purpose — came fully into its own. Corporations now drove defense decisions more than ever, which was a major factor in the readiness of both the administration and Congress to add billions to the Pentagon budget. Reagan's enthusiastic partner on Capitol Hill was Senator Jesse Helms, who followed in the steps of Senator Henry Jackson as the great booster of defense.[122] In 1982, the Pentagon was spending $21 million *an hour;* by the time Reagan left office, that sum was increased by that much again.[123] Such military spending was completely unhinged from any justifiable operational requirement.

All of this presumed that the "paranoid style in American politics"[124] had made a comeback, and it was true, but this time there was a disconnect between the leaders and the people. After years of détente, Americans were no longer consoled by the simplistic good-versus-evil of the early Cold War. The nation did long for a recovery of the prestige and power that had been squandered in Vietnam, and the new militarists were determined that the United States should come roaring back into world dominance. But where American leaders after World War II sought to build an international order based on law and agreements, the post-Vietnam leadership that came fully into power under Reagan wanted a world order based on the military might of the United States, period.[125]

Instead of leadership in the measured mode of George Marshall or the rational style of Robert McNamara, what the Pentagon offered the nation was zealotry. And the names first hung on its office doors in these post-Vietnam years — Richard Armitage, Richard Perle, Donald Rumsfeld, Richard Cheney, Colin Powell, and Paul Wolfowitz — would define zealotry for a generation. Wolfowitz had headed a study group in the late 1970s that raised dire warnings on Iraq[126] (a preoccupation to which he would cling), and it says everything about the direction in which Reagan wanted to take the country that Wolfowitz was now named director of policy planning in the State Department, the position that had launched George Kennan and Paul Nitze.[127]

The Reagan ideologues were obsessed with restoring American power, but also with restoring what they called morality in foreign policy. What they meant by that was a refusal to see the Soviet Union as anything but the devil's own outpost. Their worldview was coherent, but it was anachronistic. A large segment of the population heard the pronouncements of the Reagan circle as slightly crazy.

Haig, at the State Department, jolted Congress and the nation when he offhandedly referred to a NATO plan to fire a nuclear shot across the Soviet bow.[128] Caspar Weinberger was the most ferocious hawk ever to serve as secretary of defense, and he was quickly perceived as such (although not by his devoted young aide Colin Powell, whose own trajectory in government is better understood if attention is paid to its roots in Weinberger's rampant militarism). Among Weinberger's first declarations was a demand for an antiballistic missile system[129] — as if the nation were not prohibited by the 1972 ABM Treaty from such a thing. Was it the United States, and not the Soviet Union, that felt free to toss aside treaties? Weinberger's close aide Richard Perle would soon call for the abrogation of the treaty before Congress.[130]

Weinberger carried to a new extreme the old RAND tradition of decrying the Soviet threat as a way of justifying increases in the Pentagon budget. Fred Ikle, Weinberger's undersecretary of defense for policy, kept the tradition alive and bolstered Weinberger with orthodox nuclear theology. In October 1981, Weinberger unveiled the details of the new military buildup: he not only brought the canceled B-1 bomber back but said there would be a hundred of them. There would be a hundred MX missiles, too, and a major expansion of the Trident submarine program and a whole new fleet of stealth warplanes. In the same month, the SIOP, already expanded by Carter, was expanded again.[131]

And Weinberger depended on extremists. Richard Perle, for example, had spent a decade outfitting Senator Henry Jackson with the fangs he used to tear into every gesture of conciliation toward the Soviet Union, whether the last gasps of détente or the most carefully hedged arms control proposals. Now Perle was in the Pentagon as assistant secretary of defense for international affairs, a position that put him in charge of Weinberger's fangs.[132] In this capacity, Perle blithely declared that the Soviet Union would willingly sacrifice twenty million of its own citizens in a nuclear war with the United States, a prediction that the president had often made in after-dinner speeches as a private citizen. But these men were in charge now, and such wild characterizations had a frightening ring to them.

Appointed to run the Arms Control and Disarmament Agency was Eugene Rostow, a well-known opponent of arms control, and he lost no time, despite being the chief American negotiator, in denouncing the very idea of negotiations.[133] Rostow made news when he described the bombing of Hiroshima and Nagasaki as having been not so bad; "Japan, after all," he said, "not only survived but flourished after the nuclear attack."[134] In this assessment, Rostow, in fact, was repeating what Paul Nitze had concluded thirty-six years before, when, as a member of the Strategic Bombing Survey, he viewed the atomic bomb damage as no worse than conventional bombing. Nuclear war, the point was, should not be regarded as unthinkable.[135] There was nothing absolute about the bomb. That hard-edged view had been pushed to the margin of American attitudes as far back as Eisenhower, but now, with the arrival of the ideologues, it had moved to the center. These men liked nukes, and said so.

Unsurprisingly, Nitze was named Rostow's deputy at the ACDA. Indeed, thirty-one members of Nitze's alarmist Committee on the Present Danger were appointed to positions in the Reagan administration. As a group they were so extreme that Nitze, who clung to the romantic idea that negotiations involved at least *some* negotiating, now was in danger of being regarded as soft, even by men whom he had empowered.[136] The dominant attitude of the Reagan arms negotiators, especially Perle and Ikle, was to say to the Soviets, "We win, you lose, sign here."[137]

But Ronald Reagan did not like it when the people of the United States, who had expressed affection for him after the assassination attempt, began to look askance at him and his administration. The trouble was that Americans started believing all their militant scare talk and, recalling the failures of the Carter years, worried that nuclear war was a real possibility again. And if a new belligerence had come to the fore in Washington, it seemed no surprise that the same seemed true in Moscow. But now Americans found more to do with their fears than simply wring their hands.

Their fears became the dominant subject of public discourse. The *New Yorker* writer Jonathan Schell, for example, in a series of articles about nuclear war, "The Fate of the Earth," struck a chord that resonated much as the one John Hersey had struck in 1946 with his "Hiroshima," which appeared in the same magazine. But Schell's pieces had more immediate consequences, circulating far and wide as a call to action. Physicians began to treat the nuclear threat as a health problem, something to discuss with patients during annual checkups.[138] Lawyers, businessmen, writers, and academics formed professional groups expressly to oppose nuclear war. The cloud of "psychic numbing"[139] lifted. Denial ended. An antinuclear movement sprung up in the West, equivalent to the democracy movement in the East — a forthright popular act of moral reckoning with the truth of what society had become.

Movies and television programs, lectures by scientists, and the protests of religious leaders brought home to the public at large the harsh fact that had

hitherto barely registered — that the United States and the Soviet Union together had accumulated and deployed nearly twenty thousand strategic nuclear warheads and another thirty thousand smaller tactical nukes, with an
almost equal number stockpiled. "We have gone on piling weapon upon
weapon," wrote a deeply chastened George Kennan, with whom it had all begun three and a half decades before, "missile upon missile, new levels of destructiveness upon old ones, helplessly, almost involuntarily, like victims of
some sort of hypnotism, like men in a dream, like lemmings headed for the
sea."[140] But suddenly, frightened awake by the policies and rhetoric of their
own leaders as much as by the Soviet "threat," the American people began to
shake off that trance. Jimmy Carter had solemnly promised to do something
about this problem, and what he had done was make it worse. Now Ronald
Reagan was talking and acting as if there were no problem.[141] Hello?

10. THE FREEZE

It was into this feverish circle of political, social, and psychological anguish
that Randall Forsberg stepped, like an American Walesa. Forsberg started out
as an English major at Columbia, but by 1980 she had devoted herself to arms
control issues and was working on her Ph.D. in political science at the Massachusetts Institute of Technology. Before Reagan's election she had composed
a manifesto, "A Call to Halt the Nuclear Arms Race," but once Reagan's extreme anti-Soviet agenda had become clear, and once his administration had
abandoned even the pretense of arms control negotiations, the Freeze, as
Forsberg's campaign became known, spread like wildfire. It was an American
version of various transnational antinuclear initiatives.[142] As frightening as a
direct look at the contingencies of nuclear stalemate was, there was also the
tremendous relief of "living in the truth" at last, even this truth — not to
mention the profound existential affirmation it was to look the monster in
the eye, and have a way of spitting back.

The Freeze proposal, containing only two paragraphs, was simplicity itself, calling on both the United States and the Soviet Union to, first, "decide
when and how to achieve a mutual and verifiable freeze on the testing, production, and future deployment of nuclear warheads, missiles and other
delivery systems"; and, second, "to pursue major mutual and verifiable reductions in nuclear warheads, missiles and other delivery systems, through
annual percentages or other effective means, in a manner that enhances stability."[143] Experts in the fields of nuclear theory and arms control dismissed
the Freeze for its simple-mindedness.[144]

In March 1981, the first National Freeze Campaign Conference convened in Washington, D.C., and the prairie fire of what would become the most successful American grassroots movement of the twentieth century was ignited. Ronald Reagan was shot outside the Hilton Hotel in Washington only days after that conference, but the universal concern for him, and the esteem in which Americans held him as he recovered, did not blunt the challenge to the nuclear status quo. If anything, Reagan's vulnerability seemed to reinforce the nation's new determination to take responsibility for the earth. That spring and summer, hundreds of city councils and state legislatures voted overwhelmingly to affirm the Freeze resolution. In Vermont, 159 of 180 town meetings adopted it. Official bodies in forty-three states passed the resolution. More than a million people signed Freeze petitions in barely more than a few weeks. Two out of three congressional districts across the country had Freeze chapters. Organizations sprung up to join the movement. The membership of one, Physicians for Social Responsibility, founded in Boston by the pediatrician Helen Caldicott, grew quickly to more than twelve thousand, representing almost every state in the Union — an astonishing number, given that doctors as a group were not known for their social activism.[145]

As Americans were embracing the Freeze idea, streets in the cities of Europe began to fill with protesters who wanted no part of American cruise missiles and Pershing II's, which, approved by NATO while Carter was president, were now being deployed. Europeans demanded an end to the U.S.-Soviet arms race, which threatened to turn their continent into a charnel house. In Bonn, Amsterdam, Paris, London, Rome, and Frankfurt, the cities of the great alliance, the unthinkable began to happen: Europeans linked the United States and the Soviet Union as moral equals, sources together of the grave danger.

For a year, the grass sprouted. Then, on March 10, 1982, at the end of a week in which Ronald Reagan presided over a war games exercise — codenamed Ivy League — that simulated a limited nuclear war, the Freeze resolution was introduced in Congress. It was driven by mounting fears of precisely such a presidential doomsday flirtation. The sponsors in the House were Massachusetts's Edward J. Markey and Silvio O. Conte and New York Representative Jonathan B. Bingham; in the Senate the sponsors were Democrat Edward M. Kennedy of Massachusetts and Republican Mark O. Hatfield of Oregon.

At the end of that month, Reagan put before Congress a $4.2 billion request for a new civil defense program that would involve the relocation of whole populations of targeted cities to the countryside.[146] The program only reinforced the fear people had — not of the Soviets but of Reagan. Rather than working to prevent nuclear war, the president was preparing for it. His civil defense request went nowhere, while the Freeze resolution took off. "People want peace so much," Dwight Eisenhower had once prophesied, "that one of these days governments had better get out of their way and let them have it." By the end of Reagan's first year in office, Kennedy and Hatfield saw it happening right before their eyes. "A sleeping giant of public opinion had suddenly awakened," they wrote, "including not only peace activists, but a broad new constituency reflecting America as a whole; in the language of nuclear physics, it seemed that the freeze movement had reached the critical mass needed to start a powerful public reaction."[147]

Ever sharp at reading the mood of his audience, Reagan was more attuned to the potential strength of this newly awakened giant than his belligerent advisers were, and he moved at once to try to blunt its effect. At Eureka College, his alma mater in Illinois, he gave a speech on May 9, 1982, in which he trumped the SALT tradition by calling for a reduction of arms instead of mere limitation. Instead, that is, of a mere freeze. But it was a rhetorical ploy — Reagan was carefully proposing a reduction in land-based delivery systems, which would have left the United States with a clear advantage because of its superior submarine-based forces — and the proposal was promptly labeled as such by the Soviets.[148] But Reagan's Eureka speech marked a new dividing line between him and his most hawkish advisers. The president was now on record as wanting reduction! He could hold two contradictory positions in his mind at once, and from now on there would be a contest within this solitary man between the impulse to prepare for nuclear war and the wish to stop it.

Three months after the Freeze resolution was introduced in Congress and a month after Reagan's Eureka speech, nearly a million people[149] gathered in New York's Central Park to demand an end to the nuclear arms race. The date was June 12, 1982, and the event was tied to a U.N. session on disarmament. Reagan, just then returning from his meeting with the pope, in which he had declared himself a man with a messianic mission, could not ignore such an outpouring. Leonid Brezhnev could not ignore it, either. Indeed, on June 15, in a speech at the United Nations, the Communist leader pledged that the Soviet Union would never be the first to use nuclear weapons — a pledge that neither Reagan nor any of those who succeeded him as president would match.[150] Brezhnev announced in this speech that he supported the Freeze.[151] Reagan would have taken note of the grateful ovation Brezhnev drew in New York.

Yet anything a man from Moscow advocated had to be regarded as suspect. It was inconceivable that Communist rulers would care about something called public opinion, but as events would show, Brezhnev and his aging inner circle were already having to adjust in response to a growing restiveness among the peoples under Soviet control. This was primarily a matter of the moribund Soviet economy. In the 1970s, the USSR had outproduced the United States in coal, steel, and oil, but the shift away from heavy industries in favor of the new economic sector of high technology made advantages in smokestack manufacturing less significant, and those advantages had faded in any case. Perhaps the simplest explanation for the dramatic opening of a huge economic lead by the West over the East in the late seventies and early eighties can be summed up in one sentence: Communism discouraged the entrepreneurship that transformed America in the Silicon Valley era. By the mid-1980s computers had begun to change everything in the United States, where there were already thirty million PCs. Russia had only fifty thousand.[152]

What would become known in Moscow as the "new thinking" had been quietly taking hold in universities, research centers, and even Kremlin offices, and now it began to show itself on the world stage, however tentatively. What would later be called the democracy movement in the Soviet sphere drew energy from a growing awareness of the worldwide nuclear danger. An internal reform process was quickened by an external one. But among Western intelligence analysts and Sovietologists of the Totalitarian school, and especially among the new Reagan ideologues, "mass awareness" behind the Iron Curtain was unimaginable. "Extension of regulation and coercion," as Jeanne Kirkpatrick put it, "into all spheres of society is the meaning of totalitarianism."[153] By definition, then, regulation and coercion made anything like a democracy movement impossible, no matter what was happening on the ground. The old political categories were as absolute as they were calcified.

Thus Reagan denounced the Freeze as playing into the hands of the Soviets, and the old notion of disarmament as a Communist ploy was hauled out again. But when the Freeze resolution came to a vote in Congress that summer, it lost by only one vote. The nation's Roman Catholic bishops then issued a pastoral letter, "The Challenge of Peace," calling for "a moral about-face." The letter was read in every Catholic church in America. The bishops not only backed the Freeze, condemned outright any first use of nuclear weapons, and denounced the arms race, but questioned the moral underpinnings of the entire idea of nuclear deterrence.[154]

By the end of 1982, the open affection in which the nation had held Reagan after he was shot had been largely replaced by disdain. "An explosive coalition," in one insider's assessment, ". . . of strategic, moral and political forces,"[155] the Freeze was a political disaster for the White House. Reagan and his advisers "realized," as Frances FitzGerald wrote, "that the strategic-nuclear-weapons policies the administration had been pursuing could no longer be sustained."[156]

This is the context in which to understand the remarkable shift Reagan then made. This shift was embodied in a number of smaller changes: the acerbic ideologue Alexander Haig's replacement by the pragmatic George Shultz at the State Department, which occurred only two weeks after the huge Central Park peace gathering; the announcement in November, shortly after the death of Brezhnev, that Reagan was proposing new lines of communication with the Moscow leadership under Yuri Andropov, aimed at lowering nuclear tensions; and the decision by Reagan to finally, on February 15, 1983, meet personally (and secretly, without the knowledge of his right-wing inner circle) with Anatoly Dobrynin, the Soviet ambassador to the United States. As Reagan's biographer Edmund Morris and others point out, this meeting, arranged by Shultz, marked the beginning of Reagan's accommodating personal diplomacy with Soviet leaders. As such, it was historic, since Reagan's lifetime of Armageddon-think depended on its abstract character. Once the apocalyptic enemy was replaced by human beings, and once the absolutes of ideological conflict gave way to the warmth of handshakes — first Dobrynin's, eventually Gorbachev's — Reagan's devotion to Cold War verities would evaporate.

But the shift is even more notable for two speeches Reagan gave, only days apart, in March 1983. The first was delivered on March 8 at a convention in Orlando, Florida, of evangelical ministers, in which he so unforgettably denounced the Soviet Union as "the focus of evil in the modern world."[157]

This "evil empire" speech is commonly cited as epitomizing Reagan's Manichaean attitude toward the Soviet Union, but what is rarely remarked upon is that his worry on that occasion was not the threat posed by Moscow but the one posed by Randall Forsberg's Freeze movement. For that gathering of conservative ministers had also taken up the Freeze resolution, and that was what Reagan was addressing. "So in your discussions of the nuclear freeze proposals," he said, "I urge you to beware the temptation of pride — the temptation of blithely declaring yourself above it all and label both sides equally at fault, to ignore the facts of history and the aggressive impulses of an evil empire, to simply call the arms race a giant misunderstanding and thereby remove yourself from the struggle between right and wrong and good and evil."[158]

This language was taken at the time as an escalation of anti-Soviet rhetoric, but that misses the larger point. The Freeze movement had transformed the political landscape in which Reagan and his administration's whole approach to foreign policy were standing. The Freeze was truly moving the earth below them. The president's rhetorical extremity was a signal of how concerned Reagan and his circle were about a popular movement that was still picking up steam. Indeed, the Freeze would garner enough votes to pass the House of Representatives on May 5, 1983.

Reagan was desperate to defuse this movement, for personal as well as policy reasons, but he had to be careful of how he framed his objections. After the resolution passed in Congress, he ingeniously denounced the Freeze because it did not go far enough. Ignoring the second paragraph of the resolution, he said the Freeze would allow the superpowers to maintain their stockpiles of weapons. Reagan, that is, rejected the Freeze because it was not dovish enough.

The generals in the Pentagon and the hawks in Congress, thrown on the defensive, did not openly reject Reagan's surprising line. They saw its sly political effectiveness, but to them the idea of the Freeze's not going far enough was, of course, absurd. They understood that their entire program of open-ended weapons development and acquisition was in jeopardy. Yet they were content to stay quietly in the background as the electorate, foolishly driven by worst-case nightmares, turned against them.

The masterly Reagan, meanwhile, was having it both ways: dovish for the first time in his life, and more hawkish than ever. In denouncing the Soviet Union as evil, Reagan was also attacking the dangerous naiveté of people who failed to see that Moscow was always angling for strategic superiority, always looking for the right moment to launch its attack on the United States. Freeze advocates, assuming the possibility of a meaningful compact with such an enemy, and demanding an end to the weapons growth that the Pentagon had come to depend on, were therefore dupes. They were dupes for wanting too much, and dupes for wanting too little. But mainly they were dupes for wanting what Moscow was on record as wanting.[159] In labeling the USSR as evil, Reagan was only an inch away from labeling the Freeze as evil. The new majority of Americans was evil. He was not going to say that, of course.

The key to understanding Ronald Reagan was never his moralism. The difference between Reagan and the ideologues around him would become crystal clear — and they would end up more appalled by his actions than the peaceniks ever were. That Reagan was an actor had a political significance that was overlooked. He never defined himself by ideas, not even those of his simplistic ethical code. He did not proceed "by a train of thought," in the shrewd distinction of Frances FitzGerald, but by "a trail of applause lines."[160] Waves of appreciative applause defined his only ideal, which is why over the years he had consistently tailored his political and moral convictions in such a way as to keep that applause coming. And as an actor, it was not the skilled artfulness of dramatic invention that drove him, but the trick of being a well-liked performer. That was why he was a second-rate actor, never regarded as an artist, a man known, even onstage, not for insight but for congeniality. A performer whose stock in trade is affability knows only one reward, the affection of those who watch him work.

That affection had never flowed more generously to Reagan than in the spring and summer of 1981, after he was shot. But the Freeze movement, growing as he regained his health, and as the nation's memory of his nearly dying faded, trumped all that. Polls showed that the American people had lost confidence in his foreign policy, and the rush away from him on Capitol Hill had turned into a stampede. In January 1983, a milestone was reached when the total number of deployed nuclear weapons in the world (not counting the merely stockpiled ones) exceeded sixty thousand, destructive power capable of obliterating Hiroshima a million times over. In the United States alone, five new nuclear weapons were being produced every day.[161]

Reagan was shaken to the core to find that Americans regarded him as a warmonger, a loose cannon, a danger to the world. His rote denunciations of Communism and Moscow, once so reliable as ever-soothing crowd pleasers, were not working anymore, not even when he escalated the language of condemnation in Orlando. Later that year,[162] a Soviet missile would bring down a civilian airliner, Korean Air Lines flight 007, killing all 269 passengers and crew, and Reagan's denunciations — "a crime against humanity," "an act of barbarism" — would land with weight. But soon Americans understood that the downing of the airliner had been a tragic mistake — the Korean pilots had accidentally drifted into Soviet airspace, and an American spy plane had coincidentally been in the area. KAL 007 faded as a point of contention in a way it never would have a decade or two before. The old master's audience had changed on him. The dependable applause lines were not enough to save him this time. Indeed, those lines only made him more frightening. Ronald Reagan needed a new way into the heart of his audience.

11. THE ABOLITIONIST

Two weeks after his "focus of evil" speech on March 23, he found it. The popularity of the Freeze movement established how much the American people had come to hate nuclear weapons. Now, in a nationally televised speech that had been billed as a routine defense of the administration's huge increases in military spending, Reagan announced that he hated nuclear weapons more than anyone. And he for one was no longer going to tolerate a situation in which peace required a threatened nuclear holocaust. He was doing what the Roman Catholic bishops had just done, which was to question the entire premise of mutual assured destruction. "Wouldn't it be better to save lives than to avenge them?" he asked, as if he were a peacenik after all. The moral theory on which the idea of deterrence rested — how can it be ethical to threaten an action that, in its implementation, would necessarily be unethical? — was convoluted in the extreme, and now Reagan joined the bishops. Ironically, when the simplistic Reagan rejected the Jesuitical reasoning of deterrence theory, he was being more true to himself than ever, and his conviction on the matter carried.

In a startling bit of political sleight of hand, Reagan glided smoothly from talk of expanding military spending to a "dream" that would make such spending obsolete: "After careful consultation with my advisors, including the Joint Chiefs of Staff, I believe there is a way. Let me share with you a vision of the future which offers hope. It is that we embark on a program to counter the awesome Soviet missile threat with measures that are defensive." Reagan wanted a missile defense shield, a "strategic defense initiative," an impenetrable umbrella over the United States, a way of responding to the threat of annihilation that simply, like magic, removed it. No matter that such a thing was impossible. No matter that the very proposal would likely prompt the Soviet Union not to match such a defense but simply to increase its offense. Reagan was a believer, and what he believed in was belief. "I call upon the scientific community in this country, who gave us nuclear weapons, to turn their great talents to the cause of mankind and world peace; to give us the means of rendering these weapons impotent and obsolete."[163]

There it was. Ronald Reagan on the record not as a man who wanted war but as a nuclear abolitionist. And in some simplistic way it was true, or could easily become true. Reagan was reprising the pitchman's role he had mastered for General Electric in the 1950s, cleverly using advertising techniques to create demand for a product before the product existed.[164]

To ask where Reagan got the idea for SDI is to enter the twilight zone of his zany imagination. Strategists had long fantasized about an effective antimissile defense, and some, like Edward Teller, spoke of laser weapons as if they were readily deployable, but mainstream scientists and engineers had demonstrated the unworkability of such a system. Teller influenced Reagan, but so did movies. As Garry Wills points out, Reagan had appeared in a 1940 film called *Murder in the Air*, in which an "inertia projector" causes incoming attack planes to fall from the sky. In a 1966 film, *Torn Curtain*, a character played by Paul Newman speaks of a "defensive weapon that will make all nuclear weapons obsolete." Hollywood is as likely a source for the president's proposal as any physicist working at RAND.[165] Reagan's science adviser was himself a physicist, yet he (and Secretary of State Shultz and, despite Reagan's claim, the Joint Chiefs of Staff) was not consulted before the SDI proposal was drafted.[166]

In the March 23 speech, the president broke with the orthodoxy of Cold War martial science, but he did so because he had never accepted it, having never really understood it. Pitchmen rarely understand (nor do they have to) the intricacies of the products they sell. Reagan's childlike inability ever to have mastered the broken logic of nuclear deterrence (how the threat to destroy the world is what saves it), his failure to grasp the counterintuitive paradox, as basic to human history as the link between the spear and the shield (that defense always stimulates offense, which always stimulates new defense, and so on), his Hollywood-bred willingness to slap a happy ending on a tragedy — all of this enabled him to launch, in Frances FitzGerald's words, "his radical and utopian proposal upon a startled world."

FitzGerald's analysis of the inner logic, or lack thereof, of Star Wars is especially instructive, and her treatment of it informs mine. She points out that Reagan-era historians — and I would add the legion of commentators who "appreciated" him at his death — missed the deeper significance of SDI. Whether praising the Star Wars proposal or debunking it, their analysis omits a crucial phenomenon, which results, FitzGerald argues, in commentary that reads "like the score of a piano concerto with the piano part missing. The phenomenon is, of course, the anti-nuclear movement: the Freeze."[167]

The Freeze stimulated Reagan to find this way of aligning himself with opponents of nuclear war, but the unexpected mass movement against nuclear weapons also prompted those who were preparing to fight a nuclear war to embrace the SDI fantasy as if they believed it. The Joint Chiefs of Staff, Secretary Weinberger, Richard Perle, Paul Nitze, Fred Ikle, and other hawks grasped the usefulness of Reagan's pie-in-the-sky scheme as an undercutter of the still swelling Freeze movement and as a trap for the Soviet Union, which would have to bankrupt itself to keep up with the huge technological investment even preliminary moves toward SDI would require. And, as FitzGerald points out, for the likes of Perle, Ikle, and Wolfowitz, it could be a way to stop the detested arms control process altogether.[168]

At the same time, administration moderates like Secretary of State Shultz could see an avowed American commitment to space-based missile defense as a bargaining chip in the recently resuscitated negotiations with the Soviet Union, an imagined U.S. threat in the heavens — the "high frontier," in General Daniel Graham's phrase — to be traded away for quite real Soviet threats on the earth. For these reasons, men who had every reason to know better signed on to Reagan's Buck Rogers fantasy, and its — to them — equally fantastic corollary, the complete elimination of nuclear weapons. Paul Nitze, for example, was too hardheaded to buy into the president's "dream," but he hid his skepticism behind "a false front of support" for a defensive program he hoped could be traded for Soviet concessions on offense.[169]

No one bothered to ask Reagan why SDI would be needed if there were no nuclear weapons, or why nuclear weapons would have to be eliminated if they had been rendered impotent. No one bothered to ask the president, or any of the experts (chief among them the old avatar of nuclearism, Edward Teller) who joined the chorus to advance the space shield, why such defensive technology — whether directed-energy lasers, nuclear-armed satellites, or so-called smart pebbles — could not be used as offensive weapons. No one asked Reagan how he felt about a super-high-tech, instant-response system that effectively eliminated the president — and all other human beings, for that matter — from any role in deciding to launch a nuclear strike. Computers, satellites, sensors, the highest of high technology, would do it all.

But such basic questions were beside the point, because no one ever actually and fully believed in such wishful thinking but Reagan. He was surrounded by people who, for a range of self-interested reasons, laid aside the hard questions of science and pretended to share his dream. For an actor like Reagan, to pretend was to believe, and to believe was to make real. His coterie learned from him, that's all. Thus his function as president had been transformed: he was Tinker Bell spreading fairy dust and asking of his audience not that they believe but that they pretend to. Across much of America, they did. And in terms of what mattered most to Reagan, it worked.

When the Freeze resolution passed in the House of Representatives, two months after the SDI speech, on May 4, the vote represented the movement's high-water mark, for the Freeze soon lost its force in American politics. Because of Reagan's wily shift, citizens relaxed; fear of nuclear war abated as promptly as it had arisen. One can surmise that the House resolution was finally able to overcome diehard Republican opposition because its opponents no longer had to take the Freeze seriously as a political threat. Why settle for a mere freeze on nuclear weapons when the nation's leader was arguing to get rid of them altogether? Indeed, now that negotiations were to begin again, why settle for a SALT process (arms limitation)? Picking up on the distinction Reagan had made, however disingenuously, at Eureka College in 1982, the new arms control negotiations, once Andropov agreed to them, were dubbed START, for arms *reduction*. They opened in Geneva on June 8, 1983, almost one year after the demonstration in Central Park.

Thus Reagan's powerful new advocacy of a "dream . . . to see the day when nuclear weapons will be banished from the earth" effectively co-opted the Freeze movement. U.S. presidents had been looking forward to the ultimate elimination of nukes since Truman, and since the Nuclear Non-Proliferation Treaty of 1968, the United States had been committed by law to the eventual "general and complete disarmament."[170] But Reagan was now speaking of ridding the world of nuclear weapons as his personal crusade. Not mere limitation, but reduction. Not control, but elimination. That the goal of abolition was linked to a massive expansion of the nuclear nightmare — one month after the START talks resumed, he asked Congress to appropriate funds for the MX missile — seemed no contradiction to him. In Reagan's bipolar mind, SDI and nuclear abolition were the opposites that held each other in perfect tension.

Nor did the contradiction bother the American public, which seemed deaf to accurate and realistic Soviet characterizations of SDI as "space-strike weapons."[171] As 1983 turned into the election year of 1984, Reagan was reborn, in his own mind and, apparently, in the electorate's, as a peace candidate. On January 16, he gave a speech defining the theme of his reelection campaign when, against advisers who would have had him invoke George Orwell, he called 1984 "the year of opportunities for peace." How far he had come from 1980, when he had defined the new decade as "one of the most dangerous decades of Western civilization."[172] Of course, Reagan asserted that the opportunities depended on the bolstered military strength he had presided over, just as Big Brother, in Orwell's novel, governed under the slogan "War is peace."[173] *Peace is our profession.* Without blushing, Reagan was about to put himself forward for reelection as the antidote to the poison draught of fear that he himself had forced on the nation. In his State of the Union message on January 25, he addressed the Russian people, saying that Americans wanted only to live in peace with them.

But the co-opting worked both ways. Precisely because Reagan was a man of uncertain substance, he was changed by the new rhetorical style he had been forced to adopt as a way of keeping that applause coming. That is why, even once he was safely reelected, he did act on his newfound vocation as a kind of peacemaker. The applause depended on it. Because of the Freeze, that is, and the way it broke him out of the MAD orthodoxy of deterrence theory, and out of an Armageddon-inspired complacency about endtime horrors, Reagan embarked in his second term on a course of action that appalled his original inner circle, especially those in the Pentagon. In his second inaugural address, on January 20, 1985, Reagan boldly called for the "total elimination" of nuclear weapons.[174] This was how the hapless Jimmy Carter had talked a decade before, but this new Reagan, speaking to — or, better, out of — an ignited longing in his nation and the world, made the impossible prospect seem real.

To compare the movements on either side of the Iron Curtain: Lech Walesa's influence on the nonviolent end of the Cold War depended on the unexpected arrival at just the right moment of a Soviet leader with the moral vision and nerve it took to respond to him; Randall Forsberg's less direct but also important influence on the nonviolent end of the Cold War depended on the equally unpredicted arrival, after his reelection, of a different Ronald Reagan. The dramatic symbol of this, and a sign of how different he was from four years earlier, was something that had occurred on November 15, 1984, one week after his overwhelming reelection: Reagan wrote to Soviet leader Konstantin Chernenko[175] proposing the immediate start of arms control talks. Chernenko accepted.

Reagan's hawkish insiders had been content to be quiet during the reelection campaign; they had seen the political value of what they took as the president's peace pose. Perle, Kirkpatrick, Weinberger, Wolfowitz, and William Casey were more firmly opposed to negotiations with the Soviets than ever. At the CIA, Casey spoke about receiving reports of Soviet intrusions in Central America,[176] to which we will turn in a moment. Weinberger, for his part, wanted to make the U.S. repudiation of negotiations permanent, denouncing in particular what he claimed were Moscow's betrayals of previous treaties. American Cold War fundamentalism had revolved around such accusations, which is why what happened then is so ironic.

As a matter of plain fact, Reagan's SDI proposal violated the sacrosanct ABM Treaty of 1972: "Each party undertakes not to develop, test or deploy ABM systems or components which are sea-based, air-based, space-based or mobile-land-based." To defend against this awkward complication, the Pentagon, sparked primarily by Richard Perle, promulgated the preposterous — and patently illegal — idea that the treaty could be "reinterpreted." This notion that the meaning of the agreement could be radically adjusted long after the fact, even if the other party to the treaty, or the U.S. senators who had voted to ratify it, disagreed, was a wild notion that undercut the very ethos of international order, yet it would come to be the administration's firm position.[177]

At the outset of Reagan's second term, Shultz, with Nitze, hoped only for modest progress at the negotiating table; nevertheless, at that they were quickly outmaneuvered by the resurgent hard-liners. (Even the "moderate" Shultz and Nitze would buy into the "reinterpretation" doctrine.) But no sooner had the new arms control negotiations begun in early March than Chernenko died, to be replaced by a new kind of Soviet leader. Experts in the United States and Western Europe were ignorant of the silent revolution that had been under way in the intellectual centers of the Soviet Union and Eastern Europe since the Khrushchev era. It had shown itself powerfully, if briefly, during the so-called Prague Spring, but the tanks that had rolled against the "new thinking" in 1968 had not crushed it.

On the contrary, it had quietly flourished, in publications both authorized and underground, with a steady repudiation of the lies and crimes of the Stalin period and a rejection of Leninist orthodoxy that assumed the inevitability of war and the necessity of class conflict. "New thinking" was imbued with a broad humanism that wanted to reclaim the original socialist ideal. The vitality of this movement was confirmed and revealed by the arrival at the pinnacle of Soviet power of Mikhail Gorbachev.

12. SANCTUARY

At fifty-four, the new chairman of the Communist Party was the first Soviet leader to have been born after the October Revolution of 1917. He embodied a readiness on the far side of the Iron Curtain for things unprecedented and, even by the dreamer Reagan, undreamt of. Lech Walesa and Adam Michnik in Poland, Václav Havel and Jan Palach in Czechoslovakia — they and their anonymous cohort had prepared one path for Gorbachev by institutionalizing nonviolence as the mode of pressure for change, enabling Gorbachev to respond in kind. Similarly, the Freeze movement had prepared Ronald Reagan, turning from the thrust of his entire public career, to meet Gorbachev's stunning initiatives, when they came, with a large-hearted openness. That preparation was what enabled Reagan to break from his own inner circle and give Gorbachev what he needed to succeed, against all odds, in his unexpected project.

As a reader must already understand, I believe it was Gorbachev who "ended the Cold War," not Reagan, and he did it with a series of unilateral acts no one could have predicted, and the significance of which few grasped at the time. Not even as informed an observer of the Russian scene as George Kennan could, after the fact, account for the rise of Gorbachev.[178] No one inside the Soviet Union or outside it could have expected such a man, and even today few understand how he came to his positions.

The scholar Matthew Evangelista insists, however, that Gorbachev, as he ascended to power, paid particular attention to the nongovernmental arms reduction groups, such as the Pugwash Conferences on Science and World Affairs, which had sponsored exchanges between Soviet and Western scientists. He was instructed, in Moscow, by scientists like Evgenii Velikhov and other veterans of those discussions. In this way, Gorbachev had learned, before becoming premier, that dismantling the nuclear war system had to be among his top priorities — a lesson gleaned, not incidentally, from a movement headed by Joseph Rotblat, whom we saw earlier as the only major member of the Los Alamos team to resign from the Manhattan Project after it was clear that Hitler would not acquire the atomic bomb. Indeed, the phrase already noted as most associated with Gorbachev, "new thinking," had its origin in the original 1955 Pugwash declaration, composed mainly by Rotblat and signed by Bertrand Russell and Albert Einstein.[179] The influence of the international arms reduction movement weighed at least as much on Gorbachev's mind as the highly touted Pentagon buildup of the Reagan era.[180]

But it wasn't only what had prepared Gorbachev; it was also what he could draw on. The Soviet leader could not have worked his changes without Solzhenitsyn, Walesa, Sakharov, Havel, and their partners on one side; and without Forsberg, Markey, Hatfield, Kennedy, and the duly transformed Reagan on the other. As Jonathan Schell points out, the antinuclear cause and the transformation of the Soviet Union from within were intricately linked.[181]

But the Freeze movement, which Reagan had co-opted, might not have been enough. After his reelection with an overwhelming mandate, he could well have sunk back into the rejectionist mindset of his first instincts, the paranoid hatred of all things Soviet that still animated the hard-liners, who were reemerging from the shadows of his administration. In fact, the American national security elite had no real interest in bringing either the Cold War or its engine, the arms race, to an end. But that was not true of the people as a whole, and it was the people who forced the change, first through the Freeze, then through a widespread, inchoate, but ultimately powerful new current running counter to war.

Along with the Freeze campaign, there had arisen another popular movement that, while different and less widespread, played its crucial role in the transformation of Ronald Reagan — and in the total defeat of a major Pentagon impulse. This was the sanctuary movement, which enlisted thousands of U.S. citizens in the struggle for justice in Central America. The movement decisively changed the politics surrounding the struggle, blocking the Reagan administration's one real effort to take the nation to war and forcing him into deceitful tactics that would, when exposed, leave the beleaguered president no choice but to accept Gorbachev as the rescuer of his status as America's hero.

The story of sanctuary is hardly remembered, and is therefore a missing piece of the Reagan puzzle. It is quickly summarized. Reagan came into office just as the popular struggle against oppressive regimes in Central America reached a critical stage. More than two thirds of the region's people had been made desperately poor over three generations by an American-sponsored, single-crop, agribusiness economy that had made a mere 5 percent of the population fabulously wealthy. The Latin oligarchs were not owners, exactly, but in effect agents of such American companies as United Fruit and Domino Sugar, and multinational corporations like Gulf & Western. Dictators had been installed in these countries to protect this U.S. dominance. But finally, the vast numbers of dispossessed people were showing signs of throwing off this system, which inevitably provoked conflict with its sponsor to the north.

In Nicaragua, the brutal Somoza regime had been in power since the 1930s. FDR had called Anastasio Somoza García a son of a bitch, "but he's *our* son of a bitch."[182] One of his sons and successors, Anastasio Somoza Debayle, was overthrown by the revolutionary Sandinista Front in 1979. The Sandinistas took their name from César Sandino, whom the senior Somoza had murdered in 1934. The Nicaraguan revolution was inspired by a mix of Socialist and Catholic ideology, and the makeup of the *comandantes* of the Nicaraguan "Directorate" reflected that. Three of the eight members of the ruling junta were Catholic priests,[183] one was a hardcore Marxist, and the others were left-wing nationalists.

The Sandinistas' program included breaking up vast estates into smaller farming cooperatives and turning serfs into landowners. Yet despite the Socialist cast of Sandinista rhetoric, the postrevolution economy remained mostly in private hands; the press remained mostly uncensored. The end of Somoza meant the end of government-sponsored violence and other forms of repression. In large part because of its source in the Catholic tradition of liberation theology, the Sandinista movement represented, in the beginning, a much-needed "third way" between Marxist ideology and postcolonial economic subjugation. Eventually, the Sandinistas would organize elections, and when they were defeated by their fiercest critic, the owner of the leading opposition newspaper, they would peacefully yield power.

The Carter administration, influenced by the usual Pentagon suspicion of revolutionary movements and the U.S. economic interests that had depended on Somoza, was ambivalent about the Sandinistas. Reagan, coming into power just as the new regime was taking control in Managua, saw it in the most simplistic terms, as a Moscow-sponsored thrust against the Western Hemisphere. Reagan's views here were shaped by conservative Republicans who were longtime friends of the Latin American oligarchies, to whose defense U.S. Marines had come again and again. On becoming president, Reagan made support for the anti-Sandinista *contrarrevolucionarios,* the Contras, a priority. The Nicaraguan revolution would be his proxy enemy, a weak adversary against whom he could earn his anti-Soviet bones. It is clear from the rhetoric he adopted at the outset that he knew nothing about Nicaragua, the plight of its people, or the leaders he demonized. He regularly condemned the Sandinistas for being, among other things, hostile to religion, despite the priest members of the junta and despite the fact that Roman Catholic "base communities" were key elements of Nicaragua's social reorganization.

Seven small nations define Central America, and the Reagan administration saw the others as dominoes ripe to fall under Soviet sway, with Nicaragua acting as a new Cuba. As part of Reagan's quick expansion of Pentagon spending, military aid and U.S. "advisers" were dispatched to Guatemala, Honduras, and El Salvador, which became bases for the Contra assault against the Sandinistas. The fact that these three countries were themselves in the grip of thuggish right-wing military governments was no problem to Reagan. To him the Contras were not brutal Somoza loyalists but "the moral equivalent of our Founding Fathers and the brave men and women of the French Resistance."[184] This American support for the Contras, prompting a huge escalation in their capacity to wage war, fatally undermined the nascent Nicaraguan efforts at economic revitalization. The Reagan administration increased what had been relatively modest support to three of the most repressive regimes in the world, just as their police-state methods reached new levels of savagery, all in the name of staving off the Marxists. It was the Truman Doctrine carried to its extreme, a potential replay of Vietnam.

Since the mid-1960s, the military governments of Guatemala and El Salvador had murdered more than a hundred thousand of their own citizens,[185] and after Somoza's overthrow in 1979, an event that sparked hope in the breasts of *campesinos* throughout the region, such violence increased. The governments set death squads loose, killing people by the thousands. One effect of this terror campaign was to drive refugees north: in 1980, seventy thousand Salvadorans fled through Mexico to the United States. In time, their number would grow to half a million.[186]

On March 23, 1980, Oscar Romero, the archbishop of El Salvador and the country's leading government critic, preached a sermon addressed to the regime's soldiers. "You are killing your own peasant brothers," he said. "No soldier is obliged to obey an order that goes against the law of God . . . In the name of the Lord and of His long-suffering people whose laments are heard in Heaven every day, I beseech you, I beg you, to stop the repression."[187] The next day, Romero was shot to death at the altar as he was saying Mass. At his funeral, the government's goons attacked again, with firebombs and bullets in the cathedral itself. Forty people died. Two American bishops[188] were among those who fell to the floor amid the gunfire, a direct experience of what Washington was supporting. These prelates would return home as radicalized opponents of Reagan's policies, and their views would affect the whole American Catholic hierarchy, soon transforming one of the most conservative institutions in the nation into a center of dissent.

On December 2, 1980, four Catholic churchwomen, three nuns and a lay volunteer,[189] were raped and murdered by the same goons. Images of these women, along with that of Romero, were put up, icon-like, in Catholic churches all over North America, as priests, nuns, and bishops threw in with the *campesinos* instead of the oligarchs. I had left the priesthood in 1974 — the year of the young Daniel Ortega's escape from a Somoza prison, which marked the real start of the Sandinista revolution — but I recognized the priests and nuns of the Central American resistance as versions of the person I still hoped to be.[190] The American-sponsored war would eventually result in the deaths of many tens of thousands, casualty rates that would remain impossibly abstract in *El Norte*. But like many Americans, my identification with those religiously motivated idealists would be a source of connection with the revolution, a way to make its stakes concrete, and a way to break out of the detachment that ordinarily kept the suffering of the dispossessed far away.[191] For example, we would learn to our shame that many of the worst abusers and killers in Central America were graduates of the U.S. Army's School of the Americas, at Fort Benning, Georgia.

As it happened, two of the murdered nuns, like Ernesto Cardenal of the Nicaraguan Directorate in Managua, were members of the Maryknoll order. Unluckily for Ronald Reagan, so was the aunt of the Speaker of the House of Representatives, Thomas P. O'Neill, Jr. Differences over the struggle in Central America would lead to a confrontation between Congress and the executive branch that was far more acrimonious and, finally, more undermining of the Pentagon's agenda than anything involving the nuclear arms race. And Tip O'Neill was at the heart of this opposition. His perspective was shaped more by the Maryknoll priests and nuns, and then by the Jesuits of his own alma mater, Boston College (when colleagues of theirs were murdered, too),[192] than by the State Department or the Pentagon. The Reagan administration's attitude toward the murdered Catholics, whom many regarded as martyrs, was eloquently summed up by U.N. Ambassador Jeanne Kirkpatrick when, in testimony before Congress, she dismissed the Catholic women slain in Salvador as "not real nuns."[193] Tip O'Neill could not have disagreed more; the Speaker characterized the Contras, whom Reagan called "freedom fighters," as "marauders, murderers, and rapists,"[194] and he set out to stop Reagan's support for them cold.

The refugee flow to *El Norte* grew rapidly, as U.S.-sponsored violence increased throughout Central America. By 1984, the number of refugees to the U.S. from El Salvador alone had reached about 500,000.[195] Such growth is no wonder, considering that the Salvadoran government regarded as a subversive anyone who displayed a picture of the martyred Oscar Romero. The arrival across the Rio Grande, and then across the continent, of these terrorized people conscripted the consciences of many ordinary Americans. It was around this time that groups of flute-playing, guitar-strumming Salvadoran, Guatemalan, and Honduran boys began appearing on street corners and in subway stations. They were black-haired, cloaked in native blankets, figures out of the novels of García Márquez. Their haunting rhythms drew the attention of passersby, music that seemed like ancient tribal laments. The women sold bright woven bracelets, hand-painted crosses. *Who are these people? Where did they come from?*

The Immigration and Naturalization Service had an answer: they were illegals. The government refused to grant those coming from El Salvador, Honduras, and Guatemala status as political refugees, for the simple reason that doing so would indict the very governments that Washington was sponsoring. So these men and women were branded as fugitives. They were aliens, as if from outer space. Like slave catchers of old, INS agents rounded up the refugees and sent them back by the thousands to whatever nightmares the death squads could conjure for them. No equivalent enforcement had ever been brought to bear against illegal aliens from Ireland, say, or from other Latin American nations. The war against Communism in Central America was a war against Central Americans in Tucson, Dallas, Madison, Boston, and New York.

The patent injustice of such a policy brought a strong response, especially among American churches, which began to offer "sanctuary." In 1982, thirty religious communities — parishes, monasteries, schools, convents — offered haven to the refugees, acts of civil disobedience aimed at forcing a change in U.S. government policy. Among the first resisting centers were church groups in Tucson, Washington, D.C., and a Benedictine monastery in Vermont. By 1984, the number of sanctuaries had grown to three thousand, and they were all over the United States. Dozens of religious organizations, including Catholic orders and dioceses and mainstream denominational bodies, passed resolutions of support for sanctuary.[196] Suburban parishes declared themselves in active alliance with "sister communities" in Salvador, Honduras, Nicaragua, and Guatemala. This direct experience by a cross-section of Americans of the real effect of the Reagan war in Central America destroyed the impunity with which the Cold War fundamentalists in the administration had launched it.

The sanctuary movement spawned the related Pledge of Resistance campaign, with more than seventy thousand people pledged to engage in acts of civil disobedience to oppose any expansion of U.S. military forces in Central America. In the same period, religious bodies that denounced Washington's policies there included the U.S. Catholic Conference, the Episcopal Church, the United Methodist Church, the American Baptist Church, and a dozen others.[197] This groundswell of opposition from the heart of the establishment meshed with what O'Neill was organizing in Congress, and on October 12, 1984, a final form of the so-called Boland amendment to an appropriations bill was passed. It outlawed the use of any U.S. funds in support of the anti-Sandinista Contras. This law, born of a mass movement (like the Freeze) that culminated in antiwar legislation, is what prompted Reagan's aides John Poindexter, Robert McFarlane, and Oliver North to secretly divert money from the sale of arms to Iran into clandestine support for the Nicaraguan insurgents — the infamous Iran-Contra affair.

For our purposes, the thing to emphasize is that Iran-Contra was Ronald Reagan's one large disgrace, and as such — threatening his applause again — it became a crucial turn in the story of his response to Gorbachev. In his second term, however much Reagan entered it with the goals of a man seeking peace, he would almost certainly have been swamped by his own instincts as an anti-Communist and by the resurgence of his most paranoid aides, a combination that would surely have forced him to rebuff Gorbachev's soon-to-come overtures. But Iran-Contra made something else happen.

The timing is instructive. Congress cut off funds for the Contras in late 1984. But conservatives in the administration, now led, on the Central American front, by the anti-Communist zealot Elliott Abrams, redoubled their commitment to the Contras. "Man, if you weren't hard enough in your support of the Contras," a White House insider reported of the period, "you were a Commie." Reagan told Robert McFarlane to find ways to keep the Contras going "body and soul."[198] With the help of Oliver North, a young Marine officer on the National Security Council staff, he did. It had recently been revealed that the CIA had illegally laid mines in Nicaraguan harbors, indicating that the law now took second place to the war against Communism, even in the White House. There is every reason to believe that such zealotry against the Marxist enemy in Central America would have defined responses to overtures from the Marxist enemy in Moscow, except for what happened there.

The secret decision to trade arms for hostages, and to divert the Iranian funds to the Contras, was made on December 7, 1985. This violation of an act of Congress was exposed less than a year later, in the fall of 1986. By the following January, Reagan was himself implicated in the scheme, accused by his own underlings of having approved violations of the law. He denied it, and denied it again. He said he could not remember. He admitted that he had little or no idea what was going on in his own administration. The picture emerged of an oblivious, detached, foolish president. The historian C. Vann Woodward told an interviewer that in the history of the American presidency he knew of "nothing comparable with this magnitude of irresponsibility and incompetence."[199]

The people on whom Reagan depended most resigned in disgrace, some to go to jail. Only recently the most admired man in America, the president was suddenly seen as a buffoon at best, a villain at worst. Finally, the humiliated Reagan was forced to go on television to confess. "A few months ago I told the American people I did not trade arms for hostages. My heart and my best intentions still tell me that's true, but the facts and the evidence tell me it is not."[200]

That was March 4, 1987. In the same weeks and months that Reagan's administration was coming unraveled by the Iran-Contra debacle, he was confronted with a series of stunning challenges from Mikhail Gorbachev on the nuclear arms race. As was the case in Central America, Reagan might have been expected to have his responses shaped by the newly reempowered ideologues around him, and for a time it looked as if his fantasy Strategic Defense Initiative, having efficiently defused the threat from the Freeze, might block him from taking up Gorbachev's offers. SDI, that is, was there to give him a way to cling to his oldest idea not only of the Soviet Union but of himself. The Iran-Contra scandal made that impossible, however. It changed the nature of the Gorbachev-Reagan encounters entirely.

Reagan was savvy enough to recognize that he was in danger of joining Richard Nixon in disgrace, a president who broke the law and lied about it. Unlike Nixon, Reagan was a man who lived for the approbation of the people arrayed before him — his viewers, his fans. As that need had prompted a shift in response to the Freeze, it did something similar again. The horror of Nixon's fate emerged in Reagan's mind as a version of what awaited him. Reagan realized just in time that what the new Soviet leader was holding out to him was a lifeline, a way to rescue his reputation, his very presidency — and he took it.

13. ENTER GORBACHEV

Within a month of coming into office in March 1985, Gorbachev unilaterally stopped the deployment of Soviet missiles in Europe. He then called for a bilateral halt to nuclear weapons testing and for cuts in strategic arms in excess of anything so far discussed. Less than three months after taking office, Gorbachev summarily replaced the Cold Warrior Andrei Gromyko as foreign minister with Eduard Shevardnadze, who epitomized the "new thinking."[201] In a series of moves and speeches, Gorbachev manifested a single-minded determination to end the arms race and get the world out from under nuclear terror. "Gorbachev simply reversed Soviet doctrine," one historian writes. "Moscow had argued that only socialists would survive nuclear war; Gorbachev said it would spare no one — not even socialists."[202]

Reagan's anti-Soviet inner circle greeted such actions in a schizophrenic manner. On the one hand, they dismissed Gorbachev's overtures as the same old propaganda tricks. Weinberger was especially strident in denouncing Moscow's deceptiveness. On the other hand, they claimed that the coming to power of such a reform-minded leader showed the success of the Reagan military buildup.[203] In fact, a long-established contrary pattern held throughout the Cold War: martial belligerence in Washington always strengthened the hand of the paranoid anti-American ideologues in Moscow. Gorbachev's biggest problem, when he became party chairman, was how to outmaneuver the very people among his own elite who were steadily empowered by Reagan's militancy. Against those who claim the Reagan military buildup caused the collapse of the Soviet Union, post–Cold War evidence gathered from inside the former Soviet Union suggests that Reagan's early expansion of the Pentagon budget, together with the blatant threats of U.S. military exercises and aggressive reconnaissance overflights, bolstered the Soviet militants, delaying the thaw that came only when Gorbachev forced it.

In the first months of Gorbachev's tenure, the tone of Reagan's pronouncements was stridently anti-Soviet,[204] yet Reagan recognized in Gorbachev a personable style of leadership not unlike his own. On the same day in July that the old hard-liner Gromyko was replaced in Moscow, it was announced that Reagan and Gorbachev would meet in Geneva, the first summit of Reagan's five-year-old presidency. Reagan's own hard-liners, centered in Weinberger's Pentagon, tried to head off any possible accommodation to "new thinking," as if they saw what was coming.[205]

The most important outcome of Geneva, when the two leaders met in November 1985, was Gorbachev's recognition of the authenticity of Reagan's wish to rid the world of nuclear weapons. Gorbachev never said so explicitly, but such a judgment of Reagan was, in fact, a precondition of the initiatives Gorbachev then took. Reagan's shallow need to please an audience coexisted with a profound will to change what the audience took for granted. That paradox defined Reagan's uniqueness. Gorbachev saw it. Notwithstanding the hawks on both sides, the two leaders concluded the meeting with a simple but unusual statement for that era: "a nuclear war cannot be won and must never be fought."[206]

Gorbachev was troubled by Reagan's stubborn (and ABM Treaty–violating) insistence on his plans for the Strategic Defense Initiative, but he must have sensed that even this foolish scheme, with its potential to move the arms race into space, was grounded in Reagan's hope for a world without war. Gorbachev was attuned to the logical inconsistencies of Reagan's position: his declared readiness to share SDI technology with Moscow, his presummit statements that SDI would not be deployed until after "we do away with our nuclear missiles, our offensive missiles."[207] Gorbachev offered to lay aside a traditional reading of the ABM Treaty and accept SDI laboratory research if Reagan would agree to ban research in the field, which was a first step toward deployment. Gorbachev was drawing a line here, because of course the field in this case was outer space. Keeping the arms race from breaking through the earth's atmosphere — this was Gorbachev's concern. Reagan refused to join him in it.

Yet Gorbachev, by his own report in commentary he would offer at the time of Reagan's death in 2004, was moved by what he first saw in the president. The Russian left Geneva aware that he and his American counterpart shared the problem of being surrounded by men stuck in the old orthodoxies of nuclear stalemate — and with a feeling that he and Reagan could work together to break out of it. Gorbachev, that is, took Reagan seriously when he declared, in a television address just before leaving for Geneva, "My mission, stated simply, is a mission for peace . . . to search out, and discover common ground, where we can agree to begin the reduction, looking to the eventual elimination of nuclear weapons from the face of the earth."[208]

It was to this impulse in Reagan, and not any others, that Gorbachev addressed himself. On January 15, 1986, picking up on Reagan's own stated wish, Gorbachev unveiled in Moscow a proposal to eliminate all nuclear weapons "from the face of the earth" by the year 1999. Reagan's ideological speechwriters swung hard in rebuffing response, including in his State of the Union message two weeks later a declaration of support for the "freedom fighters" at war with Soviet imperial expansion everywhere from Nicaragua to Afghanistan to Angola. But such denunciations had become rote for Reagan by now. As his own unscripted responses to Gorbachev would steadily show, his heart was not in them. Of far more significance to him personally and politically was another experience he had just then.

On January 28, 1986, the space shuttle *Challenger* exploded about a minute after takeoff, killing all on board, including the teacher Christa McAuliffe, with whom American schoolchildren had identified. That the catastrophe was witnessed live on television by tens of millions made it a national trauma. It was an occasion to which Reagan rose with dignity and authentic feeling, giving a magnificent eulogy: "The future doesn't belong to the fainthearted; it belongs to the brave. The Challenger crew was pulling us into the future, and we'll continue to follow them."[209]

When Reagan consoled a nation that had seen the pride of its human and technological greatness explode on television, he embodied the hope for compassion and wisdom, and what he received was not mere applause but gratitude. Grief, as it always does, trumped fear, hatred, and the desire for war. First his own near assassination, now the *Challenger:* Reagan was never more himself than when soothing the stresses attached to mortality. Thirst for another draught of such experience now defined Reagan's purpose, and he could satisfy it, he knew, only by nudging the world closer to peace.

The ideologues who could not take Gorbachev's moves on the international stage as anything more than propaganda were not paying attention to what he was doing inside the Soviet Union. Frances FitzGerald helped me appreciate the significance of Gorbachev's internal maneuvering. At the Twenty-seventh Communist Party Congress, in February 1986, he reiterated his call for the abolition of nuclear weapons by the end of the century, but in this forum he coupled it with major shifts in Soviet military thinking: instead of superiority, he was aiming at "reasonable sufficiency"; instead of class conflict, he called for an "interdependent and in many ways integral world"; instead of threatened mutual destruction, he proposed that the United States and the Soviet Union seek "comprehensive mutual security." Making such abstractions real, he broke with the old-style Soviet paranoia by declaring a readiness to accept verification measures for future arms agreements, and he said progress on the quick elimination of intermediate-range nuclear weapons could be made despite American SDI plans. He stated his determination to end the misbegotten Soviet war in Afghanistan, accepting defeat.[210]

One Soviet tradition that Gorbachev kept going was in the length of his speech. It went on for hours. But he had a lot to say. What all of this reflected in a major address to the Communist establishment was Gorbachev's clear-eyed recognition that there could be no progress on his two urgent programs of internal reform, *perestroika* and *glasnost*, until the impossible burden of the arms race was lifted from the Soviet economy and from Soviet society.[211]

Reactionary power in the Soviet Union depended on keeping alive hatred and fear of the capitalist enemy abroad. It depended equally on total control of the inner lives of the Soviet citizenry, but that was breaking. On April 26, 1986, the Chernobyl nuclear reactor went into meltdown, and the Soviet scientific and political establishments went into patently dishonest denial.[212] Hundreds of rescue workers were told nothing of the risks at the doomed reactor, and dozens died immediately of radiation poisoning. Hundreds of thousands of citizens were endangered by a cloud of released radiation that the government denied was there. The catastrophe was an epiphany of calcified deception, and when ordinary Russians and Ukrainians realized that their health and lives had been imperiled by government deceit, they took their first large step as a people into Václav Havel's realm of "living in the truth."

Gorbachev himself had hesitated (he didn't speak publicly of Chernobyl until May 14),[213] but then he turned the political fallout from the disaster into new fuel for his assault on Cold War orthodoxies. There would be no change in Soviet society, no return to the pure ideal of early socialism, without a change in the Soviet Union's place in the world. That was why Gorbachev had to accomplish his reforms on the world stage, and of primary importance was transforming the United States from mortal enemy to great friend. Gorbachev, that is, had to end the Cold War. But he would succeed only if Ronald Reagan joined him.

That is what made the Gorbachev-Reagan meeting at Reykjavík, Iceland, in October 1986 momentous. Gorbachev needed a foreign policy triumph to stave off growing opposition at home. Reagan needed something of the same before the November congressional elections. (Only if he could take Tip O'Neill's House majority away could he hope to head off the mounting Iran-Contra scandal.) But both men needed far more than a diplomatic success. The myth about Reykjavík is that Reagan and Gorbachev came within an inch of an agreement to eliminate all nuclear weapons by the year 2000. "Suits me fine," Reagan said.[214] Gorbachev put that offer on the table as a way of preempting Reagan's Strategic Defense Initiative. But that historic achievement was thwarted when Reagan refused to budge on his plans to go ahead with outside-the-laboratory research on SDI. This story emphasizes Gorbachev's terror at having to compete with SDI and Reagan's bold commitment to a new vision of American defense.[215]

Gorbachev opposed Star Wars, objected to it as outlawed by the ABM Treaty, but it is wrong to say that he feared having to compete with it.[216] At the time of Reagan's death, Gorbachev rebutted the myth of his fear-driven ploy at Reykjavík. He understood the realities of strategic offense and defense better than Reagan did. He knew that the idea of a reliable defensive shield was technologically impractical, and he knew that Soviet strategic forces could compensate for any American defensive measure with a relatively inexpensive increase in offensive capability. SDI was, as Andrei Sakharov later told Gorbachev, "a Maginot line in space — expensive and vulnerable to countermeasures."[217] Indeed, Gorbachev had warned Reagan, after their Geneva negotiations and before Reykjavík, that he would counter SDI simply by developing and deploying a next-generation ICBM, the Topol-M. That is just what Gorbachev did.[218]

Why, then, did he not simply agree to Reagan's fantasy? Surely because the Soviet leader understood that allowing the development of an unreliable missile defense system at a time when the need for fundamental restructuring of nuclear assumptions was urgent would have complicated an already daunting project. Gorbachev feared that SDI would foil a build-down all along the way, empowering the paranoids on both sides — a fear that was, in fact, realized.

Reagan's attachment to SDI was irrational, but he was supported in it by his advisers, especially at Reykjavík, because they saw it as the only way to get him to say no to Gorbachev's radical proposals to end the arms race. Get rid of all nuclear weapons? Reagan said to Gorbachev, "Well, Mikhail, that's exactly what I've been talking about all along . . . That's always been my goal."[219] But at the crucial moment, when the two leaders were that inch from agreement to abolish nuclear weapons, Reagan slipped a note to George Shultz, seated next to him. It read, "Am I wrong?" Wrong to make SDI "field testing" the deal breaker? The moment, reported by Edmund Morris,[220] is heartbreakingly instructive. At that instant, with Gorbachev asking him to join in the rescue of the world from its worst nightmare, Reagan embodied in himself the argument going back to the start of the nuclear age. But now the two oppositions were in the heart of one man, Stimson versus Forrestal all over again, but within Ronald Reagan.

There is a poignancy in Reagan's having turned to his secretary of state for help in resolving this conflict. In what must have been the most fateful act of his long career in public service, Shultz, as he recounted it in his memoir, whispered, "No, you are right."[221] His reply was surely not rooted in his sharing Reagan's Star Wars fantasy, but rather in his knee-jerk realpolitik assessment that Gorbachev's proposal had to be a Soviet trick. At the crucial moment, Shultz was like Weinberger, like Forrestal.

Why? On an obvious level, the agreement to eliminate nuclear weapons would have left the United States and its European allies exposed to the superior conventional forces of the Red Army, all those brown tanks behind the Iron Curtain poised to roll west once the nuclear deterrent was removed.[222] At a subtler level, such a dramatic dismantling of the nuclear arsenals, while not necessarily destroying at a stroke the Cold War structure on which the American economy depended, would have set off tremors whose short- and long-term effects were impossible to calculate. The nuclear arsenal was the ground on which the national security system stood, and that system defined the politics, economy, and culture of the United States, indeed of the West. A stock market crash, economic dislocation, mass unemployment, loss of Washington's dominance over its allies, European outrage, the Pentagon deprived of its central place in government, the service branches demanding huge allocations for a conventional buildup — such consequences would have followed, immediately or over time, from a Gorbachev-Reagan nuclear abolition deal.

The moderate vision of a man like Shultz could foresee a slow arms control plan defusing the nuclear doomsday machine over a period of decades — no real threat to the near-term status quo, economically or diplomatically — but he could no more abide an abrupt break with the superpower contest than the right-wing ideologues whom he had bested in Washington.[223] The

national security establishment was as committed to the "stability of the strategic stalemate," as one of its architects called it,[224] as it was blind to the horrors it forever promised.

Gorbachev left Reykjavík disappointed. His foreign minister, Shevardnadze, had said, "When future generations read the transcripts of this meeting, they will not forgive us, if we let this opportunity pass."[225] But pass it had.
Gorbachev had misread Reagan's willingness to go all the way with him to the
end of the nuclear nightmare; at the very least, he had misread his own ability
to coax the old fool into following him. (Uncharitable wags at the time had it
that, in the Soviet estimate, Reagan had gone from being Rambo to being
Mister Rogers.) There is evidence that the distracted and uninformed Reagan
was already losing his mental capacity to Alzheimer's disease; at the time of
Reykjavík, he signed his name "Reagan Ronald."[226] He kept losing track of the
difference between strategic and tactical weapons systems. He was mocked
for the monumental contradiction inherent in his readiness to sacrifice the
entire existing American nuclear arsenal while refusing to sacrifice a remote
and highly technical fine point of SDI development outside the laboratory.[227]
But in Iceland, Reagan was only being true to his most deeply held prejudice
— call it conviction — about all things Soviet. "Trust but verify," he grew fond
of saying, but at this point he still could not bring himself to trust. By clinging
to the wacky dream of Star Wars, he was finding his way to do what Shultz
had done — say no to his own abolitionist impulse. In the end, his old wari-
ness of Communism prevailed. "This meeting is over," Reagan said. Indeed.

That might have been the end of the story. The Cold War might have
gone on as before. Once back from Reykjavík, Reagan resumed his hawkish
ways. On November 18, he gave a speech reiterating his support for the
Contras in Nicaragua, condemning Soviet adventurism. He chose that context to criticize Dwight Eisenhower for not having sent military aid to support the Hungarian uprising in 1956. On November 28, the United States
broke with the SALT II Treaty, exceeding its limits of strategic forces by deploying upgraded B-52s armed with cruise missiles. American nuclear testing
continued in Nevada. SDI might have prompted a major new phase of the
arms race right then.[228]

The story was not over, however, because the disappointed Gorbachev
was not finished. Inhibited by the rigid certitudes of anti-Soviet ideology, in
place since the Truman era, no one in the West could imagine what they were
dealing with in Gorbachev. Returning to Moscow, he went on with his steady,
unilateral dismantling of the structure of fear, not only of the arms race
but of the entire Cold War. A month after Reykjavík, on November 10, 1986,
he told the puppet rulers of the Soviet satellite nations in Eastern Europe

that their regimes would no longer be propped up by Soviet power,[229] a stunning move that Jonathan Schell characterizes as "nonviolence from the top down."[230] A month after that, on December 12, he let the world know that he had ordered the removal of all Soviet combat forces from Afghanistan. A week later, he ordered the end of Andrei Sakharov's internal exile and brought the famous dissident into his circle of advisers. And a month after that, at the January 1987 plenary meeting of the Communist Party, Gorbachev delivered the most brutal dissection of the Soviet system ever given by a party chairman. What made this a revolutionary act was that he was addressing not the politburo apparatchiks in front of him but the whole Soviet population, for he had grasped the essence of what was happening. Gorbachev was responding to the popular will for change that was so powerfully manifesting itself throughout the once rigidly uniform empire, from the triumphant Solidarity movement in Poland to the enraged radiation sufferers near Chernobyl to the Charter 77 phenomenon in Czechoslovakia to the *Neues Forum* in East Germany. "Listen," he pleaded after the failed talks at Reykjavík, "to the demands of the American people, the Soviet people, and the peoples of all countries."[231]

Again and again in those tumultuous months, Gorbachev was tested, but he never reacted in the old despotic way. In the spring of 1987, a young German named Mathias Rust, having flown his Cessna single-engine plane from West Germany, and having penetrated the Soviet air defense system, put down in Red Square. A photo of the small plane with the iconic onion-domed cathedral in the background appeared on front pages everywhere in the world, even in the Soviet Union. Instead of imprisoning Rust for this violation of national security — not to mention the humiliation of vaunted Soviet air defenses — Gorbachev used the incident as a pretext to remove the defense establishment, army and air ministers along with about a hundred generals and colonels who had opposed his restructuring of the military.[232] He could do this only because the people backed him.

In the midst of these revolutionary moves, and capping them, Gorbachev announced on February 28, 1987, that he was separating the question of intermediate-range nuclear missiles (INF) from other questions of arms control, including that of SDI. In other words, Gorbachev would not accept Reagan's *no.* Instead, he proposed that the United States and the Soviet Union sign an agreement "without delay" to remove all such missiles from Europe within five years. This was Moscow's acceptance without conditions of the "zero option" that Reagan's doctrinaire arms controllers had put forward five years earlier, an offer they had made assuming a Soviet rejection.

Rejection no more. The citizens of Europe, who had been harboring such a hope for half a decade, awaited Washington's response to this stunning initiative with high anxiety, for the newly belligerent Reagan could be expected to reject it. The CIA, still seeing the Gorbachev charm offensive as a ploy, warned that the Soviets were preparing ever more dangerous aggressions.[233] Paul Wolfowitz even now predicted that Moscow was aiming for first-strike capability.[234] Gorbachev's stated determination to end the Soviet war in Afghanistan was dismissed; the CIA would continue supplying weapons to various Afghan fighters (including those who would later be involved in Al Qaeda) long after Moscow's forces were gone.[235] In this spirit, U.S. arms controllers, led by the right-wing ACDA head Kenneth Adelman, registered the usual slew of objections to Gorbachev's INF proposal. No agreement without on-site inspections! But when Gorbachev stunned them by accepting inspections, the Pentagon naysayers had to acknowledge that they would not allow the Soviets to examine U.S. systems and bases. The fifty-year myth of American openness to inspections was punctured in an instant.[236]

But the Pentagon threw up other objections, like so much flak. What about the INFs based in Russia itself, still capable of hitting Europe? What about those in the east of Russia, aimed at China but able to be pointed west? And so on. To each objection, Gorbachev's ready reply was *No problem, let's get rid of them all.*

14. Answer to Forrestal

But what if Reagan simply could not get to yes? Given the negative energy field in which his advisers had sought to imprison him after Iceland, rejection might have defined his response. *No more radical arms control measures for you, Mr. President.* That did not happen for the reason we saw before, his overarching need to protect the fond esteem in which he was so widely held. By an extraordinary and fortuitous coincidence, that need was set loose in his breast again by what had happened two days before Gorbachev unveiled his INF proposal: the publication of the Tower Commission's report on the Iran-Contra scandal. This was the congressional finding that laid out the failures and crimes of the White House, which prompted Reagan's humiliating act of televised contrition. The Tower Commission cast the shadow of Richard Nixon's disgrace over Reagan. It made him desperate for a way to protect his place in the affection of the nation.

Conservatives at the time (although not later, and certainly not at the time of his death) blasted Reagan for sacrificing principle to popularity, and liberals regarded the shift that came now as mere opportunism. Both assessments miss the deeper significance of the emotional component of a leader's bond with the people who had put faith in him. Reagan, for his own psychological reasons and, one must add, for reasons of the common good (his grasp of the importance of nuclear abolition), was determined to keep that faith. This is no reason to denigrate his response to Gorbachev, since it embodied his authentically held desire to lessen the dangers of nuclear war.

The point to emphasize is that both Gorbachev and Reagan, in their moves toward peace, were responding to a great countercurrent that was running outside themselves. The elites, the weapons manufacturers, the intelligence establishments, the political centers, the academic experts, the entrenched bureaucracies, and the opinion makers on both sides were dead set against them. But "the people" represented something else, an ignited mass concern crossing the boundaries of West and East that wanted to preserve the earth and force governments of all kinds to listen and change. What the two leaders did, one in response to the initiative of the other, was not the achievement merely of great men acting in isolation. Their boldness, their heroism consisted in their willingness to step into the countercurrent of popular longing for peace and freedom, that was all.

In Reagan's case, his immediate embrace of INF elimination, clearly motivated by the jolt from the Tower Commission, amounted to a political payoff of the mass opposition to his Contra war. It is not too much to argue that that opposition, enshrined in the Boland amendment, caused the Iran-Contra machinations, the subsequent congressional rage, and therefore Reagan's shame. It was part two, after the Freeze, of the people power running through this story as the great countercurrent to the belligerence of the Cold War. Reagan, that is to say, was like Gorbachev in what mattered most: being attuned to the all-trumping will of the people. In the mid-1980s that will had shown itself in a thousand ways on both sides of the East-West divide. Gorbachev knew it, and so did Reagan.

Against the advice of the newly reempowered hawks of his inner circle who, after Reykjavík, wanted no more of arms control, against his intelligence experts, and against his own resurgent hard-liner instincts, Reagan announced that he would accept Gorbachev's INF initiative with pleasure. That announcement came on March 3, the day before he went on television to repent for the sins and crimes of Iran-Contra.[237]

On December 7, 1941, the war that consumed the second half of the twentieth century began for America. On December 7, 1987, the "cold" phase of that war ended with the arrival in Washington of Mikhail Gorbachev. The next day, with the signing of the INF Treaty, the first actual reduction of nuclear arsenals was ordered, an elimination of about two thousand warheads — an event that marked the reversal of the "armaments race of a rather desperate character" of which Henry Stimson had warned on September 11, 1945.[238]

From the end of World War II until the end of the Cold War, twenty-one million people died in superpower proxy wars,[239] but contrary to the predictions of all the military and academic experts, the political philosophers and nuclear theorists, the conflict between the United States and the Soviet Union suddenly appeared able to be ended without the ultimate conflagration that had haunted Stimson.

The men who had come into power with Reagan, especially those in the Pentagon, were appalled with what the president was accepting from Gorbachev. To them, Stimson's nemesis, James Forrestal, was still right. The vision of NSC-68, with its warning of "a new fanatic faith . . . [seeking] to impose its absolute authority over the rest of the world," still held. But they were being shunted aside. Richard Perle was gone, and Kenneth Adelman soon would be. No sooner had the INF agreement been announced than Caspar Weinberger, still shrilly warning that the Russians were coming, resigned as defense secretary.[240]

During the Washington summit meeting, instead of resting on the laurels of the INF Treaty, as Reagan assumed they would, Gorbachev continued the pressure to fully dismantle the political and military structures of the Cold War. Reagan had no idea how to respond. Gorbachev proposed that they discuss reductions in conventional forces, a concern that had drawn so much fire after Reykjavík. But Reagan had no thoughts on the subject. He told jokes, prompting the usually ingratiating Shultz, when they adjourned to the privacy of the Oval Office, to roundly rebuke him: "Mr. President, that was a disaster. That man is tough. He is prepared. And you can't just sit there telling jokes."[241] But in the end it did not matter. Gorbachev was a man on a mission now, and what the Washington summit established was that not even the president of the United States could stop him. From now on, the president, like the world itself, was a mere spectator. Reagan's contribution was essential, and it consisted in not opposing Gorbachev, which was the main support the Russian needed.[242]

One year later, on December 7, 1988, Gorbachev went before the United Nations, and in his speech that day he changed history. "Necessity of the principle of freedom of choice is clear," he said. "Denying that right of peoples, no matter what the pretext for doing so, no matter what words are used to conceal it, means infringing even that unstable balance that it has been possible to achieve. Freedom of choice is a universal principle, and there should be no exceptions."[243] Gorbachev renounced violent force and its threat

— what had enabled the Soviet empire to hold together from the beginning. He declared that the Soviet Union would cut its conventional forces by half a million men, which required the withdrawal of most Red Army units from Eastern Europe. December 7, a day of infamy no longer.

That year, the Red Army Choir, in dress uniform, performed at the Vatican. The event symbolized the pope's key role in transforming the European continent, relieving it of half a century of armed terror. The hymn the soldiers sang, at the pope's request, was "Ave Maria."[244] By now, that a moral revolution had occurred in the Soviet realm was clear to the world. Not only expressly religious sources had shown themselves — the Roman Catholic character of Solidarity and the Velvet Revolution, the Lutheran character of civic opposition to the East German regime, the Russian Orthodox and Jewish roots of resistance in the USSR — but so had a principled rejection of violence, dramatically visible in East German and Czech conscientious objection to conscription[245] and the refusal of countless Communist soldiers to fire their weapons into crowds, even when ordered to do so.

The growing demand for democracy was itself democracy. The captive nations of the Warsaw Pact responded to Gorbachev's U.N. declaration by breaking with Moscow, and so did the republics of the Soviet Union itself. Gorbachev, in other words, had accepted the idea of government by the consent of the governed, and that idea instantly took hold, ultimately in Russia itself. And over subsequent months, Gorbachev proved the truth of what he declared that day by repeatedly commanding his armies to go back to their barracks as his revolutionaries — "Gorby! Gorby!" they cried in Berlin — poured into the streets. On June 4, 1989, free elections were held in Poland, and despite Communist attempts at rigging them, Solidarity won 99 of the 100 senate seats and 160 of the 161 seats in the lower house for which it entered candidates. The new prime minister of Poland was the former editor of the Solidarity newspaper. By the end of the year, the dissident Václav Havel had been elected president of Czechoslovakia, and the Romanian dictator Nicolae Ceausescu had been executed by firing squad. Perhaps more remarkably, elections had been held in the Soviet Union, and none other than Andrei Sakharov had been elected to the new Congress of People's Deputies.

In the Pentagon, all of this evidence of Gorbachev's revolution continued to be missed because the Forrestal mindset was still firmly in place. In Hell's Bottom, on the edge of the Potomac, the antagonism between the United States and the Soviet Union was rooted in the very structure of human thought: conflict was intractable, war was inevitable, and only war would defeat the evil empire. Even in 1989, that theology remained sacred, and the Pentagon remained its holy of holies.

*   *   *

If December 7 is a mystical date, so is November 9. On that day in 1938, the horrors of the twentieth century began to mount when Nazi thugs attacked synagogues and Jewish businesses and homes throughout German-occupied Europe. On that date in 1989, *Kristallnacht* was reversed when throngs of Germans first breached, then began to break down, the Berlin Wall.[246] On June 12, 1987, Ronald Reagan, at the Wall, had cried, "Mr. Gorbachev, tear down this wall!" But what Reagan, and those who lionize him for that gesture, never understood was that Gorbachev, in response to the people who eventually gathered there, was already doing just that. Gorbachev was responding not to Star Wars, not to the economic pressure of a Reagan military buildup, but to far more basic changes in the world. Inbuilt failures of the Soviet social and economic system had finally shown themselves; the information age had dawned, inventing the global village; technology had transformed military and economic realities;[247] and, above all, a revolution of popular will had swept the globe. Astoundingly, that revolution was essentially nonviolent. Because it was, what followed from the Kremlin could be nonviolent, too. Gorbachev saw all this, and responded accordingly.

So, in his way, did Reagan. When he visited Moscow in May 1988, he mingled with everyday Russians, a people whom he had demonized over a lifetime. But now he pronounced them good. Gorbachev — "this one man," as the president himself said[248] — had put the lie to Reagan's most fiercely held conviction. Yet extraordinary as Gorbachev's responses had been, Reagan was mistaken to credit him in isolation from his nation. When a reporter asked Reagan if he considered Moscow the capital of an evil empire, the president said no. That was from another time, he said. Alas, Reagan did not seem to know, even now, that in that other time, he and all the others like him had been simply wrong. Wrong from the Long Telegram and the "X" article forward. Wrong on the Truman Doctrine, NSC-68, and the Gaither Report. Wrong when Stalin died. Wrong on Vietnam. Wrong on Nicaragua. Wrong on almost every assessment of Soviet intentions and capabilities across fifty years. Wrong, most fundamentally, about those human beings on the far side of the iron divide.

John Kennedy had said as much in 1963, in the American University speech, which pointed to a road not taken: "No government or social system is so evil that its people must be condemned as lacking in virtue." Kennedy had also said, against the conviction on which Reagan had based his career, that no government or social system is so virtuous as to be exempt from self-criticism. "For our attitude is as essential as theirs."[249]

Gorbachev was plainly pleased when Reagan finally eschewed the word "evil." He took note of where Reagan did so. "He said that within the walls of the Kremlin, next to the czar's gun, right in the heart of the evil empire. We take note of that. As the ancient Greeks said, 'Everything flows, everything changes. Everything is in a state of flux.'"[250] As Reagan boarded *Air Force One* to leave Washington after the inauguration of his successor, in January 1989, he said simply, "The Cold War is over."[251] At last, James Forrestal had his answer. But Forrestal's dialectically minded ghost stubbornly refused to accept that answer, and the ghost was coming back.

EIGHT

....

UNENDING WAR

1. INTO PLOWSHARES

In early May 1997, I drove from Boston to Portland, Maine, every morning for a week to attend a trial in federal court. A man from my past, Philip Berrigan, and five others had slipped aboard the USS *The Sullivans* three months before, taken hammers to the ship's weaponry, and poured blood. This took place at the Bath Iron Works, in Bath, Maine, where the recently completed ship was to be commissioned. Berrigan and the others[1] made their move in the early morning, and within a few minutes they were arrested by sailors armed with shotguns. *The Sullivans* is an Aegis-missile-carrying destroyer, named for five brothers who died together in World War II. The protesters damaged the casement for the nuclear-capable cruise missiles. One of the group was an artist named Tom Lewis-Borbely, who had been one of the original Catonsville Nine in 1968.

In support of the Catonsville Nine, I had mounted an exhibition of Lewis-Borbely's paintings at Boston University in 1970, and he had given me one of them, a view of the Pentagon, which has hung on my wall ever since. Speaking in the hallway of the courthouse, Tom told me that, at the Bath Iron Works, he and the others approached the ship shortly after dawn. Finding it unguarded, they simply walked aboard. "I would say," Tom added, as he recalled the ease with which they acted, "that the Holy Spirit led us."[2]

Presiding at the trial in Portland was federal district judge Gene Carter, a stern man who had been nominated to the bench by Maine's Republican senator William Cohen. Carter refused to allow the defendants to explain their actions to the jury. At that, Phil Berrigan, tall as ever but gray-haired now, his face lined, turned his back on the judge, a posture he maintained day after day. The trial was perfunctory. The defendants were found guilty. Judge Carter sentenced Phil to two years in prison, the others to lesser terms. At that, Phil was finally allowed to speak. "The United States has spent fourteen trillion dollars on arms since 1946," he said. "Our government has intervened in the affairs of fifty nations and has violated the laws of God and humanity by designing, deploying, using, and threatening to use atomic weapons."[3]

Philip Berrigan, with his brother Daniel, had been famous in America during the Vietnam War, but he had dropped from the news. We saw this. Unlike most antiwar activists of the time, however, Phil had not given up his life of protest. With his wife, Elizabeth McAlister, he had founded a peace commune in Baltimore, and from there he had launched a new campaign. It was dubbed the Plowshares movement, from Isaiah 2:4: "They shall beat their swords into plowshares, and their spears into pruning hooks: nation shall not lift up sword against nation, neither shall they learn war any more." With Berrigan at its center, a circle consisting of dozens of people carried out symbolic assaults against America's nuclear weapons manufacturing sites and military deployments, including attacks on B-52 bombers, Trident submarines, and MX missiles.

The first took place at a General Electric plant in King of Prussia, Pennsylvania, on September 9, 1980, when Philip Berrigan, with seven others, including Daniel, walked into the factory as the morning shift was changing and "beat" a number of nuclear-tipped Mark 12A reentry vehicles, which were mounted on the nose cones of MIRVed MX and Trident missiles.[4] The protesters had prepared a statement: "We commit civil disobedience at General Electric because this genocidal entity is the fifth leading producer of weaponry in the U.S. . . . We wish to challenge the lethal lie spun by G.E. through its motto, 'We bring good things to life.' As manufacturer of the Mark 12A re-entry vehicle, G.E. actually prepares to bring all things to death."[5]

Over the next twenty years, about a hundred Plowshares actions followed, in Europe as well as the United States, at manufacturing plants and at Air Force and Navy bases. More than a hundred people participated in the symbolic "beatings" of weapons, all to be promptly seized and arrested. Such acts, in the military's view, are sabotage, gravely threatening, yet no one was ever injured — not the demonstrators, workers, guards, or arresting officers. Philip Berrigan had been dismayed by the peace movement's temptations to violence late in the ever more criminal Vietnam War, but with Plowshares he had found a form of protest that was as direct and nonlethal as its objects were denied and murderous. He conducted such raids again and again, and was incarcerated again and again. By the time of his death, in December 2002, he had spent eleven years of his life in prison.

Yet most people took no note of Berrigan's life after Vietnam. Few understood that the obsessive concern about nuclear war that sparked the Freeze movement for a time had gripped Berrigan and his followers with an unrelenting extremity. The threat of nuclear war that prompted such outpourings in the early 1980s would seem to most others diminished after Ronald Reagan began to speak of eliminating weapons, but Berrigan saw through the ways that Reagan had co-opted the Freeze, and unlike most others, Berrigan knew that the nuclear arsenal was still growing. And then, when Gorbachev gave the world serious reason to hope for peace, Berrigan was one of the few to note the one-sidedness of that breakthrough.

From start to finish, the media found the Plowshares actions not newsworthy. That was especially so once the dominant story unfolding in the late 1980s and early 1990s was the thaw in the Cold War, and then the end of it.

To those who had heard of the Plowshares protests, Berrigan was a lunatic, or at best a wild-eyed idealist. He and McAlister, it was said, were frozen in time, unable to surrender the self-anointed grandeur of their Vietnam glory days. Anarchist, terrorist, fanatic — such were the words prosecutors routinely applied to Berrigan. I myself was always moved by reports of his actions, but otherwise I took little more note of them over the years than most others. But the Plowshares group that took action against *The Sullivans* in 1997 called themselves "the Prince of Peace Plowshares." They took the name, of course, from Isaiah's title for the Messiah, one Christians had applied to Jesus. As it happened, I had used the same epithet as the title of a novel I wrote, based on, among other things, the Berrigan brothers' exploits during the Vietnam War.[6] That novel was concerned with the moral problems of war and how to resist it. A loving tribute to the Berrigan wing of the antiwar movement, it also took up the question of protesters who seem to judge the actions of others from a position of ethical superiority. As the story unfolds, the fictional characters, despite heroic acts of resistance to an evil war, are themselves revealed to be flawed human beings.

At the end of the Vietnam era, which coincided with the end of my time in the priesthood, many of us had been forced to confront the "beams in our own eyes," as the Gospel of Matthew defines hypocrisy. Perhaps for that reason, or perhaps because of the usual dispersal that occurs after a time of emergency passes, the once close-knit community drifted apart, leaving many of us with feelings of unfinished business, even regret. So when I read of the Plowshares raid in Bath, and that the group had called itself Prince of Peace, I recognized a coincidence that was also a conscription. The assault against the Aegis missile had been ignored in the press, and by then I was a columnist for the *Boston Globe*. I felt compelled to write about what the Plowshares collective had done, what they were trying to tell a blithely indifferent world.

"We want to tell people what's going on in this country," Phil wrote from jail in Maine. "We want people to know that the government has entered a new phase of the arms race — we are racing with ourselves . . . The government is beating plowshares into swords, creating an entirely new arsenal of nuclear weapons."[7]

It was true. This was almost exactly ten years after Mikhail Gorbachev and Ronald Reagan had marked the supposed reversal of the arms race with the signing of the INF Treaty in Washington. It was early in the second term of Bill Clinton, who had objected to the war in Vietnam and who now had had more than four years to reshape American policy. Why had Clinton done so little to dismantle the American half of the Cold War nuclear apparatus? That is our question now.

Philip Berrigan a lunatic, a wild-eyed idealist? No, it was with shrewd realism that he looked at what had happened since the end of the Cold War — a situation from which his fellow Americans had universally turned their gaze. *We are racing with ourselves.* Here is the last legacy of the "arms race of a rather desperate character" that Stimson had warned of. Back then, Stimson had been almost alone in seeing it, and now Berrigan was, too. Ever attuned to the liturgical calendar — the raid on *The Sullivans* took place on Ash Wednesday — the former priest had taken solemn note of the fact that the flag of the Union of Soviet Socialist Republics had been lowered from above the Kremlin for the final time on Christmas Day, 1991. Feast of the Prince of Peace.

A month later, in his State of the Union address, President George H. W. Bush declared that the United States, "by the grace of God," had "won the Cold War."[8] And yet the U.S. arsenal that had been built up and justified by the threat from the Soviet Union had not been dismantled. The much-ballyhooed "peace dividend" had never come. As the Warsaw Pact disbanded, NATO expanded. The newly independent former Soviet republics of Belarus, Kazakhstan, and Ukraine had completely divested themselves of nuclear weapons and embraced the Nuclear Non-Proliferation Treaty, while the United States defied it. Clause VI of that treaty requires the nuclear powers to work toward the abolition of nuclear weapons, but in America, the weapons were still being developed, built, and deployed. For use against whom? To protect America from what? In the second Clinton term, the Pentagon budget began to climb again. And this without an enemy. Why? And why, under President Clinton, had the destruction of nuclear warheads been stalled, when thousands had been destroyed under Reagan and Bush?[9] What *had* been destroyed under Clinton, at the behest of right-wing senator Jesse Helms, was the Arms Control and Disarmament Agency, just when its work was most needed.[10] Why? These were questions no one was asking.

Except Philip Berrigan and his friends. Susan Crane, one of the Prince of Peace Plowshares defendants, said, "At some point, we must call this charade to a halt. We must say 'enough' to Judge Carter and the empire on whose behalf he seeks to send us to prison."[11] A few weeks after the Plowshares trial in Portland, I happened to be interviewing William Cohen for a magazine article.[12] Having been Judge Carter's sponsor as a U.S. senator from Maine, Cohen was by now the secretary of defense. For the article, I had met with him in his grand third-floor office above the River Entrance, the office into which my father had once ushered me to meet Secretary McNamara.

Returning to the Pentagon as a writer was to be briefly at the mercy of memory: sliding down the polished ramps in my stocking feet, wandering through the rings and corridors as if they were my magic kingdom, drinking from water fountains the very abundance of which had been designed to keep the races separate. In interviewing one Pentagon general, whose office was down the hall from Secretary Cohen's, I felt a chill on my neck as my eye went to the distinctive wall map showing a projection of the globe, the leather couch in front of it, the way the wall map's frame joined the wainscot molding, and I recognized the room as my father's old office.

A few days later, I flew with Secretary Cohen on his Gulfstream jet for a trip back to his hometown of Bangor. We departed from Andrews Air Force Base, having boarded the plane within sight of an Air Force building that had been named for my father.[13] As we flew over Portland, I gestured out the window and told Cohen that Philip Berrigan was in jail down there. An assault on the destroyer at the Bath Iron Works would have registered with Cohen. The shipyard was Maine's biggest employer; its head was a major supporter of Cohen's. As secretary of defense, he was working to make sure Maine kept the Navy contracts for the new nuclear warships. I asked him if he had heard what Philip Berrigan had done.

Cohen shrugged. He is a pleasant man, with a reflective manner not given to extremes. "I read about it in the press," he told me. "I saw a little, small story about it. I figured, that was still Phil Berrigan. It didn't strike me as being unusual. I think that there are legitimate ways to protest. Destroying or trying to destroy things aboard a destroyer is not one of them."

Cohen is something of a poet,[14] yet he seemed unaware of the irony embedded in his use of the word "destroy." He went on about Berrigan, "But that's not how he feels about it. As long as he's prepared to accept the consequences that come with it, I don't pass judgment."[15] Such benign dismissal was about as positive a response as Philip Berrigan was likely to draw from any establishment figure in post–Cold War America. Yet he and his band of crazy, ignored, denigrated peaceniks seemed to have been the only ones in the nation to have noticed the stunning anomaly. The Cold War was over for most of a decade — but not in America. The arms race had ended when one of its two competitors had simply disappeared — but the United States was still running. How could that be?

2. BACK TO STIMSON

When, on September 11, 1945, Secretary of War Henry Stimson had proposed approaching the Soviet Union with a view to working out a joint custodian-ship of the atomic bomb, in order to head off "an armaments race of a rather desperate character," Navy Secretary James Forrestal had trumped the pro-posal with a deep fear of Moscow. It is clear now, as we have seen, that early, Truman-era assessments of Soviet capacities and intentions were overblown, yet the postwar American impulse toward disarmament had grown stronger. Soldiers were sent home. Warplanes were dismantled for scrap, ships dry-docked. Stringent budgets were imposed on the new Department of Defense, even with Forrestal as its first chief. The Pentagon, with its massive invest-ment in military power, had been built to be temporary, and it might have been, but those who wanted to maintain that power, and multiply it with a previously unimagined thermonuclear arsenal, were "rescued" when the So-viet Union detonated its own atomic bomb in the summer of 1949.

Forrestal's demise by suicide in the same period suggested that the na-scent "national security state," with an enemy it defined as if it had theologi-cal and ontological reach instead of merely imperialist ambitions, was, at least in part, founded on paranoia. At the same time, owing to the competing pres-sures of postwar economic dislocation and the reemergence of an instinctive American insularity, the hugely expanded military budget called for by the agitated NSC-68 was almost certainly never going to be passed by Congress. But then, as Dean Acheson — already dean of the national security state — later affirmed with brisk understatement, the Korean War "came along and saved us."[16] To meet the threat in Asia, the military budget was quadrupled in half a year,[17] and the Defense Department was off and running. We saw all this.

A Cold War pattern was set. From then on, whenever the icy vastness be-tween Moscow and Washington began to thaw, making a lessening of ten-sions, and a related slowdown of the arms race, seem possible, one new threat or another always surfaced to drop the temperature precipitously — *Sputnik,* the so-called missile gap, the Cuban Missile Crisis, the Vietnam War, the Soviet invasion of Afghanistan, the Sandinista revolution, the Iranian hostage crisis, the downing of KAL 007, the Socialist takeover of the Caribbean island of Grenada, even the attempted assassination of a pope. Each incident "rescued" Cold War rigidities, reinforced the profitable insecurities of the military-industrial complex, and kept the Niagara current of the arms race flowing. This dynamic always assumed the permanent malevolence of a Kremlin-centered enemy.

As Soviet leaders showed themselves to be serious about dismantling their side of the East-West confrontation, entrepreneurial American custodians of the national security state fell to worrying about a sequence of insecurities. Over the years, the position of Paul Nitze, whom we first saw as a protégé of James Forrestal, then a member of the Strategic Bombing Survey in Hiroshima, was a barometer of the hardening of Cold War attitudes. Early on a hawk of hawks, Nitze had come to be regarded by the Reagan-era Pentagon (including his disciples Richard Perle and Paul Wolfowitz) as soft, without having changed a thought. One telling symbol of the Defense Department's new rigidity was the way Secretary Caspar Weinberger would openly berate the distinguished Nitze with what one chairman of the Joint Chiefs characterized as "sophomoric sarcasm."[18] As the American side willfully failed to keep up with Soviet arms control initiatives, Nitze's old age and illness — he suffered from a kind of viral rheumatism known as "devil's grip" — were taken as a metaphor, his biographer says, for the entire enterprise of arms control.[19] If Nitze could be an object of suspicion, how much more so the Soviet interlocutors with whom he had worked for a generation?

But suspicions now were countered by facts. Every American question had its answer. How could arms control treaties with congenitally duplicitous Communists be trusted? Moscow agreed to verification. What if agreed-upon reductions in nuclear stockpiles increased Soviet conventional superiority? The Soviets unilaterally made deep cuts in Red Army troop strength and eliminated the tank brigades that had disturbed the sleep of Western Europe for a generation.[20] What if Soviet reforms failed and a kind of Red fascism seized Moscow? The reformers prevailed in every contest, and the Soviet Union rejected violence even in defense of its own survival. What if the Soviet empire came apart, resulting in a host of nuclear enemies? The first thing the breakaway republics did as newly independent states was renounce nuclear weapons, ceding their arsenals to Russia, and the first thing the new Russia did with its now more than thirty thousand nuclear warheads was affirm continuity with arms control agreements of the Soviet past.[21] What if impoverished East Germany, in economic free fall, became the new source of divi-

sion in Europe? The West German government in Bonn firmly committed itself to the economic support of East Germany, and to the ideal of a reunited
Germany as a source of European unity. The primal wound of East-West conflict was, in a stroke, healed. And as every justification for Cold War fears, and
therefore armaments, took itself apart, a challenge of a wholly new kind presented itself to the United States. Moscow had changed, changed utterly.
Would Washington?

3. Operation Just Cause

George H. W. Bush became president as these developments were approaching climax. When it came to matters of war and peace, he might have been a
leader of rare self-confidence, since he was an authentic war hero.[22] But
Bush's political imagination was far more conventional than Ronald Reagan's
had been. Nothing in Bush was drawn, for example, to the utopian dream of a
nuclear-free world that, notwithstanding the contradictions of SDI, had so
motivated Reagan, and that had made Reagan the perfect partner to Gorbachev. Lacking "the vision thing," Bush found it impossible to respond with
proper gravitas to the world-historic collapse of the Berlin Wall in 1989. It is
unthinkable that either of the presidents who bookended him would have
missed the opportunity to sacralize such a pure triumph of the democratic
spirit and of a human rejection of violence.

The Berlin Wall phenomenon (recall that it came down on November 9,
the anniversary of *Kristallnacht*) was followed, in early December, by a summit meeting between Gorbachev and Bush. They met on naval vessels in the
harbor at Malta, the island nation in the Mediterranean. Bush had begun his
presidency with a "pause" in diplomacy, a freeze in contacts with Moscow, for
the sake, it was said, of "policy review." In fact, the Bush foreign policy team
was as distrustful of the accommodations Ronald Reagan had made in his
second term as they were of Gorbachev's maneuvering. Just as *perestroika* was
entering its dynamic phase, America had countered with a major stall — "status quo plus." Bush fully rejected Gorbachev's overtures in the first four
months of 1989, leaving the Soviet leader vulnerable to internal critics and
keeping Bush at the mercy of Pentagon advisers who refused to credit Gorbachev's promises. The encounter at Malta, therefore, was long overdue, and
with the Berlin Wall being joyously taken apart concrete chunk by concrete
chunk, Pentagon skepticism was beginning to seem ridiculous. The Malta
meeting advanced the cause of nuclear arms reduction[23] and forged a personal bond between Bush and Gorbachev, but it was, at the level of symbol-

ism, a disaster. A winter storm roiled the waters of the Maltese harbor, which seemed to emphasize the dangers of the new situation more than the opportunities.

Indeed, the new situation seemed to bring out something profoundly reactionary in Bush. As a congressman, he had been strident in his anti-Communism, and during Vietnam he had publicly supported the idea of using nuclear weapons.[24] Now, under Bush's leadership, America followed the Berlin triumph of democracy, nonviolence, and Communist restraint — two weeks after Malta, little over a month after Berlin — with a nasty, unprovoked, and, by traditional readings of U.S. law, illegal war against Panama.[25] On December 20, twenty-four thousand U.S. soldiers and marines swooped into the Central American nation in an unbridled violation of its sovereignty. Dubbed Operation Just Cause, it was treated by the American press and public as an event of historic proportions. Polls taken at the time showed a large majority of Americans regarding Panama as a more significant security issue for the United States than anything transpiring behind the teetering Iron Curtain, and by an overwhelming percentage, Americans approved of the invasion.[26]

The reaction abroad to Operation Just Cause was more skeptical, to say the least. A Soviet official, learning of the invasion and aware of how Moscow just then was declining to use force to shore up its empire not only in Eastern Europe but in the more vital and increasingly restive Baltic nations, said to the U.S. ambassador, "It seems we've turned the Brezhnev Doctrine [of unlimited intervention in satellite nations] over to you."[27]

That Bush pursued such a strategy is no surprise. At one level, it was the manifestation of a familiar pattern — an untested president proving his mettle with an act of war. It was what Truman did at Hiroshima, what Kennedy did at the Bay of Pigs, what Johnson and Nixon each did in Vietnam, what Carter did with the attempt to rescue hostages in Iran, what Reagan did by invading Grenada. (Note that Eisenhower, who ended a war instead of starting one, had nothing to prove about his willingness to use force.)

The question that short litany raises, of course, is about the relationship between the Cold War and the power ambitions of the United States. I just observed that George H. W. Bush found it impossible to mark the momentous fall of the Berlin Wall with an appropriate symbolic act, but perhaps that is exactly what he did with the invasion of Panama — an implicit declaration that the post–Cold War American global reach would go on unimpeded, whether the Soviet Union's counterimperialism existed as a justification or not. Was the Panama invasion, for that matter, an early declaration that the restraints imposed by the Cold War balance of the superpowers would no longer hold now that one of the two was dissolving?

But it was also true that Bush's decision to invade Panama was an early result of the influence of his decidedly belligerent inner circle. Ronald Reagan, as he left office, had proclaimed that the Cold War was over, but Bush did not think so. Reagan, after all, was a moralizing fantasist, while Bush, who took pride in his credentials as a hardheaded realist and whose doctrine focused on Soviet capabilities rather than intentions, still found endless scenarios for which massive military preparation would be required. Besides, a simple look around suggested Cold War continuity. How could it be otherwise when, no matter what had happened in Moscow, so little had changed in the United States?

The fact that the new situation had come about almost entirely through initiatives of the other side left America's realist policymakers in a vacuum, at the mercy of their inbred skepticism. They were programmed to envision the future only in terms of the worst case, and the worst case in a world still bristling with nuclear weapons remained horrible. But what had become truly unthinkable was a world *without* those weapons, and now the people in power in Washington, long at home with deterrence and the balance of terror, regarded arms reduction beyond a certain point (and perhaps we had reached that point) as dangerously destabilizing. Yet what was more destabilizing of a bipolar balance than the simple disappearance of one of the poles?

Bush's national security adviser, Brent Scowcroft, embodied this Cold War habit of mind. Scowcroft was a self-styled realist who had spent his career shoring up the U.S. side of Cold War bipolarity.[28] A retired Air Force general who had found favor with Henry Kissinger, whom he succeeded as Gerald Ford's national security adviser, Scowcroft had then been a vociferous critic of Ronald Reagan's apparent readiness to bargain away America's nuclear arsenal at Reykjavík. That Bush appointed him as his own national security adviser was a sure signal that such large reaches toward disarmament were over. Scowcroft put the new administration's attitude on display on its second day, telling an interviewer on January 22, 1989, that "the Cold War is not over . . . The light at the end of the tunnel [may be] an oncoming locomotive."[29]

Bush tapped as his secretary of state James A. Baker III, who, as Reagan's early chief of staff, had been one of his most militant advisers. Bush's secretary of defense was Richard Cheney, a right-wing congressman from Wyoming who had begun as an aide to Donald Rumsfeld and whose permanent skepticism of Soviet intentions would earn him the sobriquet "the defensive secretary."[30] Arms control would never be a priority in Cheney's Pentagon. Cheney's undersecretary of defense for policy was Paul Wolfowitz, who, beginning as a Nitze protégé, had left his more moderate mentor behind to serve as a tribune of the right in every administration since Nixon, and whose ideas by now were quite fixed. Writing in the *Wall Street Journal,* Wolfowitz trumpeted, for example, a dire warning of Soviet chicanery. Two days after this cry of Wolfowitz, Gorbachev let the Berlin Wall fall.[31] Wolfowitz had missed the significance of what Gorbachev was doing.

One highly intelligent scholar on Scowcroft's staff might have brought a more open view to bear on the Bush administration's thinking, if only because of her relative youth (she was thirty-four). But she had absorbed the rigid orthodoxies of the Cold War too well. She encouraged Bush to see Gorbachev as nothing more than "another cover for power politics."[32] Russia was up to the same old game. She said so with authority. Her specialty was Russian history. She was fluent in the language. She knew what to watch for. She, too, was wrong. Her name was Condoleezza Rice.

With advice coming from such ideologues, Bush did little to support the beleaguered Gorbachev. Starvation threatened average Russians, the ruble was worthless, bottles of vodka were being used for currency. Yet there was no sizable economic aid to Moscow in its time of testing, no loosening of trade restraints. The United States declined to grant the Soviet Union most-favored-nation status, although it did grant it to China *after* the crushing of demonstrations in Tiananmen Square in June 1989.[33]

Bush is properly credited with having continued, in response to Gorbachev's pressure, the process of nuclear arms reduction, but even here Bush's actions were not remotely like his Soviet counterpart's. On September 27, 1991, for example, Bush gave a televised address in which, in the words of one historian, he "wiped out more nuclear warheads in a single unilateral gesture than decades of negotiations over arms control [have] managed to remove."[34] Bush ordered the pullout of nukes from Europe and their removal from U.S. ships deployed around the world. Not only did Gorbachev match these cuts a week later, he surpassed them. More to the point, however, the Bush cuts were in the tactical nuclear arsenal, thousands of warheads originally slated to be used by Army commanders on the battlefield and by ship captains in offshore support. But by Bush's time, the Army had long concluded that such weapons were worse than useless. There was no way for close-range combat commanders to order up barrages of nuclear artillery, or to call in such fire from naval vessels, without endangering their own troops. Bush made his most dramatic gesture of arms reduction, that is, mainly because his military no longer wanted the weapons. The president did not explain that in his speech.[35]

To say that Bush and his inner circle were reluctant to let go of the Cold War is only to acknowledge how deeply in the American imagination its rods had penetrated. And not only the imagination. The Cold War had been the ground of nothing less than the militarization of American society — the transformation that we have been tracking in this book. I remember the day in the early sixties that my father came home from the Pentagon and said that from then on senior officers who worked in the Building had the option of wearing civilian clothes to work, an event the significance of which I understood only much later. It simply would not do to draw attention to the way in which Washington had become a war capital. All those thousands of uniforms — stars and eagles on shoulders, stripes on sleeves — said too much about fortress America. But the officer elite in business suits was also the perfect emblem of the national transformation that was well under way. The tremendous budget outlays of the Defense Department were funded by the broad tax system. After Vietnam, the volunteer Army walled off civilians (especially of the middle and upper classes) from any real concern about America's martial adventures. Ours became a garrison state that did not look like one.

American industry depended on the Pentagon not only for the contracts that funded a significant proportion of the nation's economic growth, but for the actual personnel who, moving through the infamous revolving door, administered the business of business and kept those contracts coming. That pattern was matched, with more subtlety, in academia, which, during the university boom years of the 1950s and 1960s, constructed extensive science-and-technology research facilities around resources provided by the Defense Department. That phenomenon redoubled itself in the Reagan years, when the Pentagon turned its serious gaze toward space, sending golden rockets to dozens of university research centers. And the grease that made all of these wheels turn was the vast treasure provided by lobbyists to members of Congress, a kind of recycling of defense appropriation moneys back to those who disbursed them in the first place. What threatened this cozy system, far more than the Soviet Union ever had, was the disappearance of the threat. What was the Cold War complex without the Cold War?

The ingrained thinking of key defense intellectuals reflected the inability to imagine an alternative reality, and some began to affirm the benefits of the Cold War's bipolar nuclear standoff. John Lewis Gaddis preferred to call that standoff "the long peace," and some argued that life balanced on the nuclear edge was far superior to what was coming.[36]

"It was as if true north," as David Halberstam put it, "had been erased from the compasses of the men and women who had worked all their lives in national security."[37] As they watched the Soviet system coming rapidly apart — a McDonald's opened in Moscow in 1990 — American statesmen would have understood, first, that the Kremlin's leadership had been able to maintain a rigid hold on its vast empire only because of the Cold War, and without its terrifying bipolarity that hold was bound to slip. Second, they would have understood that an American version of that collapse was equally bound to follow the end of the Cold War, even if what came apart was not a police state but the national security state, with its attendant military-industrial-academic complex at home and its projection of power abroad. That global power projection, throughout forty years, had been at the service as much of expanding markets for the U.S. economy as of blocking Moscow. In fact, Russia was the least of it. The global system itself was in danger of splintering, as the ethnic, religious, and economic differences that the Cold War had suppressed began to show themselves with power. A new kind of suppression would have to be imposed, and fast.[38] Bush and his circle, centered in Cheney's Pentagon, were implicitly charged with protecting the U.S. economic hegemony that the Cold War had made possible, and they understood that that required them to protect, above all else, "the enormous machine set in motion in the 1950's, a perpetual motion machine that was built for war."[39]

4. FOOL'S GAME

But war was threatened by global outbreaks of peace. As I learned, particularly from the writer Jonathan Schell, something positive in the human heart had shown itself to be "unconquerable."[40] Not only the bloodless revolutions behind the Iron Curtain signified a moving freshness in the human imagination. In the 1970s, autocratic regimes had been nonviolently overthrown in Greece, Portugal, and Spain. In the 1980s, military dictators had been nonviolently replaced by democratic governments in Brazil, Argentina,[41] and Chile. In 1985, the first Anglo-Irish agreement since 1921 was achieved between London and Dublin, laying the groundwork for the peace process that would finally end the bloodshed in Northern Ireland. In 1986, as the democracy movement was picking up steam in the Soviet sphere, a nonviolent democratic movement forced Ferdinand Marcos to surrender power in the Philippines. In the same years, the most unlikely nonviolent force for change was centered in a prison cell on Robben Island in South Africa, and when Nelson Mandela was released from that prison, he came to power on a program of forgiveness. Less forgiving, but equally unlikely and equally nonviolent, was the revolution against America's puppet in Iran, headed by Ayatollah Ruholla Khomeini. He was no prophet of peace, and Iran under his leadership would soon be embroiled in a savage war with Iraq, but the force Khomeini brought to bear against the shah was a whole people, which succeeded in driving out the tin-pot autocrat simply by standing in the streets.

On October 14, 1989, a month before the Berlin Wall fell, the five presidents of the nations of Central America announced a breakthrough agreement with the Sandinista government of Nicaragua, ending the region's brutal conflicts — a peace initiative spearheaded by Costa Rica's Oscar Arias and pursued despite U.S. opposition. The Arias accord would hold through fresh brutalities in the region by U.S. surrogates and through the Panama invasion. The Ortega-led Sandinistas defied a decade's worth of American demonizing by holding an open election in 1990 and, when they lost, by peacefully yielding power. Despite these events, Washington refused to deliver promised aid to Nicaragua, which remained mired in war-induced poverty. Next door in El Salvador, peace came a year later, again within the Arias framework. And again, lavish American military aid would never be matched by economic support.

The last thing the Pentagon really wanted south of its border, it seemed, was peace, and it was a powerful moment when the people imposed their will on the diehard warriors whose funds and weapons came from *El Norte*. The signal sounding from Central America, as from, in short order, Germany, parts of Africa, and a dozen other places around the globe, was that military might was no longer enough to sustain control of a people who refused to be controlled. That was the lesson that, against all odds, the Soviet Union had taken in with surprising grace. It was the people of the world themselves, in other words, who threw off the shackles of the martial system to which the two superpowers had accommodated themselves quite nicely.

At the same time, institutions that had embodied the "realist" assumptions about the necessity of armed force, as well as statesmen who had articulated such assumptions, began to sound different notes. Even the intractable Middle East would enter a new phase defined by a "peace process," with breakthroughs at Madrid and Oslo. That process, however haltingly pursued, changed the dynamic of hatred between Israelis and Palestinians. Violence would flare up again, but for increasing numbers on both sides, including many battle-hardened leaders, it seemed to illuminate a dead end. A new reality took hold, both on the ground and in the willingness to air untried ideas.

We saw, to take another example, how the Roman Catholic Church, the veritable custodian in the West of the Just War theory over the centuries, had moved away from the assumption that war can any longer be justified in the nuclear age. Pope John Paul II had emerged as an opponent of war in all its forms, and would continue to be so, condemning in particular every U.S. military adventure, from Panama to the NATO air war against Serbia to both wars against Iraq. The American Catholic bishops had called for "a moral about-face" and suggested that the foundation of U.S. defense, deterrence theory, was acceptable only if understood as temporary, in the context of serious efforts to complete nuclear disarmament — efforts that ceased after the Cold War. The bishops' clear assumption was that, absent the balance of terror, a nuclear deterrent force would no longer be justifiable. "We are the first generation since Genesis with the power to threaten the created order. We cannot remain silent in the face of such danger."[42]

One of the voices we heard early in this narrative belonged to Carl Kaysen, a man who had picked German targets for Curtis LeMay's Eighth Air Force in 1943, had imagined a nuclear strike over Berlin for John F. Kennedy, and had helped negotiate the first arms control treaty, the Partial Test Ban, in 1963. In the months after the collapse of the Berlin Wall, Kaysen wrote an article titled "Is War Obsolete?" His answer, from within the heart of the American foreign policy intelligentsia, suggested what seemed possible as the Cold War ended. "The international system that relies on the national use of force as the ultimate guarantor of security," Kaysen wrote in 1990, "and the threat of its use as the basis of order, is not the only possible one. To seek a different system with a more secure and a more humane basis for order is no longer the pursuit of an illusion, but a necessary effort toward a necessary goal."[43]

In the United States the sense grew that the end of the Cold War would offer a peace dividend, freeing up billions of dollars from military outlays, just in time to rescue the economy from the Reagan deficits.[44] The horror of nuclear war that had gripped the nation in the early 1980s lessened as Americans fully expected that their leaders would now be able to deliver on the dream of nuclear abolition that had barely eluded Ronald Reagan's grasp. The most conservative president of recent times, that is, had put on the nation's to-do list what would certainly be the most radical change in American policy since World War II. In doing so, as we saw, the exquisitely attuned Reagan was simply responding to the manifest will of the people. The dangers and the waste of the nuclear stalemate had made themselves quite clear, and not only that. The impotence that went with military power defined by an unusable nuclear arsenal had become undeniable — Vietnam's lesson on one side, Afghanistan's on the other.

The true recognition that had come to the American people, once the unlikely Ronald Reagan had broken the Cold War taboo by daring to speak aloud of nuclear abolition, was that nuclear weapons were useless. Even generals and admirals were talking that way now.[45] Victory in any conceivable war between nuclear powers would be meaningless. LeMay's successor as head of the Strategic Air Command, Thomas Power, as we saw earlier, defined victory in 1960 by saying, "At the end of the war, if there are two Americans and one Russian, we win."[46] But LeMay's further successor, General George Lee Butler, who was the last SAC commander before it became the U.S. Strategic Command in 1992, has said that the war plans over which he presided were "barbaric . . . more barbaric than . . . [anything] you'll find in the animal kingdom."

After his retirement, I spoke with General Butler. He described to me his feelings of horror, of which Generals LeMay and Power knew nothing: how he stayed up night after night poring over the SIOP, trying to picture each of the thousands of targets for whose obliteration he was to be responsible. "The elegant theory of nuclear deterrence was an intellectual mistake of cosmic proportions," he told me. "It was out of control, and I saw it. I am the only person who ever looked at all twelve thousand five hundred of our targets. And when I got through, I was horrified. Deterrence was a formula for disaster. We escaped disaster by the grace of God. If you ask one person who has lived in this arena his whole career, I have come to one conclusion. This has to end. This must stop. This must be our highest priority." Butler said that to me in 1997, more than seven years after the end of the Cold War. By then he had become, as one observer put it, "a Sakharov figure." But early Sakharov, the one regarded as a traitor by his colleagues. The rebel Butler was hated by the Pentagon.[47]

"I have arrived at the conclusion," Butler told Jonathan Schell, "that it is simply wrong, morally speaking, for any mortal to be invested with the authority to call into question the survival of the planet. That is an untenable allocation of authority, and yet it has become the central feature of the nuclear age. Nuclear weapons are irrational devices. They were rationalized and accepted as a desperate measure in the face of circumstances that were unimaginable. Now, as the world evolves rapidly, I think that the vast majority of people on the face of this earth will endorse the proposition that such weapons have no place among us. There is no security to be found in nuclear weapons. It's a fool's game."[48]

No security. The Pentagon, for all that we had invested in it, was not protecting us at all. And with the evaporation of those "circumstances that were unimaginable," the Pentagon, as an Armageddon command center, was no longer necessary in any case. Seeing that, Americans began to expect a great release. Economists talked about conversion, referring not to religion but to retooling the huge defense industry for civilian purposes. The army of lobbyists started looking for new ways to keep the money flowing, discovering, for example, the needs of the environment. As career military personnel worried for the first time about job security instead of national security, they were faced with having to lay down their lifestyles, rather than their lives, for their country. The national media, meanwhile, increasingly ignored news from abroad, closing down their foreign bureaus. All of these trends were reflected in Congress, where a new generation of politicians, on the left and right both, were less concerned with events overseas — fewer and fewer of them had passports — than with the straining domestic economy.[49] The Pentagon, in effect, found itself surrounded by a mob of looters who wanted to walk off with all its treasure.

Responding to the pressures of the new situation, the Defense Department announced in 1990 that it was cutting the size of the armed forces by a quarter. It was a drastic step, unlike anything that had occurred since before the Korean War. Such cuts were opposed by the brass, less because peak manpower levels any longer made sense than because they were clearly the beginning of the post–Cold War dismantling that they had hoped to hold off.[50] The date of the announcement was August 1. The next day, against almost all expectations — and certainly against CIA intelligence estimates — Saddam Hussein's army crossed the border into Kuwait.

5. NEW WORLD ORDER

Just as North Korea's crossing of the 38th parallel in 1950 had "rescued" the national security state, so Saddam Hussein's invasion "rescued" the Pentagon's perpetual motion machine made for war. "Just in time," the historian Bruce Cumings observes of the invasion, "it snatched defense and military production lines from the jaws of oblivion."[51]

George H. W. Bush did not hesitate to declare of Saddam's move, "This will not stand."[52] Bush immediately ordered a military response. He reacted with such firm martial will not so much because he was offended by the rank aggression (Bush had violated Panama's sovereignty every bit as readily); not because Saddam was heinous (Washington had countenanced and funded his brutality during his war with Iran); not because Bush cared for Kuwait's national integrity (Kuwait had been a province of Iraq until 1961, when it was granted independence by a British government serving the interests of British Petroleum, and the United States had since expressly "taken no position" on Iraq's territorial claims);[53] not even because the Iraqi ruler's increased control of oil was a major threat (Saddam was as bound by the rules of the oil markets as other Arab dictators). No, Bush's quick and instinctive militarizing of what could have been handled as a diplomatic crisis — and what should have been handled mainly by Arab leaders in the region — had everything to do with shoring up and justifying America's dependence on the threat and use of force.

On September 11, Bush went before a joint session of Congress to declare the dawn of a "new world order . . . a world where the rule of law supplants the rule of the jungle . . . a world where the strong respect the rights of the weak."[54] Of course, Bush's assumption was that in the new unipolar world, the United States would reign supreme. The disappearance of its competing and balancing superpower rival was right and meet, a fulfillment of the global economic, political, and technological trends that had doomed the Soviet empire while guaranteeing the triumph of the "free world," by which America always meant itself and its markets. Bush's speech, in that sense, was a first definition of the post–Cold War global system, a recognition that, in the age of information technology, instant communication, and the free market economy, the earth was small enough to be thought of as one entity, and to be controlled as one. One market, to be dominated by the American economy. One political ideal, democracy, to be realized according to an American model. A sweeping claim based so completely on unchallenged military supremacy that it did not need to be mentioned, like an officer elite in civilian clothes. Here was the new mission of garrison America. Bush's September 11 speech was "the vision thing" at last. His "new world order" was nothing less — and little more, as events in Iraq over a decade would show — than the rescue of the Pentagon.

In Bush's new world as it actually existed, some things were indeed different from the past. For example, Saddam Hussein, truly a son of a bitch, had been, in Franklin Roosevelt's words about Somoza, "*our* son of a bitch." He had taken power by force and been supported by the United States in its power plays against Moscow and Tehran. His worst crimes, including his genocidal gassing of Kurds and Shiites in the early 1980s, had never drawn protests from Washington, but now those crimes were run up the flagpole of American indignation as if committed yesterday. Suddenly Saddam Hussein was Adolf Hitler reincarnate.

Also marking a difference from the past was the fact that the Soviet Union supported the American resolution in the U.N. Security Council authorizing "all necessary means" to remove the Iraqis from Kuwait. Moscow had no use for Saddam's maneuverings, but it seems clear that this gesture of support for the American line in the Arabian sand was motivated primarily by the Soviet economy's need for capital investment from the West. This was the first U.N. vote authorizing military force since the 1950 Korean crisis, when the U.S. resolution passed because the Soviet ambassador had walked out of the session.

A deadline of January 15 was set for the removal of Iraqi forces from Kuwait. As the deadline approached, with 550,000 mainly U.S. troops poised to strike from Saudi Arabia, and with B-52s revving their engines on runways as far away as Louisiana, Mikhail Gorbachev, notwithstanding the needs of his fragile economy, pleaded with Bush not to launch his war. Gorbachev had supported Bush at the United Nations, believing in the coercive power of diplomacy, sanctions, and containment. Saddam had offered to pull out his forces in return for the removal of sanctions, guarantees of an Iraqi route to the Persian Gulf, and control of the border oil field that occasioned the dispute.[55] Negotiations on such matters were not nearly exhausted. A military threat is most successful, Gorbachev might have argued, when it is not carried out. The Soviet leader was certain that Saddam would bend to continued economic and diplomatic pressures, and that outright war would put the world on a dangerous new course — and he said as much.

Was Gorbachev's plea for another way just talk? In November 1990, as Operation Desert Storm was gathering itself in Saudi Arabia, Gorbachev and Bush met in Paris, where the Soviet leader signed the Conventional Forces in Europe Treaty, which Michael Beschloss and Strobe Talbott call "the most impressive accomplishment in arms control."[56] Most impressive because so one-sided. The Red Army essentially broke camp and went home. CFE amounted to the Soviets' sacrificing an advantage of such superiority — its ability to overrun Western Europe with little or no resistance from a conventional force — that the United States had nothing comparable with which to match it.

On the night of January 16, 1991, Gorbachev made a last appeal for peace to Bush, only to have his humiliation doubled when he learned that the bombardment of Baghdad had already begun. Gorbachev, at that very moment, was turning away from the final temptation to use force to hold his empire together. With Soviet troops confronted by armed crowds in Lithuania and Latvia, the Soviet leader was faced with far graver threats to the nation he was sworn to protect than anything Bush had faced in Panama or Iraq. Yet Gorbachev, just as Bush was ordering his forces to attack, ordered his soldiers to return to their barracks. That led to the swift unraveling of the Soviet empire and to Gorbachev's rejection by the Russian people. Picking up the spirit from those who had eschewed violence in opposing him within the Soviet Union, and extending the spirit of nonviolence that had transformed nations from South Africa to the Philippines, Gorbachev gave Bush a real example of what a "new world order" might look like. For his trouble, he was treated contemptuously by the Bush administration, a foreshadowing of the fate that awaited him in his homeland.[57]

In the end, what was most new in the new world order, as actually constructed by Bush, was a move by the United States into the ideological, political, and religious thickets of the Arab Middle East. That move had been prepared for decades before, with the collapse of British control in the region and then with the Carter Doctrine. Now the United States could maneuver in these thickets without concern for opposition from other outside powers, and it could do so with a massive military presence. In the past, American interests in the region had been advanced by surrogates — the shah, the Saud family, Israel — but now those hundreds of thousands of U.S. soldiers were bivouacked on the sands of Saudi Arabia, where many regarded the American presence as blasphemy pure and simple. And the more magnificent the performance of this fighting force turned out to be — thirty-eight days of unimpeded precision bombing, followed by a four-day rout on the ground — the more deeply humiliated the whole house of Arab Islam had to feel. All that America seemed to register during the Gulf War, with its wizard's display of stealth bombers, cruise missiles, Patriot antimissile missiles, and GIs magically equipped with night vision goggles, was a glorious recovery from a long line of military debacles.[58]

But even Arabs unfriendly to Saddam Hussein had an opposite experience. They understood very well that the new world order was fueled by the oil under their sand. Indeed, while President Bush's rhetoric was all about Kuwaiti freedom, Saddam's weapons of mass destruction, and the integrity of international borders, on the same September 11 of Bush's greatest speech, Secretary of Defense Richard Cheney gave a less high-flown but more pointed statement to the Senate Armed Services Committee. "Once [Saddam] acquired Kuwait and deployed an army as large as the one he possesses," Cheney said, he would be "in a position to be able to dictate the future of worldwide energy policy, and that [would give] him a stranglehold on our economy."[59] The Carter Doctrine held: America would go to war to protect its oil, and Cheney, who with Donald Rumsfeld had anticipated Carter, was the man to say so.

The war for Kuwait's sovereignty, in other words, made a joke of Arab sovereignty. It ended with Saddam still in place as an American-sponsored bulwark against Iran, free to savage his Shiite and Kurdish minorities without a hint of U.S. objection. American rhetoric hardly bothered to cloak American purposes. As the hundreds of thousands of GIs littered the Arabian desert with empty Evian bottles, their very presence profaned a sacred territory. One of those motivated to a new militancy by this combined experience of sacrilege and shame was a self-anointed messianic mujahideen member named Osama bin Laden. What George H. W. Bush really inaugurated on *his* September 11 was a new world *dis*order that would show itself with staggering brutality exactly eleven years later.

6. THE CHINESE WORD

The phone rang just as I took in the meaning of what I was seeing on the evening news. The screen showed the night sky over Baghdad. The voice of CNN correspondent Peter Arnett described what was happening. The flashing lights in the dark were the measure of dread. It was January 16, 1991, and the United States was at war.

In the previous months, Americans, myself included, had been transfixed by a PBS series on the Civil War. The Ken Burns documentary films featured lovingly presented, sepia-toned photographs by Mathew Brady and his imitators, accompanied by lugubrious readings of soldiers' letters home, pleas of girlfriends, and prayers of mothers, all braced by a soundtrack of plaintive fiddle music. Solemn experts, headshots against impressively ordered bookshelves, assured us that the Civil War was the noblest of enterprises. The dead had not died in vain. They had achieved an immortality like that of a great poem. Men are still singing of Troy, are they not? War, we saw with our own eyes night after night, was something beautiful. How blessed was our nation to have such a war in its past. And now, on CNN, we could have another one.

Then why was I weeping? The flashes over blacked-out Baghdad were the beginning of an air campaign that would go on for more than a month. The Air Force was set to prove that it alone, of all the armed services, had not been wounded by America's martial failures. More than that, the Air Force, in a grand unveiling on live television, was showing that what the Pentagon called the "revolution in military affairs," basically a combination of computer and satellite technologies, had finally made the dreams of Curtis LeMay and the first bomber generals come true. Viewers could see it with their own eyes, as grainy photographs of crosshairs and fire bursts displayed hit after hit, with men in blue holding pointers to explain what we were seeing. Everything but fiddle music.[60] The Blue Curtain had been drawn back, revealing nothing less than the new miracle of humanitarian bombing.

When LeMay led the first air raids against Germany in early 1943 (the week in January with which this narrative began), the best his bombardiers could do, on average, was land a bomb within twenty miles of the target; by 1945, that had been improved to about half a mile. In Baghdad, on the night of January 16, 1991, the reliable range of accuracy was six feet. "Immaculate destruction," they called it. "Virtual war."[61] Virtuous war. A new day had dawned. Collateral damage was a thing of the past. No more bombing of women and children. I did not believe a word of it. My own youthful devotion to the men in blue, once again, made me feel ashamed.

When I answered the phone, it was my brother Dennis. He and I had been together, in our youth, as opponents of the Vietnam War. He had undergone his protest arrests, and I had undergone mine. In different ways we had been alienated from our father. Although Dennis achieved a reconciliation with Dad, I never did. No one understood that pain of mine like Dennis, and at the sound of his voice now, I felt a rush of gratitude. Dennis, too, would be overcome with grief to find his nation once more at war. That was why he'd called.

Wrong. I heard the sob in his voice, but he was not weeping for the reason I was. "It's Dad," he said. "It's Dad."

There are moments in which time collapses on itself, when the present is defined by a collision of the past and the future. My past with my father, when he was all there was to me; my future without him, literally unthinkable. The past, the present, and the future all disappeared, an obliteration of temporality, time replaced, as a philosopher might put it, by simple being. Death puts us in mind of love.

"What do you mean?"

My father last appeared in this narrative as a man in his prime, in 1969, at least implicitly challenging the secretary of defense on the question of intelligence estimates corrupted for the sake of politics. President Nixon and Henry Kissinger wanted an ABM system. Melvin Laird's job was to deliver a rationale for it, and so intelligence was produced that portrayed the Soviet Union as moving toward a first-strike force. My father dissented, as I understand it, and he was fired. It was the time when I defied him on Vietnam. It may have been the rank narcissism of an Oedipally wounded man to think so, but I had nevertheless imagined all those years that I, as much as Laird, had broken my father. Over the twenty years since, Dad had swiftly declined into the netherworld of Alzheimer's, but the lies of the Pentagon were his true infirmity. I inherited it. We took our malady out on each other. If he and I had found a way at last to sit together without resentment, it was only because he no longer knew who I was. In the end, our best hours together were when I bathed him, a skill I'd acquired with my infant children. My father let me shave him, let me put a razor to his throat. His trust in me was impersonal but infinite, and that was enough. Lately he had suffered a series of strokes, had been hospitalized for weeks. I had traveled from Boston to Washington and back, it seemed, every few days. Not an hour went by that I did not think of him. Not a night passed that I did not dream of him.

"He's dying. The doctor says he's dying."

The only thing uncomplicated about me was turmoil. My father's death coterminous with the launching of America's next war and the next set of lies.

How can I explain that this was no mere coincidence for me, but entry into a new kind of time? The arrow of time found its target in my heart. It is here, in this moment, that my total preoccupation with war and peace — what drives this book — shows itself for what it is: not political, as for most others, but completely personal. And the curse of my life, too, is instantly plain: this quality of detachment, that I should be five hundred miles away from my father's deathbed, ten thousand miles away from the explosions of Baghdad, yet experiencing both as if I were there, as if my kitchen were now bursting into flame.

A dividing line in time is what I am telling you about, the absolute before and after that define the son's experience of a father's death. There is only one other such line, which is birth. That is why, after speaking to Dennis, I hung up the phone and went upstairs to find my children. The previous summer, a month before Saddam's armies crossed into Kuwait, I had taken my family to Germany. Our Lizzy was ten, Pat was eight. They had to see where I had lived as a boy, harboring my first fear of the broken world and what it might do to itself. In Wiesbaden I had shown them the general's quarters where we lived, a grand mansion up the *allee* from the one where Eisenhower had presided over the occupation. *We come not as conquerors, but as friends.* I took them to the air base from which "the LeMay Coal and Feed Company" had flown supplies to Berlin in 1948, and to which Francis Gary Powers had been aiming when he was shot down in 1960, which was my senior year at the high school on the hill. I could see a new idea forming behind my children's eyes: the thought that I had once been a teenager, which for them opened up a different meaning of time. Their father, too, has a past.

From Wiesbaden we went to Berlin, so they could see where, until the previous November, the Wall had stood as the world's barrier, the mark across the earth and across the human imagination. Now the Wall was an interrupted train of rubble, a thin line of ruin winding through an otherwise thriving city, and when Lizzy and Pat took it in as I explained and explained again, they could have no idea what I was talking about, no idea of what had made me so afraid when I was their age. Fear was the bond I had had with my father. Our defining moment was that summer night in 1961, I at the wheel, he smoking his Camel, the monuments of Washington flashing behind him through the car window. He commissioned me to be prepared to keep going, with Mom and the boys, all the way to Richmond, past Richmond, going as far as I could, to get away from the coming war. A sacred trust, constructed of existential dread. No wonder, in the end, I betrayed him.

My children knew no such fear, and their assumption that history is a friend had just been vindicated, though why should they have noticed? On October 3, 1990, between the day of Saddam's invasion of Kuwait, and the day of Bush's attack on Iraq, West Germany and East Germany became one nation, the Federal Republic of Germany. If any date marked the definitive end of the East-West conflict that stretched back across the century, that one did, the day the corrugated-iron fence along Europe's most savage border was dismantled. Iron Curtain no more. Nothing was made of the reunion of Germany because the world was poised for another war, elsewhere.

My children unafraid. They and I were at the mercy of life's contingency, the wound of mortality, but my children had not been raised to expect a man-made end of the world. The Gulf War and all its high-tech marvels, to them as to most Americans, would be a video game. A recognition of their freedom from the dark shadow that fell over me in the cave of my desk at St. Mary's School was what moved my tears away from war, away from Dad, to gratitude. And that was when I saw for myself that the Cold War was over. Simply over.

So why were we at war tonight? It was like asking, Why is my father dead? I knew the one answer to both questions: how the Pentagon had lashed itself to the century's flotsam, tugged along in the one unbroken current, the river of time, the pull of Niagara, as if war *were* as inevitable as death. *But it need not be!* That was what I wanted to scream. *This is unnecessary!* My once beloved Air Force was sending its laser-guided bombs down on the bunkers of the Republican Guard — and, no matter what they said, down on the playgrounds of nursery schools — because it could. The Pentagon was responding to Saddam's offense with the sledgehammer of Operation Instant Thunder because a sledgehammer was the only tool the United States had acquired in its decades-long spending spree. For shaping the world, a sledgehammer was apparently the only tool America wanted.

On January 20, 1991, my father died. Nearly the anniversary of the day the Pentagon was dedicated, of the week Roosevelt declared "unconditional surrender," of the week LeMay led the first air raid into Germany, and of the week the lab at Los Alamos was commissioned. Nearly my birthday. A few days later, my family sat in the front pews of the chapel at Arlington Cemetery. My wife, Lexa, and Lizzy and Pat sat behind my staggered mother. My four brothers and I were in the vestibule of the chapel. We were five of the eight pallbearers. The others were the current holders of the three senior government positions our father had held: an assistant director of the FBI, the brigadier general who was director of the Air Force Office of Special Investigations, and the lieutenant general who was director of the Defense Intelligence Agency. This last officer was named Harry E. Soyster.

Unknown to me, General Soyster had been implicated in the intelligence failure on the eve of Saddam's invasion of Kuwait, which no one in the U.S. government had expected. The general was kind to my family in our grief, and for that reason it pains me to recount what, to him, must remain a source of embarrassment. On July 30, Soyster received a memo from a DIA analyst, reporting on reconnaissance photos that showed thirty-five thousand Iraqi troops mustered at the border of Kuwait. Of Saddam's plans for that force, the analyst wrote bluntly, "He intends to use it." But Soyster did not believe his analyst's conclusion. "The DIA Director just did not find it conceivable," Bob Woodward later wrote, "that Saddam would do something so anachronistic as an old-fashioned land grab."[62] Thus, despite its own assessment, the DIA reinforced the convictions of the CIA, Secretary Cheney, National Security Adviser Scowcroft, and the chairman of the Joint Chiefs of Staff that the Iraqi dictator was bluffing. Once again U.S. intelligence had failed utterly.

We pallbearers waited as an Air Force honor guard, behind the Air Force band playing Chopin's "Funeral March," arrived at the chapel escorting the horse-drawn caisson that carried our father's coffin. Next to the caisson, a ramrod-straight handler led the riderless horse, boots reversed in the stirrups, signifying the fallen general — and, to us, the memory of John F. Kennedy. The caisson drew under the green awning that extended from the chapel entrance. In the bitter January cold, the puffy fog of breath could be seen coming from the horses' nostrils. The honor guard began to remove the coffin, but a pair of officers suddenly appeared from inside the chapel. They went immediately to General Soyster and saluted. One of them, a captain, addressing both generals, said, "Excuse us, sirs. Did anyone leave a black attaché case under the second pew?"[63]

Now the reason for the officer's barely reined alarm was clear. Even from where we stood, we could see a black object under one of the pews, and taking a cue from the officer, we knew instantly what to dread: the thing was a bomb. Then I realized it was right under the pew in which my Lexa, Lizzy, and Pat were sitting. And who was I to have assumed they were out from under the threat that had defined my life? I thought at once: Saddam has done this, the perfect counterpunch, a church full of Pentagon brass, the Blue Curtain itself, the Air Force that was wreaking such havoc in his country. I saw it all, the bomb exploding, the blast tearing down the building, just as, at St. Mary's School, I had seen footage of the atom bomb being dropped from a tower in some desert of New Mexico. Only now, instead of dummies being blown to smithereens in a shack, it was my beloved family dying in a church.

This vision lasted a second, and the nightmare did not survive the third blink of my eyes, when I saw for sure that nothing had happened.

General Soyster, having read our expressions, told the captain that the briefcase belonged to no one there. For once the DIA was right. We waited the moments it took one of the officers to go forward to remove it. He carried the black case out the side door of the sanctuary as if it were a sacrament.

There were funeral services every hour and a half at Arlington, and some previous mourner had left the thing behind.

At last we brought Dad into the chapel and said the prayers. At the graveside, after the priest had handed Dad over to the angels and we had each sprinkled his coffin with dirt, the honor guard fired its rifles, every blast of which cut through me. The war in Iraq was right behind my burning eyes. One hundred forty-six Americans would be killed, and more than a hundred thousand Iraqis, mostly conscripts and civilians.[64] That was just the beginning of a brutal war that continues as I write this, fourteen years later. I was holding my Patrick's hand, and at each rifle volley I found it possible to give him a little squeeze, which was not enough to keep him from being afraid.

One night in that season of my father's death, I went into Pat's room to find him waking from a bad dream. He was crying. I sat with him, and when he could finally talk, he explained that, in his sleep, he had just been in China. He learned there that the Chinese have a word that, when uttered, makes it possible for parents to live forever. And then Pat's sobs overtook him again, as he wailed, "But I can't remember what the word is."

I recognized the throes in which he was caught, a child feeling the impossible burden of responsibility for keeping a parent alive. When I was his age, the world's true nightmare began with the detonation of the hydrogen bomb, but my conscious version of the existential dread Pat was showing me had not come to me until I was years older, that night of my Georgetown freshman year when Dad put the weight of his nuclear fear on me. I had never been able to protect him from it. I had never gotten out from under it. And here was Pat, having seen me naked in the presence of my father's death, taking my fate on himself. His job was to know the word that would save me, only to say it, but he could not remember what it was!

The death of a parent. The primordial fear. But my generation had come to have an even more fundamental terror, one that threatened nothing less than the death of the species. The obliteration of all that we mean by future was the unfenced edge along which I had been walking all my life. And not only future, but past, for the thermonuclear war would be the end of memory, since there would be no one left to do the remembering.

Thomas Mann, in accepting the Nobel Prize in 1929, reflected on how what was still called the Great War had "forced me into an agonizing reappraisal of my fundamental assumptions." It had done so despite not having, as he put it, "made any immediate demands on me physically."[65] It may seem grandiose of me to make the claim, but the very possibility of nuclear war had done as much to me throughout the years of my growing up, culminating in the discovery of my father's fear. That discovery, which came in the summer of 1961, might have remained my dread secret, but then a year later it became the world's, when the United States and the Soviet Union pushed each other, with my dad's help, to the nuclear brink over Cuba. After that, the very idea of security, whether conceived personally or nationally, was never the same.

"No event demonstrates more clearly than the missile crisis," as Richard Neustadt and Graham Allison wrote of it, "that with respect to nuclear war there is an awesome crack between unlikelihood and impossibility."[66] It was in that crack that I found myself living my life. A sense of nuclear holocaust as a present possibility brought with it a kind of third eye, through which I and others like me perceived the violence of Vietnam and other wars of our time. Vietnam was what made the perception real. After that, the catastrophes of the twentieth century was no mere abstraction.[67] Despite its having made no immediate demands on us physically, war had become a kind of psychological tent pole, holding up the firmament of consciousness. That "awesome crack" opened, as it were, into the abyss. As my father's son, I had seen it opening in myself, and I knew it could open in the world. My basic assumptions were upended by this awareness, and upended they remain.

As I held my son, in the cold wash of my version of his fear, I understood how our terrors were different. After all, in his dream life the Chinese were a source of wisdom, however elusive. In mine, beginning also in my youth, they were the enemy. My dread, that is, was attached to the ever-coming war, which was the permanent difference — fear of war being my patrimony — between my son and his father. My job in life has been the simple one of saying the word that will establish the reign of peace once and for all. This book was supposed to be that word. That word was supposed to restore the fundamental assumptions. That word, like Patrick's, was going to save us all. But by now it is clear again: I can't remember it either.

7. GOLDWATER-NICHOLS

The short-term martial success of the Gulf War was an indirect consequence of a double-barreled failure. On October 23, 1983, a truck bomb blew up the U.S. Marines' barracks in Beirut, and 241 Marines were killed. President Reagan ordered the immediate withdrawal of American forces from Lebanon, in what was seen by many as a shameful retreat. Two days later, on October 25, Reagan ordered the invasion of Grenada, after a local uprising that cloaked itself in Socialist rhetoric overthrew the government. The American incursion, a combined attack of Army paratroopers, Navy SEALs, and Marines, was Operation Urgent Fury, and the invaders expected no resistance. Yet they found themselves humiliatingly stymied by an ill-equipped militia and a small contingent of Cuban military engineers. It took a week for the Americans to take control of the small island. Reporters accompanying the U.S. force sent back bulletins describing confusion, ineptitude, incompetence — all exacerbated by interservice rivalry, fractured chains of command, and obsessive second-guessing from the Pentagon. The Grenada operation was intended to distract from the Lebanon debacle, but it doubled the image of an American military establishment that had lost its way.

Enough was enough. Thus began the first major Pentagon reform movement since the Department of Defense was established.[68] The turf fights, bureaucratic paralysis, overlapping lines of authority, endless duplication of effort, interservice bickering, civilian trespass on strictly military matters, intrusion of politics — all the tendencies that had been corrupting the Pentagon since before they drove James Forrestal to suicide, that defied Robert McNamara's attempts at rational planning, and that reached a climax in the failure of Vietnam — were finally going to be dealt with. The pressure for reform began in Congress, and initial White House reluctance was overcome. In the Pentagon, a mandate came from Secretary of Defense Caspar Weinberger, with key responsibility given to a young military aide. The movement culminated in something called the Defense Organization Project, spearheaded by a committee consisting of six former secretaries of defense (McNamara, Clark Clifford, Melvin Laird, Elliot Richardson, James Schlesinger, and Harold Brown). A rare consensus of military and civilian power centers, of executive and legislative branches, was achieved, resulting finally in the passage of the Defense Reorganization Act, more commonly known as the Goldwater-Nichols Act.[69] A sign of the unanimous understanding of the need for major changes was its passage by the Senate, on May 7, 1986, by a vote of 95 to 0.[70]

Among the many changes that this reorganization brought about, two stand out. First, it represented a long-overdue curbing of the bitter competition between services that had corrupted American defense policy since World War II, with the service branches seeing one another as the enemy every bit as much as they saw the Soviet Union as the enemy. This parochialism was enshrined in the way the Joint Chiefs had operated, with nothing really "joint" about it. The Chiefs were first and foremost advocates of their own services, seeing the national interest through lenses that were colored blue, green, or white.[71]

But no more. Chains of command were taken away from the individual branches, with authority distributed not by milieu (air, ground, sea) but by mission, global region, and combat theater. Allocations of resources would be made not to balance competing demands of each service, but according to the actual needs of military operations. The symbol of this was the absolute authority invested in the chairman of the Joint Chiefs of Staff. No longer were the Chiefs coequal presiders over the military hierarchy, with the chairman as a kind of referee. Instead, the chairman's role was now defined as supreme. He was the single adviser to the president and the secretary of defense on military matters, and, in effect, the other Chiefs were advisers to him. The chairman's status with civilian overseers of the Defense Department was considerably enhanced by his being given a statutory position on the National Security Council. The various uniformed branches would now speak with one voice, whether they wanted to or not. More to the point, the chairman would supervise the budget process of all the branches, and he would control strategic planning across the service divides. At the first meeting of the Joint Chiefs after the new law took effect, the heads of the four services, for the first time ever, stood up when the chairman walked into the room, an unprecedented act of deference.[72]

The second major change that Goldwater-Nichols effected was in the global organization of the Pentagon's reach, but with a simultaneous undercutting of the Pentagon's command authority in the event of an actual outbreak of hostilities. The earth was divided into five geographic commands, and the functions of the military were divided into four — ultimately five — commands.[73] Each "unified" command was headed by a commander in chief (CINC), whose staff was made up of officers representing the different services. In the event of war, the authority of the theater CINC was absolute, and his chain of command could run, depending on the president's order, not to the Joint Chiefs or their chairman, but to the secretary of defense and the president. The regional CINCs, that is, had great power. They were, in effect, American proconsuls. The organization of the globe in this way amounted to the institutionalization of a worldwide system of Army, Navy, and Air Force bases. By September 11, 2001, there would be more than 725 of them outside the United States, including numerous garrisons in successor states of the former Soviet Union.[74]

Before Goldwater-Nichols, this array of military outposts overseas had been regarded as a still temporary vestige of World War II, an undefined accommodation of the demands of the Cold War. Goldwater-Nichols essentially normalized the American military occupation of the planet. And not only the planet: by designating one of the functional commands as the Space Command, the United States declared its military presence in the "high frontier" of outer space, despite ongoing international negotiations that would prevent the deployment of weapons in space.[75]

The Goldwater-Nichols Act, whether deliberately or not, and even before the Cold War ended, established the permanent structure of America's martial reach in the post–Cold War world. An ad hoc anti-Communist arrangement was institutionalized, with diplomacy subservient to an all-powerful military, and with the final repudiation of the fundamental American preference for citizens under arms in favor of a purely mercenary army, although the term of art would be "professional." This adjustment provided the legal and social underpinnings to support the maintenance of the most massive military force ever assembled.[76] This gargantuan military and its recast hierarchy enabled a reach the Pentagon now defined as "global engagement" by means of "force projection." The timing of this shift in the way America's defense establishment understood itself is full of implication, as if the Pentagon possessed an awareness of the tectonic movement that was soon to overturn the world's polity.

The date of the law's Senate passage is telling, for when those senators voted unanimously for this bill that reified what was in all but name an imperial system, the Soviet imperial system had just then begun to self-destruct. Eleven days before the Senate vote, on April 26, 1986, reactor number 4 of the nuclear power plant in Chernobyl, Ukraine, exploded. We saw what this event meant in the Soviet Union: how, after Chernobyl, the Soviet peoples began "living in truth," in Havel's phrase, and how, as a result, Gorbachev put nuclear disarmament high on his agenda. That purpose led, whether he meant it to or not, to the opening up of the black-box society Stalin had set up precisely to protect the nuclear arsenal. The Soviet arsenal, in other words, went hand in hand with iron rule: to dismantle the one was to dismantle the other. So a direct line can be drawn from the disaster in Chernobyl in 1986 to the night in November 1989 when the Berlin Wall came down.

To return again to the Niagara metaphor, these momentous events and opportunities were like changes in the geography of the current. Banks fell away, the river spread wide, became shallow, and lost direction for a time before reconstituting itself, deep and strong. In the end, on the Soviet side, the demise of the Cold War forced an important reorganization of the military and a fundamental shift in basic goals. But it did not happen on the American side. Just as the Soviet empire was becoming unglued, an imperial American military came into its own — what the Pentagon had been creating for decades, and what it would need a few years hence, when the enemyless United States suddenly found itself (because this is what it felt like) with enemies all over the place.

8. THE IMMIGRANT'S SON

The first full-term chairman of the Joint Chiefs of Staff who possessed the complete powers of the Goldwater-Nichols Act was also, in his own words, "the youngest officer, the first African-American, and the first ROTC graduate to fill this office. The immigrant's son from the South Bronx now occupied the highest uniformed military post in the land."[77] He was fifty-three years old. He was appointed, over fourteen senior four-star generals, by President George H. W. Bush in August 1989, on the recommendation of Secretary of Defense Richard Cheney. His name was Colin Powell.

The first thing the new chairman did upon moving into his office above the River Entrance was install one-way glass in his windows, so he could look out and no one could look in. The glass was bulletproof.[78]

Powell had been military assistant to Secretary of Defense Weinberger during the Grenada invasion in 1983. "I was only a fly on the wall at the time," he wrote in his memoir, "but I filed away the lessons learned."[79] Powell's office had been in the secretary's suite through the years of the momentous Pentagon reorganization, and he was able to influence it from the inside. Understanding the need for an all-powerful JCS chairman as the only check on paralyzing service parochialism, Powell had helped make the new system happen. And now the job was his. It was a remarkable turn in a remarkable career.

Having been commissioned from his City College of New York ROTC unit in 1958, Powell was among the sixteen thousand advisers sent by President Kennedy to South Vietnam in 1962. He earned a Purple Heart and the Bronze Star. In his second tour there, in 1968, Powell was injured in a helicopter crash, but more notable, perhaps, was his service as a senior staff officer of the Americal Division, which became notorious in the wake of an Americal platoon's actions in the village of My Lai. The incident occurred three months before Powell arrived in Vietnam, but he was one of the first to learn of allegations of the willful murder of civilians there, and was assigned to investigate. He found nothing to the charges. "Relations between Americal soldiers and the Vietnamese people are excellent," he wrote. It would take the work of others to bring the truth of My Lai to light.[80]

In 1972, Powell moved onto the political track when he was named a White House fellow, working in the Office of Management and Budget for Frank Carlucci, who had begun in the Nixon administration, as we saw, as one of two deputies to Donald Rumsfeld (the other was Richard Cheney). Carlucci later tapped Powell as his military assistant when he, Carlucci, went to the Pentagon as Weinberger's deputy, which led to Powell's own appointment by Weinberger as *his* military assistant. When Carlucci was named Reagan's national security adviser in the second term, after the Iran-Contra scandal, Powell joined him as deputy national security adviser. Powell succeeded Carlucci as Reagan's last national security adviser, when Carlucci moved back across the Potomac to replace Weinberger as secretary of defense.

Upon becoming president, George H. W. Bush promptly moved Powell out of the national security job (as he promptly moved Carlucci out of the Defense Department job, to be replaced, musical-chairs fashion, by Cheney).[81] But then — proof that the political track was paved with polished brass — Bush soon gave Powell his fourth star and promoted him, on Cheney's recommendation and over the fourteen senior four-star generals, to the chairmanship of the Joint Chiefs of Staff.

Exercising his unprecedented authority, Powell promulgated what became known as the fourfold Powell Doctrine: military force is to be used only when the risk to America is clear, when the public's support is strong, when the force used is "overwhelming," and when the "exit strategy" is clear. Essentially, as one defense analyst told me, the Powell Doctrine boiled down to, Don't lose.[82]

During the autumn of 1990, on the basis of his doctrine, as preparations were laid for the use of force to push Saddam Hussein out of Kuwait, Powell argued against war and in favor of sanctions; what he called, less delicately, "strangulation."[83] Powell was particularly attuned to DIA estimates (having apparently put aside General Soyster's failure to foresee the invasion, with tens of thousands of Iraqi troops on the Kuwait border) that the Iraqis would fight long and hard, producing extensive casualties on both sides, certainly including many Americans.[84] In his determination to make war an extremely difficult option for top decision makers, Powell was the avatar of the Vietnam-era military, a soldier determined, above all, to prevent unqualified and ideologically motivated civilians from ever again sending selfless young fighters into a hopeless, unnecessary war.

There were such civilians in the Pentagon, White House, and State Department, but the man on whom George H. W. Bush depended most for advice in the crucial run-up to the January 15, 1991, deadline was a retired general, also of the Vietnam era. Brent Scowcroft, President Bush's national security adviser, was an enthusiastic proponent of going to war against Saddam Hussein, but he had been an Air Force officer, and the Air Force, unlike the Army, had not been scourged in the jungles of Vietnam (although the air war against Iraq would be called Instant Thunder, in contrast with Vietnam's air war, Rolling Thunder). Unlike pilots, Powell had seen war up close, and when he thought of it, what he saw were not puffs of smoke through a bombsight, but the acne-covered faces of teenage boys, screaming.[85]

But Powell faced an argument not only from the White House but from his own Pentagon. His boss and former mentor, Richard Cheney, was not Powell's main antagonist. More strongly in favor of going to war against Saddam than anyone else was an official who had to remind Powell of the tin-soldier civilians he had so detested during Vietnam, the undersecretary of defense for policy, Paul Wolfowitz. When the president, deciding with Scowcroft and Wolfowitz, overruled Powell, the chairman of the Joint Chiefs saluted. Then he went coolly and efficiently on to preside over the deployment and use of military force against Iraq. "We will surround the enemy," he told reporters, "and kill it."

As a figure representing the public and political face of the Pentagon, as well as the military, Powell promptly surpassed Cheney. This despite provisions of the law that kept Cheney, not Powell, at the top of the wartime chain of command. The Goldwater-Nichols reforms had foreseen the chairman, not the secretary, as being on the margin of war fighting, but it played out differently with Powell. The secretary of defense became superfluous as the war was launched, a status of irrelevance that extended even to the White House. "The president did one-stop shopping with Powell," a general told me. Bypassing Cheney, and Scowcroft for that matter, Bush went to Powell, from whom he "got his military advice, got his political advice, got his policy advice, got his public support."[86] Powell saw no need to brief the secretary of defense on war plans.

Americans dropped their ambivalence about the war as quickly as Powell did. All over the United States, yellow ribbons appeared on trees and mailboxes, and American flag pins showed up on men's lapels. In contrast with Walter Cronkite, who had denounced the Vietnam War, Andy Rooney, of the CBS program *60 Minutes,* praised "the best war in history."[87] No one spoke of Iraqi victims. Another departure from Vietnam, where the "body count" had been so obsessive: Pentagon press officers let it be known that the military no longer counted enemy dead. Enemy dead, as a measure of the real cost of the campaign, didn't count.[88]

With General Norman Schwarzkopf of Central Command, the CINC who actually ran the war, Powell emerged from Operation Desert Storm a national hero. Even to opponents of the war, like me, his standing as the single most powerful African American in the nation's history had appeal. The Army, against all odds, had become the most integrated institution in the nation, and the top soldier's obvious competence was a source of universal pride. "Powell was the new Eisenhower," David Halberstam wrote, "the thoughtful, careful, tough but benign overall planner, and Schwarzkopf was the new Patton, the crusty, cigar-chomping, hell-for-leather combat commander."[89] America was back.

9. CLINTON'S HONOR

Not for long. In early 1993, Bill Clinton became the unexpected president. As the British electorate had turned Winston Churchill out of 10 Downing Street in the summer of 1945, before the Allied victory over the Axis forces was complete, American voters effectively punished George H. W. Bush, whether for his unfinished victory over Saddam Hussein or for his self-declared victory over the now gone Soviet Union — or simply for not knowing how much a gallon of milk cost at the supermarket.

Clinton had mocked Bush's claims of having won the Cold War as a version of the rooster taking credit for the sunrise,[90] but, showing his political genius, he had also mastered the same triumphalism. In his campaign, he unveiled a "New Covenant for American Security," which promised to change nothing in a U.S. military policy that was seen as having scored its greatest victory in Moscow's collapse. Indeed, Clinton, while refusing to honor Bush for winning the Cold War, claimed exactly that victory for the nation, including himself. "Thanks to the unstinting courage and sacrifice of the American people," he said, "we were able to win the Cold War."[91]

Having successfully wrapped himself in the cloak of America's victory over the USSR, deflecting attention away from his own complicated history with the military, and signaling his lack of interest in challenging the Pentagon status quo, Clinton was able to home in on Bush's vulnerability, masterfully exploiting voter anxieties about the economy. These were partly a matter of the hangover from the Reagan deficit, manifested in high interest and unemployment rates, but the subliminal worry was tied to inevitable dislocations of the post–Cold War era, symbolized by perceptions that the economic future belonged more to Germany and Japan, our old enemies, than to America. When Clinton had brought up the foreign policy question at all, it had been as a knife pointed at this one Bush weakness. "Saddam Hussein still has his job," one Clinton campaign ad had jabbed. "Do you?"[92]

But perhaps Clinton's arrival suggested a deeper level of concern at work in the American psyche. After fifty long years of fears and worries about the nation's physical survival — first Hitler, then Stalin and his successors — wasn't it time to tend to other wounds? The stolid Bush, a proper successor to the movie star Reagan, was perceived as a kind of Gary Cooper, but such stoic heroism was needed only at high noon. Later in the day, it was an ideal to fall short of. What Americans needed now was a method actor like, say, Dustin Hoffman, whose anguish was itself a source of creativity. After a generation-long fixation on national security, the time seemed to have come for a little openly admitted insecurity. Daytime television defined by Oprah Winfrey was a long way from the Army-McCarthy hearings, the Watergate hearings, or CNN's blanket coverage of the Gulf War. Clinton was chosen by a nation longing to tend its secret garden. His election, as David Halberstam put it, was "a reflection that the country no longer felt threatened by external enemies."[93]

*   *   *

To those of us who had come down on the antiwar side of the cultural divide in the Vietnam years, Clinton's election was distinctly hopeful. To be sure, he had his political and philosophical inconsistencies (passionately pro–civil rights, for example, he was also a strong death penalty backer; shockingly, he had seen to the execution of a retarded African-American man on Arkansas's death row during the election campaign). But having "despised" the war in Vietnam, Clinton had put peace at the center of his youthful identity. As such, his arrival could seem perfectly timed, an American match not only for Gorbachev and Yeltsin, but for Sadat, Rabin, Arias, Walesa, Havel, Mandela, Hume, Aquino, Pope John Paul II, all those looking for another way.

In truth, Clinton the politician rarely discussed war and peace. He wanted to be seen as honoring the American fighting man, and usually he was. Defense policy was not a subject he addressed much, and the nuclear question rarely came up in his speeches. But the moment was larger than he was, and his background seemed to provide the best preparation for stepping off in a bold direction. The new currents of history seemed to be running together, and why shouldn't they flow through the United States as well? Even Clinton's emphasis on the economy could seem like peacemaking. In the 1990s, wouldn't the prosperity wrought by the new global trading system of which he spoke so eloquently make the ancient land-grab motives of war obsolete? Right after the election, when the administration began to take shape, this fanciful thinking seemed real.

The national security team looked nothing like what had come before. Vice President Al Gore, at that point in his career, was a prophet of care for the planet. His just published book, *Earth in the Balance,* made the urgent case for, in particular, a rescue of the environment from every kind of nuclear threat. Gore made the drastic argument that the entire phenomenon of Western indifference to the growing crisis of the environment "may have begun with the realization that nuclear weaponry had introduced a new potential for an end to civilization." Gore laid blame for the nuclear arms race on both sides, and he saw both sides as pursuing it out of "an obsolete understanding of what war is all about."[94]

The secretary of state, Warren Christopher, was derided by some as "Dean Rusk, without the charisma,"[95] but his history as a key assistant to the admired Cyrus Vance, and his modest demeanor, promised a step back from the Texas-style hubris of James Baker. At Defense Clinton put Les Aspin, a former MIT professor who had served as a congressman from Wisconsin for twenty years. He had begun as one of the first generation of defense intellectuals, and from one point of view, his whole career had been preparing him for the Pentagon. From another, he seemed more like the dean of a liberal arts college than the supernumerary of warriors. Temperamentally and ideologically, Aspin was the polar opposite of his predecessor, Richard Cheney, which to us was Aspin's great virtue. But the most significant signal to be taken from Aspin's appointment involved his work as chair of the House Armed Services Committee, where his central concern had been helping Russia safely defuse its nuclear arsenal — "cooperative threat reduction." Aspin had been eloquent in his insistence that the time to rid the world of nuclear weapons had come.[96]

Clinton's national security adviser was the eminently qualified Anthony Lake, who proposed replacing the idea of containment with what was taken as the relatively spacious idea of "enlargement."[97] He had served in Carter's State Department as director of policy planning, the office in which George Kennan and Paul Nitze had won their spurs. But what endeared Lake to us was the fact that he had boldly and conscientiously resigned his position on Henry Kissinger's NSC staff in 1970, to protest the incursion into Cambodia. The incoming president's commitments, we thought, were on full display. Clinton, by his own account, was motivated by the possibilities he had glimpsed in John F. Kennedy, who had made the decisive turn, on the American side, against the Cold War tide. The completion of what Kennedy had begun was long overdue. Bill Clinton could be a fulfillment of the dream of a generation, and many of us found reasons to believe in him.

From behind the one-way glass of certain Pentagon windows, the prospect of a Clinton presidency was more ominous, and the dark possibilities soon took shape. America's foreign policy, and related missions of "global engagement," became more confused, not less. The new class of civilians appointed to run the national security establishment proved unbelievably inept.[98] But the problem transcended the particular qualifications of those in responsibility at this time of international upheaval.

During the first Clinton term, in the chaotic aftermath of Cold War stasis, three dozen wars broke out around the world, some of them exceedingly violent and a few of them obviously preventable. Terrorism came into its own as a mode of political conflict, with a stunning attack on New York's World Trade Center occurring a little over a month after Clinton took office.[99] Of greater significance than the weight or lightness of Clinton's team was the nation's new situation, which had psychological as well as political aspects. The unifying and motivating enemy of the Cold War had disappeared, and that accounted for far more of Washington's uncertainty than the flaws and foibles of the novice administration did. The bifurcated political imagination of the United States, which had for so long seen good and evil in stark relief, was useless when it came to making sense of the world coming into being now.

Soon enough, American soldiers were disgraced again, both by what they were sent abroad to do and by missions to which they were not dispatched. There was Port-au-Prince and Mogadishu, where America's fighting elite fled from mobs, and there was Bosnia and Rwanda, where genocides were allowed to unfold. Even the 1991 "triumph" over Saddam Hussein was revealed to have been exaggerated, including its much-vaunted high-tech aspect. At the time of the Gulf War, for example, Raytheon's Patriot missile was celebrated for having knocked numerous Iraqi Scud missiles out of the air. It was not true. The Patriot knocked down nothing except itself.[100] But technology was not the only source of self-destruction in a highflying America. The shocking barrage of institutional problems was tied, in the Pentagon at least, to an intensely personal problem: the commander in chief at this crucial time commanded no respect.

This was a condition the Pentagon might have deplored, but in fact it was a boon for the Building. As soon became apparent, the utter absence of credible executive authority in military matters across the Potomac River meant the Niagara current of open-ended arms procurement, force projection, nuclear swagger, and defense industry dominance of Congress could flow on unchecked. American military forces had more commitments abroad in the 1990s than in any decade since 1950. The Clinton defense budget reflected that, with totals increasing from $260 billion to more than $300 billion.[101] Under Clinton, the Pentagon would even renege on commitments that had been made under Reagan and Bush to Gorbachev and Yeltsin, most egregiously on the question of NATO expansion. A condition of Gorbachev's acceptance of a unified Germany in NATO was that the alliance — created, after all, expressly to oppose Moscow — would move no farther east. Gorbachev understood James Baker as having firmly promised as much — "not one inch eastward."[102]

But the Pentagon had never accepted that. Getting former members of the Warsaw Pact into NATO, beginning with Poland, Hungary, and the Czech Republic, was less a security question, now that Russia was in decline, than an economic one, for Moscow's former satellite nations, needing an arms buildup from scratch, represented a major new market for the Pentagon's industrial partners. That was an argument Clinton could understand, and as a politician he saw the benefit of pleasing U.S. voters with ties to Eastern Europe. Another benefit was money to the Democrats: in one year alone, American defense contractors devoted $50 million to lobbying Congress on NATO expansion, and they contributed tens of millions to Democratic (and Republican) election campaigns.[103] Instead of dismantling NATO, as the disappearance of its Cold War rationale might have suggested, an unfettered Pentagon, trumping traditional State Department concerns,[104] was free to turn it into an enriching new source of power. In the short run, NATO expansion killed nuclear arms reduction, and in the long run, it laid the groundwork for a dangerous isolation of Russia. George Kennan, the godfather of containment and of the North Atlantic alliance itself, defined NATO's expansion in the Clinton years as "the most fateful error of American policy in the entire post–Cold War era."[105]

The Pentagon's dominance of Clinton was soon revealed. Early in his term, the president visited an aircraft carrier, the USS *Theodore Roosevelt*.[106] As he was piped aboard, he passed a young sailor at the head of the gangplank. The sailor pointedly declined to salute his commander in chief. Instead of rebuking such disrespect to the office of the presidency on the spot, or afterward, Clinton let the slight pass, as if it did not matter. The president's refusal to enforce due deference to authority was a graver offense against the military ethos than the sailor's contemptuous act, and every member of the armed forces took note.

When it came to exercising authority over the military, Bill Clinton was emasculated from the start. That meant ingrained habits of mind whose time had passed would not be challenged. And it meant that new forms of Pentagon dominance could be exerted, both in Washington and abroad. In large part because of the insult (and threat) to Moscow of NATO expansion, the post–Cold War slowdown of nuclear arms reduction slowed even further, until it was effectively stalled. This was the single most grievous failure of Clinton's failure-strewn presidency.

Under Reagan and Bush, the U.S. nuclear arsenal was cut approximately in half; under Clinton, over eight years, the arsenal would be reduced almost not at all.[107] Even the firmly discredited SDI, despite the thorough debunking of antimissile performance in the Gulf War,[108] would make a comeback in the Clinton years as "National Missile Defense," with Clinton providing funds for development of a weapons system he clearly did not believe in. He would preside over the Pentagon's version of the worst of times and the best of times; what made for the former enabled the latter.

How was this possible? First, there was the matter of Clinton's self-styled status as an avatar of the sixties, which, in the Building, remained code for a decadent culture of self-indulgence, the opposite of martial virtue. After the institutional crisis of Vietnam, the Pentagon threw up walls against all that seemed to have made it possible, ironically becoming its own version of a counterculture, a center of "traditional" values. It did not matter that Clinton's achievement — his life's journey from an impoverished, broken family in the Ozarks to the White House — was, despite the junk food, a triumph of self-discipline worthy of a great general. Clinton was the first president since Franklin Roosevelt not to have served in uniform (though never in uniform, FDR had been assistant secretary of the Navy before being stricken with polio).

Worse, Clinton's Republican opponents had come close to sticking him with the label "draft dodger," although most voters, remembering the complexities of Vietnam, had concluded that was unfair. Indeed, for many of his generation, the choices Clinton had made regarding his military service in the late 1960s felt quite familiar. If there was a mystery about Clinton's record, it was why he seemed to agree with Republicans that it was something to be ashamed of. After all, history's verdict on Vietnam was already in. Clinton had recognized it as a mistaken, even an immoral, war, and had declined to serve. Clinton had been right about Vietnam.

Perhaps military people would not have held his avoidance of Vietnam against him if only he had forthrightly taken responsibility for his choices. But he never did — not during the election and not in the early months of his presidency. Clinton's apparent obfuscations about his use of an ROTC appointment to avoid the draft (he was to do his ROTC service at the University of Arkansas while in law school, after Oxford) and then his abrupt withdrawal from the ROTC appointment when he subsequently drew a high number in the Selective Service lottery (enabling his preferred track to Yale Law School) were infuriating. *Why can't this guy say that he did everything he legally could to avoid fighting in an immoral war, and that he's proud of it?*

But there was a problem. Clinton was palpably not proud, which made it impossible for him to be forthright. Whether he knew it at the time or not, his draft maneuvering in the late 1960s had apparently depended on a violation of the law.[109] At the very least, Army regulations required candidates for ROTC to be enrolled as students in the university offering the appointment, which Clinton was not. He had applied for the ROTC slot *after* he had received his draft notice, which probably made the appointment illegal — a violation belonging not to Clinton but to his draft board. As a candidate, Clinton had insisted that he had been treated like every other draft-eligible young man, but was that so? The Reserves and the National Guard were populated by men who did not want to risk being drafted, but if what Clinton did was universally permitted, no one would have had to join the Reserves or Guard until after receiving a "greetings" letter. Over the years Clinton may have been confused about these obscure but crucial points of timing and regulation, but as a presidential candidate he seemed only to be dissembling. In his biography, published in 2004, Clinton puts the timing right — he says he received his draft notice in April 1969 and made his application to ROTC in July of that year — but he steps past the question that caused him to squirm in 1992 by asserting that, after his induction notice, "I was free to make other military arrangements."[110]

Clinton's 1992 obfuscations to the reporter who had done the most to ferret out the story were missed by a good part of the electorate, but they became "a cornerstone" of distrust to journalists who knew the record.[111] If certain (though far from all) members of the press took careful notice of how Clinton dealt with this issue, their scrutiny — and judgmentalism — was nothing compared to that of members of the military. The dishonor was not in what he had done as a young man, but in what he was doing now. Colin Powell, when I interviewed him by telephone in 1997 for a *New Yorker* article, drew a direct link between the authority of the chain of command and the matter of personal honor. "Regarding good order and discipline," he said, "there is one line above all. The line that can't be crossed is the chain of command, which must be protected. Otherwise the entire mission fails. And that means two things up and down that line: you can't lie to your commander, and you can't violate the trust of those under your authority. I would evaluate all of these questions of morale, behavior, and discipline in terms of these two principles."[112]

10. GAYS IN THE MILITARY

The draft history was used to impugn Clinton's character, but the Pentagon's graver concern went to the question of its own character. When the writer Jonathan Schell asked General George Lee Butler why the Pentagon had not significantly changed its armed-to-the-teeth posture after the Cold War ended, the former Strategic Air Command chief replied, "Remember that the final whimsical act of the gods was to drive George Bush from office and force us to go through a presidential transition at the most critical juncture. Policy positions sat vacant for months. Then the next administration was caught up in the controversy over Clinton's desire to address homosexuality in the armed forces. Remember? The priceless opportunity got stepped all over."[113]

"Gays in the military" was the shorthand reference for Clinton's failure with the Pentagon. A broad consensus agreed that the new president made a large mistake in taking up the question of homosexual rights in the armed services. Across the political spectrum he was derided for it.

As the story is told, the problem began with his campaign promise to lift all discriminatory barriers against homosexual men and women — an extension of his firm commitment to civil rights. Clinton is remembered as forcing the issue on the Pentagon from his first day in office, and even his supporters, aware of all that it cost him, rue his decision. But the issue did not start with Clinton. The knot of questions having to do with sexuality had been coming untied for decades, with obvious implications for military culture. The women's movement was the needle's point in that knot, and it had already penetrated the armed services.

In 1976, the separate women's units, like the Navy's WAVES and the Army's WAC, had been disbanded. At that point, less than 2 percent of service personnel were female; by the 1990s, the number had grown to 14 percent. Even ferocious Pentagon opposition to women's serving in combat roles was being overcome.[114] Nothing signaled the change in military culture more than this admission of women to it. Especially in the era of "immaculate" high-tech violence, the warrior ethos could no longer be conceived in the macho clichés of the locker room and foxhole. And when women began to survive and master the brutal obstacles of basic training, which defined the initiation rites of a closed community, that community broke open. A symbol of this was what happened to the cadence call, the chanted rhythm by which recruits learned to march. If, in the new Army, such calls were no longer to denigrate women ("I don't know but I've been told, Eskimo pussy's mighty cold" — this line, of course, denigrates two groups at once), why should they denigrate homosexuals?

For decades, the national security establishment had barred homosexuals from government service — including the military, but not limited to it — with the rationale that a secret life of disgraceful perversity made gays subject to blackmail, and therefore made them "security risks."[115] By the 1980s and early 1990s, the social stigma was lifting. Homosexuality was increasingly seen as normal, not perverse. Psychiatric definitions changed. The AIDS epidemic became the occasion of widespread education, with gay men, in particular, being perceived as responsible, courageous, and caring. There were gay people in Congress. The Pentagon itself, under Richard Cheney (whose own daughter is a lesbian), declared that national security was no longer to be considered a justification for barring homosexuals from military service.[116]

Well, if not that, then what? The Army next offered up "unit cohesion and morale" as justification for continuing the ban. The Navy openly worried about men on ships. Military nervousness about homosexuality — a kind of institutional "gay panic," an anguish of hidden insecurities to which an organization defined by martial virtue was especially vulnerable — had been reflected in the odd fact that regulations regarding homosexuals had constantly been revised, with dozens of changes registered since World War II. By the early nineties, the Uniform Code of Military Justice forbade sexual acts defined as "unlawful carnal copulation," even if committed by heterosexuals, even married heterosexuals. A husband engaging in oral sex with his wife could be charged with a crime. But gays were *assumed* to be guilty of such acts (even if they were celibate). What was striking was the military's nervousness about such questions, a strange determination to slam the door shut on anything that might remotely suggest same-sex interest. Once women were admitted to West Point, for example, a regulation was enforced forbidding male and female cadets to dance together if the female was wearing trousers.[117]

The military's problem went deep here, because the disciplined violence of war, which goes to the core of military identity, has always had a sexual edge to it. A civilized fighting force has the challenge of breaking down the taboo against killing without breaking down all taboos. As the Balkan wars of the 1990s showed, even today, in the heart of Europe, among "people like us," the rush to battle can easily run on to mass rape.[118] Understanding the power of these dark impulses in the human psyche, honorable but practical men in authority over uniformed legions of the young do not attempt so much to suppress the sexual as to channel it. That is why military tradition even in a puritanical society like the United States — despite regulations to the contrary — assumes the sexual bravado of the brothel, condoms from the quartermaster, and the license of the weekend pass and its cry of "rings off!" In the American military, off-duty rituals, including those of the officers' mess, routinely involve sexual exploitation that is as officially sanctioned as it is illegal, a contradiction that became notorious with the Tailhook scandal in the early nineties.[119]

Clinton had brought an air of sexual recklessness to his presidency, which might have been a bond with the uniformed men under his command if he had not carried it to such excess,[120] but the president saw the question of homosexuals in the military through the lens of equal rights, basic social justice. With the disappearance of the national security rationale for discrimination against gays, nothing was left but rank bigotry. The "morale" the brass wanted to protect was cohesion based on in-group contempt for a designated out-group. When Clinton was faced with the question, he knew the position he had to take. The point, however, is that the issue belonged to the time and place, and did not begin with him.

In truth, to his opponents in the Pentagon, the question of gays in the military was a deliverance, another version of the Korean War and the Gulf War as unexpected sources of reinforcement for the martial ethos. "The high priests of the nuclear age," General Butler told me in the 1990s, "are having great difficulty letting go" of their status and the weapons on which their status depends.[121] Because of the galvanizing issue of homosexuality, they would not have to.

Colin Powell first met with President-elect Clinton on November 19,

1992. By his own account, Powell says that it was he, not Clinton, who brought up the subject of homosexuals in the military.[122] And it was the Joint Chiefs of Staff, in their first meeting with the new president, on January 25, 1993, five days after his swearing in, who did the same. *Clinton did not bring up the issue.* In his memoir, Clinton says the Chiefs expressed an "urgent" concern about it. They pushed the question to the top of his agenda. Whether consciously or not, the brass were cooperating with a wily Republican ploy, led by Senator Robert Dole, who became an early foe of Clinton's. Because of the strong showing of the third-party candidate H. Ross Perot, Clinton had been elected with a paltry 43 percent of the vote, which made him vulnerable to Republican opposition. Picking up on what had been merely one of a dozen hot-button campaign issues, Dole threw the gays-in-the-military question onto the tracks in front of the new administration, hoping for derailment. It worked. But the derailment assumed an all but overt threat from the Joint Chiefs, including the chairman, that they would not carry out an order from Clinton lifting the ban.

That threat intimidated Clinton's secretary of defense, Les Aspin. As the chair of the House Armed Services Committee, Aspin had become an expert on the "revolution in military affairs," and he seemed perfectly placed to lead the Pentagon into an era of post–Cold War adjustments. But from another point of view, the personally insecure, undisciplined, phlegmatic Aspin was in no way prepared to deal with what awaited him at the Pentagon. What he soon discovered, as one of his aides later told me, was that "Colin Powell was running the Building."[123]

Powell was a wall into which Aspin walked. Four days after the inauguration, appearing on the CBS television program *Face the Nation*, the new defense secretary was asked about the issue of gays in the military (again, Aspin did not bring it up). His reply was far from resolute. Referring to the well-known opposition in the Pentagon, Aspin said, "If we can't work it out, we'll disagree, and the thing won't happen." *The thing won't happen.* Relating this in his own account of the controversy in his memoir, Colin Powell comments, "In effect, he had publicly predicted the failure of Clinton's first presidential initiative."[124] What Powell does not say was that his own position was what had driven Aspin to that quick prediction.

The Pentagon waited for Clinton to rebuke Aspin, or at least to reaffirm his determination to see the ban on homosexuals lifted. But Clinton was avoiding the issue, not pushing it. If the military did not like Clinton's position on gays, it liked his waffling even less. As Aspin's prediction made clear, Powell held the advantage on this question, not Clinton. Powell was the most widely admired man in the government, and he did not hesitate to throw the elbows that status gave him. Though he was the sitting chairman of the Joint

Chiefs of Staff, he presumed to publish an article, in the winter 1992–93 issue of *Foreign Affairs,* under the rubric "Advice for President Clinton."[125]

Clinton was not only deferential to Powell, he was groveling. Before his arrival in Washington, he sought to enlist Powell's full support. Through his friend the African-American power broker Vernon Jordan, the president-elect had sounded out Powell on a cabinet post, and later in his administration Clinton would offer to name him secretary of state.[126] Each time, Powell declined. As events would show, he was more in tune with the foreign policy of Republicans, and the bonds he had forged with Weinberger, Cheney, and Bush would continue to define him. We have seen that in the debates after Saddam Hussein's invasion of Kuwait, Powell had opposed President Bush on launching the Gulf War, yet once Bush had decided to commit, Powell had saluted, obeyed, and made it happen. He had done the same thing late in the Bush term, when the president ordered Operation Restore Hope, the humanitarian mission to Somalia.[127] But on the question of gays, put to him by Bill Clinton, there was to be only opposition, and no salute.

Powell, of course, denies that. "My life would have been easier if he [Clinton] had simply lifted the ban by executive order. The military would have said, 'Yes, Sir.' But, as Les Aspin knew, almost immediately Congress would have enacted a ban as a matter of law, forcing the President to veto it, and confronting him with an almost certain veto override."[128] What makes this explanation disingenuous is the fact that congressional opposition was firmly braced by the prior, well-known opposition of the military Chiefs, especially their chairman. And the Chiefs, confronted at the start with Aspin's surrender, were given no reason to mitigate their opposition. The Clinton administration, that is, came into office showing that it expected not to exercise authority over the military on this question.

Clinton's short-term solution was to announce, on January 29, 1993, that Aspin would study the issue for six months, then make a recommendation. Sure enough, in July, in what was talked of as a "compromise," Clinton reiterated the ban on gays in the military, although now, theoretically, it would not be aggressively enforced.[129] This policy was called "Don't ask, don't tell, don't pursue," but it condemned gay people in the military to a further life of deception, failed to protect gays from discrimination, and undermined the cohesion and morale that was supposed to have been so threatened by lifting the ban. Military women who rebuffed the advances of their male colleagues were threatened with being perceived as lesbians. More people were discharged for being homosexuals after the policy went into effect than had been the case before.[130] And, in an additional wrinkle, when a soldier "told" on himself that he was gay, theoretically to be discharged at once, the military now required proof in the form of the implication of his or her partner. Otherwise, straight personnel could use the policy as a way of getting out of the military early.

In September 1993, three months after Clinton instituted the policy, an act approving "Don't ask, don't tell" was passed by Congress, which elevated the policy from the relatively lowly realm of military regulations to a law of the land. This was a disaster for gay people and for the honor of the military, since the policy was based on universal deception.[131] But what compounded the disaster was the way the controversy destroyed Clinton's authority with the Pentagon, and therefore his ability to shape an alternative approach to security in the post–Cold War world.

Powell's responsibility for all this was enormous. It was no coincidence that the six-month "study" period coincided with the months remaining in Powell's term as chairman. Rather than confront Powell on the question or risk the political fallout if he resigned early, Clinton let it ride. As Powell knew, that ducking of the decision itself gave him his victory, for, on an issue that, however peripheral, had taken on enormous cultural and political significance, the president of the United States deferred to the open dissent of the chairman of the Joint Chiefs. After that, no wonder the sailor aboard the *Theodore Roosevelt* felt free to refuse to salute his commander in chief. But the president's exercise of authority on gays in the military could have gone another way, and indeed, on an equivalent issue forty years before, presidential authority had.

11. THE REAL CONTRAST WITH TRUMAN

Colin Powell hated the comparison of gay rights with civil rights, and whenever Clinton's wish to lift the ban on homosexuals was compared with Harry Truman's order ending discrimination against blacks in the military, Powell became incensed. Before Truman's order,[132] blacks were not only placed in segregated units, they were overwhelmingly assigned to work as drivers, cooks, and launderers. In the Navy, black men were usually assigned to the "stewards branch," along with Filipino Americans.

Powell was quite aware that Truman's order made his own career track possible. "I need no reminders," he wrote to Representative Patricia Schroeder of Colorado, who presumed to make the comparison in 1992, "concerning the history of African-Americans in the defense of their nation." Powell went on in the letter to explain why the two issues were distinct. "Skin color is a benign, nonbehavioral characteristic. Sexual orientation is perhaps the most profound of human behavioral characteristics. Comparison of the two is a convenient but invalid argument."[133] The trouble with Powell's explanation is that in 1948, the racist opposition to Truman's order saw skin color precisely as an emblem of black people's behavioral characteristics, which to the racists were anything but benign. Racism is defined by the conviction that skin color is "the most profound" of human characteristics. That is the whole point.

As chairman of the Joint Chiefs, Powell proudly kept on the wall of his Pentagon office a painting of "Buffalo soldiers," as blacks were called in the old Army.[134] But records of the Ninety-second Buffalo Division as far back as World War I were cited by opponents of Truman's order, records that enumerated such "behavioral characteristics" as "straggling," "disorganization," "panicky retreats," and "melting away under fire" — all attributed to the race of the division's members.[135] Blacks in uniform were commonly regarded not only as intellectually inferior but as cowards, deficient in everything that matters in war. There was no way the typical midcentury white American wanted a black man in a foxhole with him. In an official assessment of the record of World War II, the chief historian of the Army wrote of blacks in 1945, "They lack self-respect, self-confidence, and initiative . . . feel very little motive for aggressive fighting."[136]

They were also innately immoral. Against Powell's blithe assertion, the entire campaign against integration was fought on the issue of character, not mere skin color. Strom Thurmond denounced the "evil" of Truman's order. Some members of Congress declined to stand when Truman appeared before them, as an act of conscientious objection.[137] Questions of virtue were at stake, of God's will, of the order of the universe. This was an intrinsic part of racist rant, and it is unimaginable that Colin Powell did not know it. In opposing Truman, Senator Richard B. Russell of Georgia said on the Senate floor, "The mandatory intermingling of the races throughout the services will be a terrific blow to the efficiency and fighting power of the armed services . . . It is sure to increase the numbers of men who will be disabled through [sexually] communicable diseases. It will increase the rate of crime committed by servicemen."[138]

When attitudes like this showed themselves in the military establishment that was to implement his order, Truman made it instantly clear that he would tolerate no resistance. Some of Clinton's critics faulted him because he made his stand against second-class status for gays in the military in the context of a political campaign, but that is exactly what Truman did, issuing his order in the summer before the 1948 presidential election. He was running on a civil rights plank, and his integration order was as much about politics as about principle.

The Colin Powell of the day, General Omar Bradley, did not like Truman's stated intention to change things, any more than Powell liked Clinton's. Bradley told an interviewer that he understood Truman's order to require not integration of blacks but a military version of "separate but equal." Truman publicly rebuked Bradley, Bradley publicly apologized, and that was the end of that.[139] Integration, full and complete, was the expectation. As the first chairman of the Joint Chiefs of Staff, Bradley went on to preside over the most successful social revolution of the day, with the result that the military was the first American institution to be authentically integrated. The racist warnings of dire consequences came to nothing, as blacks were finally able to prove themselves. As the failures of almost every other institution to match that record now show, racial equality in the military in mid-twentieth-century America was at least as problematic, "morally" as well as socially, as equality for gays at century's end.

Truman's order was carried out because the president was firm in the authority with which he issued it, and because the military commanders, putting aside their own racism and that of the entire society, made it clear that the careers of those who resisted would abruptly end.[140] Colin Powell could have provided leadership of this kind. He did not. As a black man who made it to the top, Powell honored Bradley for implementing an order he disagreed with, seeing no contradiction with his own behavior. Powell was no Omar Bradley, which was half the problem. The other half, of course, was that Bill Clinton was no Harry Truman.

The personal shortcomings of Powell and Clinton, compared with Bradley and Truman, are not the main issue, however. To observe such differences is to speak of something far deeper than individual limitations of character. To understand the troubled relationship between the Clinton administration and the Pentagon, it is crucial to recall that the military had a completely different relationship with its civilian overseers at the onset of the Cold War than it did at the end of it. Although lip service to civilian control was still paid, as we saw, by Colin Powell, the course of the Cold War we have tracked in this book had upended the real meaning of authority, shifting all practical power across the river to the Pentagon.

This becomes evident if we see the Truman integration order of 1948 in the context of the other unwanted command — unwanted by the brass — he issued to the Pentagon at the same time. Four days before he promulgated the executive order ending racial discrimination, Truman had sent, on July 21, an even more momentous order, denying the Joint Chiefs' request to take over custody and control of the atomic bomb from the Atomic Energy Commission — from civilians, that is. Truman did not trust "these terrible forces," as AEC Chairman David Lilienthal wrote at the time, "in the hands of the military establishment."[141] Truman was trying to protect a principle he had already established, that the atomic bomb was a thing apart, not to be treated like other weapons and not to be removed from his own close supervision.

But by the middle of 1948, fears of war with the Communists were roiling the Pentagon (the spring "war scare" in Czechoslovakia, the Berlin blockade, Communist advances in China). The military men hated Truman for refusing to give them control of the atomic bomb. Both the Joint Chiefs and Truman knew that this was the central symbol of real power now, and the Chiefs would not rest until (after Moscow's atomic bomb, NSC-68, and Korea) they had acquired it.

But a military establishment that, until then, accepted its marginal place in matters of the nuclear arsenal was not going to defy the president on something as relatively unimportant as racial justice. By Bill Clinton's time, of course, effective control of the "terrible forces" had long since passed into the hands of a military establishment that, beginning with LeMay and continuing through Lee Butler, did not even disclose details of the SIOP to civilians. A symbolic fig leaf of civilian authority over nuclear weapons remained in the "football," the nuclear launch codes that accompany the president everywhere to this day, but the decision to use those codes, based on information supplied by the military and on systems controlled by the military, would be incidental to any realistic scenario by which nuclear war might start. The warrant officer who tracks the president is an actor in a drama that aims mainly to foster the illusion — as much the president's as the public's — of civilian control. The military authority Clinton inherited, that is, was hollow compared to what Truman had taken for granted. This was also a matter of the power that accrued to Truman from the rise of the Soviet threat; in Clinton's case, presidential power had slipped as that threat disappeared. Questions about Clinton's draft record and about gays in the military only exposed that hollowness for all to see, including those behind the one-way windows across the river.

Illusions, though, were worth only so much. With Clinton, the Pentagon would not even pretend to salute, especially once his self-destructive promiscuity undermined what little moral authority he had, but draft dodging and gays together formed a cloak of pretense over what actually mattered most. As the (to them) frighteningly unreliable Bill Clinton entered office, the power the Pentagon was dead serious about maintaining was over nuclear weapons, not over the sexual activities of soldiers. In the odd dispensation of the warrior ethos, however, the two things soon came to be related. Routing Clinton on gays at the beginning of his administration was a harbinger of the Pentagon's total defeat of every attempt to step back from Cold War arsenals and attitudes.

"Don't ask, don't tell" was, in fact, an apt metaphor for the Pentagon's message to the American public about its own fetish with nuclear weapons, which, like the traditional ban on gays, no longer had any national security justification. The furor over homosexuality early in Clinton's term, in other words, had far more significance than is usually realized. Not only was there something vaguely homoerotic about the Pentagon's obsession with phallic nuclear missiles; there were other resonances as well. Despite some troubling consequences of sexual appetite, heterosexuality is morally acceptable in a puritan society because of its functional purpose, reproduction. Once that purpose is removed, as happens in homosexual eros, sexuality engaged in "merely for pleasure" becomes not only morally problematic but existentially threatening. "Homosexual panic," a deflecting of such unacknowledged anxiety into contempt for gay people, is a disorder that afflicts plenty of heterosexuals.

Similarly, once the functional purpose of nuclear weapons (deterring the Soviet Union) disappeared, justifications for their existence disappeared, too. In the post–Cold War period, U.S. defense policy, justifying the ongoing enormity of the military budget and the permanence of the nuclear arsenal, amounted to another form of "Don't ask, don't tell." *Don't ask us about the money we're spending. We won't tell you how our weapons still threaten the future of the human race.* A kind of nuclear panic, as powerful as it was subliminal, gripped the national psyche when the nuclear rationale ceased to exist, but this panic was deflected into contempt for gays.

At the crucial moment of transition, when basic questions about Pentagon assumptions might have — should have — been asked, homosexuals were scapegoated in an irrational institutionalization of bigotry. The surfacing and exploitation of public antigay sentiment allowed for an efficient rechanneling of the paranoia that jumped its banks once the Soviet Union dissolved. The convenient gays-in-the-military issue gave the military time to redefine (or invent) the next grave threat to American security.

12. THE NUCLEAR POSTURE REVIEW

Mogadishu. The word evokes the era in the way "gays in the military" does. Operation Restore Hope, which began, under George H. W. Bush, as a warm-hearted display of American goodness,[142] ended under Clinton as an emblem of his fecklessness. We saw that Colin Powell had opposed the deployment of American troops to Somalia as a classic violation of the Powell Doctrine. But he had supervised it, as the mission "crept" from one of delivering humanitarian relief supplies to starving Somalis, to one of preventing those supplies from being looted by warlords, to one of arresting the chief warlord, Mohammed Farah Aidid.[143] When the deployment came to a disastrous end, with the downing of two Black Hawk helicopters and the deaths of nineteen Americans in a battle on October 3, 1993, it says everything about Powell's good luck — and Clinton's bad — that the chairman had retired from the Army only days earlier. America's humiliation in having its soldiers' corpses dragged through the streets of Mogadishu[144] was compounded when Clinton ordered the immediate withdrawal of the force. The United States of Cut-and-Run. Clinton was no more going to take on wild-eyed Somali fighters than he was the Pentagon.

A week later, on October 11, a Navy warship, the USS *Harlan County*, was unable to put a contingent of American soldiers ashore in Haiti as would-be peacekeepers because of threats from an armed mob. These traumas would underwrite Clinton's reluctance to commit U.S. ground troops, but that reluctance soon boomeranged when, two months later, a genocide was launched in Rwanda, resulting in the murders of a million Tutsis by machete-wielding Hutu exterminators. A small force could have stopped this. Clinton considered dispatching such a force, but decided not to, which itself became, in short order, another humiliation.[145]

In the Pentagon, the consequences of Mogadishu followed quickly. Les Aspin, not wanting to increase the U.S. military presence in a chaotic situation, had refused Army requests for tanks and armored personnel carriers in Somalia. When the Black Hawks went down, trapping American Rangers in the midst of Aidid's militia stronghold, it took Italian and Pakistani armored vehicles to rescue them — a further humiliation. Aspin's prior decision to withhold tanks became the flashpoint, and he was soon forced to resign. But Clinton's humiliation was compounded when the man he named to replace Aspin, the retired admiral and former CIA deputy director Bobby Ray Inman, announced after his meeting with the president that it was he who had done the interviewing. Inman was an eccentric whose appointment went up in smoke.[146] Clinton named Aspin's deputy, William Perry, a low-key and competent Pentagon veteran, who had served under Harold Brown in the Carter administration. Perry, "a businessman and mathematician," succeeded in bringing some calm to the Pentagon. If he was counted a success by the military, after the undisciplined Aspin, it was more because, as one insider told me, "he fixed up Navy enlisted housing, and refused to close commissaries" than because he attended to the task of filling the strategic and conceptual vacuum. Perry simply did not pursue Aspin's agenda of fundamental reconsideration of America's relationship to the use of force.

Beneath the surface of Clinton-era *Sturm und Drang*, the Pentagon elite was steadily shoring up the banks of the great Niagara current, making certain that its Cold War flow would continue, but under new rubrics, like "over-whelming force" and "full-spectrum dominance." After the Gulf War, this meant not only protecting the existing levels of strategic nuclear forces, which was the priority of the Air Force and the Polaris Navy, but also greatly expanding new conventional technologies, which the Army and broader Navy emphasized. One of Aspin's first acts had been to commission what was called a "Bottom-Up Review," a complete assessment of America's national security requirements in the post–Cold War (and, frankly, post-Republican) era. In the autumn of 1993, a reassessment of the nuclear question, a "Nuclear Posture Review," was set in motion. The Pentagon acronym (there was always an acronym) was NPR, and jokes were made in the Building about the liberal public radio network. Aspin explained to reporters that the NPR was to "in-corporate reviews of policy, doctrine, force structure, operations, safety and security, and arms control in one look."[147] The review, in the defense historian Janne Nolan's phrase, aimed at creating "a nuclear tabula rasa."[148] (It was Nolan's work that made the review's potential significance clear to me.) The document aimed to be the basis for the first genuine change in America's re-lationship to thermonuclear weapons since the Truman administration had put them at the dead center of politics and power.

Aspin, however, ordered this comprehensive review in the weeks when his authority was in meltdown, owing to the disasters of Somalia and Haiti. Outsiders, in the press and in Congress, expected the review process to yield a blueprint for "conversion" of the massive defense establishment, but that did not happen. Aspin resigned in January 1994, and the men who succeeded him did not share his single-minded, if poorly administered, agenda for trans-forming the nuclear policies of the United States.

The result was the quick discrediting of those review participants (mostly civilians) who both advocated relatively minor change — like taking nukes off the hair trigger, declaring a policy of no first use, or vastly reducing the SIOP[149] to match the vastly reduced threat from Russia — and hoped for ma-jor change, up to and including the elimination of nuclear weapons alto-gether. Was mutual assured destruction the goal of the nuclear arsenal in this era of friendship with Russia, or was it "mutual assured safety"?[150] If the latter, then surely the thrust of America's nuclear posture should shift from strategic threat to a drastic program of denuclearization. Such a process was already under way, as we saw, on the other side: the leaders of Kazakhstan, Ukraine, and Belarus had readily renounced their nukes. Those new nations had come into being as among the eight nuclear powers of the world, yet they traded that status to join the ranks of the least powerful nations. That extraordinary fact had hardly registered in the United States, yet it was a good reason to take seriously Russian assertions of similar ambitions. Why not carry the arms reduction successes of Reagan and Bush to the next level and beyond? It seemed the inevitable question for the Clinton administration, but with Aspin suddenly gone, the assumption that such a basic issue could form an agenda for action no longer went without saying.

Authority over the nuclear review then shifted to uniformed men, including General Butler, head of the Strategic Command, whose postcareer rejection of nuclear weapons we have already noted. Butler may have been Curtis LeMay's successor, but he was that rare officer who could see through the accepted wisdom to form his own beliefs. We observed how he was haunted by his close study of the SIOP targeting list — all those millions of men, women, and children incinerated by his command — and how, as the man in charge of America's monstrous nuclear force, he resolved to do something about it. Butler would emerge as a strong critic of America's nuclear stance, but not while he was in a position to really influence it. Nolan says that, as the NPR took form, Butler did little to press his growing antinuclear views on his colleagues.[151] And he retired not long after Aspin resigned. Butler's place in the review process was taken by his successor at the Strategic Command, a Navy admiral with conventional attitudes toward nuclear security.

The bias of uniformed men in favor of maintaining the nuclear status quo was predictable. At bottom, the military custodians of the strategic forces, and their allies among the Pentagon's "samurai bureaucrats," regarded the Clinton-sponsored civilian reviewers as interlopers, typical of the newly arrived zealots that sweep into the Building every time an administration changes. Such appointees knew nothing about the real requirements of national security, and they were naïve in taking Moscow's assurances at face value. Didn't they read those hard-liners' speeches in the Duma? Hadn't they noticed that the Russian legislature had yet to ratify START II?[152] In response to the outsiders' position papers and planning documents, the Pentagon insiders would nod politely as their eyes glazed over. As always, it would simply be a matter of waiting them out.

During the Reagan and Bush administrations, the major changes in American nuclear policy — notably the dramatic arsenal reductions, the phasing out of tactical nukes fired from ships and the battlefield, the end of testing, and the halt of B-52 alerts — had been ordered by the president himself, and managed under close White House supervision. But Clinton, keeping his distance from the nuclear question, handed over the initiative for change to the nuclear bureaucracy, based in the Pentagon. The White House was never engaged. Neither Warren Christopher at State nor Anthony Lake at the NSC expressed any institutional interest in the Nuclear Posture Review — extraordinary lapses for a subject of such urgency.[153] Here the stakes of

"Don't ask, don't tell" were mortal. In effect, just as the Clinton administration signaled early on that it was not serious about seeing the ban on gays lifted, it indicated that a true revision of America's nuclear posture was not that important.

And so it did not happen. The Nuclear Posture Review, when President Clinton formally accepted its recommendations, on September 22, 1994, did not propose reductions in the SIOP target list,[154] did not suggest the withdrawal of nuclear forces from Europe, did not seek cuts in the arsenal beyond those already set by START II, did not renounce first use, refused to remove nukes from the hair trigger, and did nothing to take the inexorable Niagara of escalation out of the system. On the contrary, the NPR warned that Russia, "still armed with 25,000 nuclear weapons," could quickly reemerge as a military threat. Therefore the United States should maintain the nuclear status quo as a "hedge"[155] against the possibility that Moscow would still come after us. And far from incidentally, the NPR called for maintaining "the strategic industrial base" indefinitely, an open-ended boon to defense contractors, who could look forward to "infrastructure" sustenance far into the future. Not only was the nuclear force not to change significantly,[156] but neither would the paranoid — and, as events were even then showing, wholly fanciful — exaggeration of the threat from Moscow, which had defined Pentagon thinking since Forrestal. And as had been true since Forrestal, when America took such positions, they had the effect of strengthening the hand of the clique of paranoids in Moscow, who reliably found ways to reply in kind. The NPR "was the insurance policy," as one analyst told me, "that could start the fire."[157]

When the United States declared in 1994 that it was essentially finished with nuclear disarmament, the Russians did likewise. But now there was a real danger that had never existed before. As the Russian economy tanked and the Russian military establishment began to fall into decay, controls over the nuclear arsenal became unreliable, and so did essential Russian communications and surveillance systems. To maintain Russia's deterrence, its strategic commanders relied more and more on rapid reaction — adding, in the parlance, "hair" to the "trigger." Dangers of an accidental launch surpassed any that had loomed during the Cold War.[158]

Five days after Clinton affirmed the NPR in September 1994, the Russian president, Boris Yeltsin, arrived in Washington for a summit, but the atmosphere between them was uncertain. It became clear that further progress on arms control would depend on ratification of START II, which would be problematic to say the least. Prominent voices in the Duma would use the NPR affirmations to justify a call for a Kremlin version of the "hedge." When the Clinton administration, in that same season, sponsored the expansion of

NATO to include the former Warsaw Pact nations of Poland, Hungary, and the Czech Republic, Russians, as we noted earlier, saw a betrayal of solemn assurances Mikhail Gorbachev had been given.[159] Russians not unreasonably perceived the rise of an American policy of "neocontainment" based on nuclear threat.

The Pentagon, for its part, understandably took the Nuclear Posture Review as a signal that the era of real reductions was over. There would be a proposal, in January 1997, to move to START III negotiations, with the goal of cutting strategic warheads to a range of 2,000 to 2,500 (down from the START II level of 3,500), but the proposal was tied (again) to Russian ratification of START II, and by then it was obvious that the ever more defensive Duma would not do it.[160] So the U.S. proposers did not have to imagine that START III would ever happen, and the question of reductions beyond that fell off the table. Pentagon planners were now saying that 2,500 strategic nuclear warheads were the minimum needed to maintain deterrence.[161] Despite the dream that had motivated every American president since Truman, up to and including Ronald Reagan, and despite the mandate that had been first legally declared in the Nuclear Non-Proliferation Treaty, the goal of elimination was now, for all practical purposes, dead. Which meant, naturally, that the Pentagon could move forward with plans to expand the nuclear arsenal with a new generation of "usable" nukes, a force that would make possible nuclear combat at a "reasonable" level. As Janne Nolan observed, Les Aspin had commissioned the Nuclear Posture Review by asking, "Where do we go after START II?" The answer was in: nowhere.[162]

Not only would the arsenal be expanded, so would the philosophy. Where before the United States had resolved never to use, or threaten to use, nuclear weapons against nonnuclear states, the argument could now be advanced that the way to deter "rogue states" from deploying other kinds of weapons of mass destruction, like biological or chemical agents, was by threatening nuclear use, a position the Clinton administration would enshrine in the 1996 African Nuclear-Weapon-Free Zone Treaty. The American strategy of nuclear deterrence no longer aimed merely at giving an adversary a reason not to use nuclear weapons, but also a reason not to obtain them.[163] Furthermore, the commitment to indefinitely maintain the "hedge" of nuclear weapons meant the Pentagon could resurrect arguments in favor of a resumption of testing, which would carry special weight in Congress. And freedom to prepare for the expansion of the nuclear arsenal, always under the rubric of "modernization," meant, of course, an expanding Pentagon budget, a decisive reversal of the downturn that had begun with the end of the Cold War.

The list of ways in which President Clinton deferred to the Pentagon's reassertion of Cold War rigidities is long. On January 14, 1994, during a Clinton-Yeltsin summit in Moscow, Russia and the United States agreed to "retarget" ballistic missiles so that warheads would be pointed harmlessly at the polar ice caps. The next day, Clinton told Americans, "We no longer live in the shadow of nuclear annihilation." But he neglected to mention that custodians of the American strategic force made sure that computer memories stored the original targets, to which the weapons could be returned in about a minute.[164]

Clinton would support the Comprehensive Test Ban Treaty of 1996, but would spend no political capital in getting it ratified in the Senate. After the Senate, taking cues from the Pentagon, made plain its refusal to ratify, the way was clear for India and Pakistan to resume testing, which they did in May 1998. When the 1968 Nuclear Non-Proliferation Treaty was up for extension in 1995, numerous nonnuclear countries, having taken note of Washington's fresh embrace of nukes, had protested that the United States was in violation of clause VI, which required nuclear powers to work for elimination. It was true. But it did not matter. Washington simply bowled over the objections, with Bill Clinton's collusion. A signed and ratified treaty, according to the U.S. Constitution, has the effect of law. American law required the pursuit to eliminate nuclear weapons. The Pentagon and Clinton abandoned that requirement.[165]

The protest of nonnuclear nations over America's refusal to loosen its grip on nuclear weapons was taken up at the International Court of Justice in The Hague. The deliberations of that U.N.-sponsored body were essentially ignored in the United States — although in The Hague the Clinton administration argued firmly in favor of nukes. Thirty-five nations made submissions to the court, and petitions signed by more than three million people were registered, all concerned that the nuclear powers, led by the United States, which would soon be calling itself the "indispensable nation,"[166] had abandoned the goal of nuclear abolition. The court's rulings were ambiguous, but the proceedings themselves, coming five years after the end of the Cold War, were a cry of the heart against all that had not happened since the fall of the Berlin Wall.[167]

The Nuclear Non-Proliferation Treaty was extended in 1995, but numerous smaller nations, taking note of Washington's attitude, quietly began to go about the business of acquiring nuclear weapons of their own. Clinton, that is, was the implicit sponsor of a new proliferation, and his successor in the White House would keep that particular current flowing. As North Korea and Iran would ultimately prove, deterrence could be a two-way street, but eventually the reach for deterrence would become nearly universal, with South

Korea, for example, following in the train of North Korea.[168] The main abettor of this silent proliferation would be the Pentagon's staunch ally Pakistan.

Especially after the congressional elections held halfway through his first term, Clinton was constantly pressed by a hostile Congress. He chose his fights. What is notable is how few of those fights were over the ideology, the structure, or, for that matter, the budget of the military establishment. By 1998, the United States was spending more than $278 billion a year on the military; Russia that year spent $28 billion.[169] "We won the Cold War," Lawrence Korb, an assistant secretary of defense under Reagan, told me at the time, "but we're still spending at Cold War levels. How the hell did that happen?"[170]

A Pentagon that had seen glimmers of twenty-first-century military advances in Ronald Reagan's Strategic Defense Initiative simply reinvented it as National Missile Defense. Proponents wanted the system less for the actual defensive shield it might enable than as a permanent wedge into ever higher expenditures — and as the forerunner of the Pentagon's move into outer space. Despite seeing through the illusion of any such shield, despite a sophisticated understanding of the science that debunked every claim of NMD's backers, despite knowing that U.S. deployment of even the most basic system would violate the ABM Treaty, and despite a full grasp of its pernicious role as a stimulant for the next round of the arms race,[171] Clinton gave NMD proponents sufficient funding to keep their hopes alive.

In his reelection campaign in 1996, Clinton faced a challenge on the issue from Robert Dole, who wanted a large-scale deployment of the missile defense system. Instead of rejecting Dole's position and explaining why, Clinton embraced his own, smaller version of missile defense, and by late in his second term he signed a law that signaled America's intention to deploy National Missile Defense as quickly as the technology made it feasible to do so.[172] Clinton created the Ballistic Missile Defense Organization in the Pentagon, which his successor, George W. Bush, later turned into a freestanding entity, the Missile Defense Agency. In this way, Clinton laid the groundwork for Bush, who then abrogated the ABM Treaty and began deployment of a missile defense system.[173]

When Clinton appointed William Cohen as his second-term secretary of defense, the pattern of the relationship between the White House and the brass was set. Cohen, as one defense expert told me at the time, "doesn't have a mandate from the White House to do anything significant. Quite the contrary — 'Steady as she goes!' Whatever that means." What the brass wanted, the brass got.[174] I noted earlier that Cohen was given to comparing himself to

Ahab, and the Pentagon to Moby Dick. When I mentioned that image to a Pentagon insider, he said to me, "Who is the Moby Dick? The Building? Or the president?"[175]

The tragedy of Bill Clinton's forfeiture of responsible command authority over the Pentagon on the radioactive question of America's nuclear posture is that he showed every sign of having the temperament, intelligence, and experience to have been an excellent American respondent to Gorbachev and Yeltsin, building on the nuclear reductions Reagan and Bush had accomplished despite their limits of temperament, intelligence, and experience. Clinton was perfectly placed, politically and historically, to lay the foundation of a true alternative vision to the dead end of nuclear deterrence. Because he did not do it, deterrence — and its use as the engine of the defense industry — remains the pillar of American military and foreign policy well into the twenty-first century.

Clinton's gifts as what one veteran reporter called a "Peacemaker-in-Chief,"[176] were on full display when he threw himself into the conflicts in Northern Ireland and the Middle East. In both places he defied the advice of more cautious figures in government, took great risks, physical[177] as well as political, and scored a triumph for peace in one place and a near breakthrough to peace in the other. Northern Ireland took its decisive turn away from violence because of Clinton, and he brought the Israelis and Palestinians closer to peace than they had ever been — a first articulation of what a final agreement could be. But in those two places the obstacles to Clinton's large-minded efforts were grounded in Foggy Bottom, not Hell's Bottom. He defied the State Department (and London) to grant an American visa to the Sinn Fein leader Gerry Adams, bringing the Irish Republican Army into the peace process, and he "shot the moon," in a derisive phrase of the second Bush's administration,[178] to bring Yasir Arafat and Ehud Barak together.

Clinton could exercise such scope only because the questions raised by the Irish conflict were of no concern to the Pentagon, and the Israeli-Palestinian conflict, no longer a proxy fight with the Soviet Union, was unimportant to the Pentagon in relation to maintaining broad control of Middle East oil, which was being secured by initiatives in the Persian Gulf and by the establishment of bases in central Asia.[179] Clinton could make his moves in Ireland and Israel without regard for the opinion of the American military. But where the brass had turf to defend, especially the turf covering the nuclear source of its power, Clinton was careful not to tread.

It may also be that during the Cold War, the risks of Armageddon were such that the nuclear game had to be played very cautiously, and mostly it was. Every president knew that the nuclear responsibility was by far his gravest. Yet after the perceived threat disappeared, there was a narrowed sense of urgency, a feeling of less need for caution, which allowed Clinton to abdicate this responsibility. The man who could not stop thinking about tomorrow kept the worst part of yesterday intact, an "unsustainable legacy."[180] The former war resister, the peacemaker in chief, presided over the first, and perhaps the last, moment when significant change in America's nuclear posture, and the world's, was possible. He blew it.[181]

13. THE BALKAN WARS

Then there were the Balkans. The wars that broke out in the early 1990s in the territory of what had been Yugoslavia were the most violent in Europe since World War II. In less than five years, two hundred thousand people were killed and two million had been displaced from their homes in regions that were ethnically "cleansed." It all began two months after the collapse of the Berlin Wall, when the Yugoslav Communist Party voted itself out of existence, the first in Eastern Europe to do so.

Serbia, with its capital in Belgrade, was the dominant of five republics,[182] and having inherited the Yugoslavian arsenal, it was the best armed. The Serb leader, Slobodan Milosevic, wanted to establish a "Greater Serbia" as the Yugoslav successor state, but unleashed local enmities, going back hundreds of years to wars of religion, left Latin Christians, Orthodox Christians, and Muslims at the mercy of ancient hatreds. More recent wounds went back to World War II, when the West-East divide put Slovenian and Croatian Catholics on Nazi Germany's side, while Orthodox Serbs were with the Allies, particularly Russia. The 1990s wars began when Slovenia, Croatia, and Bosnia sought independence, in defiance of Milosevic. James Baker, Bush's secretary of state, famously said, "We don't have a dog in that fight."[183]

In running for president, candidate Bill Clinton attacked the Bush administration for doing nothing to prevent Milosevic's Serb paramilitaries from carrying out a brutal policy of "ethnic cleansing," especially in Bosnia. In the spring of 1992, as the election campaign heated up, the Serbs began a systematic shelling of Sarajevo, a deliberate attempt to destroy the center of a multiethnic polity. By the fall, the word "genocide" had appeared in news reports.[184] Photographs of Bosnian Muslims, among others, packed into freight cars evoked images of the Holocaust. By the time Clinton took office, hundreds of thousands of Bosnian Muslims had been ethnically cleansed, forced to leave their homes. Whole towns and provinces emptied, to be filled by Serbs and, in some places, Croatians. The United Nations sent in a small peacekeeping force, manned mostly by European soldiers, but there was no peace to keep. Thousands of displaced Muslims took refuge in Srebrenica, but the Serbs put that city under siege, too, and began a steady rain of artillery shells.

The new Clinton administration proposed a response called Lift and Strike: lifting the arms embargo that punished the Muslims, since the Serbs were already well armed, and sending in air strikes against Serb artillery batteries. The Europeans opposed this strategy because, in breaking the peacekeepers' neutrality, it would turn European military forces on the ground into Serb hostages. When Warren Christopher took the American proposal to European capitals, he was humiliatingly rebuffed. Where are the American ground forces? he was asked.[185]

But Clinton was faced with diehard opposition from Colin Powell, for whom Bosnia was a classic instance of all that the Powell Doctrine warned of. If Clinton was not going to defy the chairman of the Joint Chiefs on gays in the military, he was not going to defy him on the question of going to war. Implications of his own campaign promises to the contrary, Clinton refused European demands that the United States commit ground forces to the fight. After the disaster at Mogadishu in October, there was no way Clinton, or the Pentagon, was going to send troops to Bosnia.

Parallels with the Holocaust became intense, with the United States cast as the bystander nation. From the traditionally antiwar left, voices were raised in favor of "humanitarian intervention," a phrase that was used as if it embodied a new idea. Every war is justified by its initiator as humanitarian, of course — a lesson of history that interventionists seemed to forget. Human rights activists and neoconservatives found themselves on the same side, and their criticism of the administration grew shriller. Clinton had not a clue how to respond. "What would they have me to do?" he pled. "What the fuck would they have me to do?"[186]

The arrival of "human rights" as the latest justification for war represented another triumph for the Pentagon — as if human rights could now be defended only with guns. Clinton had inherited a position of world leadership that was defined almost entirely by military power. After decades of the Pentagon's dominance of government, diplomacy — a stout but nonviolent defense of human rights — was a lost art in Washington. This is what it meant that generals, from George Marshall to Alexander Haig, had taken over the State Department, and equally what it meant that diplomats, from Dean Acheson and John Foster Dulles to Henry Kissinger and Madeleine Albright, thought far more in terms of coercion than of persuasion. So the urge to "do" something in response to the mounting horror in Bosnia was conceived exclusively in military terms. A leader whose instincts ran another way, like Clinton, was powerless.

The Pentagon, as someone said at the time, had only one tool in its bag, a hammer. Clinton knew that the Bosnian situation needed a finer tool than that, but he did not have it. Ironically, the Pentagon leadership was no more eager to go to war in Bosnia than Clinton was, but neither was the Pentagon looking for military alliances elsewhere. An armed intervention on behalf of human rights could have been defended if the use of weapons was internationally supported and legally authorized, but Clinton refused to organize that support. Instead, he blamed the Europeans, who were expressly waiting for U.S. leadership.

On July 11, 1995, Serb forces finally overran Srebrenica. A contingent of U.N.-sponsored Dutch soldiers did nothing as the Serbs carried out a mass execution of Bosnian males. Eight thousand were murdered. Rape as an instrument of war came fully into its own. The world recoiled in horror when these atrocities were reported. On August 28, Serb gunners lobbed shells into the marketplace in the center of Sarajevo, and photographs of the carnage were on front pages everywhere.

At last American warplanes went after Serb positions, a bombardment carried out with a vengeance. U.S. decision makers immediately drew the "false lesson," in the words of one political scientist, that the bombing worked.[187] The Pentagon began its propaganda campaign of "clean war," a new kind of combat with no need for ground troops, a concept based on extravagant claims for precision-guided munitions (claims based on the legacy of the Pentagon's duplicitous treatment of the Strategic Bombing Survey after World War II). The threat of an unleashed NATO air war was regarded as decisive, but the advances of Croatian and, to a lesser extent, Bosnian Muslim armies on the ground were what mainly prompted Milosevic to accept the terms of a peace agreement, the Dayton Accords, signed in December 1995.[188] For a time, the war was over.

Perhaps the most important thing about the Dayton peace negotiations was who was *not* there. Only the men of violence were invited to the table, representatives of the killers Milosevic and Croatian leader Franjo Tudjman, and of the Bosnian resistance, led by Alija Izetbegovic. But there was one figure in the Balkans who had held out hope of another way, the leader of the Kosovar nonviolent resistance, Ibrahim Rugova. An Albanian professor, he was the most widely admired man in Kosovo province. He had formed the Democratic League of Kosovo in December 1989, within weeks of the fall of the Berlin Wall. In his speeches he forthrightly called for the establishment of Kosovo as an autonomous republic, which is what it had been under Communist Yugoslavia, but Milosevic was claiming Kosovo for Serbia, more firmly than he was Bosnia or Croatia. Rugova regularly cited Gandhi and

Martin Luther King, Jr. What John Hume was doing just then in Northern Ireland, what Nelson Mandela had done in South Africa, and Lech Walesa in Poland, Ibrahim Rugova was trying to do in the most blood-soaked corner of Europe. For five years, as violence mounted all around Kosovo, no one in the Clinton administration or in Europe saw fit to support the Democratic League. As Americans had missed the significance of nonviolent resistance in Poland and Czechoslovakia during the 1980s, they missed it again in the Balkans in the 1990s.

Kosovo was the center of an Albanian Muslim population that was second to none in wanting out from under Serb domination. Milosevic regarded Serb claims to Kosovo as nonnegotiable, and in this he was appeased at Dayton. Not only was Rugova not invited to participate in drafting the agreement, Kosovo was not mentioned in it. The Albanian Muslims were ignored. So much for the power of nonviolent change.

After Dayton, Milosevic felt free to tighten his grip on Kosovo. Its people, meanwhile, had taken note of the fact that their broad commitment to nonviolent change, under Rugova, had been swatted aside by Europeans and Americans alike. Lech Walesa might have been similarly swatted aside, into oblivion, but as we saw, he had a powerful sponsor in Rome. The Nobel Peace laureate John Hume, too, might have remained a marginal player in Northern Ireland, but his campaign of nonviolent resistance to the ancient injustices of British and Protestant overlords found crucial support among prominent Irish Americans, especially Tip O'Neill and Ted Kennedy. With equivalent support, perhaps, Rugova's movement could have completed the transformation of Balkan politics, but no such support came.

Instead, beginning in 1996, Kosovar resistance, under a new group calling itself the Kosovar Liberation Army, became brutally violent. The KLA was made up of an Albanian Muslim mafia, thugs and drug dealers who had no hope of forcibly freeing Kosovo from the yoke of Serbia. Its strategy was simpler: to draw down such atrocities on its own people — preferably women and children — that a horrified outside world would once again have no choice but to move against the Serbs. KLA offensives were geared not to inflicting hurt on the enemy but to goading the enemy into savage reprisal. The strategy worked, as Milosevic ordered squads of murderous paramilitaries to run rampant through Albanian towns and villages. Rape again became a military tactic. Women and children were simply thrown by the KLA fighters, if they can be called that, into the maw of Serb violence.

But the KLA program was aided by an additional stroke of luck, for the violence in Kosovo began to impinge on the troubled conscience of the West just as the presidency of Bill Clinton tilted into its grotesque phase of self-destruction. In the same issue of the *New York Times* that reported an early Serb atrocity against Kosovar Muslims ("Serbia's Police Crush Protest by Kosovo's Ethnic Albanians"), there appeared a story under the headline "Starr Inquiry Is Shifting Back to Basics."[189]

"It's like we're standing under Niagara Falls," Clinton's press secretary, Mike McCurry, told *Time,* in reference to the Starr-induced Monica Lewinsky scandal, "looking for a boat to get us out of here."[190] The Niagara of the inexorable movement toward war was joined to the Niagara of what followed in the wake of a president's recklessness. The world — and the Pentagon — would learn that President Clinton had invited the sexual services of a young woman at the very time when he had been ordering American soldiers into harm's way in Bosnia. Worse, from the Pentagon's point of view, would be the revelation that Clinton had dispatched his sexual partner to a sinecure at the Pentagon itself, from which she would continue to service him. The Pentagon as cover.[191]

As the president's political survival became the national preoccupation, and as the violence in Kosovo escalated to unheard-of levels, Clinton's already limited capacity to exercise leadership on the now urgent question of war and peace was destroyed. Serbian police and paramilitaries, under the guise of protecting the Serb minority in Kosovo, increased the pressure on the Muslim population, determined to force an exodus. The U.N. passed resolutions demanding the withdrawal of Serb forces from Kosovo. Milosevic ignored the demands. On January 15, 1999, forty-five Albanian corpses were found in a mass grave in a village called Racak. Diplomatic responses failed. Milosevic remained defiant. On March 24, a NATO air campaign began against Serbia. It would go on for seventy-eight days, involving nearly forty thousand sorties, nearly a quarter of which would target the civilian "infrastructure," a Pentagon abstraction meaning water-treatment facilities, power plants, even schools and hospitals.

Clinton announced at the outset of this war that no American ground troops would be committed to it, a restriction that enabled the Pentagon to join the humanitarian-intervention chorus. The Powell Doctrine was here joined to the idolatry of air power. But the pilots who flew NATO's high-tech planes, most of them Americans, were ordered to fly no lower than fifteen thousand feet in order to avoid Serb antiaircraft fire. As a result, NATO did not suffer a single casualty. The Pentagon liked that, too. But thousands of civilians were killed on the ground,[192] by the bombing and by Serb paramilitaries, who took advantage of the occasion to unleash their worst. These sadists could assault Kosovar citizens with impunity because, at fifteen thousand feet, the NATO warplanes were unable to target them. Absurdly, the bombardment was justified by Washington ahead of time as a way to stop genocide, but the mass killing did not begin in earnest until after the air campaign started, and the bombers, flying so high, could not stop it.

Meanwhile, the many Serbs who hated Milosevic rallied to him. NATO's war aimed not at protecting Albanian Muslims but at coercing Milosevic by attacking the civil structures of Belgrade and other Serb cities. The Pentagon claimed after the fact that the air campaign against Serb armed forces was a huge success, but the truth was that NATO's bombers "did little damage" to the Serb military.[193] The campaign that mattered was against Serbia's cities, which resulted in economic losses in the billions of dollars. The Chinese embassy in Belgrade was inadvertently bombed, and the residences of Swiss, Swedish, Spanish, and Norwegian ambassadors were damaged. NATO claimed that its air war "worked," but the terms on which Milosevic's forces finally "surrendered" included acknowledgment of Serbian claims to Kosovo not previously offered. And NATO had to yield to the United Nations in administering the settlement, which meant Serbia could still expect to be protected by Russia and China. Milosevic was eventually indicted for war crimes committed by his forces in Bosnia, but the NATO war did nothing to enable his apprehension. That would be forced by the Serbian people themselves.[194]

A new question had arisen, however. Had the NATO air war represented an absurd reversal of an age-old martial ethic, with military lives given priority over the lives of civilians? "Force protection" had been the Pentagon's organizing rubric since Mogadishu. When America had gone to war again, it was to protect the innocents whom the Serb paramilitaries were threatening, if not actually attacking yet in great numbers, but the situation of those innocents was made immeasurably more dangerous because American fighters would not put their lives at risk. How far the Air Force had come from those 1943 missions led by Curtis LeMay, when B-17s had eschewed high-altitude evasion tactics, diving through German flak for the sake of precision bombing. "You can't justify killing," Carl Kaysen said about NATO's tactics over Kosovo, "for something you aren't willing to die for."[195]

But the air war raised a graver question. The narrative of this book has concentrated on the relations between Washington and Moscow. When I visited Secretary of Defense William Cohen at his Pentagon office in 1997, he showed me a prized possession, the hat of a Russian soldier, given to him by the soldier, in Bosnia. "Here's my hat," the man said spontaneously, handing it over. Cohen took it, as he told me, as "a peace offering."[196] In the past, such a thing would have been war booty, a trophy, but now it was a personal symbol of the remarkable transformation that had occurred between the two nations. After all, in Bosnia, Russia and America had been allies. In 1997, Cohen had brought the Russian minister of defense into the Tank, the secure Pentagon room in which the Joint Chiefs meet. Cohen had spoken to his counterpart of his own Russian roots, and the bond between them was palpable, a link, as Cohen described it to me, "of an invisible web." But the large post–Cold War promise that had braced that web, what had prompted a lowly soldier's gesture, it would seem now, had been betrayed. Webs are fragile things.

In America, the 1999 war against Milosevic was discussed without reference to Russia, but in Moscow the NATO war against a Slavic people was profoundly disturbing from start to finish. Russia vigorously opposed the war at the outset, and was instrumental in persuading Milosevic to end it. Nevertheless, NATO offered Moscow no role in postconflict Kosovo. As the war was winding down, Russian troops swooped in ahead of NATO forces to seize the airport at Priština, asserting their right to a postwar presence. General Wesley Clark, NATO's supreme commander, resented the Russian intervention and gave the order to move against it with force. But Clark's British subordinate, General Sir Mike Jackson, refused, saying, "Sir, I'm not starting World War III for you."[197]

Not only did the war against Serbia appear to confirm Moscow's worst fears about NATO's unfettered belligerence, it seemed a further betrayal. Further because of a previous betrayal: when NATO admitted Poland, Hungary, and the Czech Republic into its membership on March 12, 1999, less than two weeks before the air war began. If NATO could impose its will with its high-tech superiority without regard for objections from Moscow, what was to prevent it from attempting to intimidate Russia?

Well, something would prevent that, you bet. Russia was a nation whose military had been rapidly deteriorating for a decade, yet it remained a nuclear power. Here was the lesson the air war taught every nonnuclear nation, especially those tempted to go "rogue": unlike Milosevic, you had better have something with which to match the threat from Washington. And Moscow, of course, still did. In 2000, Russia's president, Vladimir Putin, as a direct result of the NATO air war, announced "a new concept of security." Putin reversed the Russian commitment, dating to Leonid Brezhnev, of no first use of nuclear weapons, declaring that Russia would now use nukes to defend itself, even against conventional assault.[198] The only imaginable target for such a threat was NATO, effectively headquartered in Washington.

Here was the main consequence of NATO expansion, of Pentagon recalcitrance, indeed of America's entire post–Cold War military strategy, going back to the weeks after the fall of the Berlin Wall but decisively carried on through the Clinton years: we had forced the Russians to be more dependent on their nuclear arsenal than ever, an arsenal that had never been as poorly maintained or less secure. And the Russian nuclear arsenal would be an opening to such arsenals of other nations, as both a stimulant and a resource. How we were treating Russia, in other words, was how we were treating the world — and the very future. Bill Clinton had brought to completion the "new world order" that his predecessor had announced at the beginning of the decade.

It was of this turn in the story that a now aged George Kennan warned after the NATO air war. Such "new orgies of destruction" would renew Russian fears of being "contained," and even overrun. That, in turn, the one-time protégé of the suicide James Forrestal said, would "have only suicidal significance."[199]

14. APOSTOLIC SUCCESSION

Kennan was present at the creation of the worldview against which he stood by the end of the twentieth century. Ever since his "X" article had been "misinterpreted" in the late 1940s, he had been decrying the shift away from diplomacy and toward militarism. Now that the Soviet Union, America's partner in stalemate, was gone, Washington's unchallenged power was the world's great danger. Long a dissenting figure, still Kennan pointed to the existence of what might be called an apostolic succession in the militarized American establishment, a line of men who, over five decades, despite objections from the likes of Kennan, created a sanctified Cold War orthodoxy that survived the Cold War. We saw how James Forrestal, in 1946, was braced by Kennan's first articulation of anti-Russian paranoia, and how he promulgated Kennan's view.

But before Kennan, the place of honor among Forrestal's protégés was occupied by Paul Nitze, who came down to Washington from Dillon, Read in 1941. Nitze took Kennan's place at the side of Dean Acheson when Kennan went "soft" in 1950, and Kennan's fate as one shunted to the sidelines of foreign policy and defense theory would be a permanent warning against the dangers of stepping back from toughness. Nitze's career, with its shift from the State Department to the Defense Department, embodied the movement of American power away from efforts to prevent war, which define diplomacy, toward efforts to prepare for war.[200] Nitze presided over the declarations of martial resolve — NSC-68 in 1950 and the Gaither Report in 1957 — that provided the intellectual and moral justification for the embrace of thermonuclear war as a national raison d'être. Following lines marked by Nitze, the Pentagon organized itself around thermonuclear weapons.

From then on, every time the American leadership dared entertain a second thought about its inherited nuclear militarism, Nitze was there to warn of the "present danger" that made such reconsideration treasonous. Reconsideration proved impossible. In 1969, Nitze saw to the apostolic succession that would protect this orthodoxy when he laid hands on a pair of graduate students, hired to marshal arguments in favor of the antiballistic missile, but also, on a deeper level, to carry on the true belief in the proposition that government exists to prepare for war more than to prevent it. They were, as we saw, Paul Wolfowitz and Richard Perle.[201] Within a couple of years of that, Nitze's one-time nemesis Donald Rumsfeld had joined the fold, with his young deputy Richard Cheney. During the Reagan years, each of these younger men, in varying ways, came into his own, while the elder Nitze reinvented himself as an arms controller, becoming momentarily regarded as soft himself. But the huge inflow of money to the Pentagon in those years plated the arms industry's lock on the nation's purpose as a permanent garrison.

The Pentagon became the vestibule in which military officers were recruited, in retirement, to become industry executives, who in turn were appointed to be the Pentagon's civilian overseers. Under Reagan, what Eisenhower had warned of — "the conjunction of an immense military establishment and a large arms industry" — became the thing to celebrate. And always that conjunction was on the alert for justification. Nitze and his disciples were always there to provide it.

Ironically, Nitze's last public word on the subject to which he had devoted his life suggested that his true commitment had never been to any deeply held principle but to mere contrariness. In 1999, toward the end of a Clinton administration that had needlessly kept the nuclear arsenal near Cold War levels, Nitze denounced that cache of destruction in an op-ed piece in the *New York Times.* "The fact is, I see no compelling reason why we should not unilaterally get rid of our nuclear weapons . . . ," he wrote. "I can think of no circumstances under which it would be wise for the United States to use nuclear weapons, even in retaliation for their prior use against us. What, for example, would our targets be? It is impossible to conceive of a target that could be hit without large-scale destruction of many innocent people." The man who had done more than any other to justify America's dependence on nuclear weapons now reversed the entire thrust of his career. To repeat: "I see no compelling reason why we should not unilaterally get rid of our nuclear weapons."[202] *Now* you tell us.

*　　*　　*

Nitze would not be talking like that, of course, when the apostolic succession that began with Forrestal and continued with him reached a new threshold with the election in 2000 of George W. Bush. Richard Cheney had chosen Bush's national security team beforehand, naming himself as vice president, Colin Powell as secretary of state, Condoleezza Rice as national security adviser, Donald Rumsfeld as secretary of defense, and Paul Wolfowitz as Rumsfeld's undersecretary for policy.[203]

Wolfowitz's appointment, in a way, was the most emblematic of all. What Nitze was to Forrestal, Wolfowitz was to Nitze. As a strategic thinker, a civilian dominating military figures, Wolfowitz was in a position to define the Pentagon's purpose at a time when the Pentagon defined the government's. And Wolfowitz was at the center of the circle enclosed by the conviction that, after Vietnam, American power was never to be defied again. That circle, loosely known as neoconservatives, were thinkers who drew on "an odd combination of Wilsonian idealism and Reaganite muscularity"[204] to promote an American triumphalism that would be as irresistible as any empire's had ever been. In the neoconservative vision, of course, this empire would be benevolent. And now the time had come — the distilled meaning of the Soviet collapse — to assert that benevolence full-bore, brooking no opposition.

Above all, the task that fell to Wolfowitz was to give theoretical and practical expression to a post–Cold War military mission that would underwrite the continuance of a Cold War martial ethos and the institutions that depended on it. We have confronted the historic question, Why did the United States not dismantle its massive arsenal after the justification for it disappeared? The answer centrally involves the work of Paul Wolfowitz.

In 1992, just before Clinton took office, Wolfowitz wrote a document called "Defense Planning Guidance," which amounted to the first articulation of a new post–Cold War military strategy. The Pentagon's "first objective" now was "to prevent the re-emergence of a new rival."[205] The United States would become the world's permanent and preeminent military overseer, maintaining armed forces of such overwhelming superiority as to be beyond challenge.[206] American power would be exercised alone and from above. The diplomat's dream of cooperative internationalism, to which the United States had traditionally deferred, if it never fully submitted, was dashed in the Wolfowitz vision, to be replaced by nothing less than Washington's unilateral reach, also known as "forward presence." It was a vision that assumed not only the maintenance of America's global array of bases but the expansion of it. Not only the maintenance of America's huge defense budget but the expansion of it. Not only the maintenance of the nuclear arsenal, but the expansion of it. The defense industry would continue to boom. The Pentagon would continue to be the very heartbeat of government, the capital of a Pax Americana.[207]

Wolfowitz foresaw the need for a new doctrine of "preventive war," interventions aimed at removing the capacity of other nations to develop, much less use, weapons of mass destruction.[208] Rather than allow other nations to compete with us in our capacity to wreak havoc on the world — or even to develop the ability to deter us from exercising our will — we would simply act preemptively. Instead of depending on treaties and international law to establish and protect order, the United States would impose that order on its own. Here was the ultimate abandonment of diplomacy in favor of militarism. Where once optimists had looked forward to a new world polity centered in the United Nations, now there would be, in effect, a unilateralist global dominion, if not a world government, centered in Washington. "Your friends will be protected and taken care of . . . ," Wolfowitz explained. "Your enemies will be punished and . . . those who refuse to support you will live to regret having done so."[209]

To illustrate this vision, and to define its corollary, the permanent need for a massive American military, the Wolfowitz vision of 1992 described in detail an imagined war against, yes, Iraq. And the justification for such a war was blatantly identified: the protection of U.S. access to "the region's oil."[210]

For eight years, the Clinton administration kept in place the structures of military dominance necessary to realize this vision. Committed in principle to treaties and international law, Clinton did little to protect treaties or advance law.[211] By expanding NATO, and then sponsoring NATO's first war, he affirmed the primacy of war as the main mode of international organization. And so on. Then Cheney, Rumsfeld, Wolfowitz, Armitage, and Perle,[212] together with the acolytes Powell and Rice, came to power with the election of George W. Bush. Again, emphasis must be given to the fact that, with the apparent exception of Rice, it was Cheney who did the appointing, not Bush. And it was Cheney's chief of staff, I. Lewis Libby, Jr., who completed the circle of apostolic succession, having been given his first government job by his former political science professor, Paul Wolfowitz.[213]

The administrations of Bill Clinton and George W. Bush differed in significant ways, but one would hardly know that by gazing out through the one-way glass of the Pentagon. All that Cheney and company needed to begin to realize their vision of world domination through overwhelming military superiority,[214] with special emphasis on unfettered access to oil, was an overt justification for it. On the eleventh anniversary of George H. W. Bush's "new world order" speech, like a gift from the gods, that justification fell from the heavens.

15. SEPTEMBER 11, 2001

The North American Aerospace Defense Command (NORAD) was established in 1958, as a result of warnings sounded by Curtis LeMay, the Gaither Commission, and, in his own small way, my father. Jet interceptor squadrons, armed with nuclear weapons, would protect the homeland.[215] But the airspace of the North American continent had never been penetrated by enemy aircraft or missiles until September 11, 2001. That day was NORAD's first test, and despite the billions of dollars spent on "ready alert," it failed miserably, a shocking lesson in the foolishness of both America's generation-old illusion of air defense and its ludicrous hopes for a future National Missile Defense. NORAD failed on September 11 because, never imagining that enemy aircraft could attack from within, it responded to threats as defined by the Cold War, which had ended a full decade earlier.

At 9:30 A.M., forty-four and twenty-seven minutes after airliners crashed into the World Trade Center towers, two F-16s were dispatched from Langley Air Force Base in Virginia. At that moment, another hijacked airliner was on its way to Washington, and to these fighters fell the job of protecting the nation's capital. But they were incapable of doing that. As *The 9/11 Commission Report* explained, "At that point in time, the Langley pilots did not know the threat they were facing, did not know where United 93 was located, and did not have shoot-down authorization . . . The Langley pilots were never briefed about the reason they were scrambled. As the lead pilot explained, 'I reverted to the Russian threat . . . I'm thinking cruise missile threat from the sea.'"[216] The pilots were irrelevant to the outcomes that morning. The 9/11 Commission concluded that, had passengers of United 93 not brought down the airliner in Pennsylvania, the NORAD fighters would not have been able to stop it from destroying its target in Washington, assumed to be either the White House or the Capitol.

The only modus operandi that the Pentagon knew to follow in an actual emergency, however ineptly, was the default reaction of a long-anticipated world war, a reaction that proved to be glaringly inappropriate. The American government's instinctive response to the acts of nineteen suicidal militants was to initiate the "Armageddon Plan," as if the nuclear conflagration had finally come.[217] The response, symbolized by the F-16 pilot's looking for Russians, was shaped by the Niagara current of nuclear dread, which had been flowing since 1945. George W. Bush brought his own peculiar mix of insecurity and swagger to the moment of crisis — his religious fundamentalism would mesh with the political fundamentalism of neoconservatives[218] — but he was swept along in the same current. Religious and political fundamentalism would emerge as powerful new forces in the exercise of American power. The trends were set as much by consensus realists over a generation as by the fundamentalists who took Washington by storm at the millennium, but the dangers inherent in the coming to boil of this political-religious brew cannot be understated.

Bush enacted a script fifty years in the writing, without knowing he was doing so. "The Russians are coming," Forrestal had cried not long before his suicide. In truth, the imagined enemy that drove him over the ledge of his paranoia was far more menacing than Russia, and so too with the imagined American enemy after 9/11. The reason that catastrophe so traumatized the nation was that the decades-old nuclear dread seemed to have come to pass at last. When we were children, crouching under our desks, we were told not to look, but we saw the mushroom cloud in our imaginations quite clearly. At 9/11, the cloud was not mushroom-shaped, but, as we looked at it again and again in those television replays, with the ashes of New York City rising into the air, we recognized a Manhattan project after all.

As the nation's leaders, from Truman on down, defined what threatened America beginning in the late 1940s as a faceless, omnipresent, worldwide force of evil, to be fought everywhere and nowhere — Communism — they did the very thing again. Luddites, anarchists, tribal chieftains, warlords, freedom fighters, religious militants — a wildly disparate hodgepodge of miscreants were lumped together as a highly organized global network, under the command of the mythic bin Laden. Nothing aggrandized bin Laden, or empowered him, like the Bush administration's response. As had happened in the late 1940s, when we glorified our enemy in terms of such an "ism," we infinitely magnified bin Laden's capacity to do us harm. All at once the word "terrorism" acquired a capital T. Once again, America was faced with a transcendent enemy, and, as before, the contest had nothing less than religious significance. And, even if only subliminally, it was grounded in nuclear dread. It was all enough to make a man mad.

Bush's panicked flight from that schoolroom in Sarasota, Florida, where he learned of the 9/11 attacks, in stark contrast to the simultaneous rush into front-line jeopardy of New York's Mayor Rudolph W. Giuliani, or of Secretary of Defense Rumsfeld, who went to help the Pentagon wounded, was every bit as mad as Forrestal's had been. Yet Bush's daylong flight can also be seen to have served a rational purpose. The extremity of the president's reaction underscored the fear the nation felt. More to the point, it justified the governing elite's "stepping through the door to carnage," as the historian Tom

Engelhardt put it, "that Osama bin Laden had so thoughtfully left open to them."[219]

The story of the national security state, planted as it was in radical insecurity, came full circle when President Bush fled, of all places, to the underground bunker at Offutt Air Force Base in Nebraska, the hole in the earth that had been dug by Curtis LeMay. For the crucial hours of the nation's trauma, the president of the United States buried himself in the single most haunted pit on the continent, an ultimate enactment of the old Duck and Cover drills. Bush's flight to SAC headquarters was, in fact, the perfect national symbol, for the awful trauma of the terrorist attack was an unconscious fulfillment of the nuclear nightmare that had roiled our dreams since Hiroshima. Why else did we instinctively dub the place ground zero?[220]

While Bush was hunkered down, Cheney was in action. At 10:39 A.M., according to the account of *The 9/11 Commission Report*, Cheney told Secretary of Defense Rumsfeld that reports had three hijacked airliners approaching Washington, and he had given the "authorization for them to be taken out." He told Rumsfeld, "They've already taken a couple of aircraft out."[221] He was vice president now, but having served as perhaps the most hawkish secretary of defense in history, and as the CEO of a corporation, Halliburton, that defined the "conjunction" Eisenhower had warned of, Cheney was less present at the creation than a creator of this new present. It seemed somehow right that he should have been the person in control of the nation's responses at the moment when the post–Cold War era ended. What began was the new age of American imperial belligerence, for which he had done so much to prepare.

In the minutes after the airliners hit the World Trade Center, Cheney took over. Invoking what proved to be a mythical danger, the vice president told the president that *Air Force One* was targeted by "a specific threat," and, in effect, he ordered Bush not to return to Washington.[222] Cheney was later unable to say where exactly he had learned of that specific threat or what it consisted of. Despite the constitutional implications of the question, the 9/11 Commission did not press Cheney, and wrote off his usurpation as a "misunderstood communication in the hectic White House Situation Room that morning."[223] Giving orders from that room, it was Cheney who defined America's response as war mobilization pure and simple. He then went into a bunker of his own, and so did several other important members of the government, where they would remain for many months.[224]

By the time George W. Bush returned to Washington, long hours after the crisis began, Cheney had set America's belligerent response in motion, defining the trajectory it would follow for the next five years. In doing so, he was not only unleashing the impulses of trigger-happy neoconservatives and calling on three decades of his own post-Vietnam career. He was also removing the last brakes from the flywheel set running fifty-five years before, when Stimson's proposal for another way was slapped down by Forrestal. That date, recall, was September 11, 1945.

On September 11, 1941, ground was broken for the Pentagon by people who imagined that the massive building would someday serve a civilian function, perhaps as a hospital.[225] In that way, but unawares, they nodded to Gandhi, whose movement had begun with an act of nonviolent resistance on September 11, 1906. And they also nodded to Woodrow Wilson, whose first call, issued on September 11, 1916, had been for "peace without victory," which was superseded by "unconditional surrender." Early on, we took note of the significance of the confluence of dates, but that assumes a perspective that is always unavailable to actors in the here and now. Gandhi's past was as unknown to those gathered in 1941 to break ground on the Potomac floodplain as was, say, the future that included Gandhi's successors the Berrigan brothers and Lech Walesa. In 1941, they could not foresee how the Pentagon would gird the nation for its long struggle against Marxist Communism. Nor could they see how the Pentagon's eventual victory, enabled less by its weapons than by legions of Gandhi's disciples on both sides of the Iron Curtain, was a triumph over Marxist Communism, but not over the savage injustices that Marxism always warned of.[226]

Nor could those who broke ground for the Pentagon have ever imagined their building's serving as the literal, symbolic, and permanent nerve center of a global empire known as "forward presence." They never imagined, therefore, that the five-sided marvel would one day draw an assault, like a magnet drawing iron, from deracinated misfits made suicidally insane by the savage inequalities that the Pentagon, to them, existed solely to preserve and protect. The groundbreakers never imagined what would happen at almost the same moment of the same day sixty years later — 9:37:46 A.M., September 11, 2001.

American Airlines flight 77, a Boeing 757 traveling at approximately 530 miles per hour, crashed into the limestone western wall of the Building, the side facing Arlington Cemetery. On a hill not far from the gravesite where my father and mother are buried, I would later stand looking down, across perfectly dressed rows of white tablets marking thousands of graves, on my once most-favored Building. I would behold the gaping wound as if it were inflicted on the body of my own family. The plane penetrated the first three rings of the Pentagon, but caused damage to all five of the Building's concentric sections. The plane hit between the first and second floors, in an area where offices included, as it happened, those of the Defense Intelligence Agency, my father's organization. Ramps on which I had slid in my stocking feet were obliterated. Water in tanks supplying my once prized drinking fountains was set to boiling by jet fuel fires. The white noise of the Building's efficient hum, which had made me feel safe, was broken by screams. One hundred twenty-five men and women of the Pentagon died.

Within moments of that catastrophe, the two towers in New York would disintegrate, more than an hour after they had been hit. The buildings collapsed into clouds of their own dust. The first result of the disappearance of the World Trade Center was that the Pentagon, even damaged, resumed its place as the largest office building in the world. Because of choices made then and later by the Bush administration, but prepared for by the Building's long history — this history — the first result of the cumulative events of September 11, 2001, was that the Pentagon, center of a nation launched into an unnecessary war, was more itself than ever. Yet on that day, resolving in grief to tell my version of its story, I reclaimed my love for the Building. Later came, once more, the fear.

NEW WORLD ORDER

1. NATIONAL MEMORY

Memory. Memorial. Memorial Bridge. The span ties one-time mortal enemies together. From the ridge of Arlington, above the Potomac River valley,
Robert E. Lee once looked out on the city of Washington. When war broke
out between the states, he left his becolumned home, with its lovely views, in
favor of vistas from the back of his horse. At the first battle of Bull Run, fifty
miles to the southwest, Lee's army had its defining victory, a rout. Retreating
Union soldiers, crossing the Lee plantation on their panicked way back to
Washington, fell upon Mrs. Lee's rose garden as the place to bury their dead.
The Arlington National Cemetery began in this act of revenge.

Like a shot fired from Lee's mansion, the bridge leads to Abraham Lincoln, eternally brooding from his stone cathedra. The Lincoln Memorial is
the American Parthenon, with the man himself the god of national reconciliation. If Lincoln has his back to Lee, it is for the sake of the same view, defined
by the bridge's line carried forward across the city. What falls within the range
of Lincoln's gaze is the sacred axis of American memory: from Lee to Lincoln
to Washington, at his monument, to the Capitol, on the other hill that banks
the river valley.

When I was a child, my mother rejoiced to drive us along the Mall, up
one avenue named for the Constitution and down the other, known as Independence. With her pointing out the sights to my brothers and me, we were
instructed in the shape of our nation's sense of self. We saw the Washington

Monument as a giant pencil, the Capitol dome as a kind of wedding cake. In those years, the great edifices that lined the Mall were museums — Mellon's National Gallery, which made us think of cantaloupe; the Museum of Natural History with its dinosaur bones; the crenelated Smithsonian, where Ivanhoe might have lived; the Botanic Garden, a house inside of which trees could grow, because it was glass. Don't throw stones.

The axis that begins in Arlington is anchored today by the flame that burns just below Lee's mansion, an eternal illumination of John Fitzgerald Kennedy. The mythic line extends all across Washington, well beyond the Capitol, to a stadium named for John Kennedy's like-martyred brother, Robert. The Mall is different, too. In the sixty-plus years of my maturing — the span of this narrative — Lee, Lincoln, and Washington have become less muses than sentries, guardians less of North-South reconciliation than of the nation's global tragedy. The reflecting pool still mirrors from one side the soaring obelisk, and from the other the Grecian temple, but along its edges have come to stand, most notably, shrines to the dead of three wars.

The Vietnam Veterans Memorial, at Lincoln's left, is the black granite slash in the ground, dating to the 1980s. To Lincoln's right, the Korean War Veterans Memorial, erected in the 1990s, mounts a ghostly troop of ponchoed bronze giants, crossing the field where government workers once played ball. The National World War II Memorial, dedicated at the foot of the pencil in 2004, is a crude colonnade, its every pillar marking an unfinished trauma. In the same years, an Avenue of Heroes, honoring fallen military figures, was created on the line across Memorial Bridge. An American necrology.

When we brought our small daughter to this place, she stood before the Maya Lin masterpiece, silently taking in the fifty-nine thousand names. Then she said, "The Vietnam War?" Yes, we said. To which she said, "Then where are the Vietnamese names?" Her question pointed to the several realities that lay beneath the burnished surfaces of America's new memorials. Certainly the legions of foreign soldiers who died in U.S. wars are not referred to — not only enemy dead are ignored; the allied dead are missing, too. One could conclude from the stone and metal constructions on the Mall that America fought its wars alone, which is an egregious omission, especially in the case of World War II. The omission serves a purpose, of course — legitimizing the late national tendency toward unilateralism, a nation able and proud to go it alone.[1]

A stone's throw from the World War II monument is the United States Holocaust Memorial Museum, designed to resemble a death factory, producing nothing so much as reminders that, perhaps, some wars are necessary. A little farther along the Mall is the National Museum of the American Indian, a building the color of the desert. It, too, acknowledges a genocide, but without quite naming the perpetrators. Across the way, at the foot of Capitol Hill, a second reflecting pool shimmers in the light, doubling the bronze image of a mounted Ulysses Simpson Grant, his broad hat pulled down over his face against a rain that falls even in the sunshine. It was mainly Grant's soldiers who, having learned the method of total war against Johnny Reb in the South, then brought it west to fight the Indians. From Grant and Sherman to Custer and Hickok. From cavalry to Calvary: as a child, I thought the two words were one, but it never occurred to me that the flayed skin of the victim on that cross was red to begin with.

U. S. Grant — "Old Unconditional Surrender," Franklin D. Roosevelt said at Casablanca, evoking Grant to license total war again, beginning in the crucial week of 1943, with which this book began. Unconditional surrender was a decision that Roosevelt forced on Churchill, and that together they promulgated in hopes of appeasing Stalin, who found only another reason to take offense. Stalin was a connoisseur of total war, waging it as much against his own soldiers as against an enemy — which was what truly filled the enemy with fear. The Red Army seized so much of Europe in the last months of the war, past Berlin to the Elbe, because Stalin did not care how many of his soldiers died in the storming of the West. British and American commanders, on the contrary, refused to pave the roads east with the corpses of their own armies.

Today, on an edge of the Mall between the Washington Monument and the Lincoln Memorial, sprawls a multipart shrine to FDR, with open-air rooms and carved walls immortalizing his already immortal words. One statue has him in his wheelchair. The lavish memorial defies Roosevelt's stated wish — nothing larger than my desk, he said — but so, one concludes, does almost everything that has been put on the Mall since his death. Despite his function as the wartime leader, FDR did not want the sacred axis of American memory defiled by war, any more than he would have defined it with the word "axis," which referred only to Germany, Italy, and Japan. That is clear from the decision he made when, in 1941, he forced the removal of the new War Department building from its chosen site in Arlington, a defilement of the line between Lee and Lincoln. But that reluctance to mark war's centrality reflected Roosevelt's blindness to what was coming, to what, with only good intentions, he himself was even then setting in motion.

This book began with the January week in which the idea of unconditional surrender was born, together with the Pointblank strategy of bombing cities, the start-up of a desert lab in New Mexico, and the dedication of the new War Department headquarters — the Pentagon. War was an old story, and so was total war. Witness what had happened to Mrs. Lee's rose garden, to the children of Cochise and Geronimo. By January 1943, the Holocaust was well under way, and if Roosevelt and Churchill, in Casablanca, deflected what they were told of the fate of Jews under the Nazis, still their will to defeat Hitler had remained resolute. Even so, there was nothing genocidal in what the Allies wanted to do: when the Germans and the Japanese stopped, the Allies would stop. But unconditional surrender pushed the moment of stopping to the far extreme of destruction, and just then, without anyone understanding its significance, the human capacity for destruction was being revolutionized.

The Allies did not uniformly desire total destruction. The difference between Stalin's method of waging war and that of Roosevelt and Churchill forecast a moral difference that would shape Western perceptions of the Cold War. The Red Army included the rape of women and the murder of old people and children in its rolling tactics, while the British and the Americans continued to define the savaging of noncombatants as crimes — except when it occurred from the air. Now total war could fly. Americans deflected the realities of air warfare from the start, refusing to look directly at what bombardment was doing. The Red Army's terror tactics were duplicated by the British and the Americans, but impersonally, without the heat of passion and overt sadism. Terror from the air was humanly different from terror on the ground, but not morally.

That strategic bombing, especially once nuclearized, blurred the ethical norms that remained sharp on the ground was never reckoned with in Washington. The meaning of technological and bureaucratic transformations that were also a moral transformation remained on the edge of national consciousness, much as, owing to FDR's intervention, the actual headquarters of these transformations remained on the geographic margin of the American axis. The Air and Space Museum has a privileged place on the National Mall, yet the emphasis there is on astronauts and Lindbergh, the Wright brothers and *Apollo*. When, in the mid-1990s, a curator attempted to mount an exhibit about Hiroshima that included reports of American doubts expressed at the time and of what the atomic bomb did to the Japanese on the ground, the curator was fired, the exhibit canceled. Today the museum proudly displays a B-29 named *Enola Gay*, the plane that bombed Hiroshima, but it does so (with no mention of Japanese casualties) at an annex in Virginia.[2] On the Mall itself, where war is remembered as American victimhood and valor, atomic amnesia holds.

What made our starting-point week in January 1943 momentous was not the demand for unconditional surrender, not the launching of Los Alamos, not the initiation of Operation Pointblank, not the dedication of the Pentagon as the engine room of a militarized economy, but all of those events in combination. Total war, nuclear war, air war, the Department of War. To-gether they generated the critical mass, ancient elements making something new, that has been our subject: the House of War. In the House of War, who is the victim? Who the slayer? Speak. The week with which we began marked the start of an epoch, and we are still in it. The lifetime of the Pentagon coin-cides exactly, although not exactly by coincidence, with the time when the moral obsolescence of war showed itself, even as the unyielding grip of war did, too.

2. THE NORMALIZATION OF WAR

The lifetime of the Pentagon is my lifetime. I have, to repeat, the eyes of a sol-dier's son, through which, unfortunately, I see everything. That there is a re-flecting pool in the center of the Washington Mall may not justify the appar-ently narcissistic nature of this rumination, yet how else is such a son to fully grasp the hidden and forbidden meaning of his life? When I look into the pool — across the narrative arc of this book — I see reflections of war memo-rials and bomber displays all around me, but also the courage and altruism that shaped the lives of almost every person mentioned in these pages.

My unbroken love of the precious American idea took form on the acres over which hover the ghosts of Lee, Lincoln, and Washington, beginning with those exhilarating drives up Constitution Avenue and down Independence Avenue with my mother at the wheel, and continuing with my own forays, with my brothers, to the great parades of inaugurations and patriotic holi-days. As a college student, I stood here in my ROTC uniform listening to the greatest speech I ever heard, Kennedy's inaugural address, which amounted to my conscription and which, with its plea for peace, remains my creed. That the nation's axis is strung now between John Kennedy's flame in Arlington and, beyond Capitol Hill, a gathering place named for his brother Robert, whose last plea was equally for peace, seems exactly right.

Nor was there any surprise that one sacred structure or other along this line should, with the World Trade Center and the Pentagon, have been a tar-get of the terrorists who commandeered United Airlines flight 93 on Septem-ber 11, 2001. Speculation about the ultimate route of the plane that passengers brought down in Shanksville, Pennsylvania, centers on the Capitol, but a hit anywhere along the National Mall would have measurably added to the immeasurable devastation. September 11 remains the defining event of the young American century, yet if the long history recounted in this book reveals anything, it is that the U.S. responses to 9/11, while immediately defined by the administration of President George W. Bush, were prepared for by all that had been unfolding in one presidential administration after another since 1943.

That Hell's Bottom in Virginia should have instantly formed the center of the government's reactions, instead of Foggy Bottom in Washington, was the result of five decades of Pentagon ascendance over the State Department, dating back through Richard Cheney's time as secretary of defense, through Donald Rumsfeld's first tour in the office, Robert McNamara's term, all the way back to James Forrestal. That war dominated America's post-9/11 responses echoed what the United States had been doing since the end of the Cold War, when it refused to dismantle the huge military establishment it had created to oppose the now dissolved Soviet Union. In the absence of the Soviet Union's stalemating power, and with the aim of shaping the international environment, Washington repeatedly sent its troops and bombers abroad, beginning within days of the fall of the Berlin Wall.

Not noted by most Americans, a new archipelago of U.S. military bases stretched across the Middle East into the heart of the former Soviet Union — a fulfillment of the rollback fantasy at last. Officially promulgated "National Defense Strategies," under the rubric of "forward defense of freedom," did away with the once firm tradition of defensively deployed forces, linked to allies and ready to react to conflicts instead of initiate them.[3] Such forward basing of forces was designed to control, by means of "regime change" and "prevention," emerging political trends around the globe, with the unabashed goal of guaranteeing U.S. dominance everywhere. Such a strategy assumes not only the possession of unparalleled military power but the display of it and the ready use of it. Under George W. Bush, a self-styled war president, "the normalization of war" was thus established.[4]

Not incidentally, just as had happened with the Korean War in 1950, the missile gap in 1958, the Soviet invasion of Afghanistan in 1979, and the Iraqi invasion of Kuwait in 1990, President Bush's open-ended war justified urgent and massive increases in military spending just when it seemed about to decline. As with money, so with the concentration of power. In the name of the Global War on Terror (styled as GWOT), the unchecked reach of the Pentagon was greatly extended when CIA covert operations, traditionally and deliberately nonmilitary actions, were put under the control of the secretary of defense — an expansion of commando capacity for the purpose of "preparing the battlefield" all around the world. "This whole thing goes to the Fourth Deck," a Pentagon adviser told a reporter in 2004, using slang for the secretary's office. "It's a finesse to give power to Rumsfeld — giving him the right to act swiftly, decisively, and lethally. It's a global free-fire zone."[5]

3. INSTANT REPLAY

It was often said that everything had changed in 2001, but the terrorist attacks laid bare what the United States was already becoming. That Washington swatted aside the structures of international law[6] as a way to respond to Osama bin Laden was prepared for by its habit, begun in the Reagan years, of dismissing international courts, ignoring treaties, and refusing to meet obligations to the United Nations and other transnational bodies. But with the new spirit of "with us or against us — no discussion," not even NATO was exempt from Washington's contempt. This denigration of international organizations was accompanied by a new cultivation of "coalitions of the willing," a pseudo-internationalism that guaranteed U.S. dominance and put other nations in the position of accepting or rejecting nonnegotiable premises of action.

The International Criminal Court, just coming into existence as America's war on terrorism was mobilized, was an institutionalizing of ad hoc entities that had brought to justice genocidal culprits from Rwanda and the Balkans (including Slobodan Milosevic). The ICC, fulfilling the desire to replace revenge with adjudication, had its origin in the American-sponsored Nuremberg trials after World War II. Nothing embodied the genius of postwar American statesmanship more completely than this new court, and it would have been the best place to make world-historic cases against Al Qaeda, Saddam Hussein, and anyone else who defied the norms of international order. George W. Bush, in one of his first acts as president, "unsigned" the ICC Treaty (". . . a bunch of fellas over there who want to try our guys"[7]), but Bill Clinton had never argued for it. Both presidents were protective of the U.S. military.

That the Pentagon regarded itself as a ready target of ICC prosecution seemed paranoid until revelations that American soldiers routinely abused prisoners in Iraq and that high Pentagon officials unilaterally rejected norms for the treatment of prisoners of war that had been set by the Geneva Convention. The jails of Abu Ghraib and Guantánamo were emblems of a new Pentagon lawlessness, but those revelations barely scratched the surface of a system of legally dubious incarceration that involved more than eleven thousand detainees held in mostly secret locations around the world, places referred to in classified documents as "black sites."[8] Yet even these astounding American abuses were rooted in several decades' worth of dismissals of international law. America was a torture nation.[9]

Ironically, U.S. military actions, including the invasion of Iraq, were justified with the language of human rights, as if the promotion of elections and the liberation of women defined the heart of Washington's agenda. This fulfilled a trend that began when liberals and neoconservatives found common ground in the Clinton-era ideal of "humanitarian intervention," as if every war in history hadn't been justified by its perpetrator as humanitarian.[10] The true measure of humane treatment, of course, is taken by what happens on the ground in the countries at issue. In Afghanistan and Iraq, new levels of sectarianism, ethnic conflict, warlordism, drug trafficking, and radical Islamism were all evident in the broader context of destroyed infrastructure, widespread malnourishment, obliterated civil society. Bush administration officials crowed that girls could at last attend schools as equals, without acknowledging that, with rare exceptions in heavily protected enclaves in both countries, there were no schools for anyone to attend. The much-touted elections in both countries were shams carefully managed by Washington. The two countries had been human rights nightmares before Bush's wars, but the wars themselves — destroying cities and villages in order to save them[11] — hardly represented improvements in the lives of ordinary people. Even under the best of outcomes — if, say, civil war could be avoided — Afghanistan and Iraq were going to be decades in recovering.

The U.S. war in Iraq, in particular, is both the crime and the evidence. What the Bush administration has done there is to lay bare the real character of the "disastrous rise" of Pentagon power of which Eisenhower warned in 1961. In Iraq, despite America's overwhelming military might, there will be no winning, ever. Whether the U.S. occupation is terminated abruptly or is maintained for years, violence and mayhem will define Iraq indefinitely, while the rest of the Middle East copes with Iraqi-spawned waves of chaos. Radical Muslim holy warriors, meanwhile, have been multiplied by the American war, empowered by it, trained by it, and dispatched around the globe.[12] When bombs went off in London in July 2005, subways and buses represented only another front in the unnecessary war George W. Bush began (and Prime Minister Tony Blair abetted). Bush, Cheney, Rumsfeld, and the rest have on their hands the blood of those Londoners, the blood of each young American killed, and the blood of many thousands of Iraqis — all those who have died and will die in that misbegotten war. But the misbegetting was years in gestation. Bush's singular responsibility must be emphasized, but his action must not be isolated from all that led to it and enabled it. Bush's crime, to repeat, is also evidence.[13]

Bush's "humanitarian" doctrine of preventive war, as we saw, was promulgated in the National Security Strategy of 2002. "This country must go on the offense," Bush said, "and stay on the offense." Many commentators regarded this move as a break with a tradition that had emphasized defense, even to the name of the U.S. war ministry. In public discussion, war had always been treated as the last resort, but now it would be a first response to threat. Like Truman before him, Bush had his doctrine, but his was the doctrine of preventive war. Yet arguments for preventive war had defined the culture of the Pentagon since right after World War II, with Leslie Groves being the first to make them. Over the years, not even the Soviet nuclear arsenal inhibited many senior American military officials from making the case for first attack — even in the teeth of the Cuban Missile Crisis. Always, presidents had pushed such arguments to the back burner, but they were never off the stove. Under George W. Bush, a long-simmering impulse had come to a boil.

And so in other ways. The compelling but rarely admitted purpose of shoring up American control of supplies of oil and natural gas was reflected in the job histories of Bush's policy team (for example, Vice President Cheney's Halliburton years), but the explicit claim of economic hegemony over the Persian Gulf region, with the threat of military force to back it up, had begun with the Carter Doctrine. As America's Middle East wars of the first decade of the twenty-first century unfolded, the stated focus was on Arabs, Muslims, and the threat of terrorism, yet the overriding strategic issue remained the oil supply.[14] And that meant Washington's nervous gaze had to shift from the Persian Gulf to China, the world's most rapidly expanding economy and America's new rival. The inextricable link between the distant Asian nation and the Middle East is revealed in the fact that China's largest source of foreign oil is Iran, and China's dependence on Persian Gulf oil is expanding as fast as its economy, making it a direct oil competitor of the United States. In 2004, China and the United States together used one third of all the oil produced on earth, and their needs were growing exponentially.[15]

China, meanwhile, was one nation with the capacity to demolish the neoconservative dream of a unipolar world under American dominance, and as such it became the object of sharp, sudden suspicion. In the Pentagon's Quadrennial Defense Review of 2005, a Chinese military buildup drew special notice, although China's military establishment remained minuscule in comparison to America's.[16] In the spring of 2005, Donald Rumsfeld, in a distant echo of James Forrestal, warned Congress of a dangerous expansion of Chinese naval power, though experts agreed that China's navy remained concentrated in its own coastal waters, not remotely challenging U.S. dominance of the open seas. Such Bush administration alarms, twinned with policies to match, consistently pushed this new Asian rival away from economic and political competition and toward military competition, including an arms race.

It was a self-fulfilling replay of 1947. The lesson of a half century — belligerent posturing designed to intimidate adversaries only prompts belligerent posturing in return; posturing fuels escalation — remained unlearned.[17]

No sooner had the United States deployed an early stage of missile defense in 2003, for example, than China demonstrated its missile prowess by sending a man into space. The Pentagon established a "high frontier" program, aiming to put high-tech weapons in space, and China began developing antisatellite technology. The Bush administration promised, in 2004, to support Taiwan's independence from China, even to the point of war, and simultaneously pressed for the hurried rearmament of Japan as an Asian balance to Chinese military power. China responded by stepping up pressure on Taiwan and sending threatening test missiles toward Japan. The worst-case paranoia that we saw early in this book was animating Washington once again, risking another cold war, but with a new wrinkle. In addition to a hostile, nuclear-armed China, these policies could lead to the reemergence of Japan as a military power, now gone nuclear.[18]

4. NATIONAL SECURITY?

Preventing the spread of nuclear weapons — "counterproliferation" replacing "nonproliferation" — was the primary reason given for the Bush invasion of Iraq. His administration's labeling of Iran and North Korea as linked to the same "axis of evil" was also justified by concerns, especially, about nuclear proliferation. It is clear that the Bush administration will not allow Iran to deploy a nuclear arsenal, and not even the disastrous war in Iraq will deter the Pentagon from striking Iranian nuclear facilities before they are fully weaponized.[19]

Yet the concerns about weapons of mass destruction that justified the attack on Iraq, and may yet do so on Iran, are absurdly misplaced. When it comes to nuclear danger, Washington is by far the graver problem, beginning with its post–Cold War refusal to significantly downsize its own nuclear arsenal; continuing through its early-1990s failure to fully secure "loose nukes" in Russia;[20] to the Pentagon's 1994 Nuclear Posture Review, which kept a sizable nuclear arsenal as a "hedge"; to the Senate's 1996 refusal to ratify the Comprehensive Test Ban Treaty; to the Bush administration's 2003 repudiation of the Antiballistic Missile Treaty and the 2004 deployment of missile defense, which motivated Russia and China to add "hair" to the hair trigger; to the Bush administration's stated — and unprecedented — readiness to use nuclear weapons against nonnuclear states. In 2005, Jimmy Carter blasted

American-led NATO for maintaining the "same stockpiles and policies as when the Iron Curtain divided the continent."[21]

Under Donald Rumsfeld, the Pentagon embarked in 2002 on the stunning project of developing a new generation of nuclear weapons, including a burrowing device designed to go after underground targets and "mini-nukes" to be used in concert with a conventional attack.[22] Congress was skeptical, and the international arms control community was appalled, but as of 2005, Rumsfeld was still pushing for such weapons. However marginal it may seem, a new nuclear system, usable at last, amounts to an ultimate repudiation of nuclear downsizing (and a reason to restore nuclear testing facilities). Indeed, there is reason to believe that that is the system's real usefulness to military planners. In seeking "conventionalized" nukes, Rumsfeld, of course, was in the powerful tradition of Forrestal, Schlesinger, Nitze, and all the other Pentagon officials who had sought to make the absolute weapon a relative one. The Bush administration's attack dog, in charge of reviling the U.S. tradition of arms control as "decades of stillborn plans, wishful thinking, and irresponsible passivity,"[23] was the right-wing ideologue John Bolton, whom Bush appointed (without Senate approval) ambassador to the United Nations in mid-2005. Bolton was the living icon of the two most dismaying facts of global politics today: nuclear arms control is dead; America killed it.

The effect of all this, whether new weapons are actually deployed or not, is to legitimize nuclear-based power politics, giving other nations, friend and foe alike, compelling reasons to acquire a nuclear capacity, if only for deterrence, and prompting them to behave in similar ways. That pattern was fully evident in Iran and North Korea, beginning almost immediately after the launching of the Global War on Terror, and the pattern promises to show itself in "nuclear-capable states" like Brazil, Argentina, Egypt, Australia, South Africa, and others that long ago renounced nuclear ambitions. Meanwhile, Russia, China, Israel, India, and Pakistan are all furiously adding to their nuclear arsenals.[24] The Pentagon has become the engine of proliferation.

Through these ominous developments, to be sure, the Pentagon proved less than monolithic in its attitudes. Inside the Building there were dissenting notes struck on most of the great decisions arising in the era of the Global War on Terror. As was true in McNamara's time (and my father's), Pentagon intelligence agencies offered competing assessments on crucial questions, but once again the lack of coherence only supported the civilian overseers' tendency to credit data and information that confirmed their preexisting purposes. Thus the United States went to war in 2003 to thwart Iraqi weapons of mass destruction that did not exist. On that very question, for example, the Defense Intelligence Agency provided more than one hundred erroneous reports from an Iraqi defector improbably code-named Curveball. Colin Powell's decisive prewar address to the United Nations offering justifications for the attack on Saddam Hussein depended on Curveball, even though other agencies had already discredited him.[25]

But not all Pentagon assessments were wrong. Regarding Afghanistan and Iraq a year after the war began, for example, it was a 2004 Pentagon report that most directly asserted that the U.S. interventions "have not only failed . . . they may have achieved the opposite of what they intended."[26] Senior officers complained, meanwhile, that too few forces were being deployed,[27] and that the pressures on the National Guard and the Reserves were destroying America's citizen-soldier tradition. This caused a stir in the Pentagon about an exorable move to a mercenary army. Inadequate training and equipment, on the other hand, became such a point of contention that one young Marine presumed to challenge Secretary of Defense Rumsfeld during his visit to troops in Iraq in December 2004.

On larger questions, dissension could be just as loud. For example, a 2003 Pentagon report argued that the most serious threat to U.S. security was not Islamist terrorism but environmental degradation.[28] Complaints and reports like these were mostly ignored. Under Rumsfeld, the top brass by and large stifled what disagreements they had with policies set by the Pentagon civilians — even policies, like the decision to disregard Geneva Convention norms for the treatment of prisoners, that would put their troops at risk. If military commanders did not like what they were ordered to do in Iraq, still they did it. Thus the American system was a success, while pursuing what increasingly had to be counted as a grievous failure.

After the long journey of this book, we come to what amounts to an ultimate betrayal by the national security establishment of its most solemn obligation, which is to provide for national security. The probing of questions about government failures before September 11, 2001, is meaningless when measured against the new jeopardy into which America was plunged by the war that Bush embarked upon, or when measured against already evident failures to protect the nation from the attacks to which that jeopardy inexorably leads. In late 2003, Donald Rumsfeld said, in an internal Pentagon memo, "We lack the metrics to know if we are winning or losing the Global War on Terror."[29] This odd assessment from a secretary of defense (one struggles to imagine Robert McNamara making such a statement) actually reflects the Pentagon's interest in an open-ended war. Permanent war means permanent martial dominance. Never mind the jeopardy.

If Rumsfeld was not sure how to measure success, it wasn't true of the other man in the administration whose job it was to keep Americans safe. A little more than a year after Rumsfeld's remark, the metrics must have been discovered, because Attorney General John Ashcroft, in resigning, said, "The objective of securing the safety of Americans from crime and terror has been achieved." But few Americans believed that. The "color alert" systems of "homeland security," together with the shoes-off inspections that left air travelers uneasy and cowed, had nothing to do with what actually threatened. Neither did the dismal record of Ashcroft's department.[30]

While the mightiest nation in history shaped much of its twenty-first-century strategy out of twentieth-century elements, the immediate threat to which that strategy responded came from a vastly overrated lone-wolf misfit who had relatively little power to hurt America further until America's global war against Arabs and Muslims gave it to him. Osama bin Laden, in that sense, was the pathetic, if malign, Wizard of Oz, hiding behind the perceptions of those who fear him.[31] Their fear is what made him powerful. But soon enough, that power was real.

The Bush administration was surely right to recognize individuals unattached to any state — terrorists — as posing a catastrophic danger to Americans, able to come at us from any one of a dozen insurgencies in an impoverished, mainly Muslim world that feels under attack from the United States. While Washington's belligerence exacerbates tensions with hostile or potentially hostile groups and states, which might engage in or support such deadly mischief, its policies also aid and abet individuals or groups who would inflict deadly harm on the nation. Washington's policies do this over the near and the long term by making nuclear materials far easier to obtain and use than they ever needed to be.

The story of the Islamist Pakistani scientist A. Q. Khan is the great cautionary tale, like a nightmare return of his near namesake Herman Kahn. Abdul Qadeer Khan went from being hailed as the father of Pakistan's nuclear bomb to being revealed, in 2003, as a trader in nuclear secrets, with such clients as North Korea, Iran, Libya, and perhaps Saudi Arabia. Yet despite Khan's record as a single-handed nuclear proliferator at work for America's sworn enemies, the Bush administration could do little because it had held itself hostage to Pervez Musharraf, the military dictator of Pakistan and Bush's putative ally. Musharraf was disinclined to discipline Khan because, as the creator of the Islamist bomb, the scientist was a Pakistani national hero. It was also unclear whether Musharraf was somehow connected to Khan's activities. Khan essentially went unpunished, and perhaps unstopped.

How many Khans are out there, and how do Bush's policies enable them to operate? This question acquired special urgency in 2005 when it became clear that the Bush administration, still at the mercy of Musharraf, was tacitly allowing the dramatic expansion of Pakistan's nuclear arsenal[32] — as if the most dangerous post-9/11 moment of all had not been the 2002 nuclear standoff between Pakistan and India.

It remains true, as 9/11 demonstrated, that conventional attacks against vulnerable targets in an open society like the United States can be carried out to devastating effect, but the nuclear nightmare that roiled the dreams of a generation, not that long ago, is back. That it was not necessarily so makes this development a crime and an outrage. The still lively prospect of a nuclear attack on an American city, carried out by an ad hoc nihilist group or by a deranged individual, unexpectedly — and tragically — rides along the Niagara current we have tracked back to its headwaters in Hell's Bottom, Virginia.[33]

5. REVENGE

Arlington Cemetery began, as we saw, in an act of revenge. The blind impulse to respond to hurt by striking back is part of the human makeup, yet the impulse is a deep source of shame, too, opening as it does into the dark realm of the irrational, where we know we do not belong. People clothe the act of vengeance in all sorts of justifications. When we go to war, or when we behave savagely in combat, we hardly ever explain the act by saying we simply must settle the score. We saw this especially in Harry Truman's linking the Hiroshima attack to "Jap" savageries while insisting its target was military.[34]

After 9/11, the United States was in the grip of vengeance. There were plausible reasons for targeted attacks against Al Qaeda training sites in Afghanistan, but they were superseded by the need for a bigger response to the trauma of the televised World Trade Center catastrophe. Instead of going after bin Laden's cabal with an internationally coordinated law enforcement effort, nothing would do but a large-scale act of war. Something we could see on television. Our purpose was not so much the effect on the terrorist networks over there as it was the effect, mediated by the television networks back here, on our wounded psyches — a counterbalancing of trauma. "World War III" was the title of a column Thomas Friedman published in the *New York Times* within days of 9/11, and there was barely suppressed glee when America had crossed that violent threshold. (Soon commentators would be talking up World War IV.)[35]

American bombers began raining destruction on the villages and towns of the most primitive country on the globe. Meanwhile, the elusive Al Qaeda slipped away. The repressive regime of Afghanistan, the Taliban, was quickly driven from power, but the demonized bin Laden himself disappeared. George W. Bush, with a sledgehammer the only tool in his bag, had brought it down on the table, aiming at the mosquito. The mosquito got away, but the table was destroyed. Destruction was the point.

But it wasn't enough. Each of the reasons offered for the subsequent war against Iraq turned out, in succession, to be false. No weapons of mass destruction. No link between Saddam Hussein and 9/11. No authentic U.S. concern for democracy.[36] Shoring up oil reserves was an authentic, if unstated, reason for the war, but not even that was the primary issue. The unconscious and unaddressed American need for revenge had not been satisfied in Afghanistan. That alone explains not only the rush to war in Iraq[37] but the ongoing American refusal to seriously reconsider its action, even as the justifications for the war were exposed, one after the other, as lies. Even as the brutality of American methods was made plain, from torture at Abu Ghraib to the obliteration of the city of Falluja. And even as Iraq itself, the next table, was reduced to rubble, a proud society destroyed.

Washington designated a succession of "turning points" that would mark the beginning of victory in Iraq — the fall of Baghdad, the capture of Saddam Hussein, the establishment of Iraqi sovereignty, elections, the start of the ruling coalition, the trial of Saddam, the commissioning of Iraqi security forces, more elections, the constitution — and none of it worked. In addition to the destruction of any civil context within which the idea of human rights might have had resonance, tens of thousands of innocent Iraqis were killed. Some estimates put that figure at well over one hundred thousand, along with, by late 2005, well over two thousand U.S. and "coalition" soldiers. On the home front, meanwhile, more than three years after 9/11, a Gallup poll found that fully a quarter of Americans approved of the use of nuclear weapons against "terrorist facilities."[38]

All for an act of revenge? By the time the extent of Iraqi destruction became apparent, with the hype of "shock and awe" replaced by the media's steadily averted gaze, Americans could not look directly at what we had done. Something had indeed been satisfied in us, even if all we could see was disaster. The war was clearly misbegotten, yet it was not to be seriously reconsidered. That was made plain during the 2004 presidential election campaign, when the Democratic candidate, Senator John Kerry, for all his objections to the Bush administration's policies, found nothing to criticize in Bush's conduct of the war — or, for that matter, in Bush's warmongering response to 9/11. Kerry, "reporting for duty," as he put it to the convention that nominated him, showed with his staged salute that he, together with the Democratic Party, was as carried along by the irrational current toward savage violence as his Republican rival. If Kerry had been elected, the war would probably have rolled on through its "turning points" just the same. Democrats could not hold up a mirror to the nation on this question because they had no more interest in a look at the truth than anyone else. The election showed the country to be divided, but, bothered as many were by the war, it turned out not to be a decisive point of difference between red states and blue.

Despite all the talk about September 11, 2001, as the moment of transcendent change, the events of that day were not themselves transforming. Rather, they revealed the currents of an American transformation that had been set moving years before. Set moving, in fact, by the vengeful, unnecessarily savage bombing of cities late in World War II and continuing through the U.S. air wars in Southeast Asia. Aerial attacks on cities, carried out after studies had shown such attacks to be strategically futile, amounted to terror campaigns with which the nation has never reckoned. And imagined revenge was the underpinning of mutual assured destruction, the American determination to incinerate Communist cities for no more reason than, assuming the horror had come to pass, that the Communists had done it to us. Revenge, like a silently invading army, had occupied the American soul. After the United States lost the war in Vietnam, Washington imposed a punishing twenty-year embargo on that impoverished country only because of the hurt Americans felt at having lost.

We do not ordinarily see ourselves as a vengeful people. But it is what we have become. That transformation, still not reckoned with, is what showed itself after 9/11. It has been the subject of this entire book.

6. I HAVE A DREAM

And yet. The National Mall, with which this chapter began, was never more itself than on August 28, 1963, when Martin Luther King, Jr., before hundreds of thousands of people, articulated a world-changing dream of another way. It was not only a dream of racial harmony but a vision of a changed relationship to the use of violence. "Again and again," he said, "we must rise to the majestic heights of meeting physical force with soul force." Because King's vision assumed a divine bias in favor of the suffering and the oppressed, it was inevitable that it would extend from issues of civil rights to the most basic assumptions of the unspoken but powerful American consensus, which he would designate as "the giant triplets of racism, extreme materialism, and militarism."

At the time of King's speech, the dream seemed possible not only between races but between nations. John Kennedy had sent to the Senate the Partial Test Ban Treaty, agreed to by the two superpowers only three weeks before; the Senate ratified it three weeks later. The treaty marked the first triumph of negotiation, the first step away from the arms race, a step taken, Kennedy himself indicated, in response to the anguished concern of countless people, including the likes of Linus Pauling, Albert Schweitzer, and Norman Cousins. The treaty was the fulfillment of a promise the president had made two months before at American University, in a speech that Cousins had helped to write.

Stretched along the Mall before King that day, in the shadow of Abraham Lincoln, along the axis that went to Robert E. Lee, a throng of formerly isolated individuals could look around and see that in their hopes for a better world, they were not alone. On that sacred terrain and around the globe, such events happened again and again in subsequent years. In 1965, the first large peace demonstration in the nation's history convened on the Mall, an act not of protest but of petition. Tens of thousands of demonstrators marched from the Lincoln Memorial to the Capitol, to plead with Congress to take action against Lyndon Johnson's already evident mistake in Vietnam. But what they did was more than plead. They *named.*

The first act of nonviolent resistance is to name the thing being opposed. As Martin Luther King named racial discrimination as the unacceptable legacy of slavery, peace demonstrators called the war in Vietnam by its proper name: an American tragedy, an American crime. The reason the war must stop, they said, is because it's wrong. It must stop because it is not succeeding. It must stop because it is not necessary. Arguments from morality and from realism were the same thing.

Those who followed the first antiwar demonstrators on the Mall succeeded in being heard. When they massed outside the Pentagon, they called the Building by its proper name, too: the War Department, the House of War. The naming of the war led to its end. This book honors those people of peace and seeks to emulate them. The House of War, exceeding agency and intention, has mutated into the great white whale of anarchy and destruction.

The countercurrent of peace flowed through the channels of the nation's axis, and if the Pentagon was the source of an energy that swept all before it, so too, as it turned out, was the dream of peace. Escalations in Vietnam, the arms race, the death squads in Central America, the belligerence of Ronald Reagan, the Cold War itself — all fell before the expressed determination of masses of common people to find another way. In central and Eastern Europe and in the Soviet Union, as we saw, equivalent forces were at work, melting the iron in the Iron Curtain in the heat of the simple truth.

The negotiations regime, created by pressures from below and inaugurated by Kennedy and Khrushchev, proved, across a generation, to be an authentic alternative to deadly conflict. It eventually created space for Walesa, Havel, Sakharov, Charter 77, Solidarity, the millions rallied by the Polish pope, and finally for the historic decisions against violence made by Gorbachev. These were voices of truth, naming the powers as the first step toward taming them.[39] Although the dark history recounted here requires a grim reckoning with the human propensity for violence, victories of the opposite impulse must be marked and held high.

This is so because the flow of what we have been calling, with Henry Adams and Jonathan Schell, the Niagara current toward war has, in these later years, been picking up speed. The study of history shows that because the channel through which that current runs is carved, in substantial part at least, by human choices, new choices can rechannel the current in another direction. It has happened in the past. It can happen in the future. Like slavery before it, war as a legitimate activity can be left behind, and with it the prospect of nuclear war. Indeed, this is an old hope for the new age. "The hope of civilization lies in international arrangements, looking, if possible, to the renunciation of the use and development of the atomic bomb." These words were spoken to Congress by Harry Truman in October 1945.[40] For the sake of an illusory national security, Truman abandoned the hope, but as events showed, it lived on without him.

And now, real changes in the political, economic, and cultural condition of human beings can open as readily to positive outcomes as tragic ones. Despite pressures toward proliferation and new Pentagon programs, a popular consensus against nuclear weapons is stronger than ever around the globe.[41] Indeed, the entire phenomenon of globalization, with its capacity for enhanced communication, can generate new currents of cooperation. International organizations, dedicated to shoring up peace, can be revitalized. Law can be as powerful among nations as within them. Poverty can be identified as the world's most pressing security issue.

These are matters not of idealized dreams but of real politics aimed at reversing the Niagara current. Thus where the U.S. economy was yoked to weapons manufacture, now it must be adapted to global development. Where a triumphal religion of anti-Communism (and then antiterrorism) braced the American soul, now evil must be recognized as that which makes us think we are innocent of it. Where the nuclear arsenal sent out its radioactive poison, now the project of nuclear abolition must become a national priority. Where interservice rivalry spawned fearmongering and power grabbing, the military establishment must be checked and balanced by democratic procedure. Some old rules and once conventional thoughts must be restored: no weapons in space; no wars of prevention; no going it alone; no torture ever, under any circumstances; treaties are sacrosanct; the spread of international legal forums is in America's interest; the sources of violence deserve as much attention as the threat of it; diplomacy, not war, is America's primary way of being in the world.

In this book we have paid attention to the current below the surface of events, but in one generation after another we have noted the fateful role of individuals, from Truman's mythic decision to Kennedy's option against his advisers in the Cuban Missile Crisis, to Nixon's choice of bombardment instead of negotiation in Vietnam, to Clinton's decision to preserve the nuclear arsenal as a hedge, and on and on. Human choices, as much as impersonal momentum, have shaped the age.

Now choices are before us again. All that has happened until today powerfully influences what we will do next, but history is as much the record of the unexpected initiative as of the dreaded outcome. Human freedom, as much as any Niagara, remains the compelling force. Indeed, it is the more powerful one, precisely because freedom is instructed by history, which is history's point. We have come all this way, through the darkest rooms of the House of War, to stand before a threshold, one opening into a house of another kind, a better house.

This book began at such a threshold, taking note of the solemn resonances of one date, September 11. We remembered September 11, 1945, when the war-weary Henry Stimson put before his nation the invitation to cross into a new and better world by halting a "desperate" arms race. Stimson's invitation implied a choice, of course, between the two ways of heading off a lethal proliferation of nuclear weapons — either by diplomacy or by war. In the decades since, every time an American president — save George W. Bush — was presented with that choice, he decided, sometimes despite advice, against war. That tradition alone is reason for hope. The choice is still before the nation, which can remember that Stimson's generation was then animated by the determination to find alternatives to war, because war now threatened the very future. "War no more. War never again!" were words spoken at the United Nations by a pope, but they had become the cry of realists.

Stimson proposed to make an untrustworthy man trustworthy by trusting him. He did that not out of naïve hope but out of the clear knowledge that the new situation required a bold break with suspicion and fear. In the end, under the slogan "Trust but verify," Ronald Reagan thought he was trusting an untrustworthy man, only to discover, contrary to what every American expert had told him and his predecessors, that his Soviet adversary was trustworthy to begin with. The desperate arms race was at last reversed. That reversal, accomplished by Reagan and Gorbachev, was the beginning of a process that has not been completed.

In emphasizing such affirmative possibilities, we heard the "music of chance" in noting that on September 11, 1906, what Gandhi called the "new principle" of *satyagraha* was born, the first outpouring of the great counter-current that eventually swept up Martin Luther King, Jr., and all who followed him on both sides of the iron divide.[42] Just as Dr. King was beginning his work in Montgomery, Alabama, Bertrand Russell and Albert Einstein issued their milestone 1955 manifesto, which, if anything, reads more prophetically than ever: "We have to learn to think in a new way. We have to learn to ask ourselves, not what steps can be taken to give military victory to whatever group we prefer, for there no longer are such steps; the question we have to ask ourselves is: what steps can be taken to prevent a military contest of which the issue must be disastrous to all parties." Once universal physical annihilation began to threaten from the future, that is, the immediate threat of moral annihilation transformed the present. Legions of people around the globe responded, picking up the Russell-Einstein cry, "Remember your humanity, and forget the rest."[43]

King's great Washington speech was followed, only weeks later, by President Kennedy's shocking, premature death. All too soon, King himself was taken, and weeks after that, so was Robert Kennedy. When has the tide of violence ever seemed more ascendant? Yet by whom has that tide ever been more effectively turned back than by those three, as they live in memory? The stamping of their idealism with the seal of mortality — the same thing had happened to Gandhi, too — made the hope they represented all the more precious. That was partly a matter of the content of that hope — world peace at last — but it was also a matter of the all-trumping power of the fate each person shares with every other. "For in the final analysis," as President Kennedy said at American University, "our most basic common link is that we all inhabit this small planet. We all breathe the same air. We all cherish our children's future. And we are all mortal."

Up the hill from the Pentagon, such thoughts come naturally. "In a dark time," the poet Theodore Roethke says, "the eye begins to see." In a dark place, too. There is a deep irony in the Building's place beside the mythic cemetery where so many are buried, especially those who fell in the Pentagon's wars. The Building faces away from Arlington, but on 9/11, American Airlines flight 77 turned that around. Tragically, E ring was slit open to the hillsides of the dead, adding its own. That the headquarters of the Department of Defense was targeted by terrorists had a different meaning from the targeting of the World Trade Center, even if traumatized Americans were unable to articulate it. The Pentagon defines America's reach across the world, and for countless millions that reach is choking. That the terrorists of flight 77 were savage nihilists, and that the people killed in their act of murder were innocent, take nothing away from the resonance of the assault. Whether Americans can acknowledge it or not, there was a naming of the monster on 9/11: the War Department is at war. What did we think, all these years, was being done there in our behalf?

The Building's wound was soon covered over by a giant flag, and then it healed, a rebuilding that took almost as long as the initial construction. After 2001, the Building looked different. For a brief time, the Pentagon seemed frail and vulnerable. No more. The Building's hurt is being avenged, its furies are set loose. The Pax Americana[44] that followed World War II, sustained by the threat of nuclear weapons and maintained by a series of interventions, police actions, counterinsurgencies, and air strikes, has become something else. The Pentagon is now the dead center of an open-ended martial enterprise that no longer pretends to be defense. The world itself must be reshaped. Nothing less than evil must be vanquished. Its good intentions heavily armed, its scope extending from "prevention" to something called "operations other than war," the Pentagon has, more than ever, become a place to fear.

By now, the stark juxtaposition of the Building and the cemetery can only seem a missed opportunity of major proportions. One wonders how the decisions made in the past sixty years in the office of the secretary of defense and in the Tank would have been altered if, before issuing their orders, the leaders of the nation's military establishment had been required to adjourn for the few moments it would have taken to mount the ridge of Arlington, to look across the hillsides salted with headstones, each one a white signal of unnumbered others. Unconditional surrender, Operation Pointblank, Los Alamos, the Truman decision, the Truman Doctrine, the atomic bomb, NSC-68, Korea, the hydrogen bomb, the Gaither Report, the missile gap, Berlin, Cuba, mutual assured destruction, Vietnam, the antiballistic missile, the Dominican Republic, the *Mayagüez,* the Iran hostage rescue attempt, the Carter Doctrine, Lebanon, El Salvador, Grenada, Star Wars, Reykjavík, Panama, the first Gulf War, gays in the military, Somalia, the Nuclear Posture Review, the Balkan Wars, NATO expansion, Afghanistan, the Global War on Terror, preventive war, Iraq, Abu Ghraib, Guantánamo, the high frontier, nuclear resumption, force projection, mission accomplished. What if each headstone symbolized all the people, American and otherwise, buried in the break between the Pentagon's choices and their unimagined consequences? Had the secretaries, assistant secretaries, generals, and admirals been required to look into the abyss of war, what might they have seen? That this story could have gone another way; it can go another way yet. "We all cherish our children's future. And we are all mortal."

I am never far from the stone that marks the place where my mother and father are buried, a few dozen yards down the slope from the Tomb of the Unknowns. My father's rank and record of service are indicated in the granite, and so is the date he died, exactly when the Gulf War began in 1991. My father, too, was an unknown soldier — at least to me. But less and less so. Now when I look around at the adjacent gravestones of the military men of his generation — men who, for all else, found a way *not* to have the dreaded war with Moscow; men who created treaties and honored them; men who nurtured a web of international ties; men who found ways to temper and turn back the fiercest among them; men who allowed for the expression of liberal doubt; men who cooperated, in sum, with partners on the other side of the Iron Curtain to keep the Cold War cold — I see what there is to honor as well as to regret. My father and his cohort were neither religious nor political fundamentalists. Their successors may be both.[45] Beware the House of War when understood as the House of God.

I have written this book about the great Building into which my father took me as a child, before I could see anything but greatness. I have written this book as a way of honoring my parents, and loving them. Once my father warned me of the danger of a coming war, and he commissioned me to do something about it. So I have written this book. Like every other person who lives long enough to bury his father, I learned from him the ultimate lesson of my own mortality. How briefly on the earth we are. Too briefly, I insist, not to find another way to live than by killing. More than for my parents, I have written this book, in love, for my children. And for everyone's. Let us cherish their future.

ACKNOWLEDGMENTS

NOTES

BIBLIOGRAPHY

INDEX

ACKNOWLEDGMENTS

I wrote this book while a scholar-in-residence at the American Academy of Arts and Sciences in Cambridge, Massachusetts. My debt to the academy is large, beginning with its president, Patricia Spacks, and its director, Leslie Berlowitz. The officers and staff of the academy supported me in many ways, and I am grateful. Particular thanks go to Giffen Maupin, who helped me track down the photographs that appear here, to Helen Anne Curry, who supplied special expertise, and to Alexandra Oleson, whose help was constant. The academy's Committee on International Security Studies, chaired by John Steinbruner and Carl Kaysen, was a steady resource, as were members of the academy's Tuesday lunch group and its Friday Forum. Carl Kaysen generously read much of the manuscript and offered crucial advice. Over several years, Martin Malin was my consultant and friend, and his careful review of the entire manuscript proved invaluable. James Miller, the editor of *Daedalus,* read parts of the work and gave me important suggestions. I gratefully acknowledge all of the academy's visiting scholars, especially David Hollinger, whose early advice was important to me, as well as Lisa Szefel, Asif Siddiqi, and Sharon Weiner, each of whom offered criticism on large parts of the manuscript. Mistakes and errors of judgment, of course, remain mine.

During early work on the book, I was an associate of the Robert and Renée Belfer Center for Science and International Affairs at Harvard's Kennedy School of Government. I gratefully acknowledge the Belfer Center and its director, Graham Allison, and the Kennedy School dean Joseph McCarthy, who gave me early support. I drew on the research of Carl Conetta and Charles Knight at the Project on Defense Alternatives in Cambridge, and offer my thanks to them.

Parts of the book, in different forms, were previously printed in several publications. Images of the child at play in the Pentagon appeared in certain early poems I wrote while studying with the late George Starbuck, whom I remember fondly. In weekly columns for the *Boston Globe* I first tackled many of the questions addressed here, and I gratefully acknowledge my editors at the paper: Renee Loth, Robert Turner, Marjorie Pritchard, Nick King, Steve Morgan, Robert Hardman, Peter Accardi, and Glenda Buell. In two articles for *The New Yorker,* I wrote about the Vietnam War and about the Pentagon. I incorporate here much of what I learned in researching and reporting those articles; my thanks to Jeffrey Frank. Other editors to whom my debt is large are Wendy Strothman, who affirmed this project at the start, and Tom Engelhardt, whose steady voice informs mine.

Charles Davis, a longtime analyst for the Defense Intelligence Agency, read the manuscript and gave me detailed suggestions, which considerably improved the work. I was warmly received by the DIA historians Deane Allen, Richard J. Shuster, and Brian G. Shellum. The historian for the Air Force Office of Special Investigations, Christy Williamson, was generous in the support she offered. I owe a large debt of thanks to each of them.

Over a period of ten years, in researching the subjects that provided background for the book, I conducted numerous interviews. I gratefully acknowledge those who gave me the benefit of their time and expertise, especially Bernard Smith, Paul Kaufman, Theodore Postol, Eugene Skolnikoff, John P. Holdren, Janne E. Nolan, Lawrence Korb, Joseph Nye, Larry Smith, John Steinbruner, Michael O'Hanlon, Tom Lewis-Borbely, Daniel Berrigan, William Sloane Coffin, Thomas W. Simons, Thomas Halsted, Daniel Ellsberg, Philip Morrison, Robert McNamara, Theodore Sorensen, Carl Kaysen, William S. Cohen, Colin Powell, Arthur Schlesinger, Jr., General James L. Jones, Franklin Lindsay, Howard Zinn, James Podner, Dante E. Guazzo, Richard Garwin, John Kenneth Galbraith, General George Lee Butler, General Jack Sheehan, Lieutenant General James Terry Scott, General John Shalikashvili, Kenneth Bacon, Senator Edward Kennedy, Senator John McCain, Senator John Kerry, and Representatives Edward Markey and Barney Frank.

At Houghton Mifflin Company, I acknowledge a large debt to Eamon Dolan, Janet Silver, Larry Cooper, and all the dedicated publishing professionals who brought this book into the world. Lois Wasoff read the manuscript and made important recommendations, for which I am grateful. Eileen Fitzgerald helped me with fact checking. My agent, Donald Cutler, as always, supported me throughout, and I remain ever grateful to him. My most deeply felt word of thanks goes to Alexandra Marshall, my beloved wife, the pulse of my heart. Thank you, Lexa.

NOTES

Prologue. The Invisible Boy

1. Lawren, *The General and the Bomb*, 60.
2. The Ground Zero Café was the name of an outdoor snack bar in the courtyard during the 1980s and 1990s.
3. *What Is to Be Done?* is the title of a novel by the Russian social reformer N. G. Chernyshevsky, published in 1836. In 1902 Lenin used the same title: *What Is to Be Done? Burning Questions of Our Movement.*
4. Goldberg, *The Pentagon*, 44.
5. Pogue, *George C. Marshall*, 38.
6. I acknowledge Lisa Szefel, who helped me sharpen this idea.

One. One Week in 1943

1. The image originates with Norman Mailer: "He had made the grand connection between Egyptian architecture and the Pentagon. Yes, the Egyptian forms, slab-like, excremental, thick walls, secret caverns, had come from the mud of the Nile." Mailer, *Armies of the Night*, 179.
2. Goldberg, *The Pentagon*, 52.
3. Brinkley, *Washington Goes to War*, 72.
4. Goldberg, *The Pentagon*, 14.
5. Ibid., 24.
6. The concern about abandoning "the human scale for the Stalinesque" would be made explicit some decades later by Russell Baker: "Man is out of place in these ponderosities. They are designed to make man feel negligible, to intimidate him, to overwhelm him with evidence that he is a cipher, a trivial nuisance in the great institutional scheme of things. Those most likely to be affected are men who work in such arrogant surroundings." Baker, "Moods of Washington."
7. Goldberg, *The Pentagon*, 28.
8. Brice, *Stronghold*, 116.
9. Brinkley, *Washington Goes to War*, 75.

10. Richard Rhodes notes that Groves had "sufficient girth to balloon over his webbing belt above and below its brass military buckle." *The Making of the Atomic Bomb,* 425.

11. Lawren, *The General and the Bomb,* 59.

12. The man was General Miles. Ibid., 48.

13. Ibid., 47, 55.

14. Ibid., 61. The first desegregation of Virginia public schools occurred in 1957, nearly fifteen years after the Pentagon ribbon-cutting.

15. The building had been occupied as its sections were completed, with, for example, Secretary of War Stimson moving into his office in November 1942. Norris, *Racing for the Bomb,* 158. The Navy high command refused to move into the Pentagon at all, and the Joint Chiefs did not meet there in wartime. Sherry, *The Rise of American Air Power,* 219.

16. Beschloss, *The Conquerors,* 12.

17. Sifton, *The Serenity Prayer,* 268.

18. Speaking of plans for postwar Germany at the Tehran conference the following November, Stalin would tell Roosevelt and Churchill, "At least fifty thousand — and perhaps a hundred thousand — of the German command staff must be physically liquidated. I propose a salute to the swiftest possible justice for all Germany's war criminals — justice before a firing squad! I drink to our unity in killing them as quickly as we capture them. All of them! There must be at least fifty thousand." Churchill protested, "The British people will never stand for such mass murder . . . I will not be a party to any butchery in cold blood . . . I would rather be taken out in the garden, here and now, and be shot myself than sully my country's honor by such infamy." Roosevelt, "mediating," as he put it, joked that the two might be able to agree on a lesser figure, "say, forty-nine thousand, five hundred." Beschloss, *The Conquerors,* 26–27.

19. Gilbert, *Churchill,* 738.

20. O'Neill, *A Democracy at War,* 146. Ultra depended on the Enigma machine, used for mathematical computations in decoding numerical ciphers. The Germans developed it well before the war, but the British were able to obtain Enigma machines and read German codes. The story of Ultra was mostly kept secret until the 1970s, when historians were forced to revisit some of the Allied successes against Germany. See F. W. Winterbotham, "The Ultra Secret," in Friedman, *The Secret Histories.* An American version of Ultra, as it happened, was also implemented in January 1943. Code-named Verona and targeting the Soviet Union, not Germany, this cryptanalysis program, run by the Army's Signal Intelligence Service and, later, by the National Security Agency, successfully read many intercepted Soviet diplomatic messages, continuing until 1980. Verona was made public only in 1995. See "The Verona Cables," in Friedman, *The Secret Histories.*

21. Bird, *The Color of Truth,* 77, 82.

22. Churchill, *The Hinge of Fate,* 687.

23. Beschloss, *The Conquerors,* 34. Lincoln, once he heard the news of Lee's surrender, ordered federal army bands to play "Dixie." For my understanding of the implications of FDR's "unconditional surrender" demand, I acknowledge a particular debt to Michael Beschloss.

24. Langer, *World History,* 970.

25. Ibid., 970.

26. His regret on this point might have included a note of self-criticism, since he had himself been part of the British-American refusal to heed France's protests through the 1930s against Germany's rearmament. His determination to prevent Germany's reemergence as a military threat was not as extreme as Hans Morgenthau's, whose later plan for the "pastoralization" of Germany would be rejected by FDR.

27. Beschloss, *The Conquerors,* 14.

28. Quoted by Schelling, *Arms and Influence,* 45.

29. On March 13, 1943, a bomb was placed on Hitler's plane, but it failed to go off. Sifton, *The Serenity Prayer*, 269. On July 20, 1944, Claus von Stauffenberg left a suitcase bomb near Hitler. It exploded, but also failed to kill him.

30. News of Hitler's mass murder of Jews had come to Roosevelt at least two months earlier. Wyman, *The Abandonment of the Jews*, 102. On December 2, 1942, the State Department had announced "that two million Jews had perished in Europe and five million more were in danger." Rhodes, *The Making of the Atomic Bomb*, 437. Two weeks before the Casablanca meeting, on January 11, 1943, a German military communication was intercepted by Allied intelligence putting the number of Jews killed at four death camps — Lublin, Belzec, Sobibor, and Treblinka — at 1,274,166. "U.S. Study Pinpoints Near-Misses by Allies in Fathoming the Unfolding Holocaust," *New York Times*, July 31, 2005, A6.

In understanding — not justifying — the Allies' refusal to act against the genocide, several factors are relevant. U.S. military leaders had all read Clausewitz, instructing them to stick with the original battle plan. They resisted initiatives giving priority to the camps. The British, for their part, had a history of complacency, having done nothing to help the Armenians in 1915. Stalin, of course, had presided over a genocide of his own in Ukraine.

In 2005, a U.S. government analysis of when exactly the Allies first learned of the Nazis' systematic genocide of the Jewish people cites the memorandum of a British cryptanalyst: "The fact that the police are killing all Jews that fall into their hands should now be sufficiently appreciated." The memo was written in 1941 — in fact, it is dated September 11. "U.S. Study Pinpoints Near-Misses," 6.

31. Beschloss, *The Conquerors*, 24.

32. Schelling, *Arms and Influence*, 2. For his work on game theory as applied to war and other endeavors, Schelling won the 2005 Nobel Prize in economics.

33. Sifton, *The Serenity Prayer*, 271. Sifton notes that her father, Reinhold Niebuhr, "cautiously supported" unconditional surrender, but not without distress. As for the American public, its enthusiasm for unconditional surrender has always been understood as a kind of calculation — the slaughter of civilians on the enemy side as a way of avoiding U.S. casualties — but this calculation leaves out the elements of revenge, rage, and retribution.

34. Schelling, *Arms and Influence*, 9.

35. Lindqvist, *A History of Bombing*, 10. The vestige of this impulse accounts in part for the difference between Allied tactics in Europe and the far more brutal ones pursued in Japan. More than simple racism, the savaging of Japanese cities was related to Asians' status as the Other. See Dower, *War Without Mercy*, especially "Apes and Others," 77–93.

36. Sherman wrote, "If the people raise a howl against my barbarity and cruelty, I will answer that war is war . . . If they want peace, they and their relatives must stop the war." A colleague added, "Sherman is perfectly right . . . The only possible way to end this unhappy and dreadful conflict . . . is to make it terrible beyond endurance." J.F.C. Fuller comments, "For the nineteenth century this was a new conception, because it meant that the deciding factor in the war — the power to sue for peace — was transferred from government to people, and that peacemaking was a product of revolution. This was to carry the principle of democracy to its ultimate stage." Quoted by Schelling, *Arms and Influence*, 15.

37. Schelling defines terrorism as "violence intended to coerce the enemy rather than to weaken him militarily." Ibid., 17.

38. In 1941, the name of the Army Air Corps was changed to the Army Air Forces. In 1947, the AAF would be established as a separate service, the U.S. Air Force.

39. Lindqvist, *A History of Bombing*, 81. Thinking perhaps of the German campaign against cities in Spain, Roosevelt said: "The ruthless bombing from the air of civilians in unfortified centers of population during the course of hostilities which have raged in various quarters of the earth during the past few years, which has resulted in the maiming and in the death of thousands of defenseless men, women, and children, has sickened the

hearts of every civilized man and woman, and has profoundly shocked the conscience of humanity.

"If resort is had to this form of inhuman barbarism during the period of the tragic conflagration with which the world is now confronted, hundreds of thousands of innocent human beings who have no responsibility for, and who are not even remotely participating in, the hostilities which have now broken out, will lose their lives. I am therefore addressing this urgent appeal to every Government which may be engaged in hostilities publicly to affirm its determination that its armed forces shall in no event, and under no circumstances, undertake the bombardment from the air of civilian populations or of unfortified cities, upon the understanding that these same rules of warfare will be scrupulously observed by all of their opponents. I request an immediate reply."

London accepted the appeal at once, and within weeks, so had Berlin. But as Richard Rhodes points out, Roosevelt, nine months before making this urgent moral request, had himself ordered long-range bombers built for the Army Air Corps. *The Making of the Atomic Bomb,* 310.

40. Ibid., 469.

41. In addition to Rotterdam, German warplanes had bombed Warsaw in 1939, but it was Hitler, more than the Luftwaffe, who embraced bombing of cities. "The Luftwaffe learned from its experience during the Spanish Civil War that counterpopulation bombing had much less effect on civilian morale than expected and that accurate bombing of industrial targets was beyond the limits of their technology." Pape, *Bombing to Win,* 70.

42. Sven Lindqvist, for example, writes, "Churchill not only sacrificed London and other British cities, he also sacrificed those conventions for the protection of civilians that it had taken Europe 250 years to evolve." *A History of Bombing,* 82. Obviously, British aerial bombing was not the first breach of the norms protecting civilians (Guernica, for example), but now London had joined in the abandonment of such norms.

43. Quoted by Sherry, *The Rise of American Air Power,* 64. Here is how the historian of war John Keegan accounts for the change: "At the outbreak in 1939, all combatant powers, Germany as well as France and Britain, forswore the bombing of civilian targets. Then, in May 1940, the Germans bombed by mistake the German city of Freiburg im Bireisgau and, to disguise the error, blamed it on the enemy. Thereafter it was open season." *The Battle for History,* 26.

44. London, as Churchill saw it, was "the greatest target in the world, a kind of tremendous, fat, valuable cow tied up to attract the beast of prey." Quoted by Sherry, *The Rise of American Air Power,* 64.

45. Schaffer, *Wings of Judgment,* 63.

46. The RAF had tried daylight raids against Germany in 1940, but the losses they sustained were intolerable.

47. Carl Kaysen, author interview.

48. Keegan, *The Battle for History,* 26.

49. Regarding British area bombing of cities, John Kenneth Galbraith, a member of the U.S. Strategic Bombing Survey, observed, "Necessity [was] as ever the parent of belief. The Lancasters and Halifaxes of the RAF (and also the unarmed all-wood Mosquitoes) could only fly at night; by day they were hopelessly vulnerable. In the dark they could find only the cities, and from this technological imperative came the conclusion." Galbraith, *A Life in Our Times,* 204.

50. Lindqvist, *A History of Bombing,* 91.

51. The Strategic Bombing Survey showed that German industrial output, especially including military manufacture, rose dramatically and consistently through the war years. The most the air bombardment can be said to have done was to slow the rate of increase. See, for example, Galbraith, *A Life in Our Times,* 205.

52. The commanding general of the Army Air Forces, since late in 1942, was a member of the Joint Chiefs of Staff, indicating that the AAF was evolving toward an independent branch of the service.

53. Schaffer, *Wings of Judgment*, 61.

54. Rhodes, *The Making of the Atomic Bomb*, 520.

55. Galbraith, *A Life in Our Times*, 204.

56. Carl Kaysen, author interview.

57. Schaffer, *Wings of Judgment*, 38. Arnold was typical of air war leaders in his ambivalence. The airman "is handling a weapon which can be either the scourge or the savior of humanity according to how well he uses it." But also, "The way to stop the killing of civilians is to cause so much damage and destruction and death that civilians will demand that their government cease fighting." Sherry, *The Rise of American Air Power*, 151.

58. In the fall of 1942, as the Pentagon was first being occupied, Stimson offered the Navy one million square feet of office space. Since that was barely more than one fourth of the Building's total, Navy Secretary Frank Knox demanded more. Stimson refused, so Knox refused to move the Navy in. And why should he have? The Navy had been an independent entity since 1798, and would continue to be until 1947. Pogue, *George C. Marshall*, 42.

59. Quoted by Rhodes, *The Making of the Atomic Bomb*, 586.

60. Paul Kaufman, with whom I spoke in 2004, was the pilot of the *Millie Kay*, and flew, as he put it to me, "fifteen and a half missions" before being shot down over Germany. He was captured and held at Stalag 1, in Barth, Germany. A Jew, he was isolated with about three hundred other Jewish POWs until liberation in 1945. Hitler had ordered the killing of all Jewish POWs, but the senior American at Stalag 1 persuaded the camp commandant not to carry out the order. Kaufman was twenty-one when he flew.

61. Coffey, *Iron Eagle*, 36.

62. For a sense of the evolution of precision in bombing, consider that, on average in World War II, to drop one bomb in an area one half the size of a football field required the dropping of nine hundred bombs, which required the flights of hundreds of planes. By the time of the Gulf War in 1992, it required one plane to drop one bomb to be relatively assured of hitting such a target. By the Iraq War, beginning in 2003, one B-2 bomber could drop sixteen bombs on sixteen different targets, each within that same half a football field.

63. In the European theater, the AAF suffered 52,173 combat deaths in World War II, and 35,946 killed in noncombat situations. The RAF, engaged in combat twice as long as the Americans, lost 70,253 in all operations, 47,268 in its Bomber Command. Sherry, *The Rise of American Air Power*, 204–5.

64. Ibid., 212.

65. Sebald, *On the Natural History of Destruction*, 77.

66. "What 'undue fatigue' meant was fear. And it was a very rare man who didn't feel it." Coffey, *Iron Eagle*, 77.

67. Ibid., 48.

68. Sherry, *The Rise of American Air Power*, 157; Coffey, *Iron Eagle*, 90.

69. Coffey, *Iron Eagle*, 88.

70. Sherry, *The Rise of American Air Power*, 206.

71. Coffey, *Iron Eagle*, 92.

72. Galbraith, *A Life in Our Times*, 206.

73. Craven and Cate, *The Army Air Forces in World War II*, 58.

74. Robert McNamara, author interview. Daniel Ellsberg, who worked closely with McNamara in the 1960s, told me that McNamara's Pentagon colleagues were entirely unaware that he had served under LeMay during World War II.

75. Paul Hendrickson recounts at length his difficulty in getting McNamara to agree to interviews for his book *The Living and the Dead*, a process complicated by critical pieces

Hendrickson had written after earlier interviews for the *Washington Post. The Living and the Dead,* 383–85.

76. William R. Emerson, Harmon Memorial Lecture, U.S. Air Force Academy, 1962.

77. Robert McNamara, author interview.

78. Howard Zinn, author interview.

79. Emerson, Harmon Lecture.

80. LeMay, *Mission with LeMay,* 363.

81. Sherry, *The Rise of American Air Power,* 206.

82. Groves, *Now It Can Be Told,* 3–4.

83. The letter was actually written by Leo Szilard. Years later, Einstein said, "I made one great mistake in my life, when I signed the letter to President Roosevelt recommending that atom bombs be made, but there was some justification — the danger that the Germans would make them." Sherwin, *A World Destroyed,* 27.

84. "There's no doubt Hitler would have used it the minute he had it, probably against London . . . If they calmly reported on a cricket match, I would turn it right off." Philip Morrison, author interview.

85. Rhodes, *The Making of the Atomic Bomb,* 437.

86. The Manhattan Project took its name from the Corps of Engineers office in New York City, a subterfuge. The Manhattan Engineer District would soon be transferred to Tennessee.

87. Bush was director of the Office of Scientific Research and Development. Sharing responsibility were MIT President Karl T. Compton, Harvard President James B. Conant, and Bell Telephone Laboratories President Frank B. Jewett. As of early fall 1942, overall responsibility for development of the atomic bomb belonged to the War Department, with ultimate responsibility resting with Secretary of War Henry Stimson and Army Chief of Staff General George Marshall, who designated Groves.

88. "Three major installations encompassing a total of over half a million acres; thirty minor installations, employing a total workforce of 1,295,000 and dispensing an annual payroll of some $200 million. When the final tallies were in, it was calculated that the bomb had cost slightly over two billion dollars — by far the largest governmental expenditure on a single object to that time . . . 'the greatest single achievement of organized human effort in history.'" Lawren, *The General and the Bomb,* 259–60.

89. Ibid., 191.

90. Philip Morrison, author interview.

91. Lawren, *The General and the Bomb,* 137; Norris, *Racing for the Bomb,* 291.

92. Sherwin, *A World Destroyed,* 58. Morrison, who was assigned as a liaison to Groves's office, told me of his early impression that the general "was the most apt officer that could have had the job." Author interview.

93. Churchill would prevail upon Roosevelt the following August, in Quebec, to reverse this, bringing British scientists back into the project.

94. William Cohen, author interview. Ahab is lashed to the back of Moby Dick in the movie, but not in the novel.

95. Dwight Eisenhower, farewell address, January 17, 1961.

96. At 250,000 men, the U.S. Army ranked nineteenth in the world, after Belgium. Germany's 1939 invasion force in Poland was 1.5 million; its 1940 invasion force in France was almost 2 million. By the end of World War II, the American military would number around 14 million men. Parker, *John Kenneth Galbraith,* 124. See also Schmitz, *Henry L. Stimson,* 154.

97. Hodgson, *America in Our Time,* 130.

98. See, for example, Lowen, *Creating the Cold War University.*

99. Brodie, *The Absolute Weapon.*

100. Schelling, *Arms and Influence*, 19.

101. Rauch, "Firebombs over Tokyo." See also Howard W. French, "100,000 People Perished, but Who Remembers?" *New York Times,* March 14, 2002, A4. George Marshall, commenting after the war on the effect of the Tokyo bombing, said, "We had had the one hundred thousand people killed in Tokyo in one night of conventional bombs, and it had had seemingly no effect whatsoever. It destroyed the Japanese cities, yes, but their morale was not affected as far as we could tell, not at all." Rhodes, *The Making of the Atomic Bomb,* 688. One should note that Marshall's comment on the minimal psychological effects of conventional bombing were intended to contrast with the greater effects of the atomic bomb, with a view to justifying its use. John Lewis Gaddis made the point this way: "The atomic bomb's quantum jump in destructive power . . . created a psychological impression that went well beyond anything conventional operations during the war had produced." *The United States and the End of the Cold War,* 109. All of this talk of "not remembering," of course, refers to an American point of view. The devastation of Tokyo is remembered in Japan.

102. Schelling, *Arms and Influence*, 17.

103. Ibid., 23.

104. Rhodes, *The Making of the Atomic Bomb,* 742.

105. ". . . the sanctification of Hiroshima . . . the elevation of the Hiroshima event to the status of a profoundly mystical event, an event ultimately of the same religious force as biblical events." Weinberg, "The Sanctification of Hiroshima," 34.

106. Charles Davis, a former DIA official, describes a Schlesinger-era war game: "I was the leader of the Red Team (Soviet) in a Pentagon war game where the Soviets backed a Syrian invasion of Israel. The U.S. backed up Israel by bombing Syrian positions (populated with Soviet combat advisors) with tac-nukes launched by U.S. A-4 aircraft from an aircraft carrier in the Mediterranean. To the disgust of the A.F. colonels and Navy captains on my team (and probably to the disgust of those who had ordered the war game), I refused to allow our Soviet forces to retaliate in kind. While the Syrian forces were forced to retreat from their invasion, the loss in standing the U.S. suffered (in the war game) for employing nukes was overwhelming. The Red Team let the Syrians suffer their fate and refused to let Moscow be sucked in." Author correspondence.

107. Quoted by Auster, *The Invention of Solitude,* 164.

108. Sherwin and Bird, *American Prometheus,* 309.

109. Rhodes, *The Making of the Atomic Bomb,* 668.

110. Philip Morrison, author interview.

111. Ibid.

112. Morrison, "Recollections of a Nuclear War," 30.

113. Rhodes, *The Making of the Atomic Bomb,* 615.

114. Auster, *The Invention of Solitude,* 83.

115. Sebald, *On the Natural History of Destruction,* 22–23.

116. "It must be considered that there is nothing more difficult to carry out, nor more doubtful of success, nor more dangerous to handle, than to initiate a new order of things." Niccolò Machiavelli, *The Prince,* chapter 6. The words *Novus Ordo Seclorum* appear under the engraving of the pyramid on the one-dollar bill.

117. Referring to the September 11 event, Gandhi wrote, "The foundation of the first civil resistance under the then-known name of passive resistance was laid by accident . . . I had gone to the meeting with no preconceived resolution. It was born at the meeting. The creation is still expanding." Quoted by Schell, *The Unconquerable World,* 119.

118. Sherwin and Bird, *American Prometheus,* 268.

119. Gorbachev said, "Necessity of the principle of freedom of choice is clear. Denying that right of people, no matter what the pretext for doing so, no matter what words are

used to conceal it, means infringing even that unstable balance that it has been possible to achieve. Freedom of choice is a universal principle, and there should be no exceptions." Quoted by Schell, *The Unconquerable World*, 211. The fall of the Berlin Wall one year later was a direct consequence of this speech.

120. Morris, *Dutch*, 630.

121. Shattuck, *Proust's Way*, 20.

122. Lisa Szefel, author correspondence.

123. Quoted by May and Neustadt, *Thinking in Time*, 232.

124. Sebald, *On the Natural History of Destruction*, 71.

125. Carroll, *An American Requiem*.

126. Associating world-historic events with one's own birthday — the last U.S. ground forces were withdrawn from Vietnam on January 22, 1973, the day I turned thirty (also the day that Lyndon Johnson died, and the day *Roe v. Wade* was handed down by the U.S. Supreme Court) — may be the height of narcissism, but it is also a person's way of being located in time and history.

Two. The Absolute Weapon

1. Truman himself emphasizes the word "decision" in the title of the first volume of his memoirs, *Year of Decisions*.

2. The atomic bomb changed other nations almost as dramatically. To avoid Japan's fate, the great powers — and eventually smaller powers — sought to acquire nuclear weapons, but it was the United States, and then the Soviet Union, that constructed a whole new edifice of politics and economy on the nuclear platform.

3. Hodgson, *The Colonel*, 336.

4. McCullough, *Truman*, 444.

5. Powers, "History: Was It Right?," 23. In coming to sympathize with Truman, Powers describes himself as having "completed some kind of ghastly circle" (23).

6. Revisionist authors and texts include Alperovitz, *Atomic Diplomacy: Hiroshima and Potsdam*; Bernstein, *The Atomic Bomb*; Sherwin, *A World Destroyed*. For an opposing position, see Maddox, *The New Left and the Origins of the Cold War*. As the debate over the Cold War's origins unfolded, the polar positions came to be symbolized by John Lewis Gaddis on one side and Melvyn Leffler on the other. See Gaddis, *Strategies of Containment*, and Leffler's *A Preponderance of Power*. In Japan, revisionism goes the other way, with some Japanese scholars showing how the atomic bomb did break the impasse between militarists and the peace party, allowing the surrender. "We of the peace party were assisted by the atomic bomb in our endeavor to end the war," Koichi Kido, an intimate of the Emperor's, said later. A cabinet secretary, Hisatsune Sakomizu, is also cited: "The atomic bomb was a golden opportunity given by heaven for Japan to end the war." These men, of course, were offering testimony that the occupiers wanted to hear. See Nicholas D. Kristof, "Blood on Our Hands?" *New York Times*, August 5, 2003, A19.

7. Gaddis, *We Now Know*. See also Carolyn Eisenberg's review of the book.

8. Stephen S. Rosenfeld, "The Revisionists' Agenda," *Washington Post*, August 4, 1995, in Bird and Lifschultz, *Hiroshima's Shadow*, 406.

9. William O'Neill writes, "The Bomb was met with wonder and jubilation at first . . . It was only later that doubts arose." *A Democracy at War*, 420–21.

10. A Gallup poll taken in August 1945 found 85 percent approving, 10 percent disapproving. Bird and Lifschultz, *Hiroshima's Shadow*, 189.

11. "Between Hell and Reason," *Combat*, August 6, 1945, in Bird and Lifschultz, *Hiroshima's Shadow*, 260.

12. "The Decline to Barbarism," in Bird and Lifschultz, *Hiroshima's Shadow*, 263. Mac-

donald, a former Marxist, was chiefly associated with other journals, especially *Partisan Review.*

13. Fred Eastman, letter to the editor, *Christian Century,* August 29, 1945, quoted by Paul Boyer, "Victory for What: The Voice of the Minority," in Bird and Lifschultz, *Hiroshima's Shadow,* 239.

14. "The Atom Bomb," *Catholic World,* September 1945, in Bird and Lifschultz, *Hiroshima's Shadow,* 245.

15. O'Neill, *A Democracy at War,* 415. O'Neill comments: "Critics of the atomic bomb never take into account the shock felt by leaders in the United States over the rapidly escalating casualty rates. Marshall, a humane man, had been so upset by the losses on Iwo Jima that he recommended using poison gas on Okinawa, even the thought of which had been taboo until then" (416).

16. Truman, *Year of Decisions,* 417.

17. Martin J. Sherwin says Truman cited Marshall for the first figure in his memoir, but in an unpublished letter, Truman cited Marshall for the second: "I asked General Marshall what it would cost in lives to land on the Tokyo plain and other places in Japan. It was his opinion that such an invasion would cost at a minimum a quarter of a million casualties." The word "casualties," of course, refers not to dead, but to dead and wounded. Sherwin, *A World Destroyed,* xxii; McCullough, *Truman,* 437.

18. Churchill, *Triumph and Tragedy,* 638.

19. Manchester, *Goodbye, Darkness,* quoted with approval by Paul Fussell, another combat veteran who counted himself a survivor because of the bomb. "Thank God for the Atomic Bomb," in Bird and Lifschultz, *Hiroshima's Shadow,* 214. My father-in-law was a Pacific veteran who, though a Navy man, shared the sense of many of his generation that the bombing of Hiroshima and Nagasaki had spared him and friends. Aware of my questions on the subject, he chose not to discuss it with me.

20. Fussell, "Thank God for the Atom Bomb," in Bird and Lifschultz, *Hiroshima's Shadow,* 218.

21. For example, O'Neill, *A Democracy at War,* 420; McCullough, *Truman,* 456. Richard Rhodes also cites the passage: *The Making of the Atomic Bomb,* 736.

22. Fussell, *The Great War and Modern Memory.* Another writer, who was also on his way to the Pacific, reported, as he put it to me in an interview, "a feeling of elation" when he learned of the atomic bomb. But unlike Fussell, this writer had second thoughts. "I recall August 6, 1945, very clearly. I had served as a bombardier in the Eighth Air Force in Europe, flew back to the States for a thirty-day furlough before a scheduled move to the Pacific, and while on furlough picked up a newspaper telling of the bomb dropped on Hiroshima. I felt only gladness that the end of the war was imminent." But this reflection is given in the context of a critique of the American use of the bomb. Zinn, *The Politics of History,* 256.

23. Bird and Lifschultz, *Hiroshima's Shadow,* xlvii. The most influential reiteration of the high casualty defense of the decision is in McCullough's *Truman.* For discussion of the gap between scholars and the public on Truman's decision, see I. Samuel Walker, "History, Collective Memory, and the Decision to Use the Atomic Bomb," *Diplomatic History,* Spring 1995.

24. The significance of this article in shaping the American memory about the decision to use the bomb was first drawn to my attention by Kai Bird in *The Color of Truth.* Bird credits Barton J. Bernstein's "Seizing the Contested Terrain." Elsewhere, Bird wrote, "Bernstein's reconstruction of how the *Harper's* essay was written is a remarkable piece of historical detective work." Bird and Lifschultz, *Hiroshima's Shadow,* xlvii.

25. Hodgson, *The Colonel,* 19.

26. Ibid., 5.

27. Lawren, *The General and the Bomb,* 191.

28. Ibid., 191.

29. On April 13, the day after FDR's death and moments after Truman's swearing-in, Stimson indicated that there was under development a weapon of "almost unbelievable destructive power," but it was not until April 25 that he gave the new president a full briefing. Hodgson, *The Colonel*, 316. According to Stimson's own notes of this meeting, he outlined for the president the unprecedented destructive power of the new weapon and the implications for "sharing." He said, "The question of sharing it with other nations, and if so shared, upon what terms, becomes a primary question of our foreign relations . . . [The weapon] has placed [on us] a certain moral responsibility for any disaster to civilization which it would further." See Alperovitz, *The Decision to Use the Atomic Bomb*, 132.

30. Conant wrote to McGeorge Bundy, "You may be inclined to dismiss all this talk as representing only a small minority of the population . . . You will recall that it became accepted doctrine among a group of so-called intellectuals who taught in our schools and colleges that the United States had made a great error in entering World War I." Bird, *The Color of Truth*, 90.

31. Cousins, "The Literacy of Survival," in Bird and Lifschultz, *Hiroshima's Shadow*, 305. The *Saturday Review* was a high-circulation magazine for the general reader, not one of the precious journals of ex-Marxist elites. Howard Zinn, who served as a bombardier and who was en route from Europe to the Pacific when the atomic bomb fell, told me that his elation at the news was unmitigated until he read the Hersey article, which was the beginning of his criticism of the bomb and war. Author interview.

32. Stimson and Bundy, *On Active Service in Peace and War*, 633.

33. Kai Bird, McGeorge Bundy's biographer, asks, "Where did Stimson and Mac find this figure? Bundy had asked the War Department for any casualty estimates given to Stimson in the summer of 1945, but he never got them. Instead, he and Stimson simply agreed to use the nice round figure of one million casualties." *The Color of Truth*, 93.

34. Sherwin, *A World Destroyed*, xxii. The Joint War Plans Committee ultimately took the position that "while the bombing and blockade of Japan will have considerable effect upon Japanese morale and their ability to continue the war, there is little reason to believe that such action alone is certain to result in the early unconditional surrender of Japan." Quoted in Pape, *Bombing to Win*, 97.

35. Bird says that "the *Harper's* article became the source for [the] . . . central myth about the decision," i.e., the million casualties figure. *The Color of Truth*, 93.

36. Sherwin, *A World Destroyed*, xxiv.

37. Eisenhower, *Mandate for Change*, 380.

38. Sherwin and Bird, *American Prometheus*, 295.

39. See, for example, Sigal, *Fighting to a Finish*, 235. Emperor Hirohito told his top leaders to "study concrete means" of war termination and to "strive for their prompt realization." See also Galbraith, *A Life in Our Times*, 232.

40. Wainstock, *The Decision to Drop the Atomic Bomb*, 33.

41. Stimson and Bundy, *On Active Service in Peace and War*, 625.

42. Millis, *The Forrestal Diaries*, 69.

43. John Dower points out that there were no more "honor suicides" after the Japanese surrender than there had been in Germany, an astounding fact given the pronounced Japanese cult of ritual suicide. *Embracing Defeat*, 39.

44. Sherwin, *A World Destroyed*, 235.

45. George C. Marshall, "Memorandum for the Secretary of War, June 9, 1945," in Bird and Lifschultz, *Hiroshima's Shadow*, 509.

46. Stimson and Bundy, *On Active Service in Peace and War*, 626.

47. Wainstock, *The Decision to Drop the Atomic Bomb*, 73.

48. Ibid., 126.

49. Sherwin, *A World Destroyed*, 235.

50. www.randomhouse.com/features/americancentury/citadel.html.

51. Byrnes had been head of the Office of War Mobilization, a small coordinating body that operated out of the White House. Byrnes served as a kind of troubleshooter for FDR, smoothing conflicts among the vast number of businesses, military groups, and political bodies that had to work together on the war effort. This role earned for him the informal title "Assistant President."

52. "The day after Trinity," as Kai Bird and Lawrence Lifschultz write, "Stimson made a final plea to Byrnes for an explicit warning regarding the capability of the bomb and a precise assurance to the Japanese that unconditional surrender did not mean an end to the Emperor. Byrnes cut him off and unequivocally rejected both ideas, saying he spoke for the President. The plausible alternative to both an invasion and the bomb was now dead at Potsdam. Byrnes had the Soviet Union on his mind, and the manner of Japan's surrender would become a dramatic demarche in the opening phase of the post-war world." Bird and Lifschultz, *Hiroshima's Shadow*, lxi. For more on the Japanese surrender, see Dower, *Embracing Defeat*, chapter 1.

53. Sherwin, *A World Destroyed*, 72. The notion of prewar Anglo-American friendship is overblown. Roosevelt's pullback here comports with a broader animus against British arrogance — political, cultural, economic — that had percolated since World War I.

54. Ibid., 113.

55. Norris, *Racing for the Bomb*, 631.

56. This is not to say that FDR would have behaved as Truman did at Potsdam. As the one who promulgated the policy of unconditional surrender, he may also have been the one to step back from it. Indeed, at Potsdam every one of his senior advisers favored doing just that, and only Byrnes and Truman did not. And Gar Alperovitz points out, "Had Roosevelt lived, James F. Byrnes would not have become Secretary of State . . . and since only Byrnes stood strongly in the way of the recommended policy, there is a reasonable likelihood that the assurances in paragraph 12 of the Potsdam Proclamation [about the Emperor] would not have been eliminated (and that the assurances it contained would have triggered the surrender process)." *The Decision to Use the Atomic Bomb*, 663.

57. John McCloy, quoted by Bird and Lifschultz, *Hiroshima's Shadow*, lxi.

58. Sherwin, *A World Destroyed*, 228.

59. Bird and Lifschultz, *Hiroshima's Shadow*, lxiv.

60. About the bomb, Stimson wrote in his diary in May 1945, "The same rule of sparing the civilian population should be applied as far as possible to the use of any new weapon." Sherwin, *A World Destroyed*, 197.

61. Martin Sherwin comments of Stimson, "The possibility that its [the bomb's] extraordinary and indiscriminate destructiveness represented a profound qualitative difference, and so cried out for its governance by a higher morality than guided the use of conventional weapons, simply did not occur to him." *A World Destroyed*, 197.

62. Stimson and Bundy, *On Active Service in Peace and War*, 629. Kai Bird comments, "This was a startling admission which most readers in 1948 seem to have ignored then and ever since." *The Color of Truth*, 96.

63. Wainstock, *The Decision to Drop the Atomic Bomb*, 102.

64. Ibid., 103.

65. Bird, *The Color of Truth*, 87.

66. Dower, *Embracing Defeat*, 41.

67. See, for example, Sherwin, *A World Destroyed*; Bernstein, *The Atomic Bomb*; Boyer, *By the Bomb's Early Light*; Messer, *The End of an Alliance*; Wainstock, *The Decision to Drop the Atomic Bomb*; Alperovitz, *The Decision to Use the Atomic Bomb*; Dower, *War Without Mercy*; Bundy, *Danger and Survival*.

68. The term "revisionist" is misleading in the way it suggests that second thoughts about and criticism of the decision to use the bomb appeared only later, but even at the time, as was noted earlier, there were many objections to the bombings of Hiroshima and Nagasaki. Those objections are mostly forgotten, and the events of August 1945 are recalled as if they were uncontroversial at the time. That is not so.

69. Alperovitz, *The Decision to Use the Atomic Bomb*, 132.

70. Bernstein, "Understanding the Atomic Bomb and Japanese Surrender."

71. Hasegawa, *Racing the Enemy*, 5.

72. Sherwin, *A World Destroyed*, 227. For more on Stalin's reaction to news of Trinity, see Holloway, *Stalin and the Bomb*, 117.

73. Stimson and Bundy, *On Active Service in Peace and War*, 644.

74. Sherwin, *A World Destroyed*, 228.

75. The most prominent proponents of a demonstration use of the bomb in an uninhabited area were the Chicago-based atomic physicists who had helped create the bomb, but who, after Germany's defeat, opposed its use. Led by Leo Szilard, more than seventy such scientists signed the proposal. More than that number, however, continued to support its use, most prominently J. Robert Oppenheimer.

76. Joseph Rotblat, "Leaving the Bomb Project," in Bird and Lifschultz, *Hiroshima's Shadow*, 256.

77. Ibid.

78. Freeman Dyson, quoted by Sherwin and Bird, *American Prometheus*, 298.

79. Rhodes, *The Making of the Atomic Bomb*, 635.

80. Byrnes reports in his memoir that he was first made aware of the Manhattan Project as early as 1943, by FDR himself, but he would have come to fully know of the program only in the spring of 1945. Hodgson, *The Colonel*, 350.

81. Wainstock, *The Decision to Drop the Bomb*, 40–41.

82. Rhodes, *The Making of the Atomic Bomb*, 638.

83. Even as the bomb's targets were being picked, Stimson continued to imagine they could be subject to the "rule of sparing the civilian population." Ibid., 640.

84. Groves, *Now It Can Be Told*, 296.

85. Rhodes, *The Making of the Atomic Bomb*, 749.

86. Of the declining scientists, Joseph Rotblat offers this comment: "The majority were not bothered by moral scruples; they were content to leave it to others to decide how their work would be used" Rotblat, "Leaving the Bomb Project," in Bird and Lifschultz, *Hiroshima's Shadow*, 257. Here is Teller's full reply to Szilard: "Since our discussion, I have spent some time thinking about your objections to an immediate military use of the weapon we may produce. I decided to do nothing . . . The accident that we worked out this dreadful thing should not give us the responsibility of having a voice in how it is to be used." Rotblat, "Preface," *Hiroshima's Shadow*, xx.

87. Bird and Lifschultz, *Hiroshima's Shadow*, xxxvi.

88. The plane from which the Nagasaki bomb was dropped was named *Bock's Car*, which evolved in usage to *Boxcar*, a word that would later evoke the boxcars used to transport Jews to death camps. *Bock's Car* has been preserved and is on display at the museum at Wright-Patterson Air Force Base in Dayton, Ohio.

89. Leahy, *I Was There*, 441.

90. "Summary Report (Pacific War), United States Strategic Bombing Survey, July 1, 1946," 26; Galbraith, *A Life in Our Times*, 233. See also Bernstein and Matusow, *The Truman Administration*. This conclusion is rebutted by claims, for example, that it was based "on flawed post-war interviews." Buckley, *Air Power in the Age of Total War*, 196.

91. The disinvited historian was Barton Bernstein. Bird and Lifschultz, *Hiroshima's Shadow*, xlii.

92. Historian Marc Trachtenberg calls it "nuclear amnesia." *History and Strategy*, 152.

93. A follow-up to the 1995 dispute occurred in December 2003, when a new Air and Space Museum exhibit opened in Virginia, featuring the *Enola Gay*. Celebrating the plane that bombed Hiroshima, in the words of the current museum director, as "a magnificent technological achievement," the exhibit made no mention of the controversies about the atomic bombings, nor even of the casualties it caused. (In contrast, the museum's exhibit of a German V-2 rocket emphasized casualties.) Gar Alperovitz, Martin Harwit, and other veterans of the 1995 dispute, together with numerous Japanese atomic bomb survivors (*hibakusha*), protested this exhibit, but the American press ignored the entire affair. The amnesia was complete.

94. Truman, *Year of Decisions*, 419.

95. McCullough, *Truman*, 458. See also Dower, *War Without Mercy*, chapter 1.

96. McCullough, *Truman*, 442.

97. George Elsey, quoted by McCullough, *Truman*, 442.

98. Bird and Lifschultz, *Hiroshima's Shadow*, xlvii.

99. Marilyn Young, quoted in Bird and Lifschultz, *Hiroshima's Shadow*, xlviii.

100. Zinn, *The Politics of History*, 256.

101. See, for example, Alperovitz, *The Decision to Use the Atomic Bomb*, 326–27.

102. Rhodes, *The Making of the Atomic Bomb*, 691.

103. "Guardians" is Janne Nolan's term, in the title of her book *Guardians of the Arsenal*.

104. Sherry, *The Rise of American Air Power*, 341.

105. "If Arnold had not done what I wanted," Groves said, "I could have asked for Marshall to order him to do so . . . On these matters, I was controlling the situation." Norris, *Racing for the Bomb*, 414.

106. Groves, in his autobiography, attributed to General Marshall the decision to keep operational control of the bomb with the engineers, and Groves insisted it surprised him. But Marshall's sense that "operational planning officers [who] might not be able to understand the technical problems involved" had come from Groves. *Now It Can Be Told*, 267.

107. Ibid., 265.

108. Alperovitz, *The Decision to Use the Atomic Bomb*, 657.

109. Alperovitz wants to emphasize Truman's centrality to the decision and so downplays Groves's role: "The 'toboggan' metaphor, of course, is so vague as to be impossible to refute; the related argument that Truman's only choice was to say no ignores the specific issues involved in the three key decision points. Moreover, the real decisions did not involve Groves." Ibid.

110. Norris, *Racing for the Bomb*, 376.

111. Ibid., xii. Norris uses this statement as the organizing device for his biography. A measure of Groves's power is that he could ignore the will even of J. Edgar Hoover, whose requests for information the general did not hesitate to reject. Sherwin and Bird, *American Prometheus*, 511.

112. Norris, *Racing for the Bomb*, 631.

113. Philip Morrison, author interview.

114. Norris, *Racing for the Bomb*, 393.

115. Rhodes, *The Making of the Atomic Bomb*, 640.

116. Norris, *Racing for the Bomb*, 387.

117. Philip Morrison, author interview.

118. Morrison, "Recollections of a Nuclear War," 31.

119. Groves, *Now It Can Be Told*, 266.

120. Wainstock, *The Decision to Drop the Atomic Bomb*, 46–47.

121. Bird and Lifschultz, *Hiroshima's Shadow*, xxxvii.

122. Rhodes, *The Making of the Atomic Bomb*, 638; Sherwin and Bird, *American Prometheus*, 286.

123. Rotblat, "Preface," Bird and Lifschultz, *Hiroshima's Shadow*, xxiv, xix.

124. Stimson and Bundy, *On Active Service in Peace and War*, 237.

125. Ibid., 638.

126. For discussions of the complications of the bomb and its "revolutionary" character, see Jervis, *The Meaning of the Nuclear Revolution* and *The Illogic of American Nuclear Strategy*.

127. Alperovitz, *The Decision to Use the Atomic Bomb*, 240.

128. McCullough, *Truman*, 432.

129. Sherry, *The Rise of American Air Power*, 202.

130. Cohn, "Sex and Death in the Rational World of Defense Intellectuals," 701.

131. Sherwin and Bird, *American Prometheus*, 303.

132. Sherwin, *A World Destroyed*, 225.

133. Caldicott, *Missile Envy*.

134. McCullough, *Truman*, 432.

135. Rhodes, *The Making of the Atomic Bomb*, 734.

136. Ibid., 645.

137. Schmitz, *Henry L. Stimson*, 182.

138. www.trumanlibrary.org/studycollections/bomb/large/interim_committee.

139. Stimson and Bundy, *On Active Service in Peace and War*, 617.

140. Sherwin, *A World Destroyed*, 204.

141. Ralph Bard, "An Alternative to A-Bombing Japan," www.doug-long.com/bard.htm.

142. Sherwin and Bird, *American Prometheus*, 289.

143. Sherry, *The Rise of American Air Power*, 318.

144. www.trumanlibrary.org/studycollections/bomb/large/interim_committee.

145. Rhodes, *The Making of the Atomic Bomb*, 651.

146. Norris, *Racing for the Bomb*, 472.

147. Rhodes, *The Making of the Atomic Bomb*, 650.

148. Sherwin, *A World Destroyed*, 237.

149. Norris, *Racing for the Bomb*, 475.

150. Philip Morrison, author interview.

151. Lawren, *The General and the Bomb*, 267.

152. Gusterson, "Remembering Hiroshima at a Nuclear Weapons Laboratory," 264.

153. Ibid., 260. The film is based on the book by Marguerite Duras.

154. Father Tadashi Hasegawa, in Fallon and Goldfeld, *Beyond Hiroshima*, 23.

155. "Old capital" refers to Kyoto. The new capital, of course, is Tokyo.

156. McCullough, *Truman*, 444.

157. Bundy, *Danger and Survival*, 80. Bundy would say on television that Hiroshima was a military target "like New York." Bird and Lifschultz, *Hiroshima's Shadow*, lvi.

158. LeMay, *Mission with LeMay*, 383.

159. Pape, *Bombing to Win*, 10.

160. LeMay, *Mission with LeMay*, 383.

161. Ibid., 425.

162. Sherry, *The Rise of American Air Power*, 181. Michael Sherry's study of air warfare is one of the most compelling sources I have consulted. I gratefully acknowledge my large debt to him.

163. Schaffer, *Wings of Judgment*, 37.

164. Sherry, *The Rise of American Air Power*, 251. I owe the insight about rhetoric to Lisa Szefel.

165. Sebald, *On the Natural History of Destruction*, 77.

166. Ibid., 70.

167. Pape, *Bombing to Win*, 254.

168. Sebald, *On the Natural History of Destruction*, 3. Sherry puts the figure at between 300,000 and 600,000. *The Rise of American Air Power*, 260. John Buckley puts the figure at 500,000. Buckley, *Air Power in the Age of Total War*, 168.

169. After Normandy, the U.S. forces in Europe lost 583,000 dead and wounded, the British more than 250,000, and the Germans more than one million. These figures, together with "millions of civilian casualties due to aerial bombing, ground fighting, displacement of refugees, and the continuing operation of the 'final solution,'" amount to the ultimate cost of "unconditional surrender." Pape, *Bombing to Win*, 254.

170. Sebald, *On the Natural History of Destruction*, 26.

171. Ibid., 28.

172. Schaffer, *Wings of Judgment*, 64. One of the reasons so many died in Hamburg was the fact that thousands of citizens took refuge in a traffic tunnel, the mouth of which was hit, turning the shelter into an inferno. Carl Kaysen, author interview.

173. Sherry, *The Rise of American Air Power*, 156.

174. Ibid., 152.

175. Ibid., 141.

176. Schaffer, *Wings of Judgment*, 66.

177. Sherry, *The Rise of American Air Power*, 260.

178. Cabell had an intuitive reaction against terror bombing, but he offered three reasons for his rejection of the change: bombing of oil facilities and the like was more important, Germans would portray U.S. targeting of civilians as barbaric, and such tactics would harm the image of the Air Force at home. McElroy, *Morality and American Foreign Policy*, 157.

179. Schaffer, *Wings of Judgment*, 79.

180. Rumpf, *The Bombing of Germany*, 144–45.

181. Lindqvist, *A History of Bombing*, 102; Schaffer, *Wings of Judgment*, 88.

182. Carl Kaysen, author interview.

183. Schaffer, *Wings of Judgment*, 83.

184. Ibid., 84.

185. Buckley, *Air Power in the Age of Total War*, 164. Eisenhower had not fought in Europe in World War I, and so did not learn some of the wrong lessons his Allied colleagues had learned, but he was not immune to their dread of a repeat of the nightmare of the trenches.

186. O'Neill, *A Democracy at War*, 315.

187. Sherry, *The Rise of American Air Power*, 260.

188. Lindqvist puts it at 100,000; *A History of Bombing*, 102. Sherry puts it at 35,000; *The Rise of American Air Power*, 260. Schaffer calls 35,000 a "conservative figure"; *Wings of Judgment*, 97. McElroy says the raids killed 60,000; *Morality and American Foreign Policy*, 148.

189. Rhodes, *The Making of the Atomic Bomb*, 593.

190. Ibid. Vonnegut would write a best-selling novel based on his experience in Dresden, *Slaughterhouse-Five*.

191. Lindqvist, *A History of Bombing*, 102.

192. Sebald, *On the Natural History of Destruction*, 98.

193. Lindqvist, *A History of Bombing*, 104.

194. Sherry, *The Rise of American Air Power*, 263.

195. Jervis, *The Meaning of the Nuclear Revolution*, 110.

196. Lindqvist, *A History of Bombing*, 104.

197. Howard Zinn, author interview.

198. Zinn, "The Bombing of Royan," *The Zinn Reader*, 269.

199. Howard Zinn, author interview.

200. Zinn, *The Politics of History,* 262.

201. Howard Zinn, author interview.

202. Rumpf, *The Bombing of Germany,* 149.

203. May 7, 1945. See "Act of Military Surrender" in Bernstein and Matusow, *The Truman Administration,* 160.

204. Matthias Griebel, quoted by Alan Cowell, *New York Times,* February 11, 1995.

205. Schaffer, *Wings of Judgment,* 89.

206. Ibid., 103.

207. Dyson, *Disturbing the Universe,* 53.

208. Sherry, *The Rise of American Air Power,* 225.

209. Paul Fussell, "Thank God for the Atomic Bomb," in Bird and Lifschultz, *Hiroshima's Shadow,* 219. Fussell uses this perspective of combat extremity as an easy justification for the atomic bombing of Japanese cities, as well as firebombing in general. As if the berserking of soldiers in and after mortal combat — murdering of prisoners, mutilating of corpses, and so on — is a proper moral standard for the considered policies of a nation.

210. Sherry, *The Rise of American Air Power,* 245.

211. Lindqvist, *A History of Bombing,* 106.

212. Sherry, *The Rise of American Air Power,* 123.

213. Ibid., 115.

214. Ibid., 125.

215. Ibid., 230.

216. Clark, *The Role of the Bomber,* 119. John Buckley argues that Arnold remained committed to precision bombing against Japanese industrial targets, and that LeMay initiated area bombing on his own authority, taking advantage of Arnold's illness. *Air Power in the Age of Total War,* 192.

217. Coffey, *Iron Eagle,* 123.

218. Ibid., 124.

219. Schaffer, *Wings of Judgment,* 125.

220. Buckley, *Air Power in the Age of Total War,* 193.

221. Clark, *Role of the Bomber,* 119.

222. Buckley, *Air Power in the Age of Total War,* 193.

223. Sherry, *The Rise of American Air Power,* 290.

224. Carroll, "Shoah in the News," 8.

225. Sebald, *On the Natural History of Destruction,* 35.

226. Sherry, *The Rise of American Air Power,* 281.

227. Lindqvist, *A History of Bombing,* 109.

228. Pape, *Bombing to Win,* 104. Schaffer puts the figure of civilian dead at 330,000 to 900,000. *Wings of Judgment,* 148. To put these numbers in perspective, consider that U.S. combat fatalities totaled 405,399. Patterson, *Grand Expectations,* 4. John Dower puts the total of Japanese military and civilian dead at 2.7 million. *Embracing Defeat,* 45.

229. Conquest writes in his preface, "We may perhaps put this in perspective in the present case by saying that in the actions here recorded about twenty human lives were lost, not for every word, but every letter, in this book." He puts the terror-famine death toll at 14.5 million. *The Harvest of Sorrow,* 1; 306.

230. Sherry, *The Rise of American Air Power,* 288.

231. Schaffer, *Wings of Judgment,* 132. Many years later, Power would succeed LeMay as the commander of the Strategic Air Command. In a 1960 exchange with a Pentagon civilian who expressed concern about plans for an all-out nuclear strike against the cities of the Soviet Union, Power replied, "Why do you want to restrain ourselves? Restraint! Why are you

so concerned with saving their lives? The whole idea is to kill the bastards . . . At the end of the war, if there are two Americans and one Russian, we win." Janne E. Nolan, *Guardians of the Arsenal*, 258. Fred Kaplan refers to the same anecdote, and adds that the civilian, a RAND theorist named William Kaufman, responded, "Well, you'd better make sure that they're a man and a woman." Kaplan, *Wizards of Armageddon*, 246.

232. Howard Zinn, author interview.

233. Writing in the *Los Angeles Times* six months after his interview with me, McNamara reported that LeMay himself said after the Tokyo bombing, "If we lose the war we'll be tried as war criminals." McNamara commented, "I think he was right. We would have been." *Los Angeles Times*, August 3, 2003. The documentary film *The Fog of War*, directed by Errol Morris and released in the fall of 2003, has McNamara addressing the same subject: "LeMay said if we'd lost the war, we'd all have been tried as war criminals. And I think he's right. He, and I'd say I, were behaving as war criminals. LeMay recognized that what he was doing would be thought immoral if his side had lost. But what makes it immoral if you lose and not immoral if you win?"

234. Lindqvist, *A History of Bombing*, 94.

235. Groves, *Now It Can Be Told*, 283.

236. Coffey, *Iron Eagle*, 176.

237. Ibid., 179. Rather than seeing this as a remarkable admission on LeMay's part, I see it as a bid, in behalf of his bombing raids on Tokyo and other cities, for the primary glory of having delivered the decisive blows against Japan.

238. Sherry, *The Rise of American Air Power*, 330.

239. Schaffer, *Wings of Judgment*, 142. Paul Fussell salutes this conclusion as justified in the context of what those fighting the war suffered. "Why delay and allow one more American high school kid to see his own intestines blown out of his body and spread before him in the dirt while he screams and screams when with the new bomb we can end the whole thing just like that?" "Thank God for the Atomic Bomb," in Bird and Lifschultz, *Hiroshima's Shadow*, 217.

240. Sherry, *The Rise of American Air Power*, 287.

241. Ibid., 254.

242. *Encarta World English Dictionary*.

243. Buckley, *Air Power in the Age of Total War*, 168.

Three. The Cold War Begins

1. Hagerty, *The OSI Story*, 2.

2. Patterson, *Grand Expectations*, 32.

3. I provide a full account of my father's career as an FBI agent turned general in *An American Requiem*.

4. Rogow, *Victim of Duty*, 109.

5. Borklund, *Men of the Pentagon*, 11.

6. As the narrative will show, Forrestal would be defeated by the powerlessness of his position as secretary, but this shortfall in the authority of the secretary of defense would be made up for with the passage of amendments to the National Security Act, in August 1949, giving the secretary of defense clear authority over the service secretaries. It was then, for example, that the secretaries of the Army and Navy were dropped from the president's cabinet. But by then Forrestal would be dead.

7. "Atomic bombing," according to a Bell Telephone Laboratories study of 1946, "was ten to 100 times less expensive" than conventional bombing, with losses to the enemy "40 to 600 times greater than the cost of inflicting the loss." Yergin, *Shattered Peace*, 267.

8. Recall that Bard had issued the lone dissent from the decision of the Interim Committee to use the bomb against an industrial target surrounded by workers' houses. Hoopes and Brinkley, *Driven Patriot*, 212.

9. Meilinger, *Hoyt S. Vandenberg*, 125.

10. "In February 1947, the dollar value of all [aircraft] industry shipments totaled $52 million — of which the military accounted for $42 million." Yergin, *Shattered Peace*, 268.

11. Woodward, *The Commanders*, 74.

12. Stimson and Bundy, *On Active Service in Peace and War*, 632–33.

13. Referring to an intervention of Stimson's at the May 31 meeting of the Interim Committee, Oppenheimer wrote that Stimson emphasized "the appalling lack of conscience and compassion that the war had brought about . . . the complacency, the indifference, and the silence with which we greeted the mass bombings of Hamburg, of Dresden, of Tokyo . . . Colonel Stimson felt that, as far as degradation went, we had had it." Yet that was the meeting at which it was decided to drop the atomic bomb on a target "surrounded by workers' houses," to which Stimson assented. Bird and Lifschultz, *Hiroshima's Shadow*, liv. See also Rhodes, *The Making of the Atomic Bomb*, 647.

14. Stimson's connection with the first decisions about the atomic project were decisive, well before he appointed Groves to oversee the Manhattan Project. "In the fall of 1941 President Roosevelt had put him on a committee to consider the military employment of nuclear fission, and after May 1, 1943, he served as the President's senior adviser in that field." Current, *Secretary Stimson*, 229. Another biographer says that Stimson first learned of the atomic bomb project on November 6, 1941. Morison, *Turmoil and Tradition*, 614.

15. Stimson and Bundy, *On Active Service in Peace and War*, 642. The idea of sharing the atomic secret with the Soviet Union as a way of heading off an arms race went back to the Danish physicist Niels Bohr, who proposed it to Washington and London both in 1943. Sherwin and Bird, *American Prometheus*, 263.

16. "Stimson Memo on the A-Bomb," in Stimson, "The Decision to Use the Atomic Bomb," 99. Truman's taking his lead from Stimson here is far from inconceivable; he had just done the very thing in following Stimson's advice on the charged question of what to do with Nazi war criminals. Stimson was one of the few who advocated fair trials for them.

17. Stimson and Bundy, *On Active Service in Peace and War*, 646.

18. Stimson diary, September 4, 1945. Hodgson, *The Colonel*, 352.

19. Stimson and Bundy, *On Active Service in Peace and War*, 642–45. Stimson was supported in this view that the risk was necessary. That a comprehensive agreement with the Soviet Union was urgent was communicated to Stimson on August 17, 1945, by "the laboratory leaders of the Manhattan Project . . . But they wrote in secret to the U.S. secretary of war, and their views remained hidden for many years." Morrison, "Recollections of a Nuclear War," 32. This scientists' proposal effectively echoed what Niels Bohr had been pressing on Roosevelt before his death. Those who had thought about it, in other words, saw a system of international control as mandatory. Helping Stimson in drafting the September 11 memo was John McCloy, assistant secretary of war. Stimson's words about trusting an untrustworthy man are displayed at the entrance of the Stimson Center, an arms control think tank in Washington.

20. Hodgson, *The Colonel*, 344.

21. Leffler, "The Cold War," 516. The German Socialists (Social Democratic Party) hated the Communists, and from 1919 to 1933, they refused to form an alliance, preferring to have a weak but pure Socialist Party. The Communists in Germany, who took orders from Moscow, reciprocated this antipathy.

22. As recently as at Potsdam, Stimson had argued against "sharing the atomic bomb with Russia while she was still a police state." He acknowledged as much in his September 11

cover letter to Truman, but indicated his change of mind: "I have become convinced that any demand by us for an internal change in Russia as a condition of sharing the atomic weapon would be so resented that it would make the objective we have in view less probable." Stimson and Bundy, *On Active Service in Peace and War*, 642.

23. The Mexico-Munich contrast appears in Yergin, *Shattered Peace*, 80. Yergin cites Stimson: "Some Americans are anxious to hang on to exaggerated views of the Monroe Doctrine and at the same time bite into every question that comes up in Central Europe." Melvyn Leffler comments, "The president and his advisers expected the men in the Kremlin to interpret American behavior as Americans intended it. They were unwilling, however, to accept Soviet explanations of Russian behavior, even when the latter's actions resembled those of the United States." *A Preponderance of Power*, 98.

24. Hodgson, *The Colonel*, 360.

25. Millis, *The Forrestal Diaries*, 95.

26. Yergin, *Shattered Peace*, 133. Supporting Forrestal's position at this meeting were Attorney General Tom Clark, Treasury Secretary Fred Vinson, Agriculture Secretary Clinton Anderson, and the head of war mobilization, John Snyder. Hoopes and Brinkley, *Driven Patriot*, 285.

27. Morison, *Turmoil and Tradition*, 642. On September 22, 1945, a front-page headline in the *New York Times* declared, "Plea to Give Soviet Atom Secret Stirs Debate in Cabinet." The subheadline read, "No Decision Made on Wallace Plan to Share Bomb Data as Peace Insurance." And a sub-subheadline read, with eloquent understatement, "Armed Forces Opposed." Bundy, *Danger and Survival*, 139.

28. Catholics had good reason to oppose Communism. "The Russians and their allies in eastern Europe were vigorously repressing the Church and killing Catholics . . . If Communists triumphed in Italy and elsewhere, believers would be repressed and killed." Levering et al., *Debating the Origins of the Cold War*, 45.

29. Rogow, *Victim of Duty*, 115, 121.

30. "The Red Army suffered fifty-five times more casualties than did U.S. forces, and inflicted 93% of German combat losses during the three year period between Barbarossa (June 22, 1941) and D Day (June 6, 1944)." Levering et al., *Debating the Origins of the Cold War*, 92.

31. The Big Three conference at Yalta took place from February 3 to February 11, 1945. Roosevelt, Stalin, and Churchill agreed to some kind of Soviet sphere of influence in Eastern Europe and Asia, in return for a Soviet commitment to enter the war against Japan. Roosevelt's concessions here would be a point of contention among anti-Communist critics after the war.

32. Yergin, *Shattered Peace*, 68.

33. Ibid., 81.

34. Sherwin, *A World Destroyed*, 140. The subject of the meeting was Poland, and Molotov claimed the Soviets were acting in accord with agreements, which was, in fact, essentially how Stimson saw it. But not Truman. "I just gave him a straight one-two to the jaw," Truman later told an aide. Molotov protested to Truman, "I have never been talked to like that in my life." To which Truman replied, "Carry out your agreements and you won't be talked to like that." James T. Patterson calls this "one of the most fabled of Cold War contacts" (*Grand Expectations*, 106), and notes its being recounted by Stephen Ambrose, William Chafe, John Gaddis, and Michael Lacey. The anecdote also appears in Yergin, *Shattered Peace*, 82; Wolfe, *The Rise and Fall of the "Soviet Threat"*, 10; McCullough, *Truman*, 376; and Levering et al., *Debating the Origins of the Cold War*, 31. The latter reports that Averell Harriman noted that "Truman's behavior gave Molotov the excuse to tell Stalin that Roosevelt's policy was being abandoned. I regretted that Truman gave him that opportunity."

35. Reported by Charles E. Bohlen in Williams, *The Tragedy of American Diplomacy*, 203.

36. Millis, *The Forrestal Diaries*, 493.

37. Ibid., 97.

38. Chase, "After Hiroshima."

39. Clarfield and Wiecek, *Nuclear America*, 90.

40. Stimson and Bundy, *On Active Service in Peace and War*, 642. There were important differences between the Acheson-Lilienthal and Baruch plans, with the latter, unlike the former, not really aiming at Soviet agreement. But both assumed major internal change in the USSR, and so neither one was ever likely to draw Soviet approval.

41. Williams, *The Tragedy of American Diplomacy*, 263.

42. Sherwin and Bird, *American Prometheus*, 339.

43. Yergin, *Shattered Peace*, 123.

44. "Byrnes Report on Council of Foreign Ministers," in Bernstein and Matusow, *The Truman Administration*, 190.

45. Yergin, *Shattered Peace*, 127.

46. Franklin Lindsay, author interview.

47. "Justice William O. Douglas, an otherwise sensible man, told Forrestal the speech was tantamount to 'the declaration of World War III.'" Hoopes and Brinkley, *Driven Patriot*, 255. But in fact the war that Stalin predicted, following Marxist-Leninist theory, was one between capitalist nations, not between the Soviet Union and the United States. Levering et al., *Debating the Origins of the Cold War*, 38.

48. Churchill had used the words "an Iron Curtain is drawn down upon their front from Stettin to Triest" in a cable to Washington on May 12, 1945, within days of the German surrender. Hodgson, *America in Our Time*, 27.

49. A report of the Senate committee charged with oversight of the Baruch proposals stated: "The plan does not require that the United States shall discontinue such manufacture [of the bomb] either upon the proposal of the plan or upon the inauguration of the international agency. At some point in the development that is required." But what that point was to be, the plan did not say. Williams, *The Tragedy of American Diplomacy*, 263.

50. Leffler, *A Preponderance of Power*, 116.

51. Yergin, *Shattered Peace*, 266.

52. Franklin Lindsay, author interview.

53. Ibid.

54. Norris, *Racing for the Bomb*, 472. See also Schell, "The Case Against the War," 14.

55. Office of the Historian, *SAC Missile Chronology*, 3. Germany had developed the V-2 during World War II, but the missile age really began with liquid fuel. (The first, primitive liquid-propellant rocket was launched by Robert Goddard in 1926.) Ironically, the scientists who presided over the new martial technology were inclined to slow the momentum over which they presided, hence Philip Morrison's intervention with Stimson on August 17. Morrison commented, in his interview with me, "The scientists of the Manhattan Project were, broadly speaking, enlightenment figures who believed, as I did, that reason and prudent conciliation would one day lead to international control. Well, that day has not yet come. The generals' narrower views have so far won out."

56. On October 11, a newspaper headline summed up a Truman press conference: "U.S. Will Not Share Atom Bomb Secret, President Asserts." Truman was asked if that meant "that the armaments race is on." To which he replied, "Yes." Yergin, *Shattered Peace*, 140.

57. Sherwin and Bird, *American Prometheus*, 325.

58. Sherry, *The Rise of American Air Power*, 349: "It was Stimson's finest hour, but his eloquence went unheeded. As with most of the protesting scientists before Hiroshima and with Eisenhower in July, the distance from power that provided Stimson perspective also limited his persuasiveness and influence." Finest hour, perhaps, but Stimson's remarkable initiative is all but forgotten outside the closed world of scholars. In interviews for this

book, I asked both Arthur Schlesinger, Jr., and Robert McNamara what they recalled of the discussion of Stimson's September 11 proposal, and neither had ever heard of it.

59. As of this writing, there have been twenty secretaries, with Donald Rumsfeld serving twice.

60. Borklund, *Men of the Pentagon*, 45.

61. Millis, *Forrestal Diaries*, 555. As to "teeming," only a minority of Pentagon workers would actually have passed by Forrestal's bust, since most enter and exit the building from subway and bus tunnels or from parking lot entrances.

62. Simpson, *The Death of James Forrestal*, 19.

63. Arthur Schlesinger, Jr., author interview.

64. Arthur Schlesinger, Jr., in an interview with the author, was the first I knew of to make this comparison. Others compared him to tragic figures out of Theodore Dreiser or Ernest Hemingway. See Rogow, *Victim of Duty*, 289. In fact, both John O'Hara and John Dos Passos "wrote novels whose central figures were modeled on Forrestal." Hoopes and Brinkley, *Driven Patriot*, 472.

65. The friend was George Kennan. "He had, I thought, something of the ambitious tightness of the parvenu. He smacked a bit of F. Scott Fitzgerald. There was lacking, it seemed to me, the relaxation and languor of the securely well-born." Quoted in Hoopes and Brinkley, *Driven Patriot*, 274.

66. Fitzgerald, *The Great Gatsby*, 48.

67. Hoopes and Brinkley, *Driven Patriot*, 132.

68. Yergin, *Shattered Peace*, 220. For a summary of the historians' debates over the Cold War's origins, see Leffler, "The Cold War."

69. Some historians even argue whether the Cold War has actually ended. Chalmers Johnson says it has ended only in Europe, with Cold War dynamics still defining politics in Asia. *The Sorrows of Empire*, chapter 1. See also Schrecker, *Cold War Triumphalism*.

70. Leffler, "The Cold War," 501.

71. Eisenhower, *Crusade in Europe*.

72. John Lewis Gaddis is a historian for whom good and evil remain the relevant framework in which to understand the Cold War. This understanding had its political expression in Harry Truman at the beginning of the Cold War and in Ronald Reagan at the end.

73. Hixon, *George F. Kennan*, 11.

74. Kennan, "Telegraphic Message of February 22, 1946," *Memoirs*, 557.

75. "Neither Stalin's speech nor his actions were as threatening as some U.S. officials thought they were . . . [It was] no more threatening than Truman's Navy Day address the previous October." Leffler, *A Preponderance of Power*, 103, 107.

76. Kennan, "Telegraphic Message," *Memoirs*, 557.

77. Hoopes and Brinkley, *Driven Patriot*, 281.

78. Hixson, *George F. Kennan*, 3.

79. It is notable that after the collapse of his Foreign Service career, Kennan would be rescued back to Princeton by another ingenious misfit, J. Robert Oppenheimer.

80. Kennan, *Memoirs*, 16.

81. From early in the twentieth century until World War II, Princeton would supply more candidates to Protestant foreign missions than any other American college except Oberlin. David Hollinger, author interview.

82. Leffler, *A Preponderance of Power*, 109.

83. Kennan, *Memoirs*, 295.

84. Kennan, "The Sources of Soviet Conduct," 96.

85. Costigliola, "'Unceasing Pressure for Penetration,'" 1323.

86. Kennan, "The Sources of Soviet Conduct," 99.

87. Robert Donovan, cited in Hoopes and Brinkley, *Driven Patriot*, 272.

88. Manchester, *The Glory and the Dream*, 438.

89. "The Secretary of the Navy, Mr. James Forrestal, had it reproduced and evidently made it required reading for hundreds, if not thousands, of higher officers in the armed services . . . My reputation was made. My voice now carried." Kennan, *Memoirs*, 195.

90. Costigliola, "'Unceasing Pressure for Penetration,'" 1333.

91. Kennan, "Telegraphic Message," *Memoirs*, 557.

92. Leffler, *A Preponderance of Power*, 7.

93. Hoopes and Brinkley, *Driven Patriot*, the title of chapter 21.

94. Kennan, *Memoirs*, 359.

95. Manchester, *The Glory and the Dream*, 436.

96. Hoopes and Brinkley, *Driven Patriot*, 290.

97. John Kenneth Galbraith, author interview; Parker, *John Kenneth Galbraith*, 212–13.

98. Parker, *John Kenneth Galbraith*, 213.

99. "American Relations with the Soviet Union: A Report to the President by the Special Counsel to the President" (September 24, 1946), in Etzold and Gaddis, *Containment*, 64.

100. Leffler, *A Preponderance of Power*, 138.

101. Parker, *John Kenneth Galbraith*, 216.

102. Hixson, *George F. Kennan*, 35.

103. In 1949, a few months before the Soviet Union exploded its first atomic bomb, Kennan dismissed all arms control negotiations with Moscow as "useless and misleading." He looked forward to a continued American monopoly. Ibid., 38.

104. Levering et al., *Debating the Origins of the Cold War*, 130.

105. Yergin, *Shattered Peace*, 245, 255.

106. Hoopes and Brinkley, *Driven Patriot*, 280. Not even Lenin considered his philosophy "implacable and unchanging." He approved Nikolai Bukharin's New Economic Policy in the 1920s.

107. Arthur Schlesinger, Jr., author interview.

108. Kennan, *Memoirs*, 365–66.

109. Schlesinger, *A Life in the Twentieth Century*, 514. George Orwell's novel *1984* was published in 1949; Hannah Arendt's masterwork, *The Origins of Totalitarianism*, was published in 1951.

110. Here, for example, is how the editor of Forrestal's *Diaries* explains his thinking in 1946: "It is clear that from this time on he felt increasingly that policy could not be founded on the assumption that a peaceful solution of the Russian problem would be possible." Millis, *The Forrestal Diaries*, 135.

111. Hoopes and Brinkley, *Driven Patriot*, 281.

112. Millis, *The Forrestal Diaries*, 299.

113. Williams, *The Tragedy of American Diplomacy*, 240.

114. Leffler, *A Preponderance of Power*, 228.

115. *Encarta World English Dictionary*.

116. See Hofstadter, *The Paranoid Style in American Politics*.

117. "Harry S. Truman Speech to Congress, March 12, 1947," in Levering et al., *Debating the Origins of the Cold* War, 82. See also Freeland, *The Truman Doctrine*, 85–86.

118. LaFeber, *America, Russia, and the Cold War*, 55.

119. www.hpol.org/marshall.

120. Richard Holbrooke, in a speech at the Orion Foundation, in Stavanger, Norway, June 6, 1997, gave the well-known Truman quote as "two sides of the same coin."

121. Freeland, *The Truman Doctrine*, 100. Besides marking the launching of major U.S. aid to Europe, the Truman Doctrine speech was a milestone for three additional reasons: it used the fear of Communism as a political and economic goad to Congress; it made a suc-

cessful presidential demand for unprecedented power; it sanctioned American intervention in another country's civil war. LaFeber, *America, Russia, and the Cold War*, 62.

122. Freeland, *The Truman Doctrine*, 101.

123. "Executive Order on Loyalty," in Bernstein and Matusow, *The Truman Administration*, 358.

124. Hodgson, *America in Our Time*, 94.

125. He made this charge at a cabinet meeting on February 7, 1947. Freeland, *The Truman Doctrine*, 140.

126. Leffler, *A Preponderance of Power*, 14.

127. In November 1947, Clark Clifford drafted a memo to Truman that read, "There is considerable advantage to the Administration in its battle with the Kremlin . . . The nation is already united behind the president . . . The worse matters get, up to a fairly certain point — real danger of imminent war — the more there is a sense of crisis. In times of crisis, the American citizen tends to back up his president." Freeland, *The Truman Doctrine*, 192.

128. Borklund, *Men of the Pentagon*, 48.

129. Meilinger, *Hoyt S. Vandenberg*, 125.

130. Borklund, *Men of the Pentagon*, 51.

131. Meilinger, *Hoyt S. Vandenberg*, 128.

132. "Twelve ministers representing the National Socialist People's and Slovak Democratic parties resigned from the Czech government. Their departure allowed the Communists to take control of the government legally . . . Before 20 February, Czechoslovakia was a pluralist democratic state supportive of Soviet foreign policy yet knitted to the West economically; by 1 March, it had become a Communist dictatorship, a symbol of the fate that awaited any country that accepted Communists into coalition governments." Leffler, *A Preponderance of Power*, 205.

133. Millis, *The Forrestal Diaries*, 387.

134. Parker, *John Kenneth Galbraith*, 211.

135. Rogow, *Victim of Duty*, 304.

136. Millis, *The Forrestal Diaries*, 393.

137. Ibid., 395.

138. Freeland, *The Truman Doctrine*, 271.

139. Ibid.

140. Hixson, *George F. Kennan*, 75.

141. Hoopes and Brinkley, *Driven Patriot*, 374.

142. Freeland, *The Truman Doctrine*, 286.

143. Leffler, *A Preponderance of Power*, 131. But John Lewis Gaddis argues that the American role in relation to Germany was reactive, not initiating, as if Germany's partition were mainly Moscow's doing, not Washington's. Gaddis, *We Now Know*.

144. Rhine-Main Air Force Base was decommissioned as a U.S. base and returned to Germany in October 2005.

145. Coffey, *Iron Eagle*, 263.

146. Ibid., 269.

147. Ibid., 265. The war plan proposed the use of fifty atomic bombs, the entire arsenal at the time, against twenty cities in the USSR. Rosenberg, "American Atomic Strategy," 68.

148. Millis, *The Forrestal Diaries*, 538.

149. Leffler, *A Preponderance of Power*, 226.

150. Nolan, *Guardians of the Arsenal*, 38.

151. The Strategic Air Command was created in 1946, headquartered at Andrews Air Force Base in Maryland. Shortly after LeMay's arrival, SAC moved its headquarters to the then far less vulnerable Omaha, Nebraska. Offutt Field had originally been established as Camp Crook in 1888, a post for fighting Indians. Coffey, *Iron Eagle*, 275.

152. Hixson, *George F. Kennan*, 80.

153. Millis, *The Forrestal Diaries*, 463.

154. Hoopes and Brinkley, *Driven Patriot*, 382.

155. Millis, *The Forrestal Diaries*, 494.

156. Ibid., 538.

157. At $15 billion, Truman's limit represented one third of the federal budget. He would keep refusing increases until the outbreak of the Korean War, which effectively retired the very idea of a military budget ceiling. Ironically, Truman's determination to keep the military budget low led to the military's reliance on atomic bombs, not only because such weapons represented an alternative to a huge conventional army, but also because such weapons production was part of the Atomic Energy Commission's budget, not the Pentagon's. Rosenberg, "American Atomic Strategy," 71.

158. Millis, *The Forrestal Diaries*, 544.

159. McCullough, *Truman*, 738.

160. Millis, *The Forrestal Diaries*, 552.

161. Hoopes and Brinkley, *Driven Patriot*, 445.

162. Rogow, *Victim of Duty*, 3.

163. Such talk of Jews always seems insane, but reports surfaced much later that Israeli officials (if not agents) *had* monitored Forrestal, because his positions on the Middle East, mainly anti-Israel, were so influential. Just because you're paranoid . . .

164. McCullough, *Truman*, 739.

165. Ibid. Drew Pearson was the source of this report. His previous vilifications of Forrestal make the report unreliable, but Forrestal's mental illness definitely included delusions that the Soviets had invaded the United States. See also Hoopes and Brinkley, *Driven Patriot*, 451, 455.

166. Hoopes and Brinkley, *Driven Patriot*, 454.

167. Simpson, *The Death of James Forrestal*, 85. Monsignor Maurice S. Sheehy was turned away by Forrestal's doctors seven times in the last weeks of his life.

168. Ibid. Cornell Simpson's book vents the theory that Forrestal's fears were not imagined, and that he was in fact murdered by the Soviets, as Jan Masaryk was assumed to have been a little over a year before. The theory gave the word "defenestration" currency.

169. Hoopes and Brinkley, *Driven Patriot*, 475.

170. Hixson, *George F. Kennan*. After Forrestal's death, Kennan resigned his government position in 1950, repudiated the militarization of containment, criticized NATO, rejected the U.S. decision to pursue the H-bomb, saw the domino theory as folly, mocked the idea that containment applied to Asia, condemned the arms race, and eventually repudiated the Reagan-era assumption that U.S. martial resolve had "won" the Cold War. At the age of ninety-eight, in 2002, Kennan criticized the Bush administration's national security posture and called congressional Democrats "shabby and shameful" for affirming the Bush war in Iraq. *Hill Profile*, September 26, 2002.

171. Rogow, *Victim of Duty*, 9.

172. Simpson, *The Death of James Forrestal*, 13. In an odd echo of this event, President George W. Bush's nominee to become secretary of the Navy, Colin McMillan, killed himself with a gunshot to the head in 2003. "Bush's Navy Nominee Is an Apparent Suicide," *Boston Globe*, July 26, 2003, A2.

173. Rogow, *Victim of Duty*, 18.

174. Meilinger, *Hoyt S. Vandenberg*, 130.

175. McCullogh, *Truman*, 741. About the impolitic new secretary of defense, General Bradley, the Army chief, said, "Unwittingly, Truman has replaced one mental case with another" (742).

176. Kaplan, *Wizards of Armageddon*, 38.

177. Perry, *Four Stars*, 18.

178. "Square miles — that's all he [LeMay] could hit, and he figured if he hit enough of them, that would do the trick." Kaplan, *Wizards of Armageddon*, 43.

179. Leffler, *A Preponderance of Power*, 274.

180. *Congressional Record*, May 26, 1949.

181. Later, the MX missile would be called the Peacekeeper.

182. Lindqvist, *A History of Bombing*, 120.

183. Hagerty, *The OSI Story*, 47.

184. Schaffer, *Wings of Judgment*,

185. Meilinger, *Hoyt S. Vandenberg*, 240.

186. Dante E. Guazzo was a first-generation OSI agent who worked closely with my father. In a telephone interview in 2002, Guazzo, then eighty-seven, told me that he once accompanied my father to a House Appropriations Committee hearing in the early 1950s, during the McCarthy period. "We went up to the Hill. A Republican congressman of Kansas was chairman. He asked the questions. But there was another congressman off to the side. He was gnawing on a toothpick. His feet were on a wastepaper basket. He interrupted: 'General, I want to know what you are doing to keep Communists out of the Air Force.' Your father looked at him so cool, answered him so calmly. 'Mr. Congressman, I am going to answer the chairman's question first. Then I will be glad to answer any question you have.' Your father was his own man."

187. Remarks by Lieutenant General Joseph F. Carroll, USAF (Ret.), at the AFOSI Worldwide Commanders' Conference, 1978, recorded by Captain Joseph Corfield. Office of the OSI Historian, Andrews Air Force Base, Maryland.

188. Hagerty, *The OSI Story*, 47. I wrote an account of my father's role in this case in *An American Requiem*. I depended there on the memory of one of my father's associates, "Keefe" O'Keefe. Here I depend on Air Force and congressional sources, as indicated.

189. Hagerty, *The OSI Story*, 48.

190. "Investigation of the B-36 Bomber Program," Committee on Armed Services, House of Representatives, 81st Congress (Washington: Government Printing Office, 1949), 215.

191. Ibid., 220.

192. Ibid., 232.

193. Ibid., 503.

194. Hagerty, *The OSI Story*, 48.

195. *Newsweek*, August 29, 1949.

196. "Investigation of the B-36," 506.

197. Ibid., 655.

198. The strategic rivalry between the Navy and the Air Force would be reborn with the advent of the Polaris, a submarine-launched ICBM that would prove far less vulnerable than bombers or land-based missiles. And because the Polaris was far less accurate than land-based Air Force missiles, it put the Navy even more squarely in the business of indiscriminate targeting of cities. So much for the Navy's superior morality.

199. Hagerty, *The OSI Story*, 48. Two years later, in a signal of my father's acceptance, the Air Force sponsored special legislation to "regularize" his commission, bringing him in from the Reserves as a major general. In testimony before the House Armed Services Committee on July 27, 1951, the secretary of the Air Force, Thomas K. Finletter, said, "In short, my case for General Carroll rests on the fact that we have no one to replace him . . . We think of him as the Mr. Hoover of the Air Force." Kilday subcommittee hearing on HR 4692, Committee on Armed Services, House of Representatives.

200. Hagerty, *The OSI Story*, 48.

201. As we saw, on September 23, 1949, Groves predicted that the Soviet Union would

not have the atomic bomb for "ten to twenty years." That very day, Truman announced that they already had it. Lawren, *The General and the Bomb*, 267; Norris, *Racing for the Bomb*, 475–77. On September 20, just before scientists completed an analysis of radioactivity detected in Siberia, the CIA issued a report saying that the USSR would acquire the bomb in 1953. *New York Times*, May 11, 2003, A4.

202. When the Soviet A-bomb test succeeded, Vannevar Bush was about to publish a book that said of the prospect for such an event, "Opinion now indicates a longer time than it did just after the war." The Soviets, he said, lack "the resourcefulness of free men, and regimentation is ill-adapted to unconventional efforts." Bush, *Modern Arms and Free Men*, 90, 96–97; also cited in Freedman, *Evolution of Nuclear Strategy*, 28.

Four. Self-Fulfilling Paranoia

1. www.gwu.edu/-nsarchiv/coldwar/documents/episode-1/kennan.htm. For a history of Russian paranoia going back to the czars, see Pipes, *Russia Under the Old Regime*.

2. Poe, *The Russian Moment in World History*, 65.

3. Pipes, *Russia Under the Old Regime*, 338–40.

4. Poe, *The Russian Moment in World History*, 65.

5. John Lewis Gaddis (*We Now Know, The Long Peace*, etc.) is one historian who emphasizes Stalin's malevolence as the overriding cause of the Cold War. The field of Cold War history is contentious. Such figures as Robert Conquest and Richard Pipes see the USSR as a monolithic tyranny in which even small decisions were made by Stalin, whose crimes were monumental. Historians like Sheila Fitzpatrick, Robert Thurston, and Melvyn Leffler, without deemphasizing Stalin's brutality, also give importance to social forces and the complexities of postwar life, and see the regime's violence in a broader context.

6. "Both America and Russia were powerful militarily and expansionist for security and ideological reasons, and each stood firm for its vision of the postwar world. But there the similarities largely ended." Levering et al., *Debating the Origins of the Cold War*, 25.

7. Hoover's polemic against Communism had its religious component. "The danger of Communism in America," he wrote in 1953, "lies not in the fact that it is a political philosophy but in the awesome fact that it is a materialistic religion, inflaming in its adherents a destructive fanaticism. Communism is secularism on the march. It is a mortal foe of Christianity . . . The two cannot live side by side." Quoted by Whitfield, *The Culture of the Cold War*, 85.

8. O'Carroll, *Pius XII*, 154.

9. The pope's decree condemned not only joining the Communist Party but "showing favor" to it. It was forbidden to contribute to any journal that "supported Communist teaching of action." Ibid., 159.

10. The image is Osip Mandelstam's. His poem comparing Stalin's mustache to a cockroach was part of what got Mandelstam arrested and sent to the gulag, where he died in 1938.

11. Amis, *Koba the Dread*, 57. Amis is not usually a source for historical information, but as a novelist he grasps the importance of details such as the stench radiating from corpses.

12. The question of the number of children who died in Ukraine is subject to debate, but Robert Conquest puts the number of children killed between 1932 and 1934 at four million. *The Harvest of Sorrow*, 297.

13. Conquest, *Stalin*, 315.

14. Martin Amis observes that even the name of the state was false: "Union was a lie, and Soviet was a lie, and Socialist was a lie, and Republic was a lie. *Comrade* was a lie. The Revolution was a lie." *Koba the Dread*, 258.

15. Conquest, *Stalin*, 321.

16. Gaddis et al., *Cold War Statesmen Confront the Bomb*, 41.

17. Melvyn Leffler, "Inside Enemy Archives: The Cold War Reopened," *Foreign Affairs*, Summer 1996.

18. Mastny, *The Cold War and Soviet Insecurity*, 21. Another post-Soviet Russian assessment is even more unequivocal: "Stalin, notwithstanding his reputation as a ruthless tyrant, was not prepared to take a course of unbridled expansionism after World War II. He wanted to avoid confrontation with the West. He was even ready to see cooperation with the Western powers as a preferable way of building his influence and solving contentious international issues. Thus, the Cold War was not his choice or his brainchild." Zubok and Pleshakov, *Inside the Kremlin's Cold War*, 276.

19. Sherwin and Bird, *American Prometheus*, 446. For transportation, fully half the Red Army units depended on horse-drawn vehicles, and would continue to do so until around 1950. LaFeber, *America, Russia, and the Cold War*, 31.

20. The success of Stalin's armies depended on his willingness to let hundreds of thousands of his soldiers die in full frontal attacks, something Eisenhower refused to accept for his own men, which was a source of conflict between the Allies of East and West. Lisa Szefel, correspondence with the author.

21. Gaddis et al., *Cold War Statesmen Confront the Bomb*, 44; Holloway, *The Soviet Union and the Arms Race*, 19.

22. Isaacson and Thomas, *Wise Men*, 342.

23. On October 18, 1945, Beria's NKVD received from Fuchs designs of the plutonium bomb that was dropped on Nagasaki. Soviet physicists developed a version of that bomb, but they also developed one of their own design. Gaddis et al., *Cold War Statesmen Confront the Bomb*, 45, 48. See also Holloway, *Stalin and the Bomb*, 107–8.

24. Gaddis et al., *Cold War Statesmen Confront the Bomb*, 42.

25. Bundy, *Danger and Survival*, 176.

26. Ibid.

27. The ready assertion that the Soviets would have rejected any and all postwar American gestures of conciliation ignores the fluidity of history, how difficult it is to anticipate the future or to define a future that might have been. One of Stalin's most hard-line successors, former KGB head Yuri Andropov, for example, enabled the arrival of his successor, Mikhail Gorbachev, who, against all expectations, ended the Cold War.

28. Gaddis et al., *Cold War Statesmen Confront the Bomb*, 51.

29. Isaacson and Thomas, *Wise Men*, 343.

30. Groves said, for example, in late 1945, "If we were truly realistic instead of idealistic, as we appear to be, we would not permit any foreign power with which we are not firmly allied, and in which we do not have substantial confidence, to make or possess atomic weapons. If such a country started to make atomic weapons we would destroy its capacity to make them before it has progressed far enough to threaten us." Schell, "The Case Against the War," 14.

31. Isaacson and Thomas, *Wise Men*, 34.

32. Gaddis et al., *Cold War Statesmen Confront the Bomb*, 60.

33. Isaacs and Downing, *Cold War*, 75. NSC-30 also enunciated the principle that the United States should never give the Soviet Union reason to believe it would not use nuclear weapons against them.

34. Rosenberg, "The Origins of Overkill," 11. The stockpile grew from two bombs in late 1945, to nine in mid-1946, to thirteen in mid-1947, to fifty in mid-1948 (14).

35. LeMay, *Mission with LeMay*, 497.

36. Broiler would involve attacks on twenty-four Soviet cities with thirty-four atomic bombs. Subsequent LeMay-inspired atomic war plans in the late 1940s were called Frolic, Halfmoon, and Trojan, each adding more bombs and more cities. Rosenberg, "The Origins of Overkill," 16.

37. Gaddis et al., *Cold War Statesmen Confront the Bomb*, 2.

38. Lebow and Stein, "Deterrence and the Cold War," 180.

39. Pearl Harbor, as a defining trauma, had involved the deaths of 2,400 Americans. The Russian equivalent, the Nazi war on Soviet soil, had involved the deaths of millions. Melvyn Leffler observes that for American historians, like John Lewis Gaddis, who emphasize Pearl Harbor as the background to U.S. concerns about Moscow, "the Japanese attack left an indelible imprint on post-war conceptions of American national security, but the war apparently had little impact on the Kremlin." Leffler, "The Cold War," 513.

40. Snead, *The Gaither Committee*, 32. Whether estimates of Soviet strength in the late 1940s and early 1950s were exaggerated in Washington is still debated. Ernest May is one of those who believes they were not exaggerated. Writing in 1992, he commented, "Evidence of a big Soviet military build-up steadily accumulated after 1945. By 1950 the best intelligence possessed by the U.S. government indicated that the Soviets had 175 divisions, very large and rapidly improving tactical air forces, several hundred bombers on the model of the B-29 . . . and over three hundred submarines . . . Some of the estimates of Soviet military forces seemed later to have been too high. Scholars have charged that the American military deliberately exaggerated Soviet capabilities so as to improve chances of getting money. These charges do not withstand scrutiny." "U.S. Government, Legacy of the Cold War," in Hogan, *The End of the Cold War*, 221.

41. Sherwin and Bird, *American Prometheus*, 411.

42. Writing in 1989, John Newhouse, a disarmament specialist, called Truman's decision to build the H-bomb "the most significant taken by any recent President." *War and Peace in the Nuclear Age*, 10.

43. "General Advisory Committee's Majority and Minority Reports on Building the H-Bomb," www.pbs.org/wgbh/amex/bomb/filmmore/reference/primary/extractsofgeneral .html. Oppenheimer's decisive role in opposing the H-bomb, and Teller, would lead to the disloyalty charges brought against him in 1953. See *In the Matter of J. Robert Oppenheimer: Transcript of Hearing Before Personnel Security Board and Texts of Principal Documents and Letters* (Cambridge: MIT Press, 1971).

44. McCullough, *Truman*, 749.

45. For this discussion of the controversy over the H-bomb I depend in part on McCullough, *Truman*, 754–64. David Alan Rosenberg's treatment of the history is somewhat more complex. He points out that the JCS regarded the extreme explosive power of the hydrogen bomb as being useful on relatively few targets; a Nagasaki-type bomb was big enough for most. Rosenberg also points out that Truman had been kept in the dark on nuclear issues, including the size of the atomic stockpile. For Truman, despite what the scientists were saying, the defining line had apparently already been crossed, with the decisions first to build and use the atomic bomb, and then to authorize the expansion of the arsenal. "American Atomic Strategy," 66, 81–84.

46. Bundy, *Danger and Survival*, 141.

47. Isaacson and Thomas, *Wise Men*, 362. "You know, I listened as carefully as I knew how," Acheson said in reference to Oppenheimer's argument against the H-bomb, "but I don't understand what Oppie was trying to say. How can you persuade a paranoid adversary to disarm 'by example'?" Sherwin and Bird, *American Prometheus*, 418.

48. Isaacson and Thomas, *Wise Men*, 488.

49. Kennan, *Memoirs*, 473.

50. Isaacson and Thomas, *Wise Men*, 489. Acheson said, "George, if you persist in your view on this matter, you should resign from the Foreign Service, assume a monk's habit, carry a tin cup and stand on the street corner and say, 'The end of the world is nigh.'" Sherwin and Bird, *American Prometheus*, 421. The Joint Chiefs of Staff, too, warned against the invoking of morality on the question of the hydrogen bomb, arguing — rightly, I would

say — that rejection of such a weapon on moral grounds would inevitably raise moral questions about the atomic bomb. Rosenberg, "American Atomic Strategy," 82.

51. Gaddis, in noting the difference between Kennan and Nitze, points out that they always agreed on the ends of containment, if not on the means of obtaining it: "the restriction of Soviet influence within the boundaries of the USSR." Gaddis uses the phrase "Kennan-Nitze strategy of containment." *The United States and the End of the Cold War,* 27, 42.

52. Nitze was married to Phyllis Pratt. Her family shared in the ownership of Standard Oil.

53. John Kenneth Galbraith, author interview.

54. Isaacson and Thomas, *Wise Men,* 484.

55. "His task, he later recalled, was to 'measure precisely' the impact of the bomb — 'to put calipers on it instead of describing it in emotive terms.'" Ibid.

56. Ibid., 485.

57. John Kenneth Galbraith, author interview.

58. The ultimate manifestation of this trend occurred under Eisenhower, when Secretary of State John Foster Dulles epitomized American belligerence, while the secretary of defense, Charles Wilson, had little or no influence over the national debate. Making this point, Thomas Schelling pointed out in an unpublished lecture that in McGeorge Bundy's history, *Danger and Survival,* there are thirty-one index references to Dulles, two to Wilson. The martial initiative stayed with State until the Kennedy administration, when the trend was reversed. Bundy has forty-two references to Secretary of Defense Robert McNamara, twelve to Secretary of State Dean Rusk.

59. Teller is called the father of the H-bomb, but decades later he credited the physicist Richard L. Garwin as the actual creator of the design that worked. Garwin had received almost no credit for the breakthrough, although a year and a half before Teller's death on September 9, 2003 (news of his death dominated the papers on September 11), the *New York Times* told the story of Garwin's work ("Who Built the Bomb? Debate Revives," April 24, 2001, F1). I interviewed Garwin that same autumn. I asked him if he thought Truman's decision to build the bomb was necessary for national security, and he said no. "Our national security would not have suffered [without the H-bomb] because the atomic bombs are big enough to do what was needed." Author interview.

60. This aspect of the fusion weapon's difference from the fission weapon was explained to me by Richard Garwin. Author interview.

61. Churchill delivered this speech in 1955. Jervis, *The Meaning of the Nuclear Revolution,* 7.

62. Richard L. Garwin, "Enrico Fermi and Modern Physics," public lecture, Pisa, Italy, October 19, 2001. Garwin's figure is 70,000. The National Resources Defense Council put the nuclear total at about 50,000 for each side in 1976. "Archive of Nuclear Data," www.nrdc.org/nuclear/nudb/datab9.asp.

63. Isaacson and Thomas, *Wise Men,* 490.

64. McCullough, *Truman,* 762.

65. Bundy, *Danger and Survival,* 212.

66. *New York Times,* February 1, 1950, A1. Truman made his decision about the hydrogen bomb without ever having been briefed by the JCS on Pentagon war plans, with no knowledge of how the military intended to use its nuclear weapons. Rosenberg, "American Atomic Strategy," 78, 84.

67. McCullough, *Truman,* 763.

68. Nitze, *From Hiroshima to Glasnost,* xvi.

69. Ibid., 7.

70. The Committee on the Present Danger was reconstituted in 2004 to support the Global War on Terror. See its Web site, www.fightingterror.org.

71. Nitze, *From Hiroshima to Glasnost*, 78.

72. Ibid.

73. "In death, James Forrestal's wish was fulfilled. The study known as NSC-68 would be a memorial to Forrestal's unrelenting demand for military preparedness. In addition, it would come to be regarded as a blueprint for U.S. national security policy through the 1960's." Isaacson and Thomas, *Wise Men*, 490. Here is LaFeber's summary of NSC-68: no negotiations with Russia; develop the H-bomb; build up conventional forces; raise new taxes; mobilize Americans; strengthen alliances under U.S. aegis; undermine the Soviet system from within. LaFeber, *America, Russia, and the Cold War*, 103.

74. NSC-68: www.fas.org/irp/offdocs/nsc-hst/nsc-68-htm.

75. Ibid.

76. Acheson, *Present at the Creation*, 376.

77. The historian William Appleman Williams called NSC-68 "an American Papal Bull." May, *American Cold War Strategy*, 135.

78. Whitfield, *The Culture of the Cold War*, 77.

79. Carl Kaysen, in May, *American Cold War Strategy*, 117.

80. May's summary of John Lewis Gaddis. Ibid., 140. See Gaddis, *Strategies of Containment*, 90–98, 104–6.

81. For an example of a crediting of NSC-68 with winning the Cold War, see Graham Allison, in May, *American Cold War Strategy*, 16.

82. Robert R. Bowie, in May, *American Cold War Strategy*, 111.

83. Cited by Marc Trachtenberg, *History and Strategy*, 109.

84. NSC-68: www.fas.org/irp/offdocs/nsc-hst/nsc-68-htm.

85. Gaddis, *The United States and the End of the Cold War*, 54.

86. "Korea came along and saved us — [did] the job for us," a colleague of Acheson's said in a seminar at Princeton in 1953. "I think you can say that," Acheson replied. Bruce Cumings, "The Wicked Witch of the West Is Dead," in Hogan, *The End of the Cold War*, 90.

87. Peacock, *Strategic Air Command*, 19.

88. May, *American Cold War Strategy*, 14.

89. In fiscal year 1950, the military budget amounted to less than one third of all federal expenditures, and less than 5 percent of the gross national product. By fiscal year 1953, those figures had grown to more than 60 percent and more than 12 percent.

90. Peacock, *Strategic Air Command*, 19. Soon there would be 1,400 B-47s stationed around the globe. All told, there would be 3,636,000 American men under arms. Clarfield and Wiecek, *Nuclear America*, 142.

91. In testimony before the Army Ordnance Board in 1944, Charles Wilson, then head of the War Production Board, said a permanent war economy was the way to avoid a return to the Depression. Wilson famously said, "What's good for General Motors is good for the country."

92. Carl Kaysen, in May, *American Cold War Strategy*, 119.

93. NSC-68 warned of 175 Soviet divisions, with no knowledge, apparently, that two thirds of them were undermanned. The dreaded invasion of Western Europe from the east would have been impeded by the lack of railroad tracks running from Russia to Germany: the Red Army had pulled the tracks up to prevent an invasion from the west. And so on. Isaacson and Thomas, *Wise Men*, 503.

94. "Military plans had a way of giving reality to the very contingencies against which they purported to prepare." George F. Kennan, in May, *American Cold War Strategy*, 96.

95. Peacock, *Strategic Air Command*, 20.

96. Robert R. Bowie, in May, *American Cold War Strategy*, 111.

97. Bundy, *Danger and Survival*, 230.

98. Robert R. Bowie, in May, *American Cold War Strategy*, 111.

99. Office of the Historian, *SAC Missile Chronology*, 6.

100. Bundy, *Danger and Survival*, 230; Rosenberg, "The Origins of Overkill," 23. What Truman set in motion would lead, over fifty years, to the production on the U.S. side alone of more than ninety thousand nuclear weapons. Sherwin and Bird, *American Prometheus*, 423.

101. Post–Cold War archives in the Soviet Union suggest that the Acheson speech had little effect on Moscow's perceptions. Arthur Schlesinger, Jr., author interview.

102. Ibid.

103. Manchester, *American Caesar*, 613.

104. Ibid., 584.

105. Air Force History Office, *Strategic Air War*, 92.

106. By late 1950, after MacArthur had moved north, the U.S. nuclear arsenal had about doubled from the two hundred weapons early in the year, so somewhere between a quarter and a half of the stockpile was reserved for targets in the Soviet Union.

107. Air Force History Office, *Strategic Air War*, 90.

108. Nolan, *Guardians of the Arsenal*, 57.

109. Manchester, *American Caesar*, 607.

110. Ibid., 608.

111. McCullough, *Truman*, 822.

112. Ibid.

113. Acheson, *Present at the Creation*, 475.

114. Manchester, *American Caesar*, 672.

115. McCullough, *Truman*, 821.

116. New York Governor Thomas Dewey was the man Truman narrowly defeated in 1948. For an example of his belligerence during the Korean War, see *New York Times*, August 24, 1950, A6.

117. Dean Acheson told a Senate committee, in December 1950, that "the great trouble is we are fighting the wrong nation. We are fighting the second team, whereas the real enemy is the Soviet Union." Trachtenberg, *History and Strategy*, 125.

118. NSC-100, January 11, 1951. Trachtenberg, *History and Strategy*, 124. Trachtenberg notes that Truman "drafted but did not send" a note to Symington in response: "My dear Stu, this is [as] big a lot of Top Secret malarkey as I've ever read. Your time is wasted on such bunk as this. H.S.T."

119. Wittner, *One World or None*, 261–62.

120. Ernest May, "U.S. Government, Legacy of the Cold War," in Hogan, *The End of the Cold War*, 227.

121. Ibid., 223.

122. Senator Joseph McCarthy's later attacks on the Army, and on General Marshall in particular, in 1951, had their origin in the idea that MacArthur's will to "roll back" Communism in Korea with the full power of American might, including the atomic bomb, had been thwarted by Communists in the Pentagon.

123. The Korean War caused more than 4 million Korean mortalities, two thirds of them civilian (compared to about 2.3 million Japanese deaths during World War II). The U.N. forces' dead numbered more than 40,000, almost all Americans. The U.S. casualty totals approached those of the Vietnam War, but that suffering was inflicted in more than ten years. In Korea, it took three.

124. Gaddis et al., *Cold War Statesmen Confront the Bomb*, 268. Elsewhere, Gaddis says of Truman's decision not to use the bomb in Korea, "The decision was based, in part, to be sure, upon the absence of any very good targets, but the documents also show that a desire to avoid the unnecessary destruction of civilian populations — a concern rooted in considerations of both morality and expediency — played a role in it." *The United States and the End of the Cold War*, 163.

125. The decision not to carry the war to China equaled a decision for "limited war." Foot, *The Wrong War*, 120.

126. Secretary of the Navy Francis Matthews, in Trachtenberg, *History and Strategy*, 117.

127. Assistant Secretary of State Dean Rusk, Memorandum of Conversation, December 19, 1950. Ibid., 123. A few months later, in April 1951, Vandenberg asked Truman to transfer at least a few armed atomic bombs to complete military control, beyond the authority of the Atomic Energy Commission, and Truman agreed. Nolan, *Guardians of the Arsenal*, 52.

128. Trachtenberg, *History and Strategy*, 103–4.

129. Sherwin and Bird, *American Prometheus*, 441.

130. Bundy, *Danger and Survival*, 197. Sakharov, a brilliant young physicist, was one of the technical leaders of the Soviet nuclear establishment from 1949 to 1968. In 1969, his essay "Reflections on Progress, Peaceful Coexistence, and Intellectual Freedom" struck a major blow, from the Soviet side, for détente. It also made him a suspect figure in the USSR. But his influence only grew, and he was instrumental in bringing about the great internal shift that led to the reforms of Mikhail Gorbachev and then the collapse of the Soviet Union. On December 14, 1989, only weeks after the fall of the Berlin Wall, Sakharov died of a heart attack.

131. It is impossible to know what the Soviets would have done in response to an American proposal to postpone the H-bomb test, but it is clear that decisions in Moscow were influenced by those in Washington. Here David Holloway makes two points on the question: "First, although there are clear elements of reciprocal influence in the Soviet and American nuclear weapons decisions of 1949–52, the actions that are salient on one side are not necessarily so on the other. American accounts of the period highlight President Truman's announcement of 31 January 1950. The Soviet accounts, however, suggest that Truman's decision was not as important to their own decisions as the . . . Mike test of 1952. In strategic interaction the salience of actions depends not on the actor's context but on that of the observer.

"Second, Soviet decision making shows elements both of reaction to American actions and of an internal dynamic. The early thermonuclear studies were stimulated by reports of American work. The decision to proceed to development of a fusion bomb followed the first fission bomb test and was not directly triggered by American actions. The search for the superbomb was intensified by the Mike test. Yet if we can find elements both of reaction and of internal dynamic in Soviet policy, the overall effect of American actions was to speed up the Soviet effort to develop thermonuclear weapons." Holloway, "Research Note: Soviet Thermonuclear Development," 196.

132. Vannevar Bush testimony, *In the Matter of J. Robert Oppenheimer*, 562. See also Sherwin and Bird, *American Prometheus*, 443, 523.

133. Bethe, "Sakharov's H-bomb."

134. Philip Morrison, author interview.

135. Rubenstein and Gribanov, *The KGB File*, 12.

136. Teller died in 2003.

137. Clarfield and Wiecek, *Nuclear America*, 147.

138. Vannevar Bush testimony, *In the Matter of J. Robert Oppenheimer*, 562. See also York, *The Advisors*,

139. I am sure my father voted for John Kennedy, Lyndon Johnson, and Hubert Humphrey. The first time he actually admitted voting for a Republican was in 1972, for Richard Nixon, against the "kook" George McGovern.

140. There is a sizable literature on America's nuclear "culture." See, for example, Inglis, *The Cruel Peace*; Engelhardt, *The End of Victory Culture*; Scott C. Zeman and Michael A. Amundson, eds., *Nuclear Culture: How We Learned to Stop Worrying and Love the Bomb* (Boulder: University Press of Colorado, 2004). In *The Technological Society*, Jacques Ellul

offers a larger reflection on how traditional values are trumped by technology, a phenomenon that pervades the atomic culture.

141. *Saturday Evening Post,* January 7, 1950.

142. Schwartz, "Check, Please," 36.

143. Kennedy and Hatfield, *Freeze!,* 16.

144. Quoted by Ernest May, in Gaddis et al., *Cold War Statesmen Confront the Bomb,* 5. Eisenhower here strikes the same note Truman had struck at first when he described the A-bomb in 1945 as "just another piece of artillery." But Truman learned to believe otherwise. Clarfield and Wiecek, *Nuclear America,* 81.

145. Gaddis et al., *Cold War Statesmen Confront the Bomb,* 262.

146. In 1991, after the Cold War ended, the time was seventeen minutes to midnight. The *Bulletin of the Atomic Scientists* removed the clock from its cover for a time, but by 2005 it was back, standing at seven minutes to midnight again. www.thebulletin.org.

147. In addition to the various proposals for atomic use that came from NSC, military, and especially Air Force figures in June 1951, Secretary of Defense George Marshall proposed telling the Chinese leaders that "we are going to give them a taste of the atom," and by 1952 an ever more frustrated Truman had reconsidered the question. He told associates that if the enemy still refused an armistice, "the proper approach now would be an ultimatum threatening all-out war." Wittner, *One World or None,* 261.

148. Memorandum of the 131st National Security Council meeting, February 11, 1953. Neal Rosendorf in Gaddis et al., *Cold War Statesmen Confront the Bomb,* 71.

149. Eisenhower, *The White House Years,* 180.

150. Rosenberg, "The Origins of Overkill," 27.

151. See, for example, Manchester, *The Glory and the Dream,* 662. The crisis in Vietnam came in spring 1954 when a nuclear-armed U.S. aircraft carrier threatened to launch Operation Vulture, using atomic bombs against Communist forces at Dien Bien Phu. The French refused Eisenhower's offer, and the British opposed the use of atomic bombs. The crisis in Formosa came in late 1954, lasting until spring 1955. China shelled the islands of Quemoy and Matsu. The JCS formally urged use of atomic bombs against China. On March 16, Ike made his famous statement: "Atomic bombs can be used . . . as you would use a bullet." On May 1, the Chinese ceased their shelling of Quemoy and Matsu.

152. Isaacson and Thomas, *Wise Men,* 559.

153. Nitze would not last in the Eisenhower administration, but not because he didn't fit in. When Joseph McCarthy attacked "Wall Street operators" in government, Nitze was an easy target. He took up what would be a near permanent sinecure at Johns Hopkins University, establishing an academic institute that would grow into a distinguished school that bears his name. Nitze, the diplomat in the Pentagon, was a career-long instance of the old Pentagon slogan about policymakers: "Where you sit is where you stand." And, sitting outside the Eisenhower administration, Nitze became one of its firm critics when it began to veer from the recommendations he had made in NSC-68.

154. Dulles, "A Policy of Boldness."

155. Gaddis, *The United States and the End of the Cold War,* 67.

156. What Dulles actually said was "Local defenses must be reinforced by the further deterrent of massive retaliatory power." Dulles, "The Evolution of Foreign Policy," 107–10. A few days earlier, in his State of the Union address, Eisenhower had said the United States has "and will maintain a massive capability to strike back." americanpresidencnet/1954.htm.

157. Wolfe, *The Rise and Fall of the "Soviet Threat,"* 15.

158. Once this style was set, it would last. Thus John Kennedy, in the 1962 Cuban Missile Crisis, would insist that America had gotten its way by moving to the brink of nuclear war and not "blinking," when in fact, in a covert blink, the Kennedy administration had yielded to Moscow's demand for the removal of U.S. missiles in Turkey. When Kennedy insisted

that the Turkey missile deal be kept secret, of course, he was protecting the secret not from Moscow but from his Republican political opponents. And the secret was that blink. (The word is Dean Rusk's: "We were eyeball to eyeball, and the other guy blinked.")

159. See Grose, *Operation Rollback.*

160. Rosenberg, "The Origins of Overkill," 28.

161. Bundy, *Danger and Survival,* 240. For other evidence that Stalin's death was key to the Korean armistice, see Gaddis et al., *Cold War Statesmen Confront the Bomb,* 99.

162. Perret, *Eisenhower,* 453.

163. Grose, *Operation Rollback,* 211.

164. One of America's famous antiwar activists, William Sloane Coffin, Jr., began as a CIA "rollback" operative, recruiting émigré Russians and sending them back. But in 1953, "severe burnout hit William Sloane Coffin as his lovingly nurtured Russian agents flew off into the night with their parachutes and codebooks, disappearing behind the Iron Curtain, never to reappear in person or deed. Coffin left the CIA in 1953, returning to the seminary and a distinguished career in the ministry." Grose, *Operation Rollback,* 213. Also William Sloane Coffin, author interview.

165. The post-Stalin power struggle would go on for two years, until Nikita Khrushchev emerged as the dominant power in 1956. One of the first moves he made was to denounce the Stalin era, and he completed the dismantling of the Kremlin establishment's policies and personnel.

166. Gaddis et al., *Cold War Statesmen Confront the Bomb,* 264. Ethnic, racial, and ideological factors in Churchill's view of the Soviets were balanced by "great game" considerations, dating back to his time as head of the British war and air ministries from 1919 to 1921. That experience gave him a strategic understanding of Bolshevik methods and Soviet goals in Transcaucasia, the Middle East, and Eastern Europe.

167. Grose, *Operation Rollback,* 211.

168. Snead, *The Gaither Committee,* 16.

169. Carlton, *Churchill and the Soviet Union,* 179.

170. "'Chance for Peace' Speech," www.eisenhower.utexas.edu/chance.htm.

171. Perret, *Eisenhower,* 454.

172. "Atoms for Peace," www.eisenhower.utexas.edu/atom6.htm.

173. Bundy, *Danger and Survival,* 244.

174. Neal Rosendorf, in Gaddis et al., *Cold War Statesmen Confront the Bomb,* 63.

175. Bundy, *Danger and Survival,* 287.

176. It was in the context of the March 1955 crisis over Quemoy and Matsu that Eisenhower made his remark saying the use of atomic weapons was "just exactly as you would use a bullet." Ernest R. May, in Gaddis et al., *Cold War Statesmen Confront the Bomb,* 5.

177. Mao ordered the start of China's atomic bomb project in January 1955. Gaddis et al., *Cold War Statesmen Confront the Bomb,* 266.

178. Dulles wrote in 1954 that the United States "would certainly feel free to inflict heavy damage upon the aggressor beyond the immediate area which he chose for his aggression . . . It should not be stated in advance precisely what would be the scope of military action if new aggression occurred . . . That is a matter as to which the aggressor had best remain ignorant. But he can know and does know, in the light of present policies, that the choice in this respect is ours and not his." "Policy and Security for Peace," *Foreign Affairs,* April 1954, 360.

179. The "Joint Strategic Capabilities Plan" for war, drafted by the Joint Chiefs and approved by Eisenhower, anticipated that the first American strike would result in 425 to 460 million enemy dead, a figure that undoubtedly included China. Clarfield and Wiecek, *Nuclear America,* 154.

180. Bundy, *Danger and Survival,* 252. Eisenhower approved a 1954 National Security

Policy paper that said, "The United States and its allies must reject the concept of preventive war or acts intended to provoke war." Rosenberg, "The Origins of Overkill," 34.

181. Brodie, *The Absolute Weapon.*

182. Trachtenberg, *History and Strategy,* 4.

183. Kaplan, *The Wizards of Armageddon,* 10. They "move freely through the corridors of the Pentagon and the State Department rather as the Jesuits through the courts of Madrid and Vienna three centuries ago."

184. Freedman, *Evolution of Nuclear Strategy,* 44.

185. The film, directed by Stanley Kubrick, has Strangelove as Herman Kahn (with bits of Henry Kissinger and Edward Teller), and General Ripper as LeMay. When Daniel Ellsberg saw the film in 1964, he told a colleague, "That was a documentary!" Fred Kaplan, "Truth Stranger Than 'Strangelove,'" *New York Times,* October 10, 2004, 21.

186. "This conjunction of an immense military establishment and a large arms industry is new in the American experience . . . In the councils of government, we must guard against the acquisition of unwarranted influence, whether sought or unsought, by the military-industrial complex. The potential for the disastrous rise of misplaced power exists and will persist. We must never let the weight of this combination endanger our liberties or democratic processes. We should take nothing for granted." Farewell address, January 17, 1961. The "conjunction" Eisenhower foresaw was new — aspects of civilian life intricately bound to the military — but the warning was not. "Overgrown military establishments are under any form of government inauspicious to liberty, and are to be regarded as particularly hostile to Republican liberty." George Washington, farewell address, September 17, 1796.

187. The ironies and contradictions of systems theory are caught in typical phrases like "security dilemma," "prisoner's dilemma," and "suboptimal outcome." I acknowledge the insight here of Martin Malin, in conversation.

188. Trachtenberg, *History and Strategy,* 152.

189. Ibid., 43.

190. The mission statement of RAND, established under LeMay, read, "Project RAND is a continuing program of scientific study and research on the broad subject of air warfare with the object of recommending to the Air Force preferred methods, techniques and instrumentalities for this purpose." Kaplan, *Wizards of Armageddon,* 59.

191. Snead, *The Gaither Committee,* 63.

192. Peacock, *Strategic Air Command,* 22. The first eight B-52s were operational in 1955. Within a year, twenty new B-52s were being produced each month. Rosenberg, "The Origins of Overkill," 41.

193. Air Force Office of Special Investigations, Oral History Project, interview with Lieutenant General Joseph F. Carroll, USAF (Ret.), December 13, 1982.

194. Hagerty, *The OSI Story,* 58–59. The early SAC vulnerability tests had names like Operation Try Out, Watch Tower, and Fresh Approach.

195. Ibid., 60.

196. Peacock, *Strategic Air Command,* 44.

197. Air Force intelligence noted the huge number of Soviet Bison bombers flying in formation at a Moscow air show in 1955. In fact, the Soviets possessed only ten Bisons, but they flew them in broad circles, making it appear that there were many more. Clarfield and Wiecek, *Nuclear America,* 160. Kaplan, in *Wizards of Armageddon,* says that the report of the planes flying in circles was never confirmed (160). See also Rosenberg, "The Origins of Overkill," 41–50.

198. Charles Davis, author interview.

199. Clarfield and Wiecek, *Nuclear America,* 159.

200. The committee members included defense specialists, industrialists, and academics, like Jerome Wiesner of MIT and James Phinney Baxter III, president of Williams Col-

lege. The committee was served by an advisory panel of scientists, military figures, and other experts.

201. May, *American Cold War Strategy*, 100.

202. Kaplan, *Wizards of Armageddon*, 134; Rosenberg, "The Origins of Overkill," 47.

203. Franklin Lindsay, author interview.

204. Rosenberg, "The Origins of Overkill," 37.

205. The phrase is Janne Nolan's.

206. It would be formally presented to the National Security Council on November 7, 1957. The report, which remained classified for decades, was promptly leaked to the press. The main author of the report, in addition to Nitze, was the mathematician Albert J. Wohlstetter.

207. Snead, *The Gaither Committee*, 122.

208. Kaplan, *Wizards of Armageddon*, 135.

209. Talbott, *The Master of the Game*, 64.

210. Ibid.

211. *Washington Post*, December 20, 1957, cited by Kaplan, *Wizards of Armageddon*, 153.

212. Bernard Smith, the former director of the U.S. Naval Surface Weapons Laboratory, told me that after that Vanguard failure, "we were desperate to get anything up there into orbit — a hunk of concrete, anything." And to do so in any way they could. At a test site at China Lake in the Mojave Desert, Smith participated in a project to use a Navy F-4 jet fighter as the first stage of a satellite launch, with the piloted fighter screeching straight up to forty-five thousand feet, at which point it would fire a missile that would leave the stratosphere. It was, Smith said, "a joke." Author interview.

213. In 1956, the USSR had perhaps 150 intercontinental bombers. In addition to hundreds of still active B-36 bombers, the United States had 1,400 B-47s, and was beginning the deployment of 600 B-52s. Nevertheless, the bomber-gap scare worked, with Eisenhower forced by the public's reaction to approve an increase in the planned manufacture of the B-52, from seventeen aircraft a month to twenty. Clarfield and Wiecek, *Nuclear America*, 161–62.

214. Bundy, *Danger and Survival*, 337. Between 1958 and 1960, the total number of nukes in the U.S. arsenal went from 6,000 to more than 18,000. LaFeber, *America, Russia, and the Cold War*, 205.

215. Zaloga, *The Kremlin's Nuclear Sword*, 59.

216. In 1960, Kennedy would name Nitze to chair his committee of national security advisers, and after the election, Kennedy would name Nitze assistant secretary of defense for international security affairs. It was the same post he had been offered early in the Eisenhower administration. Chalmers Roberts, "Kennedy Names Policy Group to Prepare Program If He Wins," *Washington Post*, August 31, 1960, cited by Talbott, *The Master of the Game*, 78.

217. Snead, *The Gaither Committee*, 173–74. See also Kaplan, *Wizards of Armageddon*, 249. At the time Kennedy became president, the "neglected" military establishment consisted of 3,500 bases in the United States and around the globe, covering territory larger than all of New England. The arsenal included more than 20 long- and medium-range ballistic missiles, 1,700 intercontinental bombers, 1,300 supersonic fighters, the Army's tactical nuclear weapons, and "in one base alone enough nerve gas to kill the world's population several times over." Parker, *John Kenneth Galbraith*, 340.

Five. The Turning Point

1. This was when my father, as Air Force inspector general, was on a special assignment to the secretary, investigating breaches of Pentagon security (also known as press leaks).

Later, when he was head of the DIA, my father's office was some corridors, and one floor, away from McNamara's.

2. I owe the phrase to Tom Engelhardt, the author of, among other works, *The End of Victory Culture.*

3. Sebald, *On the Natural History of Destruction,* 70.

4. I acknowledge a debt to the literary scholar Rob Chodat, whose analysis of the "supra-personal mind" in Don DeLillo's work influenced me here.

5. Eugene Skolnikoff, author interview.

6. The instrument of destruction was the Army's lawyer, Joseph Welch, who faced down McCarthy with the immortal line, "Senator, you have done enough. Have you no sense of decency?"

7. William D. Cohen. "I have finally come face to face with the white whale," Cohen told me. "And I'm lashed to it." Author interview. As we saw, it is in the film, not the novel, that Ahab is lashed to Moby Dick. General John M. Shalikashvili, chairman of the Joint Chiefs under Cohen, "compared the Pentagon to a monster: the Secretary's job is to tame it, without removing its teeth." Carroll, "War Inside the Pentagon," 53. Moby Dick was the name of a CIA reconnaissance program in the early 1950s. It consisted of sending huge balloons over the Soviet Union, drifting in air currents toward Japan. Attached to the balloons were cameras. The pictures they took were useless. Rosenberg, "The Origins of Overkill," 21.

8. Farewell address, January 17, 1961.

9. Bundy, *Danger and Survival,* 319.

10. Newhouse, *War and Peace in the Nuclear Age,* 146.

11. Carl Kaysen was working for Kennedy at the time. In addition to Kennedy's courage, what he saw in the president's decision not to proceed further with air support with the Bay of Pigs invasion was his prudence. Kennedy "was a *very* cautious guy." Author interview.

12. Lasky, *JFK: The Man and the Myth,* 361.

13. Isaacs and Downing, *Cold War,* 173. Here is how James Reston of the *New York Times* summed up the Vienna encounter, describing his own meeting with Kennedy in its immediate aftermath: "He [the president] came into a dim room in the American embassy shaken and angry. He had tried, as always, to be calm and rational with Khrushchev, to get him to define what the Soviet Union would and would not do, and Khrushchev had bullied him and threatened him with war over Berlin . . . Kennedy said just enough in that room to convince me of the following: Khrushchev had studied the events of the Bay of Pigs; he would have understood if Kennedy had left Castro alone or destroyed him; but when Kennedy was rash enough to strike at Cuba but not bold enough to finish the job, Khrushchev decided he was dealing with an inexperienced young leader who could be intimidated and blackmailed." Manchester, *The Glory and the Dream,* 910.

14. I wrote about this scene in my memoir *An American Requiem.* At the time I wrote that book, I remembered the event as occurring in 1960, but in learning more about the context of the unfolding Berlin crisis, and the debate in the Pentagon on what to do about it, I have concluded that it was almost certainly 1961.

15. Isaacs and Downing, *Cold War,* 177. Also Sulzberger, *The Last of the Giants,* 860; Rusk, *As I Saw It,* 227.

16. Trachtenberg, *History and Strategy,* 187. Even George Kennan, hardly a hawk by 1958, proposed in that year that West Germany be given nukes as a way to allow the "disengagement" of the large American combat force from Germany. LaFeber, *America, Russia, and the Cold War,* 211.

17. Beschloss, *The Crisis Years,* 174.

18. Incorporating this incident, I wrote a novel based on it, *Secret Father* (Boston: Houghton Mifflin, 2003).

19. Bundy puts the figure at twelve thousand a month by the summer of 1961. *Danger and Survival*, 362.

20. Beschloss, *The Crisis Years*, 219.

21. Kahn had published a book, *Thinking About the Unthinkable*.

22. Eugene Rostow in Kennedy and Hatfield, *Freeze!*, 1.

23. The astronomer Carl Sagan popularized the term. I associate it with him.

24. The "mechanics" of escalation include accidents, failures of C³I, emotions, misperceptions, political pressures, military coups, etc. Martin Malin, author correspondence. The essence of the problem is caught by Robert Jervis: "Because escalation, which would ruin both sides, is an ever-present possibility, attempts to put pressure on the other side will also put pressure on the self." *The Illogic of American Nuclear Strategy*, 34.

25. Eden, *Whole World on Fire*, 2.

26. Beschloss, *The Crisis Years*, 225.

27. Carl Kaysen was an author of the fallout shelter proposal. "I wrote that program on the basis of my experience in England." He laughed when he told me this. "It made me an expert in civil defense." In addition to Kennedy's authentic worry about war, he was motivated in this proposal by politics. His potential Republican challenger, Nelson Rockefeller, was a big proponent of shelters. Kennedy said to Kaysen, "Rockefeller is trying to put fallout shelters up my ass." Author interview.

28. It was during the Berlin crisis of 1961 that Dean Acheson gave Kennedy private advice: "The president should himself give that question [nuclear use] the most careful and private consideration, well before the time when the choice might present itself, that he should reach his own clear conclusion in advance as to what he would do, and that he should tell no one at all what that conclusion was." Bundy, *Danger and Survival*, 375. See also Schell, *The Unconquerable World*, 57.

29. www.cs.umb.edu/jfklibrary/jfk_berlin_crisis_speech.html. Writing in the *Los Angeles Times*, Robert Hartmann observed that Kennedy was "trying very hard to be a great leader of a troubled nation, yet he conveyed the impression that he was the most troubled citizen of all." Beschloss, *The Crisis Years*, 261.

30. Reeves, *President Kennedy*, 171. The "cold winter" remark, but without the flat prediction of war, was reported, for example, in Schlesinger, *A Thousand Days*, 374, and Sidey, *John F. Kennedy, President*, 200.

31. McGeorge Bundy (*Danger and Survival*, 363) drew my attention to Lowell's poem "Fall 1961," which speaks of "the chafe and jar of nuclear war."

32. *An American Requiem*, 83.

33. Beschloss, *The Crisis Years*, 260.

34. Bundy, *Danger and Survival*, 363.

35. Eden, *Whole World on Fire*, 26. My description of the heat effects of a nuclear detonation draws on Eden.

36. At one point the United States had four hundred nuclear weapons targeting Moscow. A former commander of STRATCOM, the successor to SAC, was certain that Washington would be targeted with "several dozens" of nuclear weapons. Ibid., 16.

37. This phrase indicates a combined influence on Kennedy of the RAND analyst Albert Wohlstetter, author of "The Delicate Balance of Terror," and of Maxwell D. Taylor, author of *The Uncertain Trumpet*.

38. John F. Kennedy, inaugural address, in Safire, *Lend Me Your Ears*, 811.

39. Kennedy's phrase, in his July 1961 speech on Berlin, was between "humiliation" and "all-out nuclear action."

40. Eisenhower ordered "the construction and deployment of 255 Atlas and Titan ICBMs, as well as 450 silo based and 90 mobile Minuteman missiles. He also approved the construction of 19 Polaris type submarines each armed with 16 missiles." Ike ordered al-

most 1,100 strategic missiles. Clarfield and Wiecek, *Nuclear America*, 172. Herbert York asserts that the strategic force as eventually constituted under Kennedy and Johnson (1,000 Minutemen, 500 bombers, 656 Polaris missiles) represents essentially what Eisenhower had aimed at. York, *Making Weapons, Talking Peace*, 193–97.

41. Philip Nash, "Bear Any Burden? John F. Kennedy and Nuclear Weapons," in Gaddis et al., *Cold War Statesmen Confront the Bomb*, 124.

42. See, for example, Kennedy, "Disarmament Can Be Won," 217.

43. Kennedy's former aide Theodore Sorensen told me that Kennedy's anguished worry about nuclear weapons was the central motivating factor in his run for president and the dominant concern of his entire time in office. Author interview. McGeorge Bundy says that "the reduction of nuclear danger was his [JFK's] highest single hope." *Danger and Survival*, 356.

44. In the assessment of Michael Beschloss, "Kennedy rarely showed the magnanimity that should have been expected of a superior power. Instead he aroused the Western world to an hour of imminent danger that did not exist, provoked the adversary by exposing Soviet nuclear weakness to the world, and unwittingly caused the Soviets to fear that he was on the verge of exploiting American nuclear strength to settle the Cold War on American terms, perhaps even in a preemptive strike." *The Crisis Years*, 702.

45. Moscow had announced its suspension of testing on May 1, 1958. When JFK received word of the Soviet resumption of testing, he said to his brother Robert, "Fucked again . . . The bastards! That fucking liar!" Reeves, *President Kennedy*, 223. Kennedy was also furious at the CIA, which had offered no warning of the test, which surely reinforced him in the decision just announced to establish the competing Defense Intelligence Agency. Newhouse, *War and Peace in the Nuclear Age*, 157.

46. Manchester, *The Glory and the Dream*, 913. On April 29, 1961, the National Security Council approved the dispatch of armed "advisers" to the South Vietnamese Self-Defense Corps, the true beginning of the American war in Vietnam. Herring, *The Pentagon Papers*, 44.

47. As we saw earlier, America's overinflation of Soviet military strength began in 1945, when estimates putting the Red Army's divisions at 175 were off by a factor of two, and when half of its transportation needs were met by horse-drawn vehicles. By 1961, however, the Soviet threat was indeed real. "Khrushchev was hardly the innocent victim of American paranoia. His nuclear threats and unfounded claims of nuclear superiority were the catalyst for Kennedy's decision to increase the scope and pace of the American strategic buildup." Lebow and Stein, "Deterrence and the Cold War," 162.

48. Forrestal was a friend of Joseph Kennedy's. Beschloss, *The Crisis Years*, 281. Michael Forrestal was a thirty-five-year-old lawyer from Wall Street. After his father's suicide, the young man had been effectively adopted by Averell Harriman.

49. Recall that Nitze's tenure in that job had been cut short in 1953 when conservative Republicans went after him because of his previous service with Dean Acheson in the Truman State Department.

50. Talbott, *The Master of the Game*, 81. When the missile gap was shown to be in America's favor, Nitze refused to believe it.

51. Eisenhower provided secret briefings for Kennedy in the summer of 1960, perhaps showing him U-2 photographs of Soviet installations that suggested there was no missile gap, but Kennedy apparently accepted Air Force assessments and continued to press the issue. Nixon couldn't rebut the charge because the intelligence was secret. The U-2 photos were inconclusive in any case, as were estimates provided by various intelligence agencies.

52. Robert McNamara, author interview. One of the ways Air Force intelligence arrived at its estimate of a huge Soviet missile force was to assume that photographed factory buildings making unknown products were missile plants, calculate the square footage of

the plants, then compare those figures with the square footage of U.S. missile manufacturing facilities. The exaggerated estimate of Soviet capacity was a result of the highly dubious assumption that any unknown plant was making missiles.

53. *Discoverer* was launched in August 1960. Its photographs were not processed until November, after the election. Its sweep enabled it to cover more Soviet territory, with more accuracy, than all previous U-2 missions. Even so, the pictures were incomplete. In the beginning of the reconnaissance, canisters of photos taken by the satellite's camera were dropped from orbit with small parachutes attached, to be snagged in midair by Air Force planes.

54. Schlesinger, *A Thousand Days*, 610.

55. Kaplan, *Wizards of Armageddon*, 287. According to McGeorge Bundy, it was not only the Air Force that got this intelligence wrong. Speaking of 1958 and 1959, Bundy wrote, "The CIA continued to project the early prospect of such [Soviet] missiles in the hundreds; air force estimates were regularly higher, and the intelligence assessments of the Strategic Air Command were higher still." *Danger and Survival*, 337.

56. It is not necessary, either, to regard 2002 intelligence estimates of Saddam Hussein's weapons of mass destruction as lies. A few weeks before the United States invaded Iraq in 2003, an action justified by intelligence "proving" that Saddam Hussein had weapons of mass destruction, I interviewed Thomas Halsted, a former top-level intelligence official who began as an Army photo interpreter, working for Army intelligence in the period when Air Force intelligence was emphasizing the missile gap. He explained how such an egregious intelligence failure could happen. "Air Force intelligence officials went around Washington with a dog-and-pony show [in 1959 and 1960]. Graphics, beautiful paintings of artists' conceptions of things, some fuzzy photographs, and a glib tongue. They'd say, 'Now this is a missile and this is the launch facility.' What they're showing is maps of the Soviet Union with little dots saying 'Probable ICBM Sites' all over the place. Where are they? Well, they're near rail lines. That's reasonable. That's where we'd expect them to be. But what are the sites? They had U-2 photographs that actually showed barrow pits, a barrow pit being where gravel is taken from to make fill for a highway or a railway. Barrow pits are elongated areas near railroad tracks. They had hundreds of barrow pits — which were one candidate for launch sites. Then there were battlefield monuments, near the Crimea, where the 'Charge of the Light Brigade' took place, an area full of these vertical objects that could look like erected missiles. They were monuments. But these briefers were going crazy with these things. Missiles! And they were very smooth, and they would say, 'Now we don't know for certain what this is, but this could very well be . . .' Then, when you move that up a couple of echelons, it has gone from 'could be' to 'probably' to 'we have evidence.' And the very same thing happened at the U.N. three weeks ago when [Secretary of State Colin] Powell said, 'There are these mobile bacteriological warfare labs. This is a decontamination truck.' Powell wasn't lying. Powell was passing along — with some of the caveats removed along the way — what the zealots wanted to use to prove that the Iraqis are doing all this. It's a seamless web." Author interview.

57. Author interview. McNamara says here that he "conceived" the DIA. Actually, SecDef studies conducted by McNamara's predecessor Thomas Gates had recommended the establishment of such an interservice agency. Borklund, *Men of the Pentagon*, 203.

58. Manchester, *The Glory and the Dream*, 895.

59. Press conference, State Department, April 21, 1961. Perry, *Four Stars*, 110.

60. Prados, *The Soviet Estimate*, 124.

61. *U.S. News & World Report*, August 28, 1961, 24.

62. Defense Intelligence Agency, *Communiqué*. See also "General Carroll Saw Something," *Washington Evening Star*, November 1, 1962; Prados, *The Soviet Estimate*, 138.

63. The DIA detailed, for example, the stresses Khrushchev was under during the mis-

sile crisis, being pressed by a far more belligerent, hard-line Kremlin faction. Reeves, *President Kennedy,* 410.

64. McNamara, *In Retrospect,* 288, 294.

65. Robert McNamara, author interview. When I asked McNamara in 2003 why he had chosen my father for the DIA in the first place, he said, "I had read his background, and I concluded he was bright and independent and honest, and that's what I needed."

66. See "Questions About the Arms Race: Who's Racing Whom? A Bureaucratic Perspective," in Pfaltzgraff, *Contrasting Approaches to Strategic Arms Control.*

67. When McNamara met the systems analysts and nuclear theologians from RAND, it was "love at first sight." Kaplan, *Wizards of Armageddon,* 251. He brought men like Daniel Ellsberg, William Kaufman, Henry Rowan, Charles Hitch, and Alain Enthoven in from RAND not only to challenge the thinking of the generals but to put reins on it. These men would be dismissed, as General Thomas White put it, as "pipe-smoking, fuzzy-headed intellectuals." White, "Strategy and the Defense Intellectuals." The irony, of course, is that RAND began as a creation of those generals, having come into being in 1946 as an in-house Air Force think tank by order of Curtis LeMay.

68. After the Vietnam War, Army officers exercising in the Pentagon Officers' Athletic Club took to wearing T-shirts saying "South East Asia War Games, 1961–1973, Second Place." Charles Davis, author correspondence.

69. Coffey, *Iron Eagle,* 422–23; Perry, *Five Stars,* 122.

70. McNamara was the source of small irritations, too. He ordered the Navy and Air Force to change the designations of their warplanes, forcing them to share numbering patterns. But that was the least of it. When the F-111 came on line, both the Navy and the Air Force hated it. The plane, as one veteran told me, "was a monstrosity. It was incapable of effective carrier operations, and the Air Force used it only as a bomber, not a fighter." Pilots of both services regarded it as a flying coffin. "The F-111 had a habit of flying into hillsides." During Vietnam, Air Force flyers blamed McNamara for the more than fifty deaths associated with the plane's performance problems. As for the Chiefs, they took to calling him Robert "Very Strange" McNamara. Perry, *Four Stars,* 170, 172. Charles Davis, author interview.

71. McNamara explained the TFX dispute to a congressional committee: "I would be less than candid . . . if I did not admit that the majority of experts in the Navy and Air Force said it couldn't be done. As late as the 22nd of August 1961, after the Navy and the Air Force had been working together for almost eight months, it was reported to me by both services that development of a single TFX aircraft to fulfill stated requirements of both services was not technically feasible. While this attitude, based on years of going separate ways, was understandable, I did not consider it a realistic approach, considering the versatility and capabilities that could be built into a modern aircraft because of advances in technology . . . I believed that the development of a single aircraft of genuine tactical utility to both services in the projected time frame was technically feasible and economically desirable." Senate Subcommittee on Investigations (McClellan committee), March 21, 1963. Coffey, *Iron Eagle,* 364.

72. Only one B-70 exists, on display at the Air Force museum in Dayton, Ohio. Curtis LeMay refers in his memoir to "a saying on the fourth floor of the Pentagon [the Air Force floor] that a plane or a plan could *take off* on the fourth floor, but would get shot down on the third [the Department of Defense]" (italics in original). *Mission with LeMay,* 549.

73. Kaplan, *Wizards of Armageddon,* 256.

74. John Steinbruner, author interview.

75. Kaysen made the point that McNamara brushed LeMay aside on numerous issues, but on the all-important one of nuclear control, LeMay refused to defer to McNamara, saying, "Don't bother me with this stuff. I know what to do." Ultimately, McNamara did

change the siop, but command and control of nukes remained ambiguous. Carl Kaysen, author interview.

76. Coffey, *Iron Eagle*, 359.

77. Bottome, *The Missile Gap*, 119; Bundy, *Danger and Survival*, 343.

78. David Alan Rosenberg explains how SAC evolved to its "unique" position in U.S. operational war planning, not fully supervised even by the Joint Chiefs of Staff. Rosenberg, "The Origins of Overkill," 10.

79. Thomas B. Ross, *Chicago Sun-Times*, February 8, 1961.

80. Ibid. I have a copy of a memo written by LeMay in the same period to Air Force Secretary Eugene Zuckert protesting the fact that someone in the Joint Chiefs meeting had leaked an "interpretation" of his comment to the *Sun-Times*. LeMay did not deny having made the proposal. He demanded that the leak be investigated, and eventually my father was assigned to do that. I found the LeMay memo in my father's file in the OSI historian's office.

81. Dallek, *An Unfinished Life*, 352.

82. Roswell Gilpatrick's word, in Dallek, *An Unfinished Life*, 345. Richard Reeves, another of Kennedy's biographers, speculates that Kennedy kept LeMay on board because, in the event of nuclear war, "the general was the kind of man you want around." *President Kennedy*, 183. Reeves's guess is supported by Kaysen's memory. I asked Kaysen why LeMay was promoted to chief of staff. He told me that President Kennedy said to his science adviser, Jerome Wiesner, "I know what trouble I'll get, but he's the guy I'll have to rely on if there's a war." Author interview.

83. May and Zelikow, *The Kennedy Tapes*, 182. Not long after LeMay's "appeasement" remark, Kennedy left the room. The tape recorder captured Marine General David Shoup congratulating LeMay: "You pulled the rug right out from under him. Goddamn" (188).

84. Dallek, *An Unfinished Life*, 555.

85. McNamara misremembered the committee's name. There was a Net Evaluation Subcommittee, but the committee referred to here was almost certainly the Joint Strategic Target Planning Staff. The head of this committee was always a SAC general, with the number-two officer from the Navy.

86. Author interview.

87. Secretary of Defense Thomas Gates, McNamara's predecessor, met fifteen times with the JCS on the issue of the siop alone, without ever successfully exerting authority on the question. Rosenberg, "The Origins of Overkill," 64. See also Nolan, *Guardians of the Arsenal*, 57–58.

88. Kaplan, *Wizards of Armageddon*, 278.

89. Bird, *The Color of Truth*, 208. The number of targets in SAC's war plan was 2,997 in 1956 and 3,261 in 1957, but by 1960 it had grown to 20,000. Rosenberg, "The Origins of Overkill," 50.

90. Rosenberg, "The Origins of Overkill," 67.

91. Nolan, *Guardians of the Arsenal*, 71. Between 1958 and 1960, to repeat, the U.S. nuclear arsenal grew from 6,000 bombs and warheads to more than 18,000. Rosenberg, "The Origins of Overkill," 66.

92. It should be noted that the purpose of sparing civilians in a nuclear assault is not merely "humane." As the strategic theorists understood it, civilians are like hostages, and once a hostage taker kills his hostage, his power to coerce comes to an end. Even in a nuclear war, one hopes to get an enemy to surrender at some point or to refrain from launching its complete arsenal. If the enemy's cities have been destroyed, it is left with nothing to lose, with no motive for restraint.

93. This shift to "flexibility" and "counterforce" was indicated in JFK's 1962 State of the Union speech, when he said, "We have rejected any all-or-nothing posture which would

leave no choice but inglorious retreat or unlimited retaliation." McNamara said in a speech in Chicago in early 1962: "We may have to retaliate with a single massive attack. Or, we may be able to use our retaliatory forces to limit damage done to ourselves, and our allies, by knocking out the enemy's bases before he has time to launch his second salvos. We may seek to terminate a war on favorable terms by using our forces as a bargaining weapon — by threatening further attack." Cited in Nolan, *Guardians of the Arsenal*, 75–76. Around the same time, McNamara elaborated the "no cities" doctrine in a speech at a secret NATO meeting in Athens, and then publicly, on June 15, 1962, in a commencement address at the University of Michigan, where he said, "The U.S. has come to the conclusion that to the extent feasible basic military strategy in a possible general nuclear war should be approached in much the same way that more conventional military operations have been regarded in the past. That is to say, principal military objectives, in the event of a nuclear war stemming from a major attack on the Alliance, should be the destruction of the enemy's military forces, not of their civilian populations . . . We are giving a possible opponent the strongest imaginable incentive to refrain from striking our own cities." Cited in Clarfield and Wiecek, *Nuclear America*, 253.

94. The counterforce rhetoric introduced in 1961, reinforcing Moscow's fear of a U.S. preventive war, may have been part of what drove Khrushchev to stiffen his own deterrence posture by, in the same period, ordering the siting of Soviet missiles in Cuba.

95. Clarfield and Wiecek, *Nuclear America*, 253.

96. Author interview.

97. Trachtenberg, *History and Strategy*, 209.

98. Before a Soviet-Romanian league meeting in Moscow, Khrushchev said, "They [the imperialists] will force us, in self-defense, to deal crushing blows not only against the territories of the principal countries . . . not only the orange groves of Italy but also the people who created them . . . the cities, people and historical monuments [of Greece] . . . There will very likely be no one and nothing in Germany to unite." Bundy, *Danger and Survival*, 365.

99. Trachtenberg, *History and Strategy*, 219.

100. Wohlstetter's article "The Delicate Balance of Terror," in *Foreign Affairs*, was "probably the single most important article in the history of American strategic thought." Trachtenberg, *History and Strategy*, 19.

101. Reeves, *President Kennedy*, 230.

102. Schlesinger, *Robert Kennedy and His Times*, 483.

103. Trachtenberg, *History and Strategy*, 11.

104. On July 7, 1961, Bundy wrote to Kennedy, "All agree that the current strategic war plan is dangerously rigid and, if continued without amendment, may leave you with very little choice as to how you face the moment of thermonuclear truth. We believe that you may want to raise this question with Bob McNamara in order to have a prompt review and new orders if necessary. In essence, the current plan calls for shooting off everything we have in one shot, and is so constructed as to make any more flexible course very difficult." Galbraith, "Did the U.S. Military Plan a Nuclear First Strike for 1963?"

105. When, in a subsequent interview, I asked Kaysen about "poetry," he said he simply meant "imaginative literature," as much a matter of projection and guesswork as factual assessment.

106. Author interview.

107. Working with Kaysen was a political scientist with roots as a defense intellectual at RAND, Henry Rowen. In 1961, he was deputy assistant secretary of defense, working closely with McNamara.

108. Brodie, *The Absolute Weapon*, 46–47.

109. Bird, *The Color of Truth*, 206.

110. Trachtenberg, *History and Strategy*, 225.

111. Carl Kaysen, "Strategic Air Planning and Berlin," National Security Archives, Record Group 218, www.gwu.edu/~nsarchiv/nsaebb/nsaebb56/index2.html.

112. Quoted in Kaplan, "JFK's First-Strike Plan," 85. A few years after that meeting, General Power explained his rationale: "With such grisly tradition and shocking record in the massacre of their own people, the Soviets cannot be expected to let the risk of even millions of Russian lives deter them from starting a nuclear war if they should consider such a war to be in the best interest of the Communist cause. Nor would they be deterred by the danger of losing some cities because widespread devastation and subsequent recovery have had numerous precedents in Russia's hectic history . . . The point is that what will deter us will not necessarily deter the Soviets . . . Moral principles would deter us strongly from launching a preemptive war *unless there were no other way of averting certain aggression and still greater losses.* But moral considerations and the prospect of losing Russian lives and cities would not deter the Soviets from launching an aggressive war *if they saw no other way of achieving their objectives*" (italics mine, showing that, in attempting to contrast Soviet and American moral thinking, Power in fact equates the two). Power, *Design for Survival*, 111–13.

113. Office of the Historian, *SAC Missile Chronology*, 32.

114. Nitze, *From Hiroshima to Glasnost*, 204. While Nitze records himself in favor of a first strike here, it seems also to have been the case that he opposed the particular plan for such a strike put forward by Kaysen. He objected to that scenario because, though Kaysen imagined the American continent might well be spared, Nitze was sure the Soviets would fire their medium-range missiles at Western Europe, with many millions killed. Talbott, *The Master of the Game*, 82.

115. I found this sequence of events in Kaplan, "JFK's First-Strike Plan." Kaplan was the first journalist to learn of the existence of the Kaysen plan. Kaysen told him of it in an interview before Kaplan's 1983 book, *Wizards of Armageddon,* appeared. Once the actual document was declassified decades later, Kaplan was first to report on it, in the *Atlantic Monthly.*

116. Beschloss, *The Crisis Years*, 256; Bird, *The Color of Truth*, 207; Kaplan, *Wizards of Armageddon*, 299; Schell, "The Case Against the War."

117. Bird, *The Color of Truth*, 207.

118. Kaysen, "Strategic Air Planning and Berlin."

119. McGeorge Bundy was probably closer than anyone to Kennedy's day-to-day deliberations on the prospect of nuclear war that summer, and he said, years later, "I never heard Kennedy say what he would do at the limit on Berlin." At a press conference in mid-September 1961, as the United States was preparing to resume nuclear testing, McNamara was asked if he "might be intending to use nuclear weapons in connection with the Berlin crisis." He answered, "Yes." Newhouse, *War and Peace in the Nuclear Age*, 154, 157.

120. Kaysen, "Strategic Air Planning and Berlin."

121. Bird, *The Color of Truth*, 212, 214. Bird points out that Kaysen's proposal anticipated the rapprochement for which West German Chancellor Willy Brandt would later win the Nobel Peace Prize. When I discussed Bird's conclusion about the significance of his proposal with Kaysen, he demurred. Looking back decades after the fact, he doubted that Kennedy could actually have implemented it.

122. "Throughout his short presidency," Bird concludes, "Kennedy's political instincts persuaded him to avoid the political risks of accommodation and to accept the risks of military confrontation." Ibid., 214. The National Security Council formally resolved (NSC-109), on October 21, 1961, to use "selective nuclear attacks" up to "general nuclear war" over Berlin. LaFeber, *America, Russia, and the Cold War*, 226.

123. Sorensen, *Kennedy*, 583.

124. Bird, *The Color of Truth*, 214.

125. Nitze, *From Hiroshima to Glasnost*, 190.

126. Carl Kaysen, author interview.

127. Kaysen and Jerome Wiesner suggested that the Soviet nuclear test "would be a great propaganda opportunity for the United States." Kennedy replied, "What are you, peaceniks? They just kicked me in the nuts, and I'm supposed to say that's okay?" Reeves, *President Kennedy*, 223. It is interesting to note that the man who would become the Soviet Union's most famous "peacenik," Andrei Sakharov, began to earn that status in the same period (July 1961) by opposing Khrushchev's decision to resume nuclear testing. He was "unceremoniously" fired as chief of the Soviet nuclear program. Zubok and Harrison, "The Nuclear Education of Nikita Khrushchev," in Gaddis et al., *Cold War Statesmen Confront the Bomb*, 163.

128. Trachtenberg, *History and Strategy*, 231.

129. Kaplan, *Wizards of Armageddon*, 301.

130. For the Soviets, it almost goes without saying that the Berlin crisis was far more dangerous than the Cuban Missile Crisis, if only because Kremlin leaders would not have gone to war, in principle, over Cuba, while they certainly would have over Berlin. "Any sensible American should have understood," said Arkady Shevchenko, a former senior Soviet official, "that the Soviet Union wouldn't fight for Cuba." Newhouse, *War and Peace in the Nuclear Age*, 171. One such "sensible American" was Paul Nitze, who wrote in his memoir, "To my mind, the Berlin crisis of 1961 was a time of greater danger of nuclear confrontation with the Soviet Union than the Cuban missile crisis of 1962." *From Hiroshima to Glasnost*, 205. This point is made, too, by McGeorge Bundy in *Danger and Survival*.

131. Trachtenberg, *History and Strategy*, 231.

132. The analyst was Colonel John Wright. Prados, *The Soviet Estimate*, 138. I later heard the story from my mother of how Colonel Wright called my father at home at Bolling Air Force Base just as they were going out to dinner at the quarters of the JCS chairman. Upon their arrival at the dinner, my father took the chairman and other generals into a side room to brief them on what he'd heard from Colonel Wright. My father and the others left the dinner party. My mother did not see him again for some days.

133. Zaloga, *The Kremlin's Nuclear Sword*, 82.

134. Blight et al., *Cuba on the Brink*, 353. Some historians, like Graham Allison, see the episode as an exercise in skilled crisis management. Allison and Zelikow, *Essence of Decision*. McNamara, highlighting near-miss accidents and instances of miscommunication, sees the peaceful outcome as resulting more from pure dumb luck than anything else.

135. May and Zelikow, *The Kennedy Tapes*, 183.

136. Noteworthy is Kennedy's refusal throughout the crisis, in contrast with the Berlin crisis the year before, to order detailed plans for a nuclear war. Declassified tapes and other materials make clear that Kennedy was less concerned with threatening or coercing his Soviet counterpart than with helping him find a way out. America's overwhelming nuclear superiority was irrelevant to the outcome, and so, for that matter, was the Soviet Union's relative inferiority. A very limited nuclear exchange would have been horror enough. This was an instance of what is known as "finite deterrence," the idea that the smallest of nuclear arsenals is enough to compel the avoidance of war. See Lebow and Stein, "Deterrence and the Cold War," 170.

137. Talbott, *The Master of the Game*, 83.

138. Nitze, *From Hiroshima to Glasnost*, 223.

139. Newhouse, *War and Peace in the Nuclear Age*, 172.

140. Talbott, *The Master of the Game*, 84.

141. But controlling SAC was not so easy. When General Power ordered his forces to the high alert status known as DEFCON 2 (the acronym means "defense condition"), he did so, on his own authority, "in the clear." That is, the SAC commander issued his extremely sensitive order deliberately unencoded, so that Moscow would know. This failure to encrypt such an order was taken as an escalation of threat by the Soviets and could well have

prompted their panicked move toward a preemptive strike — which was probably what Power wanted. The Soviets had a very limited ability to launch such a strike at that point. Newhouse, *War and Peace in the Nuclear Age*, 175.

142. "The Dry Salvages," *T. S. Eliot: Collected Poems, 1909–1962* (New York: Harcourt, Brace & World, 1970), 194.

143. Talbott, *The Master of the Game*, 84. The transcripts of the early ExComm deliberations show a telling moment when the president said of the Soviet missiles in Cuba, "It's just as if we suddenly began to put a major number of MRBMs in Turkey. Now that'd be goddamn dangerous, I would think." To which McGeorge Bundy replied, "Well we did, Mister President." May and Neustadt, *Thinking in Time*, 9. It is possible that the well-informed Kennedy was being ironic here, to make a point.

144. Robert Kennedy insists that the secrecy of the Jupiter swap was essential to the offer, and in fact it was not made public at the time. The Jupiter withdrawal was announced by the Turkish government three months later. Seymour Hersh drew this point to my attention in a public lecture in 2003. His assessment of both Kennedys on this point is especially critical, not least for the destructive precedent such an appearance of toughness set for JFK's successors. Similarly, Jonathan Schell calls this secrecy an "iron rule" and relates the common anecdote that Kennedy threatened the Soviet ambassador Anatoly Dobrynin: "If you publish any document indicating a deal then it is off." *The Unconquerable World*, 60.

145. The record "shows a President taking matters into his own hands — a political animal who had decided to take the intense political heat that a public trade of missiles would generate rather than the possibly greater heat that would build up if he failed to act at once." Newhouse, *War and Peace in the Nuclear Age*, 181.

146. Bundy, *Danger and Survival*, 462.

147. "The Education of Robert McNamara" is the title of an episode in the PBS television series *The Cold War*.

148. Borklund, *Men of the Pentagon*, 222. Upon hearing that report, Kennedy ordered McNamara to take a vacation. McNamara went skiing with his family in Colorado. The secretary of defense was not the only one to register the strain. At the beginning of 1962, between Berlin and Cuba, Curtis LeMay suffered a heart attack and was hospitalized for more than a month. Coffey, *Iron Eagle*, 373.

149. Talbott, *The Master of the Game*, 86–88. Talbott says that, years later, Rumsfeld apologized to Nitze.

150. The graduated escalation of the air war against North Vietnam was a classic instance of the defense intellectuals' theory of coercion as a form of bargaining. It failed utterly, leading to the broad conclusion that "this body of thought" was now irrelevant. The Vietnamese refusal to be coerced led to the "sense that it [RAND-style strategic thinking] was out of touch with reality." Trachtenberg, *History and Strategy*, 44. This shift would be powerfully symbolized when the man who began as RAND's leading game theorist, Daniel Ellsberg, became disillusioned with the Vietnam War.

151. "Limited nuclear options" would make a comeback, particularly under Secretary of Defense James Schlesinger, who, like McNamara, sought alternatives to the SIOP war plan. Significantly, Schlesinger began at RAND, which was the source of McNamara's thinking. See Trachtenberg, *History and Strategy*, 39. There was some debate about the "survivability" of Soviet submarine-based missiles, since U.S. antisub forces became proficient at tracking them, especially in later stages of the Cold War. Theoretically, the United States could take out the Soviet subs as part of a first strike, but the operative word here is "theoretically."

152. Brodie, *The Absolute Weapon*, 46.

153. Clarfield and Wiecek, *Nuclear America*, 263.

154. Sorensen, *Kennedy*, 719.

155. Clarfield and Wiecek, *Nuclear America*, 260.

156. Borklund, *Men of the Pentagon*, 218.

157. Sorensen, *Kennedy*, 729. In 2005, it was revealed that in that same month of May Kennedy and his aides, including McNamara, Rusk, and Joint Chiefs Chairman Maxwell Taylor, seriously discussed using nuclear weapons against China, in defense of India. *New York Times*, August 26, 2005, A5.

158. Kennedy here echoes Stimson, who, in arguing for accommodation with Moscow, had written, "The face of war is the face of death." Stimson and Bundy, *On Active Service in Peace and War*, 633.

159. Theodore Sorensen was the one on whom Kennedy most depended in the drafting of this speech, but according to Sorensen's own account, McGeorge Bundy and Carl Kaysen made contributions. Sorensen, *Kennedy*, 730. John Kenneth Galbraith's biographer says Galbraith was consulted by Kennedy on the speech. Parker, *John Kenneth Galbraith*, 406. Arthur Schlesinger, Jr., told me he made suggestions for it as well. Author interview.

160. John F. Kennedy, "American University Speech," www.jfklibrary.org/speeches.htm.

161. Newhouse, *War and Peace in the Nuclear Age*, 193.

162. Clarfield and Wiecek, *Nuclear America*, 268; Sorensen, *Kennedy*, 733.

163. "Radio and Television Address to the American People on the Nuclear Test Ban Treaty," July 26, 1963, www.jfklibrary.org/speeches.htm.

164. Sorensen, *Kennedy*, 734.

165. Thomas Halsted, author interview.

166. Sorensen, *Kennedy*, 739. In his memoir, LeMay writes, "Reluctantly, we agreed that we would support a test ban treaty, *provided* certain safeguards were set up to reduce risk . . . We were to continue an extremely active underground test program within the restrictions of the treaty, so that we might accumulate as much as we could in additional knowledge on atomic subjects" (italics in original). *Mission with LeMay*, 544.

167. "Kennedy Sought Dialogue with Cuba: Initiative with Castro Aborted by Assassination, Declassified Documents Show," National Security Archives, November 24, 2003, www.gwu.edu/~nsarchiv.nsaebb/nsaebb103/index.htm.

168. Sorensen, *Kennedy*, 746.

169. Hamilton, *JFK: Reckless Youth*, xix. Hamilton helped me grasp the genius of Jacqueline Kennedy's association of her husband's death with Lincoln's instead of FDR's.

Six. The Exorcism

1. Hendrickson, *The Living and the Dead*, 300.

2. Most accounts of the march on the Pentagon put the figure at about fifty thousand, although at the time, the Pentagon itself said there were twenty thousand protesters.

3. The image is Paul Hendrickson's, *The Living and the Dead*, 299. McNamara's biographer describes him as seeing the marchers as "speckled like a long snake, winding up the drive to the lawn below his window." Shapley, *Promise and Power*, 435. Norman Mailer compared the snaking crowd to a caterpillar. *The Armies of the Night*, 128.

4. David Dellinger said, "This is the beginning of a new stage in the American peace movement in which the cutting edge becomes active resistance." Goldstein, *William Sloane Coffin, Jr.*, 200.

5. The text of the exorcism is given in Mailer, *The Armies of the Night*, 139–40.

6. I described the gradual but inexorable break in my relationship with my father over the Vietnam War in *An American Requiem*.

7. www.cs.umb.edu/jfklibrary.

8. *Pacem in Terris*, www.vatican.va.

9. *New York Times*, October 5, 1965, A1.

10. Mailer, *The Armies of the Night*, 285. About the exorcism, Mailer turned to the poet

Robert Lowell and said, "You know I like this." To which a "not untroubled" Lowell replied, "It was all right for a while, but it's so damn repetitious" (143).

11. Coffey, *Iron Eagle*, 4.

12. McPherson, *A Political Education*, 393.

13. General Emmett (Rosie) O'Donnell, Jr., not to be confused with the movie actress.

14. Jimmy Stewart had done his part for the Strategic Air Command, starring in a mythmaking movie of the same name.

15. Goodwin, *Remembering America*, 305. The line, of course, is taken from W. H. Auden's poem "September 1, 1939," although it is altered. Auden has it as "We must love one another or die."

16. The original SAC motto was "War is our profession — peace is our product." It was changed in 1958. www.centennialofflight.gov/essay/dictionary/sac.

17. Goldwater had published a celebration of SAC, a defense of LeMay, in combination with a diatribe against any talk of disarmament, against the United Nations, and against the "nuclear philosophers' . . . omnipresent implication that no matter what happens we cannot use the bomb." Goldwater, *Why Not Victory?*, 181.

18. McNamara, *In Retrospect*, 174.

19. Goodwin, *Remembering America*, 368.

20. Coffey, *Iron Eagle*, 369.

21. "And you will always — won't you? — find yourself groping / in a dark stairwell ill-lit by that feeble, dangerous lamp / while you drag along, strapped to you, the corpse of all your errors." Rosanna Warren, "Departure," *Departure* (New York: Norton, 2003), 31. Warren is quoting Max Beckmann.

22. Mailer, *The Armies of the Night*, 110.

23. Miller, *Democracy Is in the Streets*, 282.

24. Allison, *Essence of Decision*. See also the revised and updated edition of this work, Allison and Zelikow, *Essence of Decision*, and Halperin, *Bureaucratic Politics and Foreign Policy*. An early political theorist working to understand the relationship between war and the organization of states, as opposed to individual agents, is Kenneth N. Waltz. See his classic text, *Man, the State, and War*.

25. Kennan, *Memoirs*, 351. The historian Barton J. Bernstein contrasts Allison's "rational actor" analysis with that of Kennan, who "lamented virtually the opposite: that in his judgment, the influences of popular passions and of legalisms and moralisms, and of bureaucratic or personal disputes, had frequently blocked the proper formation of U.S. foreign policy." Bernstein, "Understanding Decisionmaking," 147.

26. Nolan, *Guardians of the Arsenal*, 126.

27. Shattuck, *Proust's Way*, 84.

28. McNamara, *In Retrospect*, 174.

29. "Black and hideous to me is the tragedy that gathers . . . The tide that bore us along was then all the while moving us to this as its grand Niagara . . . I avert my face from the monstrous scene." James wrote this on August 10, 1914. Schell, *The Unconquerable World*, 305. Schell uses "Niagara" as a chapter heading and an organizing idea, and in that, with full acknowledgment, I follow him. Hannah Arendt was drawn to the same metaphor. She defined the wars of the twentieth century as events "cascading like a Niagara Falls of history." *Responsibility and Judgment*, x.

30. Trachtenberg, *History and Strategy*, 219.

31. The treaty was signed in Moscow on August 5, 1963, and went into effect on October 10.

32. Lawrence, *Studies in Classic American Literature*, 137–38.

33. Melville, *Moby Dick*, 194–95.

34. "The Eighteenth Brumaire of Louis Bonaparte," in Tucker, *The Marx-Engels Reader*, 595.

35. Goodwin, *Remembering America*, 387.

36. John Kennedy as a figure of hope for the countervailing power of good choices was matched by his brother Robert, who gave the idea its most eloquent expression in South Africa, where he invoked the image of the ripple becoming a great wave, bringing change for the better.

37. Shapley, *Promise and Power*, 415.

38. "Bob's greatest concern at the beginning of 1965 was his fear that he might not be able to talk the president into the bombing. He spent all his time preparing arguments and lining up allies." Cited by Goodwin, *Remembering America*, 375.

39. The aide was John Roche, cited by Shapley, *Promise and Power*, 426. Shapley reports that McNamara dismisses Roche's characterization of his emotional state in this period as "absolutely absurd." In his memoir, McNamara rejects any comparison with Forrestal, saying he "never contemplated suicide." *In Retrospect*, 313.

40. Shapley, *Promise and Power*, 426.

41. Hendrickson, *The Living and the Dead*, 299.

42. Sheehan, *A Bright Shining Lie*, 684.

43. Polner and O'Grady, *Disarmed and Dangerous*, 171. By 1967, "all" included JFK's inner circle, men like Galbraith, Goodwin, and Schlesinger. They formed an organization called Negotiations Now.

44. *New York Times*, August 26, 1967, A1.

45. McNamara, *In Retrospect*, 228, 244, 288.

46. Quoted by Hendrickson, *The Living and the Dead*, 320.

47. *New York Times*, August 26, 1967, A5.

48. Shapley, *Promise and Power*, 432. In his memoir, McNamara states that he doubts the truth of the report that the Chiefs considered resigning. *In Retrospect*, 291.

49. Hendrickson, *The Living and the Dead*, 343.

50. Schell, *The Unconquerable World*, 95.

51. Engelhardt, *The End of Victory Culture*, 169.

52. "Deterrence advocates, all of them prepared at least to threaten mass extermination, advance arguments of several kinds. At one pole are the minority of open partisans of preventive war — who falsely assume the inevitability of violent conflict and assert the lunatic efficacy of striking the first blow, assuming that it will be easier to 'recover' after thermonuclear war than to recover now from the grip of the Cold War. Somewhat more reluctant to advocate initiating a war, but perhaps more disturbing for their numbers within the Kennedy administration, are the many advocates of the 'counterforce' theory of aiming strategic nuclear weapons at military installations — though this might 'save' more lives than a preventive war, it would require drastic, provocative and perhaps impossible social change to separate many cities from weapons sites, it would be impossible to ensure the immunity of cities after one or two counterforce nuclear 'exchanges,' it would generate a perpetual arms race . . . make outer space a region subject to militarization, and accelerate the suspicions and arms build-ups which are incentives to precipitate nuclear action." coursea.matrix.msu.edu/~hst306/documents/huron.html.

53. Polner and O'Grady, *Disarmed and Dangerous*, 144. Daniel Berrigan gives an account of the gathering: "Bobby Kennedy and his wife, the Shrivers, an ambassador, and Robert McNamara. At the end of the dinner, Shriver got up and said, 'We would like to hear from the Secretary [of Defense] and Father Berrigan on the subject of Vietnam.' We went into another room and had drinks. I said, 'The war is only about killing people, why not stop it now? End it tonight.' McNamara was cool: 'In response to Daniel Berrigan I would

say this: I think of Vietnam as Mississippi. When the law is not obeyed, we send in the troops.' I was stunned by the analogy, and didn't say anything beyond it. But when I got home I wrote it all down in my diary. I thought, in a week I won't believe this. I've remembered it thirty years" (144).

54. Daniel Berrigan, author interview.

55. Ibid.

56. The most famous would be the raid on a draft board in Catonsville, Maryland, in May 1968, for which Daniel and Philip served nearly two years in federal prison. By the time Philip died in 2003, he would have spent much of the intervening thirty-five years in prison for a succession of acts of antiwar civil disobedience.

57. On the afternoon of June 15, 1955, as Day recounted it, "we went to the park and sat down on the benches there, and when the sirens began their warning we continued to sit. At 2:05 a number of elaborately uniformed men with much brass, stars, and ribbons of past battles hung on their blue auxiliary police outfits marched upon us and told us to move. When we refused, they announced we were under arrest, and the police van was driven up inside the park." Miller, *Dorothy Day,* 438. In fact, Day's first arrest had occurred years before, in 1917, when she was jailed in Washington for participating in a suffragette protest.

58. Wittner, *One World or None,* 332.

59. The Pugwash movement would be awarded the Nobel Peace Prize in 1995.

60. Norman Cousins, editor of the *Saturday Review,* was a leading figure behind SANE, its most famous early member was Dr. Benjamin Spock, and, in the 1990s, its president was William Sloane Coffin, Jr.

61. Freedman, *The Evolution of Nuclear Strategy,* 197.

62. Ibid., 198–99. See also Bok, *Alva Myrdal,* 303f.

63. Both men contributed to the milestone "Arms Control" issue of *Daedalus.* Kahn's article was titled "The Arms Race and Some of Its Hazards." Teller's was "The Feasibility of Arms Control and the Principle of Openness." Of the two dozen articles, a dissenting note was struck by the psychologist Erich Fromm, "The Case for Unilateral Disarmament."

64. Freedman, *The Evolution of Nuclear Strategy,* 199.

65. About resuming testing at this point, Kennedy said to Adlai Stevenson, who opposed it, "Shit, I have no choice. They spit in our eye three times. I have to do this." Reeves, *President Kennedy,* 227.

66. John F. Kennedy, "Address Before the General Assembly of the United Nations, September 25, 1961," www.cs.umb.edu/jfklibrary/j092561.htm speech.

67. Thomas Halsted, author interview. "The Arms Control Agency . . . it was hard to have the word 'disarmament' in there."

68. Cook, *The Warfare State,* 251.

69. Thomas Halsted, author interview.

70. Ibid.

71. Cook, *The Warfare State,* 258.

72. Kennedy, "Address Before the General Assembly."

73. Only a few months before the October demonstration at the Pentagon, Zinn had published *Vietnam: The Logic of Withdrawal,* arguing for an immediate removal of U.S. forces.

74. In the Tet Offensive, 58,000 Communist soldiers died, along with untold numbers of civilians, and 1,100 Americans. Helms, *A Look over My Shoulder,* 331.

75. Berrigan, "My Name," *And the Risen Bread,* 117.

76. Zinn, *You Can't Be Neutral on a Moving Train,* 131. See also Berrigan, *Night Flight to Hanoi.*

77. Berrigan, *And the Risen Bread,* 114–15.

78. Or almost never. Many years later, Zinn was traveling on a commercial airliner in

the United States. When the pilot's voice greeted the passengers, Zinn recognized his name and sent a message to the cockpit with the flight attendant, asking if, by chance, the pilot remembered the name Howard Zinn. The pilot came back to Zinn's seat. "We greeted each other, but it was very awkward. He quickly went back up front, and I didn't see him again." Author interview.

79. Polner and O'Grady, *Disarmed and Dangerous*, 183.

80. To be arrested with the celebrity Berrigans was to be consigned to the status of "others." I remember a joke that made the rounds of the Catholic Left, that if the priests died in a plane crash, the newspapers would report "The Berrigan brothers and 174 others were killed . . ." The seven others at Catonsville were Tom Lewis, Mary Moylan, David Darst, Marjorie Melville, Thomas Melville, John Hogan, and George Mische.

81. Zinn, *You Can't Be Neutral on a Moving Train*, 134–35.

82. Patterson, *Grand Expectations*, 699.

83. Berrigan was arrested on Block Island, Rhode Island, at the home of the lawyer and theologian William Stringfellow, on August 11, 1970.

84. I tell it in *An American Requiem*.

85. Laird was the chairman of the House Republican Policy Committee. Talbott, *The Master of the Game*, 97.

86. Robert McNamara, author interview.

87. www.lbjlib.utexas.edu.

88. McNamara, *The Essence of Security*, 64.

89. Robert McNamara, author interview.

90. Talbott, *The Master of the Game*, 108.

91. For this service, the Navy named a destroyer after Nitze in 2004, not long before he died. Navy ships are rarely named for living persons.

92. Talbott uses the term "hairpin turn" to describe the shift in the speech. *The Master of the Game*, 97.

93. Robert McNamara, author interview. Fred Kaplan points out that when McNamara collected his speeches into a volume, *The Essence of Security*, "he placed only the first part of the San Francisco speech in the main body of the book. The last part, the part calling for an anti-China ABM, the part that served his purposes as a bureaucrat under pressure but embarrassed him as an intellectual, he buried in an obscure appendix at the back." *Wizards of Armageddon*, 348.

94. McNamara, *The Essence of Security*, 165.

95. June 17, 1966.

96. Richard Garwin, "Missile Defense," www.fas.org.rlg.

97. Halperin, *Bureaucratic Politics and Foreign Policy*, 3.

98. Ibid., 307. Since the mid-1960s, the Soviets were assumed to be working on a limited ABM system to protect Moscow (called "Galosh"), and another to be deployed in other places ("Tallinn"), but the latter was probably more an air defense system than an ABM system. A year after Kosygin's rejection of McNamara's logic at Glassboro in 1967, the Soviets — perhaps because of the "anti-Chinese" Sentinel — had changed their position and were seeking an agreement to curb the ABM. Lyndon Johnson hoped to reach it at an October 1968 summit in Moscow, but the Soviet invasion of Czechoslovakia in August made that impossible.

99. Newhouse, *War and Peace in the Nuclear Age*, 205.

100. Nolan, *Guardians of the Arsenal*, 95.

101. Bundy, "To Cap the Volcano," 1–20.

102. The aide was Richard Neustadt. Ernest R. May, in Gaddis et al., *Cold War Statesmen Confront the Bomb*, 4.

103. Talbott, *The Master of the Game*, 101.

104. These numbers define the growth of arms on both sides: In 1962, the United States had 229 ICBM launchers (as apposed to mere warheads) and 144 submarine-based launchers (SLBMs). The Soviets had 50 ICBMs and 97 SLBMs. By 1970, the U.S. had 1,054 ICBM launchers and 656 SLBMs, and was arming both with MIRVs, which would multiply the warheads. The Soviets had 1,427 ICBM launchers and 289 sub launchers, and would continue to add launchers, moving inevitably to MIRVs. Nitze, *From Hiroshima to Glasnost*, 287.

105. Quoted by Talbott, *The Master of the Game*, 99.

106. American tests began on August 16, 1968. Soviet tests began on August 28. Newhouse, *War and Peace in the Nuclear Age*, 208.

107. In 1968, an AP wire-service report quoted an American artillery officer, after the brutal shelling of the town of Ben Tre, in the Mekong Delta, as saying, "We had to destroy it in order to save it." Hodgson, *America in Our Time*, 356.

108. "The bastards have never been bombed like they're going to be bombed this time," Nixon said in early 1972. Patterson, *Grand Expectations*, 758.

109. The Non-Proliferation Treaty was signed on July 1, 1968, and took effect on March 5, 1970. Clause VI of the treaty committed the United States, along with the other nuclear powers, to work for the eventual elimination of nuclear weapons. Thus the goal of nuclear abolition, a dream of the disarmers and a joke to the realists, was now enshrined in U.S. law. In 1995, the treaty was renewed in perpetuity, with 178 nations pledged to it.

110. Robert McNamara, author interview. McNamara retired from the World Bank in 1981, and the next year, he joined with George Kennan, McGeorge Bundy, and Gerard K. Smith, a former SALT delegation chief, to issue a stirring critique of nuclear weapons. "Nuclear Weapons and the Atlantic Alliance" (a monument to Lifton's "nuclear retirement syndrome"). With this article McNamara's apostolate of nuclear disarmament began. His books, especially his Vietnam memoir, *In Retrospect*, were greeted with broad hostility, and in 2003, a documentary film about him, *The Fog of War* by Errol Morris, put his moral confusion on full display.

111. Robert McNamara, author interview.

112. Herman Melville, *Moby Dick*, 598.

113. Talbott, *The Master of the Game*, 123.

114. Ibid., 112.

115. Ibid., 120. In later years, Nitze would put the "year of maximum danger" at 1984, and then at 1994, always carrying forward the logic of NSC-68. The Soviet Union, the moment it could do so with a reasonable risk of "tolerable" losses, was certain to launch a nuclear attack against the United States.

116. SALT I, "The Interim Agreement on the Limitation of Strategic Offensive Weapons," limited submarine-launched missiles and ICBMs and forbade the conversion of older missiles to newer versions. "The only American proposal on MIRV that was put forward in SALT I was for a test ban with on-site inspections, in those days an excellent way of ensuring Soviet rejection." Bundy, *Danger and Survival*, 552.

117. Ibid., 552–53.

118. Isaacson, *Kissinger*, 322. See also Newhouse, *War and Peace in the Nuclear Age*, 223.

119. Hyland, *Mortal Rivals*, 43.

120. Richard Perle would go from his work for Nitze to a staff position with Senator Henry Jackson, who, with Perle's help, would emerge as a staunch critic of SALT I and any notion of "parity." In 2004, at an Aspen Institute ceremony in honor of Nitze (a founder of the institute), Wolfowitz gave the keynote speech. As deputy secretary of defense under Donald Rumsfeld, he had been the chief architect of the Bush administration's war on terrorism and the war in Iraq, and one of his allies was Richard Perle, by then a senior Pentagon veteran. In that speech, Wolfowitz defined himself as Nitze's protégé — he had followed

Nitze as head of policy planning at the State Department and as deputy secretary of defense, and had served as head of the Nitze School at Johns Hopkins. Wolfowitz proudly traced the lineage back to Forrestal, whom he recalled as saying "Damn you, Paul!" when Nitze told him, in 1940, that he should leave Dillon, Read to help prepare the nation for war. In his memoir, Nitze brags that the 1969 papers that Perle and Wolfowitz "helped us produce ran rings around the misinformed and illogical papers" produced by ABM opponents. *From Hiroshima to Glasnost,* 295.

121. Talbott, *The Master of the Game,* 118.

122. The Pentagon Papers were a seven-thousand-page collation of documents related to the conduct of the war, many of them classified Top Secret. McNamara had ordered the compilation in June 1967, as his disillusionment with the war was becoming complete, and one of its editors, Daniel Ellsberg, also disillusioned, leaked the documents two years later. The Supreme Court upheld the right of the press to publish the material. An infuriated Nixon put together a group called "the plumbers" to plug such leaks, leading to Watergate and his downfall.

123. Herring, *The Pentagon Papers,* 168.

124. Patterson, *Grand Expectations,* 635.

125. McNamara, *In Retrospect,* 104, 288, 294. In March 1968, to take another example of Air Force–DIA conflict, the Air Force was insisting on the effectiveness of its bombing of targets in North Vietnam as part of its bid for a major expansion of tactical fighter squadrons, but DIA reports undercut that bid, even as they contributed to Lyndon Johnson's decision that month to cut back on such bombing. Halperin, *Bureaucratic Politics and Foreign Policy,* 49.

126. Talbott, *The Master of the Game,* 99. In late 1967, McNamara had been explicit: "Does [the Soviet Union] possess a first-strike capability against the United States? The answer is that it does not. Can the Soviet Union in the foreseeable future acquire such a first-strike capability against the United States? The answer is that it cannot." Remarks in San Francisco, September 18, 1967, in "Foreign Relations, 1964–1968," document 192, www.state .gov/r/pa/ho/frus/johnson/b/x/9099.htm.

127. *Newsweek,* May 12, 1969, 18. The Laird statement depended on the assessment that the Soviet SS-9 was being outfitted with MIRV warheads that would be able to target and destroy 95 percent of the Minuteman missile force, a degree of reliability such that "they would no longer be deterred from launching a nuclear war." Prados, *The Soviet Estimate,* 210.

128. *Time,* August 29, 1969, 14.

129. In 2005, Laird published an article proposing "Vietnamization" as a model for the war in Iraq—as if Vietnamization had succeeded.

130. Richard Helms offers this definition of "first strike": The phrase "means much more than landing the first blow. A successful first-strike ICBM salvo will demolish the enemy's ability to return fire. By definition, a first strike is a knockout blow." *A Look over My Shoulder,* 386.

131. *U.S. News & World Report,* April 7, 1969, 36.

132. The Intelligence Board consisted of the directors of the CIA, the DIA, the FBI, and the National Security Agency, and representatives of the intelligence arms of the military branches, the State Department, the Treasury Department, and the Atomic Energy Commission.

133. "Foreign and Military Intelligence: Final Report of the Select Committee to Study Governmental Operations with Respect to Intelligence Activities," United States Senate, April 26, 1976. Later Laird would seize on the phrase "within the period of this estimate" to suggest that there was a disagreement because the intelligence report was "short term" while his warning was "longer term." See also Steury, *Intentions and Capabilities,* 239–61;

"Soviet Strategic Air and Missile Defenses (NIE 11-3-68, 11-8-68)," www.foia.cia.gov/browse
_docs_full.asp?doc_no=0000278480&title+soviet+str.

134. Helms, *A Look over My Shoulder*, 385. See also NIE 11-3-68, 24.

135. Hearing, Committee on Foreign Relations, United States Senate, 91st Congress, 1st session, with Melvin R. Laird, Secretary of Defense, June 23, 1969, 12.

136. *Time*, August 29, 1969, 18.

137. Hearing, Committee on Foreign Relations, June 23, 1969, 9.

138. Powers, *The Man Who Kept the Secrets*, 212.

139. Prados, *The Soviet Estimate*, 213. The memo stated that the SS-9 was being armed not with MIRV warheads but with MRVs (multiple warheads, but not independently targeted), which meant the missile would never be accurate enough to wipe out the Minuteman.

140. "Memorandum to Holders, NIE 11-8-68," June 23, 1969, www.foia.cia.gov/browse
_docs_full.asp?doc_no=0000278487&title=soviet+str, 11.

141. Powers, *The Man Who Kept the Secrets*, 212.

142. "Foreign and Military Intelligence: Final Report," 77.

143. Powers, *The Man Who Kept the Secrets*, 212.

144. Hearing, Committee on Foreign Relations, June 23, 1969, 71.

145. The deleted passage reads in full: "We believe that the Soviets recognize the enormous difficulty of any attempt to achieve strategic superiority of such order as to significantly alter the strategic balance. Consequently, we consider it highly unlikely that they will attempt within the period of this estimate to achieve a first strike capability, i.e., a capability to launch a surprise attack against the U.S. with assurance that the USSR would not itself receive damage it would regard as unacceptable. For one thing, the Soviets would almost certainly conclude that the cost of such an undertaking along with all their other military commitments would be prohibitive. More important, they almost certainly would consider it impossible to develop and deploy the combination of offensive and defensive forces necessary to counter successfully the various elements of U.S. strategic attack forces. Finally, even if such a project were economically and technically feasible the Soviets almost certainly would calculate that the U.S. would detect and match or overmatch their efforts." The only reason this text is available is that its deletion became the subject of a subsequent investigation into undue political pressure being applied to the intelligence community by the so-called Church committee. "Foreign and Military Intelligence: Final Report," 78.

146. A mild version of the deleted paragraph appeared in the final NIE, but as a footnote attributed to the State Department representative: "He believes that the Soviets would face great difficulties in any attempt to achieve strategic superiority of such an order as to significantly alter the strategic balance. In particular, he does not see how they would be able within the period of this estimate to achieve a capability to launch a surprise attack against the U.S. with assurance that the USSR would not itself receive damage it would regard as unacceptable." NIE 11-8-69, in Steury, *Intentions and Capabilities*, 261.

147. Powers, *The Man Who Kept the Secrets*, 212. In his own defense, writing in his memoir, published in 2003, Helms said, "An important factor in my decision to compromise with the Defense Department position was my long-standing conviction that it is a serious mistake for any intelligence service ever to assume it has achieved absolute wisdom. I disagreed with the Pentagon position, and could not suppress the feeling it was tainted by the Nixon administration's determination to develop an anti-ballistic missile." In Helms's account, the contradiction between Laird's position on first strike and the intelligence estimate's position did not become public until early September 1969, but the record shows that the dispute had been widely publicized in Washington from April on. *A Look over My Shoulder*, 386.

148. Prados, *The Soviet Estimate*, 218. In his account of this dispute in his memoir, Helms is circumspect. He does not distinguish between "the Pentagon" and the DIA, as if

the DIA agreed with Laird throughout the controversy instead of only at the end of it. The records cited above show the CIA and DIA consistently "concurring."

149. Joseph Carroll was relieved of duty as head of the DIA in July 1969, shortly after Senator Fulbright challenged Laird on contradictions with his own intelligence sources. The "updated" intelligence estimate on Soviet ICBM capability, removing the note of contradiction, was published in "early September." Helms, *A Look over My Shoulder,* 386.

150. Charles Davis, author interview. Davis was assigned as a Navy lieutenant to the Defense Intelligence Agency in 1962, and remained with it, in Washington, as a civilian, until 1984. Davis spent most of this time with the Directorate for Estimates and was involved in the controversial National Intelligence Estimate at issue when my father was terminated.

151. Deane Allen, author interview. Allen began as the head of the DIA's Office of History in the early 1980s. He told me that Carroll's conflicts with Laird concerned the counterintelligence function of the DIA, and the DIA's authority in relation to the Joint Chiefs. Consistent with other trends under Laird, it seems likely that the DIA's autonomy established under McNamara was to be mitigated by bringing the agency more directly under the Chiefs.

152. In *An American Requiem,* I reported that my father testified before the Senate committee. Any such hearing would have been secret. Congressional records from that period have now been declassified, and I find no reference to my father's testimony. But not all briefings were recorded. Because of his history with Symington, a member of the committee, I still assume my father's connection to the committee's challenge to Laird.

153. Keegan, *The Face of Battle,* 330.

154. Bundy, *Danger and Survival,* 550. But history can play its tricks. Nixon, Kissinger, and Laird did not know it yet, but Robert McNamara had, in fact, turned a tide against the ABM. The Soviet Union, belatedly taking up the argument McNamara had made to Kosygin at Glassboro, changed its position. Nixon's SALT negotiators, overruling their fellow member Paul Nitze, accepted the principle that defensive measures amounted to a new and dangerous escalation. "The treaty limiting ABMs to very low levels, negotiated in Moscow in May 1972," Morton Halperin observed, "was a final vindication of McNamara's position." *Bureaucratic Politics and Foreign Policy,* 310.

155. My impression is that the ceremony was presided over by a representative of the Joint Chiefs and attended only by my mother and his closest aides, but I have not been able to confirm that. My father's medical condition was given as the reason for his retirement.

156. Melville, *Moby Dick,* 614.

157. Schell, *The Unconquerable World,* 305.

158. Polner and O'Grady, *Disarmed and Dangerous,* 253.

159. In *An American Requiem,* I describe how my brother Brian was an arresting FBI agent in the case of the Camden 28, and I was a character witness for one of those he had helped arrest (235–36).

160. Polner and O'Grady, *Disarmed and Dangerous,* 239.

161. "FBI Reports Plot by Antiwar Group to Kidnap U.S. Aide," *New York Times,* November 28, 1970, A1.

162. Polner and O'Grady, *Disarmed and Dangerous,* 280.

163. The trial was held in Harrisburg, Pennsylvania. The Harrisburg Eight were Philip; a nun, Elizabeth McAlister; three other priests, Neil McLaughlin, Joseph Weneroth, and Anthony Scoblick, together with Scoblick's new wife, an ex-nun named Mary Cain Scoblick; and an antidraft organizer, John Glick. Unaccountably, a Pakistan-born scholar, Eqbal Ahmad, was indicted as well, but it would turn out that he was the one who proposed a "citizen's arrest" of Kissinger. Polner and O'Grady, *Disarmed and Dangerous,* 280.

164. McGowan, *Peace Warriors,* 26.

165. On August 22, 1970, Philip Berrigan wrote about the proposed plan to kidnap

Kissinger: "This comes off the top of my head. Why not grab the Brain Child [Kissinger], treat him decently, but tell him nothing of his fate — or tell him his fate hinges on the release of pol[itical] people or cessation of air strikes in Laos . . . One thing should be implanted in that pea brain — that respectable murderers like himself are no longer inviolable." Bill Kovach, "Berrigan Case Broadened; Letters on 'Plot' Released," *New York Times,* May 1, 1971, 1, 12; Polner and O'Grady, *Disarmed and Dangerous,* 282–83.

166. The FBI's William Sullivan, one of Hoover's top aides, was appalled at the charges. "The Berrigans and their followers dreamed up and discussed hundreds of wild schemes to break into buildings and destroy federal property," he said, "ninety-nine percent of which never got beyond the discussion stage." Polner and O'Grady, *Disarmed and Dangerous,* 269.

167. Philip Berrigan died in 2002.

168. Miller, *Democracy Is in the Streets,* 325.

169. Mailer divides the forces of evil and good as between "the witches and the fugs." *The Armies of the Night,* 135.

170. Hodgson, *America in Our Time,* 378.

171. Nixon hated it when this campaign was referred to as the "Christmas bombing," since on December 25 itself the campaign was suspended. He preferred the military name, Operation Linebacker.

172. Isaacson, *Kissinger,* 470.

173. January 22, 1973, was also the day that Lyndon Johnson died in Texas, and the day the U.S. Supreme Court handed down its *Roe v. Wade* decision.

174. Polner and O'Grady, *Disarmed and Dangerous,* 298.

Seven. Upstream

1. Newhouse, *War and Peace in the Nuclear Age,* 236.

2. In 1972, the U.S. nuclear arsenal totaled 12,363 strategic warheads and 12,615 nonstrategic warheads. The Soviet Union was approaching numerical parity by then. National Resources Defense Council, www.nrdc.org/nuclear/nudb/datab9.asp.

3. In 1960, for example, the Council for a Livable World was established by Leo Szilard and other nuclear scientists. In the 1970s, George Kennan, John Kenneth Galbraith, and others organized the American Committee on East-West Accord. In the late 1980s, Galbraith helped found Economists Allied for Arms Reduction. Parker, *John Kenneth Galbraith,* 581.

4. The ABM Treaty did allow each side to defend two sites with ABM systems, but this was a token gesture that came to nothing.

5. Newhouse, *War and Peace in the Nuclear Age,* 233.

6. Nolan, *Guardians of the Arsenal,* 106.

7. Hyland, *Mortal Rivals,* 40. The B-1's first flight was in December 1974, the Trident was authorized in November 1973, and the Abrams was deployed in 1980.

8. Ibid., 54.

9. Melvin Laird left the administration at the beginning of Nixon's second term, having "presided over one of the most difficult military operations in history — the withdrawal of a nearly shattered 500,000-man army" from Vietnam. Perry, *Four Stars,* 244. Laird was replaced by Elliot Richardson, a moderate Republican whose strong ties to Congress were expected to result in increases in the defense budget, the beginning of the post-Vietnam recovery. But Richardson was shuffled to the attorney general's office in July 1973, where Nixon, under Watergate pressure, needed him more. Nixon offered the secretary of defense post to David Packard, who turned it down. James Schlesinger, having served, after RAND, in the Bureau of the Budget and as CIA director, was named to replace Richardson. Kissinger, having been appointed national security adviser at the start of Nixon's first term

in 1969, was named secretary of state, replacing William Rogers, on August 22, 1973. His first accomplishment as holder of both positions was the coup in Chile in which President Salvador Allende was murdered on September 11.

10. Kissinger was aiming for the City College of New York, to become an accountant, when he was drafted — in January 1943, as it happens, just as the Pentagon was being dedicated. His Army service expanded his horizons, and when he returned from the war, he went to Harvard. He and Schlesinger were members of the class of 1950.

11. Isaacson, *Kissinger*, 85.

12. Kennedy, too, had substance abuse problems. At the very least, his addiction to drugs that were prescribed for his physical ailments was an issue, yet his stewardship of nuclear weapons, compared to Nixon's, was prudent. Dallek, *An Unfinished Life*, 398.

13. There has been some debate on whether deterrence "worked." For example, Richard Ned Lebow and Janice Gross Stein assembled the primary-source documentation available in the early 1990s to "test" deterrence theory against the historical record in Cuba and critical events in 1973. They found it wrong as an explanatory theory and dangerous as a strategy. The outcomes, they show, did not depend on threats but rather on reassurances. Martin Malin drew my attention to their work and made plain its significance. Their book is called *We All Lost the Cold War*. I cite their summary article "Deterrence and the Cold War."

14. Seymour Hersh wrote that the Nixon alert put American military forces at DEFCON 1. Hersh, *The Price of Power*, 124. But Henry Kissinger defined DEFCON 1 as war. DEFCON 2 is readiness for an imminent attack. DEFCON 3 is "readiness without the determination that war is likely." Normally the U.S. strategic forces are at DEFCON 4. Kissinger, *Years of Upheaval*, 588.

15. Newhouse, *War and Peace in the Nuclear Age*, 282. Soviet strategic forces would come to a heightened alert in response to Ronald Reagan's broadcast joke that he was about to "bomb Russia," but not even that was a full alert.

16. In addition to October 1969, heightened alerts of the U.S. military were ordered in September 1970, during the "Jordan crisis," and during the Yom Kippur War in 1973. Kissinger, *Years of Upheaval*, 591. In his memoir, Kissinger mentions the latter two, but not the 1969 alert.

17. Haldeman, *The Ends of Power*, 83. See also Sagan and Suri, "The Madman Nuclear Alert," 156; Isaacson, *Kissinger*, 163. Ironically, the madman theory had its origins in the game theorizing of RAND analysts. Daniel Ellsberg is often credited with the idea, something I asked him about. He said that he "used to worry that [he] was the source of the idea" — it would have come from Ellsberg through Kissinger to Nixon — "which would have been a heavy responsibility." But Ellsberg concluded that Nixon had come to the idea from other sources. Author interview.

18. Sagan and Suri, "The Madman Nuclear Alert," 150.

19. The 1969 "nuclear ploy" was revealed for the first time in the December 23, 2002, issue of the *Bulletin of the Atomic Scientists*, "Nixon's Nuclear Ploy," by the National Security Archive analyst William Burr and the Miami University historian Jeffrey Kimball. Some months later Scott D. Sagan and Jeremi Suri published "The Madman Nuclear Alert," on which I mainly depend. Sagan and Suri point out that the secrecy of this alert was maintained until 1992, when certain SAC records were declassified. When Seymour Hersh published an account of the alert in his 1983 book on Kissinger (*The Price of Power*, 124), critics dismissed it. Sagan and Suri, "The Madman Nuclear Alert," 156.

20. September 2, 1969.

21. Isaacson, *Kissinger*, 164.

22. Haldeman records the remark in his diary for October 20, 1969. Sagan and Suri, "The Madman Nuclear Alert," 173.

23. April 25, 1972. Kissinger said of the nuclear bomb, "That, I think, would just be too much."

24. Sagan and Suri comment, "There is no evidence in the available records that White House officials were even informed of this important detail of the nuclear alert operation." "The Madman Nuclear Alert," 168.

25. It had begun in March 1969.

26. Sagan and Suri, "The Madman Nuclear Alert," 179.

27. There is no way to know if the "madman alert" prompted the Soviets to begin the SALT talks, but it is likely that the U.S. Senate's having voted in favor of the ABM only weeks before, in August, played a part in it.

28. Since 1969, the American news media had cooperated in the creation of this myth, emphasizing, for example, that the Vietnam story was all about peace talks in Paris, not combat in Southeast Asia. When, before the 1972 election, Kissinger declared "Peace is at hand," Americans believed it, though the war's most savage bombing lay in the future, not the past. See Hodgson, *America in Our Time,* 378.

29. A supreme irony of this history lies in the fact that McGovern's campaign was hobbled at the outset when his designated running mate, Senator Thomas Eagleton, was revealed to have undergone shock treatments years before for psychiatric problems. If anyone should have received psychiatric help, it was Nixon.

30. Kissinger, *Years of Upheaval,* 581.

31. Ibid., 582.

32. Gerald Ford had been nominated to the vice presidency on October 12, but the Senate had not confirmed him. Ibid., 586.

33. Ibid., 589.

34. Nolan, *Guardians of the Arsenal,* 122. In his own memoirs, Nixon slides over his absence from the crucial events following the Dobrynin ultimatum: "When Haig informed me about this message, I said that he and Kissinger should have a meeting at the White House to formulate plans for a firm reaction to what amounted to a scarcely veiled threat of unilateral Soviet intervention. Words were not making our point — we needed action, even the shock of a military alert." *RN: The Memoirs of Richard Nixon,* 938.

35. Nolan, *Guardians of the Arsenal,* 122.

36. Perry, *Four Stars,* 258. See also Nolan, *Guardians of the Arsenal,* 123.

37. Waltz, *Man, the State, and War,* 222.

38. Hyland, *Mortal Rivals,* 72. Kissinger moved Nixon away from the by then absurd notion of "superiority," but Kissinger would embrace it again, once out of government, when he argued against the Carter administration's SALT II Treaty. Arleigh Burke, the chief of naval operations, had told Kissinger's Harvard seminar in 1960, "You very seldom see a cowboy, even in the movies, wearing three guns. Two is enough." Rosenberg, "The Origins of Overkill," 71.

39. Nolan, *Guardians of the Arsenal,* 120, 113.

40. Each side could have up to 2,400 long-range delivery systems, with a maximum of 1,320 of them MIRVed.

41. Newhouse, *War and Peace in the Nuclear Age,* 251.

42. Schlesinger would return to government as secretary of energy under Jimmy Carter. His payback to Rumsfeld would come many years later when, as chair of a special commission investigating the American military's abuse of prisoners in Iraq in 2004, Schlesinger found that the abuse occurred during interrogations of prisoners and were not random acts of sadism. Rumsfeld denied the Schlesinger commission's charges. "Rumsfeld Denies Details of Abuse at Interrogations," *New York Times,* August 28, 2004, A1.

43. I acknowledge James Mann for my first understanding of Rumsfeld's arrival during the Ford years. See Mann's *Rise of the Vulcans.*

44. "If past trends continue," the committee reported in 1977, "the USSR will within several years achieve strategic superiority over the United States." Bundy, *Danger and Survival*, 557. Nitze's fresh apocalyptic warning showed up quickly, in "Assuring Strategic Stability in the Era of Détente" (207). He announced the formation of the new Committee on the Present Danger in March 1976. Its members included Walt Rostow, Elmo Zumwalt (who had served Nitze as a military aide), Maxwell Taylor, Douglas Dillon (of Forrestal's Dillon, Read), and Dean Rusk. Ronald Reagan was a member, and among the dozens of other members who went to work for him when he became president were David Packer, Richard Allen, Max Kampelman, Richard Pipes, William Casey, Jeanne Kirkpatrick, Walt Rostow, Kenneth Adelman — and Nitze.

45. In 1968, the percentage of the gross national product spent on defense was 8.85. Under Nixon it steadily declined to, in 1974, 5.45 percent. In 1975, with Rumsfeld, the reversal immediately began, at 5.49 percent. Wolfe, *The Rise and Fall of the "Soviet Threat,"* 24.

46. Robert T. Hartmann, Gerald Ford's aide, observed about Cheney in 1980 that "his adult life had been devoted to the study of political science and the service of Donald Rumsfeld." Hartmann, *Palace Politics*, 283.

47. LaFeber, *America, Russia, and the Cold War*, 286, 295. The Republicans under Ford found powerful allies in so-called neoconservative Democrats, centered around the figure of Henry Jackson, who lost the military budget debates on Capitol Hill, but who then determined to make an issue of the whole idea of détente as a surrender to evil. Jackson's circle included Richard Perle, Richard Pipes, and Paul Wolfowitz, each of whom also had ties to Albert Wohlstetter, one of the original RAND conservatives, forever given to the view that Moscow's threat was far graver than credited.

48. One Rumsfeld-led assessment in the 1970s found that the failure of U.S. sonar to pick up any signals from Soviet submarines proved not the absence of submarines but the Soviets' success in inventing a system to thwart acoustic detection. It was fantasy. Bergen, "Beware the Holy War," 27. The determination of Rumsfeld et al. to avenge the disaster of Vietnam led them, decades later, to replay it in Iraq.

49. Mann, *Rise of the Vulcans*, xiii.

50. LaFeber, *America, Russia, and the Cold War*, 296.

51. Kaplan, *Wizards of Armageddon*, 380. Leslie Gelb was the main editor of the Pentagon Papers. Carter's refusal to offer Nitze a position resulted from what Carter later called Nitze's "know-it-all" attitude during what amounted to a job interview: "He was arrogant and inflexible," Carter said. "His own ideas were sacred to him. He didn't seem to listen to others, and he had a doomsday approach." Talbott, *The Master of the Game*, 149. Frances FitzGerald comments, "For defense experts Nitze's doomsday scenario appeared as the gorgeous displays of plumage in a war dance." *Way Out There in the Blue*, 97.

52. LaFeber, *America, Russia, and the Cold War*, 302. LaFeber points out that Carter's anti-Soviet absolutism on human rights was oddly narrow: Carter never made it an issue with leaders of China or with the shah of Iran.

53. Thirty-five countries agreed to the permanence of Eastern European boundaries in return for Soviet acceptance of a new human rights standard for the Eastern European nations and the USSR itself. The accords, in the words of a Soviet official, "gradually became a manifesto of the dissident and liberal movement, a development totally beyond the imagination of the Soviet leadership." Ibid., 296.

54. Newhouse, *War and Peace in the Nuclear Age*, 266.

55. Drew Gilpin Faust, "We Should Grow Too Fond of It," at the Radcliffe Institute, Harvard University, citing Freeman, *R. E. Lee*, vol. 2, 462.

56. Perry, *Four Stars*, 265–66. Perry says this meeting took place in December 1976. See also Nolan, *Guardians of the Arsenal*, 129; May and Neustadt, *Thinking in Time*, 155; Powers, "Choosing a Strategy for World War III," 84.

57. May and Neustadt put the total at 50,000, referring to deployed warheads. *Thinking in Time,* 114. But the Natural Resources Defense Council put the deployed number of U.S. warheads in 1976 at about 26,000, with stockpiled weapons at 25,956. According to the NRDC, 1976 was the peak year for the arsenal, with the numbers of both deployed and stockpiled weapons gradually declining after that. "Archive of Nuclear Data," National Resources Defense Council, www.nrdc.org/nuclear/nudb/datab9.asp.

58. Kennan would call for 50 percent reductions in the two superpower arsenals on May 19, 1981, in an address before the arms control establishment. The proposal would reshape the arms control agenda during the Reagan years. Talbott, *The Master of the Game,* 165. Kennan would be joined by McNamara and Bundy in calling for drastic nuclear reductions.

59. Perry, *Four Stars,* 266.

60. Newhouse, *War and Peace in the Nuclear Age,* 294.

61. In a speech in July 1979, Carter said, "Human identity is no longer defined by what one does, but by what one owns. But we've discovered that owning things and consuming things does not satisfy our longing for meaning. We've learned that piling up material goods cannot fill the emptiness of lives which have no confidence or purpose." "Energy and National Goals," www.jimmycarterlibrary.org/documents/speeches/index.phtml.

62. Margaret Mead, cited by Drew Gilpin Faust, at the Radcliffe Institute, Harvard University. See Mead, "Warfare Is Only an Invention," 402–5.

63. Moscow had the initiative with one weapons system, the ICBM, deploying it in 1957, one year before the U.S. ICBM.

64. Probably for that reason, Sorensen's nomination did not take.

65. One of Carter's aides, William Hyland (a holdover from Kissinger's tenure), doubted that Carter's two-hundred-missile proposal was meant seriously. "More likely, it was Carter's way of alerting the JCS that he was in charge." Hyland, *Mortal Rivals,* 210.

66. ". . . our years of the Bomb. The questions that arose out of the doom of Hiroshima were indeed late and lamely posed, frequently stifled, softened, evaded, by all manner of myth, promise, sweet talk, frictions and enmities, ignorance multiplied, frivolity and distraction. And yet, and yet, the questions held. They would not go away. They hung in the air, like a woven thread suspending the nuclear sword, unimaginably precarious in midair." Berrigan, *Testimony,* 210.

67. Remarque's *All Quiet on the Western Front* and Robert Graves's *Goodbye to All That* appeared in 1928, Hemingway's *Farewell to Arms* in 1929, Sassoon's *Memoirs of an Infantry Officer* in 1930.

68. Carter, inaugural address, in *Keeping Faith,* 21–22.

69. Eisenhower's homburg, in contrast to Truman's top hat, had itself been a relaxing of stiff formality.

70. Newhouse, *War and Peace in the Nuclear Age,* 380. With the defeat of Ford, the idea of Republican moderation was defeated, too. Ever more hawkish Republicans made new alliances with Democratic neoconservatives, in a fundamental realignment of American politics that would come into its own first under Reagan and then under George W. Bush.

71. Here is McGeorge Bundy's comment about the alarmists: "Beset by their fears . . . they pushed aside the point that Eisenhower had explained to his countrymen in 1954 — the Soviet leaders would think first of what nuclear weapons could do to their homeland and themselves." *Danger and Survival,* 565.

72. Newhouse, *War and Peace in the Nuclear Age,* 293.

73. One of them was Anatoly Shcharansky. *New York Times,* March 16, 1977, A10. Shcharansky was imprisoned for nine years and then, as part of the Gorbachev-Reagan rapprochement, was exchanged for a Soviet spy and allowed to leave the country. As Natan Sharansky, he became a leading conservative politician in Israel.

74. Hyland, *Mortal Rivals*, 206–7.

75. In reflecting on this later, Carter wrote, "In light of what I now know about the Soviet leaders, it is easier for me to understand why the boldness of some of these proposals would cause them concern." Cited by May and Neustadt, *Thinking in Time*, 130.

76. Hyland, *Mortal Rivals*, 210.

77. May and Neustadt, *Thinking in Time*, 111.

78. Hyland, *Mortal Rivals*, 215.

79. May and Neustadt, *Thinking in Time*, 112. They cite, in particular, Strobe Talbott.

80. January 12, 1977. www.ford.utexas.edu/library/speeches.

81. Newhouse, *War and Peace in the Nuclear Age*, 303–5.

82. The SALT II Treaty agreement was announced on May 9, 1979; the MX missile was approved on June 8. Carter and Brezhnev signed the SALT II Treaty at a Vienna summit meeting on June 18. The two leaders agreed that neither side would strive for strategic nuclear superiority. But during the last two years of his presidency, Carter saw to major increases in the defense budget. The last word on Carter's intention to turn the nation away from dependence on endless escalation came twenty-five years after he left office, when he presided, at Groton, Connecticut, over the commissioning of the USS *Jimmy Carter*. It is "the most heavily armed submarine ever built . . . the last of the Seawolf class of attack subs that the Pentagon ordered during the Cold War's final years." Cara Rubinsky, Associated Press, February 19, 2005.

83. After escapes and releases, fifty-two would be held hostage for more than a year.

84. Bacevich, *The New American Militarism*, 102. Obviously, U.S. contingency planning for repelling a Soviet seizure of gulf-area oil fields long preceded Carter, but he moved such planning from contingency toward actual deployment. Carter's doctrine was more than rhetorical. He established, in Tampa, Florida, a military command that would evolve into Central Command, and he ordered the buildup of forces that would make U.S. forays into the Persian Gulf possible. Klare, *Blood and Oil*, xvi, 45–47.

85. General James (Terry) Scott, author interview.

86. Rumsfeld made the remark in his testimony against the SALT agreement. Mann, *Rise of the Vulcans*, 102.

87. The ASAT story is a prime example of Carter's confused approach to arms control. He ramped up the space weapons research while pressuring the Soviets for ASAT limits. Carter's arms negotiator Paul Warnke warned of a "Brobdingnagian skeet shoot," a reference to *Gulliver's Travels*. But the Carter approach did little to head it off. The phrase appears in the title of a significant article on the subject by Donald L. Hafner, "Averting a Brobdingnagian Skeet Shoot," 41–60.

88. Perry, *Four Stars*, 277.

89. *New York Times*, August 6, 1980, A1. Janne E. Nolan's comment: "The man who had entered office promising 'to banish nuclear weapons' left behind a rich legacy of plans for the conduct of nuclear war." *Guardians of the Arsenal*, 126.

90. LaFeber, *America, Russia, and the Cold War*, 315. Another historian, writing about the Iraq wars of the late twentieth and early twenty-first centuries, declared that they amounted to "World War IV, and were started by Jimmy Carter." Bacevich, *The New American Militarism*, 185.

91. Gaddis, *The United States and the End of the Cold War*, 43.

92. Carter's Presidential Directive 59, as much as Ronald Reagan's buildup, licensed Pentagon budget increases in the billions of dollars. Boyle, *American-Soviet Relations*, 194.

93. For example: "If Gandhi's enormously powerful and successful strategy of nonviolent resistance had met with a different enemy—Stalin's Russia, Hitler's Germany, even prewar Japan, instead of England—the outcome would not have been decolonization, but massacre and submission." Arendt, *On Violence*, 53.

94. Beschloss, "The Thawing of the Cold War," 41. See also "Mountain May Be Renamed for Reagan," *Boston Globe,* June 7, 2004, A8. This article reports that the New Hampshire legislature was set to name a peak in the Presidential Range of the White Mountains for Reagan as "a tribute," in the New Hampshire governor's words, "to the man who won the Cold War and almost single-handedly caused the dramatic decline of Communism." Such praise was not showered on Reagan at the time the Cold War ended, especially not by conservatives. George F. Will wrote of Reagan's responsiveness to Gorbachev in 1988, "Reagan has accelerated the moral disarmament of the West — actual disarmament will follow." Cited by FitzGerald, *Way Out There in the Blue,* 467.

95. Todd S. Purdum, "An Impact Seen, and Felt, Everywhere," *New York Times,* June 7, 2004, A18.

96. Talbott, *The Master of the Game,* 193.

97. Arthur Schlesinger, Jr., made this point to me in conversation. See his "Lessons from the Cold War," in Hogan, *The End of the Cold War,* 54.

98. "Be not afraid," he said in his inaugural homily on October 22, 1977. "Open up — no, swing wide the gates to Christ. Open up to his saving power the confines of the state, open up economic and political systems, the vast empires of culture, civilization and development. Be not afraid! Christ knows what we have inside. Only He knows." Bernstein and Politi, *His Holiness,* 182. The refrain "Be not afraid," which would serve as John Paul II's motto, was what Jesus said to his disciples when appearing to them in the midst of a storm.

99. Kwitny, *Man of the Century,* 326–27.

100. Bernstein and Politi, *His Holiness,* 232.

101. David Remnick, "Comment," *The New Yorker,* April 11, 2005, 22.

102. Havel published an essay titled "Living in Truth" in 1978. Even as a secular man — and the nonviolent democracy movement as it spread out from Poland would be mainly secular — Havel gave full expression to John Paul II's conviction when he wrote, "Under the orderly surface of the life of lies, therefore, there slumbers the hidden sphere of life in its real aims, of its hidden openness to truth. The singular, explosive, incalculable political power of living within the truth resides in the fact that living openly within the truth has an ally, invisible to be sure, but omnipresent: this hidden sphere." Quoted by Schell, *The Unconquerable World,* 197. When John Paul II went to Prague in 1990, Havel greeted him saying, "I am not sure that I know what a miracle is. In spite of this, I daresay that I am participating in a miracle: in a country devastated by the ideology of hatred, the messenger of love has arrived." Remnick, "Comment," 22.

103. "Holy Alliance" was the title of a *Time* cover story (February 4, 1992) by Carl Bernstein, which formed the basis of his 1996 book, *His Holiness,* written with Marco Politi. For a debunking of the Bernstein thesis that Reagan and John Paul II actively collaborated against the Soviet Union, see Kwitny, *Man of the Century.*

104. Soviet leaders, Reagan told the journalist Sam Donaldson, at a press conference on January 29, 1981, "have openly and publicly declared that the only morality that they recognize is what will further their cause, meaning they reserve unto themselves the right to commit any crime, to lie, to cheat . . . And we operate on a different set of standards. I think when you do business with them, even at a détente, you keep that in mind." *Public Papers of the Presidents of the United States, Ronald Reagan, 1981,* 57. Boyle, *American-Soviet Relations,* 200. See also Matlock, *Reagan and Gorbachev,* 4. Reagan had been speaking this way of Communists for years.

105. Kwitny, *Man of the Century,* 301.

106. At the United Nations in 1979, where he repeated Paul VI's great cry "War no more!," John Paul II accused both Moscow and Washington of keeping the nuclear arms race going for the most hollow and even wicked motives: "In alleging the threat of a poten-

tial enemy, is the real intention not, rather, to keep for oneself a means of threat, in order to get the upper hand?" The arms race serves both powers, that is, as a source of dominance. "Peace tends to vanish in favor of ever new forms of imperialism." Ibid., 337.

107. After Bishop Roger Mahoney of Stockton, California, declared that "no Catholic" should have anything to do with nuclear weapons (not as a worker for a defense contractor, not as a member of the military), he was named a cardinal and appointed to the Archdiocese of Los Angeles.

108. Notwithstanding the conservative mythmakers, the only financial support that went from America to Solidarity was sent not by the U.S. government but by the U.S. labor movement, especially Lane Kirkland's AFL-CIO. Kwitny, *Man of the Century*, 451.

109. *The Gulag Archipelago* was published in the West in 1973. In 1974, Solzhenitsyn was exiled by the Kremlin. He lived in Vermont until 1994, when he returned to Russia.

110. When Ronald Reagan died, Sharansky participated in the myth of Reagan's "triumph" over Communism (see his interview in the *Weekly Standard*, June 21, 2004), but by then Sharansky was politically aligned, as a minister in Israel's Likud government, with forces whose conservative purposes were served by the lionizing of Reagan. Similarly, Lech Walesa wrote an appreciation of Reagan that week in the *Wall Street Journal* (June 1, 2004). The article celebrated Reagan for imposing trade sanctions against Poland in retaliation for the outlawing of Solidarity in 1982, but at the time Solidarity, like John Paul II, opposed those sanctions.

111. Kwitny, *Man of the Century*, 478. Kwitny calls the week of the pope's 1983 visit to Poland the "most important" of his papacy (475).

112. Bernstein and Politi, *His Holiness*, 227. As the millennium approached, John Paul II called for a "purification of memory," and made self-criticism of and by the Church a major project. In 2000, he issued "Memory and Reconciliation," an explicit, if incomplete, attempt to accomplish a moral reckoning with historic failures of the Roman Catholic Church. I have written of this in *Constantine's Sword: The Church and the Jews*.

113. It is hard to adequately quantify the enormous expansion of military spending under Reagan. Even though the buildup had begun under Carter, it was mightily accelerated under Reagan. In 1980, the defense budget amounted to $142 billion. By 1982, it was $222 billion. By 1986, it would be $376 billion. Boyle, *American-Soviet Relations*, 201. Relatively little of this expansion went to nuclear forces. Military salaries were increased. Aircraft carriers were ordered. The B-1 was brought back, and so were numerous other warplanes. Increases were determined less by military need than by the fact that Reagan had an *a priori* determination to grow the budget by 5, 7, even 10 percent, depending on what figures were used. And because figures were used inconsistently, the increases were not rational. "The generals are in Beulah land," a former secretary of defense said of Caspar Weinberger, Reagan's secretary of defense. "Anything they want, he gives them." FitzGerald, *Way Out There in the Blue*, 149, 155.

114. John Paul II, in his New Year's message of 1985, condemned "projects for global space systems." Kwitny, *Man of the Century*, 529.

115. Frances FitzGerald explains what had prompted Haig's upset. He had just raced up from the White House Situation Room, where he had learned, to his horror, that Caspar Weinberger had ineptly ordered worldwide U.S. military forces to alert, which Haig — who had watched Kissinger do the same thing in 1973 — feared would prompt a dangerous reaction from Moscow. When Haig demanded of Weinberger if he had raised the DEFCON alert, it became clear that Weinberger did not know what it was. FitzGerald, *Way Out There in the Blue*, 170.

116. Farrell, *Tip O'Neill and the Democratic Century*, 553.

117. Mehmet Ali Ağca would claim that he acted at the behest of the Bulgarian intelligence service, and a Rome-based Bulgarian state airline employee, Sergei Ivanov, would be

charged with conspiracy by Italy in 1982. He was acquitted. While few assumed that Ağca acted alone, the Vatican never openly gave credence to the theory that the Bulgarian intelligence service (and ultimately the KGB) was behind the shooting, but many people, especially in Poland, took it for granted. In 2005, Cold War–era documents found in East German secret-police files offered evidence that the KGB, operating through East Germany's Stasi and the Bulgarian secret police, had in fact organized the attempted assassination. *Agence France-Presse,* March 30, 2005.

118. Contrary to those who claim they shared a political agenda, John Paul's biographer Jonathan Kwitny says that their forty-five-minute meeting was taken up not with political discussion but with "the mystical significance Reagan saw in the fact that both had survived assassination attempts." The pope attributed such significance to his own survival, emphasizing that the event occurred on the Feast of Our Lady of Fatima, but Reagan's cosmic enthusiasm impressed people at the Vatican as "superstitious." Kwitny, *Man of the Century,* 445.

119. For a report of Reagan's invoking Armageddon, see McFarlane, *Special Trust,* 228. McFarlane repeatedly emphasized the connection in Reagan's mind between nuclear war and Armageddon. During the 1984 reelection campaign, Reagan was explicitly asked to explain his thinking on the link between Armageddon and nuclear war. He acknowledged having had "philosophical discussions" on the question, but then said "no one knows" if "Armageddon is a thousand years away or the day after tomorrow. So, I have never seriously warned and said we must plan according to Armageddon." Many who heard this were less than reassured. Cannon, *President Reagan,* 288.

120. A private remark made by George H. W. Bush to Mikhail Gorbachev in 1988. Beschloss and Talbott, *At the Highest Levels,* 4.

121. Boyle, *American-Soviet Relations,* 198.

122. As Jackson had empowered his protégé Richard Perle, Helms launched the career of John Bolton, a conservative ideologue who came into his own under George W. Bush. In 2005, Bolton was named U.S. Ambassador to the United Nations, an institution he plainly despised.

123. Farrell, *Tip O'Neill and the Democratic Century,* 608.

124. Hofstadter, *The Paranoid Style in American Politics.*

125. Mann, *Rise of the Vulcans,* 52.

126. Ibid., 79.

127. Because he had worked in the Carter administration, Wolfowitz was opposed as a "liberal" for this position by Senator Jesse Helms, which is as ludicrous as Nitze's having been opposed as a liberal in 1963 by Donald Rumsfeld.

128. Boyle, *American-Soviet Relations,* 203.

129. FitzGerald, *Way Out There in the Blue,* 119.

130. Perle testified before Congress on February 23, 1982: "I'm sorry to say that [the ABM Treaty] does not expire. That is one of its many defects. I would hope that were we to conclude that the only way we could defend our own strategic forces was by deploying defense, we would not hesitate to renegotiate the treaty, and, failing Soviet acquiescence in that renegotiation, I would hope we would abrogate the treaty." Talbott, *The Master of the Game,* 233. Perle succeeded in this ambition when George W. Bush abrogated the treaty.

131. Morris, *Dutch,* 450, 453.

132. "Perle ended up having more impact on policy in arms control than any other official in the U.S. government, an achievement that was all the more remarkable in that he held a third-echelon job." Talbott, *Deadly Gambits,* 17.

133. "I don't know anyone," Rostow said at his confirmation hearing on June 18, 1981, "who knows what it is yet that we want to negotiate about." Boyle, *American-Soviet Relations,* 203–4. Rostow would not last long in the job. He would be replaced in early 1983 by

the even more hawkish Kenneth Adelman, "a one-time protégé of Donald Rumsfeld's and a neo-conservative newcomer to arms control with close ties to Richard Perle." Talbott, *The Master of the Game*, 169.

134. Kennedy and Hatfield, *Freeze!*, 1.

135. In his memoir, Nitze wrote, for example, of his Bombing Survey experience at Hiroshima, "We also found that even in the immediate blast area, people who had taken to simple air raid tunnels emerged unscathed, indicating that the bomb's effects were largely confined, like most conventional weapons, to above-ground targets." *From Hiroshima to Glasnost*, 42. We saw that Nitze's nemesis on the survey was John Kenneth Galbraith, and he entered the fray now, to disagree again, arguing against the normalizing of nuclear war. "In the ashes," Galbraith wrote, "communism and capitalism, let it be said again, will be indistinguishable. They will also be indistinguishable and irrelevant in the ultra-primitive struggle for existence for those who are unfortunate enough to survive." Kennedy and Hatfield, *Freeze!*, 75.

136. In November, Reagan's idea of arms control negotiation came when Rostow's ACDA proposed to the Soviets the famous "zero option" on Intermediate Missile Forces. That meant Moscow would have to remove all of its missiles already deployed in the European theater, while the United States and NATO would have to refrain only from carrying out deployments that had not occurred yet. The Soviets naturally refused to consider such a one-sided proposal. When Nitze, taking a "walk in the woods" at Geneva, negotiated an unofficial compromise with his Soviet counterpart, it was Washington that slapped it down — specifically, it was Richard Perle, who began as Nitze's protégé. So arms control under the Reagan administration was not negotiation but offers made on a take-it-or-leave-it basis.

137. Eugene Carroll, cited in Perry, *Four Stars*, 294.

138. Dr. Helen Caldicott, appealing only to her authority as a physician, became a leading antiwar activist. Doctors in Boston, in league with doctors in the Soviet Union, founded International Physicians for the Prevention of Nuclear War, which would win the Nobel Peace Prize in 1985.

139. The term is Robert Jay Lifton's.

140. Kennedy and Hatfield, *Freeze!*, 98. Kennan, together with McGeorge Bundy, Robert McNamara, and other veterans of the nuclear establishment, now began to decry the arms race, and called for an end to nuclear weapons. At Kennan's death in 2005, one obituary singled out his most eloquent plea to world leaders: "For the love of God, for the love of your children, and of the civilization to which you belong, cease this madness. You are mortal men. You are capable of error. You have no right to hold in your hands — there is no one wise enough and strong enough to hold in his hands — destructive power sufficient to put an end to civilized life on a great portion of our planet." *Boston Globe*, March 18, 2005, D23.

141. In October 1981, Reagan told reporters a nuclear war could be limited with no grave consequences to a European battlefield: "I could see where you could have the exchange of tactical [nuclear] weapons against troops in the field without it bringing either one of the major parties to pushing the button." Perry, *Four Stars*, 291. Weinberger made equivalent statements in the same period.

142. In 1957, the Committee for a Sane Nuclear Policy (SANE) was organized in response to the Russell-Einstein antinuclear manifesto. Greenpeace had its beginning in 1971 as a protest against nuclear testing on an island off Alaska. The Center for Defense Information, based in Washington, Physicians for Social Responsibility, International Physicians for the Prevention of Nuclear War, and other groups were formed. Obviously, grassroots organizing on the Soviet side was not simple, yet groups sprung up there, too — the Committee of Soviet Scientists, for example. Soviet and American scientists carried on informal contacts through the Papal Academy of Sciences. Evangelista, *Unarmed Forces*, 249f.

143. Kennedy and Hatfield, *Freeze!*, 169–70.

144. McGeorge Bundy, for example, dismissed the Freeze in this way: "But the largest single effort to slow the arms race, the nuclear freeze movement, was also the least successful." *Danger and Survival*, 582.

145. Kennedy and Hatfield, *Freeze!*, 115f; FitzGerald, *Way Out There in the Blue*, 180.

146. The Reagan-sponsored proposal for civil defense was sparked, in part at least, by the "discovery" of a Soviet civil defense program by Lieutenant General Daniel O. Graham, who had been one of my father's successors as director of the Defense Intelligence Agency. The DIA assessment of a major effort to protect the Soviet population was unreal. Graham was a crackpot even among the crackpots. He retired from the DIA in 1976 and published an alarmist book in 1979, *Shall America Be Defended? SALT II and Beyond*.

147. Kennedy and Hatfield, *Freeze!*, 159, 123.

148. Morris, *Dutch*, 458.

149. Organizers of the demonstration put the number at more than a million; police estimates at the time were half that. Historians generally give the figure of three quarters of a million people.

150. Russian President Vladimir Putin renounced the no-first-use commitment in 1998, an indication that by then the Russian military no longer had significant conventional capacity. Its nuclear force was Russia's sole claim to superpower status, and after the NATO air war against Serbia, a Russian ally, Putin was relying on the nuclear threat as a deterrent against even nonnuclear moves by the United States and NATO.

151. Arms Control and Disarmament Agency, *Documents on Disarmament*, 349.

152. LaFeber, *America, Russia, and the Cold War*, 333.

153. Kirkpatrick, *Dictatorships and Double Standards*, 135.

154. The bishops wrote: "We cannot avoid our responsibility to lift up the moral dimensions of the choices before our world and nation. The nuclear age is an age of moral as well as physical danger. We are the first generation since Genesis with the power to threaten the created order. We cannot remain silent in the face of such danger . . . We need a moral about-face. The whole world must summon the moral courage and technical means to say no to nuclear conflict; no to weapons of mass destruction; no to an arms race which robs the poor and the vulnerable; and no to the moral danger of a nuclear age which places before humankind indefensible choices of constant terror or surrender." According to the bishops, deterrence was a morally acceptable policy only if it was understood as temporary, in the context of steady efforts at arms reduction and disarmament. U.S. Conference of Catholic Bishops, *The Challenge of Peace*, vii.

155. Hyland, *Mortal Rivals*, 249.

156. FitzGerald, *Way Out There in the Blue*, 191. I am especially indebted to FitzGerald for my understanding of the relationship between the Freeze and Reagan's disarmament impulse.

157. "Reagan Denounces Ideology of Soviet as 'Focus of Evil,'" *New York Times*, March 9, 1983, A1.

158. Ibid., A18.

159. For an example of the kind of panicked alarmism the Freeze prompted on the right, see Conquest and White, *What to Do When the Russians Come*.

160. FitzGerald, *Way Out There in the Blue*, 209. It is FitzGerald, above all, who helped me understand the political significance of Reagan's need for applause. The diplomat Thomas W. Simons, who worked with Reagan, thinks it a mistake to emphasize his need for audience approval. Author interview. See Simons, *The End of Cold War?*

161. Morris, *Dutch*, 471. LaFeber, *America, Russia, and the Cold War*, 330.

162. September 1, 1983.

163. "Reagan Proposes U.S. Seek New Way to Block Missiles," *New York Times,* March 24, 1983, A1.

164. This is Garry Wills's insight, how Reagan's belief in the infinite potential of American enterprise, as he represented it on television, shaped his SDI vision. Wills, *Reagan's America.*

165. Ibid., 361; FitzGerald, *Way Out There in the Blue,* 23. In the 1940 film, the Reagan character declares, "Yes, Doctor, and wait till you see it in action. It not only makes the United States invincible in war, but in so doing promises to become the greatest force for world peace ever discovered." Engelhardt, *The End of Victory Culture,* 273.

166. Morris, *Dutch,* 475–76.

167. FitzGerald, *Way Out There in the Blue,* 198, 199.

168. Ibid., 257.

169. Talbott, *The Master of the Game,* 187.

170. Article 6 of the treaty reads, "Each of the parties . . . undertakes to pursue negotiations in good faith on effective measures relating to cessation of the nuclear arms race at an early date and to nuclear disarmament, and on a treaty on general and complete disarmament under strict and effective international control."

171. Heated Soviet objections to SDI took on an alarming character when, on September 1, 1983, Korean Airlines flight 007, referred to earlier, was shot down by a Soviet fighter after it entered Soviet airspace. Reagan designated September 11, 1983, as a "national day of mourning" for the victims of the disaster — September 11 as a fate-laden date again. But Reagan refused to cancel the START talks, which continued until the normal recess in December.

172. FitzGerald, *Way Out There in the Blue,* 109.

173. Reagan's election-year claims for his actual buildup, as opposed to his spending, were mightily exaggerated, and have been exaggerated by his acolytes ever since. The MX missile tilted the balance toward the United States, but it was not deployed until 1986. The one improvement in the strategic arsenal to come in the first Reagan term was the deployment of cruise missiles on ships and bombers, but they had been ordered by Carter. See Bundy, *Danger and Survival,* 587.

174. Morris, *Dutch,* 512.

175. Chernenko replaced Andropov when the latter died, on February 10, 1984.

176. Reagan himself, on March 24, 1984, had denounced the Sandinista government in Nicaragua as a Communist dictatorship with ties to Cuba and Moscow; in the same speech he praised the right-wing government of El Salvador, whose death squads had murdered thousands. Daniel Ortega, as if in response, met with Chernenko in Moscow the following June 18, and they jointly condemned American policies in Central America. After Reagan's reelection, his administration's efforts to resume negotiations with Moscow stood in contrast to a new spirit of confrontation with the so-called Brezhnev Doctrine of support for Communist insurgencies, like those it saw in Central America.

177. The Antiballistic Missile Treaty of 1972. The reinterpretation ploy would fail because the U.S. plans for missile defense starkly contradicted the treaty, which is why George W. Bush "withdrew" from it.

178. Gaddis, *The United States and the End of the Cold War,* 126. Gorbachev, for his part, took note of Kennan. At a reception at the Soviet embassy in Washington in 1987, the Soviet leader embraced the veteran diplomat. "Mr. Kennan," Gorbachev said, "we in our country believe that a man may be the friend of another country and remain, at the same time, a loyal and devoted citizen of his own; and that is the way we view you." Mark Feeney, "George Kennan Dies at 101; Devised Cold War Policy," *Boston Globe,* March 18, 2005, D23.

179. Evangelista, *Unarmed Forces,* 3.

180. LaFeber, *America, Russia, and the Cold War,* 339. Rotblat, with Pugwash, won the Nobel Peace Prize in 1995. Another transnational group similarly devoted to arms reduction, International Physicians for the Prevention of Nuclear War, had received the prize in 1985.

181. Here is Jonathan Schell's comment on the relationship of the two movements: "The anti-nuclear cause must be seen as the second stage of a process whose first stage was the overthrow from within of the Soviet Union. Although the West did not 'win' the Cold War, there is no doubt that the modern Western system — characterized by democracy in politics, capitalism in economics, and reliance on the fruits of advanced technology and science — has in fact spread throughout the world, very much including the territories of its former adversaries. It is no secret to anyone, however, that this dominant system has profound flaws. And chief among them is the surpassingly strange fact that it holds a loaded, cocked pistol to its head and threatens to blow its brains out — that it has a profound suicidal bent." Of the "peoples of the East," Schell says, "They accomplished by far the most arduous part of our common task." *The Gift of Time,* 213.

182. Roosevelt is remembered as having said that of Somoza, although Cordell Hull is sometimes credited with having said it of Rafael Trujillo of the Dominican Republic.

183. The Jesuit fathers Miguel D'Escoto and Fernando Cardenal were ministers of foreign affairs and education, respectively. A Maryknoll father, Ernesto Cardenal, the brother of Fernando, was minister of culture. The Cardenal brothers were two of the most famous priests in the Catholic Church, Fernando a widely admired poet, Ernesto an influential theologian and a leading disciple of Thomas Merton.

184. "Remarks at the Annual Dinner of the Conservative Political Action Committee," March 1, 1985, www.reagan.utexas.edu/speech_srch.html.

185. Golden and McConnell, *Sanctuary,* 2.

186. LaFeber, *America, Russia, and the Cold War,* 328.

187. Kwitny, *Man of the Century,* 353.

188. Cardinal James Hickey of Washington and Archbishop John Quinn of San Francisco.

189. Ita Ford and Maura Clarke were Maryknoll nuns; Dorothy Kazel was an Ursuline nun; Jean Donovan was a lay volunteer.

190. In leaving the priesthood, I had left the life of a social activist behind, but I then took a job as a writer of scripts for the Packard Manse Media Project, headed by Patrick Hughes and based outside Boston. Its "slide shows" were polemical attacks on American military policies, with a focus on Central America and the arms race. I wrote, among other scripts, "Guess Who's Coming to Breakfast," an attack on Gulf and Western's exploitation of the Dominican Republic; "I Have Three Children of My Own," a profile of Dr. Helen Caldicott, founder of Physicians for Social Responsibility; and "The Hopeful Revolution," a supportive portrayal of the Sandinista revolution against Somoza.

191. After a trip to Nicaragua in early 1988, during which I interviewed leaders of the Contras, including Arturo Cruz; leaders of the anti-Sandinista opposition, including Violeta Chamorro, who would be elected president in 1990; and leaders of the Nicaraguan Directorate, including Daniel Ortega, I published an account of my experience. "Nicaragua: A Personal Response," *Boston Globe,* March 13, 1988, A26.

192. On November 16, 1989, six Jesuits at the University of Central America in San Salvador, including its president, Ignacio Ellacuría, were murdered by a government-sanctioned death squad. The killers also murdered the Jesuits' housekeeper and her daughter, Celina and Elba Ramos. Of the twenty-six soldiers subsequently identified as the killers, nineteen had been trained at the School of the Americas, at Fort Benning, Georgia. Berrigan, *Testimony,* 112.

193. Reagan had been drawn to Kirkpatrick, despite her being a Democrat, when she

published "Dictatorships and Double Standards" in *Commentary* in 1980. In that article, later included in a book with that title, she condemned President Carter for abandoning Somoza in Nicaragua because he was "positively friendly" to the United States. In this, we see the Totalitarian school at work, the assumption that anti-Communist dictators are different from the Soviet dictatorship because the latter is incapable of reform. Gorbachev, of course, showed how this was mistaken. "As for the Catholic Left," she wrote, "its interest in revolution on this earth has waxed as its concern with salvation in heaven has waned." *Dictatorships and Double Standards*, 68.

194. Farrell, *Tip O'Neill and the Democratic Century*, 620.

195. Golden and McConnell, *Sanctuary*, 20.

196. Among the sanctuary movement's supporters were the American Friends Service Committee, the Catholic Archdiocese of Milwaukee, the General Synod of the United Church of Christ, the General Assembly of the Presbyterian Church (USA), the General Conference of the United Methodist Church, the General Assembly of the Unitarian Universalist Association, the Catholic Conference of Major Superiors of Men, and the General Assembly of the American Lutheran Church.

197. Golden and McConnell, *Sanctuary*, 91–92.

198. Cannon, *President Reagan*, 381, 385.

199. *New York Times*, June 6, 2004, A31.

200. Ibid.

201. Gromyko had served as Soviet foreign minister since 1957.

202. LaFeber, *America, Russia, and the Cold War*, 338.

203. "Had it not been for Reagan, the Soviets probably would have kept in power somebody like Yegor Ligachev, believing that the Brezhnev hardline would ultimately pay off." John McLaughlin, cited by Boyle, *American-Soviet Relations*, 216. Conservatives similarly credit Reagan with forcing Gorbachev's reform, but Gorbachev himself rebutted that notion when it dominated the eulogies given Reagan at his death. "All that talk that somehow Reagan's arms race forced Gorbachev to look for some arms reductions, etcetera, etcetera." Gorbachev was dismissive, insisting, "The Soviet Union could have withstood any arms race." *Los Angeles Times*, June 12, 2004, A19. For a contrary view, see Irving Kristol, "It Wasn't Inevitable: Reagan's Military and Economic Policies Won the Cold War," *Weekly Standard*, June 21, 2004, 24–25.

204. For example, in separate speeches in spring 1985, Reagan emphasized the Soviet threat in Central America, accused Moscow of trying to drive a wedge between the United States and NATO, accused Nicaragua of atrocities that were "the natural expression" of Communism, attacked the Soviets for being hostile to religion, condemned Moscow for its treatment of Andrei Sakharov, and proclaimed "Baltic Freedom Day," emphasizing the "murderous" oppression carried out in the Baltic states since 1941. Reagan rebuffed Gorbachev on the offers to remove missiles from Europe and to halt nuclear testing. Hill, *Cold War Chronology*, 281–83.

205. Weinberger sent Reagan a letter on the eve of the summit, warning him against Gorbachev. To be sure Reagan felt its pressure, Weinberger saw that the letter was leaked to the press. Brands, *The Devil We Knew*, 195–96.

206. Joint communiqué, Soviet-American summit, Geneva, November 21, 1985. An unusual statement, but hardly unprecedented. At Geneva, as William Hyland points out, Reagan and Gorbachev were "echoing Eisenhower and Khrushchev thirty years earlier. Traveling widely different routes, the superpowers seemed to have arrived at a common destination." *Mortal Rivals*, 246. Reagan's statement of this truth, however, explicitly contradicted the order he had given to the U.S. nuclear forces in 1981, to be able "to fight and win a protracted nuclear war." Steinbruner, *Principals of Global Security*, 60.

207. FitzGerald, *Way Out There in the Blue*, 305.

208. *New York Times*, November 15, 1985, A10.

209. "Remarks at the Memorial Service for the Crew of the Space Shuttle *Challenger*," www.reagan.utexas.edu/speech_srch.html.

210. Speech at the Twenty-seventh Communist Party Congress, February 25, 1986, www.usask.ca/education/ideas/tplan/sslp/dismantl.htm.

211. Frances FitzGerald points out that former CIA director Robert Gates, in his 1996 memoir, defined the Twenty-seventh Party Congress as "an historic turning point" and "the beginning of the end of the Cold War." But neither Gates nor any of his peers in Washington recognized it as such at the time. FitzGerald, *Way Out There in the Blue*, 328–29.

212. Reagan saw Chernobyl as a sign from God. He obsessed over the passage in Revelation (8:10–11) that described how "a great star fell from heaven, blazing like a torch, and it fell on a third of the rivers and on the fountains of water. The name of the star is Wormwood. A third of the waters became wormwood, and many men died of the water, because it was made bitter." Lou Cannon comments, "When Reagan learned that 'Chernobyl' is the Ukrainian word for 'wormwood,' he was certain that the disaster at Reactor Number 4 was indeed a portent of Armageddon." Cannon notes that in later relating this awesome fact, Reagan said that "Chernobyl" was the Ukrainian word for "Wedgwood." *President Reagan*, 757.

213. FitzGerald, *Way Out There in the Blue*, 333.

214. Talbott, *The Master of the Game*, 324.

215. This is the way the Reagan biographers Edmund Morris and Lou Cannon tell the story. A more recent example of this prevailing narrative appeared at the time of Reagan's death. Michael Beschloss wrote, "In October 1986, at Reykjavik, terrified by the prospect that the Soviets would have to spend wildly to compete with the Strategic Defense Initiative, Gorbachev offered Reagan a deal to abolish nuclear weapons and nuclear missiles: 'This all depends, of course, on you giving up SDI.' Tantalized by the deal, Reagan refused the condition. When he realized that Gorbachev was serious, Reagan said, 'This meeting is over,' and flew home." "The Thawing of the Cold War," *Time*, June 14, 2004, 41.

216. The journalist Fred Barnes, in appreciating Reagan at his death, wrote of Reagan's refusal to yield on SDI at Reykjavík: "Instantly, the Soviets, especially the generals, realized they'd lost the Cold War. They couldn't keep up an arms race. Reagan had broken their will, and undermined their faith in their system. Reagan alone could have done this." "One of a Kind," *Weekly Standard*, June 21, 2004, 33.

217. Gorbachev was sure that SDI was a waste of money, easily countered. Chernyaev, *My Six Years with Gorbachev*, 57–58.

218. As Gorbachev promised, the Topol-M was developed during the late 1980s and early 1990s, and deployed by the late 1990s. It is the backbone of Russia's land-based strategic force, poised to overwhelm any imagined defense. See Uhler, "Gorbachev's Revolution," 40. So much for SDI's bankrupting Moscow, and so much for ending the arms race. "Go ahead and deploy [the SDI]," Gorbachev told Reagan in their Washington meeting in 1987. "Who am I to tell you what to do? I think you're wasting your money. I don't think it will work. But if that is what you want to do, go ahead. We are moving in another direction." Talbott, *The Master of the Game*, 364.

219. Gaddis, *The United States and the End of the Cold War*, 128.

220. Morris, *Dutch*, 599. The first proposal to which Reagan and Gorbachev almost gave assent was to cut strategic nuclear forces by 50 percent in five years and all ballistic missile forces in ten years. Paul Nitze was distressed that this deal did not come off, but not because he was by now the wild-eyed disarmer conservatives would blast Reagan as being. Nitze observes in his memoir that such an agreement would be good for the United States because "we were ahead of the Soviets in bomber and cruise missile technology and could

remain so." *From Hiroshima to Glasnost,* 434. Nitze does not comment on the move toward complete abolition that Reagan and Gorbachev made then.

221. Shultz, *Turmoil and Triumph,* 773. Shultz explains that he "admired the president for hanging in there" because Gorbachev was offering concessions only "because of the pressure of SDI" and because he was "trying to impose" a strict reading of the ABM Treaty. Neither of Shultz's assertions is true.

222. It was this fear that prompted near-universal denunciations of the deal Reagan almost agreed to, coming from Margaret Thatcher (she called Reykjavík "an earthquake") and even relatively dovish Democrats in Congress, like Les Aspin. Senator Sam Nunn declared that if SDI had not forced the breakdown, "it would have been the most painfully embarrassing example of American ineptitude in this century." Cited by Uhler, "Gorbachev's Revolution," 44. Gaddis sums up the conventional view: "It was probably just as well. The sweeping agreements contemplated at Reykjavik grew out of hasty improvisation and high-level posturing, not careful thought." Gaddis, *The United States and the End of the Cold War,* 129.

223. The actual achievements of Reykjavík were the terms of agreement, worked out on the American side by none other than Paul Nitze, which laid the groundwork for future accords, reflected in START and INF. Nitze had by then become genuinely committed to real reductions in nuclear forces, unlike the hard-liners, but he remained an incrementalist. For example, he was still committed to going ahead with a new generation of American ICBMs. Talbott, *The Master of the Game,* 326, 327.

224. Bundy, *Danger and Survival,* 583.

225. Matlock, *Reagan and Gorbachev,* 235.

226. Morris, *Dutch,* 602.

227. FitzGerald, *Way Out There in the Blue,* 355.

228. Gorbachev's comment after Reykjavik was "The arms race has not been stopped, and it is becoming increasingly clear that developments are approaching a point where a new spiral of the arms race becomes inevitable, with unpredictable political and military consequences." Gorbachev, *Reykjavík,* 15.

229. Kwitny, *Man of the Century,* 554.

230. Schell, *The Unconquerable World,* 211.

231. Gorbachev, *Reykjavík,* 27.

232. Uhler, "Gorbachev's Revolution," 44.

233. FitzGerald, *Way Out There in the Blue,* 427.

234. Thomas Halsted, author interview.

235. Kwitny, *Man of the Century,* 587.

236. Ibid., 572.

237. Hill, *Cold War Chronology,* 296. John Lewis Gaddis writes, "To the astonishment of his own hard-line supporters, what appeared to be an enthusiastic return to the Cold War in fact turned out to be a more solidly based approach to détente than anything the Nixon, Ford, or Carter administration had been able to accomplish." *The United States and the End of the Cold War,* 123.

238. Reagan's ambassador to Moscow remarked of the INF Treaty, "It's importance . . . was . . . in the precedents it set . . . With it, Reagan and Gorbachev proved that a way could be found to put the arms race in reverse." Matlock, *Reagan and Gorbachev,* 276. As things turned out, the INF Treaty had more symbolic value than real military significance. In giving up shorter-range missiles, for example, the Soviets could still target the same places with longer-range missiles. The United States did not actually remove all two thousand of the missiles covered by the treaty. In operational terms, nuclear danger was not much reduced. But the treaty marked a watershed just by reversing nuclear growth. Martin Malin, author correspondence.

239. Walter LaFeber, "An End to Which Cold War?," in Hogan, *The End of the Cold War*, 13.

240. FitzGerald, *Way Out There in the Blue*, 427.

241. Ibid., 431. In their meeting in Washington, Reagan wanted to reiterate his SDI position, but Gorbachev told him not to bother. "Let's talk about something else." Talbott, *The Master of the Game*, 364.

242. Against his own hawks, Reagan put it clearly in 1988: "My personal impression is that he is a serious man seeking serious reform. We look to this trend to continue. We must do all that we can to assist it." *New York Times*, June 6, 2004, A31. Reagan's biographer Lou Cannon concludes that Reagan's "assist" to Gorbachev "may well have been Reagan's most important contribution of his presidency." *President Reagan*, 791.

243. The title of the speech was "The Problem of Mankind's Survival." *New York Times*, December 8, 1988, A16.

244. Kwitny, *Man of the Century*, 577.

245. Denise Artaud, "End of the Cold War: A Skeptical View," in Hogan, *The End of the Cold War*, 190.

246. "They tooted trumpets and danced on top. They brought out hammers and chisels and whacked away at the hated symbol of imprisonment, knocking loose chunks of concrete and waving them triumphantly before television cameras. They spilled out into the streets of West Berlin for a champagne-spraying, horn-honking bash that continued until past dawn and then another dawn." "The Wall Crumbler," *Time*, November 20, 1989, 24.

247. "Computers, not imaginary lasers, had won the Cold War." Morris, *Dutch*, 659.

248. "It was evil, until he — until this one man made all the difference." Ibid., 647.

249. John F. Kennedy, *American University Address*, www.jfklibrary.org/speeches.htm.

250. Cannon, *President Reagan*, 788.

251. *New York Times*, January 21, 1989, A1. The *Times* declared on April 2, 1989, that the Cold War was over. Soviet and American coauthors summed up Reagan: "Having entered office denouncing the détente of the 1970s as a fraud, the arms control agreements of that decade as fatally flawed, and the Soviet Union itself as an empire that was the focus of evil in the world, Reagan prepared to leave office having met with his Soviet counterpart more often than any other president, having signed far-reaching arms control treaties, and, like Mikhail Gorbachev, having proclaimed a new era in U.S.-Soviet relations." Bialer and Mandelbaum, *The Global Rivals*, 9.

Eight. Unending War

1. The others were Steven Baggarly, Susan Crane, Steve Kelly, S. J., Tom Lewis-Borbely, and Mark Colville.

2. Tom Lewis-Borbely, author interview.

3. Wilcox, *Disciples and Dissidents*, xviii–xix. Berrigan's figure is conservative. A Brookings Institution study in the early 1990s concluded that the United States had spent more than $20 trillion on its military since World War II, of which $6 trillion was spent on nuclear weapons. http://southmovement.alphalink.com.au/southnews/980701-USnukes .htm. Berrigan's assertion that the United States had intervened in fifty nations over the course of fifty years squares with the broad average across the nation's history. A Congressional Research Service study done early in the twenty-first century counted 250 occasions when the United States engaged in "armed action abroad, from George Washington to George W. Bush — roughly one a year." www.fas.org/man/crs/index.html.

4. "We went (I believe we were led)," Daniel Berrigan wrote of that first Plowshares act, "against all expectation, straight as unbroken arrows, to our quarry . . . We walked unhindered into a 'high security' setting. There was no security worth the word . . . One cannot

but reflect that the myth that 'the weapons are secure' is matched by the myth that 'the weapons bring security.'" Berrigan, *Testimony*, 18.

5. Ibid., 21.

6. Carroll, *Prince of Peace.*

7. Wilcox, *Disciples and Dissidents*, xviii.

8. *New York Times*, January 29, 1992, A16.

9. In July 1991, the START I Treaty ordered reductions of Soviet long-range nuclear warheads from 11,012 to 6,163, and U.S. warheads from 12,646 to 8,556. The START II Treaty, agreed to in 1993, was to continue that reduction to the 3,000 to 3,500 range, but it was never ratified by the Russian Duma because of dislocations caused mainly by NATO expansion, about which we will see more. LaFeber, *America, Russia, and the Cold War,* 364.

10. Recall that the ACDA had been established by John Kennedy in 1961 as an independent agency reporting directly to him. That arms control remained a detested purpose to conservatives made the ACDA a permanent target, and Helms kept it in his sights. President Clinton showed his ambivalence by appointing Randall Forsberg, founder of the Freeze, to the ACDA in 1996 and then, a year later, abolishing the agency. On April 18, 1997, in a statement headed "The era of big government is over," Clinton ordered the "full integration" of the agency into the State Department. Arms reduction and nonproliferation responsibilities were dispersed, a deemphasis that was soon reflected in the effective end of reductions and the growth of proliferation, from Pakistan and India to North Korea and Iran.

11. Wilcox, *Disciples and Dissidents,* 72.

12. Carroll, "War Inside the Pentagon."

13. The Air Force Office of Special Investigations had named its training academy for my father.

14. He has also published three novels, and he brought his library of three thousand volumes with him to the Pentagon. When I traveled with Cohen, he was carrying a copy of Conrad's *Heart of Darkness.*

15. William Cohen, author interview. On the other hand, at least one defense expert had a different take on Berrigan. "There is a certain clarity of vision and purity of focus that you see in someone like Berrigan. It is dismissed as crazy, but it is a form of rational behavior if you have his vision of the inappropriateness of these systems. I don't see things as clearly as he does. I wouldn't risk my life against an Aegis destroyer." John Holdren, author interview. Holdren, a member of the Pugwash Conferences on Science and World Affairs, spoke for the organization in Oslo when it received the 1995 Nobel Peace Prize.

16. Cumings, "The Wicked Witch of the West Is Dead," in Hogan, *The End of the Cold War,* 90.

17. Between June and December 1950, the defense budget went from well under $4 billion to more than $13 billion.

18. Admiral William Crowe, in Talbott, *The Master of the Game,* 375.

19. Ibid., 384.

20. In his December 7, 1988, speech before the United Nations, Gorbachev undercut the last rationale of opposition to nuclear arms reduction by announcing unilateral cuts of 500,000 troops from the Red Army and 10,000 tanks from positions in Eastern Europe.

21. LaFeber, *American, Russia, and the Cold War,* 351. Kazakhstan and Belarus were prompt in yielding their nuclear arsenals. Ukraine briefly tried to use its nukes as a pressure point to get money from the United States, but quickly renounced any claim to them.

22. World War II's youngest combat pilot, Bush was shot down at the age of eighteen. After being rescued, he went on to fly more than a thousand hours of combat. He served in Congress and as U.N. ambassador, U.S. representative to China, and head of the CIA before becoming vice president.

23. At Malta, Bush and Gorbachev launched the START negotiations, which would conclude with an agreement signed in July 1991,coming into force in late 1994. When Bush and Gorbachev met, the combined total of deployed strategic warheads was about twenty-four thousand, about evenly divided. START I would halve that force to about six thousand warheads each. Michael Beschloss and Strobe Talbott say that Bush was prepared at that meeting to eliminate all MIRVed ICBMs, which, as ultimate first-strike weapons, had been the source of terrifying destabilization, but he was talked out of this step by his secretary of defense, Richard Cheney. *At the Highest Levels*, 146.

24. LaFeber, *America, Russia, and the Cold War*, 348.

25. Operation Just Cause, originally named Blue Spoon, was launched on December 20, 1989. Its purpose was to enable federal agents to arrest the Panamanian leader, Manuel Noriega, a former CIA operative and a key funneler of funds to the Contras, on charges of violating American drug laws. This enforcement of U.S. criminal law abroad, if necessary by kidnapping suspects, was unprecedented, and it was based on the Bush Justice Department's explicit change in policy — as if the United States would tolerate a British invasion of Queens, New York, to arrest wanted IRA gunmen. Of course, the enforcement of drug laws provided flimsy cover; if the Justice Department were serious, it would have invaded Colombia. Drug trafficking through Panama actually increased after the invasion. The Bush administration was acting ahead of the January 1, 1990, deadline when Jimmy Carter's hated Panama Canal Treaty was to come into force. Noriega was simply not trusted as custodian of the canal. See Woodward, *The Commanders*, 115.

26. Laurence Ingram Radway, "George Bush, Mass Nationalism, and the Gulf War," in Bose and Perotti, *From Cold War to New World Order*, 467.

27. Beschloss and Talbott, *At the Highest Levels*, 170. In 1990, Gorbachev put the question directly to congressional leaders who raised the issue of Soviet force in Lithuania: "Why did you let your administration intervene in Panama if you love freedom so much?"(272).

28. It was on the basis of an appeal to "realism" that Scowcroft wrote his famous 2002 article questioning George W. Bush's evident plan to invade Iraq. "Don't Attack Saddam," *Wall Street Journal*, August 15, 2002, op-ed page.

29. Beschloss and Talbott, *At the Highest Levels*, 17.

30. Ibid., 445. Cheney argued that Gorbachev "would ultimately fail. And when that happens, he's likely to be replaced by somebody who will be far more hostile." Blumenthal, *Pledging Allegiance*, 328. Bush's first choice as secretary of defense was Senator John Tower, a fellow Texan, but he was not confirmed by the Senate because of questions about his character and health. Thus Cheney was not sworn in until nearly two months after Bush took office.

31. Wolfowitz warned that the much-ballyhooed "new thinking" could be "a decision to pursue the same ends by less costly and less controversial means." Paul Wolfowitz, "Glasnost in Order on Regional Clashes," *Wall Street Journal*, November 7, 1989, op-ed page.

32. Beschloss and Talbott, *At the Highest Levels*, 105.

33. LaFeber, *America, Russia, and the Cold War*, 353, 363.

34. John Lewis Gaddis, "The Cold War, the Long Peace, and the Future," in Hogan, *The End of the Cold War*, 31.

35. *New York Times*, September 28, 1991, A1. Bush also announced that B-52 airborne alerts, which had been carried out since my father had helped prove them necessary in the 1950s, were to be discontinued. He announced as well that the still problematic MX missile would not be deployed. See Cumings, "The Wicked Witch of the West Is Dead," in Hogan, *The End of the Cold War*, 91.

36. Gaddis, *The Long Peace*. See, for example, Mearsheimer, "Why We Will Soon Miss the Cold War."

37. Halberstam, *War in a Time of Peace*, 74.

38. The 185 countries represented in the United Nations comprised something like 250 ethnic and religious factions, any one of which could lay claim to nationhood. LaFeber, *America, Russia, and the Cold War*, 346.

39. Cumings, "The Wicked Witch of the West Is Dead," in Hogan, *The End of the Cold War*, 91.

40. See Schell, *The Unconquerable World*, 1–63.

41. The Falklands War in 1982 undermined the military junta of Argentina, but the leaders were not replaced until elections the next year, and could have clung to power. They yielded to a clear popular will that did not resort to violence.

42. U.S. Conference of Catholic Bishops, *The Challenge of Peace*.

43. Carl Kaysen, "Is War Obsolete?," 63.

44. During the Reagan years, the federal deficit went from $59.6 billion to a high of $220 billion. The gross federal debt went from $749 billion to $2 trillion. Hurst, *The Foreign Policy of the Bush Administration*, 5.

45. Robert McNamara and James Blight provide a list of military leaders who, as the Cold War wound down and then ended, concluded that the time for the elimination of nuclear weapons had come. Those listed include General G. Lee Butler, former commander in chief of the Strategic Command; Admiral Noel Gayler, former chief of U.S. forces in the Pacific; General Larry Welch, former Air Force chief of staff; and General Charles A. Horner, chief of the Space Command. In all, dozens of retired admirals and generals signed statements calling for the elimination of nuclear weapons. *Wilson's Ghost*, 205–7.

46. Kaplan, *Wizards of Armageddon*, 246.

47. The observer was John Steinbruner. Carroll, "War Inside the Pentagon," 59. Government documents declassified in 2004 show that the SIOP (Single Integrated Operational Plan) assumed the firing of more than 3,200 nuclear weapons at more than 1,000 targets in the various Communist countries: 130 cities would be obliterated, 285 million people would be killed. See William Burr's analysis at www.gwu.edu/~nsarchiv/nsaebb/nsaebb130/index.htm.

48. Schell, *The Gift of Time*, 207–8.

49. Halberstam, *War in a Time of Peace*, 75.

50. The announcement of manpower cuts noted, however, that a whole new investment in high technology would have to be made — a prediction of the skyrocketing military budget that occurred in the Clinton years. LaFeber, *America, Russia, and the Cold War*, 357.

51. Cumings, "The Wicked Witch of the West Is Dead," in Hogan, *The End of the Cold War*, 90. Bruce Cumings makes the connection between the Korean "rescue" of U.S. military outlays in 1950 and Saddam Hussein's in 1990.

52. On August 5, less than three days after the invasion, Bush said, "This will not stand, this aggression against Kuwait." *New York Times*, August 6, 1990, A1.

53. On July 19, 1990, U.S. ambassadors in the Middle East were instructed by Washington that "the United States takes no position on the substance of bilateral issues concerning Iraq and Kuwait." On July 25, a week before Iraq's invasion, the U.S. ambassador to Iraq, April Glaspie, said as much to Saddam Hussein, a signal he could not unreasonably have taken to mean the United States would not oppose his move. Hurst, *The Foreign Policy of the Bush Administration*, 89.

54. "Address Before a Joint Session of Congress on the Crisis in the Persian Gulf and the Federal Budget Deficit," September 11, 1990, *Public Papers of the Presidents of the United States: George Bush, 1990*.

55. Radway, "George Bush, Mass Nationalism, and the Gulf War," in Bose and Perotti, *From Cold War to New World Order*, 468.

56. Beschloss and Talbott, *At the Highest Levels*, 288.

57. Gorbachev's first plea for peace before the January 15 deadline came on January 11. It was dismissed not only by the Pentagon but by historians writing after the fact. Michael Beschloss and Strobe Talbott swat Gorbachev's initiative away: "Mindful as ever of his conservative critics, he wished to put himself on the record one more time as championing a political solution." *At the Highest Levels,* 304. Between January 11 and January 19, as bombs exploded over Baghdad, Soviet troops fired into crowds in Vilnius, Lithuania, and in Riga, Latvia, killing more than twenty people. Gorbachev was blamed for this, especially by hawks in the Pentagon, who seized on the slayings as proof that he was still a threat. In fact, it was Gorbachev alone who forced the Soviet military to back down from such tactics, and he disavowed the killings on January 28. In these weeks he sealed his fate as a political loser among his own people, but in my view he was a moral hero. Much later, after he had effectively lost his battle to hold the Soviet Union together and to keep his position, he told Beschloss and Talbott of having been asked if he was happy. "Happy?" he replied. "That is a question to be asked of a woman" (454).

58. Stalemate in Korea, defeat in Vietnam, the hostage-rescue disaster of Desert One, the bombing of the Marine barracks in Beirut, the inept invasion of Grenada.

59. Klare, *Blood and Oil,* 50.

60. The television networks lacked Ken Burns's good taste in music. They contrived dramatic jingles to accompany station identifications with "America at War" logos before and after commercial breaks.

61. Halberstam, *War in a Time of Peace,* 55.

62. Woodward, *The Commanders,* 217.

63. I first recounted this incident, and my father's funeral, in *An American Requiem,* 276.

64. LaFeber, *America and Russia in the Cold War,* 359.

65. Thomas Mann, Nobel Address, 1929, http://nobelprize.org/literature/laureates/1929/mann-autobio.html.

66. Quoted by McNamara and Blight, *Wilson's Ghost,* 76.

67. The statistics of the twentieth century are only statistics, but, imagined singly, they are, as Stalin himself said, every one a tragedy. According to the best estimates, 120 million people died in wars between 1900 and 2000. Mao and Stalin each murdered another 20 million. The overwhelming majority of these victims, of course, were civilians. Ibid., 22.

68. For the connection between military failures and the Pentagon reform, see Perry, *Four Stars,* 315–39.

69. Named for Senator Barry Goldwater and Representative William Nichols. Mark Perry reports that when the bill passed unanimously in the Senate, a soon-to-retire Barry Goldwater wept. Ibid., 338.

70. Ibid., 331.

71. A military man who "goes purple" is no longer seeing things through his service's color. Powell, *My American Journey,* 410.

72. Perry, *Four Stars,* 340.

73. Atlantic Command, Central Command, European Command, Pacific Command, Southern Command, Forces Command, Space Command, Special Operations Command, Strategic Command, and Transportation Command.

74. Johnson, *The Sorrows of Empire,* 4.

75. The U.N. Conference on Disarmament, meeting periodically in Geneva since 1959, had hammered out all of the great arms control treaties. In 1967, the Outer Space Treaty established rules governing the military uses of space. From the late 1990s into the early years of the twenty-first century, the conference has been working toward an agreement called Preventing an Arms Race in Outer Space (PAROS), with China taking the lead. But American intentions for missile defense and, as the Pentagon dubs it, "full spectrum dominance,"

have led Washington to block PAROS. See Steinbruner and Lewis, "The Unsettled Legacy of the Cold War," 5–10.

76. Some examples: By 2005, the U.S. Navy was built around a fleet of twelve huge Nimitz-class aircraft carriers, the length of each one about equal to the height of the Empire State Building. They patrol every ocean on the globe. No other Navy in the world has even one ship to compare with these vessels. The Marine Corps is a fraction the size of the U.S. Army, yet it is one and a half times larger than the whole British army. The U.S. defense budget exceeds the figure spent on defense by "all other nations in the world together." Bacevich, *The New American Militarism*, 17.

77. Powell, *My American Journey*, 411–12.

78. Ibid., 412. "Over the years," Powell comments about these windows, "I found myself in an ideal position to watch the daily human drama, from little cabals of Pentagon officers to lovers arranging trysts."

79. Ibid., 292.

80. Mann, *Rise of the Vulcans*, 43.

81. Carlucci resented being forced by Bush to submit his resignation before his successor was confirmed, which became a public embarrassment for Carlucci and Bush both when the nomination of John Tower was scuttled.

82. Michael O'Hanlon, author interview.

83. Woodward, *The Commanders*, 299.

84. Pat Lang, a DIA analyst, said of the Iraqis at an Oval Office war council meeting one week before the January 15 deadline, "They won't back away. They will fight skillfully and hard. They are tough . . . They won't surrender." While Lang spoke to the president and his advisers, Powell could be seen nodding. Ibid., 359.

85. Ibid., 301. Also opposing the use of force, in favor of diplomacy and sanctions, was Powell's predecessor as JCS chairman, Admiral William J. Crowe, Jr. (332). Opposed as well were "five former secretaries of defense, two former chairmen of the Joint Chiefs of Staff [including Crowe], President Carter's National Security Adviser . . . and a large majority of European and American experts on Arab affairs." Radway, "George Bush, Mass Nationalism, and the Gulf War," in Bose and Perotti, *From Cold War to New World Order*, 470. Almost half of the Senate opposed the use of force.

86. General James (Terry) Scott, author interview. Carroll, "War Inside the Pentagon," 52.

87. Radway, "George Bush, Mass Nationalism, and the Gulf War," in Bose and Perotti, *From Cold War to New World Order*, 479.

88. To this day, it is impossible to know with precision how many Iraqis died in the Gulf War and what percentage of those were civilians. We have already cited one scholar, Walter LaFeber, who accepts a figure of 100,000. Another puts the number of "killed or wounded" at "over half a million." Ibid., 479.

89. Halberstam, *War in a Time of Peace*, 13.

90. Beschloss and Talbott, *At the Highest Levels*, 468.

91. Bacevich, *The New American Militarism*, 120.

92. Radway, "George Bush, Mass Nationalism, and the Gulf War," in Bose and Perotti, *From Cold War to New World Order*, 481.

93. Halberstam, *War in a Time of Peace*, 108. Halberstam cites Ed Rollins as linking Winfrey and Clinton, and associating Gary Cooper with the Cold War ethos.

94. Gore, *Earth in the Balance*, 4, 34.

95. Halberstam, *War in a Time of Peace*, 175.

96. In a speech at MIT in 1992, Aspin said, "A world without nuclear weapons would actually be better." Quoted by Janne Nolan, *An Elusive Consensus*, 38.

97. LaFeber, *America, Russia, and the Cold War*, 373. "Enlargement" implies the spread-

ing of democracy as a national security strategy, but this has its problems in theory and practice. George W. Bush's rhetoric about bringing democracy to Afghanistan and Iraq has its roots here, in the Clinton era. For more on problems with this idea, see Edward Mansfield and Jack Sneider, "Democratization and War," *Foreign Affairs,* May/June 1995, www.foreignaffairs.org/19950501faessay5039/edward-mansfield-jack-snyder/democratization-and-war.html.

98. Secretary of Defense Les Aspin was forced to resign in 1993. He died of a stroke in 1995. Warren Christopher was quickly shown to be, especially during the Bosnia crisis, a man without influence with other foreign ministers, or even with Clinton. He was replaced in the second term by Madeleine Albright, whose promotion of America as the "indispensable nation" seemed laughable. Anthony Lake never mastered the national security bureaucracy or won Clinton's full confidence. He was beset by ill health and personal problems, and was replaced by his deputy Samuel R. (Sandy) Berger, who later became embroiled in Clinton's scandals and was ultimately disgraced for the illegal handling of classified materials. At the Pentagon, Les Aspin's deputies were William Perry, who eventually replaced Aspin as secretary, and John Deutch, who became director of the CIA, where he was accused of working on classified material at home. Perry is regarded as having been a successful secretary of defense, but he did not serve long before being replaced, in Clinton's second term, by William Cohen.

99. LaFeber, *America, Russia, and the Cold War,* 371.

100. Postol, "Lessons of the Gulf War Patriot Experience," 119–71.

101. LaFeber, *America, Russia, and the Cold War,* 385.

102. Beschloss and Talbott, *At the Highest Levels,* 185–86. See also McNamara and Blight, *Wilson's Ghost,* 86.

103. LaFeber, *America, Russia, and the Cold War,* 382; Martin Malin, www.brown.edu/administration/news_bureau/op-eds/gottlieb.html.

104. There would be nothing to trump when Madeleine Albright became secretary of state. The Czech native and fierce anti-Communist was a champion of NATO expansion.

105. McNamara and Blight, *Wilson's Ghost,* 90. "Such a decision," Kennan wrote in 1997 of NATO's enlargement, "may be expected to inflame the nationalistic, anti-Western and militaristic tendencies in Russian opinion; to have an adverse effect on the development of Russian democracy; to restore the atmosphere of the Cold War to East-West relations, and to impel Russian foreign policy in directions decidedly not to our liking." *New York Times,* March 18, 2005, A22. A proponent of expansion, Richard Holbrooke, noted his disagreement with Kennan on the occasion of his death in 2005: "Events proved Bill Clinton right and Kennan — and the bulk of the liberal intellectual community — wrong." Richard Holbrooke, "The Paradox of George F. Kennan," *Washington Post,* March 21, 2005, A19. This assertion does nothing to address Kennan's larger concern. It is far too soon to say that Kennan was wrong. One might also note that most university-based defense intellectuals opposed NATO's expansion — hardly a group of liberals. Martin Malin, author correspondence.

106. It was on another aircraft carrier, the *Abraham Lincoln,* that George W. Bush stood before a sign emblazoned "Mission Accomplished" in May 2003, as the worst phase of the Iraq War was about to begin.

107. In 1980, the United States had 14,404 strategic warheads, 9,360 nonstrategic warheads, and 23,764 stockpiled warheads. In 1992, it had 9,444 strategic warheads, 4,287 nonstrategic warheads, and 13,731 stockpiled warheads. In 2000, 8,679 strategic, 1,936 nonstrategic, and 10,615 stockpiled warheads. "Archive of Nuclear Data," Natural Resources Defense Council, www.nrdc.org/nuclear/nudb/datainx.asp.

108. The MIT physicist Theodore Postol published findings that showed the Patriot missile had not performed successfully during the Gulf War, despite Pentagon claims.

www.fas.org/spp/starwars/docops/pl920908.htm. See also his "Lessons of the Gulf War Patriot Experience."

109. Halberstam, *War in a Time of Peace*, 114.

110. Clinton, *My Life*, 154.

111. Halberstam, *War in a Time of Peace*, 117.

112. Colin Powell, author interview.

113. Schell, *The Gift of Time*, 207.

114. Katzenstein and Reppy, *Beyond Zero Tolerance*, 5. Women moving into combat roles did not have it easy. Lieutenant Kelly Flinn was the first woman assigned to pilot a B-52. She was disgraced and forced out of the service for having had an adulterous affair with the husband of an enlisted woman. "In the end, this is not an issue about adultery," Air Force Chief of Staff Ronald R. Fogelman told the Senate Armed Services Committee. "This is an issue about an officer entrusted to fly nuclear weapons who lied. That's what this is about." Carroll, "War Inside the Pentagon," 55.

115. In the early 1960s, this concern was given vivid expression by revelations, for example, that two soldiers assigned to the National Security Agency at Fort Meade, Maryland, were serving as Soviet spies. That they were homosexual seemed to explain everything. The same was true of the notorious British spies of the same period, Kim Philby and Guy Burgess.

116. In testimony before Congress on February 5, 1992, JCS Chairman Colin Powell was asked by Congressman Barney Frank, a homosexual, if national security concerns were the reason the military barred gays, and Powell answered no. He justified the regulation by citing "good order and discipline." Powell, *My American Journey*, 546.

117. Katzenstein and Reppy, *Beyond Zero Tolerance*, 9.

118. Rape was clearly used as a weapon of war in the Balkans in the 1990s, with Bosnian Muslim women being particularly targeted by Serb paramilitaries, to shame them and drive them and their families away. Rape, that is, was a tool of ethnic cleansing.

119. At a Tailhook convention of Navy fighter pilots in 1991, dozens of women, civilian and military, were sexually harassed and even molested. The controversy escalated when the official Navy inquiry was found (by the Pentagon's inspector general and others) to have downplayed the seriousness of the offenses and to have covered up the participation of senior officers. The unspoken ethic of sexual bravado, and its acceptance in the military, was glaringly evident in this scandal.

120. The contradictions of the sexual mores of the military were reduced to the absurd in 1997, when Air Force General Joseph W. Ralston's appointment to the chairmanship of the Joint Chiefs of Staff was derailed because Ralston had committed adultery ten years before, in a period when he and his wife were separated. The chain of command could not overlook Ralston's offense while it was court-martialing Lieutenant Kelly Flinn for having had an affair with an enlisted woman's husband. At the same time, Sergeant Major of the Army Gene McKinney was being charged with sexual harassment. All of this was unfolding while the nation's commander in chief was embroiled in sexual scandals of his own, ultimately including a classic instance of workplace sexual harassment, for which most civilian as well as all military careers would have been destroyed. Why should a military career be ruined for behavior the president defended as "private"? One general said to me, with undisguised contempt, "There is no moral leadership from the White House on this. When challenged on adultery, the accused say, 'Who is it that is holding me accountable to this standard? Who?'" Carroll, "War Inside the Pentagon," 61.

121. Ibid., 59. General Butler added, "I feel empowered to say that, because I was one of them."

122. Powell, *My American Journey*, 563.

123. In December 1992, after being named as the new secretary of defense, Aspin invited

the outgoing assistant secretary of defense, Lawrence Korb, to breakfast at the Four Seasons in Washington. Aspin asked Korb if he had "any advice." As Korb related it to me when I was preparing an article for *The New Yorker* in 1997, "I said, 'You've got to get rid of Powell. He's leaving in a couple of months anyway, but you cannot restructure the military the way Clinton talked about in the campaign, or in your "Bottom-Up Review," as long as he's there.'" Author interview.

124. Powell, *My American Journey*, 570. Significantly, Powell heard the account of Aspin's comments while having dinner with his close friend Caspar Weinberger, at Weinberger's Watergate apartment.

125. "Advice for President Clinton: U.S. Forces; Challenges Ahead."

126. Powell, *My American Journey*, 603. The offer was made on December 18, 1994. Powell would have replaced Warren Christopher, who stayed on when Powell declined.

127. Looking back on Somalia and other such "Operations Other Than War," Powell told me, in a telephone interview in 1997, "We bring young men and women into the armed forces to be warriors, in a warrior culture. They are not social workers. They are warriors, and every aspect of our policy must support that." Carroll, "War Inside the Pentagon," 59.

128. Powell, *My American Journey*, 573.

129. In his memoir, Clinton sums up what happened: "On paper, the military had moved a long way, to 'live and let live,' while holding on to the idea that it couldn't acknowledge gays without approving of homosexuality and compromising morale and cohesion." With pointed understatement, Clinton adds, "In practice, it often didn't work out that way." *My Life*, 485.

130. In the ten years before "Don't ask, don't tell," an average of 1,500 people were discharged from the military each year for being homosexual. In the five years after the policy was instituted, the number of soldiers forcibly discharged increased to an average of nearly 2,000. The underground culture of violence and threats against gays grew worse. Katzenstein and Reppy, *Beyond Zero Tolerance*, 214.

131. "Don't ask, don't tell" was a disaster for military readiness, too. By 2005, 9,488 people had been expelled from the military under the Clinton policy. Of those, 757 were in "critical occupations," including hundreds of translators with knowledge of Korean, Arabic, and Farsi. With the coming of war in Iraq, the Defense Department apparently realized that some things were more important than sexual orientation. In 2004, the number of gays discharged, 653, was half what it had been in 2000 and 2001. The figures are from a General Accounting Office report, cited in the *Atlantic Monthly*, May 2005, 52.

132. On July 26, 1948, Truman issued Executive Order 9981, which required "equality of treatment and opportunity for all persons in the armed services without regard to race, color, religion, or national origin." The order also established the President's Committee on Equality of Treatment and Opportunity, which was to oversee, with the secretary of defense, implementation of the policy. Binkin et al., *Blacks and the Military*, 26. By the year 2000, with African Americans making up 13 percent of the population, they comprised 25 percent of Army personnel. Andrew J. Bacevich, *Boston Globe*, March 28, 2005, A11.

133. Powell, *My American Journey*, 546.

134. The name derives from an Indian expression, Indians having seen some similarity between the close, tight hair of Negro soldiers and the matted hair of buffalo.

135. Binkin et al., *Blacks and the Military*, 22.

136. Ibid., 23.

137. McCullough, *Truman*, 651, 667.

138. Binkin et al., *Blacks and the Military*, 26.

139. Colin Powell, in a speech delivered in 1998 to mark the anniversary of the Truman order, noted Bradley's attempt to fend off integration, and he also noted how Bradley

swung back to full compliance with the spirit of the order when Truman demanded it. In his speech, Powell made no reference to gays in the military or to his own role in undermining Clinton's authority on the issue. Powell, "President Truman and the Desegregation of the Armed Forces."

140. The Air Force's deputy chief of staff for personnel, Lieutenant General Idwal H. Edwards, for example, told his senior staff in 1948: "There will be frictions and incidents. However, they will be minimized if commanders give implementation of this policy their personal attention and exercise positive command control." Office of the Secretary of Defense, "Sexual Orientation and U.S. Military Personnel Policy" (National Defense Research Institute, 1993), 167.

141. McCullough, *Truman*, 650.

142. I myself saluted Operation Restore Hope in a column I wrote, in the *Boston Globe*, in December 1992.

143. "Aidid" means "one who tolerates no insult." Bolger, *Savage Peace*, 298. Perhaps the largest impact of the American failure in Somalia was in the encouragement Osama bin Laden took from it, as a signal of the "false courage" of the United States. Bacevich, *The New American Militarism*, 196.

144. The dead were Sergeant Thomas Field and Master Sergeant Gary I. Gordon.

145. Clinton later apologized for failing to stop the genocide in Rwanda. Clinton was "an omnidirectional apologizer," a Pentagon insider put it to me, "because he had so much to apologize for." See the interviews on PBS's *Frontline* documentary *The Triumph of Evil*. "As Philip Gourevitch, an expert on the Rwanda genocide, bitterly notes at the conclusion of this report, the Clinton administration's failure to intervene in Rwanda "wasn't a failure to act. The decision was not to act. And at that, we succeeded greatly." www.pbs.org/wgbh/pages/frontline/shows/evil.

146. Inman had also been the vice director of the Defense Intelligence Agency in the mid-1970s, a few years after my father's retirement.

147. Quoted by Nolan, *An Elusive Consensus*, 39.

148. Ibid., 40.

149. The number of targets in the SIOP would be reduced from 4,700 in 1992 to between 2,000 and 2,500 by 1998. Ibid., 44. In 2004, the number of targets in the SIOP was classified, but still thought to be counted in four figures.

150. The phrase originates with William Perry, Aspin's successor.

151. Nolan, *An Elusive Consensus*, 43.

152. START II was signed in early 1993. The U.S. Senate did not ratify it until 1996. Theoretically, it was to cut the strategic forces to a maximum of about 3,500 strategic warheads. The agreement also called for the elimination of MIRVs. But START II's limits referred to *deployed* strategic warheads. It had no effect on tactical nukes or on warheads that were "stored." Therefore, neither the United States nor Russia ever really achieved START II reduction levels. At the end of the Cold War, the U.S. arsenal had about 21,500 nuclear warheads. In 2004, with most tactical nukes gone, America's active stockpile numbered about 10,400. "U.S. Nuclear Reductions," *Bulletin of the Atomic Scientists*, September/October 2004, 70–71.

153. Nolan, *An Elusive Consensus*, 50.

154. Chinese targets had been removed from the SIOP only in the 1980s. The SIOP had last been revised under Richard Cheney in 1989. Even he was appalled to learn, for example, that Kiev, Ukraine, was to be hit with forty thermonuclear weapons. A new SIOP was approved in July 1993, but it still assumed thousands of targets, an orgasm of apocalyptic violence. Ibid., 19, 29.

155. "Lead but hedge" is the phrase the NPR uses. The idea was to have a hedge against

the chance that Russian reform would falter, after which its nuclear arsenal, in the hands of one kind of fascist government or another, would again pose a transcendent threat. www .defenselink.mil/execsec/adr95/npr_.html.

156. The NPR established the nuclear force as consisting of 14 Trident submarines, each with 24 missiles, each of which carried 5 warheads; 66 B-52 bombers carrying air-launched cruise missiles; 20 B-2 bombers carrying gravity bombs; and 500 Minuteman III missiles, each carrying a single warhead. See "Nuclear Posture Review," www.defenselink.mil/ execsec/adr95/npr.html.

157. John Holdren, author interview.

158. Steinbruner, *Principles of Global Security,* 49.

159. Poland, Hungary, and the Czech Republic were formally admitted to NATO in 1999.

160. On April 9, 1997, the Duma voted to indefinitely postpone debate on START II ratification.

161. There is a middle point between the goal of elimination and a deterrent force of thousands. Many experts say that a full-blown deterrent can be maintained by a force as small as 200 nukes. For example, the National Academy of Sciences urged a prompt decrease, first to 2,000, then to 1,000, and ultimately to "roughly 300 each." Committee on International Security and Arms Control, *The Future of U.S. Nuclear Weapons Policy,* 80. General Terry Scott put the figure needed for minimum deterrence even lower, at 200. Author interview. An arsenal in the low hundreds still threatens extraordinary destruction, but it would be far less liable to accidental launchings or security breaches.

162. Nolan, *An Elusive Consensus,* 58.

163. This is the basic logic of George W. Bush's 2002 National Security Strategy of coercive prevention, but it has antecedents. The policy of threatening nonnuclear states with nuclear weapons had begun under Richard Cheney in the George H. W. Bush administration, with the Nuclear Weapons Employment Policy of 1992, but after the NPR, there was nothing to stop the Clinton administration from adopting it, as it did in the African Treaty. Ibid., 65, 67.

164. Steinbruner, *Principles of Global Security,* 24.

165. Just as the Non-Proliferation Treaty's extension debate approached conclusion, Clinton was forced to take a position on the key issue. Janne Nolan, having interviewed a Clinton speechwriter, gives the account:. "On March 1, 1995, the president gave a speech at the Washington-based Nixon Center for Peace and Freedom calling for the nuclear weapons states 'to pursue nuclear arms control and disarmament.' The original draft of the speech had Clinton calling for the 'eventual elimination of nuclear weapons,' consistent with article 6 of the treaty, but these words were deleted in response to opposition from individuals at the Pentagon." *An Elusive Consensus,* 76. Some say the idea of being legally committed to weapons elimination is meaningless, since it is so unlikely to happen. But as one defense scholar puts it, "the commitment expresses a basic sense of fairness that has practical importance even if it cannot be fully achieved. It generates an operating principle that affects the detailed workings of international politics — if anyone is to accept restraint, then everyone must do so." Steinbruner, *Principles of Global Security,* 124. On December 5, 1996, sixty-one retired generals and admirals from seventeen nations signed a statement, spearheaded by General Lee Butler, calling for the eventual elimination of nuclear weapons. They did this because the movement away from elimination had become so powerful.

166. America is "the indispensable nation" because "we stand tall and hence see further into the future" than other nations. Madeleine Albright, NBC *Today* show, February 19, 1998.

167. For a discussion of the court's proceedings, see Lindqvist, *A History of Bombing,* 179–81.

168. A group characterized by the South Korean government as "rogue scientists" in South Korea began enriching uranium in 2000 as a first step toward manufacturing a nu-

clear weapon, but the scientists turned out to be working for the government. "The Nuclear Genie Pops Out Yet Again," *New York Times,* September 5, 2004, 2.

169. The figures are in constant 1999 dollars. *World Military Expenditures and Arms Transfers, 1999–2000* (Washington, D.C.: U.S. Department of State, Bureau of Compliance and Verification, 2002), table 1, 91, 99. www.globalsecurity.org/military/library/report/2003/wmeat9900/index.html.

170. Carroll, "War Inside the Pentagon," 53. Chalmers Johnson comments, "The frequent Republican charge that Clinton cut military spending is untrue. In the wake of the Reagan defense buildup . . . he simply allowed military spending to return to what had become its normal level." *The Sorrows of Empire,* 56. By the year 2004, the Defense Department's annual budget exceeded Russia's entire gross domestic product. *The 9/11 Commission Report,* 95.

171. William Perry, for example, warned that Taiwan, China, India, and Pakistan would all inevitably increase their nuclear forces in the wake of an American deployment of missile defense. He did that after leaving his position as secretary of defense.

172. The timing of this legislation, coming in the midst of the NATO air war in the summer of 1999 against Serbia and a direct challenge to Russia, which firmly opposed the air war, could not have been worse. Clinton, like Lyndon Johnson in 1968, was using the ABM Treaty to protect not against Moscow but against Republicans at home.

173. The Clinton administration had begun the process of "renegotiating" the ABM Treaty to legitimize missile defense. In July 2000, a key test of an ABM failed, another in a succession of failures. The scientists who had said the whole idea was flawed were proven right. Instead of canceling the system, Clinton announced he would defer the decision in favor of the next administration. Bush abrogated the ABM Treaty in 2001, and he ordered the deployment of eight missile interceptors in Alaska and California. The next proposed step will be a "constellation" of spaced-based interceptors.

174. Carroll, "War Inside the Pentagon," 61.

175. Ibid.

176. R. W. Apple used the term in reports from Clinton's visit to Northern Ireland.

177. I was present in Derry Square, in Derry, Northern Ireland, when Clinton addressed a combined crowd of Catholics and Protestants. The square was still the center of a war zone, with British troops ringing its medieval walls. A Secret Service agent told me of Clinton's bulletproof raincoat. I saw it when Clinton, emerging from his car, declined to wear the coat, tossing it onto the seat. He addressed the crowd quite movingly, a heartfelt plea for peace. They sensed, I believe, that he was making himself vulnerable with them. The Irish people mark that day as the beginning of their new, far more hopeful era.

178. See, for example, Daniel Pipes, "Camp David II and Shoot the Moon Diplomacy," *New York Post,* March 4, 2002.

179. The not-so-hidden agenda of the U.S. war on terrorism was the creation of bases in the former Soviet region, with the goal of influencing, if not controlling, the movement of Caspian Sea oil reserves. LaFeber, *America, Russia, and the Cold War,* 387.

180. Steinbruner, *Principles of Global Security,* 11.

181. We have seen that, in 2000, the United States had 8,679 strategic warheads, 1,936 nonstrategic warheads, and 10,615 stockpiled warheads. "Archive of Nuclear Data," Natural Resources Defense Council, www.nrdc.org/nuclear/nudb/datainx.asp. Chalmers Johnson says that when Clinton left office in 2001, there were 5,400 nuclear warheads on missiles; 1,750 bombs loaded on B-2 and B-52 warplanes; and 1,670 "tactical" nukes in artillery units and on ships. Ten thousand more nukes were "stored," ready to be deployed on short order. *The Sorrows of Empire,* 64.

182. The five are Serbia, Slovenia, Croatia, Bosnia, Macedonia, and Montenegro.

183. www.nwc.navy.mil/balkans/bc2m22p1.htm.

184. Roy Gutman, "There Is No Food Here. There Is No Air," *Newsday*, August 2, 1992.

185. It was U.N. Ambassador Madeleine Albright's question, too. An early advocate of armed intervention in the Balkans, she famously asked Colin Powell, "What's the point of having this superb military that you're always talking about if we can't use it?" It is an irony of how the Pentagon developed as a center of American belligerence that soldiers were reluctant to commit forces to actual combat, while civilians were often anxious to. Albright embodied this. Writing of her remark in his memoir, Powell says he nearly had an "aneurysm." *My American Journey*, 576. Albright was surrounded by men, like Powell, who saw the world through a lens labeled "Vietnam." Her lens was labeled "Munich."

186. Halberstam, *War in a Time of Peace*, 307. I was writing columns for the *Boston Globe* at the time, and I, too, was uncertain of what course to advocate. I consistently opposed military force, wishing for diplomatic alternatives that never materialized. For example, I wrote in early 1993, "We see that a humane use of American power has never seemed so necessary, yet we also see that American power is never so dangerous to itself or the world as when acting out of an unexamined sense of moral superiority." "Seeing the Balkan Chaos with Both Eyes Open," *Boston Globe*, February 2, 1993. Two of the key figures of the left calling for intervention were Susan Sontag and her son, David Rieff, both of whom wrote passionate dispatches back from Sarajevo. Rieff eventually had a change of heart, as I note below.

187. Posen, "The War for Kosovo," 60.

188. Ibid. The Dayton Accords, worked out under the leadership of the American diplomat Richard Holbrooke, created two states, a Croat-Bosnian Federation, with its capital in Sarajevo, and a Bosnian Serb Republic. In effect, the agreement accepted the results of ethnic cleansing. It was the refusal to "reward" ethnic cleansing that motivated widespread rejection of the Vance-Owen proposal of 1992, which was more or less the same as Dayton. The Dayton Accords were the occasion for the arrival of 60,000 NATO troops to enforce the truce, including 20,000 Americans. In December 2004, NATO formally handed over its peace mission to a force of about 7,000 troops led by the European Union.

189. March 3, 1998. The first story was by Chris Hedges, the second by Adam Nagourney.

190. "Clinton's Crisis: Truth or Consequences," *Time*, February 2, 1998, 22.

191. Clinton's sexual relationship with Monica Lewinsky began on November 15, 1995. On April 5, 1996, she was transferred from the White House to the Pentagon. Clinton's last sexual encounter with her occurred on March 29, 1997. www.time.com/time/daily/scandal/starr_report/files.

192. "The NATO air campaign directly caused an estimated 1,500 civilian deaths throughout Yugoslavia, and the Serbian rampage in Kosovo is judged to have killed up to 10,000 noncombatants." Steinbruner, *Principles of Global Security*, 253. Chalmers Johnson puts the total number of civilian deaths due to NATO bombing at "nearly 2000." *The Sorrows of Empire*, 75.

193. Posen, "The War for Kosovo," 64.

194. Ibid., 79. Kosovo came under the protection of the U.N. The final disposition of its status was postponed until 2005, when talks were set to begin. If Kosovo is granted independence from Serbia, nationalist pressures may well mount again in Bosnia. The last Serb-connected republic of the former Yugoslavia, Montenegro, is also expected to seek its independence from Belgrade as the Kosovo talks commence. Milosevic, meanwhile, was brought to trial for war crimes at The Hague. For a positive evaluation of Clinton's Balkan policy, see LaFeber, *America, Russia, and the Cold War*, 385.

195. McNamara and Blight, *Wilson's Ghost*, 162.

196. Carroll, "War Inside the Pentagon," 62.

197. Clark, *Waging Modern War*, 394.

198. Putin had other reasons for turning to the nuclear arsenal as a main threat against the West, not least the serious decline of Russia's conventional forces. See Miller and Trenin, *The Russian Military.*

199. McNamara and Blight, *Wilson's Ghost,* 91.

200. "Richard Gardner, a former ambassador to Spain and Italy, estimates that, by a ratio of at least sixteen to one, the United States spends more on preparing for war than on trying to prevent it." Johnson, *The Sorrows of Empire,* 63.

201. Richard Perle brought his own line of apostolic succession, having married the daughter of Albert Wohlstetter, the dean of defense theorists and progenitor of neoconservatism.

202. Paul Nitze, "A Threat Mostly to Ourselves," *New York Times,* October 28, 1999, op-ed page.

203. Rice was named secretary of state in Bush's second term, and Wolfowitz was named head of the World Bank, the position to which Robert McNamara was named in 1968. As for apostolic succession, in the spring of 2004, the Navy christened a new ship in honor of Nitze, not long before he died. It was a rare distinction for a man still living. The keynote address at the ceremony was given by Wolfowitz, who paid tribute to Nitze as the father of the movement of which he, Wolfowitz, was champion. He made no reference to Nitze's having become a nuclear abolitionist, and, of course, neither did Nitze.

204. Paul Kennedy, cited by Johnson, *The Sorrows of Empire,* 71.

205. The "guidance" would be reiterated again and again by Wolfowitz, Powell, Rumsfeld, and Cheney until it showed up in 2002 as the heart of the commencement speech President Bush delivered at West Point, and then in the "National Security Strategy" document of the same year. Armstrong, "Dick Cheney's Song of America," 76.

206. "I want to be the bully on the block," Colin Powell told the House Armed Services Committee in 1992. Enemies should know "there is no future in trying to challenge the armed forces of the United States." Ibid., 78.

207. Joseph Biden criticized "Defense Planning Guidance" as "Pax Americana." Ibid., 79. Daniel Bolger points out that the models for that reference, Pax Romana and Pax Britannica, involved savage violence against Parthians, Germans, Britons, Picts, and Jews in the Roman case, and against Crimeans, Afghans, Ashanti, Boers, Chinese, Burmese, and Irish in the British. Some Pax. Bolger, *Savage Peace,* 378.

208. To appreciate the radical character of preventive war, compare it with the Eisenhower-approved 1954 National Security Policy paper that said, "The United States and its allies must reject the concept of preventive war or acts intended to provoke war." Rosenberg, "The Origins of Overkill," 34.

209. Paul Wolfowitz, quoted by Keller, "The Sunshine Warrior," 52.

210. "In the Middle East and Southwest Asia," "Defense Planning Guidance" states, "our overall objective is to remain the predominant outside power in the region and preserve U.S. and Western access to the region's oil." Klare, *Blood and Oil,* 68.

211. We saw that it was Clinton who sought to "renegotiate" the ABM Treaty to allow National Missile Defense, a process George W. Bush completed when he abrogated the treaty. Clinton signed the Comprehensive Test Ban Treaty, but he did not press the Senate to ratify it. Similarly, he signed the treaty creating the International Criminal Court, but with such reluctance that George W. Bush had no trouble "unsigning" it as one of the first acts of his presidency.

212. Richard Armitage was undersecretary of defense in the Reagan administration and was named deputy secretary of state by George W. Bush. Perle was named to a key Pentagon oversight board. In 2003, with David Frum (a Bush speechwriter who coined the phrase "axis of evil"), Perle published a neocon manifesto, *An End to Evil.*

213. "Scooter" Libby was indicted for lying to a grand jury about his actions in relation

to the unauthorized disclosure of a CIA employee's identity. *New York Times,* October 29, 2005, A13.

214. On September 20, 2002, the Bush administration gave explicit expression to the new vision with "The National Security Strategy of the United States." The document said, "The greater the threat, the greater is the risk of inaction — and the more compelling the case for taking anticipatory action to defend ourselves, even if uncertainty remains as to the time and place of the enemy's attack. To forestall or prevent such hostile acts by our adversaries, the United States will, if necessary, act preemptively." www.whitehouse.gov/nsc/nss.html.

215. Rosenberg, "The Origins of Overkill," 32.

216. *The 9/11 Commission Report,* 44. As a result of the 9/11 trauma, NORAD reinvented its operations. In January 2005, a new high-tech operations center — the Combatant Commander Integrated Command and Control System — was opened at NORAD headquarters at Cheyenne Mountain, Colorado. Every aircraft flying over North America is tracked, with two hundred interceptors ready to go on the attack. (On 9/11 there were twenty.) See James Oberg, "NORAD Gets a Makeover," www.spectrum.iee.org/webonly/wonews/jun05/0605nnor.html.

217. James Mann, "The Armageddon Plan," *Atlantic Monthly,* March 2004, 71–74.

218. And perhaps with the quiet Christian fundamentalism of the people staffing the Pentagon itself. A defense expert told me in 1996 that among the most common computer passwords in use in the Pentagon at that time were "Jesus" and "God."

219. Tom Engelhardt, "Tomgram: September 23rd," www.tomdispatch.com/index.mhtml?pid=1814.

220. "Ground zero" was bombardiers' argot for the target in the bombsight, but the phrase had come to refer exclusively to the places where the atomic bombs exploded at Hiroshima and Nagasaki and at test sites. Now America had a ground zero of its own, which entitled us to that sense of victimhood which could alone assuage the unfinished guilt we carried as a nation for having ushered in the nuclear age. The person who first drew my attention to this new meaning of ground zero is the historian John Dower.

221. *The 9/11 Commission Report,* 43. Cheney implied to Rumsfeld, and claimed in testimony before the commission, that he had received authority for the order to shoot down hijacked aircraft in a telephone conversation with the president. The *Commission Report* makes clear that there is no record of this call having occurred.

222. I acknowledge Tom Engelhardt for drawing this detail to my attention. The *Commission Report* observes that Cheney "recalled urging the President not to return to Washington." The Secret Service and the president's staff were also against a return to Washington, while the president "only grudgingly agreed to go elsewhere." *The 9/11 Commission Report,* 39.

223. Ibid., 325.

224. Thus Osama bin Laden accomplished what the Kremlin had never done. Not even during the Cuban Missile Crisis did the American military elite take refuge in its ready bunkers. My mother told me how, throughout the ten days of that crisis, she and other generals' wives at Bolling Air Force Base had kept their eyes on the helicopters that were poised to fly their husbands to the mountain bunker in West Virginia from which they would fight World War III. My mother and her friends were proud of the fact that those helicopters never left Bolling, that their husbands never fled the Pentagon.

225. The records show that the builders imagined it as a storage facility or an archive, but the impression that the Pentagon would ultimately become a hospital took hold early. On one of my first visits to the Building in the late 1940s, my mother told me that was the plan, and even as a child I saw that the idea embodied a kind of American nobility. Which is why, no doubt, so many have believed it.

226. Implied in Marx's critique of capitalism was the harsh fact that its high living standards could be enjoyed only by a minority of the earth's people. The Pentagon now stands guard over that inequity. Taking only the most obvious example, the most impoverished fifth of humanity draws 1.4 percent of the world's income, while the wealthiest fifth draws 82.7 percent. In Somalia, in 1995, the average income was $210 a year; in El Salvador, $940. In the United States about $7,000 qualified a person as "poor," while the same income would mark a person as solidly middle class in Greece. These disparities grow more extreme by the day, and in the poorest nations they are compounded by the arsenals of weapons that were supplied by both sides during the Cold War, and that arms manufacturers continue to supply. The result is that "once Americans enter the underdeveloped world, they are at war. It only remains to be seen who will draw and fire first." Bolger, *Savage Peace*, 47, 51, 99.

Epilogue. New World Order

1. In the American narrative of World War II, Soviet forces hardly appear. But not even the Western allies show up much. D-Day, for example, is remembered as primarily a U.S. operation. Yet the number of U.S. troops to go ashore in France on June 6, 1944, was 73,000, compared with 83,000 British and Canadian. Nigel Hamilton, "We Were Allies Once: Lessons of D-Day, 1944," *New England Journal of Public Policy*, Winter 2005, 57.

2. As we saw, *Bock's Car*, the B-29 that leveled Nagasaki, is displayed at an even farther remove, in Dayton, Ohio.

3. The themes struck in "The National Security Strategy of the United States of America," published in 2002, were firmly institutionalized in "The National Defense Strategy of the United States," published in March 2005. www.globalsecurity.org/military/library/policy/dod/nds/usa_Mar2005.html. The Pentagon promulgation takes for granted the doctrine of preventive wars, waged by the United States, acting alone, against nations that do not use their sovereignty "responsibly," from military platforms in outer space, which will be denied to other nations. I owe to Tom Engelhardt the observation that "rollback" has been achieved.

4. The phrase originates with Andrew Bacevich. See his *New American Militarism*, and Johnson, *The Sorrows of Empire*. As of 2005, permanent U.S. military bases, including "enduring camps," "main operating bases," "forward operating sites," and "cooperative security locations," are in Kyrgyzstan (near the Chinese border), Uzbekistan, the former Yugoslavia, Afghanistan (which has nine bases), and Iraq (which has fourteen). Russia's borders are more constrained, and more hemmed in by potentially hostile forces, than they have been since the nineteenth century. See "The National Defense Strategy of the United States, 2005," chapter 3.

5. Seymour Hersh, "The Coming Wars," *The New Yorker*, January 24 and 31, 2005. In 2005, the State Department maintained a "watch list" of twenty-five nations where U.S. intervention might be required by various kinds of social or political disorder. www.tomdispatch.com, April 2, 2005.

6. On September 13, 2001, I published an article in the *Boston Globe*, "Law Not War," arguing that the terrorist attacks should be defined as crimes, not acts of war, and that the response should be a swift, internationally coordinated, unprecedented act of law enforcement. My argument assumed the use of force, but insisted that military force was too blunt an instrument — unlikely to succeed in capturing or stopping the terrorists, and all too likely to lead to a dangerous increase in the Arab and Muslim resentment that was the ground of the terror attacks in the first place. Anne-Marie Slaughter made a similar argument three days later with "A Defining Moment in the Parsing of War," *Washington Post*, September 16, 2001. Events proved us right. The war impulse deposed the Taliban in Af-

ghanistan, an action justified as a removal of a terrorist training center, but the U.S.-led war turned most of that nation over to warlords and a drug mafia, leaving it ripe for further exploitation by terrorists. The subsequent war against Iraq removed Saddam Hussein, but Iraq replaced Afghanistan as the world capital of terrorist recruitment and training, and, in the eyes of most Arabs and many of the world's Muslims, confirmed Osama bin Laden's hateful characterizations of the United States. Bin Laden, meanwhile, was not captured. (Neither were Mullah Omar, the Taliban leader; Ayman al-Zawahiri, bin Laden's deputy; Abu Musab al-Zarqawi, the Al Qaeda leader in Iraq — nor even the anthrax mailer in the United States.) As of 2005, those of bin Laden's lieutenants who were seized had almost all been tracked down not by military forces, American or otherwise, but by police. See the report of the New York University Center on Law and Security, "Terrorist Trial Report Card."

7. Hamilton, "We Were Allies Once," 11.

8. U.S. run black sites are in Thailand, Afghanistan, and Eastern Europe, as well as at Guantánamo Bay. "CIA Allegedly Has Secret Prisons," *Boston Globe*, November 2, 2005, A2. The organization Human Rights First filed a lawsuit in 2005 against Donald Rumsfeld, detailing illegal Defense Department–sponsored practices. See www.humanrightsfirst.org.

9. In November 2004, the International Red Cross accused the United States of using methods "tantamount to torture" at Guantánamo Bay. *New York Times*, November 30, 2004, A1. On April 23, 2005, Human Rights Watch issued a report citing "overwhelming evidence that U.S. mistreatment and torture of Muslim prisoners took place not merely at Abu Ghraib, but at facilities throughout Afghanistan and Iraq, as well as at Guantánamo, and at 'secret locations' around the world in violation of the Geneva Convention and the laws against torture." The report found no evidence that Donald Rumsfeld had ever ordered a halt to such abuse. The Pentagon conducted seven separate investigations of the abuse, not one of which examined the role of civilian leaders in the Department of Defense, even though, the report said, the abuse "resulted from decisions made by U.S. officials to bend, ignore or cast the rules aside." Only low-level personnel were ever charged in the cases. *New York Times*, April 24, 2005, A6. On April 26, 2005, the European Union issued a report accusing the United States of torture. "Europe Rights Body Accuses US of Torture," *Boston Globe*, April 27, 2005. What was new at Abu Ghraib was the overt and military character of the torture. The CIA had engaged in covert torture for decades, even if it was mainly psychological, or "no-touch," forms. Military officers from various Latin American regimes were trained in torture by CIA and U.S. military personnel at the School of the Americas, in Panama, and, after 1984, at Fort Benning, Georgia. See Alfred W. McCoy, "Cruel Science: CIA Torture and U.S. Foreign Policy," *New England Journal of Public Policy*, Winter 2005, 209–62. See also the Human Rights Watch report "Leadership Failure: Firsthand Accounts of Torture of Iraqi Detainees by the U.S. Army's 82nd Airborne Division," September 25, 2005, www.hrw.org/reports/2005/ns0905.

10. Michael Ignatieff was a leading "human rights" liberal, celebrating empire as a structure of democracy and forthrightly defending Bush's military actions. David Rieff was another human rights liberal in favor of armed actions. The son of Susan Sontag, he was the most eloquent of the humanitarian interventionists during the Balkan wars of the 1990s. But he changed his mind after seeing what the idea led to in 2003. "What I witnessed on the ground in Iraq," he wrote in 2005, "was the speed with which altruism can become barbarism . . . At the time of the Kosovo war, I had written that, if I had to make the choice, I would choose imperialism over barbarism. In retrospect, though, I did not realize the extent to which imperialism is, or at least can always become, barbarism." Rieff, *At the Point of a Gun*, 253.

11. The assault by U.S. Marines on the city of Falluja in the fall of 2004 is a case in point.

Weeks of bombardment from the air leveled most of the city. Uncounted thousands of the 300,000 residents were casualties, and all the rest were turned into refugees.

12. Against Bush's claims that America is fighting terrorists in Iraq "so that we don't have to fight them here," a 2005 study by the Saudi Arabian government established that the foreign fighters entering Iraq to resist the United States "are not former terrorists and became radicalized by the war itself." "Study Cites Seeds of Terror in Iraq: War Radicalized Most, Probe Finds," *Boston Globe*, July 17, 2005, 1.

13. On January 5, 2006, those who, over the decades covered by this book, prepared the way for Bush gathered with him at the White House — thirteen former secretaries of state and defense, going back to the Kennedy administration. Billed as a consultation about Iraq, the meeting with the president lasted ten minutes. No serious discussion occurred. The former secretaries allowed themselves to be used as props in a photo op, as if the war belonged as much to them as to Bush. Which, of course, it did. *New York Times*, January 6, 2006, A10.

14. Iran and Iraq have the largest reserves of unexploited oil and natural gas in the world. In the coming decades, the United States is going to need those sources of energy more than ever. Forty percent of the world's exported oil passes through the Strait of Hormuz in the Persian Gulf, on both sides of which is Iran. In addition, Iran's natural gas reserves put it second only to Saudi Arabia as the richest energy source on earth. That, at least as much as fear of Tehran's nuclear weapons, drives Washington's policy of regime change. The strategic necessity of preventing rivals (especially China) from controlling Iran's energy reserves is absolute. See Klare, *Blood and Oil,* especially chapter 6, "Geopolitics Reborn: The U.S.-Russian-Chinese Struggle in the Persian Gulf and Caspian Basin."

15. "Crude Politics," *Atlantic Monthly,* April 2005, 48.

16. "China Bolsters Its Force, U.S. Says" was a front-page headline forecasting the Pentagon report. *Boston Globe*, April 10, 2005. China's projected 2006 defense budget, according to the National People's Congress spokesman in 2005, was $29.9 billion. The U.S. budget for the same period was slated at $418 billion (not counting the huge overruns in Iraq). By some measures, Pentagon spending in 2005 exceeded the combined military budgets of all other countries on the globe. The Chinese buildup of most concern to U.S. analysts was its nuclear submarine fleet, but instead of a "force projection" navy threatening vital American interests, this clearly represented China's efforts to deter, and if necessary respond to, U.S. carrier intrusions into the Taiwan Strait. As was true in the 1940s, interservice rivalry was again an engine driving Pentagon budget requests. To compensate for the huge financial tilt toward the Army during the Iraq War, the Navy wanted its new armada of high-tech ships (subs at $2.5 billion each, destroyers at more than $3 billion, carriers at nearly $14 billion). The Air Force, having been humiliated by the irrelevance in Iraq of its much-touted precision bombing, pushed for dozens of new A-22 fighters at $300 million a copy, while continuing its advocacy for a space-based "high frontier" weapons system, which will ultimately represent even greater costs. The Common Aero Vehicle is an example: a suborbital space vehicle, scheduled to be deployed in 2010, it will be able to hit any target on earth within two hours. As always, the Air Force and the Navy had eyes on each other and on the Army as much as on any conceivable enemy. The Army, meanwhile, has its eye on "Future Combat Systems," which will put robots on the battlefield. See Tim Weiner, "The Navy's Fleet of Tomorrow Is Mired in Politics of Yesterday," *New York Times,* April 19, 2005, A1. For defense numbers, see Andrew Bacevich, *The New American Militarism,* and www.tom dispatch.com, April 22, 2005.

17. Lebow and Stein, "Deterrence and the Cold War," 181.

18. As of 2005, Japan's military budget was about $47 billion, but Washington wants that figure to grow, in part to balance China and North Korea, but also to create a new market for U.S. arms manufacturers. In 2004, Secretary of State Colin Powell told leaders in

Tokyo that Japan could not be admitted to the U.N. Security Council until it renounced its pacifist constitution. For further analysis of China's military emergence, and the prospect of Japan's, see Chalmers Johnson, "No Longer the 'Lone' Superpower," www.tom dispatch.com, March 15, 2005.

19. The likeliest military move against Iran (a country with triple the population of Iraq) is an air war, aimed not at "compellence" of Iran's government but at the simple obliteration of its nuclear capacity. Such a "pure" air offensive, of course, is another Pentagon fantasy. If undertaken, it will lead to a savage expansion of Middle Eastern violence and global terror.

20. The Nunn-Lugar Soviet Threat Reduction Act of 1991 successfully provided U.S. support for the transfer of 22,000 tactical nuclear warheads from the new states of the former Soviet Union back to Russia, but in subsequent years, U.S. support for Moscow's efforts to control such material dwindled. As of 2005, Russia was left with between 20,000 and 30,000 nuclear weapons in its possession, and about "44,000 potential nuclear weapons' worth of highly enriched uranium and plutonium vulnerable to theft." Experts put the cost of securing "the world's supply of fissile material" at about $30 billion, about what the United States was spending "in six months of the war in Iraq in 2005." Allison, *Nuclear Terrorism*, 147. See also James Fallows, "Success Without Victory," *Atlantic Monthly*, January/February 2005, 88, 90.

21. Jimmy Carter, "Saving Nonproliferation," *Washington Post*, March 31, 2005, op-ed page.

22. Allison, *Nuclear Terrorism*, 191.

23. John Bolton, quoted in "The Nuclear Club," *Boston Globe*, August 6, 2005, A3.

24. An Associated Press report in mid-2005 put the number of active warheads at about 9,000 for the United States and about 20,000 for Russia. Britain possessed 200, France, 350. Additionally, China had 300, Israel was estimated to have between 100 and 200, India between 45 and 95, Pakistan between 30 and 50. Iran and North Korea were each suspected to have, or to soon have, some nuclear weapons capability. Ibid.

25. Douglas Jehl, "CIA Chief Orders 'Curveball' Review," *New York Times*, April 8, 2005.

26. Defense Science Board Report, November 2004. The report warned that the struggle for "hearts and minds" was being lost, that "the dramatic narrative since 9/11 [in Afghanistan and Iraq] has essentially borne out the entire radical Islamist bill of particulars." Fallows, "Success Without Victory," 85.

27. More than one million soldiers were deployed in Afghanistan and Iraq between 2001 and the end of 2004, fighting vastly fewer numbers of "insurgents," but events showed that even this force was inadequate. Ann Scott Tyson, "Two Years Later, Iraq War Drains Military," *Washington Post*, March 19, 2005, A1.

28. Peter Schwartz and Doug Randall, "An Abrupt Climate Change Scenario and Its Implications for United States National Security," October 2003, www.innovation-enterprise.com/6.2/6.2.363.php.

29. The memo, dated October 16, 2003, was addressed to Paul Wolfowitz, Douglas Feith, and Generals Richard Myers and Peter Pace. www.thesmokinggun.com/archive/rumsfeld memo1.html.

30. For all the talk of terrorism, the Department of Justice brought to court a paltry eighteen charges of terrorism between September 2001 and October 2004. By early 2005, only six had led to convictions. Karen J. Greenberg, "Torture, the Courts, and the War on Terror," *NYU Review of Law and Security*, no. 4 (April 2005).

31. The image is Tom Engelhardt's.

32. Hersh, "The Coming Wars."

33. For a description of possible terrorist purposes with nuclear weapons, see Steve Coll, "What bin Laden Sees in Hiroshima," *Washington Post*, February 6, 2005.

34. Recall that Truman gave a radio address on the night of August 9, 1945. He offered three justifications for the atomic bombing of Hiroshima. The second was to shorten the war, the third was to save American lives. The first thing he said was that the atom bomb was used "against those who have starved and beaten American prisoners of war, against those who have abandoned all pretense of obeying international laws of warfare." This reason soon dropped away from the justifications given for the bombing.

35. Neoconservatives, especially, took to the designation. Eliot Cohen, James Woolsey, and Norman Podhoretz all wrote of "World War IV" in the early years of the Global War on Terror. Andrew Bacevich calls the Cold War World War III and the ongoing war in the Persian Gulf, initiated by Jimmy Carter, World War IV. *The New American Militarism*, 189.

36. The so-called Arab Spring of 2005 — elections in Iraq, demonstrations in Lebanon — was hailed by neoconservatives as the dawning of democracy in the Arab Middle East, but it was no such thing. U.S. allies in the region (Saudi Arabia, the United Arab Emirates, Kuwait, Bahrain, Qatar, Oman) were more in the grip of dictators than ever. Where U.S. occupation forces held control — Iraq and Afghanistan — real elections would have empowered the Islamist majorities. The United States seeks not democracy but subservience. The most democratic Muslim regime in the region, measured by elections held since its revolution in 1979, is Iran. See Dilip Hiro, "Playing the Democracy Card," *Middle East International*, no. 746 (2005).

37. When the war was launched in 2003, discussions in the Pentagon were taken up with *how* the United States would attack (through Turkey? Kuwait? standing start? rolling start? decapitation?). That no attention was paid to costs and consequences (General Eric K. Shinseki, the Army chief of staff, was fired for wanting to do that) shows how revenge, not realpolitik, was the motive. And if questions of cost and consequence were not raised, how much less so the question, Why? For an example of what the Pentagon should have undertaken in 2003, see Kaysen and Malin, *War with Iraq*.

38. USA Today/CNN Gallop Poll Results, January 9, 2005, www.usatoday.com/news/polls/tables/live/2005-01-10-poll.htm.

39. We have noted the work of the war theorist Thomas Schelling, the 2005 Nobel laureate in economics. In 1973, he contributed a foreword to *The Politics of Nonviolent Action* by Gene Sharp. The book is unabashed advocacy for nonviolence as a way of resolving international conflict. Schelling's introduction is respectful but somewhat skeptical, given his realistic sense of the challenges posed to the United States by the Soviet Union. He remarks wryly, "If the book should fall into the wrong hands, and begins to inform and enlighten our adversaries, we can be doubly thankful for the work Gene Sharp has done." In 1973, no one, including Schelling, could imagine such a thing coming to pass. Yet, in effect, that is exactly what happened. The arc of nonviolence thus came full circle, for Gandhi's sources of inspiration included the general strikes of the anticzarist movement, what he called "the Russian Remedy." The same tactics would be successful, at the end of the twentieth century, in Serbia, where the people brought down Slobodan Milosevic after the NATO air war failed to do so, and in Georgia, Ukraine, and Kyrgyzstan. Sharp, *The Politics of Nonviolent Action*, xxi; *Gandhi as a Political Strategist*, 29.

40. Quoted by Cirincione, "Lessons Lost," 42.

41. Ibid., 52.

42. King wrote in his book *Stride Toward Freedom:* "The intellectual and moral satisfaction that I failed to gain from the utilitarianism of Bentham and Mill, the revolutionary methods of Marx and Lenin, the social contracts theory of Hobbes, the 'back to nature' optimism of Rousseau, and the superman philosophy of Nietzsche, I found in the nonviolent resistance philosophy of Gandhi. I came to feel that this was the only morally and practically sound method open to oppressed people in their struggle for freedom." Sharp, *Gandhi as a Political Strategist*, x.

43. Joseph Rotblat, the last living signatory to the Russell-Einstein manifesto, lifted it up again on its fiftieth anniversary in 2005, in an op-ed piece, "The 50-Year Shadow," *New York Times,* May 17, 2005.

44. In order to maintain the Pax Romana, the Roman Empire kept about 2 percent of its citizens in the military; during the Pax Britannica of the late nineteenth century, London kept about 1 percent in the military. By the mid-1990s, the United States kept less than .7 percent of its citizens in the military. Bolger, *Savage Peace,* 391.

45. In 2005, a scandal occurred at the Air Force Academy, with Jewish and other non-Christian cadets being aggressively proselytized by Evangelical Christian cadets. It became apparent that a widespread, sanctioned Christian fundamentalism had taken root not only at the academy but among senior Air Force officials. See "Report of Americans United for Separation of Church and State on Religious Coercion and Endorsement of Religion at the United States Air Force Academy," www.au.org.

BIBLIOGRAPHY

Acheson, Dean. *Present at the Creation: My Years in the State Department.* New York: Norton, 1987.

Ackerman, Peter, and Christopher Kruegler. *Strategic Nonviolent Conflict: The Dynamics of People Power in the Twentieth Century.* Westport, Conn.: Praeger, 1994.

Air Force History Office. *Strategic Air War.* Washington: USAF Warrior Studies, 1988.

Allison, Graham T. *Nuclear Terrorism: The Ultimate Preventable Catastrophe.* New York: New York Times Books/Henry Holt, 2004.

———, and Philip Zelikow. *Essence of Decision: Explaining the Cuban Missile Crisis.* 2nd ed. New York: Longman, 1999.

Allman, T. D. *Rogue State: America at War with the World.* New York: Nation Books, 2004.

Alperovitz, Gar. *Atomic Diplomacy: Hiroshima and Potsdam: The Use of the Atomic Bomb and the American Confrontation with Soviet Power.* New York: Penguin, 1985.

———. *The Decision to Use the Atomic Bomb.* New York: Vintage Books, 1995.

Amis, Martin. *Koba the Dread.* New York: Hyperion, 2002.

Arbatov, Georgi. *Cold War or Détente: The Soviet Viewpoint.* London: Zed Books, 1983.

Arendt, Hannah. *The Origins of Totalitarianism.* New York: Meridian Books, 1958.

———. *On Violence.* New York: Harcourt, Brace, 1970.

———. *Responsibility and Judgment.* New York: Schocken Books, 2003.

Arms Control and Disarmament Agency. *Documents on Disarmament.* www.davidson.edu/administrative/library/GovDoc/gov-documents_on_disarmament.htm.

Armstrong, Anne. *Berliners: Both Sides of the Wall.* New Brunswick, N.J.: Rutgers University Press, 1973.

Armstrong, David. "Dick Cheney's Song of America: Drafting a Plan for Global Dominance." *Harper's Magazine,* October 2002.

Army Air Forces. *The Official World War II Guide to the Army Air Forces.* New York: Bonanza Books, 1988.

Auster, Paul. *The Invention of Solitude.* New York: Random House, 1982.

Bacevich, Andrew J. *The New American Militarism: How Americans Are Seduced by War.* New York: Oxford University Press, 2005.

Baker, Russell. "Moods of Washington." *New York Times Magazine*, March 24, 1974.

Barnes, Fred. "One of a Kind." *Weekly Standard*, June 21, 2004, 33.

Bergen, Peter. "Beware the Holy War." *The Nation*, June 20, 2005, 25–34.

Bernstein, Barton J. "Seizing the Contested Terrain." *Diplomatic History*, Winter 1993, 46–47.

——. "Understanding the Atomic Bomb and Japanese Surrender: Missed Opportunities, Little-Known Near Disasters, and Modern Memory." In Michael J. Hogan, ed., *Hiroshima in History and Memory*. New York: University of Cambridge Press, 1996.

——. "Understanding Decisionmaking, U.S. Foreign Policy, and the Cuban Missile Crisis: A Review Essay." *International Security* 25, no. 1 (Summer 2000), 147.

——, ed. *Towards a New Past: Dissenting Essays in American History*. New York: Vintage, 1969.

——, ed. *The Atomic Bomb: The Critical Issues*. New York: Vintage, 1976.

——, Sheldon Hackney, and James M. Banner, Jr., eds. *Understanding the American Experience: Recent Interpretations*. New York: Harcourt Brace Jovanovich, 1973.

——, and Allen J. Matusow, eds. *The Truman Administration: A Documentary History*. New York: Harper & Row, 1966.

Bernstein, Carl. "Holy Alliance." *Time*, February 4, 1992.

——, and Marco Politi. *His Holiness: John Paul II and the Hidden History of Our Time*. New York: Doubleday, 1996.

Berrigan, Daniel. *Night Flight to Hanoi: War Diary with 11 Poems*. New York: Macmillan, 1968.

——. *And the Risen Bread: Selected Poems, 1957–1997*. New York: Fordham University Press, 1998.

——. *Testimony: The Word Made Flesh*. Maryknoll, N.Y.: Orbis Books, 2004.

Beschloss, Michael. *Kennedy and Roosevelt: The Uneasy Alliance*. New York: Norton, 1980.

——. *The Crisis Years: Kennedy and Khrushchev, 1960–1963*. New York: HarperCollins, 1991.

——. *The Conquerors: Roosevelt, Truman, and the Destruction of Hitler's Germany, 1941–1945*. New York: Simon & Schuster, 2002.

——. "The Thawing of the Cold War." *Time*, June 14, 2004, 41.

——, and Strobe Talbott. *At the Highest Levels: The Inside Story of the Cold War*. Boston: Little, Brown, 1993.

Bethe, Hans. "Sakharov's H-bomb." *Bulletin of the Atomic Scientists* 46, no. 8 (October 1990), 8–9.

Bialer, Seweryn, and Michael Mandelbaum. *The Global Rivals*. New York: Knopf, 1988.

Binkin, Martin, et al. *Blacks and the Military*. Washington: Brookings Institution, 1982.

Bird, Kai. *The Color of Truth. McGeorge Bundy and William Bundy: Brothers in Arms*. New York: Simon & Schuster, 1998.

——, and Lawrence Lifschultz, eds. *Hiroshima's Shadow*. Stoney Creek, Conn.: Pamphleteers Press, 1998.

Blight, James G., Bruce J. Allyn, and David A. Welch. *Cuba on the Brink: The Missile Crisis and the Soviet Collapse*. New York: Pantheon, 1993.

Blumenthal, Sidney. *Pledging Allegiance: The Last Campaign of the Cold War*. New York: Harper & Row, 1990.

——. *The Clinton Wars*. New York: Farrar, Straus and Giroux, 2003.

Bok, Sissela. *Alva Myrdal: A Daughter's Memoir*. Reading, Mass.: Addison-Wesley, 1991.

Bolger, Daniel P. *Savage Peace: Americans at War in the 1990s*. Novato, Calif.: Presidio Press, 1995.

Borklund, Carl. *Men of the Pentagon: From Forrestal to McNamara*. New York: Praeger, 1966.

Bose, Meena, and Rosanna Perotti, eds. *From Cold War to New World Order: The Foreign Policy of George H. W. Bush*. Westport, Conn.: Greenwood, 1997.

Bottome, Edgar. *The Missile Gap: A Study of the Formulation of Military and Political Policy*. Rutherford, N.J.: Fairleigh Dickinson University Press, 1971.

Boulding, Elise, and Randall Forsberg. *Abolishing War*. Boston: Research Center for the Twenty-first Century, 1998.

Boutwell, Jeffrey, and Michael T. Klare, eds. *Light Weapons and Civil Conflict*. Lanham, Md.: Rowman and Littlefield, 1999.

Bowie, Robert R., and Richard H. Immerman. *Waging Peace: How Eisenhower Shaped an Enduring Cold War Strategy*. New York: Oxford University Press, 1998.

Boyer, Paul. *By the Bomb's Early Light: American Thought and Culture at the Dawn of the Atomic Age*. Chapel Hill: University of North Carolina Press, 1994.

Boyle, Peter G. *American-Soviet Relations: From the Russian Revolution to the Fall of Communism*. London and New York: Routledge, 1993.

Brands, H. W. "A Preponderance of Power: National Security, the Truman Administration, and the Cold War." *American Historical Review* 98, no. 2 (April 1993), 604–5.

———. *The Devil We Knew: Americans and the Cold War*. New York: Oxford University Press, 1993.

———. "The Specter of Communism: The United States and the Origins of the Cold War, 1917–1953." *Journal of American History* 82, no. 3 (December 1995), 1258–9.

Brice, Martin H. *Stronghold: A History of Military Architecture*. London: B. T. Batsford, Ltd., 1984.

Brinkley, David. *Washington Goes to War*. New York: Knopf, 1998.

Brodie, Bernard. *The Absolute Weapon: Atomic Power and World Order*. New York: Harcourt, Brace, 1946.

Brown, Seyom. *The Illusion of Control: Force and Foreign Policy in the Twenty-first Century*. Washington: Brookings Institution, 2003.

Brudny, Yitzhak M. *Reinventing Russia: Russian Nationalism and the Soviet State*. Cambridge: Harvard University Press, 1998.

Brzezinski, Zbigniew. *Game Plan: A Geostrategic Framework for the Conduct of the U.S.-Soviet Contest*. Boston: Atlantic Monthly Press, 1986.

Buckley, John. *Air Power in the Age of Total War*. Bloomington: Indiana University Press, 1999.

Bundy, McGeorge. *Danger and Survival: Choices About the Bomb in the First Fifty Years*. New York: Random House, 1988.

———. "To Cap the Volcano." *Foreign Affairs* 48, no. 1 (October 1969).

Burr, William, and Jeffrey Kimball. "Nixon's Nuclear Ploy." *Bulletin of the Atomic Scientists*, January/February 2003, 28–37, 72–73.

Burrows, William E. *By Any Means Necessary: America's Secret Air War in the Cold War*. New York: Farrar, Straus and Giroux, 2001.

Bush, Vannevar. *Modern Arms and Free Men*. London: Heineman, 1950.

Butler, George Lee. "Time to End the Age of Nukes." *Bulletin of the Atomic Scientists*, March/April 1997, 33–36.

Caldicott, Helen. *Missile Envy: The Arms Race and Nuclear War*. Toronto: Bantam, 1986.

Campbell, Kenneth. "A Profile of the First Director of DIA: Lieutenant General Joseph F. Carroll." *American Intelligence Journal*, 16, no. 1 (Spring 1995), 89–93.

———. "Lt. Gen. Joseph F. Carroll, USAF: First Director of DIA." *Defense Intelligence Journal* 8, no. 2 (1999), 49–65.

Cannon, Lou. *President Reagan: The Role of a Lifetime*. New York: Simon & Schuster, 1991.

Carlton, David. *Churchill and the Soviet Union*. Manchester, U.K.: Manchester University Press, 2000.

Carroll, James. *Prince of Peace.* Boston: Little, Brown, 1984.

——. *An American Requiem: God, My Father, and the War That Came Between Us.* Boston: Houghton Mifflin, 1996.

——. "A Friendship That Ended the War." *The New Yorker,* October 21 and 28, 1996, 130–156.

——. "War Inside the Pentagon." *The New Yorker,* August 18, 1997, 59.

——. "Shoah in the News: Patterns and Meanings of News Coverage of the Holocaust." Discussion Paper D-27, Joan Shorenstein Center for Press, Politics, and Public Policy, John F. Kennedy School of Government, Harvard University, October 1997.

Carter, Jimmy. *Keeping Faith.* New York: Bantam, 1982.

Chace, James. "After Hiroshima: Sharing the Atom Bomb." *Foreign Affairs,* January/February 1996.

Chayes, Antonia Handler, and Paul Doty, eds. *Defending Deterrence: Managing the ABM Treaty into the 21st Century.* Washington: Pergamon-Brassey's International Defense Publishers, 1989.

Chernyaev, Anatoly. *My Six Years with Gorbachev.* Translated and edited by Robert English and Elizabeth Tucker. University Park: Pennsylvania State University Press, 2001.

Churchill, Winston S. *The Second World War. Vol. 3: The Grand Alliance.* Vol. 4: *The Hinge of Fate.* Vol. 5: *Closing the Ring.* Vol. 6: *Triumph and Tragedy.* Boston: Houghton Mifflin, 1950–53.

Cirincione, Joseph. "Lessons Lost." *Bulletin of the Atomic Scientists,* November/December 2005, 42–53.

Clarfield, Gerard H., and William M. Wiecek. *Nuclear America.* New York: Harper & Row, 1984.

Clark, Ronald W. *The Role of the Bomber.* New York: Crowell, 1977.

Clark, Wesley K. *Waging Modern War: Bosnia, Kosovo, and the Future of Combat.* New York: Public Affairs, 2001.

Clinton, Bill. *My Life.* New York: Knopf, 2004.

Coffey, Thomas M. *Iron Eagle: The Turbulent Life of General Curtis LeMay.* New York: Crown, 1986.

Cohn, Carol. "Sex and Death in the Rational World of Defense Intellectuals." *Signs: Journal of Women in Culture and Society* 12, no. 4 (Summer 1987), 701.

Conquest, Robert. *The Harvest of Sorrow: Soviet Collectivization and the Terror-Famine.* New York: Oxford University Press, 1986.

——. *Stalin: Breaker of Nations.* London: Weidenfeld and Nicolson, 1991.

——, and Jon Manchip White. *What to Do When the Russians Come.* New York: Stein & Day, 1984.

Cook, Fred J. *The Warfare State.* New York: Macmillan, 1962.

Corson, William R. *The Arms of Ignorance: The Rise of the American Intelligence Empire.* New York: Dial, 1977.

Costigliola, Frank. "'Unceasing Pressure for Penetration': Gender, Pathology, and Emotion in George Kennan's Formation of the Cold War." *Journal of American History* 83, no. 4 (March 1997), 1309–39.

Craven, Wesley F., and James L. Cate, eds. *The Army Air Forces in World War II.* Washington: Office of Air Force History, 1983.

Current, Robert N. *Secretary Stimson: A Study in Statecraft.* New Brunswick, N.J.: Rutgers University Press, 1954.

Dallek, Robert. *An Unfinished Life: John F. Kennedy, 1917–1963.* New York: Little, Brown, 2003.

Defense Intelligence Agency. *Communiqué* 3, no. 2 (January 28, 1991).

Dower, John W. *War Without Mercy: Race and Power in the Pacific War*. New York: Pantheon, 1986.

———. *Embracing Defeat: Japan in the Wake of World War II*. New York: Norton/New Press, 1999.

Dulles, John Foster. "A Policy of Boldness." *Life*, May 1952.

———. "The Evolution of Foreign Policy." *Department of State Bulletin* 30 (January 25, 1962), 107–10.

Dyson, Freeman. *Disturbing the Universe*. New York: Harper & Row, 1979.

———. *Weapons and Hope*. New York: Harper & Row, 1984.

Eden, Lynn. *Whole World on Fire: Organizations, Knowledge, and Nuclear Weapons Devastation*. Ithaca, N.Y.: Cornell University Press, 2004.

Eisenberg, Carolyn. Review of *We Now Know: Rethinking Cold War History*. *Journal of American History* 84, no. 4 (March 1998), 1462–64.

Eisenhower, Dwight. *Crusade in Europe*. Garden City, N.Y.: Doubleday, 1948.

———. *Mandate for Change, 1953–1956: The White House Years*. Garden City, N.Y.: Doubleday, 1963.

Ellsberg, Daniel. *Secrets: A Memoir of Vietnam and the Pentagon Papers*. New York: Viking, 2002.

Ellul, Jacques. *The Technological Society*. Translated by John Wilkinson. New York: Knopf, 1964.

Engelhardt, Tom. *The End of Victory Culture*. New York: Basic Books, 1995.

Etzold, Thomas H., and John Lewis Gaddis, eds. *Containment: Documents on American Policy and Strategy, 1945–1950*. New York: Columbia University Press, 1978.

Evangelista, Matthew. *Unarmed Forces: The Transnational Movement to End the Cold War*. Ithaca, N.Y.: Cornell University Press, 1999.

Fallon, Jean, and Anne Goldfeld, eds. *Beyond Hiroshima*. Nyack, N.Y.: Circumstantial Productions, 1999.

Fariello, Griffin. *Red Scare: Memories of the American Inquisition*. New York: Norton, 1995.

Farrell, John A. *Tip O'Neill and the Democratic Century*. New York: Little, Brown, 2001.

FitzGerald, Frances. *Way Out There in the Blue: Reagan, Star Wars, and the End of the Cold War*. New York: Simon & Schuster, 2000.

Fitzgerald, F. Scott. *The Great Gatsby*. New York: Scribner, 1925.

Foley, Michael S. *Confronting the War Machine: Draft Resistance During the Vietnam War*. Chapel Hill: University of North Carolina Press, 2003.

Foot, Rosemary. *The Wrong War: American Policy and the Dimensions of the Korean Conflict, 1950–1953*. Ithaca, N.Y.: Cornell University Press, 1985.

Freedman, Lawrence. *The Evolution of Nuclear Strategy*. London: Macmillan, 1981.

Freeland, Richard M. *The Truman Doctrine and the Origins of McCarthyism*. New York: New York University Press, 1985.

Freeman, Douglas Southall. *R. E. Lee: A Biography*. 4 volumes. New York: Scribner, 1934.

Friedman, John S. *The Secret Histories*. New York: Picador, 2005.

Fromm, Erich. "The Case for Unilateral Disarmament." *Daedalus* 89, no. 4 (Fall 1960).

Frum, David, and Richard Perle. *An End to Evil: How to Win the War on Terror*. New York: Random House, 2003.

Fussell, Paul. *The Great War and Modern Memory*. New York: Oxford University Press, 1975.

Gaddis, John Lewis. *Strategies of Containment: A Critical Appraisal of Postwar American National Security Policy*. New York: Oxford University Press, 1982.

———. *The Long Peace: Inquiries into the History of the Cold War*. New York: Oxford University Press, 1987.

——. *The United States and the End of the Cold War.* New York: Oxford University Press, 1992.

——. *We Now Know: Rethinking Cold War History.* New York: Oxford University Press, 1997.

——. "The Devil We Knew: Americans and the Cold War." *American Historical Review* 100, no. 1 (February 1995), 263–64.

——, et al., eds. *Cold War Statesmen Confront the Bomb: Nuclear Diplomacy Since 1945.* New York: Oxford University Press, 1999.

Galbraith, James K. "Did the U.S. Military Plan a Nuclear First Strike for 1963?" *American Prospect* 5, no. 9 (September 21, 1994).

Galbraith, John Kenneth. *A Life in Our Times.* Boston: Houghton Mifflin, 1981.

Gandhi, Mohandas K. *An Autobiography: The Story of My Experiments with Truth.* Boston: Beacon Press, 1993.

Gerson, Joseph. *With Hiroshima Eyes: Atomic War, Nuclear Extinction, and Moral Imagination.* Philadelphia: New Society, 1995.

Gilbert, Martin. *Churchill: A Life.* New York: Henry Holt, 1991.

Goldberg, Alfred. *The Pentagon: The First Fifty Years.* Washington: Historical Office, Office of the Secretary of Defense, 1992.

Golden, Renny, and Michael McConnell. *Sanctuary: The New Underground Railroad.* Maryknoll, N.Y.: Orbis, 1986.

Goldstein, Warren. *William Sloane Coffin, Jr.: A Holy Impatience.* New Haven: Yale University Press, 2004.

Goldwater, Barry M. *Why Not Victory?* New York: McGraw-Hill, 1962.

Goodwin, Richard. *Remembering America.* Boston: Little, Brown, 1988.

Gorbachev, Mikhail. *Reykjavík: Results and Lessons.* Madison, Conn.: Sphinx Press, 1987.

——. *Memoirs.* Garden City, N.Y.: Doubleday, 1996.

Gore, Al. *Earth in the Balance.* Boston: Houghton Mifflin, 1992.

Graebner, Norman A. *The National Security: Its Theory and Practice, 1945–1960.* New York: Oxford University Press, 1986.

Graham, Daniel O. *Shall America Be Defended?: SALT II and Beyond.* New Rochelle, N.Y.: Arlington House, 1979.

Graubard, Stephen R. "Arms, Defense Policy, and Arms Control." *Daedalus,* Summer 1975.

Griffin, David Ray. *The New Pearl Harbor.* Northampton, Mass.: Olive Branch Press, 2004.

Grose, Peter. *Operation Rollback.* Boston: Houghton Mifflin, 2000.

Groves, Leslie R. *Now It Can Be Told.* New York: Harper & Row, 1962.

Gunston, Bill, and Mike Spick. *Modern Air Combat.* New York: Crescent Books, 1985.

Gusterson, Hugh. *Nuclear Rites: A Weapons Laboratory at the End of the Cold War.* Berkeley: University of California Press, 1998.

——. "Remembering Hiroshima at a Nuclear Weapons Laboratory." In Laura Hein and Mark Selden, eds., *Living with the Bomb.* Armonk, N.Y.: M. E. Sharpe, 1997.

Haass, Richard N. *Intervention: The Use of American Military Force in the Post–Cold War World.* Washington: Brookings Institution Press, 1999.

Hafner, Donald L. "Averting a Brobdingnagian Skeet Shoot: Arms Control Measures for Anti-Satellite Weapons." *International Security* 5, no. 3 (Winter 1980–81), 41–60.

Hagerty, Edward J. *The OSI Story: A 50-Year Retrospective.* Washington: AFOSI, 1997.

Halberstam, David. *The Best and the Brightest.* New York: Ballantine, 1992.

——. *War in a Time of Peace: Bush, Clinton, and the Generals.* New York: Scribner, 2001.

Haldeman, H. R., with Joseph DiMona. *The Ends of Power.* New York: Times Books, 1978.

Halperin, Morton H. *Bureaucratic Politics and Foreign Policy.* Washington: Brookings Institution, 1974.

Hamilton, Nigel. *JFK: Reckless Youth.* New York: Random House, 1992.

Hartmann, Robert T. *Palace Politics: An Inside Account of the Ford Years.* New York: McGraw-Hill, 1980.

Harwit, Martin. *An Exhibit Denied: Lobbying the History of the Enola Gay.* New York: Copernicus, 1996.

Hasegawa, Tsuyoshi. *Racing the Enemy: Stalin, Truman, and the Surrender of Japan.* Cambridge: Belknap/Harvard University Press, 2005.

Hastings, Max. *Victory in Europe.* Boston: Little, Brown, 1985.

Hayden, Tom. *Reunion: A Memoir.* New York: Random House, 1988.

Hein, Laura, and Mark Selden, eds. *Living with the Bomb: American and Japanese Cultural Conflicts in the Nuclear Age.* Armonk, N.Y.: M. E. Sharpe, 1997.

Heller, Mikhail, and Aleksandr M. Nekrich. *Utopia in Power: The History of the Soviet Union, 1917 to the Present.* New York: Summit, 1982.

Helms, Richard. *A Look over My Shoulder.* New York: Random House, 2003.

Hendrickson, Paul. *The Living and the Dead: Robert McNamara and Five Lives of a Lost War.* New York: Knopf, 1996.

Herring, George C., ed. *The Pentagon Papers: Selections.* New York: McGraw-Hill, 1993.

Hersey, John. *Hiroshima.* New York: Vintage, 1946.

Hersh, Seymour. *The Price of Power: Kissinger in the Nixon White House.* New York: Summit, 1983.

Hill, Kenneth. *Cold War Chronology: Soviet-American Relations, 1945–1991.* Washington: Congressional Quarterly, 1993.

Hixson, Walter L. *George F. Kennan: Cold War Iconoclast.* New York: Columbia University Press, 1989.

Hodgson, Godfrey. *America in Our Time.* New York: Vintage, 1979.

———. *The Colonel: The Life and Times of Henry Stimson, 1867–1950.* New York: Knopf, 1990.

Hofstadter, Richard. *The Paranoid Style in American Politics and Other Essays.* Chicago: University of Chicago Press, 1965.

Hogan, Michael J., ed. *The End of the Cold War: Its Meaning and Implications.* New York: Cambridge University Press, 1992.

———, ed. *Hiroshima in History and Memory.* New York: Cambridge University Press, 1996.

Holbrooke, Richard. *To End a War.* New York: Random House, 1998.

Holloway, David. *The Soviet Union and the Arms Race.* New Haven: Yale University Press, 1983.

———. *Stalin and the Bomb: The Soviet Union and Atomic Energy, 1939–1956.* New Haven: Yale University Press, 1994.

———. "Research Note: Soviet Thermonuclear Development." *International Security* 4, no. 3 (Winter 1979–80), 192–97.

Holton, Gerald. "Arms Control." *Daedalus* 89, no. 4 (Fall 1960).

Homer-Dixon, Thomas F. *Environment, Scarcity, and Violence.* Princeton, N.J.: Princeton University Press, 1999.

Hoopes, Townsend, and Douglas Brinkley. *Driven Patriot: The Life and Times of James Forrestal.* New York: Knopf, 1992.

Hurst, Steven. *The Foreign Policy of the Bush Administration: In Search of a New World Order.* New York: Cassell, 1999.

Hyland, William G. *Mortal Rivals: Superpower Relations from Nixon to Reagan.* New York: Random House, 1987.

Inglis, Fred. *The Cruel Peace: Everyday Life and the Cold War.* New York: Basic Books, 1983.

Isaacs, Jeremy, and Taylor Downing. *Cold War.* Boston: Little, Brown, 1998.

Isaacson, Walter. *Kissinger: A Biography.* New York: Simon & Schuster, 1992.

———, and Evan Thomas. *Wise Men: Six Friends and the World They Made.* London: Faber & Faber, 1986.

Jervis, Robert. *Perception and Misperception in International Politics.* Princeton, N.J.: Princeton University Press, 1976.

——. *The Illogic of American Nuclear Strategy.* Ithaca, N.Y.: Cornell University Press, 1984.

——. *The Meaning of the Nuclear Revolution.* Ithaca, N.Y.: Cornell University Press, 1989.

Johnson, Chalmers. *Blowback: The Costs and Consequences of American Empire.* New York: Henry Holt, 2000.

——. *The Sorrows of Empire: Militarism, Secrecy, and the End of the Republic.* New York: Metropolitan/Henry Holt, 2004.

Just, Ward. *Military Men.* New York: Avon, 1968.

——. *To What End: Report from Vietnam.* New York: Public Affairs, 2000.

Kahn, Herman. *Thinking About the Unthinkable.* New York: Horizon, 1962.

——. "The Arms Race and Some of Its Hazards." *Daedalus* 89, no. 4 (Fall 1960).

Kaplan, Fred. *The Wizards of Armageddon.* New York: Simon & Schuster, 1983.

——. "JFK's First-Strike Plan." *Atlantic Monthly,* October 2001, 85.

Karnow, Stanley. *Vietnam: A History.* New York: Viking, 1983.

Katzenstein, Mary Fainsod, and Judith Reppy, eds. *Beyond Zero Tolerance: Discrimination in Military Culture.* Lanham, Md.: Rowman & Littlefield, 1999.

Kaysen, Carl. "Is War Obsolete?" *International Security* 14, no. 4 (Spring 1990).

——, and Martin Malin, eds. *War with Iraq: Costs, Consequences, and Alternatives.* Cambridge: American Academy of Arts and Sciences, 2003.

Keegan, John. *The Face of Battle.* New York: Viking, 1976.

——. *The Battle for History: Refighting World War II.* New York: Vintage, 1996.

——, ed. *The Book of War.* New York: Viking, 1999.

Keller, Bill. "The Sunshine Warrior." *New York Times Magazine,* September 22, 2002, 52.

Kennan, George F. *Memoirs, 1925–1950.* Boston: Little, Brown, 1967.

——. "The Sources of Soviet Conduct." *Foreign Affairs,* July 1947, 25.

Kennedy, Edward M., and Mark O. Hatfield. *Freeze! How You Can Prevent Nuclear War.* New York: Bantam, 1982.

Kennedy, John F. "Disarmament Can Be Won." *Bulletin of the Atomic Scientists* 16 (June 1960), 217.

——. "Fallout Shelters." *Life,* September 15, 1961.

Kennedy, Robert. *Thirteen Days: A Memoir of the Cuban Missile Crisis.* New York: Norton, 1971.

Kirkpatrick, Jeanne. *Dictatorships and Double Standards.* New York: Simon & Schuster, 1982.

Kissinger, Henry. *Nuclear Weapons and Foreign Policy.* New York: Norton, 1969.

——. *Years of Upheaval.* Boston: Little, Brown, 1982.

Klare, Michael. *Blood and Oil.* New York: Henry Holt, 2004.

Knaack, Marcelle Size. *Post–World War II Bombers.* Washington: Office of Air Force History, 1988.

Koistinen, Paul A. C. *Planning War, Pursuing Peace: The Political Economy of American Warfare, 1920–1939.* Lawrence: University of Kansas Press, 1998.

Korb, Lawrence. *A New National Security Strategy in an Age of Terrorists, Tyrants, and Weapons of Mass Destruction.* New York: Council on Foreign Relations Press, 2003.

Kristol, Irving. "It Wasn't Inevitable: Reagan's Military and Economic Policies Won the Cold War." *Weekly Standard,* June 21, 2004, 24–25.

Kuhns, Woodrow J., ed. *Assessing the Soviet Threat: The Early Cold War Years.* Washington: Center for the Study of Intelligence, Central Intelligence Agency, 1997.

Kwitny, Jonathan. *Man of the Century.* New York: Henry Holt, 1997.

LaFeber, Walter. *America, Russia, and the Cold War, 1945–2000.* New York: McGraw-Hill, 2002.

——, ed. *America in the Cold War: Twenty Years of Revolution and Response, 1947–1967.* New York: Wiley, 1969.

Laird, Melvin. *A House Divided: America's Strategy Gap.* Chicago: H. Regnery, 1962.

Langewiesche, William. "The Wrath of Khan." *Atlantic Monthly,* November 2005, 62–86.

Lasky, Victor. *JFK: The Man and the Myth.* New York: Macmillan, 1963.

Lawren, William. *The General and the Bomb: A Biography of General Leslie R. Groves, Director of the Manhattan Project.* New York: Dodd, Mead, 1988.

Lawrence, D. H. *Studies in Classic American Literature.* Edited by Ezra Greenspan, Lindeth Vasey, and John Worthen. Cambridge, U.K.: Cambridge University Press, 2003.

Leahy, William D. *I Was There: The Personal Story of the Chief of Staff to Presidents Roosevelt and Truman.* New York: Whittlesley House, 1950.

Lebow, Richard Ned, and Janice Gross Stein. "Deterrence and the Cold War." *Political Science Quarterly* 110, no. 2 (Summer 1995), 157–81.

Leffler, Melvyn P. *A Preponderance of Power: National Security, the Truman Administration, and the Cold War.* Stanford, Calif.: Stanford University Press, 1992.

——. "The Cold War: What Do 'We Now Know'?" *American Historical Review* 104, no. 2 (April 1999), 501–24.

Legvold, Robert, ed. *Thinking Strategically: The Major Powers, Kazakhstan, and the Central Asian Nexus.* Cambridge: American Academy of Arts and Sciences/MIT Press, 2003.

LeMay, Curtis, with MacKinlay Kanter. *Mission with LeMay.* Garden City, N.Y.: Doubleday, 1965.

Lemkin, Rafael. *Axis Rule in Occupied Europe.* Washington: Carnegie Endowment for International Peace, 1944.

Levering, Ralph B., et al. *Debating the Origins of the Cold War: American and Russian Perspectives.* Lanham, Md.: Rowman & Littlefield, 2002.

Levin-Waldman, Oren M. "The Ban on Homosexuals in Political Context: The Clinton Administration." In *Homosexuality and the Military: A Sourcebook of Official, Uncensored U.S. Government Documents.* Upland, Pa.: Diane Publishing, 1993.

Levy, Barry S., and Victor W. Sidel, eds. *War and Public Health.* New York: Oxford University Press, 1997.

Lifton, Robert Jay. *Destroying the World to Save It.* New York: Henry Holt, 2000.

——. *Superpower Syndrome.* New York: Nation Books, 2003.

——, and Greg Mitchell. *Hiroshima in America: A Half Century of Denial.* New York: Putnam, 1995.

Lindqvist, Sven. *A History of Bombing.* New York: New Press, 2000.

Lowen, Rebecca. *Creating the Cold War University: The Transformation of Stanford.* Berkeley: University of California Press, 1997.

Macdonald, Dwight. "The Decline to Barbarism." In Kai Bird and Lawrence Lifschultz, eds., *Hiroshima's Shadow.* Stoney Creek, Conn.: Pamphleteers Press, 1998.

Maddox, Robert James. *The New Left and the Origins of the Cold War.* Princeton, N.J.: Princeton University Press, 1973.

Mailer, Norman. *The Armies of the Night.* New York: New American Library, 1969.

Manchester, William. *The Glory and the Dream: A Narrative History of America, 1932–1972.* Boston: Little, Brown, 1973.

——. *American Caesar: Douglas MacArthur, 1880–1964.* Boston: Little, Brown, 1978.

——. *Goodbye, Darkness: A Memoir of the Pacific War.* Boston: Little, Brown, 1980.

Mann, James. *Rise of the Vulcans: The History of Bush's War Cabinet.* New York: Viking, 2004.

Mansfield, Sue. *The Gestalts of War: An Inquiry into Its Origins and Meanings as a Social Institution.* New York: Dial Press, 1982.

Mastny, Vojtech. *The Cold War and Soviet Insecurity: The Stalin Years*. New York: Oxford University Press, 1996.

Matlock, Jack F., Jr. *Reagan and Gorbachev: How the Cold War Ended*. New York: Random House, 2004.

May, Ernest R., ed. *American Cold War Strategy: Interpreting NSC-68*. Boston: Bedford Books, 1993.

———, and Richard Neustadt. *Thinking in Time: The Uses of History for Decision Makers*. New York: Free Press, 1986.

———, and Philip D. Zelikow. *The Kennedy Tapes: Inside the White House During the Cuban Missile Crisis*. Cambridge: Harvard University Press, 1997.

McCullough, David. *Truman*. New York: Simon & Schuster, 1992.

McElroy, Robert W. *Morality and American Foreign Policy*. Princeton, N.J.: Princeton University Press, 1992.

McFarlane, Robert C., and Zofia Smardz. *Special Trust*. New York: Cadell & Davies, 1994.

McGowan, Edward. *Peace Warriors: The Story of the Camden 28*. Nyack, N.Y.: Circumstantial Productions Publishing, 2001.

McMillan, Priscilla J. *The Ruin of J. Robert Oppenheimer and the Birth of the Modern Arms Race*. New York: Viking, 2005.

McNamara, Robert S. *The Essence of Security: Reflections in Office*. New York: Harper & Row, 1968.

———. *In Retrospect: The Tragedy and Lessons of Vietnam*. New York: Times Books, 1995.

———, and James G. Blight. *Wilson's Ghost: Reducing the Risk of Conflict, Killing, and Catastrophe in the Twenty-first Century*. New York: Public Affairs, 2001.

———, George Kennan, McGeorge Bundy, and Gerard K. Smith. "Nuclear Weapons and the Atlantic Alliance." *Foreign Affairs*, Spring 1982.

McNeal, Patricia. *Harder Than War: Catholic Peacemaking in Twentieth-Century America*. New Brunswick, N.J.: Rutgers University Press, 1992.

McPherson, Harry. *A Political Education: A Washington Memoir*. Boston: Houghton Mifflin, 1988.

Mead, Margaret. "Warfare Is Only an Invention — Not a Biological Necessity." *Asia* 40 (1940), 402–5.

Means, Howard. *Colin Powell: Soldier/Statesman, Statesman/Soldier*. New York: Donald I. Fine, 1992.

Mearsheimer, John. "Why We Will Soon Miss the Cold War." *Atlantic Monthly*, August 1990, 35–50.

Meilinger, Phillip S. *Hoyt S. Vandenberg: The Life of a General*. Bloomington: Indiana University Press, 1989.

Melville, Herman. *Moby Dick, or The Whale*. New York: Heritage Press, 1943.

Messer, Robert L. *The End of an Alliance: James F. Byrnes, Roosevelt, Truman, and the Origins of the Cold War*. Chapel Hill: University of North Carolina Press, 1982.

Miller, James. *Democracy Is in the Streets*. New York: Simon & Schuster, 1987.

Miller, Steve, and Dmitri Trenin. *The Russian Military: Power and Policy*. Cambridge: American Academy of Arts and Sciences, 2004.

Miller, William. *Dorothy Day: A Biography*. New York: Harper & Row, 1982.

Millis, Walter, ed., with the collaboration of E. S. Duffield. *The Forrestal Diaries*. New York: Viking, 1951.

Mitford, Jessica. *The Trial of Dr. Spock*. New York: Knopf, 1969.

Morison, Elting E. *Turmoil and Tradition: A Study of the Life and Times of Henry L. Stimson*. Boston: Houghton Mifflin, 1960.

Morris, Edmund. *Dutch: A Memoir of Ronald Reagan*. New York: Modern Library, 1999.

Morrison, Philip. "Recollections of a Nuclear War." *Scientific American*, August 1995, 31–32.

Murphy, David E., et al. *Battleground Berlin: CIA vs. KGB in the Cold War.* New Haven: Yale University Press, 1997.

National Academy of Sciences, Committee on International Security and Arms Control. *The Future of U.S. Nuclear Weapons Policy.* Washington: National Academy of Sciences Press, 1997.

Newhouse, John. *War and Peace in the Nuclear Age.* New York: Knopf, 1989.

Nicosia, Gerald. *Home to War.* New York: Crown, 2001.

9/11 Commission Report, The. New York: Norton, 2004.

Nitze, Paul. "Assuring Strategic Stability in the Era of Détente." *Foreign Affairs* 54, no. 2 (January 1976).

———, with Ann M. Smith and Steven L. Rearden. *From Hiroshima to Glasnost. At the Center of Decision-Making: A Memoir.* New York: Grove Weidenfeld, 1989.

Nixon, Richard. *RN: The Memoirs of Richard Nixon.* New York: Grosset and Dunlap, 1978.

Nolan, Janne E. *Guardians of the Arsenal: The Politics of Nuclear Strategy.* New York: Basic Books, 1989.

———. *An Elusive Consensus.* Washington: Brookings Institution, 1999.

———, ed. *Global Engagement: Cooperation and Security in the Twenty-first Century.* Washington: Brookings Institution, 1994.

Noonan, Peggy. *When Character Was King: A Story of Ronald Reagan.* New York: Penguin, 2001.

Norris, Robert S. *Racing for the Bomb: General Leslie R. Groves, the Manhattan Project's Indispensable Man.* South Royalton, Vt.: Steerforth Press, 2002.

———. "U.S. Nuclear Reductions." *Bulletin of the Atomic Scientists* 60, no. 5 (September/October 2004), 70–71.

———. "U.S. Nuclear Forces, 2005." *Bulletin of the Atomic Scientists* 61, no. 1 (January/February 2005), 73–75.

———, and William M. Arkin. "U.S. Nuclear Stockpile, July 1998." *Bulletin of the Atomic Scientists* 54, no. 4 (July/August 1998), 69–71.

———, and Hans M. Kristensen. "Dismantling U.S. Nuclear Warheads." *Bulletin of the Atomic Scientists* 60, no. 1 (January/February 2004), 72–74.

———, Hans M. Kristensen, and Joshua Handler. "The B61 Family of Bombs." *Bulletin of the Atomic Scientists* 59, no. 1 (January/February 2003), 74–76.

Nye, Joseph, Jr. *Nuclear Ethics.* New York: Free Press, 1986.

———. *Soft Power: The Means to Success in World Politics.* New York: Public Affairs, 2004.

O'Carroll, Michael. *Pius XII: Greatness Dishonored.* Dublin: Laetare Press, 1980.

Office of the Historian, HQ Strategic Air Command. *SAC Missile Chronology.* Omaha: Offutt Air Force Base, 1990.

Office of the Secretary of Defense. "Sexual Orientation and U.S. Military Personnel Policy: Options and Assessment." Washington: National Defense Research Institute, 1993.

O'Malley, Padraig, ed. "War." *New England Journal of Public Policy,* Winter 2005.

O'Neill, William. *A Democracy at War.* Cambridge: Harvard University Press, 1993.

Orton, Peter K., and Arno Scholz. *Outpost Berlin.* Berlin: Arani Verlag, 1955.

Pape, Robert A. *Bombing to Win: Air Power and Coercion in War.* Ithaca, N.Y.: Cornell University Press, 1996.

Parker, Richard. *John Kenneth Galbraith: His Life, His Politics, His Economics.* New York: Farrar, Straus and Giroux, 2005.

Parrish, Thomas. *Berlin in the Balance, 1945–1949.* Reading, Mass.: Addison-Wesley, 1998.

Patterson, James T. *Grand Expectations: The United States, 1945–1974.* New York: Oxford University Press, 1996.

Peacock, Lindsay T. *Strategic Air Command.* London: Arms and Armor Press, 1988.

Pentagon Papers, The. New York: Bantam, 1971.

Perret, Geoffrey. *Eisenhower*. New York: Random House, 1999.

Perry, Mark. *Four Stars: The Inside Story of the Forty-Year Battle Between the Joint Chiefs of Staff and America's Civilian Leaders*. Boston: Houghton Mifflin, 1989.

———. "Lessons from the Cold War." *Carnegie Reporter*, Summer 2000, 41.

Pfaltzgraff, Robert, Jr. *Contrasting Approaches to Strategic Arms Control*. Lexington, Mass.: Lexington Books, 1974.

Pipes, Richard. *Russia Under the Old Regime*. London: Penguin Books, 1995.

Poe, Marshall T. *The Russian Moment in World History*. Princeton, N.J.: Princeton University Press, 2003.

Pogue, Forrest C. *George C. Marshall: Organizer of Victory*. New York: Viking, 1973.

Polner, Murray, and Jim O'Grady. *Disarmed and Dangerous: The Radical Lives and Times of Daniel and Philip Berrigan*. New York: Basic Books, 1997.

Porter, Gareth. *Perils of Dominance: Imbalance of Power and the Road to War in Vietnam*. Berkeley: University of California Press, 2005.

Posen, Barry R. "The War for Kosovo: Serbia's Political-Military Strategy." *International Security* 24, no. 4 (Spring 2000), 39–84.

Postol, Theodore. "Lessons of the Gulf War Patriot Experience." *International Security* 16 (Winter 1991–92), 119–71.

Powell, Colin, with Joseph L. Persico. *My American Journey*. New York: Random House, 1995.

———. "President Truman and the Desegregation of the Armed Forces: A Fiftieth Anniversary View of Executive Order 9981." Gauer Distinguished Lecture in Law and Public Policy, vol. III. Washington: National Legal Center for the Public Interest, 1998.

Powers, Thomas. *Design for Survival*. New York: Coward-McCann, 1964.

———. *The Man Who Kept the Secrets*. New York: Knopf, 1979.

———. "Choosing a Strategy for World War III." *Atlantic Monthly*, November 1982, 84.

———. "History: Was It Right?" *Atlantic Monthly*, July 1995, 20–23.

Prados, John. *The Soviet Estimate: U.S. Intelligence and Soviet Strategic Forces*. Princeton, N.J.: Princeton University Press, 1982.

———. *Presidents' Secret Wars: CIA and Pentagon Covert Operations Since World War II*. New York: William Morrow, 1986.

———. *Hoodwinked: The Documents That Reveal How Bush Sold Us the War*. New York: New Press, 2004.

Rauch, Jonathan. "Firebombs over Tokyo." *Atlantic Monthly*, July/August 2001.

Reeves, Richard. *President Kennedy: Profile of Power*. New York: Simon & Schuster, 1993.

Rhodes, Richard. *The Making of the Atomic Bomb*. New York: Simon & Schuster, 1986.

Rieff, David. *At the Point of a Gun: Democratic Dreams and Armed Intervention*. New York: Simon & Schuster, 2005.

Rogow, Arnold A. *Victim of Duty: A Study of James Forrestal*. London: Rupert Hart-David, 1966.

Rosenberg, David Alan. "American Atomic Strategy and the Hydrogen Bomb Decision." *Journal of American History* 66, no. 1 (June 1979), 62–87.

———. "The Origins of Overkill: Nuclear Weapons and American Strategy, 1945–1960." *International Security* 7, no. 4 (Spring 1983), 3–71.

Roth, David. *Sacred Honor: A Biography of Colin Powell*. San Francisco: HarperSanFrancisco, 1993.

Rubenstein, Joshua, and Alexander Gribanov, eds. *The KGB File of Andrei Sakharov*. New Haven: Yale University Press, 2005.

Rumpf, Hans. *The Bombing of Germany*. New York: Holt, Rinehart and Winston, 1963.

Rusk, Dean. *As I Saw It*. New York: Norton, 1990.

Safire, William, ed. *Lend Me Your Ears: Great Speeches in History*. New York: Norton, 1992.

Sagan, Scott D., and Jeremi Suri. "The Madman Nuclear Alert: Secrecy, Signaling, and Safety in October 1969." *International Security* 27, no. 4 (Spring 2003), 156.

Schaffer, Ronald. *Wings of Judgment: American Bombing in World War II.* New York: Oxford University Press, 1985.

Schell, Jonathan. *The Village of Ben Suc.* New York: Knopf, 1967.

———. *The Gift of Time: The Case for Abolishing Nuclear Weapons Now.* New York: Metropolitan/Henry Holt, 1998.

———. *The Unconquerable World: Power, Nonviolence, and the Will of the People.* New York: Metropolitan, 2003.

———. "The Case Against the War." *The Nation,* March 3, 2003, 14.

Schelling, Thomas C. *Arms and Influence.* New Haven: Yale University Press, 1966.

Schlesinger, Arthur, Jr. *A Thousand Days: John F. Kennedy in the White House.* New York: Fawcett, 1971.

———. *Robert Kennedy and His Times.* New York: Ballantine, 1996.

———. *A Life in the Twentieth Century.* Boston: Houghton Mifflin, 2000.

Schmergel, Greg, ed. *U.S. Foreign Policy in the 1990s.* London: Macmillan/Harvard International Review, 1991.

Schmitz, David F. *Henry L. Stimson: The First Wise Man.* Wilmington, Del.: SR Books, 2001.

Schrecker, Ellen, ed. *Cold War Triumphalism.* New York: New Press, 2004.

Schwartz, Stephen E. "Check, Please." *Bulletin of the Atomic Scientists,* September/October 1998, 36.

Sebald, W. G. *On the Natural History of Destruction.* New York: Random House, 2003.

Seton-Watson, Hugh. *From Lenin to Khrushchev: The History of World Communism.* New York: Praeger, 1960.

Shapiro, Andrew O., and John M. Strikes. *Mastering the Draft.* New York: Avon, 1970.

Shapley, Deborah. *Promise and Power: The Life and Times of Robert McNamara.* Boston: Little, Brown, 1993.

Sharp, Gene. *The Politics of Nonviolent Action.* Boston: P. Sargent, 1973.

———. *Gandhi as a Political Strategist.* Boston: P. Sargent, 1979.

Shattuck, Roger. *Proust's Way.* New York: Norton, 2000.

Shawcross, William. *Sideshow: Kissinger, Nixon, and the Destruction of Cambodia.* New York: Simon & Schuster, 1979.

Shay, Jonathan. *Achilles in Vietnam.* New York: Simon & Schuster, 1994.

Sheehan, Neil. *A Bright Shining Lie: John Paul Vann and America in Vietnam.* New York: Random House, 1988.

Sherry, Michael S. *The Rise of American Air Power: The Creation of Armageddon.* New Haven: Yale University Press, 1987.

Sherwin, Martin J. *A World Destroyed: Hiroshima and the Origins of the Arms Race.* New York: Vintage, 1987.

———, and Kai Bird. *American Prometheus: The Triumph and Tragedy of J. Robert Oppenheimer.* New York: Knopf, 2005.

Shriver, Donald. *An Ethic for Enemies.* New York: Oxford University Press, 1995.

Shultz, George P. *Turmoil and Triumph: My Years as Secretary of State.* New York: Scribner, 1993.

Sidey, Hugh. *John F. Kennedy, President.* New York: Atheneum, 1964.

Sifton, Elisabeth. *The Serenity Prayer: Faith and Politics in Times of Peace and War.* New York: Norton, 2003.

Sigal, Leon V. *Fighting to a Finish: The Politics of War Termination in the United States and Japan, 1945.* Ithaca, N.Y.: Cornell University Press, 1988.

Simons, Thomas W. *The End of the Cold War?* New York: St. Martin's Press, 1990.

Simpson, Cornell. *The Death of James Forrestal.* Boston: Western Islands, 1966.

Smith, Hedrick. *The Russians.* New York: Ballantine, 1976.

Smith, John Chabot. *Alger Hiss: The True Story.* New York: Holt, Rinehart and Winston, 1976.

Smith-Christopher, Daniel L., ed. *Subverting Hatred: The Challenge of Non-Violence in Religious Traditions.* Boston: Boston Research Center for the Twenty-first Century, 1998.

Snead, David L. *The Gaither Committee: Eisenhower and the Cold War.* Columbus: Ohio State University Press, 1999.

Sorensen, Theodore. *Kennedy.* New York: Harper & Row, 1965.

Steinbruner, John D. *Principles of Global Security.* Washington: Brookings Institution, 2000.

———, and Jeffrey Lewis. "The Unsettled Legacy of the Cold War." *Daedalus,* Fall 2002, 5–10.

Steury, Donald P., ed. *Intentions and Capabilities: Estimates on Soviet Strategic Forces, 1950–1983.* Washington: History Staff, Center for the Study of Intelligence, Central Intelligence Agency, 1994.

Stimson, Henry. "The Decision to Use the Atomic Bomb." *Harper's Magazine,* February 1947, 99.

———, and McGeorge Bundy. *On Active Service in Peace and War.* New York: Harper & Brothers, 1948.

Stone, I. F. *The Hidden History of the Korean War.* New York: Monthly Review Press, 1952.

Sulzberger, C. L. *The Last of the Giants.* New York: Macmillan, 1970.

Takiff, Michael. *Brave Men, Gentle Heroes.* New York: William Morrow, 2003.

Talbott, Strobe. *Deadly Gambits: The Reagan Administration and the Stalemate in Nuclear Arms Control.* New York: Vintage, 1985.

———. *The Master of the Game: Paul Nitze and the Nuclear Peace.* New York: Knopf, 1988.

Taylor, Maxwell D. *The Uncertain Trumpet.* New York: Harper & Row, 1960.

Taylor, Walt. *Waging Peace for a Living.* Victoria, B.C.: Trafford, 1999.

Teilhard de Chardin, Pierre. *The Making of a Mind: Letters from a Soldier-Priest, 1914–1919.* Translated by R. Hague. New York: Harper & Row, 1965.

Teller, Edward. "The Feasibility of Arms Control and the Principle of Openness." *Daedalus* 89, no. 4 (Fall 1960).

Thomas, Evan. *The Very Best Men. Four Who Dared: The Early Years of the CIA.* New York: Simon & Schuster, 1995.

Thompson, John A. *Revolutionary Russia, 1917.* Prospect Heights, Ill.: Waveland Press, 1989.

Thurston, Robert W. *Life and Terror in Stalin's Russia.* New Haven: Yale University Press, 1996.

Timber, Robert. *The Nightingale's Song.* New York: Simon & Schuster, 1995.

Trachtenberg, Marc. *History and Strategy.* Princeton, N.J.: Princeton University Press, 1991.

Truman, Harry S. *Memoirs.* Vol. 1: *Year of Decisions.* Garden City, N.Y.: Doubleday, 1955.

Tucker, Robert C., ed. *The Marx-Engels Reader.* New York: Norton, 1978.

Uhler, Walter C. "Gorbachev's Revolution." *The Nation,* December 31, 2001.

U.S. Atomic Energy Commission. *In the Matter of J. Robert Oppenheimer: Texts of Principal Documents and Letters of Personnel Security Board, General Manager, Commissioners. Washington, D.C., May 27, 1954 through June 29, 1954.* Washington: U.S. Government Printing Office, 1954.

U.S. Conference of Catholic Bishops. *The Challenge of Peace: God's Promise and Our Response.* Washington: U.S. Catholic Conference, 1983.

Vonnegut, Kurt. *Slaughterhouse-Five, or The Children's Crusade: A Duty-Dance with Death.* New York: Delacorte Press, 1969.

Wainstock, Dennis D. *The Decision to Drop the Atomic Bomb.* Westport, Conn.: Praeger, 1996.

Walt, Stephen M. *Taming American Power: The Global Response to U.S. Primacy.* New York: Norton, 2005.

Waltz, Kenneth N. *Man, the State, and War: A Theoretical Analysis*. New York: Columbia University Press, 1959.

———. "Structural Realism After the Cold War." *International Security* 25, no. 1 (Summer 2000).

Walzer, Michael. *Just and Unjust Wars*. New York: Basic Books, 1971.

Warren, Rosanna. *Departure*. New York: Norton, 2003.

Weinberg, Alvin M. "The Sanctification of Hiroshima." *Bulletin of the Atomic Scientists*, August 1985.

Weinberger, Caspar. *Fighting for Peace*. New York: Warner Books, 1990.

West, Rebecca. *The New Meaning of Treason*. New York: Penguin, 1964.

White, Thomas. "Strategy and the Defense Intellectuals." *Saturday Evening Post*, May 4, 1963.

Whitfield, Stephen J. *The Culture of the Cold War*. Baltimore: Johns Hopkins University Press, 1991.

Wilcox, Fred, ed. *Disciples and Dissidents: Prison Writings of the Prince of Peace Ploughshares*. Athol, Mass.: Haley's, 2001.

Williams, William Appleman. *The Tragedy of American Diplomacy*. New York: Dell, 1959.

Wills, Garry. *Reagan's America: Innocents at Home*. Garden City, N.Y.: Doubleday, 1987.

Wittner, Lawrence. *One World or None: A History of the World Nuclear Disarmament Movement Through 1953*. Stanford, Calif.: Stanford University Press, 1993.

Wohlstetter, Albert J. "The Delicate Balance of Terror." *Foreign Affairs* 37 (January 1959).

Wolfe, Alan. *The Rise and Fall of the "Soviet Threat."* Washington: Institute for Policy Studies, 1979.

Woods, Randall Bennet. "A Transforming Experience: Review of Michael J. Hogan, *A Cross of Iron*," *Diplomatic History* 24, no. 4 (Fall 2000).

Woodward, Bob. *Veil: The Secret Wars of the CIA, 1981–1987*. New York: Simon & Schuster, 1987.

———. *The Commanders*. New York: Simon & Schuster, 1991.

———. *The Choice*. New York: Simon & Schuster, 1996.

Wyman, David S. *The Abandonment of the Jews*. New York: Pantheon, 1984.

Yergin, Daniel. *Shattered Peace: The Origins of the Cold War and the National Security State*. Boston: Houghton Mifflin, 1978.

York, Herbert. *The Advisors: Oppenheimer, Teller, and the Super Bomb*. San Francisco: W. H. Freeman, 1976.

———. *Making Weapons, Talking Peace: A Physicist's Odyssey from Hiroshima to Geneva*. New York: Basic Books, 1987.

Zaloga, Steven J. *Target America: The Soviet Union and the Strategic Arms Race, 1945–1964*. Novato, Calif.: Presidio Press, 1993.

———. *The Kremlin's Nuclear Sword: The Rise and Fall of Russia's Strategic Nuclear Forces, 1945–2000*. Washington: Smithsonian Institution, 2002.

Zinn, Howard. *Vietnam: The Logic of Withdrawal*. Boston: Beacon Press, 1967.

———. *The Politics of History*. Boston: Beacon Press, 1970.

———. *You Can't Be Neutral on a Moving Train*. Boston: Beacon Press, 1994.

———. *The Zinn Reader*. New York: Seven Stories Press, 1997.

Zubok, Vladislav M., and Hope M. Harrison. "The Nuclear Education of Nikita Khrushchev." In John Lewis Gaddis et al., eds., *Cold War Statesmen Confront the Bomb: Nuclear Diplomacy Since 1945*. New York: Oxford University Press, 1999.

———, and Constantine Pleshakov. *Inside the Kremlin's Cold War: From Stalin to Khrushchev*. Cambridge: Harvard University Press, 1996.

INDEX

PHOTO CREDITS, in order of appearance: Pentagon under construction: U.S. Army Corps of Engineers. Pentagon after 9/11 (2 photos): Department of Defense. Pentagon aerial (2 photos): Department of Defense. B-17: Department of Defense. LeMay: Library of Congress. Tokyo aerial: Library of Congress. Oppenheimer and Groves: Library of Congress. Hiroshima: Ted Polumbaum/ The Newseum. Patton, Bundy, Stimson: Harry S. Truman Library. Stimson and Forrestal street photos: National Park Service/Abbie Rowe/Harry S. Truman Library. Truman and Forrestal: Harry S. Truman Library. Joseph Carroll with cigarette: courtesy of the author. Symington and Carroll: courtesy of the author. General Carroll in 1950: U.S. Air Force photo. B-52: Department of Defense. Kahn: Library of Congress. Intelligence photo: Department of Defense. Kennedy: John F. Kennedy Library. Carroll reviews troops: Joint General Staff, Republic of Vietnam Armed Forces. McNamara and Rusk: Lyndon B. Johnson Library. Ribbon cutting: Department of Defense. Protest march: Lyndon B. Johnson Library. Berrigan behind fence: Ted Polumbaum/Life/The Newseum. Kerry: Ted Polumbaum/The Newseum. Plowshares: courtesy of the author. Chile protest: Ted Polumbaum/The Newseum. Ford: Gerald R. Ford Library. Reagan and Pope John Paul II: Ronald Reagan Library. Red Square: Ronald Reagan Library. Bush and Walesa: George Bush Presidential Library. Cohen and Nitze: Department of Defense. Clinton and Joint Chiefs: Library of Congress. Rumsfeld and Bush: Department of Defense. Pentagon: Department of Defense.